R. Gupta's®

Sainik School

ENTRANCE EXAM

Previous Years' Papers

With Explanatory Answers

For Class IX

2027
EDITION

RAMESH PUBLISHING HOUSE, NEW DELHI

Published by

O.P. Gupta *for* Ramesh Publishing House

Admin. Office

12-H, New Daryaganj Road, Opp. Officers' Mess,
New Delhi-110002 ✆ 23275224, 23245124

E-mail: info@rameshpublishinghouse.com

For Online Shopping: www.rameshpublishinghouse.com

Showroom

- Balaji Market, Nai Sarak, Delhi-110006 ✆ 23282525 📱 9354373464
- 4457, Nai Sarak, Delhi-110006

Book Code: R-1653

ISBN: 978-93-5012-439-0

Price: ₹ 390

Printed at: S.K. Graphics, Delhi

CONTENTS

Previous Year Papers (Solved)

2604

Previous Years' Paper

All India Sainik Schools Entrance Exam (AISSEE)–2026

Class-IX

(Exam held on 18-01-2026)

Section A : Mathematics

1. In the following figure, $l \parallel m$ and n is a transversal. Find the value of $(x + y)$.

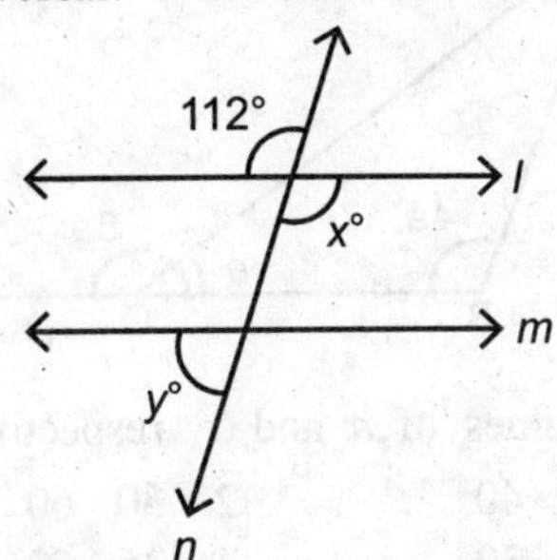

1. 154 2. 200
3. 180 4. 168

2. Which of the following statements are true?

Statement I: If two lines are parallel to a third line, then they themselves are parallel.

Statement II: All the eight angles made by a transversal with two parallel lines are always equal.

Statement III: If the alternate angles made by a transversal with a pair of lines are 80° and 100°, then the lines are parallel.

Statement IV: If the lines are parallel, then the interior angles on the same side of the transversal are supplementary.

1. only I, IV 2. only I, III
3. only II, III 4. only I, II, III

3. A, B and C can do a work in 10 days, 16 days and 20 days respectively. They started working together, but B left the work after 4 days. In how many days the work got completed?

1. $4\frac{3}{4}$ 2. 5
3. $5\frac{1}{2}$ 4. 4

4. Amit and Sunil together can do a work in 6 days. If Amit can do it in 10 days, then in how many days can Sunil do it?

1. 16 days 2. 14 days
3. 15 days 4. 12 days

5. If $5^{2x} \times 5^{x+3} \times 5^{5-x} = \left(\sqrt{5}\right)^{20}$, then the value of '$x$' is:

1. 2 2. 0
3. 1 4. –1

6. If $\sqrt{18 \times 14 \times x} = 168$, then the value of x is:

1. 117 2. 112
3. 115 4. 113

7. What is the smallest number by which 3087 must be divided, so that the number obtained is a perfect cube?

1. 13 2. 9
3. 11 4. 7

8. Karishma paid 15% of her monthly salary towards an EMI. From the remaining salary she paid 10% as internet bill and 20% as rent of the house. If after the mentioned expenses she was left with ₹ 35,105, then what was Karishma's monthly salary?

1. ₹ 59,000 2. ₹ 55,500
3. ₹ 57,000 4. ₹ 55,000

9. 76% of the students in a school are boys. If there are 204 girls in the school, then what is the total number of students?

1. 900 2. 800
3. 850 4. 760

10. A shopkeeper bought a table and a chair for ₹ 8,000 each. He sold them and made a profit of 8% on the table and incurred a loss of 4% on the chair. The gain per cent on the whole transaction is:

1. 4% 2. 3%
3. 2% 4. 5%

11. In a polyhedron, there are 18 vertices and 28 edges. The number of faces is:

1. 18 2. 12
3. 15 4. 20

12. Seven equal solid metallic spheres having radius 6 cm are melted to cast a cuboid with length 33 cm and width 24 cm. What will be the height of the cuboid so formed? (Use π = 22/7)

1. 9 cm 2. 7 cm
3. 8 cm 4. 6 cm

13. A solid metallic cuboid having dimensions 250 cm × 40 cm × 100 cm is melted and recast into a solid cube. The edge (in meter) of the cube so formed is:

1. 25 m 2. 1 m
3. 50 m 4. 100 m

14. The area of a parallelogram is 63 cm^2. If its base is 7 cm, then what is the height of the parallelogram?

1. 11 cm 2. 8 cm
3. 9 cm 4. 7 cm

15. If the diagonals of a rhombus are 8 cm and 6 cm, then perimeter of the rhombus is:

1. 25 cm 2. 15 cm
3. 20 cm 4. 10 cm

16. The angles of a quadrilateral are in the ratio 2 : 4 : 5 : 7. The measure of smallest of these angles is:

1. 60° 2. 20°
3. 40° 4. 10°

17. In the given figure.

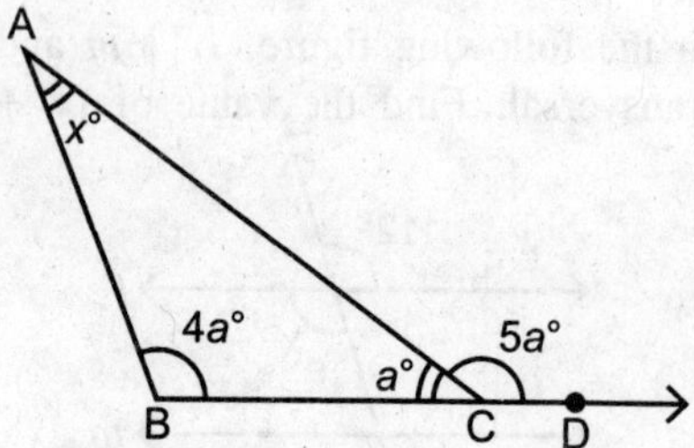

The values of a and x, respectively are:

1. 36, 40 2. 30, 60
3. 30, 30 4. 25, 50

18. A 5 m long ladder is placed against a wall. The foot of the ladder is 3 m away from the base of the wall. How far up the wall does the top of the ladder reach?

1. 2.5 m 2. 4 m
3. 3 m 4. 5 m

19. In the figure in ΔABC, $\angle A = 80°$ and $\angle ABC = 40°$. BD and CD bisect angles B and C, respectively. The values of x and y respectively are:

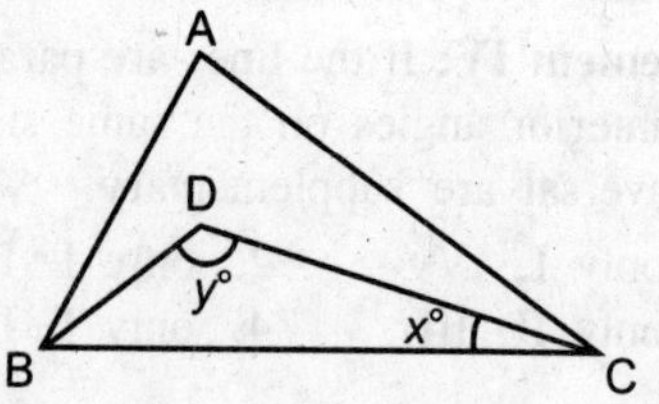

1. 20 and 125 2. 10 and 125
3. 30 and 130 4. 10 and 130

20. If P is the smallest number that should be added to 669 to get a perfect square, then what is the value of $\sqrt{3P+4}$?

1. 7 2. 5
3. 6 4. 4

21. When $(5x^2 + 70x - 160)$ is divided by $(x + 16)$, then the quotient is:

1. $(5x + 10)$ 2. $5(x - 2)$
3. $2(x + 5)$ 4. $5(x - 5)$

22. In the following bar graph, total number of students and number of boys in the school have been presented for schools A, B, C and D.

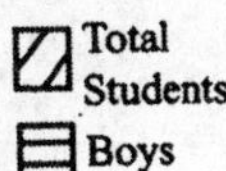

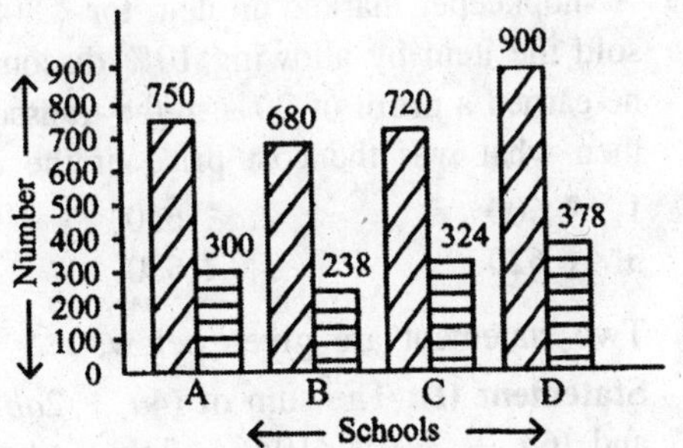

Which school has maximum number of girls and what is the percentage of girls in that school?

1. D, 44% 2. A, 62%
3. D, 58% 4. A, 40%

23. A shopkeeper sold 5 kinds of cosmetic creams A, B, C, D and E. The number of creams sold by the shopkeeper in a month is presented in the given pie chart. If the total number of creams sold by the shopkeeper is 800, then how many cream B were sold by the shopkeeper?

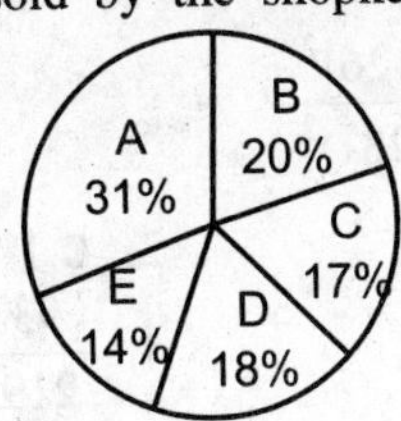

1. 182 2. 152
3. 160 4. 164

24. If the 4-digit number 48*ab* is divisible by 2, 5 and 7, then the value of $(10a - b)$ is:

1. 50 2. 30
3. 45 4. 15

25. If 7-digit number 78*3945 is divisible by 11, then value of '*' is:

1. 5 2. 1
3. 3 4. 0

26. What is the difference between the greatest and the smallest of the fractions $\frac{5}{8}, \frac{3}{4}, \frac{4}{7}, \frac{2}{3}, \frac{5}{9}$, ?

1. $\frac{5}{28}$ 2. $\frac{7}{36}$
3. $\frac{1}{9}$ 4. $\frac{5}{72}$

27. Evaluate

$$256 \div \frac{4}{3} + 5 \times \frac{4}{3} - 8 \div \frac{27}{24} \times \left(\frac{1}{3} \text{ of } 81\right).$$

1. 84 2. 3
3. $\frac{64}{3}$ 4. $\frac{20}{3}$

28. The present age of a father is five times the age of his only son. After 10 years, the age of the father will be three times the age of his son. The present age of the father is:

1. 30 years 2. 50 years
3. 40 years 4. 45 years

29. The denominator of a fraction is 5 more than twice its numerator. If the numerator is increased by 4 and the denominator is decreased by 1, the fraction becomes $\frac{2}{3}$.

The original fraction is:

1. $\frac{6}{17}$
2. $\frac{3}{11}$
3. $\frac{4}{13}$
4. $\frac{2}{9}$

30. In the figure, ABCD is a parallelogram. The measures of the angles x, y and z are:

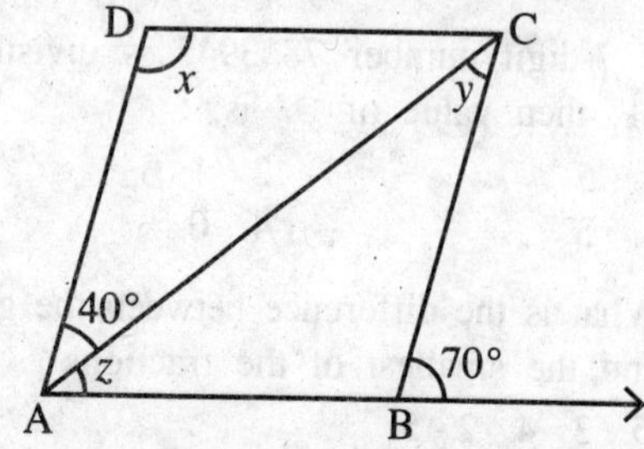

1. $x = 70°$, $y = 40°$, $z = 30°$
2. $x = 110°$, $y = 40°$, $z = 30°$
3. $x = 90°$, $y = 20°$, $z = 70°$
4. $x = 100°$, $y = 50°$, $z = 30°$

31. What is the mean of the observations 2, 5, 7, 5, 12, 16, 14, 18, 15 and 16?

1. 11.5
2. 11
3. 11.2
4. 10

32. The median of ten consecutive even natural numbers starting from 8 is:

1. 12.5
2. 16
3. 17
4. 15

33. If mode of the observations 5, 7, 11, 14, 15, 16 and $(2k + 3)$ is 11, then the value of $(k + 1)^2$ is:

1. 4
2. 16
3. 25
4. 9

34. A coin is tossed 60 times and head appears 25 times. What is the probability of getting a tail?

1. $\frac{1}{2}$
2. $\frac{1}{25}$
3. $\frac{7}{12}$
4. $\frac{5}{12}$

35. A bag contains 6 black and 8 white balls One ball is drawn at random. What is the probability that the ball drawn is white?

1. $\frac{3}{7}$
2. $\frac{4}{7}$
3. $\frac{1}{8}$
4. $\frac{3}{4}$

36. A shopkeeper was selling all his items at 25% discount. During the off season, he offered 30% discount over and above the existing discount. If an item is marked for ₹ 2,400, then how much the customer has to pay for it?

1. ₹ 1,320
2. ₹ 1,260
3. ₹ 1,080
4. ₹ 1,140

37. A shopkeeper marked an item for ₹ 800 and sold the item by allowing 10% discount. If he earned a profit of 20% in the transaction, then what was the cost price of the item?

1. ₹ 600
2. ₹ 650
3. ₹ 620
4. ₹ 680

38. Two statement are given below:

Statement (I): The sum of $(4a + 2ab - c)$ and $(6a + 3c)$ is $(10a + 2ab + 4c)$.

Statement (II): $(6a + 3c)$ when subtracted from $(4a + 2ab - c)$ gives $(-2a + 2ab - 4c)$.

Choose the ***correct*** answer from the options given below.

1. Both Statements (I) and (II) are false
2. Statement (I) is false and Statement (II) is true
3. Both Statements (I) and (II) are true
4. Statement (I) is true and Statement (II) is false

39. Which of the following is equal to

$$\frac{(312)^2 - (126)^2}{(719)^2 - (281)^2}?$$

1. 0.438
2. 0.186
3. 1
4. $\frac{93}{219}$

40. If $a^2 + \frac{1}{a^2} = 51, a > 1,$ then the value of $a - \frac{1}{a}$ is:

1. 11 2. 7
3. 9 4. 5

41. A square and a rectangle have same perimeter. If area of the square is 121 cm^2 and length of the rectangle is 18 cm, then area of the rectangle is:

1. 198 cm^2 2. 324 cm^2
3. 72 cm^2 4. 121 cm^2

42. If $x = 2 + \sqrt{3}$, then the value of $x^3 + x^{-3}$ is:

1. $18\sqrt{3}$ 2. 52
3. $52\sqrt{3}$ 4. 76

43. The value of $(3^2)^3 \times 3^{-5} \times \sqrt[3]{216} \div \sqrt{9} \times \sqrt[3]{8}$ is:

1. 24 2. 12
3. 18 4. 10

44. There are 24 men who can build a wall in 10 days. If the wall is to be built in 8 days, then how many additional men need to be employed?

1. 8 2. 5
3. 6 4. 4

45. If 5 similar pipes can fill a tank in 2 hours 8 minutes, then in how much time 8 similar pipes will fill the tank?

1. 1 hour 15 min. 2. 1 hour 45 min.
3. 1 hour 20 min. 4. 1 hour 30 min.

46. If the cost price of 14 chairs is equal to the selling price of 10 chairs, then the gain percentage is:

1. 45% 2. 33%
3. 40% 4. $28\frac{4}{7}$%

47. The simple interest on a certain sum at the rate of 8.5% for 3 years is ₹ 7,140. Find the simple interest on the same sum at the rate of 7.5% for 2 years.

1. ₹ 4,250 2. ₹ 4,140
3. ₹ 4,200 4. ₹ 3,980

48. In how many years, ₹ 1,500 will produce the same simple interest at the rate of 8% as ₹ 6,000 produce in 3 years at the rate of 4%?

1. 8 2. 6
3. 7 4. 5

49. On compound interest a certain sum of money amounts to ₹ 34,560 in 2 years and to ₹ 41,472 in 3 years at the same rate of interest, Find the rate of interest per annum.

1. 25% 2. 20%
3. 10% 4. 12%

50. The compound interest on a certain sum of money for 2 years at 10% per annum is ₹ 525. The simple interest on the same sum of money for double the time at half the rate of interest per annum is:

1. ₹ 600 2. ₹ 500
3. ₹ 515 4. ₹ 484

Section B : Intelligence

51. In the following sequence, if the first half of the alphabets are written in reverse order, then which is the 9th letter from the right?

(Left) EPMZNRBCKFGHTN (Right)

1. M 2. P
3. K 4. R

52. Choose the odd one out.

1. (12, 49, 5) 2. (14, 36, 4)
3. (13, 25, 8) 4. (11, 64, 3)

53. In a certain code language if 'SCIENCE' is written as 'RBHDMBD' then how will be 'HISTORY' written in the same language?

1. IJTUPSZ 2. GHRSPSX
3. GHTSNQX 4. GHRSNQX

54. 'Teacher' is related to 'Student' in the same way as 'Doctor' is related to:

1. Practice 2. Patient
3. Medicine 4. Hospital

55. 'A' is the father of 'D', 'D' is not his son, 'B' is the brother of 'D', 'C' is the mother of 'B'. How is 'C' related to 'A'?

1. Daughter 2. Mother
3. Wife 4. Sister

56. If the day before yesterday was Sunday, what day of the week is day after tomorrow?

1. Friday 2. Tuesday
3. Wednesday 4. Thursday

57. Which of the following groups of letters can be rearranged to get the word 'TRIANGLE'?

1. ATGRNEIL
2. GLRFTNIE
3. GRIATEMN
4. LRNTLHEA

58. In a certain code language, if 'LATE' is coded as '1234', then how is 'TALE' coded in the same language?

1. 2341 2. 2314
3. 3214 4. 1432

59. Choose the correct mirror image of the following figure (X). If the mirror is kept as shown at line AB.

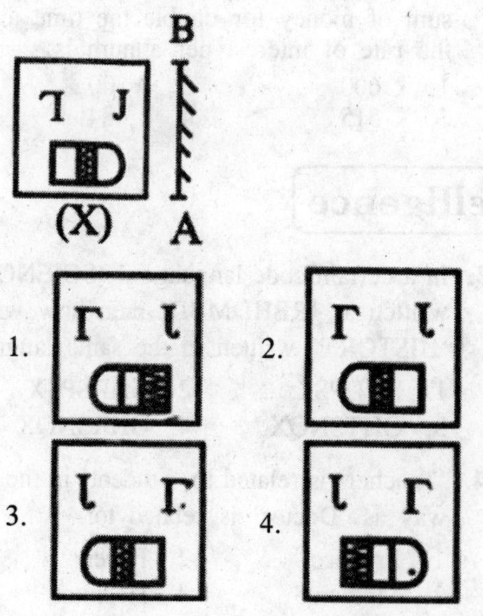

60. One term in the following series is wrong. Find the wrong term.

2483, 3584, 4685, 5786, 6898, 7988

1. 6898 2. 4685
3. 7988 4. 5786

61. Ram goes straight 40 m towards North. He turns left and covers 50 metres and then again turns left. In which direction is he facing now?

1. West 2. South
3. East 4. North

62. If the boy's position in a row is seventh from left end and eighth from right end. How many boys are there in that row?

1. 14 2. 17
3. 15 4. 18

63. Which number will come in the place of question mark (?) to complete the following matrix?

3	5	7	9	11	13
8	23	46	?	116	163

1. 75 2. 78
3. 77 4. 80

64. Find the missing number in the following series:

3, 12, 36, 72, 72, 36, ?

1. 42 2. 48
3. 9 4. 6

65. If 'P' denotes multiplied by, 'T' denotes subtracted by, 'M' denotes added to and 'B' denotes divided by, then 28B7P8T6M4 is equal to:

1. 30 2. 1
3. 25 4. 0

66. A, B, C and D are four friends. A and C like Computer Science while others do not. B and C like Physics while others do not. Who does not like any of these subjects?

1. C 2. A
3. D 4. B

67. Choose the figure from given alternatives which contains figure (X) as it's part.

fig. (X)

1. 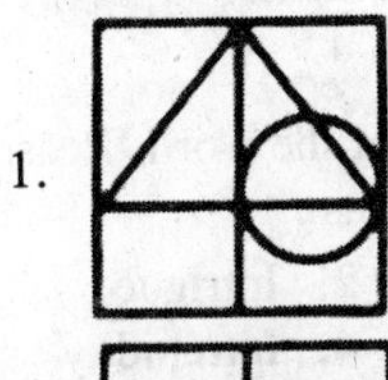

2. 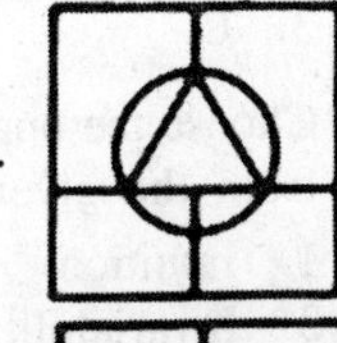

3. 

4. 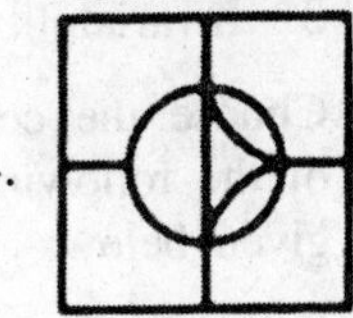

68. Choose the odd one out:

1. WUS   2. NLJ
3. KIG   4. TQN

69. Complete the following analogy:

CAT : 24 :: MAN : ?

1. 25   2. 28
3. 26   4. 22

70. Arrange the given words as they appear in the dictionary.

A. Broucher   B. Brother
C. Broadcast   D. Brought
E. Broadband

1. E, C, B, A, D   2. D, E, C, B, A
3. A, B, C, D, E   4. C, D, E, A, B

71. Complete the following analogy.

Circle : Diameter :: Rectangle : ?

1. Angle   2. Perimeter
3. Diagonal   4. Radius

72. 'Cyclone' is related to 'Anti cyclone' in the same way as 'Flood' is related to:

1. Sea   2. River
3. Drought   4. Operation Flood

73. The members in each figure follow a similar pattern. Find the missing number.

1. 18   2. 17
3. 19   4. 20

74. Amit is faster than Bobby but slower than Dharam. Chetan is the slowest. Who is the fastest among these?

1. Chetan
2. Amit
3. Dharam
4. Bobby

75. The first two figures are related in same way. To establish the similar relation with third figure.

Choose the correct option.

1. 

2. 

3. 

4. 

Section C : English

76. Choose the sentence from the options given below that has the correct usage of transitive verb:

1. The glass broke
2. The elephant walks
3. She burnt with revenge
4. She walks the dog

77. Choose the sentence with the correct "Present Continuous Tense" usage from the options given below:

1. I have known her for a long time
2. I think you are right
3. I am thinking you are right
4. Pawan received his letter a week ago

78. Identify the tense of the following sentence.

"They have been building the stadium for several years".

1. Present Perfect Continuous Tense
2. Present Continuous Tense
3. Present Perfect Tense
4. Simple Present Tense

79. Choose from the options which best describes the underlined idiom:

As usual he is blowing his own trumpet.

1. praising himself and others
2. playing a tune on the trumpet
3. praising himself
4. refusing to use anybody else's trumpet

80. Choose the correct meaning of the underlined idiom from the options given below:

Sukriti and Sara are at cross-purposes.

1. are each others sworn enemies
2. misunderstanding each other
3. are pursuing different things in life
4. are continuously harming each other

81. Choose the correct option to improve the underlined part of sentence:

Krishna is stronger than all students.

1. all the students
2. any other student
3. all student
4. any other students

82. Spot the error in the following sentence:

(A) None of the/ (B) two boys/ (C) could complete/ (D) the job.

1. D
2. B
3. C
4. A

83. Choose the opposite of the word 'Reasoning' from the given options:

1. Intuition
2. Intrigue
3. Invariability
4. Intrepidity

84. Choose the correct passive transformation of the following sentence from the options given below:

It is time to close the office.

1. It is time that the office be closed.
2. It is time that the office is to be closed.
3. It is time for the office to be closed.
4. It is time the office be closed.

85. Choose the correct indirect transformation of the following sentence from the options given below:

My mother said, "You should take proper diet".

1. My mother told me that I should take proper diet.
2. My mother said that I must take the proper diet.
3. My mother told me that I must take the proper diet.
4. My mother said that I should take proper diet.

Directions (Qs. No. 86-90): *Read the passage carefully and answer the questions given below:*

Diagnosing disease and prompting treatment options is one thing, but can artificial intelligence really design new drugs to tackle the source of antimicrobial resistance? Apparently it can, right down to the atom.

Massachusetts Institute of Technology (MIT) has used generative A.I. to structure two new antibiotics that have shown much promise in mice models, killing super bugs that cause drug resistance and MSRA, a bacterial infection many antibiotics fail to cure.

Antimicrobial resistance has become a global public health threat. In 2019, it led to around 5 million deaths, according to World Health Organisation estimates. Excessive use of antibiotics has made bacteria mutate to resist the drug, but very few new antibiotics have been launched over the decades. The MIT study, published in the journal 'cell', aims to bridge the gap.

86. The passage does not talk about
1. use of homeopathy to cure bacterial disease
2. drug resistance
3. bacterial mutation
4. generative A.I.

87. Out of the given options, choose the synonym of 'generative'.

1. generation   2. destructive
3. creative   4. generous

88. According to the passage, around 5 million people lost their lives in 2019 due to:
1. mice models
2. antimicrobial resistance
3. new antibiotics
4. generative A.I.

89. According to the passage, which of the following shows the utility of A.I. in providing treatment options?
1. decoding the journal published by various organisations
2. promoting excessive use of antibiotics
3. providing generative A.I. feature to structure new antibiotics
4. helping bacterial mutation to resist the drug

90. According to the passage, what is the cause of bacterial mutation to resist the drug?

1653 (Sainik Sch

bal public health
ssive use of antibiotics
of 5 million people
enerative A.I.

91. Fil nks with the correct pair of prepo ase from the options given below:

She accepte her settlement claim that wa_____ the insurance company _____ ed by

1. on behalf of, inent.
2. in lieu of, on behaf
3. in event of, in lieu
4. by way of, in lieu of

92. Fill in the blanks with the correct unctions:

She will help you _____ you ask r but he will be penalised _____ that the rges of aiding and abetting are proved beyond doubt.

1. lest, unless   2. provided, if
3. if, provided   4. unless, supposing

93. Choose the correct conjunction to fill in the blank:

_____ she is clever, she often makes mistakes.

1. Yet   2. Since
3. Although   4. Despite

94. Choose the correct spelling from the following options:

1. conspicouous   2. congrous
3. connosseur   4. conjuncture

95. Find out the correctly spelt word from the options:

1. Discrepansy   2. Descrepancy
3. Discripancy   4. Discrepancy

96. Fill in the blank with the suitable question tag:

Somebody has called, _____?

1. haven't they   2. hasn't they
3. have they   4. has they

...estion

...7. Fill in the blank with th... tag:

They haven't come ...

1. hadn't they
2. has they
3. have they
4. haven't the...

98. Choose the conjunction to fill in the blank.

____, my father has always been involved ...ublic affairs.

1. As well as 2. Similarly
3. No matter 4. In addition

99. Fill in the blank with the correct modal verb:

____ you show me the way to the station.

1. May 2. Shall
3. Might 4. Could

100. Fill in the blank with the correct verb:

Five thousand rupees ____ charged by him.

1. were 2. is
3. was 4. am

Section D : General Science

101. ...at is the full form of ORS?
1. Oral Rehydration Solvent
2. Oral Rehydration Solute
3. Oral Rehydration Solution
4. Oral Rehydration Salt

102. What is the range of temperature of laboratory thermometer?
1. 10°C to 110°C 2. –10°C to 110°C
3. –10°C to 90°C 4. 10°C to 90°C

103. Choose the incorrect statement.
1. Fossil fuels can be made in the laboratory.
2. Coal and natural gas are fossil fuels.
3. Fossil fuels are formed from the dead remains of living organisms.
4. Fossil fuels are exhaustible resources.

104. The process of depositing a layer of any desired metal on another material by means of electricity is called ____.
1. Electrostatic 2. Electrophoresis
3. Electroplating 4. Electrolysis

105. The distance - time graph for the motion of an object moving with a constant speed will be ____.
1. Straight Line
2. Elliptical
3. Hyperbolic
4. Parabolic curve

106. The animals such as frog, lizard which lay eggs are called:
1. Carnivorous 2. Oviparous
3. Ovoviviparous 4. Viviparous

107. Distinctive colour of the human eyes are due to which part of the eye?
1. Lens 2. Iris
3. Cornea 4. Pupil

108. Match the micro-organisms given in Column-A with their action given in Column-B:

Column-A	Column-B
A. Rhizobium	*(i)* Causing Malaria
B. Lactobacillus	*(ii)* Rust of Wheat
C. A protozoan	*(iii)* Setting of curd
D. A fungi	*(iv)* Nitrogen fixation

Choose the ***correct*** answer from the options given below.
1. A-(*ii*), B-(*i*), C-(*iv*), D-(*iii*)
2. A-(*iii*), B-(*iv*), C-(*i*), D-(*ii*)
3. A-(*iv*), B-(*iii*), C-(*i*), D-(*ii*)
4. A-(*i*), B-(*ii*), C-(*iii*), D-(*iv*)

109. Choose the correct order for the processing of fibre into wool.
1. Sorting → Rolling → Scouring → Shearing
2. Shearing → Scouring → Sorting → Rolling
3. Scouring → Shearing → Rolling → Sorting
4. Rolling → Scouring → Shearing → Sorting

110. Micro-organisms act upon the dead plants to produce ____.

1. Humus 2. Wood
3. Sand 4. Mushrooms

111. Which of the following relation is correct?

1. $\text{Speed} = \dfrac{1}{\text{Distance} \times \text{Time}}$
2. Speed = Distance × Time
3. $\text{Speed} = \dfrac{\text{Distance}}{\text{Time}}$
4. $\text{Speed} = \dfrac{\text{Time}}{\text{Distance}}$

112. Which of the following statement is NOT true?

1. The process of conversion of water vapour into its liquid state is called condensation.
2. Water changes its state on heating or cooling.
3. Water is found in different states-solid, liquid and gas.
4. Evaporation causes heating effect.

113. The number of oscillations per second of a vibrating object is called as:

1. Velocity 2. Frequency
3. Wavelength 4. Amplitude

114. Which of the following statement is incorrect?

1. Aquatic animals use dissolved oxygen in water for respiration.
2. Air is present in water and soil.
3. We cannot see air, but we can feel it.
4. Air does not occupy space.

115. Which of the following statement is incorrect?

1. A cylindrical magnet has only one pole.
2. Iron, Nickel and Cobalt are magnetic material
3. A freely suspended magnet always aligns in N—S direction.
4. Magnetite is a natural magnet.

116. What is the chemical name of milk of magnesia?

1. Ammonium hydroxide
2. Magnesium hydroxide
3. Calcium hydroxide
4. Sodium hydroxide

117. Choose the correct arrangement of different forces of friction.

1. static friction → sliding friction → rolling friction
2. rolling friction → sliding friction → static friction
3. sliding friction → static friction → rolling friction
4. rolling friction → static friction → sliding friction

118. Match the objects mentioned in Column-I with their action mentioned in Column-II:

Column-I	Column-II
(*i*) Opaque objects	(*a*) allow light to pass through them partially
(*ii*) Transparent objects	(*b*) do not allow light to pass through them
(*iii*) Translucent objects	(*c*) allow light to pass through them and we can see through these objects easily

Choose the ***correct*** answer from the options given below:

1. (*i*)-(*b*), (*ii*)-(*a*), (*iii*)-(*c*)
2. (*i*)-(*c*), (*ii*)-(*b*), (*iii*)-(*a*)
3. (*i*)-(*b*), (*ii*)-(*c*), (*iii*)-(*a*)
4. (*i*)-(*c*), (*ii*)-(*a*), (*iii*)-(*b*)

119. Different types of interactions occurs between organisms.

Match Column-I and Column-II.

Column-I	Column-II
(*a*) Parasitism	1. Both organisms benefit
(*b*) Commensalism	2. One organism benefits while other is harmed

(*c*) Mutualism	3. One organism benefits while the other is not affected

Choose the ***correct*** answer from the options given below.

1. (*a*)-2, (*b*)-1, (*c*)-3
2. (*a*)-1, (*b*)-2, (*c*)-3
3. (*a*)-3, (*b*)-1, (*c*)-2
4. (*a*)-2, (*b*)-3, (*c*)-1

120. Which of the following mirror is used by dentists to see an enlarged image of the teeth?

1. Plane lens
2. Concave mirror
3. Convex mirror
4. Plane mirror

121. What is the function of Alveoli? Choose the correct one.

1. To filter the air
2. To exchange gases
3. Air reaches our lungs through this part
4. To protect lungs

122. What is the function of bile in digestion?

1. Digestion of Fats
2. Digestion of Carbohydrates
3. Digestion of Amino acid
4. Digestion of Proteins

123. Name the process by which heat is transferred from the hotter end to the colder end of an object.

1. Insulation
2. Radiation
3. Conduction
4. Convection

124. Richter scale is used to measure ______.

1. Earthquake
2. Tsunami
3. Lightning
4. Thunder

125. Which of the following is NOT a part of Pistil?

1. Stigma
2. Ovule
3. Anther
4. Style

Section E : Social Science

126. Which among the following is correct in the context of Himalayas?

1. The Himadri have a more moderate climate, allowing rich diversity and human habitation
2. The Shivalik hills are the lowest ranges of the Himalayas
3. Mount Everest is the part of Himachal ranges of Himalayas
4. The Himachal are the highest and most rugged part of the Himalayas

127. Identify the correctly matched pair.

1. Atmospheric Pressure – Hygrometer
2. Atmospheric Pressure – Thermometer
3. Atmospheric Pressure – Anemometer
4. Atmospheric Pressure – Barometer

128. Choose the appropriate option to fill in the blank.

The ______ is a landform that rises up from the surrounding land and has a more or less flat surface, some of its sides are often steep slopes. They have been called 'store house of minerals'.

1. Desert
2. Mountain
3. Plateau
4. Plain

129. Puneet called up his friend who resides in another country. He was surprised to know when his friend told him that it was 6 pm there. While he was calling at 9 pm local time. What is the longitudinal difference between the given two countries?

1. 120°
2. 60°
3. 90°
4. 45°

10. Total CP = 8000 + 8000 = 16000
Table SP = 8000 × 1.08 = 8640
Chair SP = 8000 × 0.96 = 7680
Total SP = 8640 + 7680 = 16320
Profit = 16320 − 16000 = 320

$$\text{Gain } \% = \frac{320}{16000} \times 100 = 2\%.$$

11. V − E + F = 2
18 − 28 + F = 2
F − 10 = 2
F = 12.

12. Volume of 7 spheres $= 7 \times \frac{4}{3}\pi r^3$

$$= 7 \times \frac{4}{3} \times \frac{22}{7} \times 6^3$$

$$= \frac{4}{3} \times 22 \times 216$$

$= 88 \times 72 = 6336 \text{ cm}^3$

Let height of cuboid = h.
$33 \times 24 \times h = 6336$
$792h = 6336$
$h = 8$ cm.

13. Volume of cuboid = 250 × 40 × 100
$= 1000000 \text{ cm}^3$

Let edge of cube = a
$a^3 = 1000000$
$a = 100$ cm = 1 m.

14. Area of parallelogram = base × height
$63 = 7 \times h$
$h = 9$ cm.

15. Half of diagonals $= \frac{8}{2} = 4, \frac{6}{2} = 3$

Side of rhombus:

$$s = \sqrt{4^2 + 3^2}$$

$$= \sqrt{16+9} = \sqrt{25} = 5 \text{ cm}$$

Perimeter = $4s$ = 4 × 5 = 20 cm.

16. Sum of angles of a quadrilateral = 360°
Given ratio: 2 : 4 : 5 : 7

Total parts:
2 + 4 + 5 + 7 = 18

$$\text{One part} = \frac{360}{18} = 20°$$

Smallest angle = 2 × 20° = 40°.

17. At point C, the angles $a°$ and $5a°$ lie on a straight line:
$a + 5a = 180°$
$6a = 180°$
$a = 30°$

In ΔABC:
$x + 4a + a = 180°$
$x + 5a = 180°$
$x + 5(30) = 180°$
$x + 150 = 180°$
$x = 30°$.

18. Right triangle is formed with ladder as hypotenuse.
Hypotenuse = 5 m, Base = 3 m
Using Pythagoras theorem:
$\text{Height}^2 = 5^2 - 3^2$
$= 25 - 9 = 16$

$\text{Height} = \sqrt{16} = 4$ m.

19. In ΔABC:
∠A = 80°, ∠B = 40°
∠C = 180° − (80° + 40°) = 60°

BD bisects ∠B:

$$\angle CBD = \angle ABD = \frac{40°}{2} = 20°$$

CD bisects ∠C:

$$x = \frac{60°}{2} = 30°$$

Now in ΔBDC:
$y + 20° + 30° = 180°$
$y + 50° = 180°$
$y = 130°$.

20. 669 lies between the perfect squares
$25^2 = 625$
and, $26^2 = 676$

So the smallest number to be added to 669 is

$$P = 676 - 669 = 7$$

Now,

$$= \sqrt{3P+4} = \sqrt{3\times7+4}$$

$$= \sqrt{21+4} = \sqrt{25} = 5.$$

21. $x + 16)5x^2 + 70x - 160(5x - 10$

$$\begin{array}{l} 5x^2 + 80x \\ \underline{- \quad -} \\ -10x - 160 \\ -10x - 160 \\ \underline{+ \quad\quad +} \\ \times \quad\quad \times \end{array}$$

Quotient:

$$5x - 10 = 5(x - 2).$$

22. From the bar graph:

School A = 750 − 300 = 450
School B = 680 − 238 = 442
School C = 720 − 324 = 396
School D = 900 − 378 = 522

Maximum number of girls is 522 in School D

Percentage of girls in D:

$$\frac{522}{900}\times100 = 58\%.$$

23. From the pie chart,

percentage of cream B = 20%.

Total number of creams = 800.

$$\text{Number of B creams} = \frac{20}{100}\times800 = 160.$$

24. For divisibility by 2 and 5, the last digit must be 0:

$$b = 0$$

Number becomes $48a0 = 4800 + 10a$

Check divisibility by 7:

$$4800 \div 7 = 685, \text{ remainder } = 5$$

So,

$$4800 + 10a \equiv 5 + 10a \equiv 0 \pmod 7$$

$$10a \equiv -5 \equiv 2 \pmod 7$$

Since $10 \equiv 3 \pmod 7$:

$$3a \equiv 2 \pmod 7$$

Multiplying inverse of 3 (which is 5):

$$a \equiv 2 \times 5 = 10 \equiv 3 \pmod 7$$

$$a = 3,\ b = 0$$

$$10a - b = 30.$$

25. Using divisibility rule of 11:

$$(7 + * + 9 + 5) - (8 + 3 + 4)$$
$$= (21 + *) - 15 = 6 + *$$

For divisibility by 11:

$$6 + * = 11$$
$$* = 5.$$

26. Fractions given:

$$\frac{5}{8}, \frac{3}{4}, \frac{4}{7}, \frac{2}{3}, \frac{5}{9}$$

Convert to decimal form:

$$\frac{5}{8} = 0.625,\ \frac{3}{4} = 0.75,\ \frac{4}{7} \approx 0.571$$

$$\frac{2}{3} \approx 0.667,\ \frac{5}{9} \approx 0.556$$

$$\text{Greatest fraction} = \frac{3}{4}$$

$$\text{Smallest fraction} = \frac{5}{9}$$

$$\text{Difference} = \frac{3}{4} - \frac{5}{9}$$

$$= \frac{27}{36} - \frac{20}{36} = \frac{7}{36}.$$

27. $256 \div \frac{4}{3} + 5\times\frac{4}{3} - 8 \div \frac{27}{24} \times \left(\frac{1}{3} \text{ of } 81\right)$

$$256 \div \frac{4}{3} = 256 \times \frac{3}{4} = 192$$

$$5 \times \frac{4}{3} = \frac{20}{3}$$

$$\frac{1}{3} \text{ of } 81 = 27$$

$$8 \div \frac{27}{24} = 8 \times \frac{24}{27} = \frac{64}{9}$$

$$\frac{64}{9} \times 27 = 64 \times 3 = 192$$

$$192 + \frac{20}{3} - 192 = \frac{20}{3}.$$

28. Let son's present age $= x$

Father's present age $= 5x$

After 10 years:

Father's age $= 5x + 10$

Son's age $= x + 10$

Given:

$$5x + 10 = 3(x + 10)$$
$$5x + 10 = 3x + 30$$
$$5x - 3x = 30 - 10$$
$$2x = 20$$
$$x = 10$$

Father's present age:

$$5x = 5 \times 10 = 50 \text{ years.}$$

29. Let numerator $= x$, then denominator $= 2x + 5$

After changes:

$$\frac{x+4}{(2x+5)-1} = \frac{2}{3}$$
$$\frac{x+4}{2x+4} = \frac{2}{3}$$

Cross multiplication:

$$3(x + 4) = 2(2x + 4)$$
$$3x + 12 = 4x + 8$$
$$4x - 3x = 12 - 8$$
$$x = 4$$

Original fraction:

$$\frac{x}{2x+5} = \frac{4}{13}.$$

30. At B, given exterior angle 70°:

$$\angle ABC = 180° - 70° = 110°$$

In a parallelogram, opposite angles are equal:

$$x = \angle ADC = 110°$$

Adjacent angles are supplementary:

$$\angle DAB = 180° - 110° = 70°$$

At A, the diagonal divides the angle:

$$z + 40° = 70°$$
$$z = 30°$$

In ΔABC:

$$\angle A + \angle B + \angle C = \angle 180°$$
$$z + 110° + y = 180°$$
$$30° + 110° + y = 180°$$
$$y = 40°.$$

31. Mean

$$= \frac{2+5+7+5+12+16+14+18+15+16}{10}$$
$$= \frac{110}{10} = 11.$$

32. Numbers: 8, 10, 12, 14, 16, 18, 20, 22, 24, 26

$$\text{Median} = \frac{16+18}{2} = 17.$$

33.

$$\text{Mode} = 11$$
$$2k + 3 = 11$$
$$2k = 8 \Rightarrow k = 4$$
$$(k + 1)^2 = (4 + 1)^2 = 25.$$

34. Total tosses = 60, heads = 25

$$\text{Tails} = 60 - 25 = 35$$
$$\text{Probability of tail} = \frac{35}{60} = \frac{7}{12}.$$

35. Total number of balls:

$$6 + 8 = 14$$

Number of white balls = 8

$$\text{Probability} = \frac{8}{14} = \frac{4}{7}.$$

36. Marked price = ₹ 2400

First discount = 25%

$$2400 \times \frac{5}{100} = 1800$$

Additional discount = 30% on the reduced price

$$= 1800 \times \frac{70}{100} = 1260$$

So the customer has to pay ₹ 1260.

37. Marked price = ₹ 800

Discount = 10%

$$\text{Selling Price} = 800 \times \frac{90}{100} = 720$$

Profit = 20%

Selling Price = 120% of Cost Price

$$720 = \frac{120}{100} \times CP$$

$$CP = 720 \times \frac{100}{120} = 600$$

So the cost price is ₹ 600.

38. **Statement (I):** $(4a + 2ab - c) + (6a + 3c)$

$= 4a + 6a + 2ab - c + 3c$

$= 10a + 2ab + 2c$

Given result is $(10a + 2ab + 4c)$, which is incorrect.

So Statement (I) is false.

Statement (II): $(4a + 2ab - c) - (6a + 3c)$

$= 4a + 2ab - c - 6a - 3c$

$= -2a + 2ab - 4c$

This matches the given result.

So Statement (II) is true.

39. $$\frac{(312)^2 - (126)^2}{(719)^2 - (281)^2}$$

Using identity:

$$a^2 - b^2 = (a - b)(a + b)$$

Numerator $= (312 - 126)(312 + 126)$

$= 186 \times 438$

Denominator $= (719 - 281)(719 + 281)$

$= 438 \times 1000$

$$= \frac{186 \times 438}{438 \times 1000}$$

$$= \frac{186}{1000} = 0.186.$$

40. Given:

$$a^2 + \frac{1}{a^2} = 51$$

Use identity:

$$\left(a - \frac{1}{a}\right)^2 = a^2 + \frac{1}{a^2} - 2$$

$= 51 - 2 = 49$

$a - \frac{1}{a} = \sqrt{49} = 7$(since $a > 1$).

41. Area of square $= 121$ cm^2

Side $= \sqrt{121} = 11$

Perimeter of square:

$4 \times 11 = 44$

For rectangle:

$2(l + b) = 44 \Rightarrow l + b = 22$

Given $l = 18$:

$18 + b = 22 \Rightarrow b = 4$

Area $= 18 \times 4 = 72$ cm^2.

42. Given:

$$x = 2 + \sqrt{3}$$

$$\frac{1}{x} = 1/(2+\sqrt{3}) = 2 - \sqrt{3}$$

$$x + \frac{1}{x} = (2 + \sqrt{3}) + (2 - \sqrt{3}) = 4$$

Use identity:

$$x^3 + \frac{1}{x^3} = \left(x + \frac{1}{x}\right)^3 - 3\left(x + \frac{1}{x}\right)$$

$= 4^3 - 3 \times 4$

$= 64 - 12 = 52.$

43. $(3^2)^3 \times 3^{-5} \times \sqrt[3]{216} \div \sqrt{9} \times \sqrt[3]{8}$

$(3^2)^3 = 3^6$

$3^6 \times 3^{-5} = 3^{6-5} = 3$

$\sqrt[3]{216} = 6$, $\sqrt{9} = 3$, $\sqrt[3]{8} = 2$

Now, $3 \times 6 \div 3 \times 2$

$= 18 \div 3 \times 2$

$= 6 \times 2 = 12.$

44. Work $\propto$ men $\times$ days

$24 \times 10 = 240$ man-days

Required men for 8 days:

$$\text{Men} = \frac{240}{8} = 30$$

Additional men:

$30 - 24 = 6.$

45. Time for 5 pipes:

2 h 8 min = 128 min

Work rate $\propto$ number of pipes:

$$\text{Time with 8 pipes} = \frac{5}{8} \times 128$$

= 80 min = 1 h 20 min.

46. Let CP of 1 chair = C

CP of 14 chairs = 14C

SP of 10 chairs = 14C

SP of 1 chair = $\frac{14C}{10}$ = 1.4C

Profit = 1.4C − C = 0.4C

Gain % = $\frac{0.4C}{C} \times 100$ = 40%.

47. $SI = \frac{P \times R \times T}{100}$

Given:

$7140 = \frac{P \times 8.5 \times 3}{100}$

$7140 = \frac{P \times 25.5}{100}$

$P = \frac{7140 \times 100}{25.5} = 28000$

Now, required simple interest:

$SI = \frac{28000 \times 7.5 \times 2}{100}$

$= 28000 \times \frac{15}{100} = 4200.$

48. Simple interest on ₹ 6000 for 3 years at 4%:

$SI = \frac{6000 \times 4 \times 3}{100} = 720$

Now for ₹ 1500 at 8%, let time = *t* years.

$\frac{1500 \times 8 \times t}{100} = 720$

$120t = 720$

$t = 6.$

49. Amount after 2 years:

$A_2 = 34560$

Amount after 3 years:

$A_3 = 41472$

So, $\frac{A_3}{A_2} = 1 + \frac{R}{100}$

$\frac{41472}{34560} = 1 + \frac{R}{100}$

$1.2 = 1 + \frac{R}{100}$

$\frac{R}{100} = 0.2$

R = 20%.

50. For 2 years at 10%,

$CI = P\left[\left(1 + \frac{10}{100}\right)^2 - 1\right]$

$525 = P[(1.1)^2 - 1]$

$525 = P(1.21 - 1)$

$525 = 0.21P$

$P = \frac{525}{0.21} = 2500$

Now simple interest for double time = 4 years and half rate = 5%:

$SI = \frac{2500 \times 5 \times 4}{100}$ = ₹ 500.

51. The given sequence is:

E P M Z N R B C K F G H T N.

Total letters = 14,

So, first half = E P M Z N R B

and second half = C K F G H T N.

Reversing the first half gives B R N Z M P E.

New sequence becomes B R N Z M P E C K F G H T N.

Counting from the right: N(1), T(2), H(3), G(4), F(5), K(6), C(7), E(8), P(9).

Hence the required letter is P.

52. In the other three groups, the pattern is:

first number − third number

= square root of the middle number.

For (12, 49, 5),

we get $12 - 5 = 7 = \sqrt{49}$;

for (13, 25, 8), $13 - 8 = 5 = \sqrt{25}$;

for (11, 64, 3), $11 - 3 = 8 = \sqrt{64}$.

But in (14, 36, 4), 14 − 4 = 10, whereas $\sqrt{36}$ = 6, so it does not follow the pattern.

53. In SCIENCE → RBHDMBD, each letter is replaced by the letter just before it in the alphabet:
S → R, C → B, I → H, E → D, N → M.
Applying the same rule to HISTORY
Gives H → G, I → H, S → R, T → S, O → N, R → Q, Y → X.
Therefore the coded form is GHRSNQX.

54. A teacher teaches a student, so the relation is between the professional and the person receiving the service. In the same way, a doctor treats a patient. Hence "Doctor" is related to "Patient" in the same manner as "Teacher" is related to "Student".

55. A is the father of D, and D is not a son, so D is A's daughter. B is the brother of D, so B and D are children of the same parents. Since C is the mother of B, C is also the mother of D. Therefore A and C are the parents of B and D, so C is the wife of A.

56. If day before yesterday was Sunday, then yesterday was Monday and today is Tuesday. Therefore tomorrow will be Wednesday and day after tomorrow will be Thursday. Hence the required day is Thursday.

57. The word TRIANGLE contains the letters T, R, I, A, N, G, L, E. In option 1, the letters A, T, G, R, N, E, I, L can be rearranged exactly to form TRIANGLE. The other groups do not contain the exact required set of letters. Hence option 1 is correct.

58. From LATE = 1234,
We get L = 1, A = 2, T = 3, E = 4.
Therefore, TALE = T A L E = 3 2 1 4.
So the code for TALE is 3214.

59. The mirror is placed along line AB on the right side, so a horizontal reflection (left-right reversal) occurs.
Letter T will appear reversed horizontally (its top bar shifts direction).
Letter J will also flip left-right.
The capsule shape at the bottom will also reverse, so its filled/dotted portion shifts from right to left.
Checking options:
Only Option 3 correctly shows:
both letters properly mirrored,
and the bottom figure reversed in left-right direction.
Hence, the correct mirror image is Option 3.

60. In the series, each digit except 8 increases by 1 from one term to the next: 2483 → 3584 → 4685 → 5786. So the next term should be 6887, and after that 7988. Since 6898 is given instead of 6887, it is the wrong term.

61. Ram initially faces North. A left turn from North makes him face West. After moving, another left turn from West makes him face South. Hence, his final direction is South.

62. Total number of boys = (position from left + position from right − 1)
= (7 + 8 − 1) = 15 – 1 = 14.
Hence, there are 14 boys in the row.

63. Observe the pattern column-wise. Each number in the lower row is obtained by squaring the number above it and then subtracting consecutive natural numbers.

$3^2 = 9,\ 9 - 1 = 8$
$5^2 = 25,\ 25 - 2 = 23$
$7^2 = 49,\ 49 - 3 = 46$
$9^2 = 81,\ 81 - 4 = 77$
$11^2 = 121,\ 121 - 5 = 116$
$13^2 = 169,\ 169 - 6 = 163$

So the missing number is 77, which is option 3.

64. The pattern is ×4, ×3, ×2, ×1, ÷2, ÷4.

Thus, $3 \times 4 = 12$,

$12 \times 3 = 36$,

$36 \times 2 = 72$,

$72 \times 1 = 72$,

$72 \div 2 = 36$,

and $36 \div 4 = 9$.

Hence, the missing number is 9.

65. Replacing the symbols, 28B7P8T6M4 becomes $28 \div 7 \times 8 - 6 + 4$.

Now, $28 \div 7 = 4$,

$4 \times 8 = 32$,

$32 - 6 = 26$,

and $26 + 4 = 30$.

Therefore, the value is 30.

66. A and C like Computer Science. B and C like Physics. So A likes only Computer Science, B likes only Physics, C likes both subjects, and D likes neither of them. Therefore, D does not like any of these subjects.

67. The given figure (X) consists of a central circle intersected by vertical and horizontal lines, along with a triangular shape inside the circle. The required option must contain all these elements in the same relative arrangement.

On careful observation:

Option 2 clearly includes the circle at the center,

the vertical and horizontal dividing lines, and the triangular structure aligned similarly within the circle.

Other options either distort the triangle, shift the circle, or do not preserve the exact intersection pattern. Hence, option 2 correctly contains figure (X) as its part.

68. In WUS, NLJ and KIG, each letter is followed by a letter 2 places behind in the alphabet:

W → U → S, N → L → J, K → I → G.

But in TQN, the pattern is T → Q → N, that is 3 places behind each time.

Hence TQN is the odd one out.

69. The value is obtained by adding the alphabetical positions of the letters.

For CAT,

C = 3, A = 1, T = 20,

So $3 + 1 + 20 = 24$.

Similarly, for MAN,

M = 13, A = 1, N = 14,

So $13 + 1 + 14 = 28$.

Therefore the required number is 28.

70. In dictionary order, the words are arranged by comparing letters from left to right. Among the given words, Broadband comes first, then Broadcast. After that comes Brother, then Broucher, and finally Brought. Therefore the correct arrangement is E, C, B, A, D.

71. A diameter is a line segment that passes through the center of a circle and joins two points on the circle. In the same way, a diagonal is the important line segment inside a rectangle joining two opposite corners. Hence Rectangle is related to Diagonal.

72. Cyclone and anti-cyclone are opposite weather conditions. In the same manner, flood and drought are opposite conditions related to water availability. Hence the correct analogy is Flood : Drought.

73. Observe the pattern in each circle: the bottom number = (product of the two top numbers) ÷ 2.

First circle: $8 \times 3 = 24$, $24 \div 2 = 12$

Second circle: $7 \times 6 = 42$, $42 \div 2 = 21$

Third circle: $9 \times 4 = 36$, $36 \div 2 = 18$

Hence, the missing number is 18.

74. Amit is faster than Bobby, so Amit > Bobby. Amit is slower than Dharam, so Dharam > Amit. Chetan is the slowest, so he is below all of them. Therefore the order is Dharam > Amit > Bobby > Chetan.

Hence, the fastest is Dharam.

75. In the first pair, the figures are transformed by changing the positions of the symbols with respect to the diagonal. Applying the same pattern to the third figure, the @ moves to the upper left region, the black circle shifts to the right side, and the triangle comes to the lower left region. Among the given alternatives, only Option 3 shows all three symbols in the required corresponding positions.

Hence, the answer is Option 3.

76. A transitive verb requires a direct object. In this sentence, "walks" acts on the object "the dog," making it a correct example of a transitive verb usage.

77. Present continuous tense is formed using "am/is/are + verb-ing." Among the options, only the sentence 'I am thinking you are right' follows that structure, even though it is not commonly preferred in standard usage.

78. The structure "have been building" shows an action that started in the past and is continuing in the present, which is characteristic of the present perfect continuous tense.

79. The idiom "blowing his own trumpet" means boasting or praising oneself. Hence, it refers to self-praise.

80. The idiom "at cross-purposes" means people are not understanding each other correctly, often due to miscommunication.

81. In comparative degree, one is compared with the rest excluding itself. "All students" includes Krishna, so the correct form is "any other student."

82. "None" is used for more than two. Sinc only two boys are mentioned, "neither should be used. Hence error is in part A

83. Reasoning involves logical thinking, whi intuition means understanding without logic reasoning, making it the opposite.

84. Passive transformation requires shifting focu to "the office" using "for + object + t be + past participle."

85. My mother told me that I should tak proper diet/My mother said that I shoul take proper diet: Both are acceptable. "Tol me" is appropriate for advice with an object while "said that" is also grammatically correct in indirect speech.

86. The passage discusses generative A.I., drug resistance, bacterial mutation, and antimicrobial resistance, but it does not mention anything about homeopathy.

87. "Generative" refers to producing or creating something new. Hence, the closest synonym among the options is "creative."

88. The passage clearly states that in 2019, around 5 million deaths were caused due to antimicrobial resistance.

89. The passage highlights that MIT used generative A.I. to design new antibiotics, showing its role in treatment development.

90. The passage explicitly mentions that excessive use of antibiotics has caused bacteria to mutate and develop resistance.

91. "In lieu of" means in place of. Here, she accepted the offer in place of her settlement claim, which fits logically. "On behalf of" means representing someone, so the insurance company acted on behalf of their client, making the sentence correct and meaningful.

92. "If" is used to introduce a simple condition — she will help you if you ask her. "Provided" means on the condition that, and it fits the second clause where punishment depends on proof. Thus, both parts form a grammatically correct and logically consistent sentence.

93. The sentence shows contrast — she is clever, yet she makes mistakes. "Although" is the correct conjunction used to express such contrast. Other options do not properly convey this relationship.

94. Among the options, only "conjuncture" is correctly spelt. The others contain spelling errors such as extra or misplaced letters.

95. "Discrepancy" is the correct spelling meaning difference or inconsistency. All other options are incorrect spellings.

96. "Somebody" is grammatically singular but takes plural pronoun "they" in tags. The auxiliary "has" in the statement changes to "haven't" in the question tag, making it correct.

97. The sentence is negative ("haven't"), so the question tag must be positive. Hence "have they" is correct.

98. This phrase is used to add information. It correctly connects "teaching" with "being involved in public affairs," maintaining proper grammatical structure.

99. "Could you show me..." is the most polite and commonly used form when asking for directions. Other options are less appropriate in tone.

100. "Five thousand rupees" represents a single amount, so it is treated as singular. Therefore, the correct verb is "was."

101. ORS is a mixture of salts and glucose dissolved in water used to treat dehydration, especially in diarrhoea. It helps restore lost fluids and electrolytes in the body.

102. A laboratory thermometer is designed to measure a wider range of temperatures compared to a clinical thermometer. Its usual range extends from –10°C to 110°C, making it suitable for experiments.

103. Fossil fuels take millions of years to form from dead organisms under high pressure and temperature. They cannot be artificially produced in laboratories, making this statement incorrect.

104. Electroplating is the process of depositing a thin layer of metal over another material using electric current. It is commonly used to prevent corrosion and improve appearance.

105. When an object moves with constant speed, equal distances are covered in equal intervals of time. Hence, the distance-time graph is a straight line with constant slope.

106. Animals that lay eggs are called oviparous. Frog and lizard reproduce by laying eggs, so they fall under this category.

107. The iris is the coloured part of the eye. The variation in pigments in the iris determines the colour of a person's eyes.

108. Rhizobium fixes nitrogen, Lactobacillus helps in setting curd, protozoans like Plasmodium cause malaria, and fungi cause diseases like rust of wheat.

Hence the correct matching is option 3.

109. Wool processing starts with shearing (removing fleece), then scouring (cleaning), followed by sorting and finally rolling into fibres.

110. Micro-organisms decompose dead plants and animals into simpler substances, forming humus, which enriches soil fertility.

111. Speed is defined as the distance travelled per unit time. Mathematically, it is expressed as distance divided by time.

Therefore, the correct relation is:

$$\text{Speed} = \frac{\text{Distance}}{\text{Time}}.$$

112. Evaporation actually causes a cooling effect because higher-energy particles escape from the liquid, lowering the temperature of the remaining liquid. Hence this statement is not true.

113. Frequency is the number of oscillations completed in one second. It is measured in Hertz and defines how fast an object vibrates.

114. Air is matter and occupies space. This statement is incorrect, while the other statements correctly describe air.

115. Every magnet has two poles—north and south. Hence this statement is incorrect.

116. Milk of magnesia is chemically magnesium hydroxide and is commonly used as an antacid.

117. Static friction is the maximum, followed by sliding friction, and rolling friction is the least. Option 1 shows decreasing order, while option 2 shows increasing order. Both represent the correct relationship among the three types of friction.

118. Opaque objects do not allow light to pass, transparent objects allow light fully, and translucent objects allow light partially.

119. Parasitism harms one organism, commensalism leaves one unaffected, and mutualism benefits both organisms.

120. A concave mirror forms an enlarged image when the object is placed within its focal length, which helps dentists examine teeth clearly.

121. Alveoli are tiny air sacs in the lungs where the exchange of gases takes place. Oxygen from inhaled air diffuses into the blood, and carbon dioxide from the blood diffuses into the alveoli to be exhaled.

122. Bile does not directly digest fats but helps in their digestion by emulsifying them into smaller droplets. This increases the surface area for enzymes to act, aiding fat digestion.

123. Conduction is the process by which heat is transferred from the hotter end to the colder end of an object through direct contact of particles without movement of the material.

124. The Richter scale is used to measure the magnitude or intensity of earthquakes by quantifying the energy released during seismic activity.

125. The pistil consists of stigma, style, and ovary (which contains ovules). Anther is part of the stamen, not the pistil.

126. The Shivalik range forms the outermost and lowest part of the Himalayas. The Himadri are the highest, while Himachal are middle ranges.

127. Atmospheric pressure is measured using a barometer. Other instruments measure different parameters like humidity (hygrometer), temperature (thermometer), and wind speed (anemometer).

128. A plateau is an elevated flat landform with steep sides in many cases and is rich in mineral resources, hence called the "storehouse of minerals."

129. The time difference between the two places is 9 pm – 6 pm = 3 hours. The Earth rotates 360° in 24 hours, so in 1 hour it rotates 15°. Therefore, in 3 hours the longitudinal difference is $3 \times 15 = 45°$. Hence, the required longitudinal difference is 45°.

130. The Non-Cooperation Movement started in 1920, not 1928. Other pairs are correctly matched with their respective years.

131. The Lok Sabha consists of 543 elected members, directly chosen by the people through elections. The Rajya Sabha has 233 elected members, who are elected by the elected members of State Legislative

Assemblies. In addition, 12 members are nominated to the Rajya Sabha by the President for their expertise in fields like art, literature, science, etc. Hence, the correct matching is I-C, II-A, III-B.

132. The Parliament of India is composed of the President, Lok Sabha (Lower House), and Rajya Sabha (Upper House). Panchayat Samiti is part of the three-tier local self-government system at the block level, not a component of Parliament. Therefore, it is not part of the Indian Parliament.

133. Terrace farming is practiced in hilly regions where land is sloped. Steps or terraces are created to reduce the speed of water flow, which prevents soil erosion. It also helps in retaining water and nutrients, making cultivation possible on slopes.

134. Gram Panchayat is the lowest level of rural local self-government, functioning at the village level. It is responsible for basic civic administration, sanitation, water supply, and development activities. The other options are part of higher legislative bodies, not local governance.

135. The Indian Constitution divides powers into three lists. The Concurrent List allows both Union and State governments to legislate on the same subjects like education, forests, etc. In case of conflict, the Union law prevails over the State law.

136. Lothal is a prominent site of the Indus Valley Civilization located in Gujarat, known for its dockyard. Ropar is in Punjab (not Himachal), Kalibangan is in Rajasthan (not Punjab), and Dholavira is in Gujarat (not Rajasthan). Hence, only option 1 is correct.

137. The Subsidiary Alliance system was introduced by Lord Wellesley in 1798. Under this system, Indian rulers accepted British protection and maintained British troops. Hyderabad was the first state to accept this alliance, marking the beginning of British political control expansion.

138. Harisena was the court poet and minister of Samudragupta. He composed the Prayaga Prashasti (Allahabad Pillar Inscription), which describes the achievements and conquests of Samudragupta in detail.

139. The Chinese traveller Fa-Hien visited India during the reign of Chandragupta II of the Gupta Empire (4th–5th century CE). He came to study Buddhist texts and practices and described the social and religious conditions of India.

140. In the Lok Sabha, seats are reserved to ensure representation of Scheduled Tribes. As per constitutional provisions, 47 constituencies are reserved for Scheduled Tribes, enabling their participation in the democratic process and governance.

141. Sustainable development focuses on judicious use of resources, maintaining a balance between present needs and future requirements. It emphasizes conservation so that resources are available for future generations. Unlimited use of resources contradicts sustainability, so B is incorrect.

142. The Thar region is a hot desert located in western India, mainly Rajasthan. It is characterized by low rainfall, sandy terrain, and sparse vegetation, which are typical desert features.

143. Wind is correctly defined as the movement of air from high pressure to low pressure areas. Statement II is incorrect because wind is also influenced by factors like temperature and Earth's rotation. Statement III is incorrect as a hygrometer measures humidity, not wind direction.

144. Agricultural runoff leads to loss of water and soil nutrients, causing environmental damage. It is not a conservation method,

whereas sprinkler, drip irrigation, and rainwater harvesting help conserve water.

145. The equator lies at 0° latitude and divides the Earth into two equal halves. It is the longest latitude because it has the maximum circumference compared to all other latitudes.

146. Rani Lakshmibai led the revolt from Jhansi, Nana Saheb from Kanpur, Kunwar Singh from Bihar, and Birjis Qadr from Lucknow. Hence, the correct matching is option 1.

147. Lord Cornwallis introduced the Permanent Settlement in 1793 in Bengal. It fixed land revenue permanently and recognized zamindars as landowners responsible for revenue collection.

148. The Battle of Plassey in 1757 was fought between the British East India Company and Siraj-ud-Daulah, leading to British political control in Bengal.

149. Krishnadeva Raya of the Vijayanagara Empire authored 'Amuktamalyada', a famous Telugu literary work reflecting devotion and statecraft.

150. The time difference is calculated as 2024 – 330 = 1694. Therefore, the event dates back 1694 years from 2024.

Previous Paper (Solved)

All India Sainik Schools Entrance Exam (AISSEE)–2025*

Class-IX

Section A : Mathematics

1. If surface area and volume of a cube are numerically equal, then the side of the cube is:

1. 4 unit
2. 5 unit
3. 6 unit
4. 8 unit

2. Which one of the following options is a top view of the below given figure?

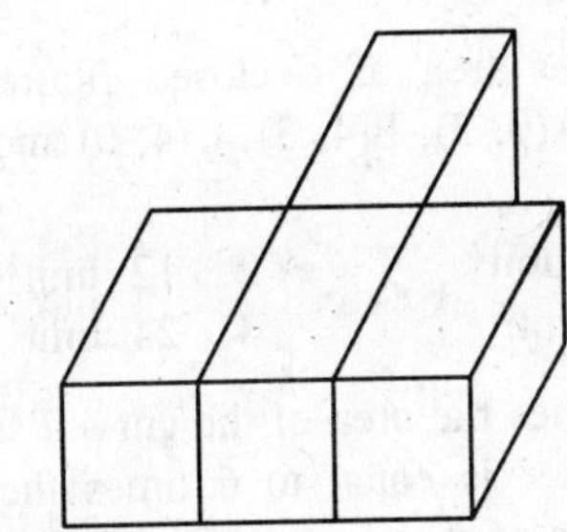

A.
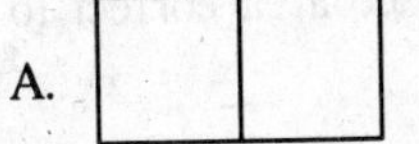

B.
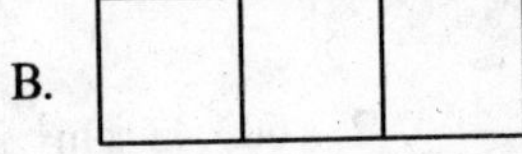

C.
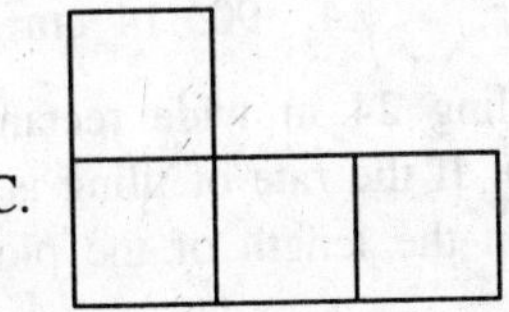

D.
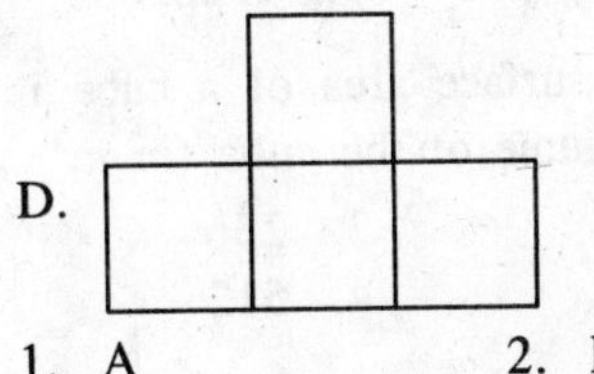

1. A 2. B
3. C 4. D

3. Following Bar-graph represents the manufacture and sale of an item by a firm in 4 months:

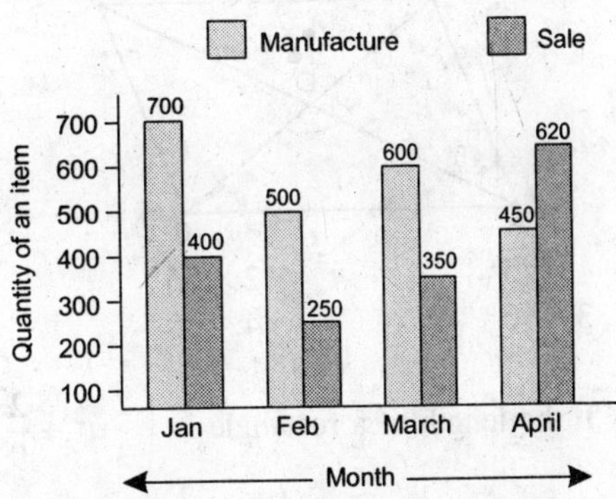

Total sale during the given months is what per cent of the total manufacture during the month?

1. 70% 2. 72%
3. 74% 4. 75%

4. Suresh earns ₹ 72000 per month. Distribution of his monthly earning is presented in the following pie-chart:

*Exam held on 05/04/2025

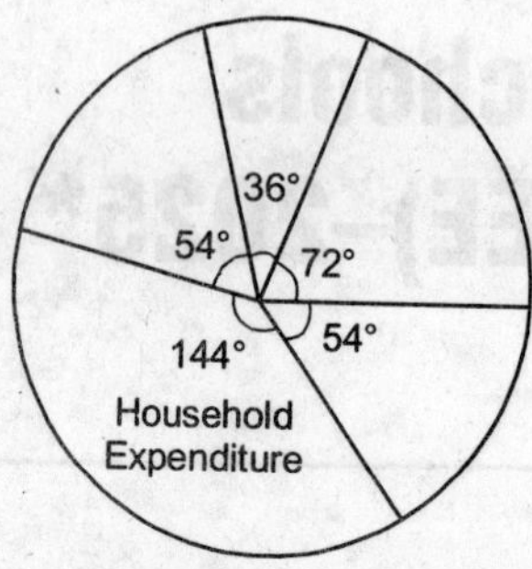

How much money he spends on household expenditures every month?

1. ₹ 32000
2. ₹ 30800
3. ₹ 28800
4. ₹ 28500

5. The lateral surface area of a cube is 256 m^2. The volume of the cube (in m^3) is:

1. 64
2. 256
3. 216
4. 512

6. In the figure, diagonals AC and BD of a parallelogram ABCD intersect each other at point O, such that $\angle DAC = 45°$ and $\angle AOB = 110°$. The measure of $\angle DBC$ is:

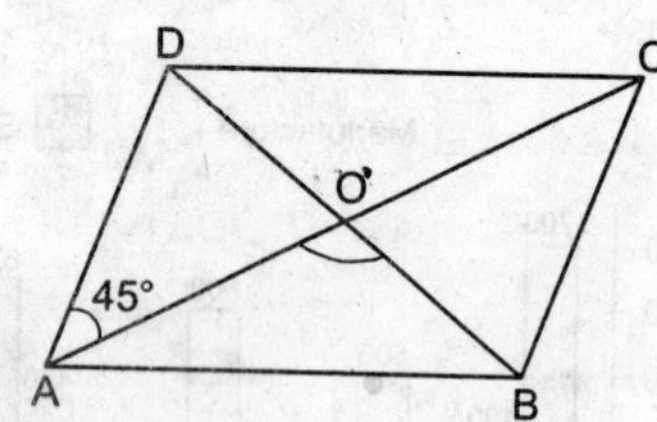

1. 45°
2. 55°
3. 50°
4. 65°

7. If the length of a rectangle is $\left(\frac{2}{3}a^2 + \frac{2}{9}\right)$ m and its breadth is $\left(a^2 + \frac{1}{6}\right)$ m, then the area of the rectangle (in m^2) is:

1. $\frac{2}{3}a^4 + \frac{1}{3}a^2 + \frac{2}{27}$
2. $\frac{2}{3}a^4 + \frac{1}{18}a^2 + \frac{1}{27}$
3. $\frac{2}{3}a^4 + \frac{1}{3}a^2 + \frac{1}{27}$
4. $\frac{2}{3}a^4 + \frac{2}{9}a^2 + \frac{1}{27}$

8. A wall of length $(5x + 2)$ unit and height $6x$ unit has a square window of side $2x$ unit and a door of width $2x$ unit and height $3x$ unit. Which of the following algebraic expressions gives the area of the wall to be painted?

1. $4x(5x + 2)$
2. $5x(2x + 3)$
3. $20x^2 + 3$
4. $4x(5x + 3)$

9. If the height of a triangle is $(4x^2 + 6)$ unit and the base of that triangle is $(3x^2 - 4)$ unit, then the area of the triangle in sq. unit is:

1. $2(6x^4 + x^2 - 6)$
2. $6x^4 + x^2 - 12$
3. $12x^4 - 2x^2 - 6$
4. $6x^2 + x - 12$

10. What should be added to $4c(-a - 2b + c)$ to obtain $3c(a - b + c) - 2c(a + b - c)$?

1. $5ac - 3bc + 9c^2$
2. $5ac + 3bc + c^2$
3. $-3ac - 13bc + 9c^2$
4. $-3ac - 3bc - c^2$

11. Find the area of a closed figure ABCO, where A(0, 3), B(4, 3), C(4, 0) and O is the origin:

1. 18 $unit^2$
2. 12 $unit^2$
3. 6 $unit^2$
4. 24 $unit^2$

12. Four times the area of the curved surface of a cylinder is equal to 6 times the sum of the areas of its bases. If its height is 12 cm then its curved surface area correct to two decimal places is:

$\left(\text{use } \pi = \frac{22}{7}\right)$

1. 301.71 cm^2
2. 603.43 cm^2
3. 452.57 cm^2
4. 905.14 cm^2

13. The cost of tiling 24 m wide rectangular plot is ₹ 39000. If the rate of tiling is ₹ 25 per sq. m, then the length of the plot is:

1. 49 m
2. 63 m
3. 60 m
4. 65 m

14. A square of side 60 m and rectangle of length 80 m have the same perimeter. The difference in their areas is:

1. 200 m^2 2. 600 m^2
3. 400 m^2 4. 500 m^2

15. By what number should $(-8)^{-3}$ be multiplied so that the product is equal to $(-6)^{-3}$?

1. $\frac{3^2}{2^4}$ 2. $\frac{2^4}{3^2}$
3. $\frac{3^3}{4^3}$ 4. $\frac{4^3}{3^3}$

16. In the following three-digit numbers, values of A and B are:

$$\begin{array}{r} B\ A\ A \\ +\ B\ A\ A \\ \hline 3\ A\ 8 \\ \hline \end{array}$$

1. A = 9, B = 2
2. A = 3, B = 2
3. A = 4, B = 1
4. A = 9, B = 1

17. A three-digit number 2a3 is added to the number 326 to give a three-digit number 5b9 which is divisible by 9. The value of $(b - a)$ is:

1. 4 2. 2
3. 1 4. 3

18. Read the following statements carefully and choose the correct option:

Statement I: Number of the form 3N + 2 will leave remainder 2 when divided by 3.

Statement II: If N upon dividing by 5 leaves remainder 3 and N upon dividing by 2 leaves remainder 0, then N upon dividing by 10 leaves remainder 4.

1. Statement I is false and statement II is true
2. Statement I is true and statement II is false
3. Both statements I and II are true
4. Both statements I and II are false

19. Read the following statements carefully and choose the correct option:

Statement I: Triangle is a polygon whose sum of exterior angles is double the sum of its interior angles.

Statement II: If the sum of interior angles of a polygon is double the sum of its exterior angles, then it is a hexagon.

Statement III: If the interior angles of a triangle are in the ratio 1 : 2 : 3, then the ratio of its exterior angles is 3 : 2 : 1.

1. Only statement III is true
2. Only statement III is false
3. All statements I, II and III are true
4. All statements I, II and III are false

20. 7 men can do a piece of work in 16 days. The number of men required to do double the work in 8 days is:

1. 14 2. 24
3. 28 4. 32

21. A jar contains 6 red, 5 green, 4 blue and 5 yellow marbles of the same size. What is the probability that a red colour marble is chosen at random?

1. $\frac{3}{5}$ 2. $\frac{3}{10}$
3. $\frac{2}{5}$ 4. $\frac{7}{10}$

22. A bag contains 16 cards bearing numbers from 1 top 16. One card is chosen at random. The probability that the chosen card bears a prime number is:

1. $\frac{5}{8}$ 2. $\frac{7}{16}$
3. $\frac{5}{16}$ 4. $\frac{3}{8}$

23. Read the following statements carefully and choose the correct option:

Statement I: For all rational numbers x and y, $x - y = y - x$.

Statement II: For all rational numbers x, y and z, $x + (y \times z) = (x + y) \times (x + z)$.

1. Statement I is true and statement II is false
2. Statement I is false and statement II is true
3. Both statements I and II are true
4. Both statements I and II are false

24. A can dig a trench in 12 days, B can dig it in 16 days and C can dig it in 18 days. If they dig the trench, working together and get a sum of ₹ 5800 for it, then share of A in the sum is:

1. ₹ 2000 2. ₹ 1600
3. ₹ 2400 4. ₹ 2800

25. A wire of length 88 cm was bent into the shape of a circle and then into a square. Which figure encloses more area and by how much? $\left(\text{Use } \pi = \frac{22}{7}\right)$

1. Square by 640 cm^2
2. Square by 320 cm^2
3. Circle by 132 cm^2
4. Circle by 264 cm^2

26. There is a circular garden and a path runs outside it along its boundary. A man walks around it only once keeping close to the edge. His each step is 66 cm long and he takes exactly 400 steps to go around the garden. The diameter of the garden is: $\left(\text{Use } \pi = \frac{22}{7}\right)$

1. 840 cm 2. 42 m
3. 420 cm 4. 84 m

27. A train runs between two stations A and B. While running from A to B its average speed is 60 km/h and when running from B to A, its average speed is 90 km/h. The average speed of the train during the two-way journey is:

1. 72 km/h 2. 75 km/h
3. 78 km/h 4. 60 km/h

28. The weights (in kg) of 8 children are 13.4, 10.6, 12.7, 17.2, 14.3, 15, 16.5, 9.8. Their median weight (in kg) is:

1. 13.5 2. 15.75
3. 13.85 4. 15.5

29. The average height of 30 boys was calculated to be 150 cm. It was found later that for one boy 165 cm was wrongly copied as 135 cm during computation of the average. The correct average is:

1. 149 cm 2. 151 cm
3. 153 cm 4. 152 cm

30. A polyhedron has 40 faces and 60 edges. The number of vertices of the polyhedron is:

1. 18 2. 20
3. 22 4. 24

31. The population of a city was 66,150 in 2005. If the population increased at the rate of 5% per annum, then the population in 2003 was:

1. 61,250 2. 60,000
3. 62,150 4. 63,400

32. A sum of money invested at $8\frac{1}{3}\%$ per annum simple interest, amounted to ₹ 2475 in 1 year 9 months. What will it amount to in 2 years at 5% per annum?

1. ₹ 2260 2. ₹ 2160
3. ₹ 2376 4. ₹ 2476

33. For the given figure, which of the following is true?

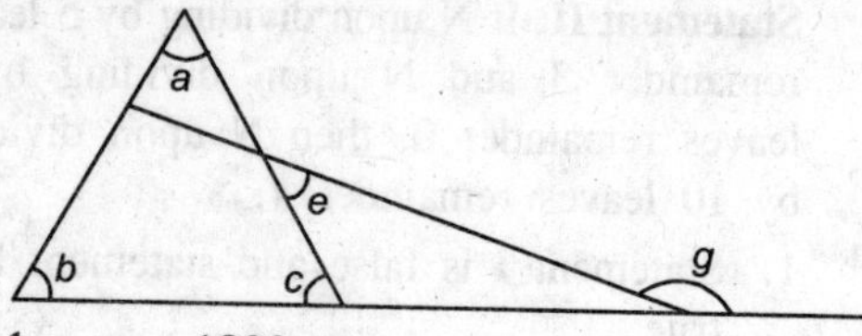

1. $c = 180° - e - g$
2. $c = e + g$
3. $c = e + (180° + g)$
4. $c = 180° - e + g$

34. $\sqrt{\sqrt[3]{343}+3\times\sqrt{289}-\sqrt[3]{729}}=$

1. 8
2. 3
3. 7
4. 9

35. The least square number which is exactly divisible by 3, 4, 5, 6 and 8 is:

1. 5184
2. 1444
3. 1600
4. 3600

36. The difference of two numbers is 988. If the cube root of the smaller of the two numbers is 7, then the cube root of the larger number is:

1. 12
2. 13
3. 11
4. 25

37.

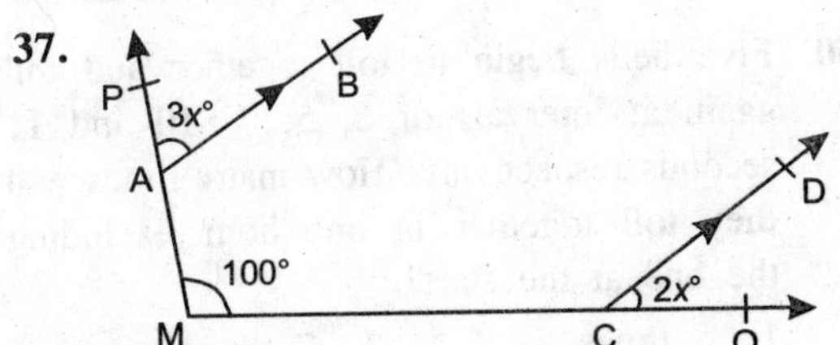

In the above figure. AB || CD. The value of x is:

1. 30
2. 20
3. 10
4. 40

38. In the given figure, FD || BC || AE and AC || ED.

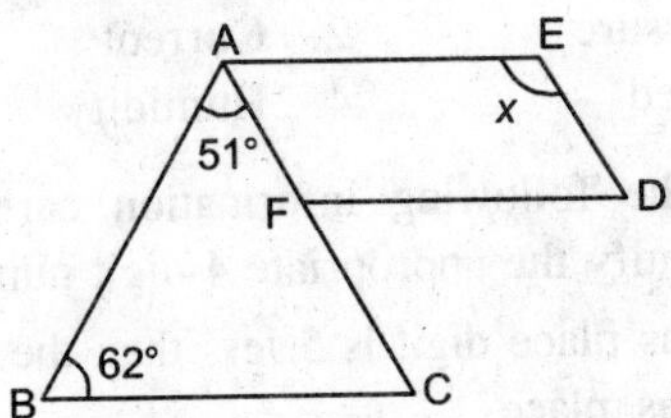

The value of x is:

1. 129°
2. 67°
3. 62°
4. 113°

39. Rahul walks 12 m towards North from his house and turns West to walk 35 m to reach the market. While returning, he walks diagonally from market to reach back to his house. The distance he travelled while returning is:

1. 39 m
2. 37 m
3. 47 m
4. 43 m

40. The sum of ₹ 300 is divided between A and B such that twice of A's share is less than 3 times B's share by ₹ 300. B's share is:

1. ₹ 160
2. ₹ 180
3. ₹ 120
4. ₹ 150

41. The perimeter of a rectangle is 240 cm. If its length is increased by 10% and its breadth is decreased by 20%, the perimeter remains the same. The length and breadth of the original rectangle respectively are:

1. 75 cm, 45 cm
2. 80 cm, 40 cm
3. 90 cm, 30 cm
4. 100 cm, 20 cm

42. A man bought a refrigerator for ₹ 15200 and spent ₹ 300 as labour charges and ₹ 500 on its transportation. At what price should he sell it to make a gain of 15%?

1. ₹ 18355
2. ₹ 16560
3. ₹ 18400
4. ₹ 18640

43. In a city, 40% of the adults are uneducated while 85% of the children are educated. If the ratio of the number of adults to that of the children is 2 : 3, then what per cent of the population is educated?

1. 60%
2. 75%
3. 65%
4. 80%

44. Beena bought 160 kg apples at ₹ 50 per kg. She sold 70% of the apples at ₹ 70 per kg and the remaining at ₹ 35 per kg. Beena's gain per cent on the whole is:

1. 21%
2. 19%
3. 30%
4. 16%

45. If $a:b:c=\frac{1}{3}:\frac{1}{6}:\frac{1}{9}$, then the value of $\frac{a^2+b^2}{b^2-c^2}$, is:

1. 12
2. 6
3. 3
4. 9

46. The marked price of an article is ₹ 1500. A shopkeeper gives a discount of 5% and still makes a profit of 25%. The cost price of the article is:

1. ₹ 1180
2. ₹ 1260
3. ₹ 1140
4. ₹ 1240

47. In a camp with 200 persons, there is enough food for 42 days. How long the food will last if 40 more persons join the camp on the first day?

1. 40 days
2. 35 days
3. 32 days
4. 36 days

48. Study the following tables carefully and choose the correct option:

Table A

x	3	6	15	20	30
y	12	24	45	60	120

Table B

x	4	7	10	16	6
y	24	42	60	96	36

1. In table A, x and y are in direct proportion and in table B, x and y are not in direct proportion
2. In table A, x and y are not in direct proportion and in table B, x and y are not in direct proportion
3. In both tables A and B, x and y are in direct proportion
4. In both tables A and B, x and y are in direct proportion

49. Which of the following vary inversely?

1. Speed and distance covered
2. Speed and time taken
3. Distance covered and taxi fare
4. Distance travelled and time taken

50. Five bells begin to toll together and toll again at intervals of 6, 5, 7, 10 and 11 seconds respectively. How many times will they toll together in one hour excluding the one at the start?

1. 8 times
2. 7 times
3. 11 times
4. 9 times

Section B : Intelligence

51. Find the missing number (?) in the given series:

1, 2, 3, 5, 8, 13, 21, ?

1. 28
2. 32
3. 33
4. 34

52. Find the missing term (?) in the following letter-number series:

3F, 6G, 11I, 18L, ?

1. 25N
2. 27P
3. 25P
4. 27N

53. There is a certain relationship between two given words on the left side of (::). Choose correct alternative for the missing term (?) having the similar relationship with the third term.

Thermometer : Temperature :: Odometer : ?.

1. Pressure
2. Current
3. Speed
4. Humidity

54. Study the following information carefully and identify the appropriate 4-digit number:

- Its tens place digit is 5 less than the digit at ones place.
- Its ones place digit is the largest 1-digit even number.
- Its hundreds place digit is the ones place digit of (758 – 354).
- Its thousands place digit is the sum of the digits at its tens place and hundreds place.

1. 9548
2. 8358
3. 7438
4. 7348

55. Find the odd one out among the following words:

1. Rain 2. River
3. Pond 4. Lake

56. Complete the following analogy:

DE : 9 :: FG : ?

1. 11 2. 13
3. 15 4. 14

57. Arrange the following in a logical and meaningful order:

A. Doctor B. Recovery
C. Illness D. Consultation
E. Treatment

Choose the correct option from the following alternatives:

1. B, A, E, D, C 2. C, A, E, D, B
3. C, A, D, E, B 4. C, A, D, B, E

58. How many triangles are there in the given figure?

1. 15 2. 10
3. 12 4. 14

59. Find the missing term in the series:

cba, cbaa, cbbaa, ?, ccbbbaaa.

1. ccbaaa 2. cbbaaa
3. ccbbaa 4. ccbbba

60. Dheekshitha is making this calendar for the bulletin board. Which day of the week should be January 20xx?

January 20xx

Sun	Mon	Tue	Wed	Thu	Fri	Sat
	1	2	3	4	5	6
7	8	9	10	11	12	

1. Monday 2. Tuesday
3. Wednesday 4. Thursday

61. Arrange the following words as per order in the dictionary:

A. Conservation B. Conscience
C. Consequence D. Consume
E. Consciousness

Choose the correct option from the following:

1. B, C, E, A, D
2. B, E, C, D, A
3. B, E, C, A, D
4. B, C, E, D, A

62. Find the missing number-pair (?, ?) in the given series:

(2, 3), (3, 5), (5, 7), (7, 11), (11, 13), (?, ?)

1. (13, 15) 2. (13, 19)
3. (13, 17) 4. (17, 19)

63. Find the odd one out among the following terms:

1. IFC 2. NKH
3. PMJ 4. ROM

64. Complete the following analogy:

3 : 30 :: 6 : ? :: 7 : 346

1. 36 2. 39
3. 216 4. 219

65. If the code for 'RIGHT' is 'SJHIU', then what is the code for 'FINDS'?

1. GJOET 2. GINET
3. GIOET 4. GJMEU

66. In the following arrangements of letters, how many 'G' are there which are followed by 'K' and preceded by N?

A K G L M N D N K G C S N G K T G K G N D Z P U N G K X

1. 4 2. 3
3. 2 4. 1

67. Choose the number-group which is different from others:

1. [26, 4, 22] 2. [45, 9, 36]
3. [64, 14, 54] 4. [99, 25, 74]

68. Replace the question mark (?) in the following figural series:

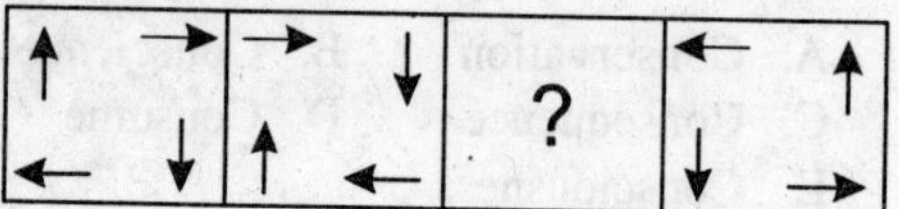

Choose the *correct* answer from the options given below:

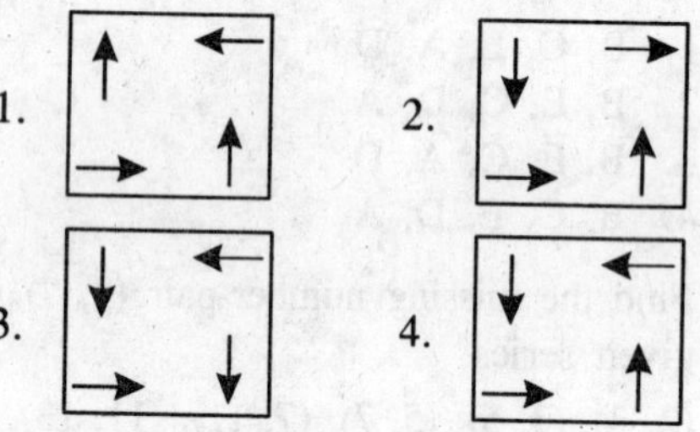

69. Select the correct mirror image of the following figure, where the mirror is placed on the line AB as shown below:

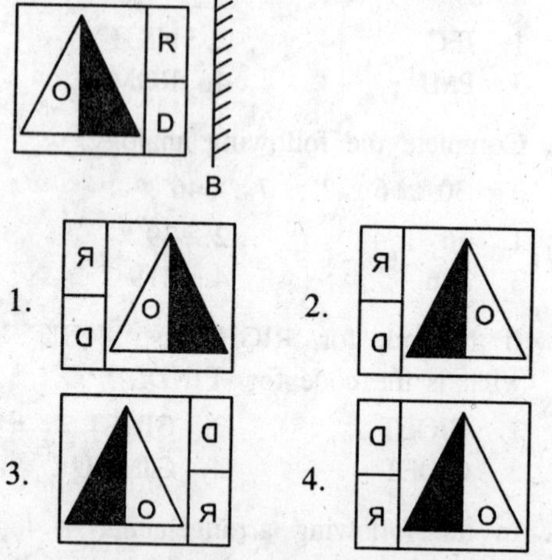

70. A set of figures carrying certain numbers is given. The numbers in each set follow a similar pattern, based on that pattern find the value of 'P'.

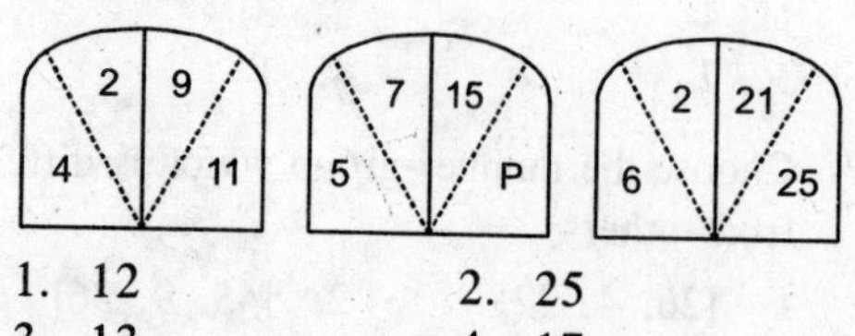

1. 12
2. 25
3. 13
4. 17

71. Replace the question mark (?) in the following figural series:

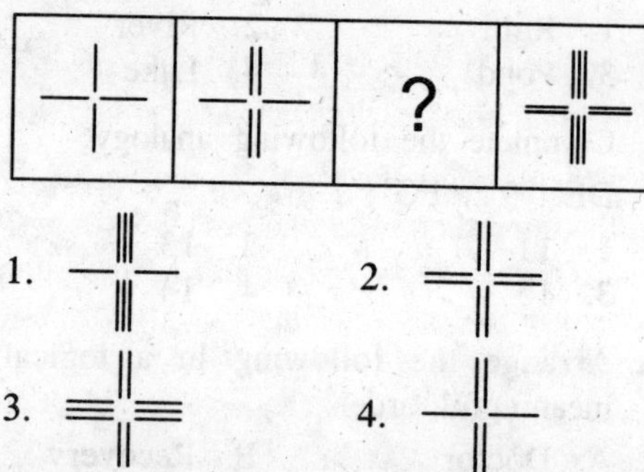

72. According to a certain code if, PEDESTRIAN = 30, ACCIDENT = 24, and DRIVER = 18, then TRAFFIC is equal to:

1. 7
2. 14
3. 28
4. 21

73. If the cost of 3 pencils and 1 sharpener is ₹ 25, the cost of 2 sharpeners and 2 erasers is ₹ 14 and the cost of 3 erasers is ₹ 9, then the cost of 1 pencil is:

1. ₹ 4
2. ₹ 7
3. ₹ 3
4. ₹ 5

74. How many ways can Mr. X reach his home?

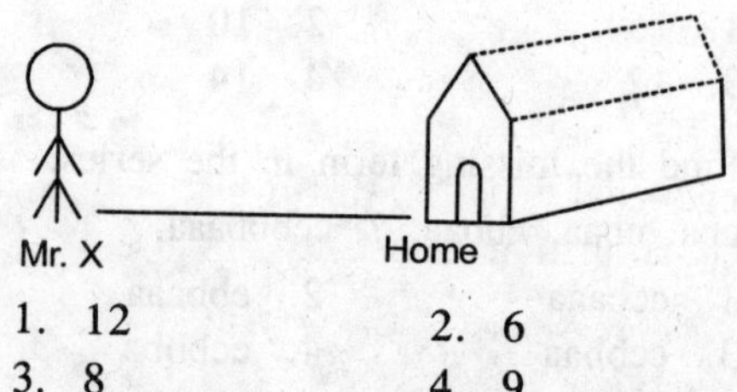

1. 12
2. 6
3. 8
4. 9

75. Anita is older than Chetna. Babita is older than Chetna but younger than Anita. Erric is younger than Divya and Chetna. Chetna is older than Divya. Who is in the middle with respect to their ages?

1. Babita
2. Divya
3. Chetna
4. Erric

Section C : English

Directions (Qs. No. 76-80): *Read the passage given below and answer the questions that follow:*

Mountain climbers are unanimous in agreeing that the unpredictable weather is what they fear the most. There may be sunshine one moment and a snowstorm the other. At higher altitudes, snow is a regular feature and being decisive about setting up camps or proceeding further is crucial. The icy sheets after ice storms make walking treacherous, while the powdery snow makes a mountaineer sink deep into the snow. Up there, where the intention is to embrace Nature's wonder, one realises that it cannot be done without facing its formidable glory. A true mountaineer may challenge the mountain, yet is always respectful to the powerful forces of nature.

Summiting mountains carries its own health risks such as oxygen and altitude sickness problems, frost bites, swelling of hands and feet, fluid collection in brain or lungs and exhaustion. Yet, the gratification mountaineers feel from mastering something that is so frightening, urges them to undertake these endeavours. We may think that the mountaineers are fearless, experts say, "Not at all. It"s feat that keeps them so intrigued with such arduous journeys." Impulse and brazenness can be deadly foes. In the words of the Indian mountaineer, Bachendri Pal, "The biggest risk ... is to not take the risk at all. Remember that."

76. The reason given for calling the weather 'unpredictable' on the mountain, as given in the passage is:

1. Sunshine as well as snowstorm in short intervals
2. Icy sheets after ice storms
3. Forces of Nature
4. High altitude resulting in less oxygen

77. The reason a true mountaineer is respectful to the forces of nature up in the mountains is:

1. Directive 2. Challenge
3. Experience 4. Survival

78. Choose the **inappropriate** reason for the feeling of exhilaration on reaching a summit, that the mountain-climbers experience:

1. Achievement of a seemingly impossible feat
2. Spectacular panoramic view
3. Application of the inculcated survival instinct
4. Opportunity to use sophisticated mountaineering equipment

79. The word from the passage that can be used to fill in the blank:

His ______ opponent beat him in no time in the boxing ring.

1. unanimous 2. unpredictable
3. treacherous 4. formidable

80. The word from the passage that means same as:

Involving a lot of effort and energy, especially over a period of time.

1. Treacherous 2. Exhaustion
3. Endeavour 4. Arduous

81. Organize the parts to form a meaningful sentence:

A. Than I expected
B. Our players
C. Was rather worse
D. The performance of

1. BCAD 2. CBDA
3. ABDC 4. DBCA

82. Choose the word opposite in meaning to the given word:

Abandon

1. Adopt 2. Continue
3. Solicit 4. Chastise

83. Find the correctly spelt word:

1. Renaissance 2. Reccomendation
3. Irrepereble 4. Meagere

84. Change the gender in the sentence:
He is a father and a teacher.
1. She is a mother and a teacheress.
2. She is a mother and a teacher.
3. She is a father and teacheress.
4. She is a father and teacher.

85. Change the sentence from passive voice to active voice:
By whom was this beautiful glass broken?
1. Who has broken this beautiful glass?
2. Who had broken this beautiful glass?
3. Who broke this beautiful glass?
4. This beautiful glass has been broken by whom?

86. Choose the appropriate word for the blank to complete the sentence:
Today is the ______ day of my life nothing seems to go as planned.
1. best 2. bad
3. worse 4. worst

87. Choose the word **opposite in meaning** of 'permit':
1. Allow 2. License
3. Present 4. Prevent

88. Choose the correct conjunction from the options given below to complete sentence:
Thought she worked hard, ______ failed.
1. but 2. yet
3. although 4. nevertheless

89. Fill in the blanks with the correct article:
It was such ______ foolish decision to accept ______ impossible task.
1. an, the 2. a, a
3. a, an 4. the, a

90. Choose the word **similar in meaning** to the given word:
'Bleak'
1. Balmy 2. Ugly
3. Gloomy 4. Bemoan

91. Fill in the blank with appropriate adverb:
______ we escaped unhurt.
1. Fortunately 2. Certainly
3. Accidently 4. Wisely

92. Change the given sentence to Passive Voice:
Your behaviour annoyed me.
1. I were annoyed on your behaviour.
2. Your behaviour was annoying me.
3. I was annoyed at your behaviour.
4. I was annoyed on your behaviour.

93. Fill in the correct adverb from the following options to make a meaningful sentence:
We cannot play music ______ in this park.
1. aloud 2. loudly
3. audibly 4. aloudly

94. Change the given sentence to Indirect Narration:
Pawan said, "How beautiful the scene is!"
1. Pawan exclaimed that how that scene was beautiful.
2. Pawan exclaimed how beautiful is the scene.
3. Pawan exclaimed that the scene was very beautiful.
4. Pawan exclaimed that the scene is indeed beautiful.

95. Spot the error in the following sentence:
(A) She asked/ (B) me that/ (C) what/ (D) had happened.
1. A 2. C
3. B 4. D

96. Change the given sentence to Direct narration by choosing the correct option:
He said that Mangal would be working hard.
1. He said, "Mangal would work harder."
2. He said, "Mangal will work hard."
3. He said, "Mangal would be working hard."
4. He said, "Mangal will be working hard."

97. Comparative degree of the adjective 'Most' is:

1. More
2. Much
3. Many
4. Foremost

98. Fill in the blanks with appropriate choice:
I wrote a line on the sand with ______ that she could not ______ before the waves washed it away.

1. read, read
2. reed, reed
3. read, reed
4. reed, read

99. Choose the correct idiom for the blank.
Mediocre artists like Sheena are found _____.

1. all and sundry
2. at every shop
3. a dime a dozen
4. in rain or shine

100. Choose the appropriate question.
We are going to the movie tonight ______.

1. are we?
2. aren't we
3. isn't it?
4. is it?

Section D : General Science

101. The major component of compressed natural gas (CNG) is:

1. Carbon monoxide
2. Nitrogen dioxide
3. Methane
4. Oxygen

102. Combustion is the chemical process in which substance reacts with ______ and produces heat.

1. Oxygen
2. Nitrogen
3. Carbon dioxide
4. Carbon monoxide

103. Which of the following is **NOT** a part of the animal cell?

1. Cell membrane
2. Cell wall
3. Cytoplasm
4. Nucleus

104. The animals which give birth to the young ones are called:

1. Oviparous
2. Viviparous
3. Ovoviviparous
4. Parthenogenic

105. Special shapes are given to the objects moving in fluid to:

1. Minimise fluid friction
2. Maximise fluid friction
3. Restore fluid friction
4. Keep fluid friction unchanged

106. Identify the measures used to limit noise pollution:

A. Minimise the use of automobile horns
B. Planting trees along the roads
C. Installing silencing devices in aircraft engines
D. Cutting trees around the residential buildings

Choose the correct option from the following:

1. B, C and D only
2. A, B and C only
3. B and D only
4. A and C only

107. Image formed by a plane mirror is:

1. Virtual, behind the mirror and enlarged
2. Virtual, behind the mirror and the same size as the object
3. Real, at the surface of the mirror and enlarged
4. Real, behind the mirror and the same size as the object

108. Which of the following is the most reactive with water?

1. Phosphorus
2. Zinc
3. Sodium
4. Cobalt

109. Select the correct statements from the following:

When the electric current passes through a conducting solution:

A. Bubbles of the gas may be formed on the electrodes

B. Deposits of metal may be seen on the electrode

C. There is no change in colour of the solution

D. Change in colour of the solution may occur

Choose the correct option from the following:

1. A, B and C only
2. A and C only
3. A, B and D only
4. B and C only

110. Match the following:

(Member of Solar System)	(Example)
A. Satellite	I. Cassiopeia
B. Constellation	II. Sirius
C. Comet	III. Moon
D. Star	IV. Halley

Choose the ***correct*** answer from the options given below:

1. A-III, B-IV, C-I, D-II
2. A-IV, B-I, C-III, D-II
3. A-III, B-I, C-IV, D-II
4. A-I, B-III, C-IV, D-II

111. The percentage of different gases in air is:

1. 78% nitrogen, 21% oxygen and other gases
2. 20% nitrogen, 20% oxygen and other gases
3. 60% nitrogen and 40% oxygen
4. 10% nitrogen, 50% oxygen and other gases

112. Which is NOT a naturally occurring greenhouse gas?

1. Methane
2. Carbon dioxide
3. Nitrous oxide
4. Ethane

113. Match the organisms in Column A with their action in Column B:

(A)	(B)
A. Bacteria	I. Fixing Nitrogen
B. Rhizobium	II. Malaria
C. Protozoa	III. AIDS
D. Virus	IV. Tuberculosis

Choose the ***correct*** answer from the options given below:

1. A-IV, B-I, C-II, D-III
2. A-III, B-II, C-I, D-IV
3. A-I, B-II, C-III, D-IV
4. A-II, B-I, C-IV, D-III

114. Microorganisms are classified into four major groups as:

1. Bacteria, Aspergillus, Amoeba, Spirogyra
2. Bacteria, Fungi, Protozoa, Algae
3. Virus, Paramecium, Antibodies, Antibiotics
4. Fungi, Bacteria, Pathogens, Rhizobium

115. Tremors are caused by the disturbance in the ______ of earth.

1. mantle
2. outer core
3. crust
4. inner core

116. The amount of heat energy produced on complete combustion of 1 kg of a fuel is called ______ value.

1. fuel
2. ideal fuel
3. energy
4. calorific

117. Match the substances given in Column A with their uses given in Column B:

(A)	(B)
A. Gold	I. Thermometer
B. Iron	II. Electric wires
C. Mercury	III. Machinery
D. Copper	IV. Jewellery

Choose the *correct* answer from the options given below:

1. A-IV, B-I, C-II, D-III
2. A-IV, B-III, C-I, D-II
3. A-IV, B-II, C-III, D-I
4. A-IV, B-III, C-II, D-I

118. The force exerted by a magnet is an example of:

1. Contact force
2. Non-contact force
3. Electrostatic force
4. Force of gravity

119. Which of the following is NOT a Kharif crop?

1. Paddy 2. Soyabean
3. Mustard 4. Cotton

120. Which of the following may NOT a cause of passing HIV virus from infected person to a normal person?

1. Sharing the syringes used injecting drugs
2. Sexual contact with an infected person
3. Shaking hands with an infected person
4. Through the milk of an infected mother to her infant

121. Which of the following hormones helps the body to adjust to stress when one is very angry, embarrassed or worried?

1. Adrenalin 2. Thyroxine
3. Insulin 4. Estrogen

122. The method of preparing compost with the help of redworms is called:

1. Composting
2. Worming
3. Vermicomposting
4. Decomposing

123. The variety of organisms existing on the earth, their interrelationships and their relationship with the environment is called:

1. Biosphere
2. Biodiversity
3. Biosphere Reserve
4. Biology

124. Which of the following is the first Reserve forest of India?

1. Satpura National Park
2. Kaziranga
3. Jim Corbett National Park
4. Tawa Reservoir

125. Many young people get acne and pimples on the face during adolescence due to:

1. Increased activity of sebacious glands
2. Increased activity of sweat glands
3. Increased activity of salivary glands
4. Increased activity of sweat glands and sebacious glands

Section E : Social Science

126. The power of the judiciary to strike down particular laws passed by the Parliament if it belives them to be in violation of the basic structure of the Constitution is called ______.

1. Judicial activism
2. Separation of powers
3. Amendment
4. Judicial review

127. Which one among the following statements is NOT correct about the Gram Sabha?

1. The ward Panchs and the Sarpanch form the Gram Sabha.
2. Anyone who is 18 years old or more and lives in the area covered by a Panchayat is a member of the Gram Sabha.
3. The work of the Gram Panchayat has to be approved by the Gram Sabha.

4. The Gram Sabha prevents the Panchayat from misusing money.

128. Which of the following statements are correct?

A. Public facilities relate to people's basic needs.

B. Public facilities are only for those who can afford them.

C. The responsibility to provide public facilities lie with the government.

D. The responsibility to provide public facilities lie with private companies.

Choose the ***correct*** answer from the options given below:

1. A and B only
2. B and C only
3. A and C only
4. A and D only

129. The Employment of Manual Scavengers and Construction of Dry Latrines (Prohibition) Act, was passed by the Government of India in which year?

1. 1989
2. 1990
3. 1992
4. 1993

130. The difference between the birth rate and the death rate of a country is called the ____.

1. Natural growth rate
2. Average density of population
3. Population distribution
4. Life expectancy

131. Which one of the following is a Renewable Resource?

1. Natural gas
2. Coal
3. Solar energy
4. Petroleum

132. The book titled "Amar Jiban" was written by:

1. Rokeya Sakhawat Hossain
2. Pandita Ramabai
3. Tarabai Shinde
4. Rashsundari Devi

133. What is the full form of "PIL"?

1. Public Interrogation Litigation
2. Private India Limited
3. Public Interest Litigation
4. Public Information Litigation

134. The Azad Hind Fauj was raised by:

1. Mahatma Gandhi
2. Bhagat Singh
3. Jawaharlal Nehru
4. Subhas Chandra Bose

135. Which of these is NOT a function of the Municipal Corporation?

1. Prevents outbreak of diseases in the city
2. Running schools
3. Providing defense services
4. Garbage collection

136. Sahara, the world's largest desert, is located in which of the following continents?

1. Africa
2. North America
3. South America
4. Antarctica

137. Which one of the following is NOT a factor of soil formation?

1. Time
2. Parent Rock
3. Precipitation
4. Climate

138. Which crop is also known as 'Golden Fibre'?

1. Cotton
2. Jute
3. Wheat
4. Millets

139. Gandhiji carried out the Dandi March to oppose which of the following?

1. Rowlatt Act
2. Salt Law
3. Simon Commission
4. Partition of Bengal

140. The last Mughal emperor was:

1. Bahadur Shah Zafar
2. Nawab Wajid Ali Shah
3. Bakht Khan
4. Ahmadullah Shah

141. Which one of the following is an example of Marine based industry?

1. Cotton textile
2. Sea food processing
3. Iron ore
4. Pharmaceuticals

142. Which Article of the Constitution of India states that the practice of untouchability has been abolished?

1. Article 14 2. Article 17
3. Article 19 4. Article 21

143. Which country is the largest producer of "Bauxite" in the world?

1. South Africa 2. Brazil
3. Australia 4. Russia

144. Match List-I with List-II:

List-I	List-II
A. Diwan	I. Financial Officer
B. Bakhshi	II. Military Paymaster
C. Faujdar	III. Military Commander
D. Kotwal	IV. Police Commander

Choose the ***correct*** answer from the options given below:

1. A-I, B-II, C-III, D-IV
2. A-II, B-III, C-I, D-IV
3. A-IV, B-I, C-II, D-III
4. A-III, B-I, C-II, D-IV

145. The full form of "CITIES" is:

1. The Contract on International Trade in Endangered Species
2. The Convention on International Trade in Endangered Species
3. The Convention on Indiscriminate Trade in Endangered Species
4. The Contract on Indiscriminate Trade in Endangered Species

146. Ibn Battuta, a fourteenth century traveller, was from which of the following countries?

1. Afghanistan 2. China
3. Iran 4. Morocco

147. According to the Constitution of India, there are ______ organs of the government.

1. Two 2. Three
3. Four 4. Five

148. Which of the following is a method for conservation of land resource?

1. Overgrazing
2. Use of chemical pesticide
3. Land degradation
4. Afforestation

149. Which of the following is NOT a feature of a shopping complex?

1. Branded stores
2. Buying and selling takes place between traders
3. Multiple products under a roof
4. Entertainment facilities

150. The magnitude of the Earthquake is measured on:

1. Digital scale 2. Victor scale
3. Nichter scale 4. Richter scale

ANSWERS

1. (3): Given,

Surface area of a cube = Volume of a cube

$\Rightarrow \quad 6(\text{side})^2 = (\text{side})^3$

$\Rightarrow \quad 6 = \text{side}$

$\therefore$ the side of the cube is 6 unit.

2. (4)

3. (2): From given Bar-graph

Total sale during the month

$= 400 + 250 + 350 + 620 = 1620$

and total manufacture during month

$= 700 + 500 + 600 + 450 = 2250$

$\therefore$ Required per cent $= \frac{1620}{2250} \times 100$

$$= \frac{162}{225} \times 100 = \frac{162 \times 4}{9}$$

$= 18 \times 4 = 72\%$.

4. (3): Suresh earn per month = ₹ 72000

In Pie-chart

360° = ₹ 72000

$\Rightarrow$ 1° = ₹ $\frac{72000}{360}$ = ₹ 200

$\therefore$ He spends money on household expenditures every month

= 144° = 144 × ₹ 200

= ₹ 28,800.

5. (4): Given, the lateral surface area of a cube

$= 256 \text{ m}^3$

$\Rightarrow 4\,(\text{side})^2 = 256$

$\Rightarrow (\text{side})^2 = 64 = (8)^2$

$\Rightarrow \text{side} = 8$

$\therefore$ The volume of the cube = $(\text{side})^3$

$= (8)^3 = 512 \text{ cm}^3$.

6. (4): From given parallelogram ABCD

$\angle DAC = 45°$ and $\angle AOB = 110°$

$\because \angle AOB = \angle COD = 110°$

(vertically opposite angle)

and $\angle AOB + \angle AOD = 180°$ (linear pair angle)

$\Rightarrow 110° + \angle AOD = 180°$

$\Rightarrow \angle AOD = 70°$

and $\angle DAC + \angle AOD + \angle ADO = 180°$

$\Rightarrow 45° + 70° + \angle ADO = 180°$

$\Rightarrow \angle ADO = 180° - 115° = 65°$

$\Rightarrow \angle ADO = 65°$

$\Rightarrow$ ADB = 65°

$\because$ AD || BC

$\therefore \angle ADB = \angle CBD = 65°$

(Alternate angle)

$\Rightarrow \angle DBC = 65°$.

7. (3): The area of the rectangle = length × breadth

$$= \left(\frac{2}{3}a^2 + \frac{2}{9}\right)\text{m} \times \left(a^2 + \frac{1}{6}\right)\text{m}$$

$$= \frac{2}{3}a^4 + \frac{1}{9}a^2 + \frac{2}{9}a^2 + \frac{1}{27}$$

$$= \frac{2}{3}a^4 + \frac{1}{3}a^2 + \frac{1}{27}$$

8. (4): The area of the wall to be painted

= area of wall – area of a window – area of a door

$= (5x + 2) \times 6x - 2x \times 2x - 2x \times 3x$

$= 30x^2 + 12x - 4x^2 - 6x^2$

$= 30x^2 + 12x - 10x^2$

$= 20x^2 + 12x = 4x(5x + 3)$.

9. (2): The area of the triangle = $\frac{1}{2}$ × base × h

$= \frac{1}{2} \times (3x^2 - 4) \times (4x^2 + 6)$

$= (3x^2 - 4) \times (2x^2 + 3)$

$= 6x^4 + 9x^2 - 8x^2 - 12$

$= 6x^4 + x - 12$.

10. (2): Let x should be added

Then, $4c(-a - 2b + c) + x = 3c(a - b + c) - 2c(a + b - c)$

$\Rightarrow x = 3c(a - b + c) - 2c(a + b - c) - 4c(-a - 2b + c)$

$\Rightarrow x = 3ac - 3bc + 3c^2 - 2ac - 2bc + 2c^2 + 4ac + 8bc - 4c^2$

$\Rightarrow x = 5ac + 3bc + c^2$.

11. (2): The area of a closed figure ABCO

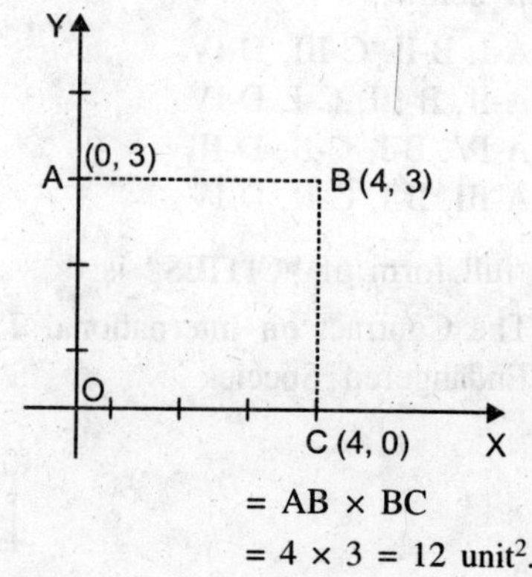

= AB × BC

$= 4 \times 3 = 12 \text{ unit}^2$.

12. (2): Given, 4 (area of the C.S. of a cylinder) = 6(the sum of the area of its bases)

$\Rightarrow 4(2\pi rh) = 6(2\pi r^2)$

$\Rightarrow 8\pi rh = 12\pi r^2$

$\Rightarrow 8h = 12r$ (given $h = 12$ cm)

$\Rightarrow 8 \times 12 = 12r$

$\Rightarrow r = 8$ cm

$\therefore$ Curved surface area of a cylinder $= 2\pi rh$

$$= 2\times\frac{22}{7}\times 8\times 12 \text{ cm}^2$$

$$= \frac{4224}{7}$$

$$= 603.4285 = 603.43 \text{ cm}^2.$$

13. (4): Let the length of the plot $= l$

then, the area of a rectangular plot $= l \times 24$ m

$$\Rightarrow \quad \frac{39000}{25}\text{ m}^2 = 24l \text{ m}$$

$$\Rightarrow \quad 1560 \text{ m}^2 = 24l \text{ m}$$

$$\Rightarrow \quad l = \frac{1560}{24}\text{ m}$$

$$\Rightarrow \quad l = 65 \text{ m}.$$

14. (3): Perimeter of a square = Perimeter of a rectangle

$$\Rightarrow \quad 4 \times 60 \text{ m} = 2(l + b)$$

$$\Rightarrow \quad 240 \text{ m} = 2(80 + b) \Rightarrow 120 = 80 + b$$

$$\Rightarrow \quad b = 40 \text{ m}$$

$\therefore$ Area of rectangle $= l \times b = 80 \times 40 \text{ m}^2$

$$= 3200 \text{ m}^2$$

and area of square $= (60)^2 = 3600 \text{ m}^2$

$\therefore$ The difference in their area

$$= 3600 - 3200 = 400 \text{ m}^2.$$

15. (4): Let x should be multiplied

Then, $(-8)^{-3} \times x = (-6)^{-3}$

$$\Rightarrow \quad x = \frac{(-6)^{-3}}{(-8)^{-3}} = \frac{(-8)^3}{(-6)^3}$$

$$= \left(\frac{8}{6}\right)^3 = \left(\frac{4}{3}\right)^3$$

$$\Rightarrow \quad x = \frac{4^3}{3^3}.$$

16. (4):

$$\begin{array}{r} \text{B A A} \\ +\,\text{B A A} \\ \hline \text{3 A 8} \end{array}$$

From given options

A = 9, B = 1

$$\therefore \quad \begin{array}{r} 1\,9\,9 \\ +\,1\,9\,9 \\ \hline 3\,9\,8 \end{array} \quad \Rightarrow \quad \begin{array}{r} 1\,9\,9 \\ +\,1\,9\,9 \\ \hline 3\text{ A }8 \end{array}$$

$\therefore$ Values of A and B are 9 and 1.

17. (2): $\because$ $5b9$ is divisible by 9

$$\therefore \quad \frac{5+b+9}{9} = \frac{14+b}{9} = \frac{14+4}{9} = 2,$$

when $b = 4$

$\therefore$ $5b9 = 549$ is divisible by 9

$$\text{Now,} \quad \begin{array}{r} 3\,2\,6 \\ +\,2\,a\,3 \\ \hline 5\,b\,9 \end{array} \quad \Rightarrow \quad \begin{array}{r} 3\,2\,6 \\ +\,2\,a\,3 \\ \hline 5\,4\,9 \end{array}$$

when $a = 2$

$$\therefore \quad (b - a) = 4 - 2 = 2$$

$\therefore$ The value of $(b - a)$ is 2.

18. (2)

19. (2): Statement I: Triangle is a polygon

Sum of exterior angles $= 2\pi$

and Sum of its interior angles $= (3 - 2)\pi = \pi$

$\therefore$ Statement I is correct.

Statement II: It is a hexagon.

Sum of interior angle $= (6 - 2)\pi = 4\pi$

and Sum of its exterior angle $= 2\pi$

$\therefore$ Statement II is correct.

Statement III: Let the interior angles of a triangle are x, $2x$, and $3x$ then $x + 2x + 3x = 180° \Rightarrow x = 30°$

$\therefore$ interior angles are 30°, 60° and 90°

$\therefore$ exterior angles are 150°, 120° and 90°

$\therefore$ ratio of its exterior angle is 5 : 4 : 3

This ratio is not 3 : 2 : 1

$\therefore$ Statement III is not correct. (false)

20. (3): More Men, Less day $\rightarrow$ Indirect proportion

Let required number of Men be x

Then, Men days

$$7 : x :: 8 : 16$$

$$\Rightarrow \quad 7 \times 16 = 8x$$

$$\Rightarrow \quad x = 14$$

$\therefore$ The number of men required to double

$$= 2 \times 14 = 28.$$

21. (2): Let S be the sample space.

Then, $n(\text{S})$ = Number of ways to chosen 1 marble out of $(6 + 5 + 4 + 5) = {}^{20}\text{C}_1 = 20$

Let E = Event of chosen 1 red marble

Then, $n(\text{E}) = {}^{6}\text{C}_1 = 6$

$$\therefore \quad \text{P(E)} = \frac{n(\text{E})}{n(\text{S})} = \frac{6}{20} = \frac{3}{10}.$$

22. (4): Let S be the sample space.

Then, $n(S) = {}^{16}C_1 = 16$

Let E = Event of chosen 1 card bears a prime number

∵ Prime numbers from 1 to 16 are 2, 3, 5, 7, 11, 13

Then, $n(E) = {}^{6}C_1 = 6$

∴ $P(E) = \frac{n(E)}{n(S)} = \frac{6}{16} = \frac{3}{8}$

Hence, required probability $= \frac{3}{8}$.

23. (4)

24. (3): Ratio of days of work

A : B : C = 12 : 16 : 18

∴ Ratio of efficiency of work

$A : B : C = \frac{1}{12} : \frac{1}{16} : \frac{1}{18}$

$= 12 : 9 : 8$

they get a sum = ₹ 5800

∴ Share of A in the sum $= 5800 \times \frac{12}{12+9+8}$

$= 5800 \times \frac{12}{29}$

$= 200 \times 12 =$ ₹ 2400.

25. (3): ∵ Perimeter of the shape of a circle = 88 cm

⇒ $2\pi r = 88$

⇒ $2 \times \frac{22}{7} r = 88$

⇒ $r = 14$ cm

∴ Area of a circle $= \pi r^2 = \frac{22}{7} \times (14)^2$

$= \frac{22}{7} \times 14 \times 14$

$= 44 \times 14 = 616 \text{ cm}^2$

And perimeter of the shape of square = 88 cm

⇒ 4 × side = 88 ⇒ side = 22 cm

∴ Area of a square = $(\text{side})^2 = (22)^2 = 484 \text{ cm}^2$

Hence, area of a circle – area of a square

$= 616 - 484 = 132 \text{ cm}^2$

Hence, circle is more area and by 132 cm².

26. (4): Perimeter of a circular garden = 400 × 66 cm

⇒ $2\pi r = 26{,}400$

⇒ $2r \times \frac{22}{7} = 26400$

⇒ $2r = 26400 \times \frac{7}{22}$

$= 1200 \times 7 = 8400$ cm

⇒ $2r = 84$ m

∴ The diameter of the garden is 84 m.

27. (1): The average speed of the train during the two-way journey

$= \frac{2xy}{x+y}$

$= \frac{2 \times 60 \times 90}{60 + 90} = \frac{2 \times 60 \times 90}{150}$

$= \frac{2 \times 2 \times 90}{5} = 4 \times 18 = 72$ km/h.

28. (3): Arranging the weight of 8 children in ascending order:

9.8, 10.6, 12.7, 13.4, 14.3, 15, 16.5, 17.2

Here, $n = 8$ (even no.)

∴ Median $= \frac{1}{2}\left[\frac{n}{2}\text{th term} + \left(\frac{n}{2}+1\right)\text{th term}\right]$

= [4th term + 5th term]

$= \frac{1}{2}[13.4 + 14.3]$

$= \frac{1}{2}[27.7] = 13.85$

∴ Required Median = 13.85.

29. (2): The total height of 30 boys

= 30 × 150 cm = 4500 cm

Correct height of 30 boys = 4500 + 165 – 135

= 4665 – 135 = 4530

∴ The correct average is $\frac{4530}{30} = 151$.

30. (3): From Euler's formula (polyhedron)

F + V – E = 2

⇒ 40 + V – 60 = 2

⇒ V – 20 = 2

⇒ V = 20 + 2

⇒ V = 22.

31. (2): Here, Population in 2005 = 66,150

Increasing rate = r = 5%

∴ The population in 2003 $= \frac{P}{\left(1 + \frac{r}{100}\right)^n}$

$$= \frac{66,150}{\left(1+\frac{5}{100}\right)^2} = \frac{66,150}{\left(\frac{21}{20}\right)^2}$$

$$= 66,150 \times \frac{400}{441}$$

$$= 150 \times 400 = 60,000.$$

32. (3): $\because$ $A = P + S.I.$

Given, $A = ₹\ 2475$

$$r = 8\frac{1}{3}\% = \frac{25}{3}\%$$

and t = 1 year 9 months

$$= 1\frac{9}{12} = \frac{7}{4} \text{ years}$$

$\therefore$ $$2475 = P + \frac{Prt}{100}$$

$\Rightarrow$ $$2475 = P + \frac{P \times \frac{25}{3} \times \frac{7}{4}}{100}$$

$\Rightarrow$ $$2475 \times 100 = 100P + \frac{175}{12}P$$

$\Rightarrow$ $$247500 = \frac{1200P + 175P}{12}$$

$\Rightarrow$ $1375P = 247500 \times 12$

$\Rightarrow$ $P = ₹\ 2160$

Now, Again, t = 2 years and $r = 5\%$

$\therefore$ $$S.I. = \frac{Prt}{100} = \frac{2160 \times 5 \times 2}{100} = 216$$

$\therefore$ Required amount = P + S.I.

$= 2160 + 216 = ₹\ 2376.$

33. (3): From the given figure:

$a + b = 180 - c$ ...(*i*)

$a + e + b = g$

$\Rightarrow$ $a + b + e = g$ ...(*ii*)

$\Rightarrow$ $180 - c + e = g$

$\Rightarrow$ $c = e + (180 - g).$

34. (3): $\sqrt{\sqrt[3]{343} + 3 \times \sqrt{289} - \sqrt[3]{729}}$

$$= \sqrt{(7^3)^{1/3} + 3 \times 17 - (9^3)^{1/3}}$$

$$= \sqrt{7 + 51 - 9} = \sqrt{58 - 9}$$

$$= \sqrt{49} = 7.$$

35. (4): The LCM of 3, 4, 5, 6 and 8 = 120

$\therefore$ The least square number = 120×30

$= 3600 = (60)^2$

which is exactly divisible by 3, 4, 5, 6 and 8

$\therefore$ Required number = 3600.

36. (3): Let the two numbers be a and b

Then, $a - b = 988$ ...(*i*)

and $\sqrt[3]{b} = 7$

$\Rightarrow$ $b = (7)^3 = 343$

$\Rightarrow$ $b = 343$ ...(*ii*)

from (*i*) and (*ii*), we get

$a - 343 = 988$

$\Rightarrow$ $a = 343 + 988 \Rightarrow a = 1331$

$\therefore$ $(a)^{1/3} = (1331)^{1/3}$

$\Rightarrow$ $\sqrt[3]{a} = (11^3)^{1/3}$

$\Rightarrow$ $\sqrt[3]{a} = 11$

$\therefore$ The cube root of the largest number = 11.

37. (2)

38. (4): In the given figure, FD || BC || AE and AC || ED

$\because$ In ΔABC

$\angle A + \angle B + \angle C = 180°$

$\Rightarrow 51° + 62° + \angle C = 180°$

$\Rightarrow$ $\angle C = 180° - 113°$

$\Rightarrow$ $\angle C = 67°$

$\because$ FD || BC || AE and AC || ED

$\therefore$ $\angle C = \angle D$ [corresponding angles]

$\therefore$ $\angle D = 67°$

$\Rightarrow$ $\angle EDF = \angle EAF = 67°$

and $\angle AED = \angle AFD = x°$

In ||gm AEDF

$\angle A + \angle E + \angle D + \angle F = 360°$

$\Rightarrow 67° + x + 67° + x = 360°$

$\Rightarrow$ $2x + 134 = 360°$

$\Rightarrow$ $2x = 360° - 134°$

$\Rightarrow$ $2x = 226° \Rightarrow x = 113°.$

39. (2): Here, Starting point = H

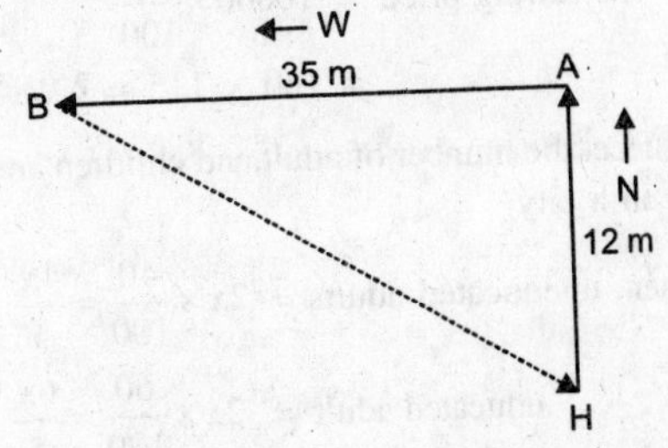

$$HA = 12 \text{ m}, \ AB = 35 \text{ m}$$

$$\therefore \quad BH = \sqrt{HA^2 + AB^2}$$

$$= \sqrt{12^2 + 35^2}$$

$$= \sqrt{144 + 1225}$$

$$= \sqrt{1369} = 37 \text{ m}$$

∴ The distance returning is 37 m.

40. (2): ∵ $A + B = ₹\ 300$

$\Rightarrow \quad 2A + 2B = ₹\ 600$ ...(*i*)

and $\quad 3B - 2A = 300$ ...(*ii*)

from adding (*i*) and (*ii*), we get

$$5B = 900 \Rightarrow B = 180°$$

∴ B's share is ₹ 180.

41. (2): The perimeter of a rectangle = 240 m

$\Rightarrow \quad 2(l + b) = 240$ cm

$\Rightarrow \quad l + b = 120$ ...(*i*)

Again, $2\left(l \times \frac{110}{100} + b \times \frac{80}{100}\right) = 240$

$\Rightarrow \quad 110l + 80b = 120 \times 100$

$\Rightarrow \quad 11l + 8b = 1200$ ...(*ii*)

from (*i*) and (*ii*), we get

$11(120 - b) + 8b = 1200$

$\Rightarrow 1320 - 11b + 8b = 1200$

$\Rightarrow \quad 1320 - 3b = 1200$

$\Rightarrow \quad 3b = 1320 - 1200$

$\Rightarrow \quad 3b = 120 \Rightarrow b = 40$ cm

Putting the value of b in (*i*), we get

$$l = 80 \text{ cm}$$

∴ The length and breadth of the original rectangle respectively are 80 and 40 cm.

42. (3): Total cost price of a refrigerator

$= ₹\ 15{,}200 + ₹\ 300 + ₹\ 500$

$= ₹\ 16000$

and $\quad$ gain = 15%

∴ Its selling price $= 16000 \times \frac{115}{100}$

$= 160 \times 115 = ₹\ 18400.$

43. (2): Let the number of adult and children are $2x$ and $3x$ in a city

Then, uneducated adults $= 2x \times \frac{40}{100} = \frac{4x}{5}$

educated adult $= 2x \times \frac{60}{100} = \frac{6x}{5}$

and uneducated children $= 3x \times \frac{100-85}{100}$

$= 3x \times \frac{15}{100} = \frac{9x}{20}$

educated children $= 3x \times \frac{85}{100} = \frac{51}{20}x$

∴ Per cent of educated population

$$= \frac{\frac{6x}{5} + \frac{51x}{20}}{5x} \times 100$$

$$= \frac{24x + 51x}{20 \times 5x} \times 100$$

$$= \frac{75x}{100x} \times 100 = 75\%.$$

44. (2): Cost price of 160 kg apples

$= 160 \times ₹\ 50 = ₹\ 8000$

and selling price of 160 kg apples

$= 160 \times \frac{70}{100} \times ₹\ 70$

$+ 160 \times \frac{30}{100} \times ₹\ 35$

$= ₹\ 16 \times 7 \times 70 + ₹\ 48 \times 35$

$= ₹\ 7840 + ₹\ 1680$

$= ₹\ 9520$

∴ $\quad$ Profit = S.P. – C.P.

$= 9520 - 8000 = ₹\ 1520$

∴ Beena's gain % $= \frac{\text{Profit} \times 100}{\text{C.P.}}$

$= \frac{1520 \times 100}{8000} = 19\%.$

45. (4): Given,

$$a : b : c = \frac{1}{3} : \frac{1}{6} : \frac{1}{9} = 6 : 3 : 2$$

Let, $\quad a = 6x,\ b = 3x$ and $c = 2x$

Then, $\quad \frac{a^2 + b^2}{b^2 - c^2} = \frac{(6x)^2 + (3x)^2}{(3x)^2 - (2x)^2}$

$$= \frac{36x^2 + 9x^2}{9x^2 - 4x^2} = \frac{45x^2}{5x^2} = 9.$$

46. (3): Let the cost price of the article = ₹ x

Then, $\quad x \times \frac{125}{100} = ₹\ 1500 \times \frac{100-5}{100}$

$\Rightarrow \quad x \times \frac{5}{4} = 1500 \times \frac{95}{100}$

$\Rightarrow \quad x \times \frac{5}{4} = 1425$

$\Rightarrow \quad x = 1425 \times \frac{4}{5}$

$= 285 \times 4$

$= ₹\ 1140$

$\Rightarrow \quad x = ₹\ 1140.$

47. (2): More persons, less days → Indirect proportion

Let required days be x

Then, persons days

$200 : 240 :: x : 42$

$\Rightarrow \quad 200 \times 42 = 240 \times x$

$\Rightarrow \quad x = \frac{200 \times 42}{240} = 5 \times 7 = 35$

$\Rightarrow \quad x = 35$ days.

48. (*) **49. (2)** **50. (1)**

51. (4): Given series: 1, 2, 3, 5, 8, 13, 21, 34

Here, $1 + 2 = 3$,

$2 + 3 = 5$,

$3 + 5 = 8$,

$5 + 8 = 13$,

$8 + 13 = 21$,

$13 + 21 = 34$

∴ The missing number = ? = 34.

52. (2):

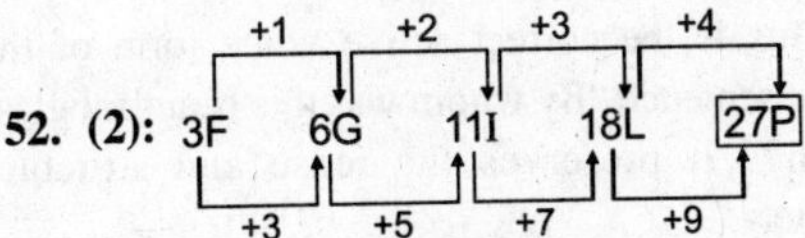

Here, ? = the missing term = 27P.

53. (*)

54. (3): From given information... and from given options.

4-digit number

Its ones place digit = 8

Its tens place digit = 8 − 5 = 3

Its hundreds place digit = 4

and Its thousands place digit = 3 + 4 = 7

∴ Required, 4-digit number = 7438.

55. (1)

56. (2): DE : 9 ⇒ D + E = 4 + 5 = 9,

Similarly,

FG = 6 + 7 = 13

∴ FG : 13

∴ DE : 9 :: FG : 13

57. (3): Logical and meaningful order:

Illness → Doctor → Consultation → Treatment → Recovery

∴ Option (3) is correct.

58. (4) **59. (3)** **60. (4)**

61. (3): Arranging the word, according to english dictionary.

Conscience → Consciousness → Consequence → Conservation → Consume

∴ Option (3) is the correct option.

62. (3):

(2, 3), (3, 5) (5, 7) (7, 11), (11, 13), (13, 17)

+1 +2 +2 +4 +2 +4

Here, the missing number pair = ? = (13, 17).

63. (4): 1. I F C (−3 −3) 2. N K H (−3 −3)

3. P M J (−3 −3) 4. R O M (−3 −2)

Here, Option (4) is the odd one among the given terms.

64. (4): 3 : 30 :: 6 : ? :: 7 : 346

$\Rightarrow \quad 3^3 + 3 = 27 + 3 = 30$

$6^3 + 3 = 216 + 3 = 219$

Similarly,

$7^3 + 3 = 343 + 3 = 346$

Here, ? = the missing number = 219.

65. (1): Given, R I G H T

+1↓ +1↓ +1↓ +1↓ +1↓

S J H I U

Similarly, F I N D S

+1↓ +1↓ +1↓ +1↓ +1↓

G J O E T

∴ The code for FINDS is GJOET.

66. (3): In given arrangement of letter.

NGK, NGK

There are 2 'G', which are followed by 'K' and preceded by N.

67. (3): 1. [26, 4, 22] ⇒ 26 − 4 = 22
2. [45, 9, 36] ⇒ 45 − 9 = 36
3. [64, 14, 54] ⇒ 64 − 14 = 50
4. [99, 25, 74] ⇒ 99 − 25 = 74

Here, option (3) is different from others.

68. (4) **69. (2)**

70. (3): From given,
First figure ⇒ 4 + 9 = 13 and 2 + 11 = 13
Second figure ⇒ 5 + 15 = 20 and 7 + P = 20
⇒ P = 13
Third figure ⇒ 6 + 21 = 27 and 2 + 25 = 27
∴ the value of 'P' = 13.

71. (2)

72. (4): Given, PEDESTRIAN = 30
⇒ (Number of letter) × 30 = 10 × 3 = 30
ACCIDENT = 24
⇒ 8 × 3 = 24
DRIVER = 18
⇒ 6 × 3 = 18
Similarly,
TRAFFIC = 7 × 3 = 21
⇒ TRAFFIC = 21.

73. (2): Given, Cost of 3 erasers = ₹ 9
⇒ 1 eraser = ₹ 3
and 2 sharpeners + 2 erasers = ₹ 14
⇒ 2 sharpeners + 2 × 3 = 14
⇒ 2 sharpeners = 14 − 6 = 8
⇒ 2 sharpeners = 8
⇒ 1 sharpener = ₹ 4
and 3 pencils + 1 sharpener = ₹ 25
⇒ 3 pencils + 4 = 25
⇒ 3 pencils = 25 − 4 = 21
⇒ 1 pencil = ₹ 7
∴ The cost of 1 pencil is ₹ 7.

74. (4)

75. (3): Anita > Babita > Chetna > Divya > Erric
Here, Chetna is in the middle with respect to their ages.

76. (1): The passage clearly mentions that "There may be sunshine one moment and a snowstorm the other", highlighting the rapid and contrasting changes in weather, thus justifying the term 'unpredictable'.

77. (4): The mountaineer respects nature not just out of admiration but because of the real threats it poses. The phrase "formidable glory" and the context suggest that survival depends on respecting nature's power.

78. (4): The feeling of exhilaration comes from emotional and physical accomplishments like overcoming fear and danger, not from using tools. This makes option 4 the inappropriate reason.

79. (4): The sentence "His formidable opponent beat him in no time in the boxing ring" uses the same word from the passage "formidable glory", meaning strong, fearsome, or challenging.

80. (4): The passage says "arduous journeys" and later explains how such journeys involve great effort and energy, matching the meaning described in the question.

81. (4): Reconstructing: "The performance of our players was rather worse than I expected" - this is the most grammatically correct and meaningful sequence.

82. (2): 'Abandon' means to leave or give up something; 'continue' is the opposite, meaning to persist or carry on.

83. (1): It is correctly spelled. The other options contain spelling errors: "Recommendation", "Irreparable", and "Meagre" are the correct spellings.

84. (2): This option changes both the gender-specific words - "father" to "mother" and maintains the gender-neutral "teacher".

85. (3): This is the correct active voice form of the passive sentence "By whom was this beautiful glass broken?" It preserves the tense and structure accurately.

86. (4): The sentence talks about everything going wrong, so the most appropriate word is "worst" - "Today is the worst day of my life..."

87. (4): 'Permit' means to allow. The opposite is 'prevent', which means to stop or disallow.

88. (2): Correct sentence: "Though she worked hard, yet she failed."
Here, the conjunction "yet" is used to indicate contrast between two clauses: effort and failure. In formal usage, "though" can be paired with "yet" to emphasize a contradiction. While "but" and

"although" are also contrastive, "yet" fits the given sentence structure best and is grammatically correct in this context.

89. (3): The sentence becomes: "It was such a foolish decision to accept an impossible task". - both are correct as per the sound of the following words.

90. (3): 'Bleak' means cold, barren, or hopeless - very close in meaning to 'gloomy'.

91. (1): "Fortunately we escaped unhurt" implies good luck or a positive outcome, fitting the context.

92. (3): This is the correct passive form and grammatically appropriate usage.

93. (2): "Loudly" is the correct adverb to describe the manner of playing music. "Aloud" is used for speaking, not general sound.

94. (3): This correctly transforms the exclamatory sentence into indirect speech, changing the present tense to past.

95. (3): Error: "me that" is incorrect. It should be "me what" or "asked me what had happened." So the error lies in part B.

96. (3): This is the exact sentence in direct speech, matching the given indirect form without any change in tense or meaning.

97. (1): 'Most' is the superlative degree. Its comparative form is 'more'. Example: much - more - most.

98. (4): Correct sentence: "I wrote a line on the sand with reed that she could not read before the waves washed it away".

'Reed' refers to a thin stick-like plant often used to write in olden times. 'Read' is the verb in past tense here.

99. (3): The idiom "a dime a dozen" means something is very common or easily available, which fits the sentence.

100. (2): Correct question tag: "We are going to the movie tonight, aren't we?" - Statement is positive, so the tag is negative.

101. (3): Compressed Natural Gas (CNG) is primarily composed of methane (CH_4) - usually 85% to 95%. Methane is a clean-burning hydrocarbon, making CNG an environmentally friendly fuel alternative. It produces fewer greenhouse gases and pollutants compared to petrol or diesel. The other gases mentioned (carbon monoxide, nitrogen dioxide, oxygen) may be present in trace amounts or as by-products but are not major components of CNG.

102. (1): Combustion refers to a chemical reaction in which a substance (usually a fuel) reacts with oxygen, producing heat and often light (as in flames). This process is essential for burning fuels like wood, coal, and gasoline. Oxygen is the critical reactant in this process - without it, combustion cannot take place.

103. (2): In biology, animal cells lack a cell wall - they only have a flexible cell membrane that encloses the cell contents. In contrast, plant cells have a rigid cell wall made of cellulose in addition to the cell membrane. The presence of cytoplasm and nucleus is common to both plant and animal cells.

104. (2): Animals that give birth to live young ones are called viviparous. Mammals, including humans, cats, and dogs, are viviparous. In contrast, oviparous animals lay eggs that hatch outside the mother's body (e.g., birds, reptiles). Ovoviviparous animals lay eggs that hatch within the body, and parthenogenic species reproduce without fertilization.

105. (1): Objects that move through fluids (liquids or gases) are given streamlined shapes to reduce fluid friction or drag. This helps them move more efficiently. For example, cars, airplanes, and fish have streamlined shapes to minimize resistance from air or water.

106. (2): To limit noise pollution, effective measures include:

A. Minimising use of automobile horns reduces traffic noise.

B. Planting trees helps absorb and block sound waves.

C. Using silencing devices in aircraft engines reduces engine noise.

Cutting trees (D) increases noise pollution, hence it is not a valid measure.

107. (2): A plane mirror forms a virtual image (not formed on a screen), which appears behind the mirror and is of the same size as the object. The image is also laterally inverted (left-right reversed), but maintains the same dimensions.

108. (3): Sodium (Na) is highly reactive with water. When it comes in contact with water, it reacts violently to produce sodium hydroxide and hydrogen gas, releasing a lot of heat. This can even ignite the hydrogen gas. The other elements listed (phosphorus, zinc, cobalt) are less reactive in comparison.

109. (3): When electric current passes through a conducting solution (like saltwater), various effects can occur:

A. Gas bubbles form due to electrolysis (e.g., hydrogen or oxygen).

B. Metal deposits form at electrodes (e.g., copper plating).

D. The solution's color may change depending on the ions present.

(C) is incorrect because a color change can occur, depending on the reaction.

110. (3): Matching:

A. Satellite → III. Moon (The Moon is Earth's natural satellite)

B. Constellation → I. Cassiopeia (a group of stars forming a recognizable pattern)

C. Comet → IV. Halley (Halley's Comet is the most famous periodic comet)

D. Star → II. Sirius (Sirius is the brightest star in the night sky)

111. (1): Air is a mixture of gases where:

- Nitrogen is about 78%
- Oxygen is about 21%
- The remaining 1% includes argon, carbon dioxide, neon, helium, etc.

This composition is crucial for respiration, combustion, and maintaining life on Earth.

112. (4): Greenhouse gases trap heat in the atmosphere. Naturally occurring ones include:

- Methane (CH_4)
- Carbon dioxide (CO_2)
- Nitrous oxide (N_2O)

Ethane (C_6H_6) is not a major natural greenhouse gas; it is a hydrocarbon often released through human activities (like natural gas leaks), but not considered a primary natural greenhouse gas.

113. (1): Matching:

A. Bacteria → IV. Tuberculosis (*Mycobacterium tuberculosis*)

B. Rhizobium → I. Fixing Nitrogen (a nitrogen fixing symbiotic bacterium in legumes)

C. Protozoa → II. Malaria (caused by Plasmodium, a protozoan)

D. Virus → III. AIDS (caused by HIV virus)

Correct pairings show the role or disease caused by each microorganism group.

114. (2): These are the four major groups of micro-organisms:

- Bacteria (unicellular prokaryotes)
- Fungi (like yeast and mold)
- Protozoa (e.g., Amoeba, Plasmodium)
- Algae (e.g., Chlamydomonas, Spirogyra)

This classification is widely used in microbiology.

115. (3): Tremors or earthquakes are primarily caused by disturbances or sudden movements in the Earth's crust. The crust is the outermost solid layer, and when tectonic plates shift or fault lines slip, seismic waves are generated.

116. (4): The calorific value is defined as the amount of heat energy produced on complete combustion of 1 kg of fuel. It is measured in kilojoules per kilogram (kJ/kg) and helps determine fuel efficiency.

117. (2): Matching substances with their uses:

A. Gold → IV. Jewellery (due to its luster and non-reactivity)

B. Iron → III. Machinery (because of its strength and durability)

C. Mercury → I. Thermometer (due to uniform expansion and visibility)

D. Copper → II. Electric wires (due to high conductivity and ductility)

These matches reflect common and practical applications of materials.

118. (2): A magnet exerts a force (attraction or repulsion) without touching the object, which makes it a non-contact force. Other examples of non-contact forces include gravitational force and electrostatic force.

119. (3): Mustard is a Rabi crop, sown in winter and harvested in spring.

Kharif crops like Paddy, Soyabean, and Cotton are sown with the onset of monsoon (June-July) and harvested around October.

120. (3): HIV is not spread by casual contact such as shaking hands, hugging, or sharing food. It is mainly transmitted through:

- Unprotected sex with an infected person
- Sharing needles/syringes
- From mother to child during birth or breast-feeding

121. (1): Adrenalin (also called epinephrine) is the "fight or flight" hormone. It helps the body deal with stress, anger, fear, or embarrassment by increasing heart rate, blood flow, and alertness.

Other hormones listed have different functions:

- Thyroxine regulates metabolism
- Insulin regulates blood sugar
- Estrogen is a female reproductive hormone.

122. (3): Vermicomposting is the process of making compost using redworms (earthworms). These worms break down organic waste into nutrient-rich compost, useful for farming and gardening.

123. (2): Biodiversity refers to the variety of life - different species of animals, plants, and microorganisms, their genetic differences, and their ecosystems. It emphasizes the interdependence of living beings and their relationship with the environment.

124. (1): Satpura National Park (in Madhya Pradesh) includes India's first Reserve Forests. It is significant for conservation and ecosystem protection.

- Jim Corbett is India's first National Park, not Reserve Forest.
- Kaziranga is famous for rhinoceroses.
- Tawa Reservoir is a dam, not a reserve forest.

125. (4): During adolescence, hormonal changes increase the activity of both sebaceous and sweat glands. Overactive sebaceous glands cause excess oil production, leading to acne and pimples, while sweat gland activity also rises. Hence, both contribute during this stage.

126. (4): Judicial review is the power of the judiciary (especially the Supreme Court and High Courts) to review laws passed by the legislature and declare them invalid or unconstitutional if they violate the basic structure of the Constitution. This principle was firmly established in the Kesavananda Bharati case (1973).

127. (1): This is NOT correct. The Gram Sabha includes all adult residents (18 years and above) of a village or villages covered by a Gram Panchayat. It is a general body of citizens, not elected representatives. The Sarpanch and ward Panchs are elected representatives and form the Gram Panchayat, not the Gram Sabha.

128. (3):

A. Public facilities (like water, healthcare, electricity) are linked to basic needs - Correct.

B. Saying they are only for those who can afford them is incorrect; public facilities are for everyone.

C. Providing these facilities is primarily the government's responsibility - Correct.

D. While private companies may be involved, the primary responsibility lies with the government, not with private companies - Incorrect.

129. (4): The Employment of Manual Scavengers and Construction of Dry Latrines (Prohibition) Act was enacted in 1993. It aimed to prohibit manual scavenging and the construction or use of dry latrines, to promote human dignity and sanitation.

130. (1): The natural growth rate of a population is the difference between the birth rate and the death rate in a given year, excluding migration.

- If births exceed deaths, the natural growth rate is positive.
- It is a key indicator of population change in demography.

131. (3): Solar energy is a renewable resource because it is naturally replenished and inexhaustible on a human timescale.

In contrast:

- Natural gas, coal, and petroleum are non-renewable fossil fuels that take millions of years to form and are depleting due to extensive use.

132. (4): "Amar Jiban" (translated as My Life) was the first known autobiography written by an Indian woman, Rashsundari Devi, in Bengali in 1876. It offers a glimpse into the life of a 19th-century housewife and her deep desire for literacy and self-expression.

133. (3): PIL stands for Public Interest Litigation - a legal mechanism that allows any individual or group to file a petition in court on behalf of those whose rights are being violated, even if they are not directly affected.

It is an important tool to promote social justice and hold authorities accountable.

134. (4): The Azad Hind Fauj or Indian National Army (INA) was raised by Subhas Chandra Bose in 1943 to fight the British for India's independence.

It was supported by Japan and consisted mainly of Indian prisoners of war and expatriates.

135. (3): Defense services (like the Army, Navy, and Air Force) are the responsibility of the Central Government.

Municipal Corporations are local bodies responsible for:

- Garbage collection,
- Maintaining public health,
- Running schools,
- Controlling disease outbreaks, etc.

136. (1): The Sahara Desert is the largest hot desert in the world and is located in northern Africa. It spans multiple countries including Algeria, Egypt, Libya, Mali, Mauritania, Morocco, Niger, Sudan, Chad, and Tunisia. It covers approximately 9.2 million square kilometers.

137. (3): The main factors of soil formation include:

- Time
- Parent rock (bedrock)
- Climate
- Organisms (plants, microbes)
- Topography (relief)

Precipitation alone is not considered a direct factor of soil formation, although it may influence climate and weathering indirectly. Therefore, it is not counted among the core factors.

138. (2): Jute is known as the "Golden Fibre" due to its natural golden shine and its economic importance as a biodegradable, eco-friendly fibre used for making bags, ropes, mats, etc. India and Bangladesh are leading producers.

139. (2): The Dandi March (1930), led by Mahatma Gandhi, was a non-violent protest against the British Salt Law, which imposed a monopoly and tax on salt production. Gandhi walked from Sabarmati Ashram to Dandi (about 390 km) to produce salt and defy the law.

140. (1): Bahadur Shah Zafar was the last Mughal emperor. He was a symbolic leader during the Revolt of 1857. After the failure of the revolt, he was exiled to Rangoon (Burma) by the British, marking the formal end of the Mughal Empire.

141. (2): Marine-based industries are those that use products from the sea and oceans as raw materials. Seafood processing involves cleaning, packaging, and preserving fish and other marine products, making it a perfect example of a marine-based industry.

Other options:

- Cotton textile is agriculture-based
- Iron ore is mineral-based
- Pharmaceuticals is chemical/biotech-based

142. (2): Article 17 of the Indian Constitution abolishes untouchability and forbids its practice in any form. It also declares that the enforcement of any disability arising out of untouchability shall be an offence punishable by law.

143. (3): Australia is the largest producer of bauxite in the world.

Bauxite is the primary ore of aluminium, and Australia has vast deposits, particularly in Queensland and Western Australia.

Other major producers include China, Brazil, and India.

144. (1): Matching:

A. Diwan → I. Financial Officer - Diwan was in charge of revenue and finance in Mughal administration.

B. Bakhshi → II. Military Paymaster - Bakhshi was responsible for military payments and records.

C. Faujdar → III. Military Commander - Faujdar maintained law and order and military control in a region.

D. Kotwal → IV. Police Commander - Kotwal was the chief of police and responsible for civic administration.

145. (2): CITES stands for "The Convention on International Trade in Endangered Species of Wild Fauna and Flora."

It is an international agreement between governments, aimed at ensuring that international trade in wild animals and plants does not threaten their survival. It was signed in 1973 and came into force in 1975.

146. (4): Ibn Battuta was a famous 14th-century Muslim traveler and scholar from Tangier, Morocco. He traveled across Africa, the Middle East, India, and China, and wrote an account of his journeys titled "Rihla", providing valuable insights into medieval cultures.

147. (2): According to the Constitution of India, the government is divided into three main organs:

- Legislature - Makes laws (e.g., Parliament)
- Executive - Implements laws (e.g., President, Prime Minister, Cabinet)
- Judiciary - Interprets laws (e.g., Supreme Court, High Courts)

148. (4): Afforestation is the process of planting trees on barren land, which helps prevent soil erosion, restores fertility, and conserves land resources.

The other options contribute to land degradation, not conservation.

149. (2): This is not a feature of a shopping complex, which is designed for direct retail between sellers and consumers.

Buying and selling between traders typically happens in wholesale markets or mandis, not in shopping malls or complexes.

150. (4): The Richter scale is used to measure the magnitude (energy released) of an earthquake.

- It is a logarithmic scale introduced by Charles F. Richter.
- The scale ranges from 0 upwards, with each increase of 1 representing 10 times more amplitude.

Other options like "Victor scale" and "Nichter scale" are incorrect or fictitious.

YOUR SPACE

Previous Years' Paper

All India Sainik Schools

Entrance Examination (AISSEE)—2024* Class-IX

Section-A : MATHEMATICS

1. If $\left(a^8+\frac{1}{a^8}\right)\left(a^4+\frac{1}{a^4}\right)\left(a^2+\frac{1}{a^2}\right)$

$\left(a+\frac{1}{a}\right)\left(a-\frac{1}{a}\right)=a^b-\frac{1}{a^b}$,

then value of b, is:

A. 8

B. 16

C. 32

D. 64

2. In a fruitstore, there are $4\left(a^2-\frac{2}{3}b^2\right)$ boxes and in each box there are $\left(\frac{3}{4}a^2+3b^2\right)$ apples. How many apples are there in the store?

A. $3a^4 + 10a^2b^2 - 8b^4$

B. $3a^4 + 12a^2b^2 + 8b^4$

C. $12a^4 + 10a^2b^2 + 6b^4$

D. $12a^4 + 12a^2b^2 - 6b^4$

3. If $x=\frac{4ab}{a+b}$, then the value of $\frac{x+2a}{x-2a}+\frac{x+2b}{x-2b}$, is:

A. $\frac{2ab}{(a+b)^2}$

B. 2

C. 4

D. $\frac{4ab}{(a+b)^2}$

4. If 8 is multiplied with 7 more than a number, it becomes the same as 15 is added to 3 times the same number. This can be represented by which of the following equations?

A. $7(8 + x) = 3x + 15$

B. $56 + x = 3x + 15$

C. $8(7 + x) = 15 + 3x$

D. $56x + 1 = 3(x + 5)$

5. $\{44(x^4 - 5x^3 - 24x^2)\} \div \{11x(x - 8)\} =$

A. $4x(x + 3)$

B. $7x(x + 2)$

C. $5x(x + 4)$

D. $(x + 2)(x + 3)$

6. In the figure, l_1 is parallel to l_2 and $\angle 1 = 115°$, $\angle 2 = 40°$, then $\angle 3$ is equal to:

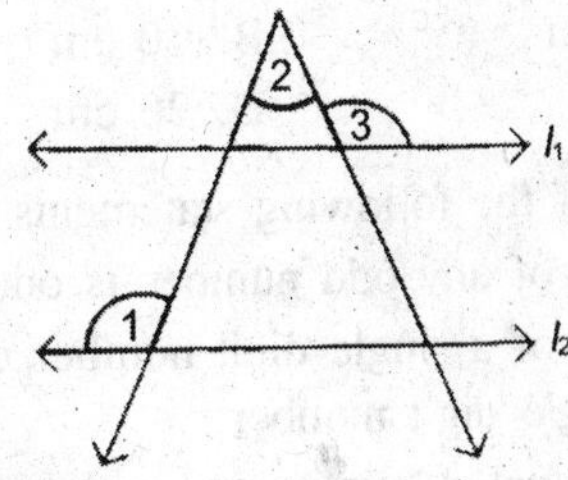

A. 115°

B. 110°

C. 105°

D. 100°

1. B	2. A	3. B	4. C	5. A	6. C

*Exam held on 28/1/2024

7. Survey was done on 900 schools children about their choice of TV programmes:

(*a*) Sports (*b*) Comedy shows
(*c*) Serials (*d*) News

Their choices are shown in the Pie chart.

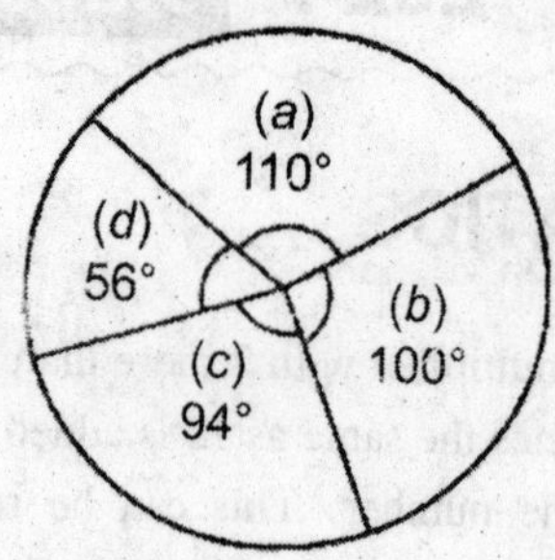

How many children showed interest for Comedy shows?

A. 235 B. 250
C. 265 D. 275

8. ABCD is a trapezium in which AB || DC and DE ⊥ AB. If AB = 2DC, DE = 12 cm and area of ABCD = 144 cm^2, then the length of AB, is:

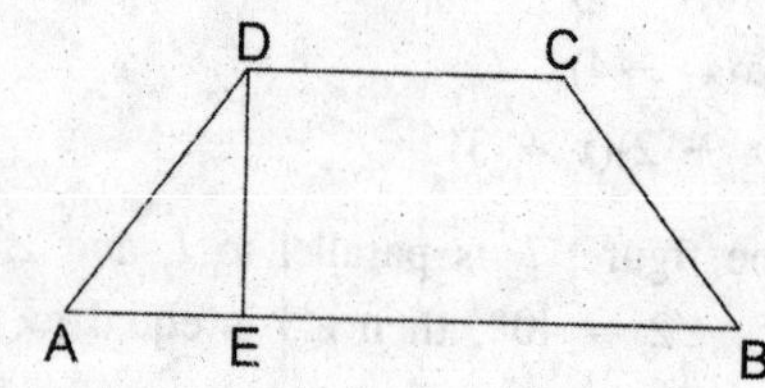

A. 16 cm B. 10 cm
C. 8 cm D. 20 cm

9. Which of the following statements are true?

(*a*) Cube of any odd number is odd.
(*b*) Cube of a single digit number cannot be a single digit number.
(*c*) A perfect cube may end with exactly two zeroes.
(*d*) Cube of a 2-digit number has at least 3 digits.

A. (*a*), (*b*), (*c*) only B. (*b*), (*c*), (*d*) only
C. (*a*), (*b*), (*d*) only D. (*a*), (*d*) only

10. The value of x from the following figure is:

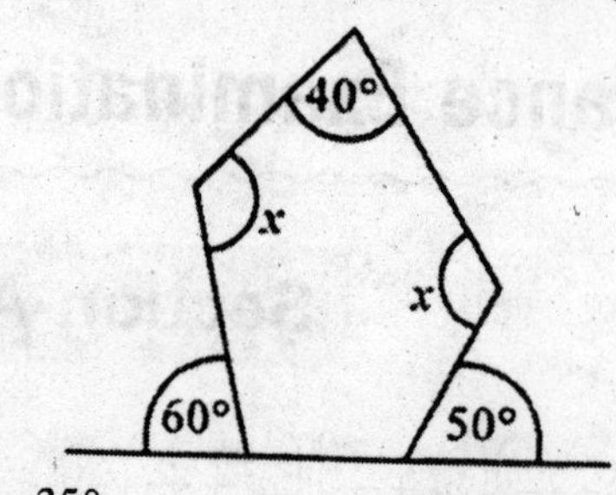

A. 35° B. 70°
C. 125° D. 250°

11. Madan scored marks given in the following table. Every paper was of 100 marks.

Maths	English	Hindi	Science	Social Science
95	72	80	68	65

His average marks per subject is:

A. 72 B. 74
C. 75 D. 76

12. Which of the following triangles with given sides is not a right-angled triangle?

(*a*) 3, 4, 5
(*b*) 5, 12, 13
(*c*) 6, 7, 8
(*d*) 6, 8, 10

A (*a*) B (*d*)
C. (*b*) D. (*c*)

13. $\sqrt{\sqrt[3]{27} - 2 \times \sqrt[3]{8} + \sqrt[3]{125}} =$

A. 4 B. 3
C. 2 D. 1

14. The average of first five prime numbers is:

A. 3.6 B. 5
C. 5.2 D. 5.6

7. B	8. A	9. D	10. C	11. D	12. D	13. C	14. D

15. Two cubes have their surface areas in the ratio 4 : 9. What is the ratio of their volumes?

A. 64 : 729 B. 8 : 27
C. 9 : 4 D. 2 : 3

16. 4 equal cuboids with dimensions 6 cm × 10 cm × 4 cm are joined side by side. The volume of the solid so formed, is:

A. 240 cubic cm B. 480 cubic cm
C. 864 cubic cm D. 960 cubic cm

17. Ritu is four years younger than her brother Varun. After 5 years, the sum of their ages will be 70 years. What is the present age of Ritu?

A. 30 years B. 25½ years
C. 28 years D. 32 years

18. Out of a certain number of marbles, $\left(\frac{3}{5}\right)^{th}$ are red and half of the remaining are green. If the number of green marbles is 12, then how many are red marbles?

A. 24 B. 36
C. 9 D. 18

19. How many sides does a regular polygon have if each of its interior angle is 156°?

A. 9 B. 12
C. 15 D. 20

20. If two perpendicular sides of a triangle are 9 cm and 40 cm and length of the side opposite to right angle is x cm, then the value of x, is:

A. 39 B. 40
C. 41 D. 42

21. The value of a car depreciates at 10% per annum. Jayant bought the car for ₹ 8,00,000. What will be its value after 3 years?

A. ₹ 5,83,000 B. ₹ 5,83,890
C. ₹ 5,92,000 D. ₹ 5,83,200

22. The median of the data set 3, 11, 8, 9, 6, 7, 12, is:

A. 6 B. 7
C. 8 D. 9

23. The average height of 6 boys is 5′ 3″. If one boy is 6′ 1″ tall, then the average height of remaining boys, is:

A. 5′ B. 5′ 1″
C. 5′ 2″ D. 5′ 4″

24. By which smallest number, 2700 must be multiplied so that the new number is a perfect cube?

A. 6 B. 10
C. 15 D. 18

25. The number of zeros at the end of number 1 × 2 × 3 × 4 × ____ × 20, is:

A. 6 B. 4
C. 5 D. 3

26. If $a : b : c : d = 1 : 2 : 3 : 5$, then the value of $\frac{a^2+b^2+c^2}{b^2+c^2+d^2}$, is:

A. $\frac{7}{19}$ B. $\frac{19}{5}$
C. $\frac{8}{17}$ D. $\frac{4}{21}$

27. Atul drives a car at a speed of 48 km/h and starts his journey for his hometown 132 km away from residence at 9 am. At what time, will he reach his hometown?

A. 11 am B. 11:20 am
C. 11:40 am D. 11:45 am

28. If the points A(3, 0) and B(0, 4) are joined, then what will be the area of the triangle formed by AB and the coordinate axes?

A. 5 unit^2 B. 6 unit^2
C. 7 unit^2 D. 12 unit^2

15. B	16. D	17. C	18. B	19. C	20. C	21. D
22. C	23. B	24. B	25. B	26. A	27. D	28. B

29. If in polyhedron, V stands for number of vertices, F stands for number of faces and E stands for number of edges, then which of the following cannot be true for a polyhedron?

A. V = 8 F = 6 E = 12
B. V = 5 F = 5 E = 8
C. V = 6 F = 5 E = 10
D. V = 4 F = 4 E = 6

30. All faces of a cube of side 5 cm are red painted and is cut into smaller cubes of side one cm. What is the total volume of smaller cubes formed, which have no face with red colour?

A. 54 cm^3 B. 45 cm^3
C. 34 cm^3 D. 27 cm^3

31. What is the greatest value of A for which the 6 digit number 326A50 is divisible by 3?

A. 2 B. 6
C. 8 D. 9

32. $\frac{7}{3}+\frac{7}{3}\div\frac{14}{3}-\frac{1}{7}\div\left(-\frac{14}{49}\right)=$

A. $\frac{7}{3}$ B. $\frac{3}{2}$
C. $\frac{10}{3}$ D. $\frac{1}{2}$

33. The cost of 5 kg apples is ₹ 425, the cost of 12 dozen oranges is ₹ 744 and the cost of 4 kg mangoes is ₹ 480. What is the total cost of 8 kg apples, 8 dozen oranges and 8 kg mangoes?

A. ₹ 1,416 B. ₹ 2,136
C. ₹ 1,826 D. ₹ 2,756

34. Pawan bought a second hand TV for ₹ 4,300. He spent ₹ 500 on its repair and sold it for ₹ 5,856. In this transaction, his gain was:

A. 20% B. 21%
C. 22% D. 24%

35. There are 120 students in a hostel and there is food provision for 25 days. How long would these provisions last out if 30 more students join the group?

A. 30 days B. 22 days
C. 20 days D. 17 days

36. If an item is sold at ₹ 1,292 after giving a discount of 15%, then the marked price of the item is:

A. ₹ 1,480 B. ₹ 1,500
C. ₹ 1,520 D. ₹ 1,530

37. 6 kg of metal A and 24 kg of metal B are melt together to form an alloy. The percentage of metal A in the alloy is:

A. 20% B. 25%
C. $33\frac{1}{3}\%$ D. 30%

38. What smallest number should be subtracted from 3142 to get a perfect square?

A. 5 B. 6
C. 7 D. 8

39. If alphabets A, B, C, ... are represented by numbers 1, 2, 3, ..., then the value of $\sqrt{Z-A}$, is:

A. 5 B. 4
C. 7 D. 11

40. In a polygon, sum of interior angles is 360°. Its diagonals are equal but not all the sies. What is the polygon?

A. Parallelogram B. Rhombus
C. Rectangle D. Square

41. If circumference of circle is 88 cm, then the area of the circle (in cm^2) is (use π = 22/7):

A. 600 B. 612
C. 616 D. 620

29. C	**30.** D	**31.** C	**32.** C	**33.** B	**34.** C	**35.** C
36. C	**37.** A	**38.** B	**39.** A	**40.** C	**41.** C	

42. Numbers 1 to 40 are written on different cards (one number on one card) and kept in a box. One card is picked up from the box. What is the probability that the card shows a perfect square number?

A. $\frac{1}{8}$

B. $\frac{1}{5}$

C. $\frac{3}{20}$

D. $\frac{1}{10}$

43. 6 identical pipes cm fill a tank in one hour and 30 minutes. How long will it take to fill the tank if 3 pipes stop working after filling half the tank?

A. 135 minutes B. 125 minutes
C. 110 minutes D. 130 minutes

44. A certain number of men can complete a work in 50 days. If there were 6 men more, the work can be finished in 10 days less. The number of men originally working are:

A. 36 B. 30
C. 28 D. 24

45. If one angle of a triangle is 63° and remaining two angles are in the ratio 1 : 2, then the measure of the largest angle of the triangle, is:

A. 63° B. 70°
C. 78° D. 82°

46. If the area of a circle is 2464 cm^2, then the radius of the circle (in cm), is (use π = 22/7):

A. 24 B. 26
C. 28 D. 56

47. The given line graph shows the number of articles sold by a company in the first 8 weeks of a particular year.

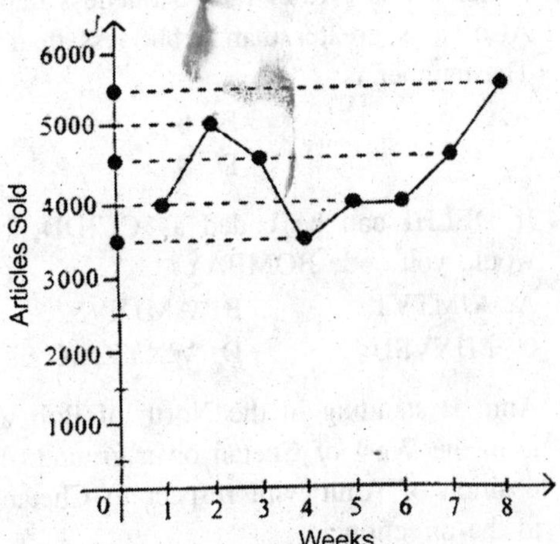

What is the average number of articles sold in 8 weeks?

A. 5892 B. 4875
C. 4375 D. 2945

48. If $a = \sqrt{2} + 1, b = \sqrt{3} - \sqrt{2}$ and $c = \sqrt{6} + 2\sqrt{2}$ then the value of $a^2 + b^2 - c$, is:

A. 8

B. $8 - 3\sqrt{6}$

C. $8 + 4\sqrt{2}$

D. $11 - 3\sqrt{6}$

49. $(2.5a - 3.5b)^2 - (3.5a - 2.5b)^2 =$

A. $-6a^2 - 6b^2$

B. $6b^2 - 6a^2$

C. $6a^2 + 6b^2$

D. $6a^2 - 6b^2$

50. If 30% of (A + B) = 50% of (A – B), then A : B is:

A. 3 : 5 B. 5 : 3
C. 4 : 1 D. 1 : 4

42. C	43. A	44. D	45. C	46. C	47. C	48. B	49. B	50. C

Section-B : INTELLIGENCE

51. A number is greater than 3 but less than 8. Also, it is greater than 6 but less than 10. The number is:

A. 5 B. 6
C. 7 D. 8

52. If DELHI can be coded as CCIDD, how would you code BOMBAY?

A. AJMTVT B. AMJXVS
C. MJXVSU D. WXYZAX

53. Amit is standing in the North of Bob who is in the West of Chetan on a ground. The position of Amit with respect to Chetan is in the direction:

A. East B. North-West
C. North-South D. North

54. Complete the analogy.

MAN : PDQ :: WAN : ?

A. NAW B. ZDQ
C. YDQ D. YQD

55. Complete the analogy.

25 : 125 :: 36 : ?

A. 126 B. 206
C. 216 D. 318

56. Find the next pattern in the sequence.

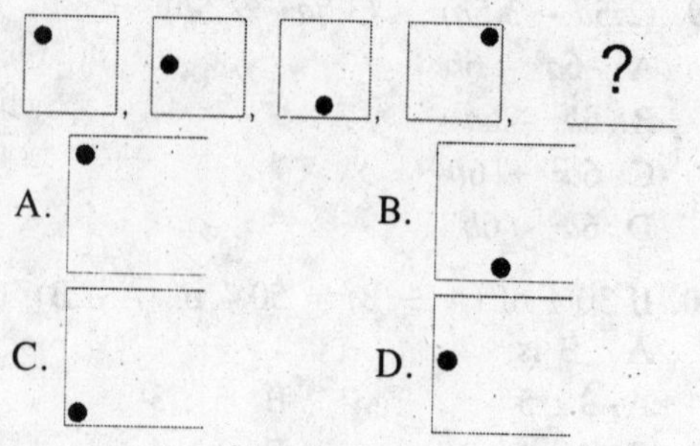

57. Replace the question mark in the following series:

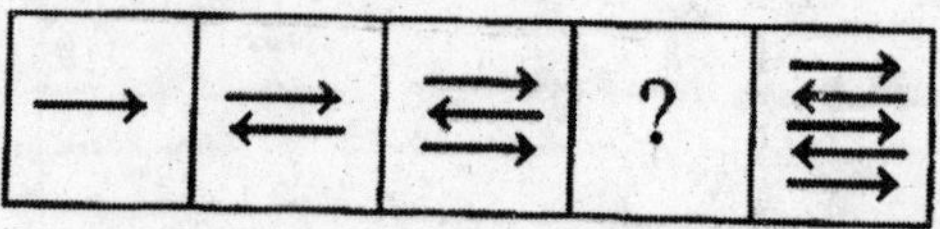

Choose the correct answer from the options given below.

A. B.

C. D.

58. Arrange the following words as per order in the dictionary.

(*a*) Consume (*b*) Consciousness
(*c*) Conscience (*d*) Conservation
(*e*) Consequence

Choose the correct answer from the options given below:

A. (*c*), (*b*), (*a*), (*e*), (*d*)
B. (*c*), (*a*), (*b*), (*e*), (*d*)
C. (*c*), (*e*), (*b*), (*d*), (*a*)
D. (*c*), (*b*), (*e*), (*d*), (*a*)

59. Find the odd one out:

A. 13 B. 17
C. 37 D. 63

60. Find the missing number:

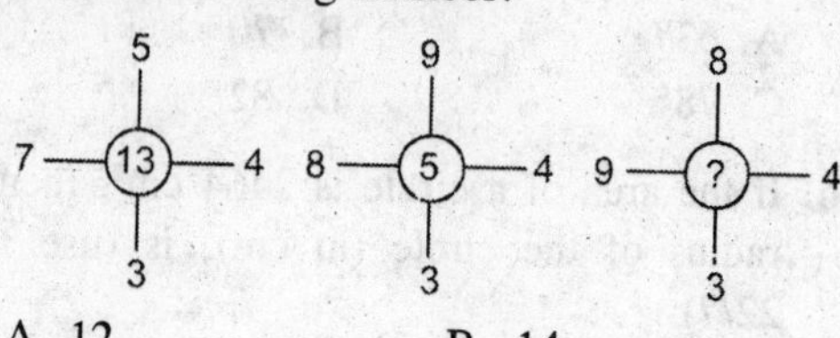

A. 12 B. 14
C. 15 D. 18

51. C	**52.** B	**53.** B	**54.** B	**55.** C	**56.** C	**57.** C	**58.** D	**59.** D	**60.** A

61. Find the next pattern in the sequence.

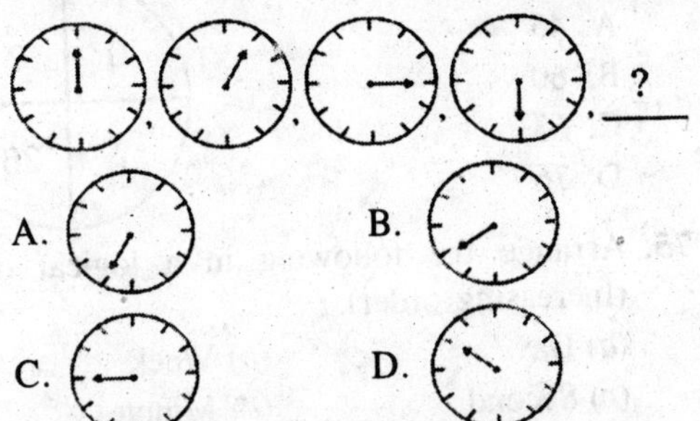

A. B.

C. D.

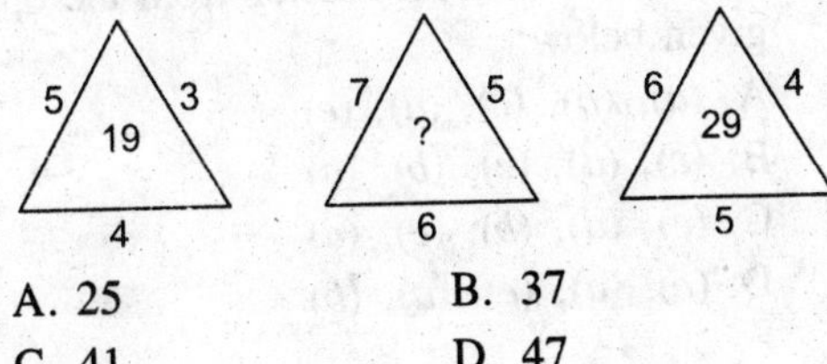

62. Find the missing number:

5, 3, 4, 19   7, 5, 6, ?   6, 4, 5, 29

A. 25   B. 37
C. 41   D. 47

63. Complete the analogy:

3 : 11 :: 7 : ?

A. 42   B. 29
C. 38   D. 51

64. Complete the following analogy:

Y : 2 :: T : ?

A. 9   B. 7
C. 8   D. 12

65. Complete the analogy.

Lizard : Reptile :: Whale: ?

A. Rodent   B. Amphibian
C. Mammal   D. Ocean

66. Find the missing number in the following series:

1, 9, 25, 49, ?, 121

A. 64   B. 81
C. 91   D. 100

67. Arrange the following in the chronological order.

(*a*) Birth   (*b*) Death
(*c*) Funeral   (*d*) Marriage
(*e*) Education

Choose the correct answer from the options given below:

A. (*a*), (*e*), (*d*), (*c*), (*b*)
B. (*a*), (*c*), (*d*), (*e*), (*b*)
C. (*a*), (*e*), (*d*), (*b*), (*c*)
D. (*a*), (*e*), (*b*), (*d*), (*c*)

68. Find the odd one out:

A. BCD   B. KMN
C. GHI   D. WXY

69. Anil, Bobby, Chetan, Deepak and Elen are five friends. Anil is shorter than Bobby but taller than Elen. Chetan is the tallest. Deepak is shorter than Bobby and taller than Anil. Who is in the middle with respect to their heights?

A. Bobby   B. Chetan
C. Deepak   D. Anil

70. If February 1, 2024 was Wednesday, what day was March 12th 2004?

A. Sunday   B. Saturday
C. Tuesday   D. Monday

71. Find the odd one out:

A. Pen   B. Sharpener
C. Scale   D. Stationery

72. How many such 5's are there in the following number sequence each of which is immediately preceded by 3 or 4 but not immediately followed by 8 or 9?

3 5 9 5 4 5 5 3 5 8 4 5 6
7 3 5 7 5 5 4 5 2 3 5 1 0

A. 3   B. 4
C. 5   D. 6

61. D	**62.** C	**63.** D	**64.** B	**65.** C	**66.** B
67. C	**68.** B	**69.** C	**70.** D	**71.** D	**72.** C

73. Identify the correct water image of the following figure.

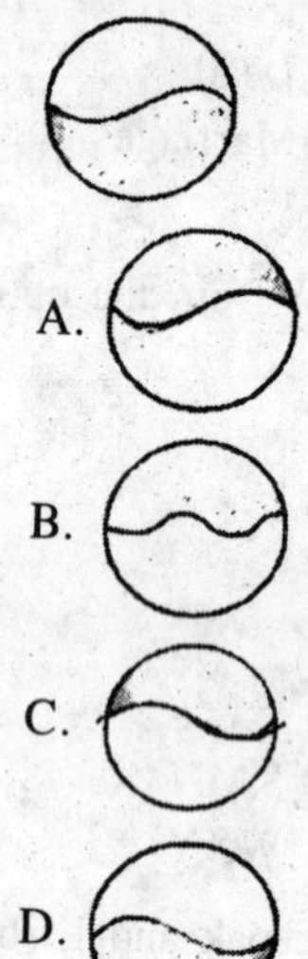

74. Find the missing number out of the options given below:

A. 45

B. 60

C. 63

D. 76

0	7
?	26

75. Arrange the following in a logical order (Increasing order).

(*a*) Day (*b*) Week

(*c*) Second (*d*) Minute

(*e*) Hour

Choose the correct answer from the options given below:

A. (*a*), (*b*), (*c*), (*d*), (*e*)

B. (*c*), (*d*), (*e*), (*b*), (*a*)

C. (*c*), (*d*), (*b*), (*e*), (*a*)

D. (*c*), (*d*), (*e*), (*a*), (*b*)

Section-C : ENGLISH

Directions (Qs. No. 76-81): *Read the passage carefully and answer the questions given below:*

The Walt Disney Company became the first major media company to ban advertisement for candy bars and junk food on its television channels, radio stations and websites, to stop food manufacturers from peddling nutritionally challenged fattening junk for kids. The ban covers foods with too much sugar, to much salt or a full meal more than 600 calories. Predictably, the outraged public said that banning smoking in public places and artery-blocking trans fats in food was bad enough, but stopping them from guzzling comfort drinks by the litres was almost a human rights violation.

It seems most people are not just happy choosing their own poison. They also want it in super-sized doses, guaranteed to kill sooner than later, for after tobacco use, obesity is the biggest public health bugbear that triggers more avoidable diseases and deaths than malnutrition. Overweight and obesity are the leading causes for global deaths, killing 2.8 million adults each year. Worldwide obesity has more than doubled since 1980. The reasons for poor lifestyle choices are many, with almost all driven by socio-economic causes such as low education and limited income. Like killer infections, obesity and the resultant type-2 diabetes affect the poor more than the affluent, largely because processed and fast food are cheaper and take less or no time to prepare than healthy home-cooked meals. Limiting food choices, however, is not enough.

The need is to get children off their chairs and into the playgrounds. Too much screen time,

73. C **74.** C **75.** D

largely social - networking followed by online and video gaming and television, are making healthy children fat and putting them at risk of type-2 diabetes in the second decade of their lives. The lifestyle disease that interferes with the way the body metabolises glucose typically affects people in their fifties and sixties and is linked with a host of complications.

The official measure of obesity in adults in Body Mass Index (BMI), which is calculated by dividing a person's weight in kilograms by the square of his height in metres (kg/m^2). The WHO definition is: a BMI greater than or equal to 25 is overweight, 30 is obese, but the cut-offs for the South Asians are 23 for overweight and 25 for obese.

76. What did the Walt Disney Company ban?

A. Candy bars

B. Junk food

C. The foods were healthy

D. Advertisement for candy bars and junk food

77. What was purpose behind the ban?

A. The foods were unhealthy

B. The foods were healthy

C. The foods were cheap

D. The foods were costly

78. Overweight and obesity are the leading causes for global deaths, killing ______ adults each year.

A. 2.6 million B. 8 million

C. 8.2 million D. 2.8 million

79. Obesity affects ______ more than the affluent.

A. the middle class

B. the educated

C. the poor

D. the sick

80. '<u>Limiting</u> food choices, however, isn't enough.'

Choose the synonym of underlined word.

A. Restricting B. Calculating

C. Ignoring D. Restructuring

81. Choose the correct option:

The antonym of 'miser' is

A. Rich B. Strong

C. Popular D. Generous

82. Choose the correct option from the following:

Her uncle who ______ to her was ______.

A. had been kind, dead

B. was dead, kind

C. is dead, kind

D. has been kind, dead

83. Fill in the blank with correct preposition:

I saw him climbing ______ the tree to pluck mangoes.

A. upon B. on

C. up D. over

84. Choose the correct spelt word:

A. Autonomus B. Autonomous

C. Autonemous D. Autenomus

85. Choose the correct sentence having an adverb:

A. He waited long for me.

B. He went on a long journey.

C. He came by an early flight.

D. He is of my near relation.

86. Change into passive voice:

'Please don't disturb me.'

A. You are requested not to disturb me.

B. You are requested not disturb me.

C. Please do not disturb me.

D. You are requested do not disturb me.

76. D	77. A	78. D	79. C	80. A	81. D	82. A	83. C	84. B	85. A	86. A

87. Fill in the blank with correct conjunction:

She is rich ______ she is not contented.

A. since B. yet
C. as D. while

88. Change the given sentence to Passive Voice:

People speak different languages all over the world.

A. Different languages are spoken all over the world.
B. Different languages were being spoken all over the world.
C. Different languages was spoken all over the world.
D. Different languages were spoken all over the world.

89. Choose the correct meaning of the given Idiom/Phrase:

'Helter skelter'

A. Natural and simple
B. Here and there
C. Merits and demerits
D. Arrogant and naughty

90. Choose the correct meaning of the following idiom:

'A wolf in a sheep's clothing'

A. A very relatable person
B. A weak person
C. A fair and honest person
D. A dangerous person pretending to be a harmless person

91. Choose the correct conjunction for the following:

This is the ring ______ she gifted me.

A. beside B. where
C. that D. if

92. Fill in the blank:

Neither she ______ he was present in the class.

A. nor B. or
C. and D. but

93. Fill in the blank:

______ she lost her daughter.

A. Hello! B. Alas!
C. Hurrah! D. Look!

94. Choose the most appropriate option:

Reema is too generous not to help the needy.

A. Reema is so generous not to help the needy.
B. Reema is so generous that she can help the needy.
C. Reema is so generous enough to help the needy.
D. Reema is so generous she will help.

95. Superlative degree of 'Top' is:

A. Topest B. Topmost
C. Toppest D. Most Top

96. Choose the correct option indicating the meaning of the given sentence:

She is too slow to be a runner.

A. She is so slow to be a runner.
B. She is slow to run.
C. She is so slow that she cannot be a runner.
D. She is too slow, she couldn't be a runner.

97. Choose the correct Question Tag for the following sentence:

It is quite hot outside today, ______?

A. is it B. isn't it
C. doesn't it D. aren't it

87. B **88.** A **89.** B **90.** D **91.** C **92.** A **93.** B **94.** B **95.** B **96.** C **97.** B

98. Spot the error:

(*a*) He is/ (*b*) the carpenter/ (*c*) who/ (*d*) made my chair.

A. (*a*)

B. (*b*)

C. (*d*)

D. No error

99. Change the given sentence to indirect narration:

Rita said to me, "I never eat junk food."

A. Rita told me that she never ate junk food.

B. Rita said to me that she never eats junk food.

C. Rita said that she never ever eats junk food.

D. Rita told me that I never ate junk food.

100. Change the given sentence to indirect narration:

They said to Rahul, "We are watching cricket."

A. They said Rahul that they are watching cricket.

B. They told Rahul that they were watching cricket.

C. They told Rahul that they are watching cricket.

D. They told Rahul that they have been watching cricket.

Section-D : GENERAL SCIENCE

101. Which source book keeps a record of all endangered animals and plants?

A. Blue Data Book B. Green Data Book

C. Red Data Book D. White Data Book

102. Identify the endemic flora of the Pachmarhi Biosphere Reserve from the following:

A. Bison and flying squirrel

B. Bison and sal

C. Sal and wild mango

D. Flying squirrel and wild mango

103. When fertilisation does not occur then the released egg and thickened lining of the uterus is shed off. It is called:

A. Pregnancy B. Menarche

C. Menopause D. Menstruation

104. Increase in height during puberty depends on:

A. Genes inherited from mother only

B. Eating right kind of food and exercise

C. Exercise and genes inherited from parents

D. Eating right kind of food and genes inherited from parents

105. Consider the following statements:

(*a*) Endocrine glands release hormones into the blood stream to reach a target site.

(*b*) Hormones are not chemical substances.

Select the correct answer using the code given below:

A. Only (*a*) is correct

B. Only (*b*) is correct

C. (*a*) and (*b*) are correct

D. Neither (*a*) nor (*b*) is correct

106. The magnitude of the power of an earthquake is expressed on a scale called:

A. Richter scale B. Vernier scale

C. Ratio scale D. Graphic scale

98. D	99. A	100. B	101. C	102. C	103. D	104. D	105. A	106. A

107. Calorific value of a fuel is expressed in:

A. Joule

B. Kilo Joule per kg (kJ/kg)

C. Kilo Joule

D. Kilo Joule/m^2

108. Tin cans are made by electro plating tin on to iron because Tin:

A. is less reactive than Iron

B. is more reactive than Iron

C. does not react with Iron

D. and Iron both are least reactive

109. Arrange the rolling, sliding and static friction in increasing order of friction and choose the correct option.

A. Rolling, Static, Sliding

B. Rolling, Sliding, Static

C. Static, Sliding, Rolling

D. Static, Rolling, Sliding

110. Which of the following is ***not*** a Rabi crop?

A. Wheat B. Pea

C. Mustard D. Paddy

111. Identify the methods for replenishing the soil with nutrients from the following:

(*a*) Growing different crops alternately.

(*b*) Usage of manures.

(*c*) Sowing healthy seeds.

(*d*) Growing legumes as fodder in one season and wheat crop in the next season.

Choose the correct option from the following:

A. (*a*), (*c*) and (*d*) B. (*a*), (*b*) and (*d*)

C. (*a*) and (*d*) D. (*b*) and (*c*)

112. When electric current is passed through the Copper Sulphate solution?

A. Copper gets deposited on the electrode connected to the positive terminal of the battery.

B. Copper gets deposited on the electrode connected to the negative terminal of the battery.

C. No reaction takes place.

D. Copper gets deposited either on positive or on negative terminal of the battery.

113. Match the following:

(Heavenly body)	**(Characteristics)**
(*a*) Orion	(*i*) Small objects revolving around Sun between Mars & Jupiter
(*b*) Comet	(*ii*) Brightest star in the sky located close to Orion.
(*c*) Sirius	(*iii*) A constellation can be seen during winter time in late evenings.
(*d*) Asteroid	(*iv*) An object which revolves around Sun in elliptical orbit and has a bright head and a tail.

Choose the correct option from the answers given below:

	(*a*)	(*b*)	(*c*)	(*d*)
A.	(*iii*)	(*iv*)	(*i*)	(*ii*)
B.	(*iii*)	(*iv*)	(*ii*)	(*i*)
C.	(*iv*)	(*iii*)	(*ii*)	(*i*)
D.	(*iii*)	(*ii*)	(*iv*)	(*i*)

114. Which of the following gases has the highest concentration in the atmosphere?

A. Oxygen B. Carbon dioxide

C. Nitrogen D. Sulphur dioxide

115. Global Warming is ***not*** responsible for:

A. Increase in sea level

B. More severe storms

C. Increased droughts

D. More earthquakes

107. B **108.** A **109.** B **110.** D **111.** B **112.** B **113.** B **114.** C **115.** D

116. Identify the multicellular microorganism from the following:
(*a*) Bacteria
(*b*) Aspergillus
(*c*) Paramaecium
(*d*) Penicillium

Choose the correct option from the following:
A. (*a*) only
B. (*a*) and (*b*) only
C. (*b*), (*c*) and (*d*) only
D. (*b*) and (*d*) only

117. The bulb of the dropper, immersed in water is pressed. When the pressure is released, water gets filled in the dropper. This happens due to:
A. Force of water
B. Force of gravity
C. Pressure of water
D. Atmospheric pressure

118. An oscillating body is making 360 oscillations in 3 minutes. Its frequency in hertz will be:
A. 120 B. 2
C. 20 D. 12

119. A person who is standing 2 m in front of a plane mirror, seems to be ______ m away from his image.
A. 2 m B. 4 m
C. 0.5 m D. 1 m

120. Which of the following statements are ***not true*** for metals?
(*a*) Metals are good conductor of heat and electricity.
(*b*) The property of metals by which they can be beaten into thin sheets is called ductility.
(*c*) Metals produce ringing sounds so they are said to be Sonorous.
(*d*) In general metallic oxides are acidic in nature.

Choose the correct option from below:
A. (*b*) and (*c*)
B. (*c*) and (*d*)
C. (*b*) and (*d*)
D. (*a*), (*b*) and (*d*)

121. Polythene and PVC are examples of:
A. Thermoplastics
B. Thermosetting plastics
C. Melamine
D. Bakelite

122. Match List-I with List-II:

List-I	List-II
(*a*) Coke	(*i*) Obtained during the processing of coal to get coke.
(*b*) Coal Tar	(*ii*) Almost pure form of carbon
(*c*) Coal Gas	(*iii*) Petroleum
(*d*) Petrol	(*iv*) Naphthalene balls

Choose the correct option from the answer given below:

	(*a*)	(*b*)	(*c*)	(*d*)
A.	(*i*)	(*ii*)	(*iii*)	(*iv*)
B.	(*ii*)	(*iv*)	(*iii*)	(*i*)
C.	(*ii*)	(*iv*)	(*i*)	(*iii*)
D.	(*iii*)	(*ii*)	(*iv*)	(*i*)

123. A combustible substance catches fire/burn as long as its temperature is ______, its ignition temperature.
A. Higher than
B. Lower than
C. Equal to or higher than
D. Equal to or lower than

116. D	**117.** D	**118.** B	**119.** B	**120.** C	**121.** A	**122.** C	**123.** C

124. Which of the following is/are present only in plant cell?

(*a*) Cell membrane
(*b*) Cell wall
(*c*) Chloroplast
(*d*) Nuclear membrane

Select the correct answer using the code given below:

A. (*b*) and (*c*) B. (*a*) and (*d*)
C. (*b*) D. (*c*)

125. Given below are the different stages in the life cycle of frog. Arrange them in order of occurrence.

(*a*) Fertilisation
(*b*) Tadpole
(*c*) Laying of eggs
(*d*) Development of embryos

Choose the correct option from the following:

A. (*a*), (*c*), (*b*), (*d*) B. (*c*), (*a*), (*d*), (*b*)
C. (*c*), (*b*), (*d*), (*a*) D. (*d*), (*a*), (*c*), (*b*)

Section-E : SOCIAL SCIENCE

126. Who began a campaign against the practice of Sati?

A. Rammohan Roy
B. Ishwarchandra Vidyasagar
C. Jyotirao Phule
D. Shri Narayana Guru

127. Where is The Tata Iron and Steel Company situated?

A. On the banks of Hooghly river
B. On the banks of Son river
C. On the banks of Ganges
D. On the banks of Subarnarekha

128. When was The English Education Act introduced?

A. 1735 B. 1800
C. 1835 D. 1870

129. Match List-I with List-II:

List-I	List-II
(*a*) Sukta	(*i*) Slave
(*b*) Chariots	(*ii*) Sacrifice
(*c*) Yajna	(*iii*) Used in battles
(*d*) Dasa	(*iv*) Well said

Choose the correct option from the answers given below:

	(*a*)	(*b*)	(*c*)	(*d*)
A.	(*ii*)	(*iv*)	(*iii*)	(*i*)
B.	(*iv*)	(*i*)	(*iii*)	(*ii*)
C.	(*iii*)	(*ii*)	(*iv*)	(*i*)
D.	(*iv*)	(*iii*)	(*ii*)	(*i*)

130. Where is Gangri glacier?

A. Assam B. Mizoram
C. Ladakh D. Uttarakhand

131. Which of the following soldiers was hanged to death on 29 March, 1857?

A. Bhagat Singh B. Rajguru
C. Sukhdev D. Mangal Pandey

132. Where were the Mughal emperor Bahadur Shah Zafar and his wife Begum Zinat Mahal sent to prison?

A. Delhi B. Meerut
C. Rangoon D. Lucknow

133. Which of the following books contain the ideas of Chanakya?

A. Upnishads B. Arthashastra
C. Yogdarshan D. Prashasti

124. A **125.** B **126.** A **127.** D **128.** C **129.** D **130.** C **131.** D **132.** C **133.** B

134. Who created the sacred space Dharmsal?
A. Baba Guru Nanak B. Kabir
C. Tukaram D. Eknath

135. What is the place where a river flows into another water body called?
A. River's mouth B. Delta
C. Basin D. Tributary

136. Arrange the following steps of terrace farming in chronological order:
(*a*) The sides of each plot are raised to retain water.
(*b*) They cultivate rice on it.
(*c*) The land on a hill slope is made into flat plots.
(*d*) Plots are carved out in steps.
A. (*a*), (*b*), (*c*), (*d*) B. (*b*), (*c*), (*d*), (*a*)
C. (*d*), (*b*), (*c*), (*a*) D. (*c*), (*d*), (*a*), (*b*)

137. For how many years is a Gram Panchayat elected?
A. 1 B. 3
C. 2 D. 5

138. Which one of the following may be called a 'dwarf' planet?
A. Pluto B. Saturn
C. Mercury D. Venus

139. Where was the Harappan city of Dholavira located?
A. Rajasthan B. Rann of Kutch
C. Gulf of Khambhat D. Punjab

140. Which of the following is a conventional source of energy?
A. Biogas B. Firewood
C. Solar energy D. Wind energy

141. Ox bow lakes are found in:
A. Mountains B. Deserts
C. Glaciers D. River valleys

142. Match List-I with List-II:

List-I	List-II
(*a*) Biotic	(*i*) Rivers, Lakes, Seas, Oceans
(*b*) Hydrosphere	(*ii*) Thin layer of air
(*c*) Atmosphere	(*iii*) Hard top layer of the earth
(*d*) Lithosphere	(*iv*) The world of living organisms

Choose the correct option from the answers given below:

	(*a*)	(*b*)	(*c*)	(*d*)
A.	(*i*)	(*ii*)	(*iii*)	(*iv*)
B.	(*ii*)	(*iii*)	(*i*)	(*iv*)
C.	(*iii*)	(*i*)	(*ii*)	(*iv*)
D.	(*iv*)	(*i*)	(*ii*)	(*iii*)

143. Where are mushroom rocks found?
A. Valleys B. Glaciers
C. Hills D. Deserts

144. Which of the following is formed by the material carried by glaciers?
A. Flood plains B. Moraines
C. Beach D. Loess

145. Which of the following are the key features of the Constitution of India?
(*a*) Federalism
(*b*) Parliamentary form of Government
(*c*) Separation of Powers

Select the correct answer using the code given below:
A. (*a*) and (*b*) only B. (*b*) and (*c*) only
C. (*a*) and (*c*) only D. (*a*), (*b*) and (*c*)

146. Which of the following is a human made resource?
A. Technology B. Water
C. Copper D. Natural gas

134. A	**135.** A	**136.** D	**137.** D	**138.** A	**139.** B	**140.** B
141. D	**142.** D	**143.** D	**144.** B	**145.** D	**146.** A	

147. Which of the following is NOT a component of maps?

A. Distance B. Direction
C. Plan D. Scale

148. Which of the following is NOT a natural ecosystem?

A. Forest B. Sea
C. Aquarium D. Desert

149. Match List-I with List-II:

List-I	List-II
(*a*) Prejudice	(*i*) Difference in language, food, dress, customs etc.
(*b*) Stereotype	(*ii*) Judging people negatively.
(*c*) Discrimination	(*iii*) Fixing people into one image
(*d*) Diversity	(*iv*) Inequality

Choose the correct option from the answers given below:

	(*a*)	(*b*)	(*c*)	(*d*)
A.	(*i*)	(*ii*)	(*iii*)	(*iv*)
B.	(*ii*)	(*iii*)	(*iv*)	(*i*)
C.	(*iii*)	(*ii*)	(*i*)	(*iv*)
D.	(*iv*)	(*iii*)	(*ii*)	(*i*)

150. Which of the following is the main work of Patwari?

A. Maintaining law and order
B. Measuring land and keeping land records
C. Maintaining accounts of the village
D. Settles disputes of the villagers

EXPLANATORY ANSWERS

1. (B): $\because \left(a+\frac{1}{a}\right)\left(a-\frac{1}{a}\right) = a^2-\frac{1}{a^2}$

$$\left(a^2-\frac{1}{a^2}\right)\left(a^2+\frac{1}{a^2}\right) = a^4-\frac{1}{a^4}$$

$$\left(a^4-\frac{1}{a^4}\right)\left(a^4+\frac{1}{a^4}\right) = a^8-\frac{1}{a^8}$$

$$\left(a^8-\frac{1}{a^8}\right)\left(a^8+\frac{1}{a^8}\right) = a^{16}-\frac{1}{a^{16}}$$

$$\therefore \quad a^{16}-\frac{1}{a^{16}} = a^b-\frac{1}{a^b}$$

$$\Rightarrow \quad a^{16} = a^b \Rightarrow b = 16.$$

2. (A): Number of apples in the store

$$= \left(4a^2-\frac{8}{3}b^2\right)\left(\frac{3}{4}a^2+3b^2\right)$$

$$= 3a^4 + 12a^2b^2 - 2a^2b^2 - 8b^4$$

$$= 3a^4 + 10a^2b^2 - 8b^4.$$

3. (B): $\because \quad x = \frac{4ab}{a+b} \Rightarrow \frac{x}{2a} = \frac{2b}{a+b}$

$$\Rightarrow \quad \frac{x+2a}{x-2a} = \frac{2b+a+b}{2b-a-b} = \frac{3b+a}{b-a}$$

and $\frac{x}{2b} = \frac{2a}{a+b}$

$$\Rightarrow \quad \frac{x+2b}{x-2b} = \frac{2a+a+b}{2a-a-b} = \frac{3a+b}{a-b}$$

Now, $\frac{x+2a}{x-2a}+\frac{x+2b}{x-2b} = \frac{3b+a}{b-a}-\frac{(3a+b)}{b-a}$

$$= \frac{3b+a-3a-b}{b-a}$$

$$= \frac{2b-2a}{b-a}$$

$$= \frac{2(b-a)}{(b-a)} = 2.$$

147. C	148. C	149. B	150. B

4. (C): Let, Number = x

$$8(x + 7) = 3x + 15$$

Required equation = $8(7 + x) = 15 + 3x$.

5. (A): $\left\{\frac{44x^2(x^2-5x-24)}{11x(x-8)}\right\}$

$$= \frac{4x[x^2-8x+3x-24]}{(x-8)}$$

$$= 4x\frac{[x(x-8)+3(x-8)]}{x-8}$$

$$= \frac{4x(x-8)(x+3)}{x-8}$$

$$= 4x(x + 3).$$

6. (C):

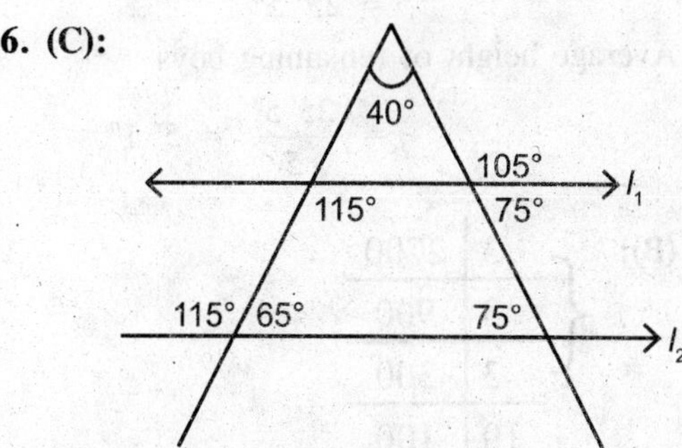

Hence, $\angle 3 = 105°$.

7. (B): Number of children showed interest for comedy shows

$$= \frac{100}{360}\times 900 = 250.$$

8. (A): Area of ABCD = $\frac{1}{2}(AB+CD)\times DE$

$\Rightarrow$ $144 = \frac{1}{2}(2CD+CD)\times 12$

$\Rightarrow$ $3CD = 24 \Rightarrow CD = 8$ cm

$\therefore$ $AB = 2 \times 8 = 16$ cm.

9. (D): (*a*) Cube of any odd number is odd. (True) ($3^3 = 27$, $5^3 = 125$)

(*d*) Cube of a 2-digit number has at least 3 digit (True)

Hence, (*a*) and (*d*) only true.

10. (C): $x + 40 + x + 130 + 120 = 540°$

$\Rightarrow$ $2x + 290 = 540°$

$\Rightarrow$ $2x = 250$

$\Rightarrow$ $x = 125°$

Hence, the value of $x = 125°$

11. (D): Total marks obtained

$$= 95 + 72 + 80 + 68 + 65$$

$$= 380$$

Average = $\frac{380}{5} = 76$.

12. (D): A. $3^2 + 4^2 = 5^2$

B. $5^2 + 12^2 = 13^2$

C. $6^2 + 7^2 \neq 8^2$

D. $6^2 + 8^2 = 10^2$

Hence, (C) is not right angle triangle.

13. (C): $\sqrt{3-2\times 2+5} = \sqrt{8-4} = \sqrt{4} = 2.$

14. (D): First-five prime numbers are 2, 3, 5, 7, 11

Sum = 2 + 3 + 5 + 7 + 11

Average = $\frac{28}{5} = 5.6$.

15. (B): $\frac{4a^2}{4b^2} = \frac{4}{9} \Rightarrow \frac{a^2}{b^2} = \frac{4}{9} \Rightarrow \frac{a}{b} = \frac{2}{3}$

Hence, ratio of their volumes

$$= \frac{a^3}{b^3} = \frac{8}{27} = 8 : 27.$$

16. (D): l = 24 cm, b = 10 cm, h = 4 cm

Required volume = $l \times b \times h$

$= 24 \times 10 \times 4$

$= 960$ cm^3.

17. (C): Let present age of Ritu = x years

$\therefore$ Varun's age = $x + 4$ years

After 5 years,

$x + 5 + x + 9 = 70$

$\Rightarrow$ $2x + 14 = 70$

$\Rightarrow$ $2x = 56 \Rightarrow x = 28$

Hence, present age of Ritu = 28 years.

18. (B): Let number of marbles = x

Number of red marbles = $\frac{3x}{5}$

Number of remaining marbles = $x - \frac{3x}{5} = \frac{2x}{5}$

According to the question

$$\frac{2x}{5} = 24$$

$\Rightarrow \quad 2x = 120 \Rightarrow x = 60$

Hence, number of red marbles = $\frac{3 \times 60}{5} = 36.$

19. (C): Required number of sides

$$= \frac{360}{180-156}$$

$$= \frac{360}{24} = 15.$$

20. (C):

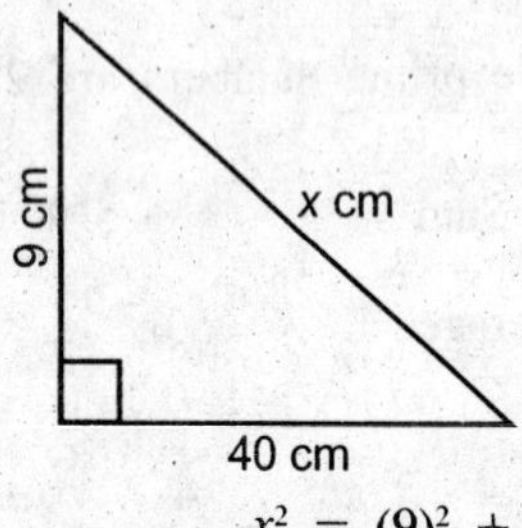

$$x^2 = (9)^2 + (40)^2$$

$\Rightarrow \quad x^2 = 81 + 1600 = 1681$

$\Rightarrow \quad x = \sqrt{1681} = 41$ cm

Hence, the value of x = 41 cm.

21. (D): After 1 year

$$\frac{10}{100} \times 800000 = 80000$$

$$\text{Value} = 800000 - 80000 = 720000$$

After 2 years

$$\frac{10}{100} \times 720000 = 72000$$

$$\text{Value} = 720000 - 72000 = 648000$$

After 3 years

$$\frac{10}{100} \times 648000 = 64800$$

$$\text{Value} = 648000 - 64800 = 583200$$

Hence, the value after 3 years will be ₹ 583200.

22. (C): 3, 6, 7, 8, 9, 11, 12

Here, n = 7 which is odd number

$\therefore \quad$ Median = $\left(\frac{n+1}{2}\right)$th term

= 14th term = 8..

23. (B): Total height of 6 boys = 31′ 6″

Total height of 5 boys = 31′ 6″ – 6′ 1″

= 25′ 5″

Average height of remaining boys

$$= \frac{25' \, 5''}{5} = 5' \, 1''.$$

24. (B):

3	2700
3	900
3	300
10	100
10	10
	1

Hence, the smallest no. = 10.

25. (B): 1 × 2 × 3 × 4 × ... × 20

1 × 2 × 3 × ... × 10

number of zeroes = 2

11 × 12 × 13 × ... × 20

number of zeroes = 2

∴ 1 × 2 × 3 × 4 × ... × 20

The number of zeros at the end of number = 4.

26. (A): ∵ $a : b : c : d = 1 : 2 : 3 : 5$

Then the value of $\frac{a^2+b^2+c^2}{b^2+c^2+d^2} = \frac{1+4+9}{4+9+25}$

$$= \frac{14}{38} = \frac{7}{19}.$$

27. (D): Distance = 132 km

Speed = 48 km/hr.

$$\text{Time} = \frac{132}{48} = \frac{11}{4} \text{ hrs.}$$

$$= 2\frac{3}{4} = 2 \text{ hrs. } 45 \text{ min}$$

Hence, Atul will reach his hometown

= 9 + 2 hr. 45 min

= 11:45 am.

28. (B): Area of triangle $= \frac{1}{2} \times 3 \times 4 = 6 \text{ unit}^2$.

29. (C): Euler's formula

$V - E + F = 2$

$V = 6$, $F = 5$, $E = 10$ is not true for a polyhedron because

$V - E + F \neq 2$

$6 - 10 + 5 = 1$.

30. (D): Total number of smaller cubes of side 1 cm cut from 5 cm cube = 125

Number cubes of faces painted red = 3 faces painted + 2 faces painted + 1 face painted

= 8 corners cubes + (12 edges × 3)

+ (6 faces × 9 cubes)

= 8 + 36 + 54 = 98

Number cubes of faces which are not painted red = 125 − 98 = 27 cm^3.

31. (C): 326A50 is divisible by 3

∴ 3 + 2 + 6 + 8 + 5 = 24 which is divisible by 3

Hence the greatest value of A = 8.

32. (C): $\frac{7}{3} + \frac{7}{3} \div \frac{14}{3} - \frac{1}{7} \div \frac{-14}{49}$

$$= \frac{7}{3} + \frac{7}{3} \times \frac{3}{14} - \frac{1}{7} \times \frac{-79}{14}$$

$$= \frac{7}{3} + \frac{1}{2} + \frac{1}{2} = \frac{14+3+3}{16}$$

$$= \frac{20}{6} = \frac{10}{3}.$$

33. (B): Cost of 5 kg apples = ₹ 425

Cost of 8 kg apples $= ₹ \frac{425}{5} \times 8$

= ₹ 85 × 8 = ₹ 680

Cost of 12 dozen oranges = ₹ 744

Cost of 8 dozen oranges $= ₹ \frac{744}{12} \times 8$

= ₹ 248 × 2 = ₹ 496

Cost of 4 kg mangoes = ₹ 480

Cost of 8 kg mangoes $= ₹ \frac{480}{4} \times 8$ = ₹ 960

Total cost of 8 kg apples, 8 dozen oranges and 8 kg mangoes

= 680 + 496 + 960

= ₹ 2136.

34. (C): C.P. of the TV = 4300 + 500

= ₹ 4800

S.P. of the TV = 5856

Gain = 5856 − 4800

= ₹ 1056

$$\text{Gain } \% = \frac{1056}{4800} \times 100 = 22\%.$$

35. (C): ∵ 120 students food provision = 25 days

∴ 150 students food provision

$$= \frac{25}{150} \times 150$$

= 20 days.

36. (C): 100 − 15 = 85

When S.P. ₹ 85 then M.P. = ₹ 100

When S.P. ₹ 1292 then M.P.

$$= ₹ \frac{100}{85} \times 1292$$

= ₹ 1520.

37. (A): % of metal A in the alloy

$$= \frac{6}{30} \times 100 = 20\%.$$

38. (B):

5	3142	56
	25	
106	642	
	636	
	××6	

When 6 is subtracted from 3142 then we get a perfect square

$56 \times 56 = 3136.$

39. (A): $\because$ A = 1, B = 2, C = 3, ..., Z = 26

Then, $\sqrt{Z-A} = \sqrt{26-1} = \sqrt{25} = 5.$

40. (C): The diagonals are equal of a polygon.

Sum of interior angles = 360°

This polygon may be square or rectangle.

But all sides are not equal.

Hence, the given polygon is rectangle.

41. (C): $C = 2\pi r$

$\Rightarrow \quad 88 = 2\times\frac{22}{7}\times r$

$\Rightarrow \quad r = 14$ cm

Area of the circle $= \pi r^2$

$= \frac{22}{7}\times 14\times 14$

$= 22 \times 28 = 616$ cm².

42. (C): Total no. = 40

Number of perfect square

= 1, 4, 9, 16, 25, 36 = 6

Required probability $= \frac{6}{40} = \frac{3}{20}.$

43. (A): $\because$ 6 pipes can fill a tank in 90 minutes

$\therefore$ 1 pipe can fill that tank in 6 × 90 min.

$\therefore$ 3 pipes can fill that tank in $\frac{6\times 90}{3}$ min.

= 180 minutes

Half portion of the tank was filled by 6 pipes

$\therefore$ Required time taken = (180 – 45) min.

= 135 minutes.

44. (D): Let number of men originally working = x

$\because$ x men can complete a work in 50 days

$\therefore$ 1 man can complete that work in $x \times 50$ days

$\therefore$ $(x + 6)$ men can complete that work in

$\frac{x\times 50}{x+6}$

According to the question,

$\frac{50x}{x+6} = 40$

$\Rightarrow \quad 50x = 40x + 240$

$\Rightarrow \quad 10x = 240$

$\Rightarrow \quad x = 24$

Hence, the number of men originally working = 24.

45. (C): $\because$ One angle of a triangle = 63°

Let remaining two angles

= 180 – 63 = 117°

$\Rightarrow \quad 1x + 2x = 117°$

$\Rightarrow \quad 3x = 117°$

$\Rightarrow \quad x = \frac{117}{3} = 39°$

$2x = 2 \times 39 = 78°$

Hence, the largest angle of the triangle = 78°.

46. (C): Area of the circle $= \pi r^2$

$\Rightarrow \quad 2464 = \frac{22}{7}r^2$

$\Rightarrow \quad r^2 = \frac{2464\times 7}{22}$

$= 112 \times 7 = 784$

$\Rightarrow \quad r = 28$ cm

Hence, the radius of the circle = 28 cm.

47. (C): Total number of articles sold in 8 weeks

= 4000 + 5000 + 4500
+ 3500 + 4000 + 4000
+ 4500 + 5500 = 35000

$\therefore$ Average number of articles sold in 8 weeks

$= \frac{35000}{8} = 4375.$

48. (B): Value of $a^2 + b^2 - c$

$= (\sqrt{2}+1)^2 + (\sqrt{3}-\sqrt{2})^2 - \sqrt{6} - 2\sqrt{2}$

$= 2+1+2\sqrt{2}+3+2-2\sqrt{6}-\sqrt{6}-2\sqrt{2}$

$= 8-3\sqrt{6}.$

49. (B): $(2.5a - 3.5b)^2 - (3.5a - 2.5b)^2$

$= [6.25a^2 + 12.25b^2 - 2(2.5a)(3.5b)]$

$- [12.25a^2 + 6.25b^2 - 2(2.5a)(3.5b)]$

$= 6.25a^2 - 12.25a^2 + 12.25b^2 - 6.25b^2$

$= 6b^2 - 6a^2.$

50. (C): $\because \frac{30}{100}(A+B) = \frac{50}{100}(A-B)$

$\Rightarrow \quad 30A + 30B = 50A - 50B$

$\Rightarrow \quad 80B = 20A$

$\Rightarrow \quad \frac{A}{B} = \frac{80}{20} = \frac{4}{1}$

$\Rightarrow \quad A : B = 4 : 1.$

51. (C): Let the number $= x$

$x > 3$ but < 8

and $x > 6$ but < 10

Clearly, $x > 6 < 8$

Hence, the number = 7.

52. (B): Given,

D	E	L	H	I
−1↓	−2↓	−3↓	−4↓	−5↓
C	C	I	D	D

Similarly,

B	O	M	B	A	Y
−1↓	−2↓	−3↓	−4↓	−5↓	−6↓
A	M	J	X	V	S

Hence, BOMBAY will be coded as AMJXVS.

53. (B): Clearly, the position of Amit with respect to Chetan is in the North-West direction.

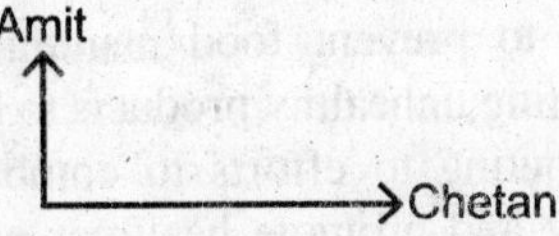

54. (B): M A N : P D Q :: W A N : Z D Q

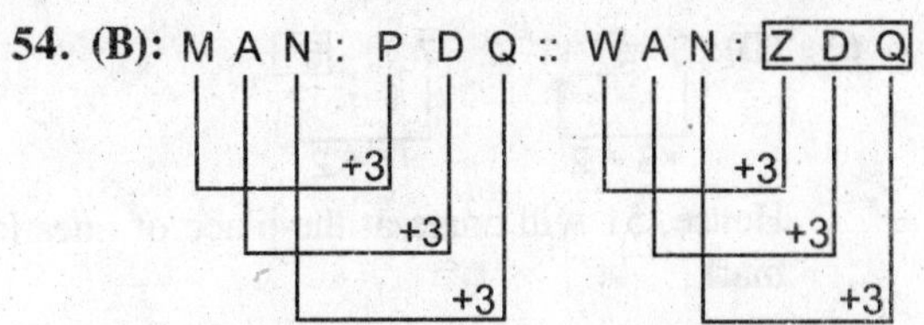

Hence, ZDQ will come at the place of question mark.

55. (C): 25 : 125 :: 36 : 216

$5^2 \quad 5^3 \quad 6^2 \quad 6^3$

Hence, 216 will come at the place of question mark.

58. (D): Conscience, Consciousness, Consequence, Conservation, Consume

The above words are arranged in the dictionary order.

59. (D): 13, 17, 37 are prime numbers.
63 is not prime number
Hence, 63 is odd one out.

60. (A):

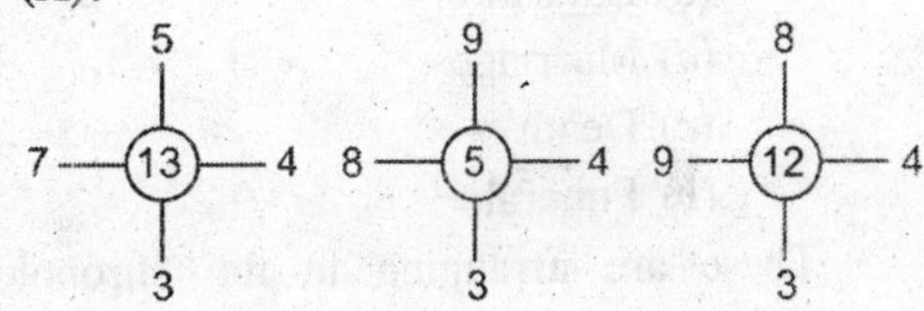

$7 \times 4 - 5 \times 3 \Rightarrow 28 - 15 = 13$

$8 \times 4 - 9 \times 3 \Rightarrow 32 - 27 = 5$

$9 \times 4 - 8 \times 3 \Rightarrow 36 - 24 = 12$

Hence, 12 will come at the place of question mark.

62. (C):

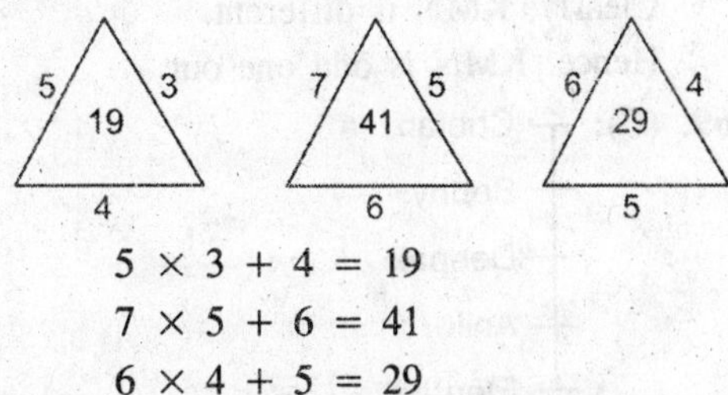

$5 \times 3 + 4 = 19$

$7 \times 5 + 6 = 41$

$6 \times 4 + 5 = 29$

Hence, 41 will come at the place of question mark.

63. (D): 3 : 11 :: 7 : 51

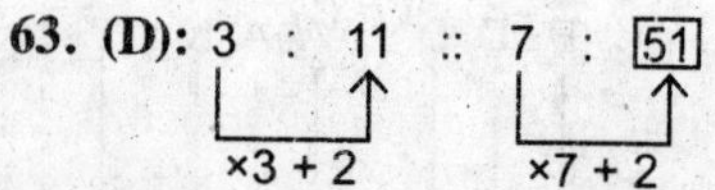

Hence, 51 will come at the place of question mark.

64. (B): Y : 2 :: T : 7

Hence, 7 will come at the place of question mark.

65. (C):

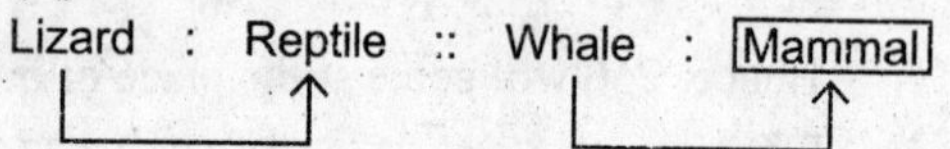

Hence, mammal will come at the place of question mark.

66. (B): 1 9 25 49 81 121

↓ ↓ ↓ ↓ ↓ ↓

1^2 3^2 5^2 7^2 9^2 11^2

Hence, 81 will come at the place of question mark.

67. (C): (*a*) Birth

(*e*) Education

(*d*) Marriage

(*c*) Death

(*b*) Funeral.

These are arranging in the chronological order.

68. (B):

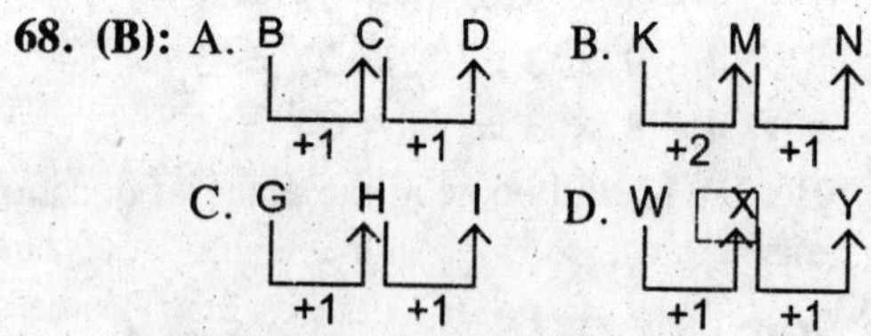

Clearly, KMN is different.

Hence, KMN is odd one out.

69. (C): Chetan

Bobby

Deepak

Anil

Elen

Hence, Deepak is in the middle with respect to their heights.

70. (D): Total days = 28 + 12 = 40 days

∵ February 1, 2004 was Wednesday

∴ March 12th 2004 was Monday

$$40 \div 7 = 5\frac{5}{7}$$

Remainder is 5.

Hence, after 5 days, the day was Monday.

72. (C): 35954553584567357554523510

Hence, There are five such 5's in the given number sequence.

74. (C):

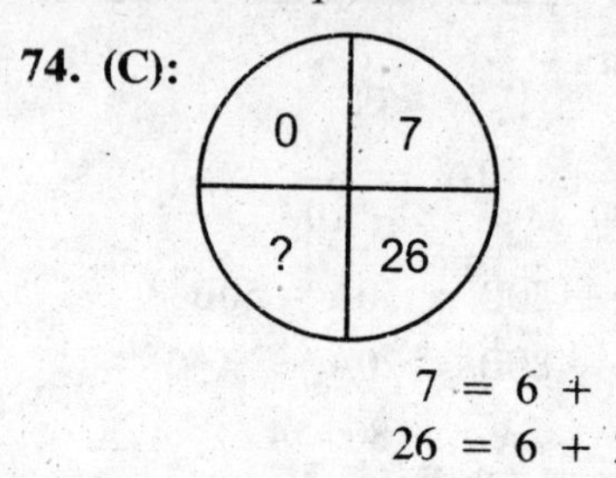

$$7 = 6 + 1 = 7$$
$$26 = 6 + 2 = 8$$
$$63 = 6 + 3 = 9$$

Hence, 63 will come at the place of question mark.

75. (D): Second, Minute, Hour, Day, Week are arranging in a logical order (increasing order). Hence, (D) is the correct answer of the given option.

76. (D): The Walt Disney Company implemented a ban on advertising specifically targeting candy bars and junk food across its various media platforms, including television channels, radio stations, and websites. This means that the company prohibited the promotion or advertisement of these unhealthy food products to children through their media outlets.

77. (A): The purpose behind the ban was to address concerns about the promotion of unhealthy food products, specifically candy bars and junk food, to children. By prohibiting advertisements the company aimed to prevent food manufacturers from marketing unhealthy products to kids, thereby contributing to efforts to combat childhood obesity and promote healthier eating habits.

78. (D): Overweight and obesity contribute significantly to global mortality rates, resulting in the deaths of approximately 2.8 million adults each year. This statistic highlights the severe impact of obesity-related complications on public health worldwide.

79. (C): Obesity tends to affect the poor more than the affluent. This is often attributed to socio-economic factors such as limited access to healthy food options, lower levels of education, and higher levels of food insecurity among low-income populations.

80. (A): The word "limiting" in the context suggests the action of placing constraints or boundaries on food choices. In this passage, the author is implying that simply restricting or regulating food choices is not sufficient to address the complex issue of obesity and unhealthy eating habits.

81. (D): The antonym of "miser" is generous, meaning they are willing to share their resources, whether it be money, time, or other assets, with others. A generous person is known for their willingness to give and help others without expecting anything in return. Therefore, "generous" is the antonym of "miser."

82. (A): This option indicates that the uncle was kind to the person in the past (before his death). The past perfect tense "had been kind" is used to show an action that occurred before another action in the past, which in this case is the uncle's death. The word "dead" indicates the current state of the uncle, which is that he is no longer alive.

83. (C): Up is the most natural preposition to use when describing climbing something that goes vertically, like a tree. This is because "up" inherently indicates movement in an upward direction, which aligns perfectly with the action of climbing.

86. (A): When changing an imperative sentence (a command or request) to the passive voice, we typically use the following structure: You are requested + infinitive (to + verb). In the original sentence, "don't disturb me" is the imperative part. "You" is the implied subject (the person being requested). "To disturb" is the infinitive form of the verb "disturb."

87. (B): The conjunction "yet" is used to indicate contrast between two clauses. In this sentence, it shows the contradiction between being wealthy and not feeling satisfied or content.

90. (D): This idiom refers to someone who appears innocent or harmless on the outside but is actually deceitful, cunning, or malicious underneath. It suggests that the person is hiding their true intentions or nature behind a facade of innocence or benevolence, much like a wolf disguising itself as a sheep to deceive others.

91. (C): In this context, "that" is used as a conjunction to introduce a defining or restrictive clause, specifying which ring is being referred to – the one that she gifted.

92. (A): In this sentence, "neither…nor" is a correlative conjunction used to indicate that both subjects ("she" and "he") were absent.

93. (B): "Alas!" is an interjection used to express sorrow, regret, or disappointment. In this context, it indicates a feeling of sadness about the situation described in the sentence.

94. (B): The sentence "Reema is too generous not to help the needy" implies that Reema's generosity compels her to help those in need. This option effectively conveys this meaning by stating that Reema's generosity is so great that she is capable of helping the needy.

97. (B): The question tag "isn't it" is used because the main clause is in the affirmative form ("It is quite hot outside today"), so the question tag should be in the negative form to create a balance.

99. (A): In indirect narration, the reporting verb changes from "said" to "told" because there is a direct object ("me"). Additionally the tense of the reporting verb changes according to the sequence of tenses rule. Therefore, "never eat" becomes "never ate" to maintain past tense in the reported speech.

100. (D): In indirect narration, the reporting verb changes from "said" to "told" because there is a direct object ("Rahul"). Additionally the tense of the reporting verb changes according to the sequence of tenses rule. Therefore, "are watching" becomes "were watching" to shift from present tense to past tense in the reported speech.

101. (C): The Red Data Book, also known as the Red List, is a comprehensive record or compilation of endangered and threatened species of animals and plants. The purpose of the Red Data Book is to assess the conservation status of various species, categorizing them based on the level of threat they face, such as critically endangered, endangered, vulnerable, or near threatened.

102. (C): Endemic flora refers to plant species that are native or restricted to a specific geographic area, such as a particular region or ecosystem. Sal (*Shorea robusta*) and wild mango are examples of endemic flora found in the Pachmarhi Biosphere Reserve. The term "endemic" typically applies to plant and animal species that are unique to a particular area and are not found naturally anywhere else in the world.

103. (D): Menstruation, also known as a period, is the shedding of the uterine lining (endometrium) along with the unfertilized egg from the ovaries. This process typically occurs approximately once a month in reproductive-age females who are not pregnant. During menstruation, the uterus contracts to expel its lining, resulting in bleeding that lasts for a few days.

104. (D): Genes inherited from parents play a major role in determining height, accounting for around 60-80% of your final height. Eating right kind of food provides the nutrients your body needs to support growth during puberty, including protein, calcium, and vitamins.

105. (A): Endocrine glands release hormones into the bloodstream, and these hormones travel through the bloodstream to reach specific target tissues or organs where they exert their effects.

106. (A): The Richter scale is a logarithmic scale used to measure the magnitude of earthquakes. The Richter scale is one of several scales used to describe the size of earthquakes, with each unit increase on the scale representing a tenfold increase in measured amplitude and approximately 31.6 times more energy release.

107. (B): Calorific value, also known as heating value or energy value, of a fuel is typically expressed in kilojoules per kilogram (kJ/kg).

108. (A): Tin cans are made by electroplating tin onto iron because tin is less reactive than iron. This means that tin is less likely to undergo chemical reactions, such as oxidation or corrosion, compared to iron. By electroplating tin onto iron, the tin layer acts as a protective barrier, preventing the underlying iron from corroding when exposed to air or moisture.

109. (B): Rolling friction is the least resistance encountered when an object rolls over a surface. Sliding friction is greater than rolling friction as it involves more contact and resistance between surfaces. Static friction is the greatest among the three types, preventing motion until a sufficient force is applied to overcome it.

110. (D): Paddy is another term for rice, which is a Kharif crop. Kharif crops are sown during the monsoon season (June-September) and harvested in September-October. They require warm and humid conditions for growth. Therefore, paddy is not a Rabi crop.

112. (B): When electric current is passed through a copper sulphate solution during the process of electrolysis, copper ions (Cu^{2+}) in the solution migrate towards the negative electrode (cathode) due to their positive charge. At the cathode, the copper ions gain electrons from the electrode and are reduced to form solid copper metal (Cu). This causes copper to be deposited on the electrode connected to the negative terminal of the battery.

113. (B):

(*a*) **Orion:** This is a group of stars forming a recognizable pattern, visible in the night sky during winter (*iii*).

(*b*) **Comet:** These icy objects have a characteristic head (made of gas and dust) and tail (formed when the Sun heats the comet) as they orbit the Sun (*iv*).

(*c*) **Sirius:** This is a single star, the brightest one we can see from Earth, located in the constellation Canis Major near Orion (*ii*).

(*d*) **Asteroid:** These are small, rocky objects that orbit the Sun, mostly found in a belt between Mars and Jupiter (*i*).

114. (C): Nitrogen makes up approximately 78% of Earth's atmosphere by volume, making it the most abundant gas in the atmosphere. Oxygen is the second most abundant gas, followed by trace amounts of other gases like argon, carbon dioxide, and others. Therefore, while oxygen is crucial for supporting life, nitrogen is the most prevalent gas in the Earth's atmosphere.

115. (D): Global warming, primarily driven by human activities such as the burning of fossil fuels, deforestation, and industrial processes, has been linked to various environmental changes. However, it is not responsible for an increase in earthquakes. Earthquakes are caused by the movement of tectonic plates beneath the Earth's surface, not by changes in the Earth's climate.

117. (D): When the bulb of the dropper, immersed in water, is pressed, the pressure inside the bulb decreases. This decrease in pressure creates a pressure difference between the inside of the bulb and the surrounding atmospheric pressure. As a result, the higher atmospheric pressure outside the dropper pushes water into the dropper to equalize the pressure difference.

118. (B): First, let's convert the time from minutes to seconds because frequency is measured in oscillations per second (hertz).

Given that the body makes 360 oscillations in 3 minutes: Number of oscillations = 360

$$\text{Time} = 3 \text{ minutes}$$
$$= 3 \times 60 \text{ seconds}$$
$$= 180 \text{ seconds}$$

Now, let's calculate the frequency using the formula:

$$\text{Frequency} = \text{Number of oscillations/Time}$$
$$\text{Frequency} = 360/180 = 2\,\text{Hz}.$$

120. (C):

(*b*) The property of metals by which they can be beaten into thin sheets is called malleability, not ductility. Ductility refers to the property of metals by which they can be drawn into wires.

(*d*) In general metallic oxides are acidic in nature. This statement is not generally true. Metallic oxides can be acidic, basic, or amphoteric (depending on the metal).

121. (A): Polythene (polyethylene) and PVC (polyvinyl chloride) are both examples of thermoplastics. Thermoplastics are a type of polymer that can be repeatedly softened by heating and hardened by cooling. This property allows them to be molded and reshaped multiple times without undergoing any significant chemical change.

122. (C):

(*a*) **Coke:** This is almost pure carbon, left behind after the volatile components of coal are removed during processing (coking). So, it matches with (*ii*).

(*b*) **Coal Tar:** A byproduct of processing coal to get coke. It contains various chemicals, including naphthalene, used to make mothballs. So, it matches with (*iv*).

(*c*) **Coal Gas:** A mixture of gases obtained during the processing of coal. So, it matches with (*i*).

(*d*) **Petrol:** A refined product of petroleum, not coal. So, it matches with (*iii*).

123. (C): A combustible substance catches fire or burns as long as its temperature is equal to or higher than its ignition temperature. For a substance to ignite and sustain combustion, its temperature must reach or exceed its ignition temperature. Once ignited, combustion will continue as long as the temperature remains at or above the ignition temperature and there is a sufficient supply of oxygen or oxidizing agent.

124. (A):

(*b*) **Cell wall:** The cell wall is a rigid structure present only in plant cells (and some other organisms like fungi and bacteria). It provides structural support and protection to the cell.

(*c*) **Chloroplast:** Chloroplasts are organelles found only in plant cells (and some algae). They are responsible for photosynthesis, the process by which plants convert light energy into chemical energy.

126. (A): Raja Rammohan Roy was a Bengali social reformer who campaigned against the practice of Sati in India. He was a strong advocate for women's rights and believed that Sati was a barbaric and inhumane practice. He wrote extensively against Sati and lobbied the British government to ban it. In 1829, the British government passed a law that made Sati illegal.

127. (D): The Tata Iron and Steel Company, also known as Tata Steel, is headquartered in Mumbai, Maharashtra, India, but its main steel plant is situated on the banks of the Subarnarekha River in Jamshedpur, Jharkhand, India. Established in 1907, Tata Steel is one of the oldest and largest steel-producing companies in India.

128. (C): The English Education Act was introduced in 1835 by the Governor-General of India, Lord William Bentinck. It aimed to shift the focus of education in India from traditional subjects like Sanskrit and Persian to Western education with English as the medium of instruction.

130. (C): The Gangri Glacier is located in the Ladakh region of northern India, nestled amidst the majestic peaks of the Karakoram mountain range. It is one of the longest glaciers in the Himalayas, stretching for about 60 kilometers (37 miles) and reaching a width of up to 6 kilometers (3.7 miles) in some areas.

131. (D): Mangal Pandey was an Indian soldier in the British East India Company's army who played a key role in the events leading up to the Indian Rebellion of 1857. He was hanged to death on March 29, 1857, after attacking British officers in Barrackpore. His actions are considered to be one of the sparks that ignited the rebellion.

132. (C): After the Indian Rebellion of 1857, also known as the Sepoy Mutiny or the First War of Indian Independence, the British captured Bahadur Shah Zafar and exiled him to Rangoon (present-day Yangon) in Burma (now Myanmar). This marked the end of the Mughal Empire's direct political rule in India.

133. (B): Arthashastra is an ancient Indian treatise on statecraft, economic policy, and military strategy attributed to Chanakya, also known as Kautilya or Vishnugupta. It is one of the most important texts in Indian political thought and covers various aspects of governance, administration, diplomacy, warfare, and economics.

134. (A): Baba Guru Nanak, the founder of Sikhism, established Dharmsal as a place for spiritual worship and congregation. Dharmsal, or Dharamsala, is a term commonly used to refer to Sikh temples or places of religious gathering in Sikhism. Guru Nanak emphasized the importance of community worship and established such spaces for the Sikh community to come together for prayers, meditation, and discussions on spiritual matters.

135. (A): The river's mouth is the point where the river empties its water into another body of water, marking the end of its journey. It is also known as the river's outlet or the river's estuary, depending on the specific geographical context.

137. (D): Gram Panchayats, which are local self-government institutions at the village or small town level in India, are elected for a term of five years. After the completion of the term, elections are held again to constitute a new Gram Panchayat.

138. (A): Pluto is classified as a dwarf planet by the International Astronomical Union (IAU). In 2006, the IAU redefined the criteria for what constitutes a planet, and Pluto no longer met all the criteria. As a result, it was reclassified as a dwarf planet.

139. (B): Dholavira is one of the five largest Harappan sites and is situated in the Rann of Kutch area of Gujarat, India. It is known for its well-planned urban infrastructure, sophisticated water conservation system, and monumental architecture, reflecting the advanced civilization of the Harappan or Indus Valley Civilization.

140. (B): Firewood is considered a conventional source of energy because it has been used for heating and cooking purposes since ancient times. It is derived from trees and biomass, and its combustion releases heat energy, making it a traditional and widely used form of energy in many parts of the world.

141. (D): Ox-bow lakes are formed in river valleys as a result of the meandering or looping of rivers over time. As a river meanders, it erodes the outer banks of its curves (meanders) and deposits sediment on the inner banks. Eventually, the river may cut through the narrow neck of a meander, leaving behind a crescent-shaped lake called an ox-bow lake.

142. (D):

(*a*) **Biotic:** Biotic refers to living things or those derived from living organisms. Option (*iv*), "The wood of living organisms," best represents biotic components.

(*b*) **Hydrosphere:** The hydrosphere refers to all the water on Earth, including rivers, lakes, seas, and oceans. So, it matches with option (*i*).

(*c*) **Atmosphere:** The atmosphere is the gaseous layer surrounding the Earth. So, it matches with option (*ii*).

(*d*) **Lithosphere:** The lithosphere is the solid, outermost layer of the Earth. So, it matches with option (*iii*).

143. (D): Mushroom rocks are found in deserts. These landforms are created by erosion. Wind erosion wears away the lower portion of a soft rock formation, leaving a harder, more resistant cap on top. This creates the distinctive mushroom shape. Deserts are particularly prone to this type of erosion due to the arid climate and strong winds.

144. (B): Moraines are accumulations of rock debris, sediment, and till that are deposited by glaciers as they advance and retreat. Glaciers transport vast amounts of rock and sediment, which they scrape and pluck from the ground as they move. When the glacier melts or retreats, it deposits this material, forming various landforms including moraines.

145. (D):

(*a*) **Federalism:** The Indian Constitution establishes a federal system of government, dividing power between the central government and the states. While the central government holds authority over certain subjects, states have autonomy over others.

(*b*) **Parliamentary form of Government:** India follows a parliamentary system where the executive branch derives its legitimacy from the legislature. The Prime Minister, who leads the majority party or coalition in the parliament, heads the government.

(*c*) **Separation of Powers:** The Constitution divides the government's power among three branches: the legislature (lawmaking), the executive (implementation), and the judiciary (interpretation and application of laws).

146. (A): Technology is a human-made resource that encompasses tools, machinery, systems, and processes developed through human innovation and creativity to enhance productivity, efficiency, and convenience in various aspects of life.

147. (C): While distance, direction, and scale are essential components of maps, a "plan" is not typically considered a component of maps. Plans generally refer to detailed, systematic arrangements or strategies for achieving specific objectives, rather than elements of a map.

148. (C): An aquarium is a man-made environment designed to house aquatic organisms, often for display or research purposes. While it may contain elements of natural ecosystems such as water, plants, and animals, an aquarium is an artificial enclosure and does not occur naturally in the environment.

149. (B)

(*a*) **Prejudice:** Prejudice is a preconceived opinion about a group of people that is not based on reason or experience. It can be positive or negative, but it often leads to negative attitudes and behaviours. So, it matches with (*ii*) - Judging people negatively.

(*b*) **Stereotype:** A stereotype is a simplified belief about a group of people that is often over generalized and inaccurate. Stereotypes can be positive or negative, but they can be harmful because they don't reflect the individuality of people. So, it matches with (*iii*) - Fixing people into one image.

(*c*) **Discrimination:** Discrimination is the act of treating a person or group differently, negatively, based on some characteristic such as race, religion, or gender. So, it matches with (*iv*) - Inequality.

(*d*) **Diversity:** Diversity refers to the variety of human experiences, backgrounds, and characteristics. It includes things like race, ethnicity, religion, gender, sexual orientation, ability, and socioeconomic status. So, it matches with (*i*) - Difference in language, food, dress, customs etc.

150. (B): A Patwari is a government official in India responsible for maintaining land records and land-related documents. Their primary duties include surveying and measuring land, updating land records, maintaining records of ownership and cultivation, and resolving land-related disputes.

Previous Paper (Solved)

All India Sainik Schools Entrance Exam (AISSEE)–2023*

Class-IX

Section A : Mathematics

1. Arun bought binder clips at the rate of 5 for a rupee. He had to sell them at the rate of 6 for a rupee. Find his loss per cent in the transaction.

A. $\frac{40}{3}\%$ B. $\frac{50}{3}\%$

C. $\frac{10}{3}\%$ D. $\frac{20}{3}\%$

2. For what value of m

$$xy^2m = (2xy + 5y)^2 - (2xy - 5y)^2$$

A. –100 B. 100

C. 40 D. –40

3. Which is the like term as $84xy^2z^2$?

A. $-3 \times 8 \times x \times y \times z \times z$

B. $12 \times 7 \times x \times x \times y \times z \times z$

C. $-5 \times 6 \times x \times x \times y \times y \times z$

D. $6 \times 4 \times x \times z \times y \times z \times y$

4. ABC is a right angled triangle, which is right angled at B. If AB = $\sqrt{12^2 + 4^2}$ cm, BC = 3 cm, then find out the perimeter of the given figure:

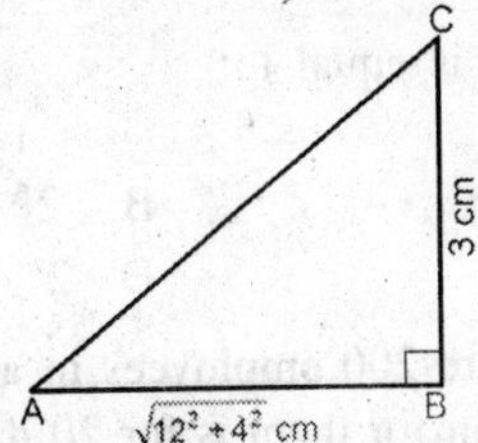

A. $(4\sqrt{10}+16)$ cm B. $(16\sqrt{10}+4)$ cm

C. $(8\sqrt{10}+2)$ cm D. $(2\sqrt{10}+8)$ cm

5. A bicycle wheel makes 1000 revolutions in moving 2 km. Find the diameter of the wheel.

A. 1.57 m B. 1.27 m

C. 6.036 m D. 0.636 m

6. If $a = 5+2\sqrt{6}$ and $b = \frac{1}{a}$, then what will be the value of $a^2 + b^2$?

A. 100 B. 96

C. 102 D. 98

7. Gauransh has 290 cards. Tanya has 150 cards. How many cards must Gauransh give to Tanya so that Tanya may have 3 times as many cards as Gauransh?

A. 180 B. 40

C. 140 D. 80

8. A's present age is twice that of B. If B's age 5 years ago was b, then what is A's present age?

A. $2b + 5$ B. $2b - 5$

C. $2b - 10$ D. $2b + 10$

9. If ABCD is a parallelogram, then find the value of x and y, where OC = $x + y$, OD = 18, OB = $y - 5$ and OA = 25.

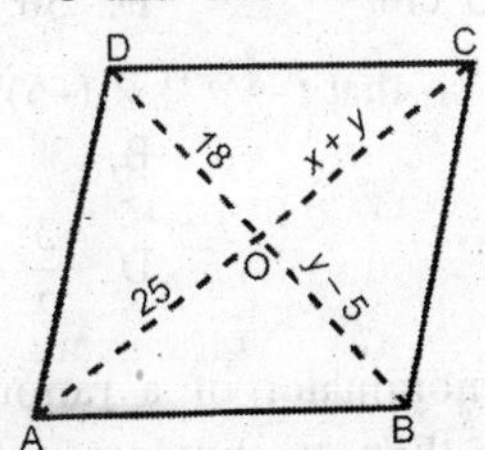

*Exam held on 08/01/2023

A. $x = 13, y = 12$ B. $x = 2, y = 23$
C. $x = 23, y = 2$ D. $x = 12, y = 13$

10. Statement A: Every parallelogram is a trapezium and every rhombus is a kite.

Statement B: Every rectangle is a square but every square is not a rectangle.

A. Both A and B are true
B. A is true and B is false
C. A is false and B is true
D. Both A and B are false

11. Find the area of Rhombus ABCD having each side equal to 13 cm and one of its diagonal is 24 cm.

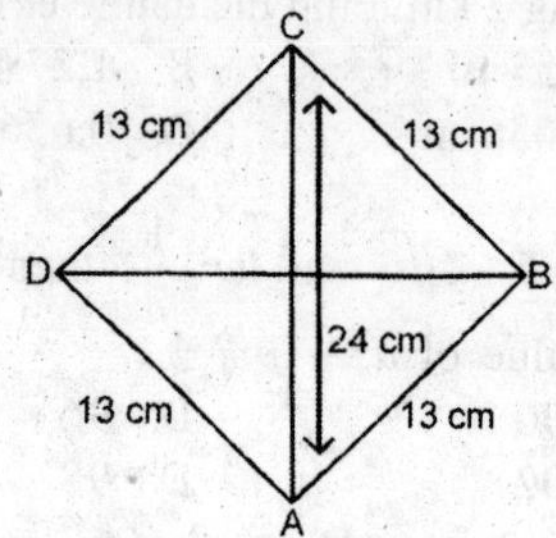

A. 80 cm^2 B. 140 cm^2
C. 100 cm^2 D. 120 cm^2

12. A rectangle ABCD is inscribed in a circle having sides 8 cm and 6 cm. Find the area of the shaded region.

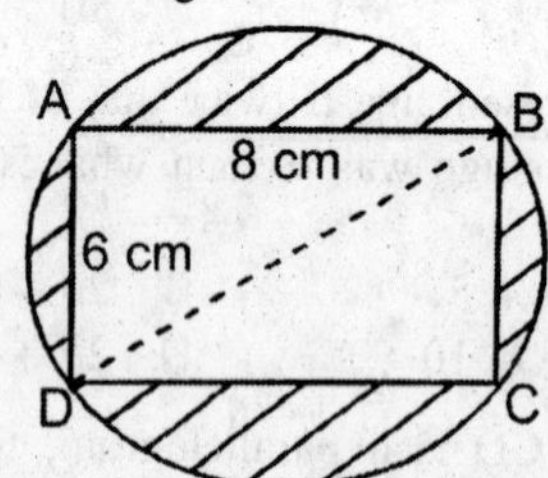

A. 32 cm^2 B. 30.5 cm^2
C. 40.5 cm^2 D. 36 cm^2

13. Find m so that $(-5)^{m+1} \times (-5)^{m-1} = (-5)^3$.

A. 1 B. 3
C. 5 D. $\frac{3}{2}$

14. The denominator of a rational number is greater than its numerator by 2. If the denominator is increased by 5 and the numerator is decreased by 2, the number obtained is $\frac{1}{10}$. The rational number is:

A. $\frac{25}{8}$ B. 3
C. 1 D. $\frac{3}{5}$

15. Which one of the following is a pythagorean triplet in which one side differs from the hypotenuse by two units?

A. $(2n + 1, 4n, 2n^2 + 2n)$
B. $(2n, 4n, n^2 + 1)$
C. $(2n^2, 2n, 2n + 1)$
D. $(2n, n^2 - 1, n^2 + 1)$

16. The ratio of the circumference of 2 wheel is 5 : 3. Find the ratio of the radii of the 2 wheels.

A. 5 : 3
B. 3 : 5
C. 9 : 10
D. 10 : 9

17. The following marks are obtained by a student in different subjects during formative assessment in 8 subjects. Find median.

7, 3, 8, 0, 9, 10, 8, 7

A. 7.5 B. 9
C. 6.5 D. 8, 7

18. Factorize $4a^2 - 9b^2 - 2a - 3b$. Identify the correct factorize answer.

A. $(2a - 3b)(2a - 3b - 1)$
B. $(2a - 3b)(2a + 3b + 1)$
C. $(2a + 3b)(2a + 3b + 1)$
D. $(2a + 3b)(2a - 3b - 1)$

19. $\sqrt[4]{\sqrt[3]{2^2}}$ is equal to:

A. $2^{-\frac{1}{6}}$ B. $2^{\frac{1}{6}}$
C. 2^{-6} D. 2^6

20. There are 200 employees in an office. Food provision for them is for 20 days. How long will this provision last if 90 of them leave the group?

A. 16 days B. 25 days
C. 17 days D. 30 days

21. 5 pipes are required to fill a tank in 1 hour 36 minutes. How long will it take if 2 pipes stopped working?
A. 57.40 minutes B. 2 hours
C. 48 minutes D. 2 hour 40 minutes

22. The Curved surface area of a cylindrical pipe is $2\pi(x^2 + x - 132)$ metres and its radius is $(x + 12)$ metres. What will be the height of the pipe?
A. $(x + 12)$ sq. m B. $(x - 11)$ sq. m
C. $(x - 11)$ m D. $(x + 12)$ m

23. Match List-I with List-II:

List-I	*List-II*
(a) $(7a + 6b)(7a - 6b)$	(i) $49a^2 + 84ab + 36b^2$
(b) $(7a + 6b)^2$	(ii) $49a^2 + 21ab - 18b^2$
(c) $(7a - 6b)^2$	(iii) $49a^2 - 36b^2$
(d) $(7a + 6b)(7a - 3b)$	(iv) $49a^2 - 84ab + 36b^2$

Choose the correct answer from the options given below:

	(a)	(b)	(c)	(d)
A.	(i)	(ii)	(iii)	(iv)
B.	(ii)	(iii)	(iv)	(i)
C.	(iii)	(i)	(iv)	(ii)
D.	(iv)	(iii)	(ii)	(i)

24. Match List-I with List-II:

List-I	*List-II*
(a) $3m \times 2m$	(i) $16a^2$
(b) $-9m \times -3n$	(ii) $6m^2$
(c) $4a^2 \times 4a^2$	(iii) $27mn$
(d) $2a \times 8a$	(iv) $16a^4$

Choose the correct answer from the options given below:

	(a)	(b)	(c)	(d)
A.	(iv)	(i)	(ii)	(iii)
B.	(iii)	(ii)	(i)	(iv)
C.	(ii)	(iii)	(iv)	(i)
D.	(ii)	(iii)	(i)	(iv)

25. If a 4-digit number $2xy8$ is exactly divisible by 3, then which of the following is the least value of $(x + y)$?
A. 2 B. 4
C. 6 D. 5

26. Find the digits A and B if

$$\begin{array}{r} BA \\ \times A4 \\ \hline 13A0 \end{array}$$

A. 5, 4 B. 5, 2
C. 4, 5 D. 2, 5

27. One of the factors of $6x^2 + 5x - 6$ is:
A. $2x - 3$ B. $3x + 2$
C. $2x + 3$ D. $2x - 2$

28. A tree broke at a height of 6 m from the ground and its top touched the ground at the distance of 8 m from the foot of the tree. Find the height of the tree.
A. 10 m B. 14 m
C. 16 m D. 2 m

29. 15 boys earn ₹ 900 in 5 days. How much will 20 boys earn in 7 days?
A. ₹ 1680 B. ₹ 1720
C. ₹ 1420 D. ₹ 2008

30. If AB || CD and EF || GH then find ∠QRH:

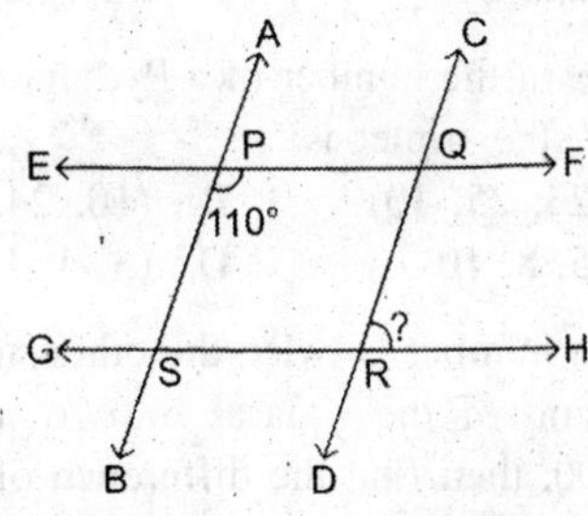

A. 105° B. 50°
C. 110° D. 70°

31. In what time will ₹ 160000 amount to ₹ 176400 at 5% per annum compounded annually?
A. 4 years B. 3 years
C. 2 years D. 1 year

32. Anita borrows ₹ 1000 at 10% p.a. simple interest for 3 years. She immediately lends this money at compound interest at the same rate and for the same time. What is her gain at the end of 3 years?
A. ₹ 40 B. ₹ 41
C. ₹ 30 D. ₹ 31

33. Mohan can do a picce of work in 25 days alone and Rohan can finish it in 20 days. They work together for 5 days & then Mohan left the work. In how many days will Rohan finish the remaining work?

A. 20 days B. 9 days
C. 14 days D. 11 days

34. The following bar graph shows the average daily hours of sunshine in two cities during the year. Observe the double bar graph and answer the following question.

In which months is the difference between average hours of sunshine of two cities least?

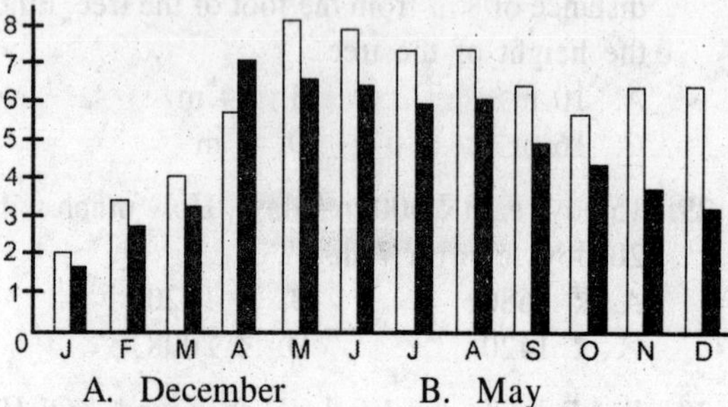

A. December B. May
C. January D. February

35. If one of the number of a Pythagorean triplet is 10, the triplet is:

A. (23, 25, 10) B. (10, 24, 26)
C. (5, 8, 10) D. (3, 4, 10)

36. If one number is twice the other number and the sum of the squares of two numbers is 50,000, then find the difference of numbers.

A. 10000 B. 50
C. 100 D. 10

37. Evaluate: $\sqrt[3]{1372} \times \sqrt[3]{1458}$.

A. 126 B. 136
C. 116 D. 106

38. If $a = 12$, $b = -5$ and $c = -7$, then the value of $a^3 + b^3 + c^3$ is:

A. 1360 B. 420
C. 1260 D. −1260

39. The value of a smart phone depreciates every year by 40%. Find out its value after 2 years if its present value is ₹ 70000.

A. ₹ 28000 B. ₹ 16800
C. ₹ 25200 D. ₹ 35000

40. Which of the following cannot be true for a polyhedron?

A. V = 4, F = 4, E = 6
B. V = 6, F = 8, E = 12
C. V = 20, F = 12, E = 30
D. V = 4, F = 6, E = 6

41. Consider the following distribution:

Class	Frequency
0 – 20	17
20 – 40	28
40 – 60	32
60 – 80	*f*
80 – 100	19

If the mean of the above distribution is 50, what is the value of *f*?

A. 24 B. 34
C. 56 D. 96

42. The mean of 20 observations is 19. On checking it was found that the two observations were wrongly copied as 3 & 6. If wrong observations are replaced by correct values 8 and 9, then what is the correct mean?

A. 19.4 B. 16.6
C. 15.8 D. 14.2

43. A person has 2 bags. First bag has 3 black and 4 white balls. Second bag has 4 black and 3 white balls. A bag is selected at random and then a ball is selected from it. Find the probability of the ball to be black.

A. $\frac{1}{3}$ B. $\frac{1}{4}$
C. $\frac{1}{7}$ D. $\frac{1}{2}$

44. What is the probability that the number selected from the numbers, 1, 2, 3, ..., 30 is a prime number.

A. $\frac{1}{29}$ B. $\frac{5}{6}$

C. $\frac{1}{3}$ D. $\frac{2}{3}$

45. Identify the correct coordinate of the vertices of rectangle OABC from the adjoining figure.

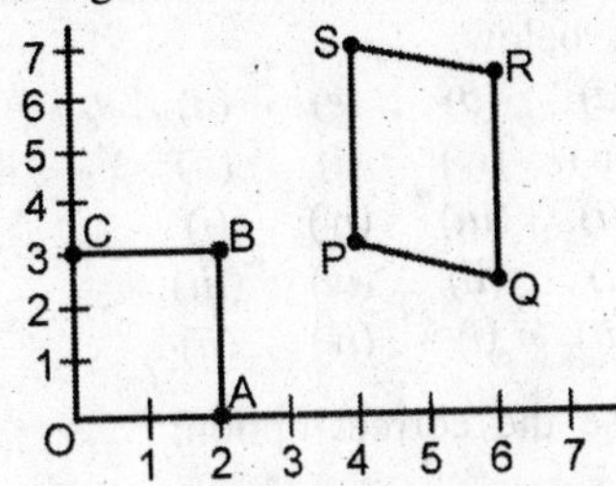

A. O(0, 0), A(2, 0), B(2, 3), C(0, 3)
B. P(4, 3), Q(6, 1), R(6, 5), S(4, 7)
C. O(0, 0), A(0, 2), B(3, 2), C(3, 0)
D. O(1, 1), A(0, 2), B(2, 3), C(3, 3)

46. A cistern can be filled by one tap in 4 hours and by another tap in 3 hours. How long will it take to fill it, if both taps are opened together?

A. $\frac{11}{7}$ hours B. $\frac{12}{7}$ hours

C. $\frac{7}{12}$ hours D. $\frac{7}{11}$ hours

47. Choose the correct remainder when $p(x) : 3x^2 + 4x + 5$ is divided by $g(x) : x - 2$:

A. 20 B. 25
C. 30 D. 35

48. In the Fig. ∠QAP = 35° and ∠ACD = 100°. Find ∠ABC:

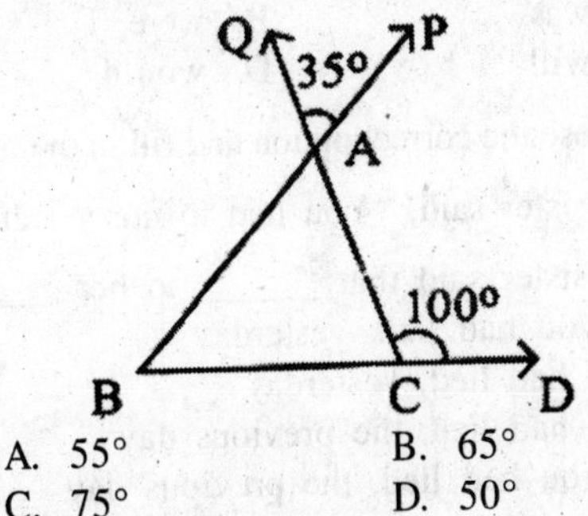

A. 55° B. 65°
C. 75° D. 50°

49. In India people speak different languages. Choose the correct option in degrees which represent the number of people speaking Tamil using the information given in the chart.

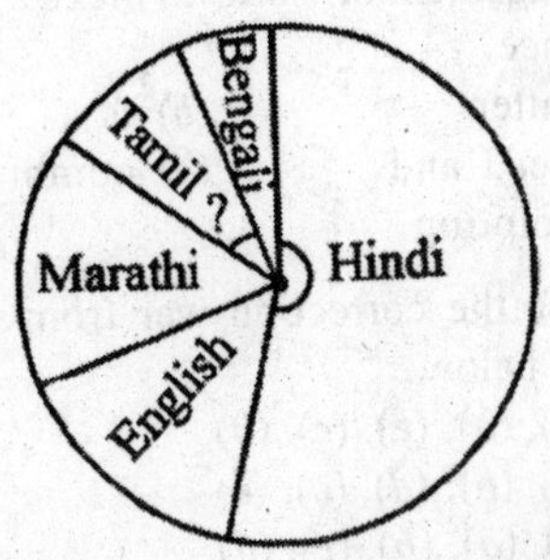

Language	Number of People
(*i*) Hindi	40
(*ii*) English	12
(*iii*) Marathi	9
(*iv*) Tamil	7
(*v*) Bengali	4
Total	**72**

A. 45° B. 35°
C. 20° D. 60°

50. The following line graph shows the yearly sales figures for a manufacturing company. Study the line graph and answer the following question.

The average sales of the company of the even years will be:

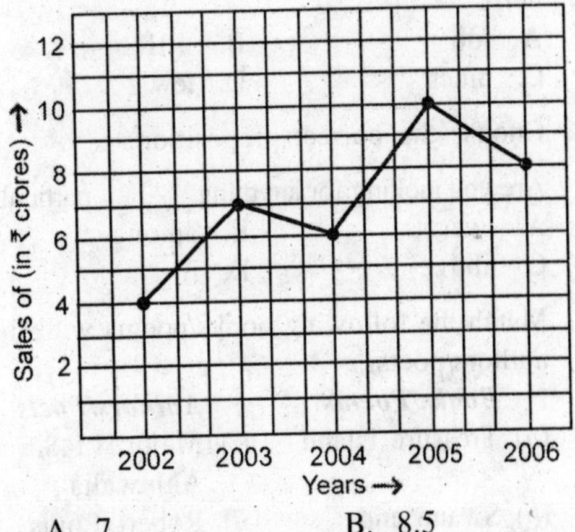

A. 7 B. 8.5
C. 6 D. 18

Section B : English

51. Choose the correct option that has the right rearrangement of words to make a meaningful sentence.

(*a*) butter (*b*) is a
(*c*) bread and (*d*) combination
(*e*) tempting

Choose the correct answer from the options given below:

A. (*d*), (*a*), (*e*), (*c*), (*b*)
B. (*a*), (*b*), (*d*), (*c*), (*e*)
C. (*c*), (*a*), (*b*), (*e*), (*d*)
D. (*a*), (*b*), (*e*), (*c*), (*d*)

52. Choose the correct option that has the right rearrangement of words to make a meaningful sentence.

(*a*) is important (*b*) rules
(*c*) it (*d*) to observe
(*e*) traffic

Choose the correct answer from the options given below:

A. (*c*), (*a*), (*d*), (*e*), (*b*)
B. (*d*), (*a*), (*b*), (*c*), (*e*)
C. (*e*), (*b*), (*a*), (*c*), (*d*)
D. (*a*), (*b*), (*c*), (*e*), (*d*)

53. Choose the correct option to fill in the blanks.

The patient was ______ weak to walk without help.

A. too B. little
C. much D. few

54. Choose the correct preposition:

Are you looking for anything ______ particular?

A. over B. among
C. above D. in

55. Match the following books/poems with their authors/poets:

Books/Poems	***Authors/Poets***
(*a*) Treasure Island	(*i*) Major H.P.S. Ahluwalia
(*b*) Swami and Friends	(*ii*) Robert Louis Stevenson
(*c*) Harry Potter	(*iii*) R.K. Narayan
(*d*) The Summit Within	(*iv*) J.K. Rowling

Choose the correct answer from the options given below:

	(*a*)	(*b*)	(*c*)	(*d*)
A.	(*iii*)	(*iv*)	(*i*)	(*ii*)
B.	(*ii*)	(*iii*)	(*iv*)	(*i*)
C.	(*i*)	(*ii*)	(*iv*)	(*iii*)
D.	(*iii*)	(*i*)	(*iv*)	(*ii*)

56. Choose the correct option:

The mason is building the wall.

The above sentence would be written in passive form as:

A. The wall are being built by the mason.
B. The wall is being built by the mason.
C. The mason is being built by the wall.
D. The wall was being built by the mason.

57. Choose the correct option.

His ______ is in the ascendant.

A. galaxy B. universe
C. star D. luckily

58. Identify the error and choose the correct option.

Energy is very essential in succeed in life.

A. in-to B. is-was
C. in-for D. is-were

59. Choose the correct option:

Ramesh and his brother ______ dancing.

A. was B. were
C. will D. would

60. Choose the correct option and fill in the blanks:

My sister said, "You lied to me yesterday."

My sister said that ______ to her ______.

A. you had lied, yesterday
B. I had lied, yesterday
C. I had lied, the previous day
D. you had lied, the previous day

61. Identify the subject in the following sentence:

The Board of Directors has arrived.

A. The Board
B. The Board of Directors
C. Directors
D. The Board of

62. Choose the correct option:

Sam is a ______ man.

A. first B. handsome
C. half D. delicious

63. Choose the correct option of fill in the blank:

The ______ man died in the hospital.

A. injury B. injure
C. to injure D. injured

64. Identify the positive degree from the following options:

A. Hottest B. Hot
C. Hotter D. Hotters

65. Choose the correct option to complete the following sentence:

Did ______ see her paintings?

A. her B. them
C. you D. him

Directions (Qs. Nos. 66-70): *Read the passage given below:*

Valentin Hauy developed a system of reading for the blind. He printed normal letters in relief that could be felt by a touch of finger. He also started a school for the blind children. Hauy's system of reading for the blind was very useful. But it was quite difficult to learn. Moreover, it was only a reading system. There was no way for the blind to write in this system. In 1819, a ten-year-old blind boy named Louis Braille entered Hauy's school. He was an intelligent student and quickly learnt to read with the help of embossed letters. But he soon realised the disadvantages in Hauy's system. He made up his mind to develop an easier method of reading and writing for the blind. And in 1824, when he was only 15, Braille invented a system of writing which has been accepted all over the world. He was yet a student in Hauy's school. This school is now known as the National Institute for Blind Children. It is supported by the French government.

On the basis of your understanding of the passage, answer the following questions:

66. What according to the passage was the major disadvantage in Hauy's system?

A. It was difficult to comprehend.
B. Hauy's system was difficult for the blind to use for writing.
C. It was easy to learn.
D. It was a regular reading and writing system.

67. What according to you is Louis Braille known for?

A. A blind boy
B. A general student in Hauy's school
C. The inventor of a system of reading and writing for the blind
D. A ten year old boy

68. He printed letters in relief.

Here the word – 'relief' means ______.

A. engraved
B. in a depressed form
C. normal form
D. in a raised form

69. Give the *synonym* of the word – 'invent'.

A. create B. realize
C. discover D. unearth

70. Give the *antonym* of the word – 'develop'.

A. grow B. decline
C. overweight D. ripe

71. Choose the correct option:

The synonym of 'take' is ______.

A. except B. accept
C. ignore D. refuse

72. Choose the correct option:

The antonym of 'Stiff' is ______.

A. bland B. dark
C. limp D. bright

73. Choose the correct option to fill in the blank:

They aren't good scuba divers, ______?

A. could they? B. are they?
C. can they? D. will they?

74. Which of the following is an assertive sentence?

A. Do you enjoy Idli Sambhar?
B. You are requested to stand in line.
C. The Taj is a beautiful monument.
D. Hurrah ! the school team has won the match.

75. Match the poems/books with poets/authors:

Poems/Books	***Poets/Authors***
(*a*) Vocation	(*i*) Rabindranath Tagore
(*b*) Christmas Carol	(*ii*) Jawaharlal Nehru
(*c*) Geography Lesson	(*iii*) Charles Dickens
(*d*) Discovery of India	(*iv*) Zulfikar Ghose

Choose the correct answer from the options given below:

	(*a*)	(*b*)	(*c*)	(*d*)
A.	(*iii*)	(*iv*)	(*i*)	(*ii*)
B.	(*iv*)	(*i*)	(*ii*)	(*iii*)
C.	(*ii*)	(*iv*)	(*iii*)	(*i*)
D.	(*i*)	(*iii*)	(*iv*)	(*ii*)

Section C : General Science

76. Identify the correct sequence of process that results in lightning:

(*a*) Magnitude of accumulated charge becomes large
(*b*) Accumulation of negative charge near the lower edges of cloud.
(*c*) Air becomes conductor of charges
(*d*) Accumulation of positive charge near the upper edges of cloud.
(*e*) Negative and positive charge meet producing streaks of bright light and sound called as lightning.

Choose the correct answer from the options given below:

A. (*a*), (*c*), (*b*), (*d*), (*e*)
B. (*d*), (*b*), (*c*), (*a*), (*e*)
C. (*d*), (*b*), (*a*), (*c*), (*e*)
D. (*a*), (*c*), (*b*), (*d*), (*e*)

77. The calorific value of a fuel is expressed in the unit:

A. g/J B. kg/J
C. kJ/kg D. J/g

78. To electroplate silver (Ag) on a metal object, what will you choose as cathode, anode and electrolyte?

A. Cathode – metal object, Anode – silver bar, Electrolyte – copper salt
B. Cathode – silver bar, Anode – metal object, Electrolyte – silver salt
C. Cathode – metal object, Anode – silver bar, Electrolyte – silver salt
D. Cathode – copper rod, Anode – silver bar, Electrolyte – copper salt

79. Rashi was unable to hold the greasy tumbler of milk in her hand. It would be because:

A. Greasing has made the surface smooth, increasing the friction
B. Greasing has made the surface rough, decreasing the friction
C. Greasing has made the surface smooth, reducing the friction
D. Greasing has made the surface rough, increasing the friction

80. 'Combine' is a machine. Identify from the following for which it is used?

A. For harvesting and threshing
B. For sowing and harvesting
C. For threshing and sowing
D. For irrigation and sowing

81. Tadpole develops into an adult frog by the process of:

A. Fertilisation B. Metamorphosis
C. Budding D. Adaptation

82. Force acting opposite to the direction of motion of a body is:

A. Gravitational Force
B. Electrical Force
C. Friction Force
D. Atmospheric Pressure

83. Human ears are sensory organs that help to hear sound. Its outer portion can be seen. The rest of the delicate ear is buried deep inside the skull. Identify the correct sequence from Outer ear to Inner ear:

(*a*) Auditory Nerve
(*b*) Ear drum
(*c*) Pinna
(*d*) Ear tube
(*e*) INNER EAR

Choose the correct answer from the options given below:

A. (*c*), (*d*), (*b*), (*e*), (*a*)
B. (*b*), (*c*), (*d*), (*e*), (*a*)
C. (*a*), (*b*), (*c*), (*d*), (*e*)
D. (*d*), (*e*), (*a*), (*b*), (*c*)

84. Match List-I with List-II:

List-I	***List-II***
(*a*) Braille	(*i*) Splitting of white light into seven colours
(*b*) Kaleidoscope	(*ii*) Left of the object appears right and right appears left
(*c*) Dispersion	(*iii*) Resource for visually (Blind) challenged person
(*d*) Lateral inversion	(*iv*) Beautiful patterns are formed because of multiple reflection

Choose the correct answer from the options given below:

	(*a*)	(*b*)	(*c*)	(*d*)
A.	(*i*)	(*iv*)	(*iii*)	(*ii*)
B.	(*i*)	(*ii*)	(*iii*)	(*iv*)
C.	(*iii*)	(*iv*)	(*i*)	(*ii*)
D.	(*iv*)	(*ii*)	(*iii*)	(*i*)

85. Which of the following statements is incorrect for CNG?

A. It can be easily transported through pipes.
B. It is more polluting.
C. It is stored under high pressure.
D. It is used as fuel for transport vehicles.

86. Amish has to demonstrate a Science Activity on Ignition temperature from the objects given to him like paper sheets, candle, matchbox and water. The correct sequence for the activity to work will be:

(*a*) Light the candle.
(*b*) Pour the water in one of the cups.
(*c*) Continue heating both the cups.
(*d*) Make two paper cups by folding a sheet of paper.
(*e*) Heat both the cups separately with a candle.

Choose the correct answer from the options given below:

A. (*d*), (*c*), (*b*), (*e*), (*a*)
B. (*d*), (*b*), (*e*), (*a*), (*c*)
C. (*d*), (*b*), (*a*), (*e*), (*c*)
D. (*b*), (*d*), (*e*), (*a*), (*c*)

87. Match List-I with List-II:

List-I (Cell organelles)	***List-II (Function)***
(*a*) Nucleus	(*i*) Contains cell organelles
(*b*) Cell membrane	(*ii*) Control centre of all activities of cell
(*c*) Chromosomes	(*iii*) Transfer of characters
(*d*) Cytoplasm	(*iv*) Provide shape and protection

Choose the correct answer from the options given below:

	(*a*)	(*b*)	(*c*)	(*d*)
A.	(*ii*)	(*iv*)	(*iii*)	(*i*)
B.	(*i*)	(*ii*)	(*iii*)	(*iv*)
C.	(*iii*)	(*iv*)	(*ii*)	(*i*)
D.	(*iv*)	(*iii*)	(*ii*)	(*i*)

88. Identify the name of a book carrying information about endangered species from the following:
A. Red Data Book
B. Record Data Book
C. Record Book
D. Observation Book

89. Identify the traditional methods of Irrigation:
(*a*) Chain pump
(*b*) Lever system
(*c*) Sprinkler system
(*d*) Drip system
A. Both (*a*) and (*c*)
B. Both (*a*) and (*b*)
C. Both (*c*) and (*d*)
D. Both (*d*) and (*a*)

90. Name a National Park situated in Pachmarhi Biosphere Reserve from the following:
A. Satpura National Park
B. Bori National Park
C. Jim Corbett National Park
D. Tawa National Park

91. Ankush has just entered his adolescence years. He wishes to know what should be eaten to remain healthy. Which of the following set of food should he consume to remain fit and healthy?
A. Milk, rice, dal, leafy, vegetables
B. Chips, leafy vegetables, milk, burger
C. Milk, dal, leafy vegetables, fried snacks
D. Dal, rice, burger, chips

92. At puberty which hormone is secreted by ovaries?
A. Estrogen
B. Growth hormone
C. Testosterone
D. Insulin

93. Metamorphosis in frog is controlled by this hormone:
A. Insulin
B. Thyroxine
C. Estrogen
D. Adrenaline

94. Choose the feasible displacement reaction from the options given below:
A. Copper sulphate + Zinc granules
B. Iron sulphate + Copper turnings
C. Zinc sulphate + Iron nails
D. Zinc sulphate + Copper turnings

95. Plastic containers or boxes are mostly preferred to store food items because these are:
A. non biodegradable
B. non reactive
C. poor conductor of heat and electricity
D. more expensive

96. If current is passed through copper sulphate solution copper gets deposited on the plate connected to:
A. positive terminal of battery
B. negative terminal of battery
C. when battery is not connected
D. copper deposited on both plates

97. ISRO stands for:
A. Indian Science Research Organisation
B. International Science Research Organisation
C. Indian Space Research Organisation
D. Interstate Research Organisation

98. Identify which is not a water pollutant from the following:
A. Sewage
B. Algae
C. Fertilisers
D. Weedicides

99. Which of these gases are responsible for global warming?
A. CO_2, methane and water vapour
B. CO_2, sulphur dioxide, water vapour
C. CO, CO_2 and water vapour
D. CO_2, ozone and methane

100. The bread or idli dough becomes fluffy because of:
A. Heat
B. Grinding
C. Growth of yeast cells
D. Kneading

Section D : Social Studies

101. The neighbourhood markets are the ones which ______.
A. are far from our house
B. are very expensive
C. provide all necessary items
D. provide less items

102. The source of fresh water available for human use is:
A. Rivers B. Rain
C. Drains D. Water vapour

103. The Khilafat Movement was led by whom, from the following?
A. Mahatma Gandhi
B. Mohammad Ali and Shaukat Ali
C. C.R. Das
D. Mahamud Ali

104. The Veda Samaj established in Madras in 1864 worked for which of the following causes?
A. Promotion of man
B. To abolish caste distinctions and for improving the conditions of women
C. Poor people
D. Against child marriage

105. The Ladakh desert is mainly inhabited by:
A. Christians and Muslims
B. Buddhists and Muslims
C. Christians and Buddhists
D. Only Buddhists

106. From the following options, choose which is not true about the Internet?
A. Provides worldwide information
B. Provides interaction
C. Allows moving physically from one place to another
D. Enhances E-Commerce

107. From the following, choose the region that is known as 'Orchards of the World'.
A. Coniferous region
B. Tropical region
C. Mediterranean region
D. Temperate region

108. Sandstone is an example of ______ rock.
A. Igneous
B. Metamorphic
C. Sedimentary
D. Extrusive igneous rock

109. Match List-I with List-II:

List-I	*List-II*
(*a*) Right to Equality	(*i*) Prohibits human trafficking
(*b*) Right to Freedom	(*ii*) Equal before law
(*c*) Right to Freedom of Religion	(*iii*) The right to form associations
(*d*) Right against Exploitation	(*iv*) The right to practise any religion of their choice

Choose the correct answer from the options given below:

	(*a*)	(*b*)	(*c*)	(*d*)
A.	(*iii*)	(*i*)	(*iv*)	(*ii*)
B.	(*ii*)	(*iii*)	(*iv*)	(*i*)
C.	(*i*)	(*ii*)	(*iii*)	(*iv*)
D.	(*iv*)	(*iii*)	(*ii*)	(*i*)

110. Identify the crop which is not classified as a plantation crop?
A. Rice B. Tea
C. Sugarcane D. Cashew

111. Who founded the "Brahmo Samaj"?
A. Dayanand Saraswati
B. Raja Rammohan Roy
C. Ishwar Chandra Vidyasagar
D. Pandita Ramabai

112. Choose the correct meaning of 'Patent'.
A. It means adding the value of any commodity.
B. It means enhancing the usability of any thing.
C. It means reducing cost of production.
D. It means the exclusive right over any idea or invention.

113. Who am I?

I am founder of Sur dynasty.

A. Humayun
B. Sher Shah
C. Alauddin
D. Genghis Khan

114. Identify the source of funds for the Gram Panchayats.

A. Income tax
B. Government school's fee
C. Taxes on national highways
D. Taxes on houses, market places etc.

115. Choose the landform, which is not formed by the river?

A. Ox-bow B. Levees
C. Meanders D. Loess

116. Iron made from iron ore is the product of ______.

A. Marine industry
B. Mineral based industry
C. Agro based industry
D. Forest based industry

117. When and to whom the British Parliament transferred their powers in order to ensure a more responsible management of Indian affairs?

A. 1857, East India Company
B. 1859, Lawrence – The Viceroy
C. 1858, Governor General with the title of Viceroy
D. 1887, Dinshaw Wacha

118. Which Article of the Constitution of India provides every citizen the Fundamental Right to life including the Right to health?

A. Article 15
B. Article 360
C. Article 12
D. Article 21

119. Choose the meaning of the word Metamorphic from the following:

A. Fire
B. Settle down
C. Change of form
D. Air

120. Match List-I with List-II:

List-I	***List-II***
(*a*) The Brahmo Samaj	(*i*) Jyotirao Phule
(*b*) The Ramkrishna Mission	(*ii*) Swami Dayanand
(*c*) Gulamgiri	(*iii*) Raja Rammohan Roy
(*d*) Arya Samaj	(*iv*) Swami Vivekananda

Choose the correct answer from the options given below:

	(*a*)	(*b*)	(*c*)	(*d*)
A.	(*iii*)	(*iv*)	(*i*)	(*ii*)
B.	(*iv*)	(*iii*)	(*ii*)	(*i*)
C.	(*iv*)	(*i*)	(*ii*)	(*iii*)
D.	(*iv*)	(*i*)	(*iii*)	(*ii*)

121. Choose the correct definition of 'birth rate' from the following options:

A. The number of births per year
B. The change in total population during a specific time
C. The number of live births per 1,000 people
D. The number of live births per year, per 10,000 people

122. Match List-I with List-II:

List-I	***List-II***
(*a*) Intensive subsistence	(*i*) Slash and burn
(*b*) Shifting cultivation	(*ii*) Amount of capital use is large
(*c*) Nomadic herding	(*iii*) Prevalent in the thickly populated areas
(*d*) Commercial farming	(*iv*) Move from place to place with their animals

Choose the correct answer from the options given below:

	(*a*)	(*b*)	(*c*)	(*d*)
A.	(*i*)	(*ii*)	(*iv*)	(*iii*)
B.	(*iii*)	(*i*)	(*iv*)	(*ii*)
C.	(*ii*)	(*iii*)	(*i*)	(*iv*)
D.	(*iv*)	(*i*)	(*ii*)	(*iii*)

123. Which of the following is a public sector company?

A. Maruti Suzuki India Limited

B. Anand Milk Union Limited

C. Steel Authority of India Limited

D. Pesticide Factory of Union Carbide

124. Arrange in chronological order:

(*a*) Tughlaq Dynasty

(*b*) Early Turkish

(*c*) Khalji Dynasty

(*d*) Rajput Dynasty

(*e*) Lodi Dynasty

Choose the correct answer from the options given below:

A. (*d*), (*c*), (*a*), (*e*), (*b*)

B. (*d*), (*b*), (*c*), (*a*), (*e*)

C. (*c*), (*a*), (*b*), (*e*), (*d*)

D. (*b*), (*d*), (*c*), (*e*), (*a*)

125. Match List-I with List-II:

List-I	*List-II*
(*a*) Khilafat Agitation	(*i*) Mohammad Ali Jinnah
(*b*) Rowlatt Act	(*ii*) Viceroy Curzon
(*c*) Salt March	(*iii*) Shaukat Ali
(*d*) Partition of Bengal	(*iv*) Mahatma Gandhi

Choose the correct answer from the options given below:

	(*a*)	(*b*)	(*c*)	(*d*)
A.	(*iv*)	(*i*)	(*ii*)	(*iii*)
B.	(*iii*)	(*i*)	(*iv*)	(*ii*)
C.	(*ii*)	(*iii*)	(*i*)	(*iv*)
D.	(*iii*)	(*iv*)	(*ii*)	(*i*)

Section E : Intelligence

126. $\frac{2}{5} : \frac{8}{25} :: \frac{11}{15} : \_\_\_\_$.

A. $\frac{1331}{225}$

B. $\frac{121}{3375}$

C. $\frac{111}{155}$

D. $\frac{128}{55}$

127. If word MATH is coded as 26, 2, 40, 16, then code for the word BOOK is:

A. 2, 15, 15, 11

B. 10, 20, 20, 44

C. 4, 30, 30, 22

D. 1, 12, 12, 14

128. A, B, C, D are four friends. A is shorter than B but taller than C who is shorter than D. Who is shortest among all:

A. A

B. B

C. C

D. D

129. Choose the correct alternative from the given options:

If 8th of April falls on Monday, what Day would be the 30th May of that year?

A. Sunday

B. Monday

C. Tuesday

D. Wednesday

130. If the English alphabets are divided into two equal halves from A to M and N to Z such as A corresponds to N, then which letter in the later half would be corresponding to letter K.

A. X

B. Y

C. Z

D. W

131. Arrange the given response in meaningful sequence:

(*a*) Leaf

(*b*) Fruit

(*c*) Stem

(*d*) Root

(*e*) Flower

Choose the correct answer from the options given below:

A. (*c*), (*d*), (*a*), (*e*), (*b*)

B. (*d*), (*c*), (*e*), (*a*), (*b*)

C. (*c*), (*d*), (*e*), (*a*), (*b*)

D. (*d*), (*c*), (*a*), (*e*), (*b*)

132. Choose the option that will replace question mark (?) in the following:

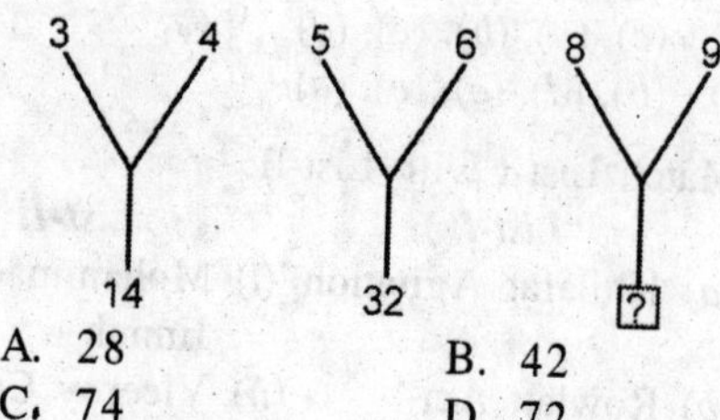

A. 28
B. 42
C. 74
D. 72

133. Find the odd one out.

A. Alphonso
B. Kesar
C. Malgova
D. Sherbati

134. Find the odd one out.

A. Rhombus
B. Square
C. Rectangle
D. Kite

135. Choose the odd one out.

A. Scissors
B. Knife
C. Axe
D. Hammer

136. Complete the analogy

36 : 225 :: 1225 : ____.

A. 7929
B. 6929
C. 5929
D. 4929

137. Find the missing number, which has same relationship with the other number on the basis of the relation between the numbers in the given pair.

16 : 41 :: 20 : ____.

A. 71
B. 53
C. 44
D. 67

138. Complete the analogy.

Thermometer : Temperature :: ____ : Current.

A. Ammeter
B. Voltmeter
C. Anemometer
D. Berometer

139. Arrange the given words in the sequence in which they occur in the dictionary.

(*a*) Aaerstd
(*b*) Aaersted
(*c*) Amquarine
(*d*) Acgledhi
(*e*) Acgledih

Choose the correct answer from the options given below:

A. (*a*), (*b*), (*c*), (*d*), (*e*)
B. (*a*), (*b*), (*d*), (*c*), (*e*)
C. (*a*), (*b*), (*d*), (*e*), (*c*)
D. (*a*), (*b*), (*c*), (*e*), (*d*)

140. Find the missing word, which has the same relationship with the other word as that between words of different pair.

Pie : Cake :: π : ____.

A. Pasta
B. Pastry
C. Mathematics
D. Noodles

141. Complete the analogy.

Work : Joule :: ____ : Watt.

A. Volume
B. Area
C. Time
D. Power

142. Complete the analogy.

Chennai : Tamil Nadu :: Kohima : ____.

A. Nagaland
B. Gujarat
C. Orissa
D. Meghalaya

143. Choose the odd one out.

ZXV, LJH, IGE, UTR, PNL

A. PNL
B. IGE
C. UTR
D. ZXV

144. Find the missing number:

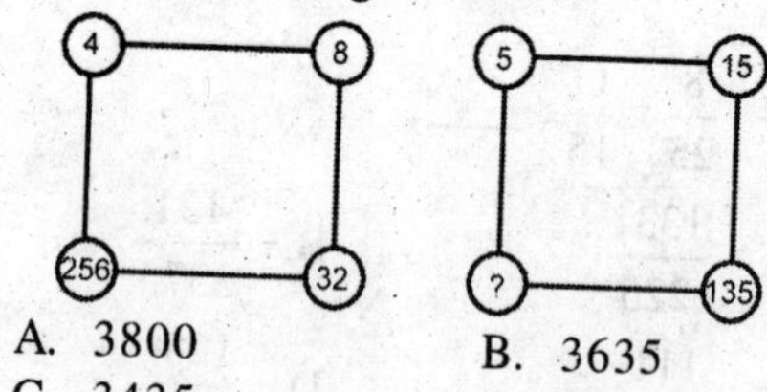

A. 3800
B. 3635
C. 3435
D. 3400

145. Find the missing term out of the options given below after studying the relationship among the given figures.

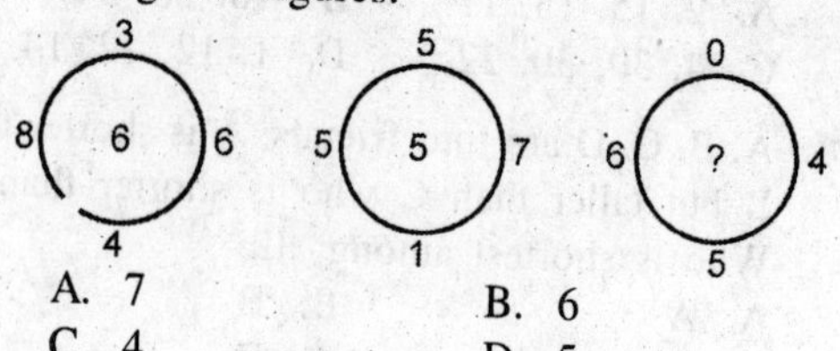

A. 7
B. 6
C. 4
D. 5

146. Decipher the pattern (study the pattern and fill in the blank)

5	40	7
11	77	6
3	?	9

A. 29 B. 43
C. 52 D. 30

147. Which letter will come in the place of '?'

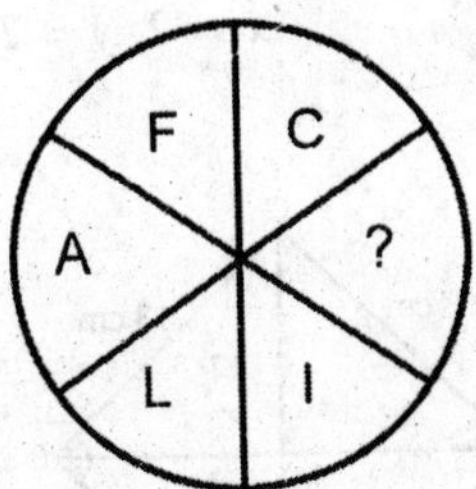

A. M B. N
C. O D. P

148. Which of the following is the water image of the given figure?

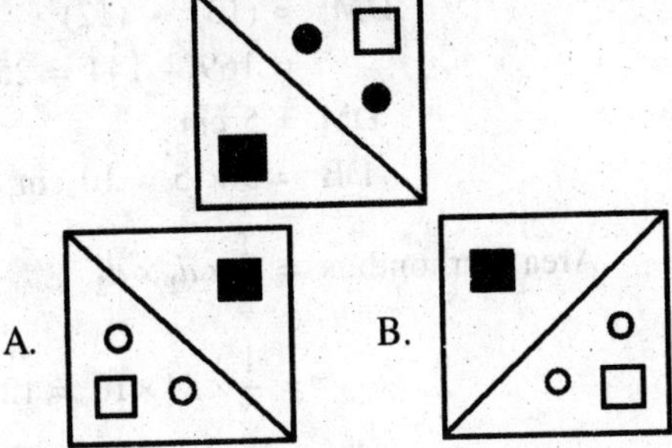

A. B.

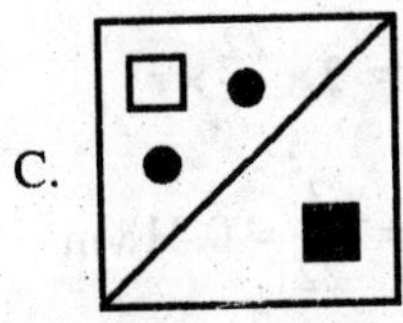

C.

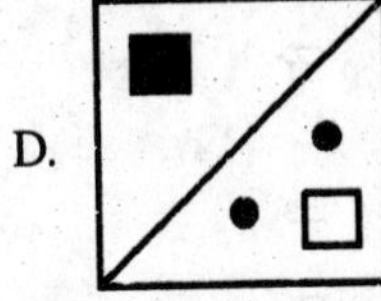

D.

149. Identify the correct mirror image of word BLINK $\overset{X}{\underset{Y}{\updownarrow}}$ along the line XY.

A. ꓘИI⅃ꓭ B. ꓭ⅃IИꓘ
C. ꓘNIꓶB D. BꓶINꓘ

150. Find the next pattern in the sequence.

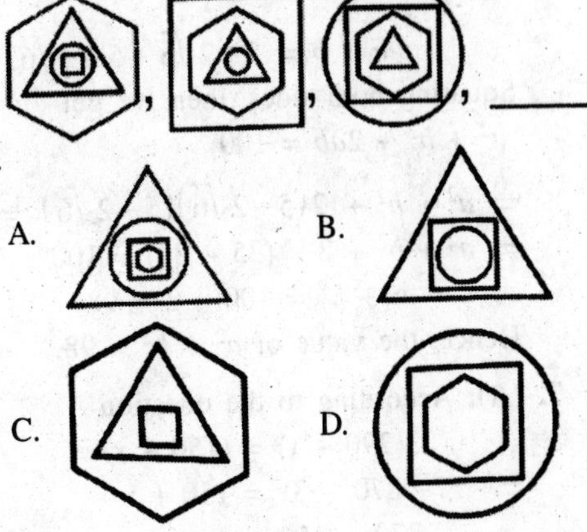

A. B.
C. D.

ANSWERS

1. **(B):** Loss% $= \frac{1}{6} \times 100 = \frac{50}{3}$%.

2. **(C):** $xy^2m = (2xy + 5y)^2 - (2xy - 5y)^2$
$= (2xy + 5y + 2xy - 5y)(2xy + 5y - 2xy + 5y)$
$= (4xy)(10y)$
$\Rightarrow \quad xy^2m = 40xy^2$
$\Rightarrow \quad m = 40.$

3. **(D):** $84xy^2z^2$
Hence, like term of $84xy^2z^2$
$= 6 \times 4 \times x \times z \times y \times z \times y$
$= 24xy^2z^2$.

4. **(A):** $(AC)^2 = (3)^2 + \left(\sqrt{12^2 + 4^2}\right)^2$

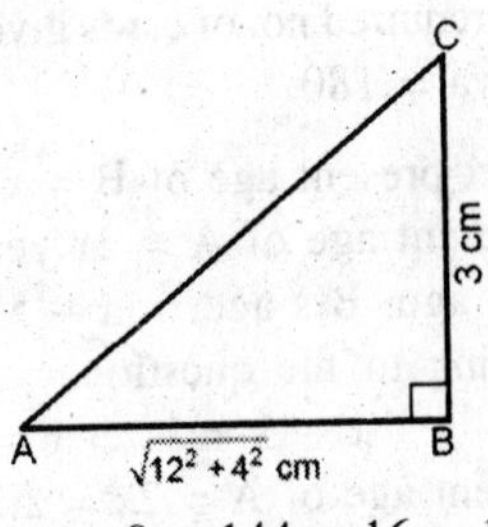

$= 9 + 144 + 16 = 169 = (13)^2$

$\therefore \quad AC = 13$ cm

Perimeter of the given figure
$= \left(4\sqrt{10} + 16\right)$ cm.

5. **(D):** $\because$ 1000 revolutions = 2000 m
$\Rightarrow$ 1 revolution = 2 m
C = 2

$\Rightarrow \quad 2 = 2\times\frac{22}{7}\times r$

$\Rightarrow \quad r = \frac{7}{22} = 0.318$ m

Hence, the diameter of the wheel = 0.636 m.

6. (D): $\because \quad a = 5+2\sqrt{6}$

$\therefore \quad \frac{1}{a} = \frac{1}{5+2\sqrt{6}}\times\frac{5-2\sqrt{6}}{5-2\sqrt{6}}$

$= \frac{5-2\sqrt{6}}{1}$

$a + b = 5+2\sqrt{6}+5-2\sqrt{6} = 10$

Squaring both sides, then we get

$a^2 + b^2 + 2ab = 100$

$\Rightarrow a^2 + b^2 + 2(5+2\sqrt{6})(5-2\sqrt{6}) = 100$

$\Rightarrow a^2 + b^2 + 2 \times (25 - 24) = 100$

$\therefore \quad a^2 + b^2 = 100 - 2 = 98$

Hence, the value of $a^2 + b^2 = 98$.

7. (A): According to the question

$3(290 - x) = (150 + x)$

$\Rightarrow \quad 870 - 3x = 150 + x$

$\Rightarrow \quad 870 - 150 = 4x$

$\Rightarrow \quad 720 = 4x$

$\therefore \quad x = \frac{720}{4} = 180$

Hence, required no. of cards given by Gauransh to Tanya = 180.

8. (D): Let present age of B = x years and Present age of A = $2x$ years

5 years ago, B's age = $(x - 5)$

According to the question,

$x - 5 = b \Rightarrow x = b + 5$

$\therefore$ Present age of A = $2x = 2(b + 5)$

$= 2b + 10.$

9. (B):

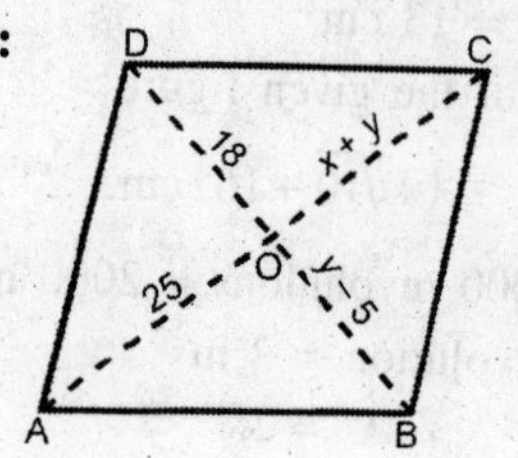

$\because$ Diagonals of || gm bisect each other.

$\therefore \quad y - 5 = 18 \Rightarrow y = 23$

and $\quad x + y = 25 \Rightarrow x = 25 - 23 = 2$

Hence, $\quad x = 2, y = 23.$

10. (D)

11. (D):

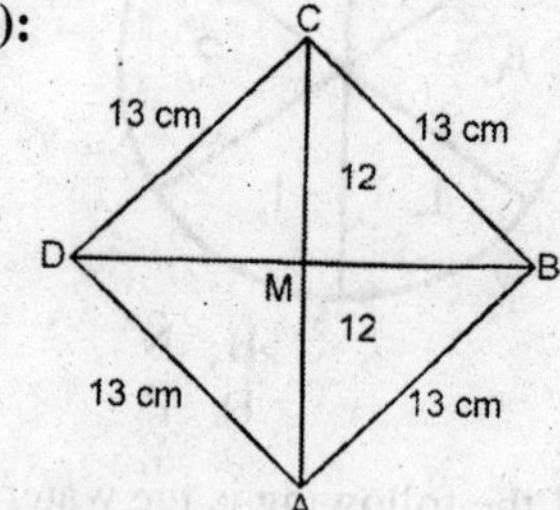

In ΔADM,

$DM^2 = (13)^2 - (12)^2$

$= 169 - 144 = 25$

$\therefore \quad DM = 5$ cm

$DB = 2 \times 5 = 10$ cm

Area of rhombus $= \frac{1}{2}\times d_1 \times d_2$

$= \frac{1}{2}\times 24\times 10 = 120$ cm^2.

12. (B):

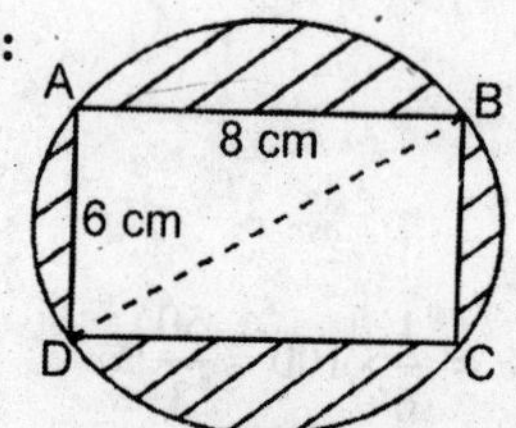

$BD^2 = 8^2 + 6^2 = 64 + 36 = 100$

$\therefore \quad BD = 10$ cm

$\therefore$ radius of circle = 5 cm

Area of rectangle = 8 × 6 = 48 cm^2.

Area of shaded region = Area of circle − Area of rectangle

$= \frac{22}{7}\times 5\times 5 - 48$

$= \frac{550}{7} - 48$

$= \frac{550-336}{7} = \frac{214}{7}$

$= 30.5$ cm^2.

13. (D): $(-5)^{m+1} \times (-5)^{m-1} = (-5)^3$

$\Rightarrow \quad (-5)^{m+1+m-1} = (-5)^3$

$\Rightarrow \quad 2m = 3 \Rightarrow m = \frac{3}{2}.$

14. (D): Let numerator = x

$\therefore$ Denominator = $x + 2$

$\therefore$ Fraction = $\frac{x}{x+2}$

According to the question

$$\frac{x-2}{x+2+5} = \frac{1}{10}$$

$\Rightarrow \quad \frac{x-2}{x+7} = \frac{1}{10}$

$\Rightarrow \quad 10x - 20 = x + 7$

$\Rightarrow \quad 9x = 27 \Rightarrow x = 3$

$\therefore$ Fraction = $\frac{3}{5}.$

15. (D): $(n^2 + 1)^2 = (2n)^2 + (n^2 - 1)^2$

$\Rightarrow \quad n^4 + 2n^2 + 1 = 4n^2 + n^4 - 2n^2 + 1$

$= n^4 + 2n^2 + 1$

Hence, $(2n, n^2 - 1, n^2 + 1)$ is a pythagorean triplet.

16. (A): $\frac{C_1}{C_2} = \frac{2\pi r_1}{2\pi r_2}$

$\Rightarrow \quad \frac{5}{3} = \frac{r_1}{r_2}$

Hence, $r_1 : r_2 = 5 : 3.$

17. (A): First write in ascending order

0, 3, 7, 7, 8, 8, 9, 10

Here $n = 8$ which is even number

$\therefore$ Median = $\frac{\text{4th term} + \text{5th term}}{2}$

$= \frac{7+8}{2} = \frac{15}{2} = 7.5.$

18. (D): $4a^2 - 9b^2 - 2a - 3b$

$= (2a)^2 - (3b)^2 - 1(2a + 3b)$

$= (2a + 3b)(2a - 3b) - 1(2a + 3b)$

$= (2a + 3b)(2a - 3b - 1).$

19. (B): $\sqrt[4]{\sqrt[3]{2^2}} = 2^{\frac{2}{12}} = 2^{\frac{1}{6}}.$

20. (*)

21. (D): Here, 1 hour 36 minutes = $1\frac{36}{60}$ hr.

$= 1\frac{3}{5} = \frac{8}{5}$ hr.

given, 2 pipes stopped working

$\therefore$ remaining pipes = 5 – 2 = 3 pipes

$\because$ 5 pipes fill a tank in $\frac{8}{5}$ hr.

$\therefore$ 5 pipes' 1 hour's work = $\frac{5}{8}$

$\therefore$ 1 pipe's 1 hour's work = $\frac{5}{8} \times \frac{1}{5} = \frac{1}{8}$

$\therefore$ 3 pipes' 1 hour's work = $\frac{3}{8}$

Hence, 3 pipes fill a tank in $\frac{8}{3}$ hours

$= 2\frac{2}{3}$ hours

$= 2 \text{ hour} \frac{2}{3} \times 60$ min.

= 2 hour 40 minutes

22. (C): The curved surface area of a cylindrical pipes

$= 2\pi(x^2 + x - 132)$

$= 2\pi(x^2 + 12x - 11x - 132)$

$= 2\pi[x(x + 12) - 11(x + 12)]$

$= 2\pi(x - 11)(x + 12)$

$\Rightarrow \quad 2\pi rh = 2\pi(x - 11)(x + 12)$

$\Rightarrow 2\pi(x + 12)h = 2\pi(x - 11)(x + 12))$

$\Rightarrow \quad h = (x - 11)$ m.

23. (C): (A) $(7x + 6b)(7a - 6b)$

= (III) $49a^2 - 36b^2$

(B) $(7a + 6b)^2$

= (I) $49a^2 + 84ab + 36b^2$

(C) $(7a - 6b)^2$

= (IV) $49a^2 - 84ab + 36b^2$

(D) $(7a + 6b)(7a - 3b)$
$= \text{(II) } 49a^2 + 21ab - 18b^2$.

24. (C): (A) $3m \times 2m$ = (II) $6m^2$
(B) $-9m \times -3n$ = (III) $27mn$
(C) $4a^2 \times 4a^2$ = (IV) $16a^4$
(D) $2a \times 8a$ = (I) $16a^2$

25. (A): A number is divisible by 3 only when the sum of its digit is divisible by 3.
Given, $2xy8$ is exactly divisible by 3

$$\therefore \frac{2+x+y+8}{3} = \frac{10+x+y}{3}$$

$$= \frac{10+2}{3} = 4, \text{ when } x + y = 2.$$

26. (B)

27. (C): $6x^2 + 5x - 6$

$$= 6x^2 + 9x - 4x - 6$$
$$= 3x(2x + 3) - 2(2x + 3)$$
$$= (2x + 3)(3x - 2)$$

$\therefore$ $(2x + 3)$ is one of the factor.

28. (C): Let AC be the height of the tree
then, AC = AB + BC
given, AB = 6 m
AC = 8 m
by pythagoras theorem
In ΔABC

C
B
6 m
A
C
8 m

$$AB^2 + AC^2 = BC^2$$
$$\Rightarrow 6^2 + 8^2 = BC^2 \Rightarrow BC^2 = 36 + 64$$
$$\Rightarrow BC^2 = 100 = (10)^2$$
$$\Rightarrow BC = 10 \text{ m}$$

$\therefore$ the height of the tree = AC = AB + BC
= 6 + 10 = 16 m.

29. (A): $$\frac{M_1 d_1 h_1}{w_1} = \frac{M_2 d_2 h_2}{w_2}$$

$$\Rightarrow \frac{15\times5\times1}{900} = \frac{20\times7\times1}{w_2}$$
$$\Rightarrow 15 \times 5 \times w_2 = 20 \times 7 \times 900$$
$$\Rightarrow w_2 = \frac{20\times7\times900}{15\times5}$$
$$= 4 \times 7 \times 60$$
$$\Rightarrow w_2 = 1680$$

$\therefore$ 20 boys earn ₹ 1680 in 7 days.

30. (D): Given, AB || CD and EF || GH
$\because$ PQRS is a parallelogram
$\therefore$ $\angle QPS = \angle QRS = 110°$
$\Rightarrow$ $\angle QRS = 110°$
and $\angle QRS + \angle QRH = 180°$
(Linear pair of Angles)
$\Rightarrow$ $110° + \angle QRH = 180°$
$\Rightarrow$ $\angle QRH = 180 - 110°$
$\Rightarrow$ $\angle QRH = 70°$.

31. (C): $\because$ $$A = P\left(1+\frac{r}{100}\right)^n$$

$$\therefore 176400 = 160000\left(1+\frac{5}{100}\right)^n$$
$$\Rightarrow \frac{176400}{160000} = \left(1+\frac{1}{20}\right)^n$$
$$\Rightarrow \frac{441}{400} = \left(\frac{21}{20}\right)^n$$
$$\Rightarrow \left(\frac{21}{20}\right)^2 = \left(\frac{21}{20}\right)^n$$
$$\Rightarrow n = 2$$

$\therefore$ Required time = 2 years.

32. (D): Simple Interest $= \frac{prt}{100}$

$$= \frac{1000\times10\times3}{100} = ₹\ 300$$

and compound interest

$$= P\left(1+\frac{r}{100}\right)^n - P$$

$$= 1000\left(1+\frac{10}{100}\right)^3 - 1000$$

$$= 1000\left(\frac{11}{10}\right)^3 - 1000$$

$$= 1000 \times \frac{1331}{1000} - 1000$$

$$= 1331 - 1000 = ₹\ 331$$

∴ Anita gain at the end of 3 years

$$= 331 - 330 = ₹\ 31.$$

33. (D): (Mohan + Rohan)'s 1 day's work

$$= \frac{1}{25} + \frac{1}{20}$$

$$= \frac{4+5}{100} = \frac{9}{100}$$

⇒ (Mohan + Rohan)'s 5 day's work

$$= 5\left(\frac{9}{100}\right) = \frac{9}{20}$$

∴ Remaining work $= 1 - \frac{9}{2} = \frac{11}{20}$

Hence, Rohan will finish the remaining work in

$$= \frac{\frac{11}{20}}{\frac{1}{20}} = 11 \text{ days.}$$

34. (C) **35. (B)**

36. (C): Let two numbers are x and $2x$.

Then, $x^2 + (2x)^2 = 50{,}000$

⇒ $x^2 + 4x^2 = 50{,}000$

⇒ $5x^2 = 50{,}000$

⇒ $x^2 = 10{,}000$

⇒ $x^2 = (100)^2$

⇒ $x = 100$

∴ The difference of numbers $= 2x - x$

$= x = 100.$

37. (A): $\sqrt[3]{1372} \times \sqrt[3]{1458}$

$= (4 \times 7 \times 7 \times 7)^{1/3} \times (2 \times 9 \times 9 \times 9)^{1/3}$

$= (4 \times 7^3 \times 2 \times 9^3)^{1/3}$

$= (8 \times 7^3 \times 9^3)^{1/3}$

$= (2^3 \times 7^3 \times 9^3)^{1/3}$

$= 2 \times 7 \times 9 = 126.$

38. (C): ∵ $(a^3 + b^3 + c^3 - 3abc)$

$= (a + b + c)(a^2 + b^2 + c^2 - ab - bc - ac)$

When, $a + b + c = 0$

then, $a^3 + b^3 + c^3 = 3abc$

Given, $a = 12,\ b = -5$ and $c = -7$

∴ $a + b + c = 12 - 5 - 7$

$= 12 - 12 = 0$

⇒ $a + b + c = 0$

∴ $a^3 + b^3 + c^3 = 3abc$

$= 3 \times 12 \times -5 \times -7$

$= 1260.$

39. (C): Here, P = ₹ 7000,

depreciation = 40%, $n = 2$

Value after n years $= P\left(1-\frac{r}{100}\right)^n$

⇒ Value after 2 years $= 70000\left(1-\frac{40}{100}\right)^2$

$$= 70000\left(1-\frac{2}{5}\right)^2$$

$$= 70000\left(\frac{3}{5}\right)^2$$

$$= 70000 \times \frac{9}{25}$$

$$= 2800 \times 9$$

$$= ₹\ 25200.$$

40. (D): Euler's formula for a polyhedron.

$F + V - E = 2$

(A) $4 + 4 - 6 = 8 - 6 = 2$

(B) $8 + 6 - 12 = 14 - 12 = 2$

(C) $12 + 20 - 30 = 32 - 30 = 2$

(D) $6 + 4 - 6 = 4$

∴ Option (D) V = 4, F = 6, E = 6 can not be true for a polyhedron.

41. (A):

Class	Mid-value (x)	Frequency (f)	fx
0 – 20	10	17	170
20 – 40	30	28	840
40 – 60	50	32	1600
60 – 80	70	f	$70f$
80 – 100	90	19	1710
		$\Sigma f = 96 + f$	$\Sigma fx = 4320 + 70f$

$$\because \quad \text{Mean} = \frac{\Sigma fx}{n}, \quad \Sigma f = n$$

$$\therefore \quad 50 = \frac{4320 + 70f}{96 + f}$$

$$\Rightarrow \quad 50(96 + f) = 4320 + 70f$$

$$\Rightarrow \quad 4800 + 50f = 4320 + 70f$$

$$\Rightarrow \quad 4800 - 4320 = 70f - 50f$$

$$\Rightarrow \quad 20f = 480$$

$$\Rightarrow \quad f = 24.$$

42. (A) **43. (D)**

44. (C): Let $S = \{1, 2, 3, ..., 30\}$

then $n(S) = 30$

Let E be the even of prime number

then E = {2, 3, 5, 7, 11, 13, 17, 19, 23, 29}

$\therefore \quad n(E) = 10$

$\therefore$ Prob. of prime number $= \frac{n(E)}{n(S)} = \frac{10}{30} = \frac{1}{3}$.

45. (A)

46. (B): Part filled by both taps in 1 hour

$$= \frac{1}{4} + \frac{1}{3} = \frac{7}{12}$$

$\therefore$ It will take $\frac{12}{7}$ hour to fill it.

47. (B): Given, $p(x) = 3x^2 + 4x + 5$

$g(x) = x - 2$

$$\because \quad p(x) = 3x^2 + 4x + 5$$

$$= (x - 2)(3x + 10) + 25$$

$\therefore$ When $p(x)$ is divided by $g(x)$

then, remainder = 25.

48. (B): Given, In a figure

$\angle QAP = 35°$ and $\angle ACD = 100°$

From given figure

$\angle QAP = \angle BAC = 35°$,

[vertically opposite angle]

By exterior angle theorem:

$$\angle BAC + \angle ABC = \angle ACD$$

$$\Rightarrow 35° + \angle ABC = 100°$$

$$\Rightarrow \quad \angle ABC = 100 - 35°$$

$$\Rightarrow \quad \angle ABC = 65°.$$

49. (B): From given in the chart:

Number of people = 72

$360° = 72$

$$\Rightarrow \quad 1 = \frac{360}{72}$$

$$\Rightarrow \quad 1 = 5°$$

$\because$ The number of people speaking Tamil = 7

$\therefore$ degrees represent $= 7 \times 5° = 35°$.

50. (C): From the given line graph

The average sales of the company of the even years

$$= \frac{4 + 6 + 8}{3}$$

$$= \frac{18}{3} = 6 \text{ crores.}$$

51. (C)	**52. (A)**	**53. (A)**
54. (D)	**55. (B)**	**56. (B)**
57. (C)	**58. (A)**	**59. (B)**
60. (C)	**61. (B)**	**62. (B)**
63. (D)	**64. (B)**	**65. (C)**
66. (B)	**67. (C)**	**68. (D)**
69. (A)	**70. (B)**	**71. (B)**
72. (C)	**73. (B)**	**74. (C)**
75. (D)	**76. (C)**	**77. (C)**
78. (C)	**79. (C)**	**80. (A)**
81. (B)	**82. (C)**	**83. (A)**
84. (C)	**85. (B)**	**86. (C)**

87. (A) 88. (A) 89. (B)

90. (A, B) 91. (A) 92. (A)

93. (B) 94. (A) 95. (B)

96. (B) 97. (C) 98. (B)

99. (A, B, C, D)

100. (C)

101. (C): The neighbourhood markets are the ones which provide all necessary items. There are many shops that sell goods and services in our neighbourhoods. We may buy milk from the dairy, groceries from departmental stores, stationery, eatables or medicines from other shops. Many of these are permanent shops, while others are roadside stalls such as that of the vegetable hawker, the fruit vendor, the mechanic, etc. Shops in the neighbourhood are useful in many ways. They are near our home and we can go there on any day of the week. Usually, the buyer and seller know each other and these shops also provide goods on credit.

102. (A)

103. (B): The Khilafat Movement, (1919-1920) was a movement of Indian Muslims, led by Muhammad Ali and Shaukat Ali, that demanded the following: The Turkish Sultan or Khalifa must retain control over the Muslim sacred places in the erstwhile Ottoman empire; the jazirat-ul-Arab (Arabia, Syria, Iraq, Palestine) must remain under Muslim sovereignty; and the Khalifa must be left with sufficient territory to enable him to defend the Islamic faith. The Congress supported the movement and Mahatma Gandhi sought to conjoin it to the Non-cooperation Movement.

104. (B): The Veda Samaj: Established in Madras (Chennai) in 1864, the Veda Samaj was inspired by the Brahmo Samaj. It worked to abolish caste distinctions and promote widow remarriage and women's education. Its members believed in one God. They condemned the superstitions and rituals of orthodox Hinduism.

105. (B): Ladakh is a cold desert lying in the Great Himalayas, on the eastern side of Jammu and Kashmir. The Karakoram Range in the north and the Zanskar mountains in the south enclose it. Several rivers flow through Ladakh, Indus being the most important among them. The rivers form deep valleys and gorges. Several glaciers are found in Ladakh, for example the Gangri glacier. The day temperatures in summer are just above zero degree and the night temperatures well below –30°C. It is freezing cold in the winters when the temperatures may remain below -40°C for most of the time.

The people here are either Muslims or Buddhists. In fact several Buddhists monasteries dot the Ladakhi landscape with their traditional 'gompas'. Some famous monasteries are Hemis, Thiksey, Shey and Lamayuru.

106. (C)

107. (C): Mediterranean forest:

- For their fruit production, Mediterranean forests are renowned as the "Orchards of the World."
- Citrus fruits like oranges, figs, olives, and grapes are widely grown here.
- Mediterranean woodlands are found in the Mediterranean Sea region, Central Chile, the Southwest United States, Australia, and Africa.
- They feature thick barks and waxy leaves that aid in reducing transpiration.
- Mediterranean plants adapt to dry summers.

108. (C): Sedimentary rocks are formed by deposition, sedimentation, and lithification of sediments over a long period of time.

Sedimentary rocks may also contain fossils of plants, animals that once lived on them. The word 'sedimentary' is derived from the Latin word "sedimentum". Shale, limestone, and conglomerate are some other examples of sedimentary rocks.

109. (B)

110. (A): Rice is not grown in plantations. Rice is the staple food crop of a majority of the people in India. Our country is the second largest producer of rice in the world after China. It is a kharif crop which requires high temperature, (above 25°C) and high humidity with annual rainfall above 100 cm. In the areas of less rainfall, it grows with the help of irrigation. It grows best in alluvial clayey soil, which can retain water. China leads in the production of rice followed by India, Japan, Sri Lanka and Egypt. In favourable climatic conditions as in West Bengal and Bangladesh two to three crops are grown in a year.

111. (B): Raja Rammohan Roy (1772 AD-1883 AD): Born in 1772 AD, founded Atmiya Sabha in Calcutta in 1815 AD, that was named Brahmo Sabha and finally Brahmo Samaj in 1828 AD. His journal was named Sabad Kaumudi. Debender became the leader of the Brahmo Samaj after Raja Rammohan Roy. He founded Tattvabodhini Sabha in 1839 and published Tattvabodhini Patrika. He compiled selected passages from the Upanishads, which came to be known as Brahma Dharma.

112. (D): A patent is an exclusive right granted for an invention. In other words, a patent is an exclusive right to a product or a process that generally provides a new way of doing something, or offers a new technical solution to a problem. To get a patent, technical information about the invention must be disclosed to the public in a patent application. The patent owner may give permission to, or license, other parties to use the invention on mutually agreed terms. The owner may also sell the right to the invention to someone else, who will then become the new owner of the patent.

113. (B): Sher Shah Suri (1540-1545) started his career as the manager of a small territory for his uncle in Bihar and eventually challenged and defeated the Mughal emperor Humayun (1530-1540, 1555-1556). Sher Shah captured Delhi and established his own dynasty. Although the Suri dynasty ruled for only fifteen years (1540-1555), it introduced an administration that borrowed elements from Alauddin Khalji and made them more efficient. Sher Shah's administration became the model followed by the great emperor Akbar (1556-1605) when he consolidated the Mughal Empire.

114. (D): The sources of funds for the Gram Panchayat are as follows:

- Collection of taxes on houses, market places etc.
- Government scheme funds received through various departments of the government - through the Janpad and Zila Panchayats.
- Donations for community works etc

115. (D): Erosional landforms by rivers are gorges, canyons, V-shaped valleys, waterfalls, levees, potholes, meanders and oxbow lakes. **Loess** is a clastic, predominantly silt-sized sediment that is formed by the accumulation of wind-blown dust. Ten percent of Earth's land area is covered by loess or similar deposits. Loess is a periglacial or aeolian (windborne) sediment, defined as an accumulation of 20% or less of clay and a balance of roughly equal parts sand and silt, often loosely cemented by calcium carbonate. Usually it is homogeneous and highly porous; it is traversed by vertical capillaries which permit the sediment to fracture and form vertical bluffs.

116. (B) **117. (C)**

118. (D): Right to Health is a part and parcel of Right to Life and therefore right to health is a fundamental right guaranteed to every citizen of India under Article 21 of the Constitution of India.

119. (C): The word metamorphic means 'change of form'. These rocks form under the action of pressure, volume and temperature (PVT) changes. Metamorphism occurs when rocks are forced down to lower levels by tectonic processes or when molten magma rising through the crust comes in contact with the crustal rocks or the underlying rocks are subjected to great amounts of pressure by overlying rocks. Metamorphism is a process by which already consolidated rocks undergo recrystallisation and reorganisation of materials within original rocks.

120. (A)

121. (C): The birth rate for a given period is the total number of live human births per 1,000 population divided by the length of the period in years. The number of live births is normally taken from a universal registration system for births; population counts from a census, and estimation through specialized demographic techniques. The birth rate (along with mortality and migration rates) is used to calculate population growth. The estimated average population may be taken as the mid-year population.

122. (B)

123. (C): Steel Authority of India Limited (SAIL) is a central public sector undertaking based in New Delhi, India. It is under the ownership of Ministry of Steel, Government of India. Incorporated on 24 January 1973, SAIL has 60,766 employees (as of 1 October 2022). SAIL operates and owns five integrated steel plants at Bhilai, Rourkela, Durgapur, Bokaro and Burnpur (Asansol) and three special steel plants at Salem, Durgapur and Bhadravathi. It also owns a Ferro Alloy plant at Chandrapur.

124. (B) **125. (B)**

126. (A): $\frac{2}{5}:\frac{8}{25} \Rightarrow \frac{2^3}{5^2} = \frac{8}{25}$

and $\frac{11}{15}: \ldots\ldots \Rightarrow \frac{11^3}{15^2} = \frac{1331}{225}$

$\therefore \frac{2}{5}:\frac{8}{25}::\frac{11}{15}:\boxed{\frac{1331}{225}}$.

127. (C): Given,

M	A	T	H
×2↓	×2↓	×2↓	×2↓
26	2	40	16

Similarly,

B	O	O	K
×2↓	×2↓	×2↓	×2↓
4	30	30	22

∴ The code for the word Book is 4303022.

128. (C): $B > A > C, D > C \Rightarrow B > A > D > C$
Here, C is shortest among all.

129. (*)

130. (A):

A B C D E F G H I J K L M

N O P Q R S T U V W X Y Z

Here, X would be corresponding to letter K.

131. (D): A meaningful sequence
Root → Stem → Leaf → Flower → Fruit.

132. (C): From given figure:
1st: $3 \times 4 + 2 = 12 + 2 = 14$
2nd: $5 \times 6 + 2 = 30 + 2 = 32$
Similalry,
3rd: $8 \times 9 + 2 = 72 + 2 = \boxed{74}$
$\therefore$? = 74.

133. (D) **134. (D)** **135. (D)**

136. (C): $36 : 225 \Rightarrow (6)^2 : (15)^2$
$1225 : \_\_\_\_ \Rightarrow (35)^2 :$
from given options
only option (C) $5929 = (77)^2$
1225 : 5929
$\therefore (35)^2 : (77)^2$
Hence, $36 : 225 :: 1225 : \boxed{5929}$.

137. (B): 16 : 41

$\Rightarrow 16 \times 3 - 7 = 48 - 7 = 41,$

20 : ___

$\Rightarrow 20 \times 3 - 7 = 60 - 7 = 53$

$\therefore$ 16 : 41 :: 20 : 53.

138. (A)

139. (C): According to English dictionary
Aaerstd → Aaersted → Acgledhi → Acgledih → Amquarine.

140. (C) **141. (D)** **142. (A)**

143. (C): Z X V, L J H, I G E, U T R, P N L
(differences: −2, −2; −2, −2; −2, −2; −1, −2; −2, −2)

Here, (C) UTR is odd.

144. (*)

145. (C): From given figure:

1st: $(8 + 6) - (3 + 4 + 1) = 14 - 8 = 6$

2nd: $(5 + 7) - (5 + 1 + 1) = 12 - 7 = 5$

Similarly,

3rd: $(6 + 4) - (0 + 5 + 1) = 10 - 6 = \boxed{4}$

$\therefore$? = the missing number = 4.

146. (D): From given pattern:
Row

1st: $5 \times 7 + 5 = 35 + 5 = 40$

2nd: $11 \times 6 + 11 = 66 + 11 = 77$

3rd: $3 \times 9 + 3 = 27 + 3 = \boxed{30}$

$\therefore$? = the missing number = 30.

147. (B):

A	B	C	D	E	F	G
|	|	|	|	|	|	|
N	M	L	K	J	I	H

C → L

F → I

Similarly, A → N

$\therefore$? = N

148. (D) **149. (B)** **150. (A)**

Previous Paper (Solved)

All India Sainik Schools Entrance Exam (AISSEE)–2022*

Class-IX

Section A : Mathematics

1. A wrist watch with MRP ₹ 5000 is available in two showrooms at different offers. First one is offering additional 40% off after a discount of 50% on MRP. Second is offering 80% discount on MRP ₹ 5000. The difference in two selling prices is:

A. ₹ 400 B. ₹ 500
C. ₹ 1000 D. ₹ 1500

2. There are 42 students in a class. Out of these, 3/4 of the boys and 2/3 of the girls come to school by bus. The total number of boys and girls of the same class who come to school by bus is 30. How many boys are there in the class?

A. 20 B. 24
C. 26 D. 16

3. If $\sqrt{1+\frac{27}{169}}=1+\frac{x}{13}$ then x equals:

A. 1 B. 3
C. 5 D. 7

4. If

$$\begin{array}{r} 1\ \ y \\ +x\ \ y \\ \hline z\ \ 6 \\ \hline \end{array}$$

when z and y are single-digit numbers such that $z - y = 3$ then the value of y and z respectively are:

A. 3, 6 B. 6, 9
C. 5, 4 D. 4, 5

5. The sum of three consecutive multiples of 7 is 357. The smallest multiple is:

A. 112 B. 126
C. 119 D. 116

6. Which of the following can give the result as 'the square of a natural 'n''?

A. Sum of the squares of first n natural numbers.
B. Sum of the first n natural numbers.
C. Sum of the first $(n - 1)$ natural numbers.
D. Sum of the first 'n' odd natural numbers.

7. When two unbiased dice are rolled together, the probability of getting both same outcomes is:

A. 0 B. $\frac{1}{36}$
C. $\frac{5}{36}$ D. $\frac{6}{36}$

8. Which of the following cannot be true for a polyhedron?
(where F = number of faces, V = number of vertices, E = number of edges)

A. V = 4, F = 4, E = 6
B. V = 6, F = 8, E = 12
C. V = 20, F = 12, E = 30
D. V = 4, F = 6, E = 6

9. The angles of a quadrilateral are in the ratio 6 : 7 : 8 : 9, then which of the following can be concluded?

A. Exactly two angles are obtuse.
B. Two pairs of angles are supplementary.

*Exam held on 09/01/2022

C. Both (A) and (B)
D. One of these angles is a right angle.

10. A card is drawn at random from a well shuffled deck of 52 cards. The probability that it is neither a heart nor a red king is:
A. 37/52 B. 19/26
C. 19/52 D. 26/52

11. If a square with each side 'a' is joined from opposite sides to form a cylinder, then area of each circular end (ignoring units) is:
A. a^2 B. $a^2/4\pi$
C. a^2/π D. $a^2/4$

12. A well with 10 m inside diameter is dug 14 m deep. Earth taken out of it is spread all around it to make an embankment of height $4\frac{2}{3}$ m. The width of the embankment is:
A. 5 m B. 4 m
C. 4.3 m D. 6 m

13. Which of the following is not a random experiment?
A. Tossing a coin.
B. Rolling a dice.
C. Choosing a card from a deck of 52 cards.
D. Throwing a stone from a roof of a building.

14. Radha invested ₹ 1600 on compound interest for 2 years. She received ₹ 1764 after the specified period. Find the rate of interest per annum.
A. 7% B. 6%
C. 5% D. 4%

15. X is a two-digit number. Y is the number obtained or reversing the digits of X. Which of the following is true?
A. X + Y is divisible by 10.
B. X – Y is divisible by 6.
C. X – Y is divisible by 9.
D. X + Y is divisible by 8.

16. Which of the following is true?
A. 0.09 > 7/8 B. 6% < 0.09
C. 8.0×10^{-3} > 6% D. $7/8 < 9 \times 10^{-3}$

17. A contractor can complete a certain piece of work, with certain number of men, in 9 days. But 6 of them remained absent from the very first day, so the rest could finish the work in 15 days. How many men were originally employed?
A. 12 B. 15
C. 18 D. 24

18. The number of sides of a regular polygon with interior angle 162° will be:
A. 18 B. 20
C. 25 D. 24

19. Shally buys some chocolates at the rate of ₹ 10 per chocolate. She also buys an equal number of candies at the rate of ₹ 5 per candy. She makes 20% profit on chocolates and 8% profit on candies. At the end of the day, all chocolates and candies are sold out and her profit is ₹ 240. The number of chocolates she had purchased is:
A. 100 B. 90
C. 150 D. 200

20. Two right circular cones of equal curved surface areas have their slant heights in the ratio of 3 : 5. Find the ratio of their respective radii.
A. 5 : 3 B. 5 : 7
C. 8 : 3 D. 3 : 5

21. If x, y and z are positive real number and a, b and c are rational numbers, then the value of $\frac{1}{1+x^{b-a}+x^{c-a}}+\frac{1}{1+x^{a-b}+x^{c-b}}+\frac{1}{1+x^{b-c}+x^{a-c}}$ is:
A. 1 B. x^{abc}
C. 0 D. x

22. Two complementary angles are in the ratio 13 : 5, then the angles respectively are:
A. 13°, 5° B. 125°, 25°
C. 65°, 25° D. 65°, 35°

23. A cistern has two inlets A and B which can fill it in 12 minutes and 15 minutes respectively. An outlet C can empty the full cistern in 10 minutes. If all the three pipes are opened together in the empty cistern, then the time taken to fill the cistern completely is:
A. 20 minutes B. 10 minutes
C. 15 minutes D. 5 minutes

24. The coordinates of a point on the *y*-axis which is at perpendicular distance of 4 units in the positive direction from origin are:
A. (0, 0) B. (0, –4)
C. (4, –4) D. (0, 4)

25. If $2^x + 2^x + 2^x = 192$, then the value of *x* is:
A. 2 B. 6
C. 5 D. 3

26. The pie chart below shows the percentages of blood types for a group of people.

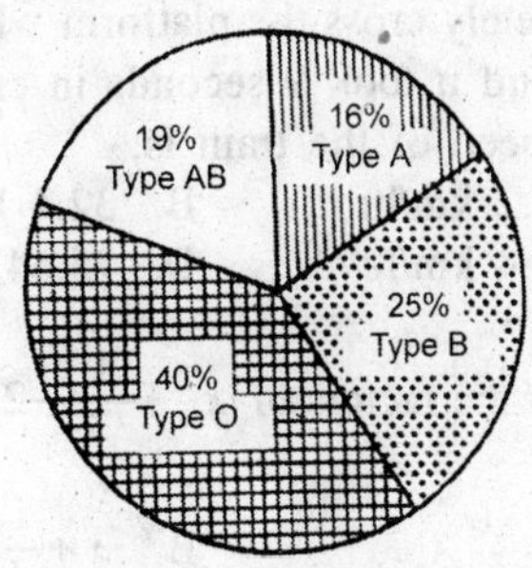

If total number of people with blood types A or B is 82, then the number of people with blood types AB or O is:
A. 100 B. 80
C. 108 D. 118

27. If the side of a chess board is smaller than its perimeter by 42 cm, then find the area of the chess board.
A. 100 cm^2 B. 144 cm^2
C. 196 cm^2 D. 180 cm^2

28. The sum of additive inverse and multiplicative inverse of 2/9 is:
A. 9/2 B. 2/9
C. 18/77 D. 77/18

29. The standard form for 0.000064 is:
A. 64×10^4 B. 64×10^{-4}
C. 6.4×10^5 D. 6.4×10^{-5}

30. In the number A4*b*, A is the smallest two digit perfect cube and A's unit place digit exceeds *b* by 3. Then the sum of the number and its cube root is:
A. 2713 B. 2754
C. 2750 D. 2758

31. Which of the following graphs cannot be a time-temperature graph?

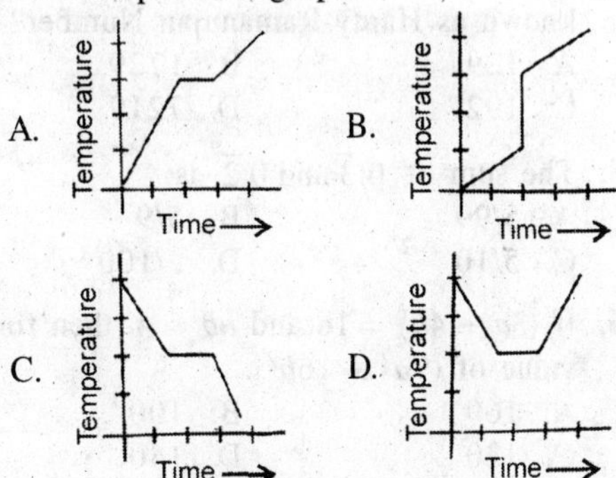

32. The following bar graph shows the number of students studying various subjects in a college. Study the bar graph carefully and answer the following question.

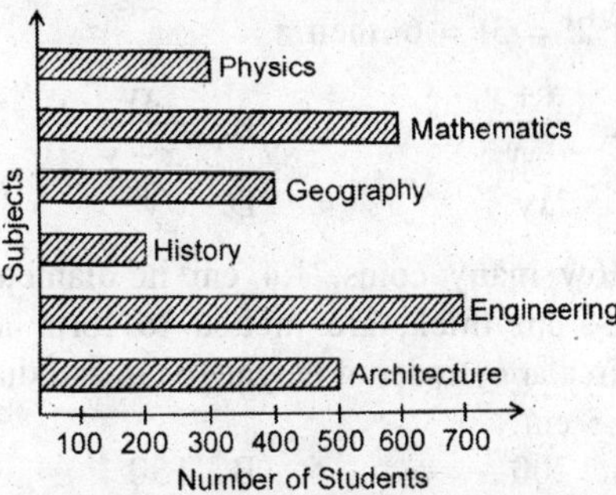

The ratio of the number of students studying History to that of the students studying Architecture is:
A. 1 : 2 B. 3 : 4
C. 2 : 7 D. 2 : 5

33. In the given figure, ABCD is a square. A line segment DX cuts the side BC at X and the diagonal AC at O such that ∠COD = 115° and ∠OXC = *x*°

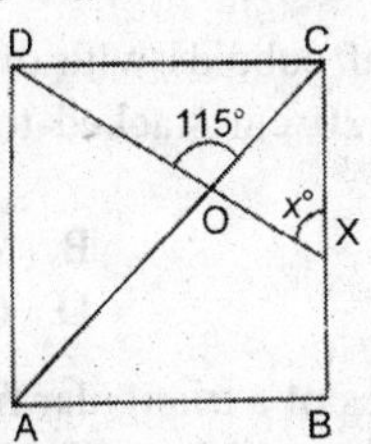

The value of *x* is:
A. 40 B. 70
C. 80 D. 85

34. Out of the following numbers which one is known as Hardy-Ramanujan Number?
A. 1297 B. 1729
C. 1927 D. 7219

35. The sum of $0.\overline{3}$ and $0.\overline{2}$ is:
A. 5/99 B. 5/9
C. 5/10 D. 5/100

36. If $(3a + 4b) = 16$ and $ab = 4$, then find the value of $(9a^2 + 16b^2)$.
A. 160 B. 100
C. 120 D. 140

37. The number of non-perfect square numbers between $(698)^2$ and $(699)^2$ is:
A. 1397 B. 1398
C. 1395 D. 1396

38. If $2^x = 3^y = 6^z$ then $z =$
A. $\frac{x+y}{xy}$ B. $\frac{xy}{x+y}$
C. $2xy$ D. x/y

39. How many coins, 1.4 cm in diameter and 0.4 cm thick, are melted to form a right circular cylinder of height 16 cm and diameter 3.5 cm?
A. 200 B. 150
C. 250 D. 300

40. Select the INCORRECT statement.
A. Every rectangle is a parallelogram.
B. A quadrilateral can be drawn if all four sides and one angle is known.
C. Triangle is a polygon whose sum of exterior angles is double the sum of interior angles.
D. If diagonals of a quadrilateral are equal, it must be a square.

41. Number of cuboids with dimensions 8 cm × 15 cm × 20 cm stacked together to form a cube is:
A. 100 B. 90
C. 80 D. 60

42. Three sides of a triangular field are of lengths 15 m, 20 m and 25 m. Find the cost of sowing seeds in the field at the rate of ₹ 5 per sq. m.
A. ₹ 600 B. ₹ 150
C. ₹ 750 D. ₹ 450

43. Which of the following rational numbers is greater than p, if $p = \frac{5}{7}$?
A. $\frac{1}{p-1}$ B. $\frac{1+p}{p}$
C. $\frac{p}{p-1}$ D. $\frac{p-1}{p+1}$

44. A person, standing on a railway platform, noticed that a train took 21 seconds to completely cross the platform which is 84 m long and it took 9 seconds in crossing him. The speed of the train is;
A. 25.2 km/hr B. 32.4 km/hr
C. 50.4 km/hr D. 75.64 km/hr

45. One of the factors of $x^2 + \frac{1}{x^2} + 2 - 2x - \frac{2}{x}$ is:
A. $x - \frac{1}{x}$ B. $x + \frac{1}{x} - 1$
C. $x + \frac{1}{x}$ D. $x^2 + \frac{1}{x^2}$

46. In the given figure, PQ ∥ RS, ∠PXM = 50° and ∠MYS = 120°, find the value of x if reflex ∠XMY is $x - 20°$.

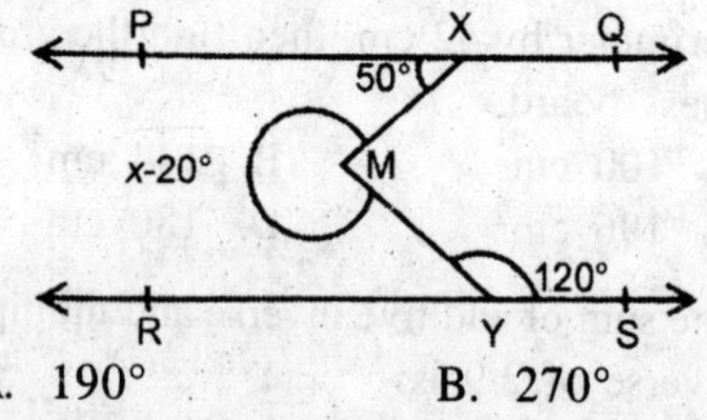

A. 190° B. 270°
C. 280° D. 250°

47. Which of the following can be another name of a cylinder?
A. A triangular prism
B. A rectangular prism
C. A pentagonal prism
D. A circular prism

48. The mean of 1, 3, 4, 5, 7 and 10 is m. The observations 3, 2, 4, 2, 3, 3 and p have mean $(m - 2)$ and median q. Find q.
A. 2 B. 3
C. 4 D. 3.5

49. Divya purchased 11 books for ₹ 10 and sold all books at 10 for ₹ 11. Her profit/loss per cent is:

A. 10% B. 11%
C. 21% D. 100%

50. If HCF and LCM of two terms a and b are x and y respectively and $a + b = x + y$, then $x^2 + y^2 = ?$

A. $a^2 - b^2$ B. $2a^2 + b^2$
C. $a^2 + b^2$ D. $a^2 + 2b^2$

Section B : English

Directions (Qs. No. 51-55): *Read the poem given below.*

A Minor Bird

I have wished a bird would fly away,
And not sing by my house all day;
Have clapped my hands at him from the door
When it seemed as if I could bear no more.

The fault must partly have been in me.
The bird was not to blame for his key.
And of course there must be something wrong
In wanting to silence any song.

—Robert Frost

On the basis of your understanding of the poem, answer the following questions.

51. The use of the word 'minor' bird in the title shows:

A. the size of the bird was small
B. insignificance with which man regards nature
C. the bird was under age
D. bird's existence in nature is of less significance

52. The rhyme scheme of the poem is:

A. abab B. aabb
C. abca D. abbb

53. Choose the quote that best captures the central idea of the poem.

A. "A bird doesn't sing because it has an answer. It sings because it has a song."
B. "Like a bird singing in the rain, let grateful memories survive in times of sorrow". — R.L. Stevenson.
C. "People are not disturbed by things but by the view they take of them". — Epictetus.
D. "People who are innately funny are innately disturbed." — Keenen Ivory Wayans.

54. Which of the following statement is NOT TRUE for the poem?

A. The poem is written in First person and a narrative style.
B. The poem ends with a philosophical idea that acceptance of Nature and its elements is a must.
C. The poem gives a message that insignificant things leave a deep impact on one's soul.
D. The poem is rich in imagery.

55. Which of the following emotions are expressed in the first stanza?

A. excitement B. arrogance
C. irritation D. elation

Directions (Qs. No. 56-65): *Choose the correct options to fill in the blanks.*

56. Some of these facts ______ incorrect.

A. is B. are
C. has been D. had been

57. "Don't waste your money", she said.
She told the boys ______

A. don't waste your money
B. not to waste any money
C. to not waste their money
D. not to waste their money

58. Everybody ______ keen to participate is the Nukkad Natak.

A. is B. are
C. were D. has

59. You ______ consult the Thesaurus if you need synonyms for those words.

A. had to B. need to
C. used to D. might

60. I have seen ______ of his work to know that he is ready for a promotion.

A. few B. a few
C. several D. enough

61. At this time tomorrow, we ______ our project details to our teacher.

A. will have presenting
B. have been presenting
C. shall be presenting
D. had been presenting

62. Only one of the boys ______ not done the homework.

A. can B. could
C. has D. have

63. The boy said to them, "Let me work now."

The boy requested them ______.

A. to let him work now
B. to let him work then
C. if he could work then
D. let me work now

64. Each of the suspected men ______ arrested.

A. was B. were
C. have D. had

65. A lot of people want to become successful entrepreneurs, but only ______ make the grade.

A. few B. not much
C. very little D. any

66. Choose the option that has the right rearrangement of the following words to make a meaningful sentence.

pollution health noise both affects behaviour and

A. Health affects both behaviour and pollution.
B. Behaviour affects health and noise pollution.
C. Pollution affects both behaviour, noise and health.
D. Noise pollution affects both behaviour and health.

67. In which of the following sentences does the verb agree with its subject?

A. What time does the news starts?
B. What time does the news start?
C. What time do the news start?
D. What time do the news starts?

68. Which of the given options has the words in an alphabetical order?

A. Peruvian, Parisian, Portuguese, Prussian, Polish, Paraguayan
B. Parisian, Paraguayan, Peruvian, Portuguese, Polish, Prussian
C. Paraguayan, Parisian, Peruvian, Polish, Portuguese, Prussian
D. Peruvian, Polish, Portuguese, Paraguayan, Parisian, Prussian

69. Identify the predicate in the following sentence.

He thinks that he has finished the course.

A. He
B. thinks
C. that he has finished the course
D. thinks that he has finished the course

70. Choose the option that has the right rearrangement of the following words to make a meaningful sentence.

planning poor rise urban give may pollution to noise

A. Poor planning may give rise to urban noise pollution.
B. Urban noise pollution may give rise to poor pollution.
C. Poor urban planning may give rise to noise pollution.
D. Noise pollution may give rise to poor urban planning.

71. The phrase 'weather the storm' means:

A. a difficult situation
B. to go out on a stormy day
C. to face challenges
D. an easy situation

72. Which of the following is an imperative sentence?

A. May God bless you, my friend!
B. They were not invited to the party.

C. Open the windows.
D. Creativity is allowing yourself to make mistakes.

73. Analogy is a comparison between one thing and another, typically for the purpose of explanation or clarification. Which of the following is the correct analogy?
A. Composer is to music as flowers are to poem.
B. Paw is to dog as hoof is to horse.
C. Branch is to tree as day is to hour.
D. Inside is to house as pale is to bright.

74. Which of the following sentences is in simple past tense?
A. The baby broke the glass.
B. The baby breaked the glass.
C. The baby has broken the glass.
D. The baby had broken the glass.

75. Ramesh knocked at the door thrice but no one answered. The word 'but' as used in the sentence is a/an:
A. preposition B. conjunction
C. verb D. adverb

Section C : General Science

76. Loudness of sound is measured in units of:
A. decibel (dB) B. hertz (Hz)
C. metre (m) D. metre/second (m/s)

77. Which type of organisms, live in the body of termites and digest wood cellulose converting it to soluble carbohydrates?
A. Algae B. Fungi
C. Protozoa D. Nematoda

78. Crop rotation is performed to:
(*a*) Improve the fertility of soil
(*b*) Save nitrogenous fertilizers
(*c*) Help in weed control and pest control
A. Only (*a*) and (*b*) B. Only (*a*) and (*c*)
C. Only (*b*) and (*c*) D. (*a*), (*b*) and (*c*)

79. It is easier to swim in sea water than in river water because:
A. Sea water is more dense than river water
B. Sea water has waves
C. Sea has large quantity of water
D. Sea water is less dense than river water

80. Read the following statements carefully and identify X, Y and Z respectively.
(*i*) X is stored under kerosene
(*ii*) Y catches fire on exposure and stored in water.
(*iii*) Z reacts with water slowly.
A. Na, Mg, Cu B. Na, P, Fe
C. Cu, Zn, K D. Zn, Cu, Na

81. The full form of LED is:
A. Light emitting diode
B. Light emission diode
C. Layer emission diode
D. Layer electron device

82. I am the source of synthetic polymer. I am a mixture of a number of carbon compounds, which can be separated by fractional distillation. I am:
A. Petrol B. Diesel
C. Petroleum D. Kerosene

83. Metals are generally hard. Which of the following metals is an exception and can be cut with a knife ?
A. Iron B. Sodium
C. Gold D. Magnesium

84. Study the given correlation.
Heat treatment : sterilization :: Vaccination : X
What would be 'X' here ?
A. Pasteurisation B. Immunisation
C. Fertilisation D. Inoculation

85. The sex determining system in which males are XY and females are XX is found in all:
A. Multicellular organism
B. Animals
C. Vertebrates
D. Mammals

86. When an object moves closer to a concave lens, the image formed by it shifts:
A. Away from the lens
B. First away and then towards the lens
C. Towards the lens
D. First towards and then away from the lens

87. A toy car released with the same initial speed will travel farthest on:
A. Muddy surface
B. Polished marble surface
C. Cemented surface
D. Brick surface

88. The loudness of sound depends on its:
A. Amplitude B. Time period
C. Frequency D. Speed

89. A small hole P is made in a piece of cardboard. The hole is illuminated by a torch as shown in the figure. The ray of light coming out of the hole falls on a mirror.

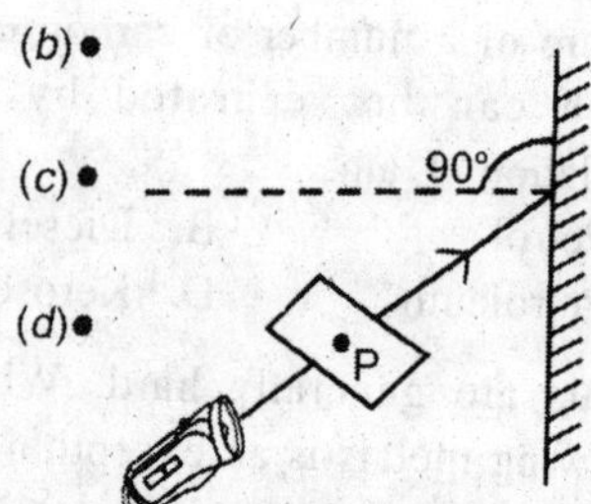

At which point should the eye be placed, so that the hole can be seen?
A. (*a*) B. (*b*)
C. (*c*) D. (*d*)

90. Which of the following statements is true?
(*i*) Yellow flame are ideal for heating.
(*ii*) The substances which vaporize during burning give flames.
(*iii*) Luminous zone contains unburnt carbon particles.
(*iv*) The non luminous zone has highest temperature.
A. (*i*), (*ii*) and (*iii*) B. (*i*), (*ii*) and (*iv*)
C. (*ii*), (*iii*) and (*iv*) D. (*i*), (*iii*) and (*iv*)

91. A cell converts:
A. Electrical energy into chemical energy
B. Chemical energy into electrical energy
C. Magnetic energy into electrical energy
D. Electrical energy into mechanical energy

92. Which of the following on reshuffling gives the term that refers to the process of sowing seeds manually by sprinkling them on soil by hand?
A. lnigtil B. glnopuihg
C. atnbrdocaigs D. ngiownwin

93. Which of the following statements about plastics is true?
(*i*) All plastics do not have same arrangement of monomer units.
(*ii*) Melamine resist fire and can tolerate heat better than other plastics.
(*iii*) Plastics with cross-linked monomers are also known.
(*iv*) The application of plastics is limited.
A. (*i*) and (*iii*) B. (*iii*) and (*iv*)
C. (*i*), (*ii*) and (*iii*) D. (*i*), (*iii*) and (*iv*)

94. A rubber sucker when pressed on a surface sticks to it because:
A. Gravitational pull acts on it.
B. Atmospheric pressure acts on it.
C. Rubber sucker has some glycerine in it.
D. Atmospheric pressure does not act on it.

95. A cube of side 0.2 m rests on the floor, as shown. Given that the cube has a mass of 50 kg, the pressure exerted by the cube on the floor is (take g = 10 N kg^{-1}).

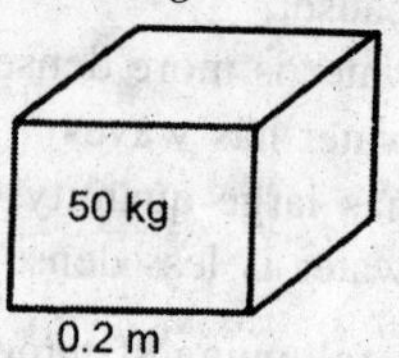

A. 25 Nm^{-2} B. 250 Nm^{-2}
C. 1250 Nm^{-2} D. 12500 Nm^{-2}

96. When the applied force is doubled on an object and the object is still at rest, then friction becomes:
A. Doubled B. Halved
C. Quadrupled D. Zero

97. Which of the following is a mismatched pair?
A. Ovaries – Oestrogen
B. Testes – Testosterone
C. Pancreas – Calcitonin
D. Adrenal glands – Corticosteroids

98. Which of the following statements is incorrect regarding metamorphosis?
A. It is the process of transformation of larva into an adult through drastic changes.
B. In human beings, metamorphosis does not occur because the young ones resembles the adults at the time of birth.
C. Life cycle of butterflies is completed in the four stages involving egg, larva, pupa, adult.
D. A tadpole that hatches out the egg resembles the adult frog in almost all respects.

99. The substance expected to have the highest ignition temperature out of the following is:
A. Kerosene B. Petrol
C. Coal D. Alcohol

100. Refer to the given figures (P and Q). How do reproductive cells produce in P differ from those produced in Q in terms of production and their modes of storage?

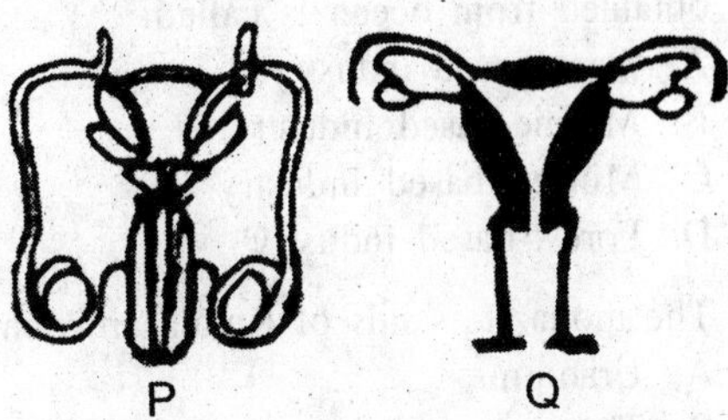

A. Mature cells of P can get stored for longer periods in reproductive tract whereas in Q only immature cells remain stored.
B. P produces fewer reproductive cells than Q does.
C. Reproductive cells produced by P do not show mobility.
D. Q produces reproductive cells for longer period in an individual's life span than P does.

Section D : Social Science

101. An FIR is filed with the ______.
A. Police B. Court
C. Army D. Chief Minister

102. Growing vegetables, flowers, fruits and decorative plants for commercial use is known as:
A. Viticulture B. Sericulture
C. Horticulture D. Pisciculture

103. Give an example of shaft mining.
A. Surface mining B. Deep bores
C. Off-shore drilling D. None of these

104. MLAs are the elected representatives of ______.
A. State Legislature B. Rajya Sabha
C. Lok Sabha D. Zila Parishad

105. Rourkela steel plant is located in which state of India?
A. Jharkhand B. West Bengal
C. Odisha D. Bihar

106. Civil law does not deal with ______.
A. Property matters B. Theft
C. Robbery D. Murder

107. The CHILD MARRIAGE RESTRATION ACT was passed in the year ______.
A. 1926 B. 1928
C. 1927 D. 1929

108. The President appoints ______ members of Rajya Sabha.
A. 12 B. 15
C. 14 D. 20

109. The method used to extract oil from the earth is called ______.
A. Shaft Mining B. Drilling
C. Open-cast mining D. Quarrying

110. Forests help in maintaining a balance of ______.
A. Nitrogen and Carbon dioxide
B. Oxygen and Carbon dioxide

C. Argon and Carbon dioxide
D. Nitrogen and Oxygen

111. Industry which processes raw material obtained from ocean is called:
A. Agro-based industry
B. Marine-based industry
C. Mineral-based industry
D. Forest-based industry

112. The monazite sands of Kerala are rich in:
A. Uranium
B. Thorium
C. Platinum
D. Coal

113. Who was the first Governor General of free India?
A. C. Rajagopalachari
B. Dr. Rajendra Prasad
C. Sardar Vallabhbahi Patel
D. Pt. Jawahar Lal Nehru

114. Which of the following is not an example of group water?
A. Water flowing in rivers
B. Water through hand pumps
C. Water through submersible pumps
D. Water through wells

115. Who gave the call 'Back to Vedas'?
A. Raja Rammohan Roy
B. Tara Bai Shinde
C. Jyotiba Phule
D. Swami Dayanand Saraswati

116. Which one of the following is not a characteristics of minerals?
A. They are created by natural processes
B. They have definite chemical composition
C. They are inexhaustible
D. Their distribution is even

117. Which level of judiciary cannot send a person to jail ______.
A. Supreme Court
B. Nyaya Panchayat
C. High Court
D. Subordinate Court

118. What makes an object a substance or a resource?
A. Utility
B. Quantity
C. Usability
D. Both (A) and (C)

119. Separation of religion from the State is referred to as ______.
A. Monarchy
B. Democracy
C. Secularism
D. Monotheism

120. What are the devotees of Vishnu called?
A. Vaishnavas
B. Nayanmars
C. Lingayats
D. Chishti

121. Which of the following are Fundamental Rights?
A. Right to equality
B. Right to freedom
C. Right against exploitation
D. All of the above

122. Justice Sachar Committee was set-up to look into the marginalization of ______.
A. Hindu B. Muslims
C. Sikhs D. Parsis

123. What was the reason for the hanging of sepoy Mangal Pandey?
A. For refusing to use the greased cartridges
B. For attacking the British or his officers
C. For disobeying orders
D. For killing the soldiers

124. Contaminated water causes ______.
A. Malaria
B. Dengue
C. Swin Flu
D. Jaundice

125. The first successful modern textile mill in India was established in:
A. Mumbai
B. Chennai
C. Ahmedabad
D. Kanpur

Section E : Intelligence

126. Select the option which satisfies the same conditions of placement of the dots as in the Figure.

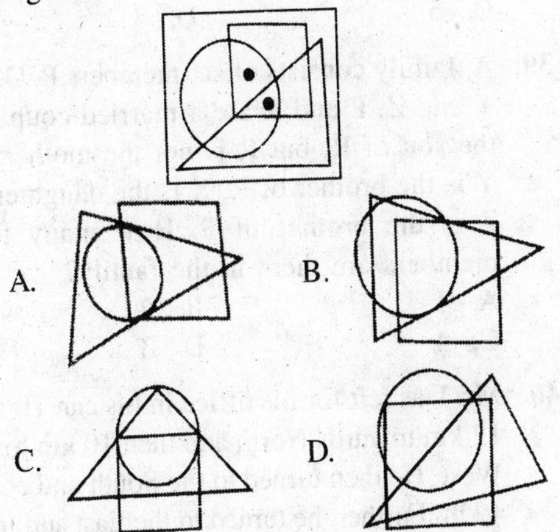

127. The question given below contains three items. These items may or may not have some relation with one another. The group of items may fit into one of the diagrams (A), (B), (C), (D). Indicate the diagram in which the group of items correctly fits into.

Boys, Class, Girls

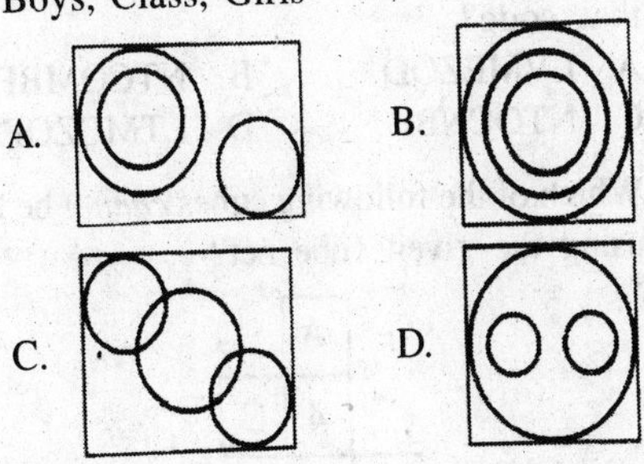

128. Which figure will come next to continue the series?

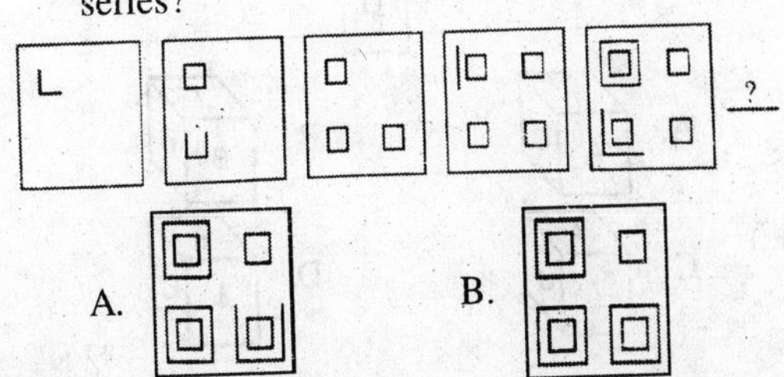

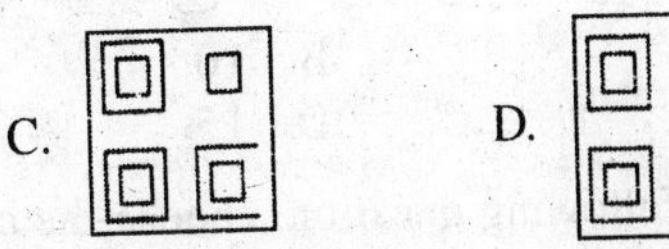

129. If P + R = 2Q and Q + S = 2P, which of the following is correct?

A. P + Q = R + S B. P + S = R + Q
C. P + Q = 2R D. P + Q = 2S

130. Observe the die. If the surfaces of the below given die are reconstructed to form a perfect die as shown in the fig. How many dots lie opposite to the face having three dots?

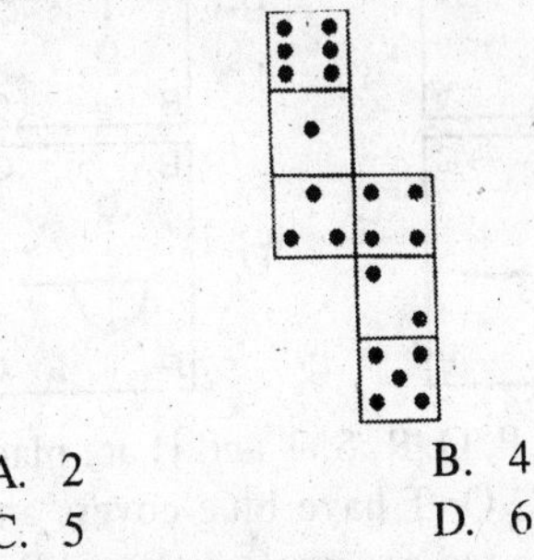

A. 2 B. 4
C. 5 D. 6

131. Complete the pattern.

6, 11, 21, 36, 56, (___)

A. 42 B. 51
C. 81 D. 91

132. In the following question, there is a certain relationship between the two given numbers on one side of (::) and one number is given on another side of (::) where another number is to be found from the given alternatives, having the same relationship with this number as the numbers of the given pair bear. Choose the best alternative.

100 : 121 :: 144 : ?

A. 160 B. 93
C. 169 D. 196

133. Which one of the following numbers will replace the question mark (?) in the number pattern given below?

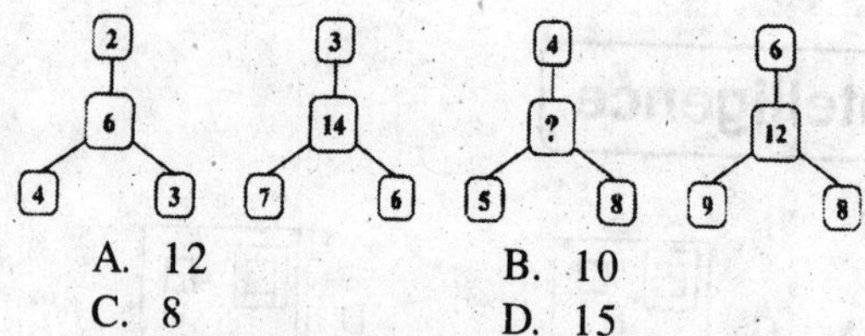

A. 12 B. 10
C. 8 D. 15

134. In the following question, choose the correct mirror image from the answer figures.

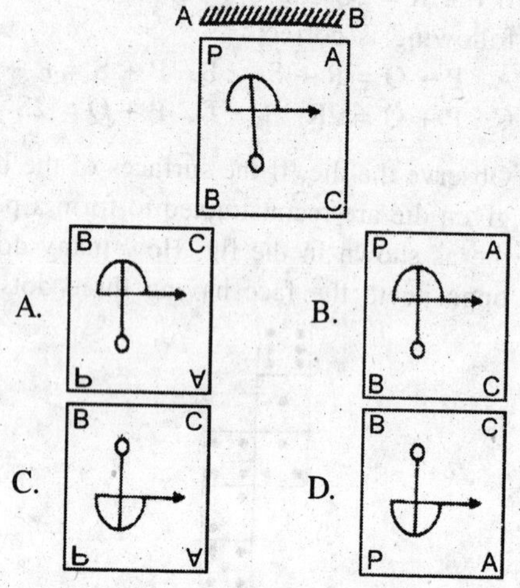

135. Six books P, Q, R, S, T and U are placed side by side. R, Q, T have blue covers and other books have red covers. Only S and P are new books and the rest are old. P, R, S are law reports, the rest are Gazetteers. Which two books are old Gazetteers with blue covers?

A. Q and U B. T and U
C. Q and T D. Q and R

136. If the seventh day of a month is three days earlier than Friday, what day will it be on the nineteenth day of the month?

A. Wednesday B. Monday
C. Friday D. Sunday

137. If 'PARK' is coded as '5394', 'SHIRT' is coded as '17698' and 'PANDIT' is coded as '532068' then how is 'NISHAR' written in that code?

A. 891560 B. 261739
C. 268539 D. 151738

138. Arrangement of numbers in the following question follow a common logic. Find out the missing number.

	49	
3	?	4
9	25	16
	36	

A. 2 B. 3
C. 5 D. 4

139. A family consists of six members P, Q, R, X, Y and Z. P and R are a married couple Q is the son of R, but R is not the mother of Q. Y is the brother of R. X is the daughter of P. Z is the brother of P. How many female members are there in the family?

A. 1 B. 2
C. 4 D. 3

140. Mr. Das left for his office in his car. He drove 12 km towards North and then 10 km towards West. He then turned to the South and covered 4 km. Further, he turned to the East and moved 8 km. Finally, he turned right and drove 8 km. How far and in which direction is he from his point?

A. 2 km, West B. 2 km, East
C. 4 km, North D. 2 km, South

141. In a certain code, 'CERTAIN' is coded as 'BFQUZJM'. How is 'MUNDANE' coded in that code?

A. LVMEZOD B. NTCOMBF
C. NTOCNBF D. LTMCZOF

142. Which of the following cubes *cannot* be formed using the given cube net?

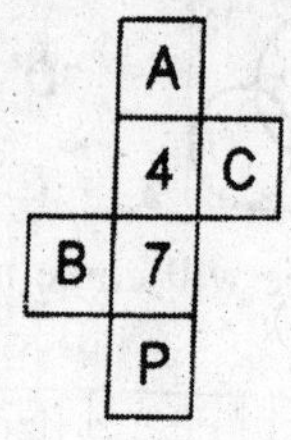

A. (P, A, C) B. (7, B, P)

C. 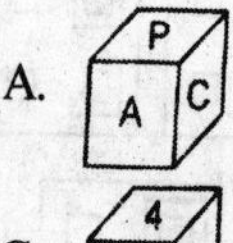

D. (B, 4, C)

143. A person is standing on a staircase. He walks down 4 steps, up 3 steps, down 6 steps, up 2 steps, up 9 steps and down 2 steps. Where is he standing in relation to the step on which he started?

A. 2 steps above B. 1 step above
C. The same place D. 1 step below

144. Freya is on the left of the person sitting in middle but is on the right of Bella. Sara is on the right of Jamie and Austin is on the right of Sara. Austin is the second person form the person sitting in the middle. Who is sitting in the middle?

A. Freya B. Jamie
C. Bella D. Sara

145. Find the missing number in the figure below.

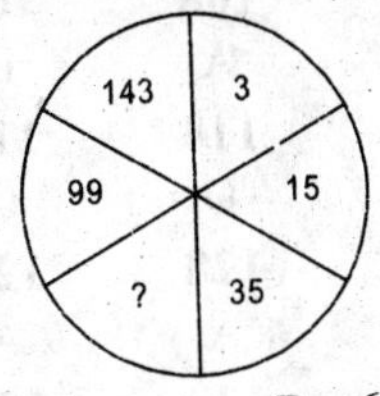

A. 56 B. 60
C. 63 D. 65

146. Given pair of figures on the either side of :: has a certain relationship. Identify the relationship between pair of figures and choose the missing figure.

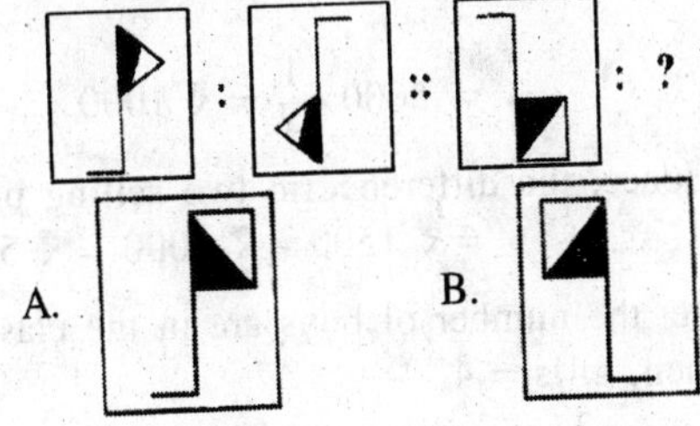

C. 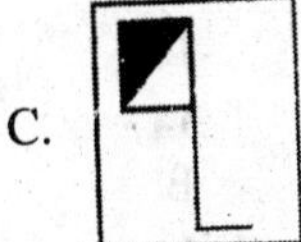 D.

147. Find the minimum number of line segment used in forming the given figure.

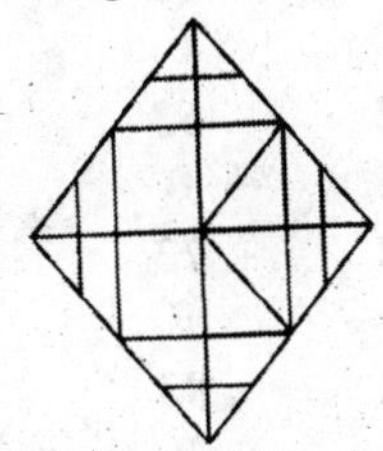

A. 24 B. 20
C. 18 D. 16

148. Using the table given below, identify the correct expression.

P	Q	R	S
×	÷	+	−

A. 2 P 9 S 24 Q 8 R 1 = 32
B. 2 R 9 S 24 Q 8 P 1 = 8
C. 2 P 8 S 24 R 9 Q 1 = 4
D. 2 P 8 S 24 Q 8 S 1 = 16

149. In a code language, SUGAR is written as BCDZF and WATER is written as PZQMF. Put the word TEARS into the same code.

A. QCMPB
B. QZFBD
C. QMZFB
D. QBDPM

150. From the given options, find the pair which is similar to the given pair 8 : 4.

A. 27 : 9 B. 216 : 32
C. 72 : 24 D. 45 : 5

ANSWERS

1	2	3	4	5	6	7	8	9	10
B	B	A	A	A	D	D	D	C	B
11	**12**	**13**	**14**	**15**	**16**	**17**	**18**	**19**	**20**
B	A	D	C	C	B	B	B	A	A

21	22	23	24	25	26	27	28	29	30
A	C	A	D	B	D	C	D	D	D
31	32	33	34	35	36	37	38	39	40
B	D	B	B	B	A	D	B	C	D
41	42	43	44	45	46	47	48	49	50
B	C	B	A	C	B	D	B	C	C
51	52	53	54	55	56	57	58	59	60
B	B	C	C	C	B	D	A	B	D
61	62	63	64	65	66	67	68	69	70
C	C	B	A	A	D	B	C	D	C
71	72	73	74	75	76	77	78	79	80
C	C	B	A	B	A	C	D	A	B
81	82	83	84	85	86	87	88	89	90
A	C	B	B	D	C	B	A	A	D
91	92	93	94	95	96	97	98	99	100
B	C	C	B	D	A	C	D	C	A
101	102	103	104	105	106	107	108	109	110
A	C	B	A	C	B, C, D	D	A	B	B
111	112	113	114	115	116	117	118	119	120
B	B	A	A	D	C, D	B	D	C	A
121	122	123	124	125	126	127	128	129	130
D	B	B	D	A	D	D	A	A	D
131	132	133	134	135	136	137	138	139	140
C	C	B	C	C	D	B	C	B	A
141	142	143	144	145	146	147	148	149	150
A	D	A	B	C	B	D	B	C	A

EXPLANATORY ANSWERS

1. Selling price of watch in first showroom

$$= ₹\ 5000 \times \frac{100-50}{100} \times \frac{100-40}{100}$$

$$= ₹\ 5000 \times \frac{50}{100} \times \frac{60}{100}$$

$$= ₹\ 5000 \times \frac{1}{2} \times \frac{3}{5}$$

$$= ₹\ 5000 \times \frac{3}{10} = ₹\ 1500.$$

and selling price of watch in second showroom

$$= ₹\ 5000 \times \frac{100-80}{100}$$

$$= ₹\ 5000 \times \frac{20}{100}$$

$$= 5000 \times \frac{1}{5} = ₹\ 1000$$

Hence, the difference in two selling price

$$= ₹\ 1500 - ₹\ 1000 = ₹\ 500.$$

2. Let the number of boys are in the class $= x$
then, girls $= 42 - x$

$$\therefore \quad \frac{3}{4}x + \frac{2}{3}(42 - x) = 30$$

$$\Rightarrow \quad \frac{3}{4}x + 28 - \frac{2}{3}x = 30$$

$$\Rightarrow \quad \frac{9x - 8x}{12} = 30 - 28$$

$$\Rightarrow \quad \frac{x}{12} = 2 \Rightarrow x = 24$$

Hence, the number of boys = 24.

3. Given, $\sqrt{1+\frac{27}{169}} = 1+\frac{x}{13}$

$\Rightarrow \quad \sqrt{\frac{169+27}{169}} = 1+\frac{x}{13}$

$\Rightarrow \quad \sqrt{\frac{196}{169}} = 1+\frac{x}{13}$

$\Rightarrow \quad \frac{14}{13} = 1+\frac{x}{13}$

$\Rightarrow \quad \frac{x}{13} = \frac{14}{13}-1 = \frac{1}{13}$

$\Rightarrow \quad \frac{x}{13} = \frac{1}{13}$

$\Rightarrow \quad x = 1$

4. Given, 1 y and 2 – y = 3 ...(*i*)

+ x y

z 6

$\because \quad 2y = 6$

$\therefore \quad y = 3$

Putting the value of *y* in (*i*), we get

$\therefore \quad z = 3 + y$

$\Rightarrow \quad z = 3 + 3$

$\Rightarrow \quad z = 6$

Hence, the value of *y* and *z* are 3 and 6.

5. Let three consecutive multiples of 7 are $7x$, $7(x + 1)$ and $7(x + 2)$

Then, $7x + 7(x + 1) + 7(x + 2) = 357$

$\Rightarrow \quad 21x = 21 = 357$

$\Rightarrow \quad 21x = 336$

$\Rightarrow \quad x = \frac{336}{21} = \frac{48}{3} = 16$

$\Rightarrow \quad x = 16$

Hence, the smallest multiple $= 7x$

$= 7 \times 16 = 112.$

7. When two unbiased dice are rolled together then, sample space

S = {(1, 1), (1, 2), (1, 3), (1, 4), (1, 5), (1, 6), (2, 1), (2, 2), (2, 3), (2, 4), (2, 5), (2, 6), (3, 1), (3, 2), (3, 3), (3, 4), (3, 5), (3, 6), (4, 1), (4, 2), (4, 3), (4, 4), (4, 5), (4, 6), (5, 1), (5, 2), (5, 3), (5, 4), (5, 5), (5, 6), (6, 1), (6, 2), (6, 3), (6, 4), (6, 5), (6, 6),}

$\therefore \quad n(S) = 36$

Let E is the event of getting same outcomes.

Then, E = {(1, 1), (2, 2), (3, 3), (4, 4), (5, 5), (6, 6)}

$\therefore \quad n(E) = 6$

Hence, required probability

$= \frac{n(E)}{n(S)} = \frac{6}{36}.$

9. Let the angles of a quadrilateral are $6x$, $7x$, $8x$ and $9x$ then,

$6x + 7x + 8x + 9x = 360°$

$\Rightarrow \quad 30x = 360° \Rightarrow x = 12$

$\therefore \quad 6x = 72°,\ 7x = 84°,\ 8x = 96°$

and $\quad 9x = 108°$

Hence, exactly two angles are obtus: 96°, 108° and two pairs of angles (72°, 108°) and (84°, 96°) are supplementary.

10. A pack of cards has 52 cards

$\therefore \quad n(S) = 52$

The number of hearts = 13

and red king = 1

Let E = event neigher a heart nor a red king

Then, $n(E) = 52 - (13 + 1)$

$= 52 - 14 = 38$

Hence, $p(E) = \frac{n(E)}{n(S)} = \frac{38}{52} = \frac{19}{26}.$

11. Given, Side of a square = *a*

Square is joined from opposite sides to form a cylinder.

$\therefore$ Perimeter of circular and = *a*

$2\pi r = a$

$\Rightarrow \quad r = \frac{a}{2\pi}$

Hence, area of each circular end $= \pi r^2$

$= \pi\left(\frac{a}{2\pi}\right)^2$

$= \pi \times \frac{a^2}{4\pi^2} = \frac{a^2}{4\pi}.$

12. Here, diameter of a well = 10 m

$\therefore \quad 2r = 10$ m

$\Rightarrow \quad r = 5$ m

and $\quad h = $ deep $= 14$ m

$\therefore$ Volume of well = V(Earth taken out)

$= \pi r^2 h$

$= \pi(5)^2 \times 14 \text{ m}^3$

$= \pi \times 25 \times 14 \text{ m}^3$

$= 350\pi \text{ m}^3$

Let the width of the embankment = x,

given, $\quad h = \frac{14}{3}$ m

Then, volume of the embankment

$$= \pi(5+x)^2 \times \frac{14}{3} - \pi \times 5^2 \times \frac{14}{3}$$

$$\Rightarrow \quad 350\pi = \pi(5+x)^2 \times \frac{14}{3} - \pi \times 5^2 \times \frac{14}{3}$$

$$\Rightarrow \quad 350\pi = \pi\frac{14}{3}[(5+x)^2 - 5^2]$$

$$\Rightarrow 350 \times \frac{3}{14} = (5 + x + 5)(5 + x - 5)$$

$\Rightarrow \quad 25 \times 3 = (10 + x)x$

$\Rightarrow \quad 75 = x^2 + 10x$

$\Rightarrow \quad x^2 + 10x - 75 = 0$

$\Rightarrow \quad x^2 + 15x - 5x - 75 = 0$

$\Rightarrow \quad x(x + 15) - 5(x + 15) = 0$

$\Rightarrow \quad (x - 5)(x + 15) = 0$

$\Rightarrow \quad x = 5, x = -15$

Hence, the width of the embankment = 5 m.

14. Given, P = ₹ 1600, n = 2 years, A = ₹ 1764

On compound interest

$$A = p\left(1+\frac{r}{100}\right)^n$$

$$\Rightarrow \quad 1764 = 1600\left(1+\frac{r}{100}\right)^n$$

$$\Rightarrow \quad \frac{1764}{1600} = \left(1+\frac{r}{100}\right)^2$$

$$\Rightarrow \quad \left(\frac{42}{40}\right)^2 = \left(1+\frac{r}{100}\right)^2$$

$$\Rightarrow \quad \frac{42}{40} = 1+\frac{r}{100}$$

$$\Rightarrow \quad \frac{21}{20} = 1+\frac{r}{100}$$

$$\Rightarrow \quad \frac{r}{100} = \frac{21}{20} - 1$$

$$\Rightarrow \quad \frac{r}{100} = \frac{1}{20}$$

$\Rightarrow \quad r = 5\%$

Hence, the rate of interest per annum = 5%.

16. A. $0.09 > \frac{7}{8}$

$\Rightarrow 0.09 > 0.875$ (not true)

B. $6\% < 0.09$

$\Rightarrow \frac{6}{100} < 0.09$

$\Rightarrow 0.06 < 0.09$ (true)

C. $8.0 \times 10^{-3} > 6\%$

$\Rightarrow 8.0 \times \frac{1}{1000} > 6\%$

$\Rightarrow \frac{8}{100} > \frac{6}{100}$

$\Rightarrow 0.008 > 0.06$ (not true)

D. $\frac{7}{8} < 9 \times 10^{-3}$

$\Rightarrow \frac{7}{8} < 9 \times \frac{1}{1000}$

$\Rightarrow 0.875 < 0.009$ (not true)

Hence, option (B) 6% < 0.09 is true.

17. Let certain number of men = x

More men, less day → indirect proportion

and less men, more day → indirect proportion

men day

$x : x - 6 :: 15 : 9$

$\Rightarrow \quad 9x = 15(x - 6)$

$\Rightarrow \quad 9x = 15x - 90°$

$\Rightarrow \quad 15x - 9x = 90°$

$\Rightarrow \quad 6x = 90°$

$\Rightarrow \quad x = 15°.$

18. A regular polygon with interior angle 162°

$\therefore \quad \theta = \left(\frac{n-2}{n}\right)180°$

$\Rightarrow \quad 162° = \left(\frac{n-2}{n}\right)180°$

$\Rightarrow \quad \frac{n-2}{n} = \frac{162°}{180°}$

$\Rightarrow \quad \frac{n-2}{n} = \frac{18}{20} \Rightarrow \frac{n-2}{n} = \frac{9}{10}$

$\Rightarrow \quad 10n - 20 = 9n$

$\Rightarrow \quad n = 20$

Hence, the number of side of regular polygon $= n = 20$.

19. Let the number of chocolates she had purchased is x

Then, cost price = ₹ $10x$ + ₹ $5x$ + ₹ $15x$

and selling price = ₹ $10x \times \frac{120}{100}$ + ₹ $5x \times \frac{108}{100}$

$= \frac{1200x}{100} + \frac{540x}{100} =$ ₹ $\frac{1740x}{100}$

Profit = S.P. – C.P.

$\therefore$ ₹ 240 = ₹ $\frac{1740x}{100} - 15x$

$\Rightarrow \quad 240 = \frac{1740x - 1500x}{100}$

$\Rightarrow \quad 240 = \frac{240x}{100}$

$\Rightarrow \quad x = 100.$

20. Let slant height of two right-circular cones are $3x$ and $5x$

Then, $\quad \pi r_1 3x = \pi r_2 5x$

$\Rightarrow \quad 3r_1 = 5r_2$

$\Rightarrow \quad \frac{r_1}{r_2} = \frac{5}{3}$

$\Rightarrow \quad r_1 : r_2 = 5 : 3.$

21. $\frac{1}{1+x^{b-a}+x^{c-a}} + \frac{1}{1+x^{a-b}+x^{c-b}} + \frac{1}{1+x^{b-c}+x^{a-c}}$

$= \frac{1}{1+\frac{x^b}{x^a}+\frac{x^c}{x^a}} + \frac{1}{1+\frac{x^a}{x^b}+\frac{x^c}{x^b}} + \frac{1}{1+\frac{x^b}{x^c}+\frac{x^a}{x^c}}$

$= \frac{x^a}{x^a+x^b+x^c} + \frac{x^b}{x^b+x^a+x^c} + \frac{x^c}{x^c+x^b+x^a}$

$= \frac{x^a+x^b+x^c}{x^a+x^b+x^c} = 1.$

22. Let the two complementary angles are $13x$ and $5x$

Then, $\quad 13x + 5x = 90°$

$\Rightarrow \quad 18x = 90°$

$\Rightarrow \quad x = 5°$

Hence, angles are $13x = 65°$ and $5x = 25°$.

23. The part filled in 1 minute by all the 3 pipes

$= \frac{1}{12} + \frac{1}{15} - \frac{1}{10}$

$= \frac{5+4-6}{60} = \frac{3}{60} = \frac{1}{20}$

Hence, all the 3 pipes will fill the cistern in 20 minutes

25. Given, $2^x + 2^x + 2^x = 192$

$\Rightarrow \quad 3(2^x) = 192$

$\Rightarrow \quad 2^x = 64$

$\Rightarrow \quad 2^x = 2^6$

$\Rightarrow \quad x = 6.$

26. Given, total number of people with blood types A or B = 82

$x \times \frac{16+25}{100} = 82$

$\Rightarrow \quad x = \frac{8200}{41} = 200$

Hence, total number of people will all blood types

$= x = 200$

Hence, the number of people with blood types AB or O

$= x \times \frac{19+40}{100}$

$= 200 \times \frac{59}{100} = 118.$

27. Let the side of a chess board = x cm

then, perimeter = $4x$ cm

According to question

$4x - x = 42$ cm

$\Rightarrow \quad 3x = 42$ cm

$\Rightarrow \quad x = 14$ cm

Hence, the area of the chess board = $(\text{side})^2$

$= x^2 = (14)^2 = 196 \text{ cm}^2$.

28. Additive inverse of $\frac{2}{9} = -\frac{2}{9}$

and Multiplicative inverse of $\frac{2}{9} = \frac{9}{2}$

Hence, the required sum $= -\frac{2}{9} + \frac{9}{2}$

$= -\frac{4+81}{18} = \frac{77}{18}$.

29. The standard form for 0.000064

$= \frac{64}{1000000} = \frac{6.4}{100000}$

$= \frac{6.4}{10^5} = 6.4 \times 10^{-5}$.

33. In the given figure,

ABCD is a square

$\therefore \quad \angle BOD = 90°$ and $\angle BCA = \angle DCA$

$\angle BCA = \angle DCA = 45°$

In ΔCOX,

$\angle COX = 180° - 115° = 65°$

$\Rightarrow \quad \angle COX = 65°$

$\because \angle COX + \angle OXC + \angle XCO = 180°$

$\therefore 65° + x° + 45° = 180°$

$\Rightarrow \quad x° + 110° = 180°$

$\Rightarrow \quad x° = 180° - 110°$

$\Rightarrow \quad x° = 70°$

Hence, the value of x is 70°.

35. $0.\overline{3} + 0.\overline{2} = \frac{3}{9} + \frac{2}{9} = \frac{5}{9}$.

36. Given, $3a + 4b = 16$ and $ab = 4$

$\because (3a + 4b)^2 = (16)^2$

$\therefore 9a^2 + 16b^2 + 2 \times 3a \times 4b = 256$

$\Rightarrow 9a^2 + 16b^2 + 24ab = 256$

$\Rightarrow 9a^2 + 16b^2 + 24 \times 4 = 256$

$\Rightarrow 9a^2 + 16b^2 = 256 - 96$

$\Rightarrow 9a^2 + 16b^2 = 160$.

38. Given, $2^x = 3^y = 6^z$

$\therefore \quad 2 = 6^{\frac{z}{x}}$ and $3 = 6^{\frac{z}{y}}$

$\therefore \quad 6^z = (2 \times 3)^z$

$\Rightarrow \quad 6^z = \left(6^{\frac{z}{x}} \times 6^{\frac{z}{y}}\right)^z$

$\Rightarrow \quad 6^z = \left(6^{\frac{z}{x}} \times 6^{\frac{z}{y}}\right)^z = 6^{z\left(\frac{z}{x}+\frac{z}{y}\right)}$

$\therefore \quad z = \left(\frac{z}{x} + \frac{z}{y}\right)^z$

$\Rightarrow \quad 1 = \frac{z}{x} + \frac{z}{y}$

$\Rightarrow \quad 1 = z\left(\frac{y+x}{xy}\right)$

$\Rightarrow \quad z = \frac{xy}{x+y}$.

39. Volume of a coin $= \pi r^2 h$

$= \pi\left(\frac{1.4}{2}\right)^2 \times 0.4 \text{ cm}^3$

and volume of a right-circular cylinder

$= \pi\left(\frac{3.5}{2}\right)^2 \times 16 \text{ cm}^3$

Hence, the number of coins

$= \frac{\text{Volume of a cylinder}}{\text{Volume of a coin}}$

$= \frac{\pi\left(\frac{3.5}{2}\right)^2 \times 16}{\pi\left(\frac{1.4}{2}\right)^2 \times 0.4} = \frac{\left(\frac{3.5}{4}\right)^2 \times 16}{\left(\frac{1.4}{4}\right)^2 \times 0.4}$

$= \frac{(3.5)^2 \times 4}{(1.4)^2 \times 0.1}$

$= \left(\frac{3.5}{1.4}\right)^2 \times \frac{4}{.1}$

$= \left(\frac{5}{2}\right)^2 \times 40 = \frac{25}{4} \times 40$

$= 25 \times 10 = 250$.

41. Volume of a cuboid = 8 cm × 15 cm × 20 cm

$= 2400 \text{ cm}^3$

$= 2^3 \times 2^2 \times 5^2 \times 3$

∵ To form a cube

∴ Volume $= 2^3 \times 2^3 \times 5^3 \times 3^3$

Hence, number of cuboid with stacked together

$$= \frac{2^3 \times 2^3 \times 5^3 \times 3^3}{2^3 \times 2^2 \times 5^2 \times 3}$$

$= 2 \times 5 \times 9 = 90.$

42. Let three sides of a triangular field are $a = 15$ m, $b = 20$ m and $c = 25$ m

Then, $S = \frac{a+b+c}{2} = \frac{15+20+25}{2}$

$= \frac{60}{2} = 30$ m

∴ Area of a triangular field

$= \sqrt{S(S-a)(S-b)(S-c)}$

$= \sqrt{30(30-15)(30-20)(30-25)}$

$= \sqrt{30 \times 15 \times 10 \times 5}$

$= \sqrt{22500} = 150 \text{ m}^2$

∴ The cost of sowing seeds in the field at the rate of ₹ 5 per sq. m.

= ₹ 5 × 150 = ₹ 750.

43. Given, $P = \frac{5}{7}$

A. $\frac{1}{P-1} = \frac{1}{\frac{5}{7}-1} = \frac{1}{-\frac{2}{7}} = -\frac{7}{2}$

B. $\frac{1+P}{P} = \frac{1+\frac{5}{7}}{\frac{5}{7}} = \frac{12}{7} \times \frac{7}{5} = \frac{12}{5}$

C. $\frac{P}{P-1} = \frac{\frac{5}{7}}{\frac{5}{7}-1} = \frac{\frac{5}{7}}{-\frac{2}{7}} = -\frac{5}{2}$

D. $\frac{P-1}{P+1} = \frac{\frac{5}{7}-1}{\frac{5}{7}+1} = \frac{-\frac{2}{7}}{\frac{12}{7}} = -\frac{1}{6}$

Hence, $\frac{12}{5} > \frac{5}{7}$

Hence, Option (B) $\frac{1+P}{P}$ is greater than P.

44. Let the length of train is x m.

then, $\frac{x+84}{21} = \frac{x}{9}$ $\left[\text{Speed} = \frac{\text{distance}}{\text{time}}\right]$

$\Rightarrow \frac{x+84}{7} = \frac{x}{3}$

$\Rightarrow 3x + 252 = 7x$

$\Rightarrow 4x = 252$

$\Rightarrow x = 63$

Hence, the speed of the train $= \frac{x}{9}$ m/s

$= \frac{63}{9} \times \frac{18}{5}$ km/hr.

$= 7 \times \frac{18}{5}$ km/hr.

$= 7 \times 3.6 = 25.2$ km/hr.

45. $x^2 + \frac{1}{x^2} + 2 - 2x - \frac{2}{x}$

$= x^2 + \frac{1}{x^2} + 2 \cdot x \cdot \frac{1}{x} - 2\left(x + \frac{1}{x}\right)$

$= \left(x + \frac{1}{x}\right)^2 - 2\left(x + \frac{1}{x}\right)$

$= \left(x + \frac{1}{x}\right)\left(x + \frac{1}{x} - 2\right)$

Hence, one of the factors $= \left(x + \frac{1}{x}\right)$.

50. ∵ HCF × LCM = Multiplication of two terms

∴ $x \times y = a \times b$

$\Rightarrow ab = xy$

and given, $a + b = x + y$

∴ $x^2 + y^2 = (x+y)^2 - 2xy$

$= (a+b)^2 - 2ab$

$= a^2 + b^2 + 2ab - 2ab$

$= a^2 + b^2$.

129. Given, $P + R = 2Q$ ...(*i*)
and $Q + S = 2P$ ...(*ii*)
Adding (*i*) and (*ii*), we get
$P + R + Q + S = 2Q + 2P$
$\Rightarrow R + S = 2Q + 2P - P - Q$
$\Rightarrow R + S = P + Q$
$\Rightarrow P + Q = R + S.$

131. 6 (+5) 11 (+10) 21 (+15) 36 (+20) 56 (+25) 81

Hence, the next number = 81.

132. $(\sqrt{100}+1)^2 = (10 + 1)^2 = (11)^2 = 121$
Similarly, $(\sqrt{144}+1)^2 = (12 + 1)^2 = (13)^2 = 169$
Hence, 100 : 121 :: 144 : 169
Hence, ? = 169.

133. From first figure $\frac{4\times 3}{2} = \frac{12}{2} = 6$

From second figure $\frac{7\times 6}{3} = \frac{42}{3} = 14$

From third figure $\frac{5\times 8}{4} = \frac{40}{4} = \boxed{10}$

From fourth figure $\frac{9\times 8}{6} = \frac{72}{6} = 12$

Hence, ? = missing number = 10.

135.

Books	Colour		
P	red	new	law reports
Q	blue	old	gazetteers
R	blue	old	law reports
S	red	new	law reports
T	blue	old	gazetteers
U	red	old	gazetteers

Hence, two books Q and T are old Gazetteers with blue covers.

136. Given, 7th day of a month = Friday – 3 days
= Tuesday
$\Rightarrow$ 14th day of the month = Tuesday
$\therefore$ 19th day of the month = Tuesday + 5 day
= Sunday.

137. Given,

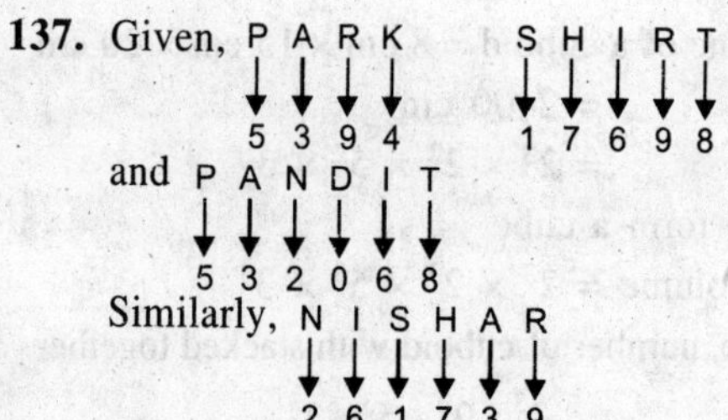

Hence, 'NISHAR' is written as 261739.

141. Given,

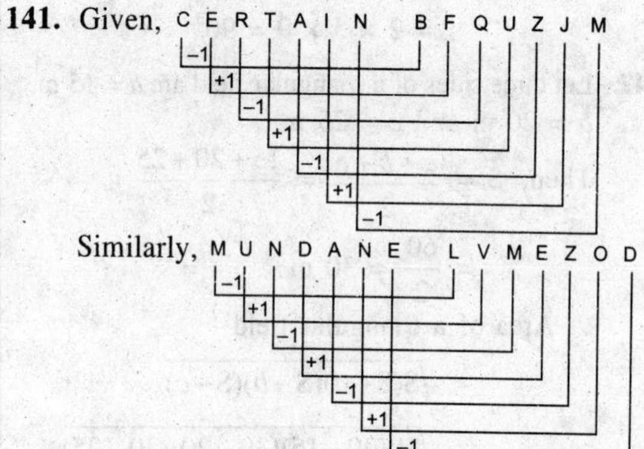

Hence, 'MUNDANE' is coded as 'LVMEZOD'.

143. Required answer
= down 4 steps + up 3 steps + down 6 steps + up 2 steps + up 9 steps + down 2 steps
= down 12 steps + up 14 steps = –12 + 14 = 2
= up 2 steps = 2 steps above.

144. Sitting arrangement:

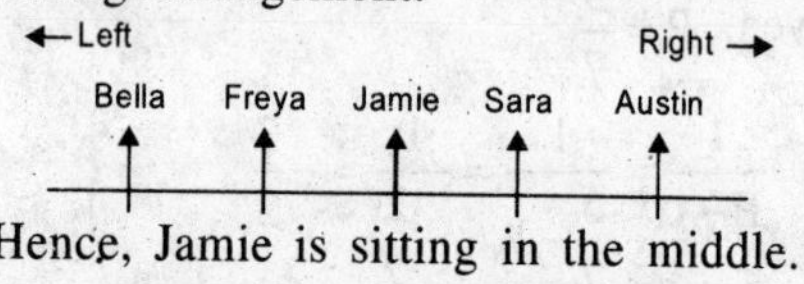

Hence, Jamie is sitting in the middle.

145.

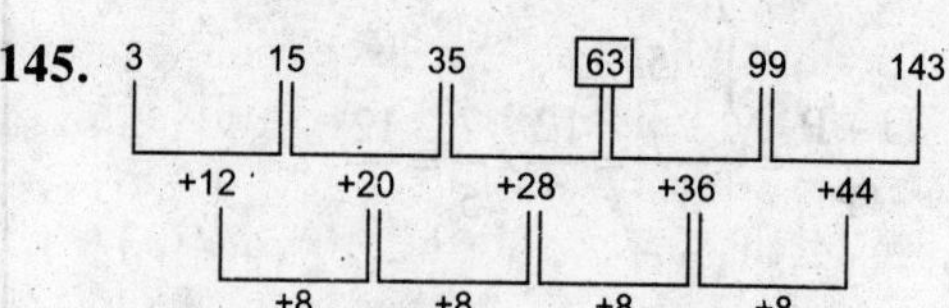

Hence, ? = Missing number = 63.

150. Given, pair = 8 : 4 = $2^3 : 2^2$
A. 27 : 9 = $3^3 : 3^2$
B. 216 : 32 = $6^3 : 2^5$
C. 72 : 24
D. 45 : 5
Hence, the pair 27 : 9 is similar to the given pair 8 : 4.

Previous Paper (Solved)

All India Sainik Schools Entrance Exam (AISSEE)–2021*

Class-IX

Section A : Mathematics

1. The value of $1+\dfrac{1}{1+\dfrac{1}{1+\dfrac{1}{9}}}$ is:

A. $\frac{29}{19}$ B. $\frac{10}{19}$
C. $\frac{29}{10}$ D. $\frac{10}{9}$

2. Find the sum of $3.\overline{2}$ and $5.\overline{4}$.

A. $\frac{78}{3}$ B. $\frac{58}{3}$
C. $\frac{58}{9}$ D. $\frac{78}{9}$

3. What should be added to $-\frac{7}{3}$ to get $\frac{3}{7}$?

A. $\frac{21}{58}$ B. $\frac{58}{21}$
C. $\frac{47}{21}$ D. $\frac{50}{21}$

4. The difference between two whole numbers is 66. The ratio of the two numbers is 5 : 2. The two numbers are:

A. 60 and 6 B. 100 and 33
C. 110 and 44 D. 99 and 33

5. If angle A and angle C are two opposite angles of a parallelogram, then

A. angle A > angle C
B. angle A = angle C
C. angle A < angle C
D. None of these

6. The lengths of the diagonals of a rhombus are 16 cm and 12 cm respectively. Find the length of each of its sides.

A. 30 cm B. 10 cm
C. 20 cm D. 28 cm

7. If the mean of the following data is 8, then find the value of x:
2, 4, 8, 6, x, 5

A. 17 B. 23
C. 48 D. 25

8. Data collected in a survey shows that 40% of the buyers are interested in buying a particular brand of toothpaste. The central angle (in degrees) of the sector of the pie chart representing this information is:

A. 120 B. 150
C. 144 D. 40

9. The monthly salary of a person is ₹ 15,000. The central angle of the sector representing his expenses on food and house rent on a pie chart is 60°. The amount he spends on food and house rent is:

A. ₹ 5,000 B. ₹ 2,500
C. ₹ 6,000 D. ₹ 9,000

10. The mid value of a class interval is called its:

A. class limit B. class mark
C. width D. range

11. If the mode of a distribution is 12 and the mean is 3, then the median is:

A. 8 B. 36
C. 4 D. 6

*Exam held on 07/02/2021

12. The square root of 0.00000121 is;

A. 0.011 B. 0.00011

C. 0.0011 D. 0.11

13. Which least number should be subtracted from 108245 so as to get a perfect square?

A. 3 B. 4

C. 5 D. 6

14. Find the one's digit of the cube root of 6,859.

A. 2 B. 3

C. 9 D. 1

15. The smallest natural number by which 1296 must be divided to get a perfect cube is:

A. 16 B. 6

C. 60 D. 26

16. 72% of 25 students are good in Mathematics. How many are ***not*** good in Mathematics?

A. 18 B. 7

C. 15 D. 9

17. I purchased 1 dozen pencils at the rate of 5 paise per pencil. For how much should I sell a pencil to make 20% profit?

A. 4 paise B. 10 paise

C. 6 paise D. 8 paise

18. A sum amounts to ₹ 4,410 after two years at 5% compound interest per annum. What is the principal?

A. ₹ 3,000 B. ₹ 4,100

C. ₹ 4,000 D. ₹ 4,200

19. What will you get when you subtract $3x - 4y - 7z$ from the sum of $x - 3y + 2z$ and $-4x + 9y - 11z$?

A. $-6x + 10y - 2z$ B. $6x + 10y - 2z$

C. $-6x - 10y - 2z$ D. $-6x + 10y + 2z$

20. Find the remainder when $5x^2 - 4x + 3$ is divided by $(x - 2)$.

A. 14 B. 15

C. 18 D. 12

21. If $x - \frac{1}{x} = 3$, then the value of $x^4 + \frac{1}{x^4}$ is:

A. 194 B. 119

C. 114 D. 116

22. The area of the square having diagonal of length '*d*' is given by:

A. $\frac{d}{2}$ B. $\frac{d^2}{2}$

C. $\frac{d^2}{4}$ D. $2d$

23. The perimeter of a circle having area 154 sq. cm is:

A. 22 cm B. 44 cm

C. 88 cm D. 66 cm

24. Find the area of a rhombus having perimeter 80 cm and one diagonal 24 cm.

A. 354 sq. cm B. 364 sq. cm

C. 384 sq. cm D. 480 sq. cm

25. What is the ratio of the volume of a cylinder and that of a cone on the same base and of the same height?

A. 1 : 2 B. 1 : 4

C. 4 : 3 D. 3 : 1

26. If the height and the radius of a cone are doubled, the volume of the cone becomes:

A. 2 times B. 4 times

C. 6 times D. 8 times

27. The total surface area of the hemisphere of volume 19404 cu. cm is:

A. 4158 sq. cm B. 2772 sq. cm

C. 5544 sq. cm D 4258 sq. cm

28. The value of $125^{-\frac{1}{3}}$ is:

A. $\frac{1}{3}$ B. $\frac{1}{5}$

C. 3 D. 5

29. The value of $(64^{\frac{2}{3}})^{\frac{1}{2}}$ is:

A. 5 B. 4

C. 3 D. 8

30. What is the value of $\left(\frac{1}{2}\right)^{-2} + \left(\frac{1}{3}\right)^{-2} + \left(\frac{1}{4}\right)^{-2}$?

A. $\frac{1}{29}$ B. $\frac{1}{9}$

C. $\frac{1}{5}$ D. 29

31. The additive identity for integers is:
A. 0 B. 1
C. –1 D. does not exist

32. Associative property of multiplication of integers:
A. exists B. does not exist
C. holds without 0 D. None of these

33. If ABC is an equilateral triangle of side a, then its altitude is equal to:
A. $\frac{\sqrt{3}}{4}a$ B. $\frac{\sqrt{3}}{2}a$
C. $\sqrt{3}a$ D. $\frac{\sqrt{3}}{5}a$

34. What is the number of possible outcomes in throwing two dice simultaneously?
A. 6 B. 12
C. 36 D. 4

35. Two coins are tossed simultaneously. The probability of getting at most one head is:
A. $\frac{1}{2}$ B. $\frac{3}{4}$
C. $\frac{2}{3}$ D. 1

36. There is food provision for 100 men for 30 days. If the number of men is reduced to 80, then the number of days the food could last for is:
A. 28 B. 35
C. $37\frac{1}{2}$ D. 37

37. A vertical pole 14 m high casts a shadow of 10 m. What will be the height of a tree that casts a shadow of 15 m under similar conditions?
A. 15 m B. 20 m
C. 21 m D. 24 m

38. If 15 workers can build a wall in 48 hours, how many workers will be required to do the same work in 30 hours?
A. 15 B. 14
C. 24 D. 30

39. If $a + b + c = 5$ and $ab + bc + ca = 10$, then $a^3 + b^3 + c^3 - 3abc$ is:
A. –25 B. 25
C. –50 D. –75

40. If $\frac{a}{b}+\frac{b}{a}=2$, then $a^3 - b^3 =$
A. 1 B. –1
C. 0 D. 2

41. Factorisation of $3\sqrt{3}x^3-8$ is:
A. $\left(\sqrt{3}x-2\right)\left(3x^2+2\sqrt{3}x+4\right)$
B. $\left(\sqrt{3}x+2\right)\left(3x^2+2\sqrt{3}x+4\right)$
C. $\left(\sqrt{3}x-2\right)\left(3x^2+2\sqrt{3}x+8\right)$
D. $\left(\sqrt{3}x-2\right)\left(3x^2-2\sqrt{3}x+4\right)$

42. At what distance does the point (12, 5) lie from the origin?
A. 17 B. 7
C. 13 D. 60

43. A can do a work in 25 days and B can do the same work in 20 days. If they work together for 5 days and then A leaves, in how many days can B finish the remaining work?
A. 10 B. 11
C. 12 D. 14

44. The difference of a two-digit number and the number obtained by reversing the digits is always a multiple of:
A. 11 B. 9
C. 7 D. 10

45. In a triangle, if two of the angles are complementary, then the measure of the third angle is:
A. 40° B. 45°
C. 75° D. 90°

46. If the exterior angle of a triangle is 60° and the interior opposite angles are in the ratio 1 : 3, then the angles of the triangle are:
A. 15°, 45°, 110° B. 120°, 10°, 50°
C. 120°, 45°, 15° D. 60°, 90°, 30°

47. If a transversal intersects two parallel lines, then the consecutive interior angles on the same side of the transversal are:
A. complementary B. supplementary
C. equal D. None of these

48. Line l is perpendicular to line m and line m is perpendicular to line n. Then the lines l and n are:
A. parallel to each other.
B. perpendicular to each other.
C. intersecting.
D. None of the above

49. From the pie chart, the shares of central angle for food and fuel, respectively, are:

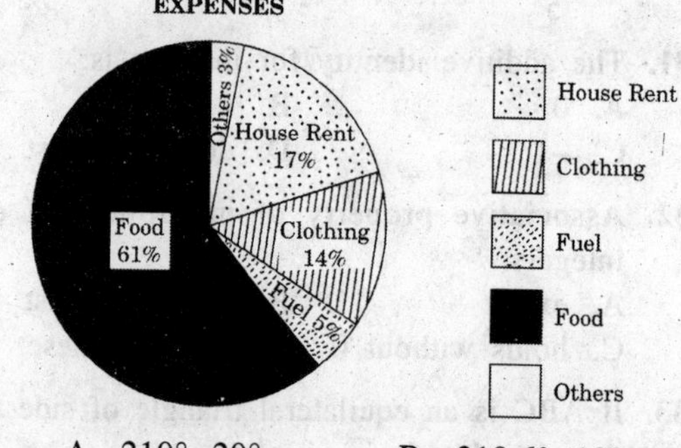

A. 210°, 20° B. 219.6°, 18°
C. 209.6°, 20° D. 209.6°, 18°

50. What is alternate name of a pie chart?
A. Pictograph B. Histograph
C. Circle chart D. None of these

Section B : English

Directions (Qs. No. 51-53): *Read the following passage and answer the following questions by choosing the most appropriate option.*

Marie Curie

Marie Curie grew up in Warsaw, Poland where she was born on November 7, 1867. Her parents were both teachers. The child of two teachers, Marie, was taught to read and write early in life. She was a very bright child and did well in school. She had a sharp memory and worked hard on her studies. As Marie grew older, her family came upon tough times. Poland was under the control of Russia at that time. People were not even allowed to read or write anything in the Polish language. Her father lost his job because he was in favour of Polish rule. Marie lost her elder sister and mother to typhus and tuberculosis respectively. After graduating from high school, Marie wanted to attend a university, but this wasn't something that young women did in Poland during the years covering the period 1800 – 1900. The university was for men. However, there was a famous university in Paris, France called the Sorbonne that women could attend. Marie did not have the money to go there, but agreed to work to help pay for her sister Bronislawa to go to school in France, if she would help Marie after she graduated. It took six years, but, after Bronislawa graduated and became a doctor, Marie moved to France and entered the Sorbonne. Marie arrived in France in 1891. Marie lived the life of a poor college student, but she loved every minute of it. She was learning so much. After three years she earned her degree in Physics.

51. A lot of emphasis was laid on Marie's education because:
A. Marie was the sole earning member of the family.
B. Marie was born into a family of teachers.
C. education of girls was very important in Poland.
D. she was the only member of the family who could read.

52. Which of the following statements about the passage is ***not*** true?
A. Marie's elder sister died of tuberculosis and mother of typhus.

B. Marie's father was a patriotic man.
C. Marie passed out of the University of Sorbonne.
D. The Polish universities discriminated against girls.

53. Marie thoroughly enjoyed the university years:
A. while her sister worked hard to pay the fees.
B. although she did not want to study medicine.
C. despite living on meagre funds.
D. but was denied the university degree.

54. Choose the correct spelling.
A. Benevolent
B. Benovalent
C. Benovolent
D. Benovelent

55. The correct synonym of the word Zenith is:
A. Infinite B. Bottom
C. Pinnacle D. Medium

56. The room was filled by the wizard's shrieks of fiendish laughter.
(Select the correct antonym of the underlined word)
A. cunning B. vicious
C. loud D. pleasant

57. I am doing hardwork to get to the college of my choice.
(Identify the incorrect part of the sentence)
A. I am
B. doing hardwork
C. to get to
D. the college of my choice

58. She speaks __________ all of us when she says that we are grateful for your kindness.
(Choose the most appropriate preposition)
A. about B. to
C. for D. of

59. Between his cat and his dog, his cat is __________ more loyal of the two.
(Choose the correct answer)
A. a B. an
C. the D. No article

60. After the school was dismissed, she said with pretended casualness that she wanted to go and meet the new teacher.
(Identify the type of verb)
A. Intransitive verb B. Participle
C. Transitive verb D. Infinitive

61. You __________ an accident if you go on driving like that.
(Choose the most appropriate option)
A. should have B. will have
C. have had D. are having

62. "Would you like some tea or coffee?" the assistant asked me.
(Choose the correct reported form of the sentence)
A. The assistant asked me whether I would like some tea or coffee.
B. The assistant asked me whether would I like some tea or coffee.
C. The assistant asked me would I like some tea or coffee.
D. The assistant asked me if I would like some tea or coffee.

63. Someone has lit the fire.
(Choose the correct passive form of this sentence)
A. You are requested to light the fire by someone.
B. The fire has been lit by someone.
C. The fire had been lit by someone.
D. The fire was lit by someone.

64. Weather forecasts aren't very reliable and __________.
A. nor should be B. not ought to be
C. nor will D. never will be

65. The Princess was very generous. Everyone liked her for her __________ innocence.
(Choose the most appropriate word)
A. childish B. childhood
C. childlike D. child

66. Neither of the girls __________ to collect their certificates.
(Choose the correct answer)
A. have come B. has come
C. are coming D. has came

67. Rearrange the following words/phrases to make a meaningful sentence. Choose the correct sequence.
into the water (A)/ everyone crowded (B)/ to see (C)/ jump (D)/ around (E)/ him (F)
A. ABCDEF B. ABCFDE
C. BEFCDA D. BECFDA

68. Rearrange the following words/phrases to make a meaningful sentence.
Choose the correct sequence.
cold (A)/ a (B)/ it was (C)/ beautiful (D)/ day (E)
A. CBDAE B. DCBAE
C. CBEDA D. CDABE

69. Answer by choosing the most appropriate option:
'To tie yourself in knots' means:
A. to get into trouble.
B. to get confused.
C. to lie.
D. to get stuck between strangers.

70. The price of this mobile phone is higher than yours.
(Choose the edited form of the underlined words from the options given)
A. are higher than yours
B. is higher than you
C. is higher than yourself
D. is higher than that of yours

71. The young teacher was brimming with confidence.
(Identify the adjective in this sentence)
A. young B. teacher
C. was brimming D. confidence

72. I need to check ________ I have brought my umbrella.
(Choose the correct conjunction)
A. provided B. whether
C. lest D. until

73. She has now organised her documents in properly labelled files.
(Change to passive voice)
A. Her documents were now being organised in properly labelled files.
B. She had organised her documents then in properly labelled files.
C. Her documents have now been organised in properly labelled files.
D. Her documents had been organised then in properly labelled files.

74. It is late and ________ to get any sleep, I must go.
A. if I am B. unless I am going
C. if I am got D. should I

75. He acted ________ at the dinner table.
A. seldom B. lately
C. clumsily D. hardly

Section C : General Science

76. Naphthalene balls used to repel moths and insects are derived from:
A. Petroleum B. Sugar
C. Coal tar D. LPG

77. The slow process of conversion of dead vegetation into coal is called:
A. Decomposition B. Evolution
C. Carbonification D. Carbonisation

78. Which amongst the following is a petroleum product which can be used for metalling of roads?
A. Coke B. Bitumen
C. Coal tar D. Coal

79. A person suffering from ________ should always cover his mouth and nose with a handkerchief while sneezing.
A. Common cold B. Cancer
C. Asthma D. Malaria

80. Which of these traps air the most?
A. Nylon B. Cotton
C. Wool D. Polyester

81. Which non-metal is highly reactive and is used in making matchsticks?
A. Phosphorus B. Sulphur
C. Carbon D. None of these

82. What is the product formed when a metal reacts with water?
A. Metal oxide B. Metal hydroxide
C. Salt D. Acid

83. Which of the following pairs of organelles does ***not*** contain DNA?
A. Mitochondria and Lysosomes
B. Chloroplast and Vacuoles
C. Lysosomes and Vacuoles
D. Nuclear envelope and Mitochondria

84. Which of the following features helps in distinguishing a plant cell from an animal cell?
A. Cell wall B. Cell membrane
C. Mitochondria D. Nucleus

85. A set of terms pertaining to reproduction are given below. Choose the set that has an ***incorrect*** combination.
A. Sperm, testis, sperm duct, penis
B. Menstruation, egg, oviduct, uterus
C. Sperm, oviduct, egg, uterus
D. Ovulation, egg, oviduct, uterus

86. The larva of frog changes its form by a sudden and drastic process called
A. Embryogenesis B. Hatching
C. Layering D. Metamorphosis

87. Cloning is similar to which of the following modes of reproduction?
A. Sexual reproduction
B. Cyst formation
C. Asexual reproduction
D. Both sexual and asexual reproduction

88. Which of the following correctly represents the value for the normal atmospheric pressure?
A. 75.3 Kilopascals
B. 76 mm of mercury
C. 101325 Pascals
D. 76 cm of mercury

89. Loudness of sound is proportional to:
A. Square of the amplitude
B. Amplitude
C. Square of frequency
D. Frequency

90. A man stands 10 m in front of a large plane mirror. How far must he walk before he is 5 m away from his image?
A. 5 m B. 7.5 m
C. 10 m D. 12.5 m

91. Which of the following metals is used in electroplating to make metal objects appear shining on car surfaces?
A. Iron B. Copper
C. Chromium D. Aluminium

92. What are the two gases mainly responsible for acid rain?
A. Sulphur dioxide and Nitrogen dioxide
B. Carbon dioxide and Sulphur dioxide
C. Nitrogen dioxide and Carbon dioxide
D. Carbon dioxide and CFC

93. The process of conversion of sugar into alcohol is called:
A. Fixation B. Moulding
C. Fermentation D. Degradation

94. Identify the correctly matched pair from the following:
A. Sunderban – Rhino
B. Ranthambore – Lion
C. Gir – Lion
D. Kaziranga – Sea Turtle

95. "Water harvesting" means:
A. Collection of water from rivers
B. Harvesting of water from tubewells
C. Collection of rainwater in storage tanks
D. Collecting water from oceans

96. The process of zinc lamination (coating) on iron is called:
A. Ionization B. Electrolysis
C. Galvanization D. None of these

97. Conditions for good electroplating are:
A. High current density
B. Low temperature
C. High concentration of metal in electrolyte
D. All of these

98. Electroplating is the application of:
A. Hydrolysis B. Electrolysis
C. Crystallization D. Recrystallization

99. An earthquake measuring 6 on the Richter scale is more powerful than another of magnitude 4 by:
A. 3/2 times
B. 100 times
C. 2/3 times
D. 10 times

100. Rabi crops are:
A. sown in winter and harvested in summer.
B. sown during rainy season and harvested in winter.
C. sown in summer and harvested in winter.
D. sown in rainy season and harvested in summer.

Section D : Social Studies

101. Which of the following is a Fundamental Right?
A. Right to Work
B. Right to Freedom of Religion
C. Right to Property
D. Right to Protection of Forest and Wildlife

102. Dikus are:
A. Outsiders
B. Insiders
C. Children
D. Senior citizens

103. 29th March 1857 is a significant date because:
A. Mangal Pandey was hanged to death.
B. Mangal Pandey was sent to prison.
C. Mangal Pandey fled prison.
D. Mangal Pandey killed his officers.

104. Which of the following is not categorised under the Himalayan earthquakes?
A. Uttarkashi Earthquake
B. Kangra Earthquake
C. Bhuj Earthquake
D. Delhi Earthquake

105. ____________, a great scholar of Sanskrit, felt that Hinduism was oppressive towards women.
A. Sri Narayan Guru
B. Raja Ram Mohan Roy
C. M.G. Ranade
D. Pandita Ramabai

106. Burning of fossil fuels:
A. Causes global warming
B. Reduces global warming
C. Releases oxygen
D. None of these

107. Which incident in the history of the Indian Freedom Movement made Tagore angry and made him renounce his knighthood?
A. Partition of Bengal
B. Jallianwala Bagh Massacre
C. Simon Commission
D. Morley-Minto reforms

108. Where did Gandhiji launch the Mill-Workers' Strike of 1918?
A. South Africa
B. Kheda
C. Andaman and Nicobar Islands
D. Delhi

109. Which of the following was termed as "devilish and tyrannical" by Gandhiji and Jinnah?
A. Ilbert Bill
B. Jallianwala Bagh Massacre
C. Rowlatt Act
D. Government of India Act, 1921

110. The Supreme Court of India has laid down specific requirements and procedures that the police and other agencies have to follow for the arrest, detention and interrogation of any person. These guidelines are also known as:
A. M.M. Basu guidelines
B. D.K. Basu guidelines
C. Procedural guidelines
D. Rules of procedure for arrest guidelines

111. Name the Indian revolutionary who threw a bomb in the Central Legislative Assembly on 8th April, 1929.
A. Subhash Chandra Bose

B. Bal Gangadhar Tilak
C. Bhagat Singh
D. Chandrashekhar Azad

112. Who is the founder of the Khudai Khidmatgars, a powerful non-violent movement among the Pathans?
A. Khan Abdul Ghaffar Khan
B. Mohammed Ali Jinnah
C. Maulana Azad
D. None of these

113. What is the meaning of the Japanese term 'Tsunami'?
A. Ocean wave B. Tidal wave
C. Current wave D. Harbour wave

114. Air pressure ________ as the height increases.
A. increases
B. decreases
C. first increases and then decreases
D. remains constant

115. Viticulture is the cultivation of:
A. Grapes B. Fish
C. Silkworms D. Apples

116. A motion of no-confidence against the government can be introduced in the ______.
A. Rajya Sabha B. Lok Sabha
C. Both A and B D. Neither A nor B

117. Ministry of Human Resource Development was created in:
A. 1951 B. 1953
C. 1985 D. 1987

118. Who were the European artists appointed by Muhammad Ali Khan of Arcot?
A. Tilly Kettle and George Willison
B. Francis Hayman and William Daniell
C. Thomas Daniell and William Daniell
D. Joham Zoffany and Tilly Kettle

119. The temperate grasslands of South Africa are called the ____________.
A. Velds B. Downs
C. Prairies D. Pampas

120. Thinnest layer of the Earth is __________.
A. Crust B. Mantle
C. Core D. None of these

121. Which of the following is an example of non-metallic mineral?
A. Bauxite B. Manganese
C. Lead D. Mica

122. The emperor who ascended the throne at 13 years of age was __________.
A. Shah Jahan B. Akbar
C. Humayun D. Jehangir

123. The number of seats reserved for Scheduled Tribes in the Lok Sabha is:
A. 35 B. 37
C. 79 D. 47

124. What is referred to as the supreme law of land?
A. Parliament B. President
C. Constitution D. Assembly

125. The breaking up and decaying of exposed rocks, by temperature changes, frost action, plants, animals and human activity is called:
A. Climate change B. Breaking
C. Weathering D. Decay

Section E : Intelligence

126. What comes next in the series:
7, 14, 42, 168,?
A. 1008 B. 840
C. 504 D. 672

127. Michael is 14th from the left end in a row of 40 boys. What is his position (rank) from the right end?
A. 21st B. 24th
C. 25th D. 27th

128. P is the brother of Q and R. S is R's mother. T is P's father. Which of the following statements cannot be definitely true?
A. T is Q's father. B. S is P's mother.
C. P is S's son. D. Q is T's son.

129. Choose the correct option in place of question mark (?) to complete the given series:
21, 25, 33, 49, 81,?
A. 145 B. 132
C. 113 D. 101

130. 'Tiger' is related to 'Cub' in the same way as 'Elephant' is related to ______.
Tiger : Cub : : Elephant :?
A. Chick B. Hatchling
C. Joey D. Calf

131. If in the year 2012, January 1st is Sunday, then which day is the Indian Republic Day in the year 2012?
A. Saturday B. Monday
C. Thursday D. Friday

132. What is the angle between the hour hand and the minute hand when it is 5:10 pm?
A. 150 degrees B. 120 degrees
C. 115 degrees D. 95 degrees

133. From his house, Ramesh goes 15 km to North. Then he turns West and covers 20 km. Then he turns South and covers 5 km. Finally he turns East and covers 30 km. Looking from his house, in which direction is he standing?
A. North-west B. North-east
C. South-east D. South-west

134. In a list, if Shikha is 15th from the upper end and 17th from the lower end, then find the total number of people in the list.
A. 41 B. 33
C. 31 D. 32

135. Find the fourth proportional of 4, 5 and 16.
A. 25 B. 16
C. 30 D. 20

136. 'Pitch' is related to 'Cricket' in the same way as 'Arena' is related to:
A. Tennis B. Gymnastics
C. Badminton D. Wrestling

137. The time in the clock is quarter past twelve. If the hour hand points to the East, which is the direction opposite to the minute hand?
A. South-west B. South
C. West D. North

138. Five boys A, B, C, D and E are sitting in a row. A is to the right of B and E is to the left of B but to the right of C. A is to the left of D. Who is second from the left end?
A. B B. E
C. A D. C

139. A word has been given, followed by four other words, one of which can be formed by using the letters from the given word: PREPARATION.
Find the word.
A. PAMPER B. REPEAT
C. PARTITION D. PARROT

140. Find the odd one that does ***not*** belong to the group.
A. KQNN B. DWFU
C. EVHS D. HSKP

141. Five friends are standing in a row. Amar is taller than Sameer. Prabhat is taller than Umesh but not as tall as Sameer. Ashok is shorter than Umesh. Who among them is the shortest?
A. Ashok B. Umesh
C. Sameer D. Amar

142. Insert the missing number.

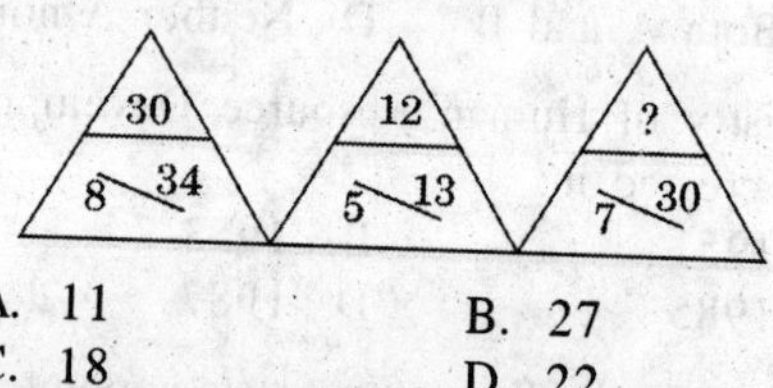

A. 11 B. 27
C. 18 D. 22

143. Choose the alternative that best represents a relationship similar to the one expressed in the original pair:
F : 216 : : L : ?
A. 1728 B. 1700
C. 1600 D. 1723

144. In a certain code, 'TERMINAL' is written as 'NSFUMBOJ' and 'TOWERS' is written as 'XPUTSF'. How is 'MATE' written in the same code?
A. FUBN B. UFNB
C. BNFU D. BNDS

145. Arrange the following words as per order in the dictionary:
1. Quilt
2. Quite
3. Queen
4. Queue

A. 1, 4, 2, 3
B. 4, 3, 1, 2
C. 2, 3, 4, 1
D. 3, 4, 1, 2

146. Choose the letter group that represents a relationship similar to the one expressed in the original pair of letter groups.
UNDERSTAND : DASENNTRDU : : RETIREMENT :?
A. TEEIENMRTR
B. TNEMERITER
C. EMENTRETIR
D. ERITEREMTN

147. Complete the series:
3, 10, 101,?
A. 10101
B. 10201
C. 10202
D. 11012

148. Select the related word from the given alternatives.
Hirakud : Mahanadi : : Tehri Dam :?
A. Damodar
B. Bhagirathi
C. Yamuna
D. Sone

149. In the following question, select the missing number from the given series.

25	144	60
81	225	135
49	289	?

A. 119
B. 120
C. 170
D. 190

150. Fill with a suitable word.
Quarantined : Separated : : Radical : ?
A. Unfriendly
B. Bad
C. Fundamental
D. Dreary

ANSWERS

1	2	3	4	5	6	7	8	9	10
A	D	B	C	B	B	B	C	B	B
11	**12**	**13**	**14**	**15**	**16**	**17**	**18**	**19**	**20**
D	C	B	C	B	B	C	C	A	B
21	**22**	**23**	**24**	**25**	**26**	**27**	**28**	**29**	**30**
B	B	B	C	D	D	A	B	B	D
31	**32**	**33**	**34**	**35**	**36**	**37**	**38**	**39**	**40**
A	A	B	C	B	C	C	C	A	C
41	**42**	**43**	**44**	**45**	**46**	**47**	**48**	**49**	**50**
A	C	B	B	D	C	B	A	B	C
51	**52**	**53**	**54**	**55**	**56**	**57**	**58**	**59**	**60**
B	A	C	A	C	D	B	C	D	B
61	**62**	**63**	**64**	**65**	**66**	**67**	**68**	**69**	**70**
B	D	B	D	C	B	D	A	B	D
71	**72**	**73**	**74**	**75**	**76**	**77**	**78**	**79**	**80**
A	B	C	A	C	C	D	B	A	C
81	**82**	**83**	**84**	**85**	**86**	**87**	**88**	**89**	**90**
A	A	C	A	C	D	C	C & D	A	B
91	**92**	**93**	**94**	**95**	**96**	**97**	**98**	**99**	**100**
C	A	C	C	C	C	D	B	B	A

101	102	103	104	105	106	107	108	109	110
B	A	A	C	D	A	B	*	C	B
111	**112**	**113**	**114**	**115**	**116**	**117**	**118**	**119**	**120**
C	A	D	B	A	B	C	A	A	A
121	**122**	**123**	**124**	**125**	**126**	**127**	**128**	**129**	**130**
D	B	D	C	C	B	D	D	A	D
131	**132**	**133**	**134**	**135**	**136**	**137**	**138**	**139**	**140**
C	D	B	C	D	D	D	B	D	B
141	**142**	**143**	**144**	**145**	**146**	**147**	**148**	**149**	**150**
A	B	A	C	D	A	C	B	A	A

EXPLANATORY ANSWERS

1. $1+\cfrac{1}{1+\cfrac{1}{1+\cfrac{1}{9}}} = 1+\cfrac{1}{1+\cfrac{1}{\frac{9+1}{9}}}$

$= 1+\cfrac{1}{1+\frac{9}{10}} = 1+\cfrac{1}{\frac{10+9}{10}}$

$= 1+\frac{10}{19} = \frac{19+10}{19} = \frac{29}{19}.$

2. Sum of $3.\overline{2}$ and $5.\overline{4}$

$= 3.\overline{2}+5.\overline{4} = 3\frac{2}{9}+5\frac{4}{9}$

$= \frac{29}{9}+\frac{49}{9} = \frac{78}{9}.$

3. Here, $\frac{-7}{3}+x = \frac{3}{7}$

$\Rightarrow \quad x = \frac{3}{7}+\frac{7}{3} = \frac{9+49}{21} = \frac{58}{21}.$

4. Let the two numbers are $5x$ and $2x$

Then, $5x - 2x = 66$

$\Rightarrow \quad 3x = 66$

$\Rightarrow \quad x = 22$

$\therefore \quad 5x = 5 \times 22 = 110$

$2x = 2 \times 22 = 44$

Hence, the two numbers are 110 and 44.

6. Given, the length of the diagonals of a rhombus

$d_1 = 16$ cm, $d_2 = 12$ cm

$\because$ Diagonals of a rhombus bisect each other at right angle

$\therefore$ Side of a rhombus

$= \sqrt{\left(\frac{d_1}{2}\right)^2+\left(\frac{d_2}{2}\right)^2}$

$= \sqrt{\left(\frac{16}{2}\right)^2+\left(\frac{12}{2}\right)^2}$

$= \sqrt{8^2+6^2} = \sqrt{64+36}$

$= \sqrt{100} = 10$ cm

Hence, the length of each side = 10 cm.

7. Given that,

$\frac{2+4+8+6+x+5}{6} = 8$

$\Rightarrow \quad 25 + x = 48$

$\Rightarrow \quad x = 48 - 25 = 23.$

8. $\because \quad 100\% = 360°$

$\therefore \quad 1\% = \frac{360}{100} = \frac{18}{5}$

$\Rightarrow \quad 40\% = \frac{18}{5}\times 40$

$= 18 \times 8 = 144.$

9. Here, From Pie chart

$\because$ $360° = ₹\ 15000$

$\therefore$ $1° = \dfrac{15000}{360}$

$\therefore$ $60° = \dfrac{15000}{360} \times 60$

$= \dfrac{15000}{6} = 2500$

Hence, the amount he spends on food and house rent is ₹ 2500.

11. Given that, mode = 12, mean = 3

We know that,

Mode = 3 Median − 2 Mean

$\Rightarrow$ 12 = 3 Median − 2 × 3

$\Rightarrow$ 12 + 6 = 3 Median

$\Rightarrow$ 3 Median = 18

$\Rightarrow$ Median $= \dfrac{18}{3} = 6$

Hence, median = 6.

12. The Square root of 0.00000121

$= \sqrt{0.00000121}$

$= \sqrt{(.0011)^2}$

$= 0.0011.$

13. $\sqrt{108245}$ = 3 $\sqrt{108245}$ = 329

```
 3 | 108245 | 329
+3 | -9
62 | 182
+2 | -124
649| 5845
 9 | -5844
   |    4
```

$\because$ 108445 − 4 = 108441 = $(329)^2$

Hence, least number = 4.

14. $\because$ $6859 = 19 \times 19 \times 19 = (19)^3$

$\therefore$ The Cube root of 6859 = $\sqrt[3]{6859}$

$= (6859)^{\frac{1}{3}}$

$= \left[(19)^3\right]^{\frac{1}{3}} = 19$

Hence, the one's digit = 9.

15. A. $\dfrac{1296}{16} = 81$

B. $\dfrac{1296}{6} = 216 = (6)^3$

C. $\dfrac{1296}{60} = \dfrac{216}{10} = \dfrac{108}{5}$

D. $\dfrac{1296}{26} = \dfrac{648}{13}$

Hence, the smallest natural number = 6.

16. Here, the number of students are not good in Mathematics

$= 25 \times \dfrac{100-72}{100}$

$= 25 \times \dfrac{28}{100} = \dfrac{28}{4}\% = 7\%.$

17. The cost price of 1 dozen pencils

= 12 × 5 = 60 paise

Selling price of 20% profit

$= 60 \times \dfrac{120}{100} = 60 \times \dfrac{6}{5}$

= 12 × 6 = 72 paise

$\therefore$ Selling price of a pencil

$= \dfrac{72}{12} = 6$ paise.

18. Here, A = ₹ 4310, $n = 2$, $r = 5\%$

$\because$ $A = P\left(1+\dfrac{r}{100}\right)^n$

$\therefore$ $4410 = P\left(1+\dfrac{5}{100}\right)^2$

$\Rightarrow$ $4410 = P\left(1+\dfrac{1}{20}\right)^2$

$\Rightarrow$ $4410 = P\left(\dfrac{21}{20}\right)^2$

$\Rightarrow \quad P\left(\frac{441}{400}\right) = 4410$

$\Rightarrow \quad P = 4410 \times \frac{400}{441}$

$= 10 \times 400$

$= ₹\ 4000.$

19. $(x - 3y + 2z) + (-4x + 9y - 11z) - (3x - 4y - 7z)$

$= x - 3y + 2z - 4x + 9y - 11z - 3x + 4y + 7z$

$= -6x + 10y - 2z.$

20.

$$\begin{array}{r|l|l} (x-2) & 5x^2 - 4x + 3 & 5x + 6 \\ & \underline{\begin{array}{l} 5x^2 - 10x \\ - \quad + \end{array}} & \\ & 6x + 3 & \\ & \underline{\begin{array}{l} 6x - 12 \\ - \quad + \end{array}} & \\ & 15 & \end{array}$$

Hence, the remainder = 15.

21. Given that, $x - \frac{1}{x} = 3$

$\Rightarrow \quad \left(x - \frac{1}{x}\right)^2 = (3)^2$

$\Rightarrow \quad x^2 + \frac{1}{x^2} - 2.x.\frac{1}{x} = 9$

$\Rightarrow \quad x^2 + \frac{1}{x^2} - 2 = 9$

$\Rightarrow \quad x^2 + \frac{1}{x^2} = 9 + 2$

$\Rightarrow \quad \left(x^2 + \frac{1}{x^2}\right)^2 = 11^2$

$\Rightarrow x^4 + \frac{1}{x^4} + 2.x^2.\frac{1}{x^2} = 121$

$\Rightarrow \quad x^4 + \frac{1}{x^4} = 121 - 2$

$\Rightarrow \quad x^4 + \frac{1}{x^4} = 119.$

22. $\because$ Diagonal of the square = d

$\therefore \quad$ Side $\sqrt{2} = d$

$\Rightarrow \quad$ Side = $\frac{d}{\sqrt{2}}$

$\Rightarrow \quad (\text{Side})^2 = \left(\frac{d}{\sqrt{2}}\right)^2 = \frac{d^2}{2}$

Hence, the area of the square = $\frac{d^2}{2}$.

23. The area of a circle = 154 sq.cm

$\therefore \quad \pi r^2 = 154$ sq. cm

$\Rightarrow \quad \frac{22}{7} r^2 = 154$ sq. cm

$\Rightarrow \quad r^2 = 154 \times \frac{7}{22}$ sq. cm

$= 14 \times \frac{7}{2}$ sq. cm

$\Rightarrow \quad r^2 = 7 \times 7 = 7^2$ sq.cm

$\Rightarrow \quad r = 7$ cm

Hence, the perimeter of a circle = $2\pi r$

$= 2 \times \frac{22}{7} \times 7 = 44$ cm.

24. Here, The perimeter of a rhombus = 80 cm

$\therefore \quad 4 \times$ Side = 80 cm

$\Rightarrow \quad$ Side = $\frac{80}{4}$ = 20 cm

and one diagonal, $d_1 = 24$

and other diagonal = d_2

$\because \quad \left(\frac{d_1}{2}\right)^2 + \left(\frac{d_2}{2}\right)^2 = 20^2$

$\therefore \quad \left(\frac{24}{2}\right)^2 + \left(\frac{d_2}{2}\right)^2 = 400$

$\Rightarrow \quad \left(\frac{d_2}{2}\right)^2 = 400 - 144$

$$\Rightarrow \quad \left(\frac{d_2}{2}\right)^2 = 256 = (16)^2$$

$$\Rightarrow \quad \frac{d_2}{2} = 16$$

$$\Rightarrow \quad d_2 = 32$$

Hence, the area of a rhombus

$$= \frac{1}{2} \times d_1 \times d_2$$

$$= \frac{1}{2} \times 24 \times 32 \text{ sq. cm}$$

$$= 12 \times 32 = 384 \text{ sq. cm.}$$

25. $\because$ Cylinder and a cone on the same base and of the same height

$\therefore$ The Volume of a cylinder $= \pi r^2 h$

and the volume of a cone $= \frac{1}{3}\pi r^2 h$

Hence, the ratio $= \dfrac{\pi r^2 h}{\frac{1}{3}\pi r^2 h} = \dfrac{1}{\frac{1}{3}} = \dfrac{3}{1} = 3:1.$

26. $\because$ The volume of the cone $= \frac{1}{3}\pi r^2 h$

Given, height $= 2h$ and radius $= 2r$

$\therefore$ The volume of the cone $= \frac{1}{3}\pi(2r)^2 \times 2h$

$$= \frac{1}{3}\pi 4r^2 \times 2h$$

$$= \frac{8}{3}\pi r^2 h$$

Hence, the volume of the cone becomes

$$= \frac{\frac{8}{3}\pi r^2 h}{\frac{1}{3}\pi r^2 h} = 8 \text{ times.}$$

27. Here, The volume of the hemisphere

$$= 19404 \text{ cu.cm}$$

$$\therefore \quad \frac{2}{3}\pi r^3 = 19404$$

$$\Rightarrow \frac{2}{3} \times \frac{22}{7} r^3 = 19404$$

$$\Rightarrow \quad r^3 = 19404 \times \frac{7 \times 3}{2 \times 22}$$

$$= 441 \times 21$$

$$\Rightarrow \quad r^3 = (21)^3$$

$$\Rightarrow \quad r = 21$$

$\therefore$ The total surface area of the hemisphere

$$= 2\pi r^2 + \pi r^2$$

$$= 3\pi r^2$$

$$= 3 \times \frac{22}{7} \times (21)^2$$

$$= 3 \times \frac{22}{7} \times 21 \times 21$$

$$= 3 \times 22 \times 3 \times 21$$

$$= 9 \times 22 \times 21$$

$$= 4158 \text{ sq. cm.}$$

28. $125^{-\frac{1}{3}} = \dfrac{1}{125^{\frac{1}{3}}} = \dfrac{1}{\left[(5)^3\right]^{\frac{1}{3}}} = \dfrac{1}{5}.$

29. $\left(64^{\frac{2}{3}}\right)^{\frac{1}{2}} = 64^{\frac{1}{3}} = \left(4^3\right)^{\frac{1}{3}} = 4.$

30. $\left(\frac{1}{2}\right)^{-2} + \left(\frac{1}{3}\right)^{-2} + \left(\frac{1}{4}\right)^{-2}$

$$= 2^3 + 3^2 + 4^2$$

$$= 4 + 9 + 16$$

$$= 29.$$

34. $\because$ Throwing two dice simultaneously

$\therefore$ S = Sample Space

= {(1, 1), (1, 2), (1, 3), (1, 4), (1, 5), (1, 6)
(2, 1), (2, 2), (2, 3), (2, 4), (2, 5), (2, 6)
(3, 1), (3, 2), (3, 3), (3, 4), (3, 5), (3, 6)
(4, 1), (4, 2), (4, 3), (4, 4), (4, 5), (4, 6)
(5, 1), (5, 2), (5, 3), (5, 4), (5, 5), (5, 6)
(6, 1), (6, 2), (6, 3), (6, 4), (6, 5), (6, 6)}

Hence, the number of possible outcomes

$$= 6 \times 6 = 36.$$

35. Two coins are tossed

$\therefore$ $S = \{HH, TT, HT, TH\}$

$n(S) = 4$

e = at most one head

$= \{HH, HT, TH\}$

$\therefore$ $n(e) = \frac{n(e)}{n(S)} = \frac{3}{4}$

Hence, the probability of getting at most one head $= \frac{3}{4}$.

36. Here, More men, less Day → Indirect proportion

Men Day

100 : 80 : : x : 30

$\Rightarrow$ $80 \times x = 100 \times 30$

$\Rightarrow$ $x = \frac{3000}{80}$

$= \frac{300}{8} = \frac{75}{2}$

$\Rightarrow$ $x = 37\frac{1}{2}$

Hence, the number of boys $= 37\frac{1}{2}$.

37. More height, more Shadow → Direct proportion

Let the height of a tree = x

$\therefore$ height Shadow

14 : x : : 10 : 5

$\Rightarrow$ $14 \times 15 = x \times 10$

$\Rightarrow$ $x = \frac{14 \times 15}{10} = \frac{14 \times 3}{2}$

$= 7 \times 3$

$= 21$ m

Hence, Height of the tree = 21 m.

38. Let the number of workers = x

More workers, less time → Indirect proportion

$\therefore$ Workers time

15 : x : : 30 : 48

$\Rightarrow$ $15 \times 48 = x \times 30$

$\Rightarrow$ $x = \frac{15 \times 48}{30} = 24$

Hence, the number of workers = 24.

39. Given that, $a + b + c = 5$ and

$ab + bc + ca = 10$

$\because$ $(a + b + c)^2 = (5)^2$

$\therefore$ $a^2 + b^2 + c^2 + 2(ab + bc + ca) = 25$

$\Rightarrow$ $a^2 + b^2 + c^2 + 2 \times 10 = 25$

$\Rightarrow$ $a^2 + b^2 + c^2 = 25 - 20$

$\Rightarrow$ $a^2 + b^2 + c^2 = 5$

$\because$ $a^3 + b^3 + c^3 - 3abc$

$= (a + b + c)(a^2 + b^2 + c2 - ab - bc - ac)$

$= 5(5 - 10)$

$= 5 \times -5 = -25.$

40. Given, $\frac{a}{b} + \frac{b}{a} = 2$

$\Rightarrow$ $\frac{a^2 + b^2}{ab} = 2$

$\Rightarrow$ $a^2 + b^2 = 2ab$

$\Rightarrow$ $a^2 + b^2 - 2ab = 0$

$\Rightarrow$ $(a - b)^2 = 0$

$\Rightarrow$ $(a - b) = 0$

$\therefore$ $a^3 - b^3 = (a - b)(a^2 + ab + b^2)$

$= 0(a^2 + ab + b^2)$

$= 0.$

41. $3\sqrt{3}x^3 - 8$

$= 3^{1+\frac{1}{2}} . x^3 - 2^3$

$= 3^{\frac{3}{2}} . x^3 - 2^3$

$= \left(\sqrt{3}\right)^3 . x^3 - 2^3$

$= \left(\sqrt{3}x\right)^3 - 2^3$

$= \left(\sqrt{3}x - 2\right)\left(\left(\sqrt{3}x\right)^2 + \sqrt{3}x.2 + 2^2\right)$

$= \left(\sqrt{3}x - 2\right)\left(3x^2 + 2\sqrt{3}x + 4\right)$

42. Distance $= \sqrt{(0-12)^2+(0-5)^2}$

$= \sqrt{(12)^2+(5)^2}$

$= \sqrt{144+25}$

$= \sqrt{169} = 13.$

43. A's 1 day's work $= \frac{1}{25}$

B's 1 day's work $= \frac{1}{20}$

$\therefore$ (A + B)'s 1 day's work

$= \frac{1}{25}+\frac{1}{20}$

$= \frac{4+5}{100}$

$= \frac{9}{100}$

$\Rightarrow$ (A + B)'s 5 day's work

$= 5\times\frac{9}{100} = \frac{9}{20}$

Remaning work $= 1-\frac{9}{20}$

$= \frac{20-9}{20} = \frac{11}{20}$

The number of days can B finish the remaining work

$= \frac{11/20}{1/20} = 11.$

46. Let the interior opposite angles are x and $3x$

$\because$ The sum of interior opposite angles = the exterior angle

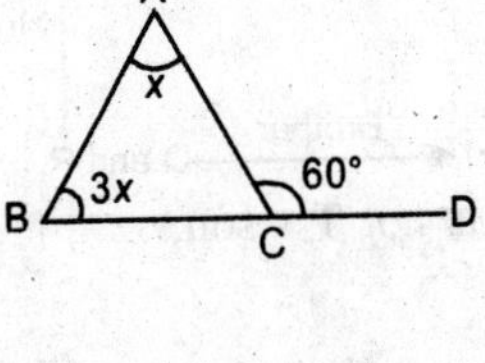

$\therefore \quad x + 3x = 60°$

$\Rightarrow \quad 4x = 60°$

$\Rightarrow \quad x = 15°$

$\therefore$ The interior angles are $x = 15°$ and $3x = 45°$

Hence, the angles of the traingle are $180° - (45° + 15°)$, $45°$, $15°$

$= 120°, 45°, 15°.$

49. From the pie chart

$\because \quad 100\% = 360°$

$\therefore \quad 1\% = \frac{360}{100} = \frac{18}{5}$

Central angle for food = 61%

$= \frac{18}{5}\times 61 = 219.6°$

and central angle for fuel

$= 5\% = 5\times\frac{18}{5} = 18°.$

76. Naphthalene balls are also known as moth balls. Naphthalene balls are obtained from coal tar and used as a moth repellent.

77. As coal mainly contains carbon, the slow process of conversion of dead vegetation into coal is called carbonisation.

78. Bitumen is used for metalling the roads these days in place of coal tar.

80. Wool traps the most air. The effect of this is that clothes made of wool act as insulating medium because air is an insulator. And as a result, these clothes trap the heat given out by the body, this keeping warm inside the clothes.

81. In matchstick, phosphorus is present which makes the matchstick to ignite instantly and it is a non-metal.

82. Metals react with water and produce a metal oxide and hydrogen gas. Metal oxides that are soluble in water dissolve in it to further form metal hydroxide.

83. Lysosomes and vacuoles do not contain DNA. Lysosomes are bounded membrane organelles which are found in the cells of animals and plants. Vacuoles are bounded, multifunctional membrane organelles that mostly found in plant cells and some protists and bacteria.

84. A plant cell contains a large, singular vacuole that is used for storage and maintaining the shape of the cell. In contrast, animal cells have many, smaller vacuoles. Plant cells have a cell wall, as well as a cell membrane. Animal cells simply have a cell membrane.

85. Sperm is male gamete, the egg is female gamete, oviduct and uterus are part of the female reproductive system. Hence option (C) is an incorrect combination.

86. The transformation of the larva into an adult through drastic changes is called metamorphosis. Metamorphosis is a biological process which involves sudden and abrupt changes in the body structure of the animal by cell growth and differentiation. It is generally observed in amphibians and insects.

87. Cloning is a mode of asexual reproduction. It refers to the process of developing an embryo with the DNA from an adult animal.

89. Intensity of the sound waves is directly proportional to the square of the amplitude of the waves meaning loudness of sound is directly proportional to the square of the amplitude so, if the amplitude of the sound is double, then the sound will become 4 times louder.

90. Initially, the distance between the man and the mirror is 10 m.
The image formed by plane mirror is the same distance behind the mirror as it between object and mirror.
The distance between the man and his image is 5 m, when the man is
2.5 m away from the mirror.
Therefore, he has to walk
10 m – 2.5 m = 7.5 m

91. Chromium is a very shining metal and it is scratch resistant. Because of the shining property of the chromium, we use this metal in electroplating.

92. Acid rain is caused by a chemical reaction that begins when compounds like sulphur dioxide and nitrogen oxides are released into the air.

95. In general, water harvesting is the activity of direct collection of rainwater. The rainwater collected can be stored for direct use or can be recharged into the groundwater. Rain is the first form of water that we know in the hydrological cycle, hence is a primary source of water for us.

96. Galvanisation is a process of protecting iron or steel from rusting by coating them with a thin layer of zinc.

98. Electroplating is a process that uses electric current to reduce dissolved metal ions by the use of electrolysis, to obtain the dissolved metal ions at the other electrode, mostly in the form of a uniform coating.

100. Rabi crops are known as winter crops. They are grown in October or November. The crops are then harvested in spring. These crops require frequent *irrigation* because these are grown in dry areas. Wheat, gram, barley are some of the rabi crops grown in India.

126.
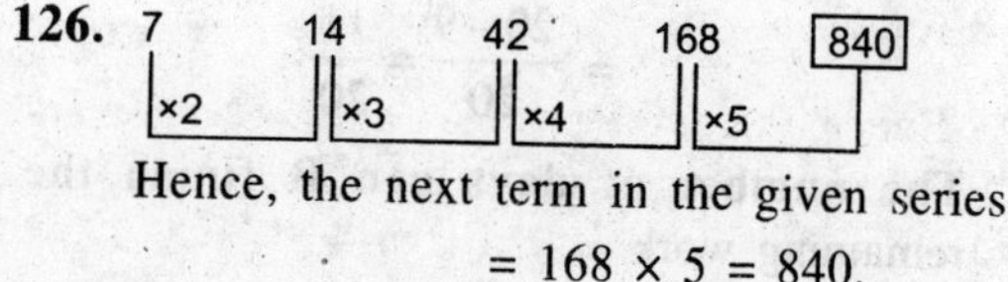

Hence, the next term in the given series
= 168 × 5 = 840.

127. Position of Michael from the right end
= 40 – 14 + 1
= 41 – 14 = 27th.

128.
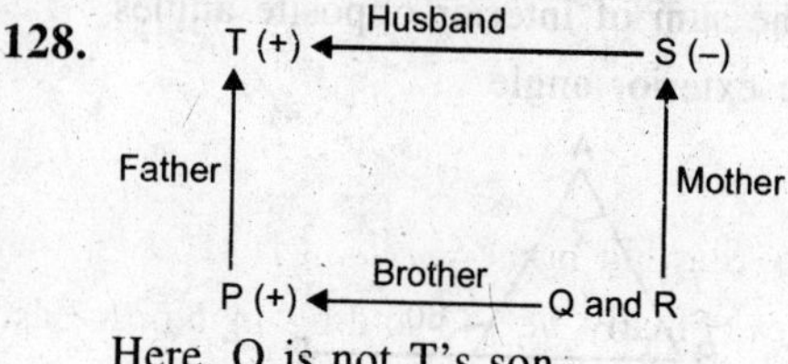

Here, Q is not T's son.

129. 21 25 33 49 81 [145]

+4 +8 +16 +32 +64

? = The next term in the given series
= 81 + 64 = 145.

131. ∵ 1st January = Sunday
8th January = Sunday
15th January = Sunday
22nd January = Sunday
26th January = Sunday + 4 days
= Thursday

Hence, the Indian Republic Day
= 26th January
= Thursday.

132. Minute hand,

60 minutes = 360°

1 minute = 6°

5 minutes = 5 × 6 = 30°

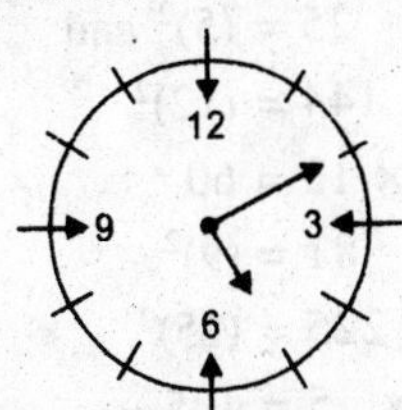

Hour hand,

Angle in 60 minutes = 30°

Angle in 10 minutes = $\frac{30}{60} \times 10 = 5°$

Hence, the angle between the hour hand and the minute hand when it is 5 : 10 pm
= 30° + 30° + 30° + 5°
= 95° = 95 degrees.

133.

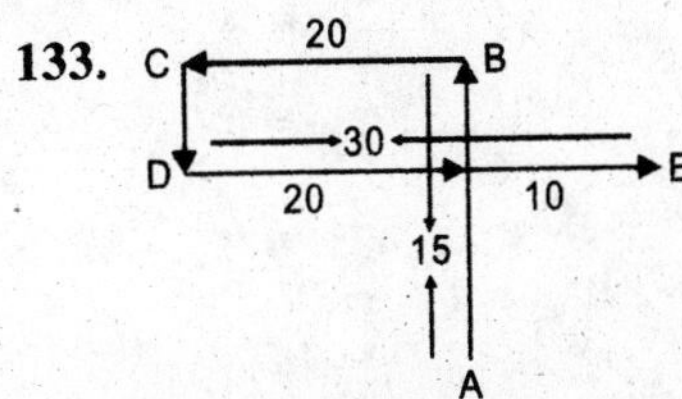

Here, Starting point = A

Hence, Finally he is standing in North-East direction from his house (A).

134. Here, the total number of people in the list
= 15 + 17 − 1
= 32 − 1
= 31.

135. Let the fourth proportional = x

Then, 4 : 5 : : 16 : x

$\Rightarrow \quad 4 \times x = 5 \times 16$

$\Rightarrow \quad x = \frac{5 \times 16}{4}$

$= 5 \times 4$

$= 20$

$\Rightarrow \quad x = 20.$

137. The time in the clock is quarter past twelve
= 12 : 15 pm

Given, the hour hand point to the East

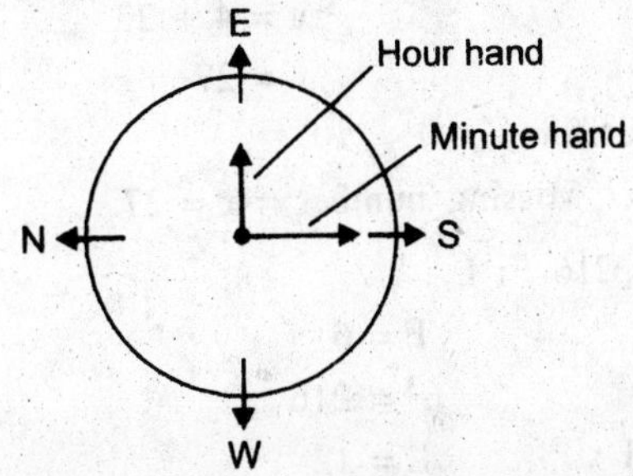

∴ The minute hand point to the South

Hence, North is the direction opposite to the minute hand.

138. Here,

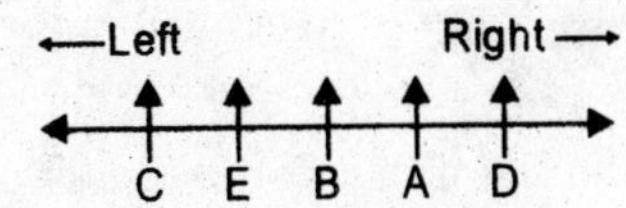

E is second from the left end.

140. A.

B.

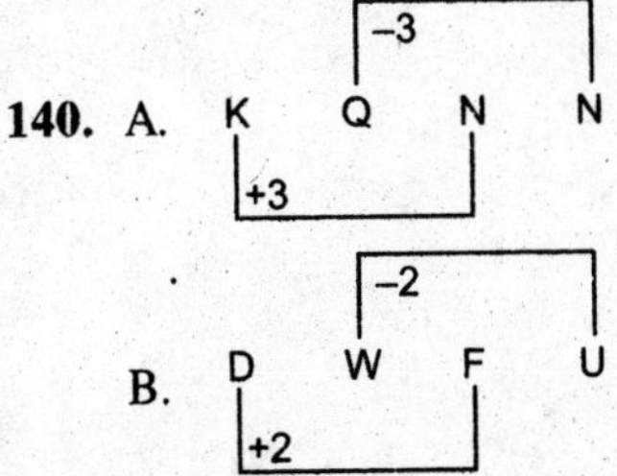

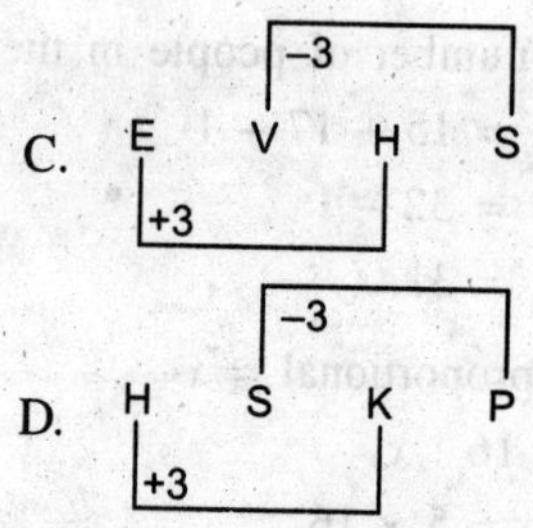

141. Here, Amar > Sameer,

Prabhat > Umesh > Ashok

⇒ Amar > Sameer > Prabhat > Umesh > Ashok

Ashok is the shortest among them.

142. Here, $30 - (34 - 8) = 30 - 26 = 4$

$12 - (13 - 5) = 12 - 8 = 4$

and $x - (30 - 7) = 4$

⇒ $x - 23 = 4$

⇒ $x = 4 + 23$

⇒ $x = 27$

Therefore,

Missing number $= x = 27$.

143. F : 216 : : L : ?

∵ F = 6

∴ $6^3 = 216$

and ∵ L = 12

∴ $(12)^3 = 1728$

Therefore, F : 216 : : 12 : 1728.

145. According to the dictionary:

Queen → Queue → Quilt → Quite.

146. U N D E R S T A N D : D A S E N N T R D U

1 2 3 4 5 6 7 8 9 10 10 8 6 4 2 9 7 5 3 1

Similarly

R E T I R E M E N T : T E E I E N M R T R

1 2 3 4 5 6 7 8 9 10 10 8 6 4 2 9 7 5 3 1

147. 3 → $3^2 + 1$ → 10 → $10^2 + 1$ → 101 → $101^2 + 1$ → 10202

Here, $? = (101)^2 + 1$

$= 10201 + 1$

$= 10202$.

149.

25	144	60
81	225	135
49	289	?

In every row:

$25 = (5)^2$ and

$144 = (12)^2$

∴ $5 \times 12 = 60$

and $81 = (9)^2$

and $225 = (15)^2$

∴ $9 \times 15 = 135$

and $49 = (7)^2$

and $289 = (17)^2$

∴ $7 \times 17 = 119$.

Previous Paper (Solved)

Sainik School Entrance Exam, 2020*

(Class-IX)

Section A : Mathematics

1. The value of

$$\left(-\frac{3}{2}\times\frac{4}{5}\right)+\left(\frac{9}{5}\times-\frac{10}{3}\right)-\left(\frac{1}{2}\times\frac{3}{4}\right)?$$

A. $\left(-\frac{503}{40}\right)$ B. $\left(-\frac{203}{40}\right)$

C. $\left(-\frac{403}{40}\right)$ D. $\left(-\frac{303}{40}\right)$

2. The abscissa of a point is its distance from the

A. Origin B. X-Axis

C. Y-Axis D. None

3. What is the value of m, if

$$\left(\frac{2}{9}\right)^3\times\left(\frac{2}{9}\right)^{-6}=\left(\frac{2}{9}\right)^{2m-1}$$

A. $m = 1$ B. $m = -2$

C. $m = -1$ D. $m = 2$

4. "If a number when divided by 4 leaves remainder 2 or 3", then which one is the correct statement?

A. The number is not a perfect square

B. The number is a perfect square

C. The number is a prime number

D. None of these

5. The value of $\dfrac{\sqrt{0.2304}+\sqrt{0.1764}}{\sqrt{0.2304}-\sqrt{0.1764}}$

A. 15 B. 16

C. 5 D. 150

6. Three numbers are in the ratio 2 : 3 : 4. The sum of their cubes is 33957. The numbers are

A. 16, 24 and 32

B. 12, 18 and 24

C. 14, 21 and 28

D. 18, 27 and 36

7. Find the least square number divisible by each one of 8, 9 and 10:

A. 360 B. 36

C. 3600 D. 3.6×10^2

8. If $\overline{148101a095}$ is a multiple of 11, where a is a digit, the value of a is

A. 0 B. 4

C. 1 D. 2

9. Find the value of A and B in

$$\begin{array}{r} B\ A \\ \times\ B\ 3 \\ \hline 5\ 7\ A \end{array}$$

A. A = 5 and B = 2

B. A = 5 and B = 5

C. A = 2 and B = 2

D. A = 2 and B = 5

10. Find the value of Z for which the number 471Z8 is divisible by 9.

A. 4 B. 5

C. 7 D. 8

*Exam held on 05/01/2020

11. If the area of an equilateral triangle is $64\sqrt{3}$ cm^2, then the side of the triangle is ______.

A. $18\sqrt{3}$ cm B. 9 cm

C. 16 cm D. $3\sqrt{2}$ cm

12. The value of $\frac{4m^2 - a^2 + 2ab - b^2}{2m + a - b}$ is:

A. $(2m - a + b)$ B. $(2m - a - b)$

C. $(2m + a + b)$ D. $(2m + a - b)$

13. The ratio between the speeds of two trains A and B is 3 : 5. If train B runs 300 km in 4 hours, the speed of train A will be

A. 40 km/h B. 60 km/h

C. 30 km/h D. 45 km/h

14. Two years ago, Dilip was three times as old as his son and two years hence, twice his age will be equal to five times that of his son. The present age of son and Dilip are:

A. 14, 38 years B. 16, 40 years

C. 12, 36 years D. None

15. The probability of getting a 7 in a single throw of a dice is:

A. 1 B. 0

C. 1/6 D. ½

16. A's income is 60% more than that of B. By what per cent is B's income less than A's?

A. 37% B. 37.5%

C. 36.5% D. 36%

17. By joining (–3, 2), (–3, –3) and (–3, 4), which of the following is obtained?

A. A triangle

B. A straight line parallel to x-axis

C. A straight line parallel to y-axis

D. A straight line passing through origin

18. The number of times a particular observation occurs in a given data is called its

A. Frequency

B. Range

C. Mean

D. None of these

19. By selling 33 m of cloth, a draper loses an amount equal to the selling price of 3 m of cloth. Find his gain or loss per cent.

A. gain $8\frac{1}{3}\%$ B. loss $8\frac{1}{3}\%$

C. gain 7% D. loss 7%

20. Three cubes of metal whose edges are 6 cm, 8 cm and 10 cm respectively are melted to form a single cube. The edge of the new cube is ______.

A. 24 cm B. 20 cm

C. 18 cm D. 12 cm

21. Find the single discount equivalent to two successive discounts of 20% and 10%.

A. 25% B. 30%

C. 28% D. 10%

22. Which of the following is not a case of direct variation?

A. Number of sheets of some kind are increased when their total weight is increased

B. More quantity of petrol is required to travel more distance with a fixed speed

C. More fees would be collected if number of students increase in a class

D. Time taken will be less, if number of workers is increased to complete the same work

23. If $a + b + c = 9$ and $ab + bc + ca = 23$, then the value of $a^2 + b^2 + c^2$ equals to

A. 35

B. 81

C. 127

D. 217

24. On dividing 200 into two parts, $\frac{1}{3}$ of the first part and $\frac{1}{2}$ of the second part are equal. The larger of the parts is ______.

A. 80 B. 120

C. 40 D. 150

25. On selling a fan for ₹ 810, Sunil gains 8%. For how much did he purchase it?

A. ₹ 700 B. ₹ 675
C. ₹ 650 D. ₹ 750

26. Find the value of x: $3^{2x} \times 3^{x+3} \times 3^{4-x} = (\sqrt{3})^{10}$

A. –1 B. 0
C. 1 D. 2

27. $\sqrt[3]{\frac{(-a^6 \times b^3 \times c^{21})}{c^9 \times a^{12}}} =$ ______

A. $-\frac{bc^3}{a^2}$ B. $\frac{bc^4}{a^2}$
C. $-\frac{ab^4}{c^2}$ D. $-\frac{bc^4}{a^2}$

28. If n is a perfect cube, then every prime factor of 'n' occurs ______

A. One time B. Two times
C. Three times D. Four times

29. Find the greatest number of four digits which is a perfect square?

A. 9800 B. 9864
C. 9999 D. 9801

30. If the ratio of the ages (in years) of x and y, 8 years ago is 7 : 6, then which of the following can be the sum of their ages 8 years from now?

A. 82 B. 97
C. 75 D. 94

31. The age of the boy is one-fifth of the age of his mother and sum of the ages of the son and the mother is equal to the age of the father. After 15 years, the sum of the ages of the son and his mother will be four-third of his father's age. Find the ratio of the persent ages of son, mother and father respectively.

A. 1 : 5 : 7 B. 2 : 10 : 10
C. 1 : 5 : 6 D. 2 : 8 : 9

32. The ratio of the income of P and Q is 5 : 4. The ratio of expenditure is 4 : 3. The saving of P is more than that of Q by $16\frac{2}{3}$%. What % of his income does P spend?

A. $53\frac{2}{3}$% B. $53\frac{1}{3}$%
C. $54\frac{1}{3}$% D. $51\frac{2}{3}$%

33. Mohan invested a sum of ₹ 12,500 at 12% per annum compound interest. He received an amount of ₹ 15,680 after x year. Then the value of x is ______.

A. 1
B. 4
C. 3
D. 2

34. Find the compound interest on ₹ 1,25,000 for 9 months at 8% per annum, compounded quarterly.

A. 7551
B. 7651
C. 7650
D. 7655

35. Pipe A can fill a tank in 12 hours and pipe B can empty the tank is 18 hours. Both pipes are opened at 6 AM and after some time, pipe B is closed and tank is full at 8 PM. At what time was the pipe B closed?

A. 10 AM
B. 8 AM
C. 9 AM
D. 11 AM

36. A car covers 300 kms at a constant speed. If its speed was 10 kmph more, it would have taken 1 hour less to travel the same distance. Find the speed of the car.

A. 60 kmph
B. 50 kmph
C. 40 kmph
D. 75 kmph

37. Two trains are travelling in opposite direction with speed of 25 m/s and 30 m/s respectively. If the length of one train is 300 m and that of the other train is 250 m, then find the time taken by the trains to cross each other.

A. 8 s B. 10 s
C. 12 s D. 14 s

38. The sum of the digits of a two digit number is 9. If 27 is subtracted from the number then the digits get reversed. Find the number.

A. 81 B. 72
C. 36 D. 63

39. There are some four-wheelers and six-wheelers in a garage. The total number of wheels of these vehicles is 120. The number of four-wheelers is 3/2 times the number of six-wheelers. Find the number of six-wheelers in the garage.

A. 20 B. 5
C. 15 D. 10

40. What is the minimum interior angle possible for a regular polygon?

A. 60° B. 75°
C. 90° D. None

41. What is the number of diagonals in a hexagon?

A. 4 B. 6
C. 9 D. 10

42. In the adjacent figure, the bisectors of ∠A and ∠B meet at a point P. If ∠C = 100° and ∠D = 60° find the measure of <APB.

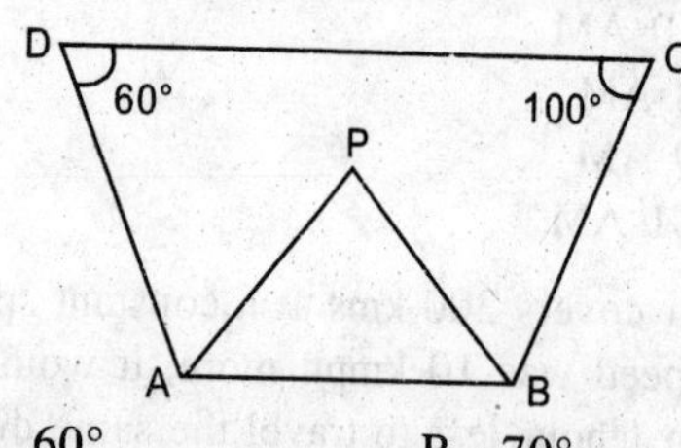

A. 60° B. 70°
C. 90° D. 80°

43. A square and a rectangle each have a perimeter of 40 m. The difference between areas of the two figures is 9 m^2. What are the possible dimensions of the rectangle?

A. 13 m, 7 m B. 14 m, 6 m
C. 108 m, 1 m D. 15 m, 5 m

44. In a parallelogram ABCD, AB = 6 cm, BC = 5 cm and AC = 7 cm. Find the perpendicular distance between $\overline{AB}$ and $\overline{CD}$.

A. $6\sqrt{6}$ cm B. $12\sqrt{6}$ cm
C. 5 cm D. $2\sqrt{6}$ cm

45. Some cubic metres of earth is dug out to sink a well which is 16 m deep and which has a radius of 3.5 m. If that amount of earth when taken out is spread over a rectangular plot of dimensions 25 m × 16 m, what is the height of the platforms so formed?

A. 1.54 m B. 1.50 m
C. 1.52 m D. 1.53 m

46. What is the difference between the total surface area and curved surface area of a cylinder whose radius is equal to 10 cm?

A. 200π cm^2
B. 300π cm^2
C. 100π cm^2
D. 10π cm^2

47. The mean of six numbers is 15. If 2 is taken away from every number, the new mean would be

A. 13 B. 4
C. 17 D. 8

48. The sides of the triangle are 45 cm, 60 cm and 75 cm. Find the length drawn to the longest side from its opposite vertex.

A. 27 cm B. 21 cm
C. 39 cm D. 36 cm

49. In the following figure, find the value of Y.

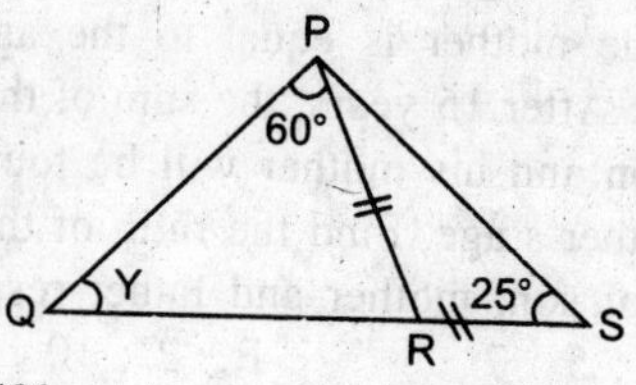

A. 50° B. 65°
C. 60° D. 70°

50. A cylindrical tank has a capacity of 5632 m^3. If the diameter of its base is 16 m, find its depth.

A. 28 m B. 25 m
C. 16 m D. 29 m

Section B : English

51. Candidates must ______ the general conditions for admission.
A. do B. prepare
C. satisfy D. create

52. He resorts ______ sharp practice in his dealings.
A. at B. to
C. in D. for

53. ______ English is an international language.
A. No article B. The
C. A D. An

54. The word 'Industrious' means.
A. Working in industry
B. Labour in factory
C. Hard working
D. Laid back

55. Choose the correct order to make the sentence below meaningful:
Wear / these / people / almost / a / majority /
1 2 3 4 5 6
of / days / a watch
7 8 9
A. 4 5 6 7 3 1 9 2 8
B. 4 5 7 6 1 3 8 2 9
C. 4 5 6 7 9 2 3 1 8
D. 4 5 6 7 3 1 2 8 9

56. Select the word closest in meaning to "Mortal".
A. Recurrent
B. Trivial
C. Fatal
D. Eternal

57. Mark the word with the correct spelling.
A. Maintenance B. Maintennance
C. Maintanance D. Maintainance

58. The coach insisted that Ronaldo ______ the centre position, even though he's too short for that position. (Use the correct verb)
A. play B. played
C. plays D. None of these

59. ______ King of Scotland saw ______ spider trying to climb up to ______ ceiling of the cave. (Use Articles)
A. The, a, the
B. A, a, the
C. No article, a, no article
D. The, a, no article

60. Raju relishes not only Chinese ______ continental food. (Use appropriate Conjunction)
A. also B. but
C. but also D. rather

61. You must learn ______ English every day to improve it. (Use appropriate determiner)
A. a few B. a little
C. a lot of D. None of these

62. Arrange the jumbled words to form a meaningful sentence
most/inventor/world/Thomas/Alva/Edison/the/in/is/remarkable/the
A. The remarkable inventor in the most world in Thomas Alva Edison.
B. Thomas Alva Edison is the most remarkable inventor in the world.
C. Is the most remarkable inventor in the world Thomas Alva Edison.
D. In the world most remarkable inventor is Thomas Alva Edison.

Directions (Qs. No. 63 to 67): *Read the following passages and answer the questions that follow:*

The moon's role in causing tides is much more high and important than that of the Sun. The reason is that the moon enjoys more proximity to the earth than the sun. As such its force is greater than that of the sun in attracting the surface water. Tides are of immense importance. In trade, navigation and fishing, tides are very useful. During the high tide, the water depth near the coast goes up and helps big ships to reach the ports. Kandla port in Gujarat and Diamond Harbour in West Bengal owe their very existence to the tides only. The significance of both London and Kolkata also depends on the tides. Tides also keep the harbours clear of refuse and mud brought down by rivers and thus they do not allow the harbours to be silted. Commonly, the tidal rivers are navigable. For the purpose of generating electricity, tidal waves are harnessed. Tides do not allow the sea water to be frozen by keeping the sea water in motion. Tides are also made use by the fishermen for sailing into the sea and returning to the harbour. In countries like Canada, U.K., France and Japan, tidal power stations are set up.

63. Why does the moon play a greater role than the sun in causing tides?
A. The moon is closer to the earth as compared to the sun.
B. The moon has greater gravitational pull.
C. The moon shines in night.
D. None of the above.

64. How are tides useful for the economy of the country?
A. Tides bring treasure of sea with them.
B. During high tides, big ships can reach the ports thus opening new vistas for business.
C. Tides destroy enemies of the country.
D. None of the above.

65. How are tides useful in cold countries?
A. They bring fish for eating.
B. They bring water for drinking.
C. They don't allow sea water to be frozen.
D. They keep the port silted.

66. How can tides solve the power problem of the world?
A. Electricity is being produced through tidal waves.
B. Tidal waves keep the steamers in motion.
C. Tidal waves melt the ice and save power.
D. None of the above.

67. Which word in the passage means 'to bring under control'?
A. Proximity
B. Silted
C. Immense
D. Harness

68. She plays better than _____ do. (Choose appropriate pronoun)
A. I B. my
C. may D. myself

69. I ______ in a school in Delhi since 2017. (Choose appropriate form of tense)
A. has studied
B. has been studying
C. have been studying
D. will study

70. There isn't any smog in the Highlands of Scotland, ______? (Choose appropriate question tag)
A. aren't it B. isn't it
C. is there D. there isn't

71. Choose the best meaning of the Idiom "to play to the gallery".
A. to watch the play with interest
B. to enact the play in the gallery
C. to endeavour to gain cheap popularity
D. to sit comfortably

72. The speckled tortoise walks steadfastly towards his goal? (Choose the adverb)
A. speckled B. steadfastly
C. towards D. goal

73. I wrote an article for the school magazine. (Change from active to passive voice)
A. An article for the school magazine I had written.
B. An article was written by me for the school magazine.
C. I have written an article for the school magazine.
D. The school magazine and an article I wrote for.

74. Empty vessels ______ much noise. (Select the correct form of verb)
A. make B. are making
C. have made D. makes

75. Gullible (Choose the word with opposite meaning)
A. trusting B. cynical
C. clever D. resourceful

Section C : General Science

76. The metal present in Chlorophyll is:
A. Iron
B. Calcium
C. Oxygen
D. Magnesium

77. Name the gas present in LPG:
A. Hydrogen
B. Oxygen
C. Methane
D. Butane

78. Which gas is used to replace CFC?
A. HCFC
B. RCFC
C. DHFC
D. HHFC

79. The first Menstrual flow at puberty is termed:
A. Menopause
B. Menstruation
C. Puberty flow
D. Menarche

80. Which among the following statement is incorrect about all organelles?
A. They are found in all Eukaryotic cells.
B. They are found in Multi cellular organisms only.
C. They coordinate to produce new cell.
D. They are small sized and mostly internal.

81. The boy is pulling a cart by a force of 100 N. The frictional force experienced by the cart is 20 N. The force causing the motion of the cart is:
A. 100 N
B. 120 N
C. 80 N
D. 5 N

82. The cans used for storing food are made by electroplating:
A. Silver onto iron
B. Chromium onto iron
C. Gold onto iron
D. Tin onto iron

83. The impression of an image does not vanish immediately from the retina. It persists for:
A. $(1/60)^{th}$ of a second
B. $(1/12)^{th}$ of a second
C. $(1/6)^{th}$ of a second
D. $(1/16)^{th}$ of a second

84. The Sun appears to rise in the East and set in the West because:
A. Earth rotates from East to West on its axis.
B. Earth rotates from West to East on its axis.
C. The Sun is at the centre of universe.
D. None of these

85. Pressure is equal to
A. Area/force on which it acts
B. Force/area on which it acts
C. Volume/force on which it acts
D. Force/volume on which it acts

86. An ultrasound equipment works at a frequency.
A. Higher than 20,000 Hz
B. Higher than 10,000 Hz
C. Lower than 20,000 Hz
D. Lower than 10,000 Hz

87. When electrodes are immersed in water and electricity is passed, the bubbles formed on the negative terminal is actually ______ gas.
A. Hydrogen
B. Carbon dioxide
C. Oxygen
D. Nitrogen

88. If light falls perpendicularly on a plane mirror, the angle in which light will be reflected is ______.
A. 45 degrees
B. 90 degrees
C. 180 degrees
D. 360 degrees

89. All non-living things are known as ______
A. Biotic Resource
B. Exhaustible Resource
C. Abiotic Resource
D. Human Resource

90. Malarial parasite is carried by
A. Culex mosquito
B. Male anopheles mosquito
C. Female anopheles mosquito
D. Aedes mosquito

91. Internal fertilisation does not occur in
A. Dog
B. Cow
C. Parrot
D. Frog

92. Regeneration is observed in
A. Planaria
B. Spyrogyra
C. Yeast
D. Amoeba

93. Rapid combustion is
A. When gas burns, it produces heat and light
B. When material suddenly burst into flames
C. When there is evolution of heat
D. None of these

94. A student is carrying out distillation process in a lab. Water is boiling in distillation flask. Water that is collected in the receiver flask is refrigerated and ice cubes are formed. Ice cubes are then kept outside the refrigerator and they start melting. Arrange following phases of water in ascending order of their total (PE + KE) energy considering that the mass of water remains the same.
(*i*) Water collected in the receiving flask
(*ii*) Water boiling in the distillation
(*iii*) Steam passing through the delivery tube
(*iv*) Ice cubes formed in the refrigerator
A. (*iv*), (*iii*), (*ii*), (*i*)
B. (*iv*), (*i*), (*ii*), (*iii*)
C. (*iii*), (*iv*), (*ii*), (*i*)
D. (*iv*), (*i*), (*iii*), (*ii*)

95. The different samples of CO_2 were found to contain carbon and oxygen in the same ratio of their mass. This illustrates
A. Law of conservation of mass
B. Law of definite proportions
C. Law of multiple proportions
D. Law of reciprocal proportions

96. An atlas of India is drawn by taking scale 100 cm = 50,000 km. The actual distance between the city of Bhopal and Cochin is 1,500 km, the distance between the two places in the atlas will be ______ cm.
A. 3
B. 1
C. 10
D. 2

97. Both sound and light waves can be propagated through
A. Vacuum
B. Air
C. Both (A) and (B)
D. None of the above

98. A man stands in front of a mirror and finds that his image is larger than himself. The mirror is a ______ mirror.
A. Convex
B. Concave
C. Plane
D. Both (A) and (B)

99. Each lung is enclosed in a double membrane called as pleura. The membrane which covers the surface of each lung is
A. Visceral pleura
B. Lung pleura
C. Peritoneal pleura
D. Parietal pleura

100. Nitrogenous waste products are eliminated mainly as ______
A. Urea in tadpole and ammonia in adult frog
B. Ammonia in tadpole and urea in adult frog
C. Urea in tadpole and adult frog
D. Urea in tadpole and uric acid in adult frog

Section D : Social Science

101. Who granted East India Company the sole right to trade with the East?
A. Robert Clive
B. Queen Elizabeth I
C. John Richardson
D. Queen Elizabeth II

102. The first Indian woman to become President of the Indian National Congress was:
A. Sarojini Naidu
B. Kamla Nehru
C. Kasturba Gandhi
D. Begum Rokeya Shakhawat Hossain

103. Land covered with grass shrubs on which animals can graze freely is known as:
A. Fallow land B. Overgrazing
C. Pasture D. Agricultural land

104. Name of the first country in the world to develop hydroelectricity.
A. Norway B. Pakistan
C. India D. Switzerland

105. Breeding of fish in specially constructed tanks and ponds is known as:
A. Agriculture
B. Sericulture
C. Pisciculture
D. Viticulture

106. Ahmedabad is referred as the ______ of India.
A. Ruhr B. Manchester
C. Boston D. Chicago

107. How many members are nominated by the President to the Rajya Sabha?
A. 233 B. 12
C. 22 D. 250

108. The Industrial Revolution started in ______ around 1750.
A. France
B. Britain
C. Russia
D. None of these

109. The British conquest of Bengal began with the Battle of ______.
A. Buxar
B. Plassey
C. Seringapatam
D. Saraighat

110. The architect of New Delhi was ______
A. Edwin Lutyens & H Baker
B. King George V
C. Lord Lytton
D. Queen Elizabeth

111. The existence of more than one level of government is known as
A. Federalism B. Secularism
C. Marginalism D. Communalism

112. Money Bill is introduced
A. Only in Rajya Sabha
B. Only in Lok Sabha
C. In both the Houses
D. By the Speaker of Rajya Sabha

113. In which state of India is the "Jim Corbett National Park" situated?
A. Uttarakhand B. Gujarat
C. Assam D. Uttar Pradesh

114. Which state of India is the highest producer of Jute?
A. Assam B. West Bengal
C. Bihar D. Odisa

115. A form of government where people enjoy equal political right, elect their ruler and hold them accountable is known as:
A. Secular B. Democratic
C. Socialist D. Republic

116. In order to prevent religion based exclusion and discrimination of 'lower castes', the Indian Constitution bans
A. Untouchability
B. Religious practices
C. Religion
D. Religious institutions

117. Sustainable development seeks to prevent _____.

A. Wastage of resources
B. Pollution
C. Loss of biodiversity
D. All of these

118. Of the earth's total water resources, the fresh water easily accessible for our use is

A. More than 90% B. 50%
C. 1% D. Less than 1%

119. These are made to protect our natural vegetation and wild life

A. National park
B. Wildlife sanctuaries
C. Biosphere reserves
D. All of these

120. The largest producer and exporter of mica in the world is

A. Australia B. India
C. USA D. Russia

121. Resources which can be renewed or reproduced are known as _____

A. Exhaustible resource
B. Non renewal source
C. Renewal source
D. Useful resource

122. The Act on the "Protection of Women from Domestic violence" finally became a law in the year:

A. 2003 B. 2004
C. 2005 D. 2006

123. Right to Information (RTI) act guarantees people's right to

A. Know governmental proceedings
B. Get universal primary education
C. Speak out their discontent freely
D. Hold meetings and public gathering

124. At the village level, the judicial functions are performed by the

A. Nyaya Panchayat
B. Gram Panchayat
C. District Judge
D. Munsif

125. Many of India's most important mining and industrial centre are located in

A. Jamshedpur B. Rourkela
C. Bokaro D. All of these

Section E : Intelligence Test

Directions (Qs. No. 126-129): *Choose the letters group that best represents a relationship similar to the one expressed in the original pair of letters group in the following.*

126. FILM : ADGH :: MILK : ?

A. ADGF B. HDGE
C. HDGF D. HEGF

127. EIGHTY : GIEYTH :: OUTPUT : ?

A. TUOTUP B. TUOUTP
C. UTOPTU D. UOTUPT

128. CAT is to DDY as BIG is to

A. CLL B. CLM
C. CML D. CEP

129. Bag is related to Luggage in the same way as Ship is related to _____?

A. Coal B. Stock
C. Cargo D. Weight

Directions (Qs. No. 130 & 131): *Which number completes the second pair in the same way as the first pair.*

130. 3 : 243 :: 5 : ___?

A. 425 B. 465
C. 546 D. 3125

131. 6 : 24 :: 5 : ?

A. 23 B. 20
C. 26 D. 22

132. Find the missing character from among the given alternatives.

A2	C4	E6
G3	I5	?
M5	O9	Q14

A. J15 B. K8
C. K15 D. L10

133. Choose the figure, which is different from others

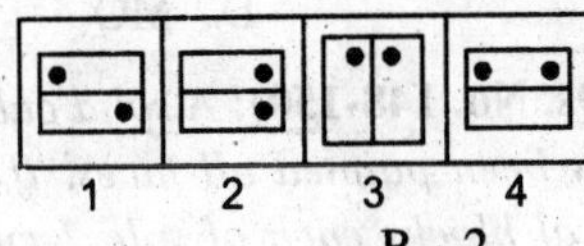

A. 1 B. 2
C. 3 D. 4

134. Arrange the following words as per order in the dictionary.

1. Live 2. Litter
3. Little 4. Literacy
5. Living

A. 3, 4, 2, 1, 5 B. 3, 2, 4, 5, 1
C. 4, 3, 5, 2, 1 D. 4, 2, 3, 1, 5

135. In a certain code, TEACHER is written as VGCEJGT. How is CHILDREN written in that code?

A. EJKNEGTP B. EGKNFITP
C. EJKNFGTO D. EJKNFTGP

136. If 30th January, 2003, was Thursday, what was the day on 2nd March, 2003?

A. Sunday B. Monday
C. Saturday D. Tuesday

137. In the following series, how many KGN occur in such a way that 'G' is in the middle and 'K' and 'N' are adjacent to it on both sides?

A K G L M N D Q K G C S N G K T G K G N D Z P U X G K E

A. 5 B. 3
C. 1 D. 2

138. Which word can't be formed by using the letters of the DISTRIBUTION word? Find that word.

A. TRUST B. SITUATION
C. TUITION D. DISTURB

139. Select the figure from the answer set that would come in place of the question mark (?).

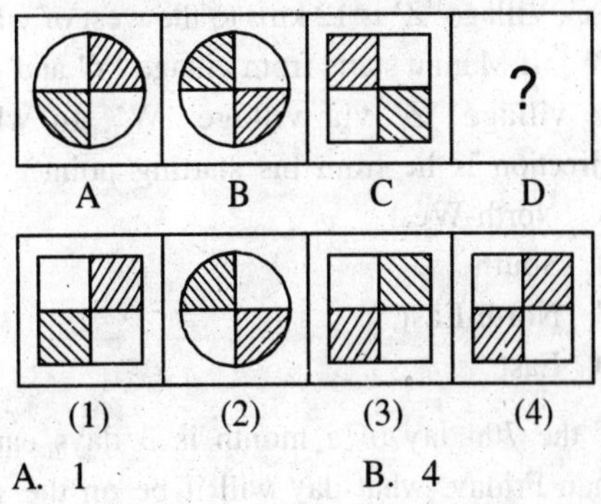

A. 1 B. 4
C. 3 D. 2

140. If Maya is the only daughter of Richa's grandmother's brother, how is Maya's daughter related to Richa?

A. Niece B. Cousin
C. Aunt D. Mother

141. It is 3 O'clock in a watch and it is rotated by 10 degrees in a manner such that if the minute hand points towards the North-East, then hour hand will point towards which direction?

A. South
B. South-West
C. North-West
D. South-East

142. Which one does not belong to the group?

A. 63 B. 65
C. 84 D. 91

143. Which square should replace the question mark?

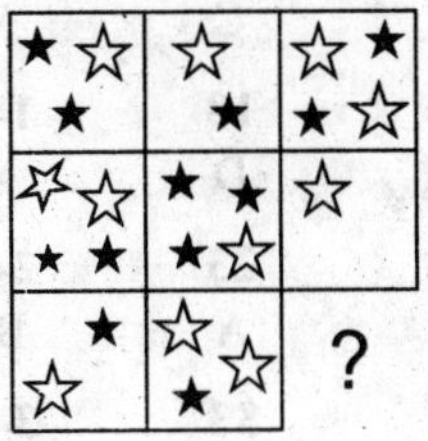

A. 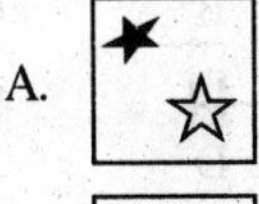 B. 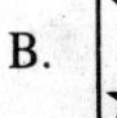

C.  D. 

144. Village 'W' is 20 kms to the north of village 'X'. Village 'Y' is 18 kms to the east of village 'X'. Village 'Z' is 12 kms to the west of village 'W'. If Mannu starts from village 'Y' and goes to village 'Z' via village 'W', in which direction is he from his starting point?

A. North-West
B. South
C. North-East
D. East

145. If the 7th day of a month is 3 days earlier than Friday, what day will it be on the 19th day of the month?

A. Monday
B. Sunday
C. Wednesday
D. Friday

146. Gaurav said to Tarun, "That boy playing with the football is the younger of the two brothers of the daughter of my father's wife". How is the boy playing football related to Gaurav?

A. Son
B. Brother
C. Cousin
D. Brother-in-law

Directions (Qs. No. 147): *Study the following arrangement of the English alphabet and answer the question given below:*

F J M P O W R N B E Y C K A V L D G X U H Q I S Z T

147. Which of the following pairs of letters has as many letters between them in the above arrangement as there are between them in the English alphabet?

A. AI B. EL
C. LS D. MO

Directions (Qs. No. 148-150): *A solid cube of each side 4 cm has been painted all faces. If it is then cut into cubical blocks each of side 2 cm, answer the question:*

148. How many cubes are there in all of a edge 2 cm?

A. 2 B. 4
C. 8 D. 16

149. How many cubes have no face painted?

A. 0 B. 2
C. 4 D. 8

150. How many cubes have only one face painted?

A. 0 B. 2
C. 4 D. 8

ANSWERS

1	2	3	4	5	6	7	8	9	10
D	C	C	A	A	C	C	B	A	C
11	**12**	**13**	**14**	**15**	**16**	**17**	**18**	**19**	**20**
C	A	D	A	B	B	C	A	B	D
21	**22**	**23**	**24**	**25**	**26**	**27**	**28**	**29**	**30**
C	D	A	B	D	A	D	C	D	B
31	**32**	**33**	**34**	**35**	**36**	**37**	**38**	**39**	**40**
C	B	D	B	C	B	B	D	D	A
41	**42**	**43**	**44**	**45**	**46**	**47**	**48**	**49**	**50**
C	D	A	D	A	A	A	D	D	A
51	**52**	**53**	**54**	**55**	**56**	**57**	**58**	**59**	**60**
C	B	A	C	A	C	A	A	A	C

61	62	63	64	65	66	67	68	69	70
B	B	A	B	C	A	D	A	C	C
71	**72**	**73**	**74**	**75**	**76**	**77**	**78**	**79**	**80**
C	B	B	A	B	D	D	A	D	B
81	**82**	**83**	**84**	**85**	**86**	**87**	**88**	**89**	**90**
C	D	D	B	B	A	A	C	C	C
91	**92**	**93**	**94**	**95**	**96**	**97**	**98**	**99**	**100**
D	A	A	B	B	A	B	B	A	B
101	**102**	**103**	**104**	**105**	**106**	**107**	**108**	**109**	**110**
B	A	C	A	C	B	B	B	B	A
111	**112**	**113**	**114**	**115**	**116**	**117**	**118**	**119**	**120**
A	B	A	B	B	A	D	C	D	B
121	**122**	**123**	**124**	**125**	**126**	**127**	**128**	**129**	**130**
C	C	A	A	D	C	A	A	C	D
131	**132**	**133**	**134**	**135**	**136**	**137**	**138**	**139**	**140**
B	B	D	D	D	A	*	B	A	B
141	**142**	**143**	**144**	**145**	**146**	**147**	**148**	**149**	**150**
D	B	D	A	B	B	D	C	A	A

EXPLANATORY ANSWERS

1. $\left(-\frac{3}{2}\times\frac{4}{5}\right)+\left(\frac{9}{5}\times-\frac{10}{3}\right)-\left(\frac{1}{2}\times\frac{3}{4}\right)$

$$= -\frac{6}{5}+(3\times-2)-\frac{3}{8}$$

$$= -\frac{6}{5}-6-\frac{3}{8} = -\left(\frac{6}{5}+6+\frac{3}{8}\right)$$

$$= -\left(\frac{48+240+15}{40}\right) = \left(-\frac{303}{40}\right)$$

3. Given, $\left(\frac{2}{9}\right)^{3}\times\left(\frac{2}{9}\right)^{-6} = \left(\frac{2}{9}\right)^{2m-1}$

$$\therefore \quad \left(\frac{2}{9}\right)^{3-6} = \left(\frac{2}{9}\right)^{2m-1}$$

$$\Rightarrow \quad \left(\frac{2}{9}\right)^{-3} = \left(\frac{2}{9}\right)^{2m-1}$$

$$\Rightarrow \quad -3 = 2m - 1$$

$$\Rightarrow \quad 2m = -3 + 1 = -2$$

$$\Rightarrow \quad m = -\frac{2}{2} = -1$$

$\therefore$ the value of $m = -1$

5. $\frac{\sqrt{0.2304}+\sqrt{0.1764}}{\sqrt{0.2304}-\sqrt{0.1764}} = \frac{.48+.42}{.48-.42}$

$$= \frac{.90}{.06} = \frac{90}{06} = \frac{90}{6} = 15$$

6. Let three numbers are $2x$, $3x$ and $4x$

Then, $(2x)^3 + (3x)^3 + (4x)^3 = 33957$

$\Rightarrow 8x^3 + 27x^3 + 64x^3 = 33957$

$\Rightarrow \quad 99x^3 = 33957$

$\Rightarrow \quad x^3 = \frac{33957}{99} = \frac{3087}{9}$

$= 343 = 7 \times 49$

$\Rightarrow \quad x^3 = 7 \times 7 \times 7 = (7)^3$

$\Rightarrow \quad x = 7$

The numbers are $2x = 14$, $3x = 21$ and $4x = 28$

i.e., 14, 21, 28

7. LCM of 8, 9 and 10 = 360

The least square number divisible by 360

$= 360 \times 10 = 3600 \Rightarrow (60)^2$

$= 3600$

$\therefore$ Least square number = 3600

8. Given, $\overline{148101a095}$ is multiple of 11, where a is a digit

We have to find a = ?

A number is divisible by 11 if the difference between the sum of its digit at odd places and the sum of its digits at even places is either 0 or a number divisible by 11

$\therefore$ (Sum of digit of odd place)

$-$ (Sum of digit at even place)

$= (5 + 0 + 1 + 1 + 4)$

$- (9 + a + 0 + 8 + 1)$

$= 11 - (18 + a)$

$= 11 - 18 - a = -7 - a$

$= -(7 + a)$

where, $\quad a = 4$

then $-(7 + a)$ is divisible by 11

Hence, the value of a is 4.

9. Checking the option (A), A = 5 and B = 2

$$\begin{array}{r} B\ A \\ \times\ B\ 3 \\ \hline 5\ 7\ A \\ \hline \end{array} \qquad \therefore \qquad \begin{array}{r} 2\ 5 \\ \times\ 2\ 3 \\ \hline 7\ 5 \\ 5\ 0\ \ \\ \hline 5\ 7\ 5 \end{array}$$

10. As, 471Z8 is divisible by 9

So, the sum of its digits is divisible by 9

$\therefore$ (4 + 7 + 1 + Z + 8) is divisible by 9

$\therefore$ (20 + Z) is divisible by 9,

$\therefore \quad$ Z = 7

$\therefore$ (20 + 7) = 27 is divisible by 9

Hence, the value of Z = 7

11. Given, the area of an equilateral triangle

$= 64\sqrt{3}\,\text{cm}^2$

$\Rightarrow \frac{\sqrt{3}}{4} \times (\text{side})^2 = 64\sqrt{3}\,\text{cm}^2$

$\Rightarrow (\text{side})^2 = 64 \times 4$

$\Rightarrow (\text{side})^2 = (8 \times 2)^2$

$\Rightarrow \quad \text{side} = 8 \times 2 = 16$ cm

12. $\frac{4m^2 - a^2 + 2ab - b^2}{2m + a - b}$

$= \frac{4m^2 - (a^2 - 2ab + b^2)}{2m + a - b}$

$= \frac{4m^2 - (a - b)^2}{2m + a - b}$

$= \frac{(2m)^2 - (a - b)^2}{2m + a - b}$

$= \frac{(2m - a + b)(2m + a - b)}{2m + a - b}$

$= 2m - a + b$

13. Let the speed of two trains A and B is $3x$ and $5x$

Given, speed of train B $= \frac{300}{4}$ km/h

$= 75$ km/h

$\Rightarrow \quad 5x = 75$

$\Rightarrow \quad x = 15$ km/h

$\therefore$ The speed of train A

$= 3x = 3 \times 15 = 45$ km/h

14. Let two years ago, age of his son = x years

Then, Dilip's age = $3x$ years

$\therefore$ Present age of his son = $x + 2$, and Dilip's age = $3x + 2$

Two years hence,

$2(3x + 4) = 5(x + 4)$

$\Rightarrow \quad 6x + 8 = 5x + 20$

$\Rightarrow 6x - 5x = 20 - 8$

$\Rightarrow \quad x = 12$ years

$\therefore$ The present age of son

$= x + 2 = 12 + 2 = 14$ years

and present age of Dilip

$= 3x + 2 = 3 \times 12 + 2$

$= 38$ years

15. A single throw of a dice,

$\therefore$ Sample space = {1, 2, 3, 4, 5, 6}

Hence, not getting 7, P(getting 7) = 0

16. Required per cent = $\frac{60}{100+60} \times 100\%$

$= \frac{60}{160} \times 100\%$

$= \frac{3}{8} \times 100 = \frac{3}{2} \times 25$

$= \frac{75}{2}\% = 37.5\%$

19. Let price of 1 m cloth is ₹ 1

Then, Selling price of 33 m cloth = ₹ 33

and loss = ₹ 3 (S.P. of 3 m)

$\therefore$ Cost price = ₹ (33 + 3) = ₹ 36

$\therefore$ loss % = $\frac{\text{loss} \times 100}{\text{cost price}} = \frac{3 \times 100}{36}$

$= \frac{100}{12} = \frac{25}{3} = 8\frac{1}{3}\%$

Hence, loss $8\frac{1}{3}\%$.

20. Volume of a cube (edge = 6 cm)

$\therefore \quad V_1 = (6 \text{ cm})^3 = 216 \text{ cm}^3$

Volume of a cube (edge = 8 cm)

$\therefore \quad V_2 = (8 \text{ cm})^3 = 512 \text{ cm}^3$

and, Volume of a cube (edge = 10 cm)

$\therefore \quad V_3 = (10 \text{ cm})^3 = 1000 \text{ cm}^3$

Form a single cube

$V = V_1 + V_2 + V_3$

$\Rightarrow \quad V = 216 + 512 + 1000 \text{ cm}^3$

$\Rightarrow \quad V = 1728 \text{ cm}^3$

$\Rightarrow \quad (\text{edge})^3 = 64 \times 27 = (4 \times 3)^3$

$\Rightarrow \quad \text{edge} = 4 \times 3 = 12$ cm

21. Two successive discount of 20% and 10%

$\therefore 100 \times \frac{80}{100} \times \frac{90}{100} = 100 \times \frac{4}{5} \times \frac{9}{10}$

$= 2 \times 4 \times 9 = 72$

A single discount = 100 − 72 = 28%

23. Given, $a + b + c = 9$ and, $ab + bc + ca = 23$

We know that

$(a + b + c)^2 = a^2 + b^2 + c^2 + 2(ab + bc + ac)$

$\Rightarrow \quad 9^2 = a^2 + b^2 + c^2 + 2(23)$

$\Rightarrow \quad 81 = a^2 + b^2 + c^2 + 46$

$\Rightarrow a^2 + b^2 + c^2 = 81 - 46 = 35$

Hence, $a^2 + b^2 + c^2 = 35$

24. Let the first part is x

Then, the second part is $(200 - x)$

$\therefore \quad \frac{1}{3}(x) = \frac{1}{2}(200 - x)$

$\Rightarrow \quad \frac{1}{3}x = 100 - \frac{1}{2}x$

$\Rightarrow \frac{1}{3}x + \frac{1}{2}x = 100$

$\Rightarrow \quad \frac{5x}{6} = 100$

$\Rightarrow \quad x = \frac{100 \times 6}{5} = 120$

$\therefore$ First part = x = 120,

Second part = 200 − 120 = 80

Hence, the larger of the parts = 120

25. Here, selling price ₹ 810, gain = 8%

$\therefore$ Cost price = ₹ $810 \times \frac{100}{100+8}$

$=$ ₹ $810 \times \frac{100}{108} = \frac{810}{27} \times 25$

$= 30 \times 25 =$ ₹ 750

26. $3^{2x} \times 3^{x+3} \times 3^{4-x} = (\sqrt{3})^{10}$

$\Rightarrow 3^{2x+x+3+4-x} = [(3)^{1/2}]^{10}$

$\Rightarrow \quad 3^{2x+7} = 3^5$

[base is equal $\therefore$ exponent is equal]

$\Rightarrow \quad 2x + 7 = 5$

$\Rightarrow \quad 2x = 5 - 7 = -2$

$\Rightarrow \quad x = -\frac{2}{2} = -1$

$\therefore \quad x = -1$

27. $\sqrt[3]{\frac{(-a^6 \times b^3 \times c^{21})}{c^9 \times a^{12}}} = \left(\frac{-a^6 \times b^3 \times c^{21}}{c^9 \times a^{12}}\right)^{\frac{1}{3}}$

$= \left(\frac{-a^6 \times b^3 \times c^{12} \times c^9}{c^9 \times a^6 \times a^6}\right)^{\frac{1}{3}}$

$= \left(\frac{-b^3 \times c^{12}}{a^6}\right)^{\frac{1}{3}}$

$= \left[\frac{(-b)^3 \times (c^4)^3}{a^6}\right]^{\frac{1}{3}} = -\frac{bc^4}{a^2}$

29. Greatest number of four digits = 9999

9	9999	99
9	81	
189	1899	
9	1701	
	198	

Greatest number of four digit (perfect square)
= 9999 − 198 = 9801

30. Let 8 years ago, ages of x and y are $7x$ years and $6x$ years

Then, present age of $x = 7x + 8$ years

and, present age of $y = 6x + 8$ years

$\therefore$ Sum of their ages 8 years from now

$= 7x + 8 + 8 + 6x + 8 + 8$ years

$= 13x + 32$ years

Checking Options

(*a*) $13x + 32 = 82$

$\Rightarrow \quad 13x = 50 \quad \therefore \quad x = \frac{50}{13}$

50 is not divisible by 13

(*b*) $13x + 32 = 97$

$\Rightarrow \quad 13x = 97 - 32$

$\Rightarrow \quad 13x = 65$

$\Rightarrow \quad x = 5$

(*c*) $13x + 32 = 75$

$\Rightarrow \quad 13x = 43 \quad \therefore \quad x = \frac{43}{13}$

43 is not divisible by 13

(*d*) $13x + 32 = 94$

$\Rightarrow \quad 13x = 62 \quad \therefore \quad x = \frac{62}{13}$

62 is not divisible by 13.

31. Let the present age of the mother = $5x$ years

Then, the present age of the son (boy)

$= x$ years

$\therefore$ the present age of the father

$= (x + 5x)$ years

$= 6x$ years

After 15 years

$x + 5x + 15 = \frac{4}{3}(6x)$

$\Rightarrow 6x + 15 = 8x$

$\Rightarrow 8x - 6x = 15$

$\Rightarrow \quad 2x = 15 \therefore x = \frac{15}{2}$

$\therefore$ The ratio of the present ages of son, mother and father respectively

$= x : 5x : 6x$

$= \frac{15}{2} : \frac{5 \times 15}{2} : \frac{6 \times 15}{2}$

$= \frac{15}{2} : \frac{75}{2} : 45$

$= 15 : 75 : 90$

$= 1 : 5 : 6$

32. Let the income of P and Q is $5x$ and $4x$ and the expenditure of P and Q is $4y$ and $3y$

Then, the saving of P = $5x - 4y$

and, the saving of Q = $4x - 3y$

According to question

The saving of P is more than Q by $16\frac{2}{3}\%$

$\therefore\ 5x - 4y = 100 + \frac{50}{3}$

$\Rightarrow 5x - 4y = \frac{350}{3}$

$\Rightarrow 15x - 12y = 350$ ...(*i*)

and $4x - 3y = 100$

$\Rightarrow 16x - 12y = 400$ ...(*ii*)

Subtracting (*i*) from (*ii*), we get

$x = 50$

from (*ii*), $y = \frac{100}{3}$

$\therefore$ The income of P = $5x = 5 \times 50 = 250$

and, the expenditure of P = $4y$

$= 4 \times \frac{100}{3} = \frac{400}{3}$

$\therefore$ Required percentage, P spend his income

$= \frac{\frac{400}{3}}{250} \times 100 = \frac{400}{3 \times 250} \times 100\%$

$= \frac{40 \times 4}{3} = \frac{160}{3}\% = 53\frac{1}{3}\%$

33. Here, P = ₹ 12,500, $r = 12\%$

A = ₹ 15,680, $n = x$ years

$\therefore\ A = P\left(1 + \frac{r}{100}\right)^n$

$\Rightarrow$ ₹ 15,680 = ₹ 12,500$\left(1 + \frac{12}{100}\right)^x$

$\Rightarrow \left(1 + \frac{3}{25}\right)^x = \frac{15680}{12500} = \frac{1568}{1250}$

$\Rightarrow \left(\frac{28}{25}\right)^x = \frac{784}{625} = \left(\frac{28}{25}\right)^2$

$\Rightarrow \left(\frac{28}{25}\right)^x = \left(\frac{28}{25}\right)^2$

$\therefore\ x = 2$ years

34. Here, P = ₹ 1,25,000, time = 9 months, $r = 8\%$ per annum compounded quarterly

$\therefore\ n = 3$ and $r = 2\%$

$\therefore$ Compound interest $= P\left(1 + \frac{r}{100}\right)^n - P$

$=$ ₹ 1,25,000$\left(1 + \frac{2}{100}\right)^3 -$ ₹ 1,25,000

$=$ ₹ 1,25,000$\left[\left(1 + \frac{1}{50}\right)^3 - 1\right]$

$=$ ₹ 1,25,000$\left[\left(\frac{51}{50}\right)^3 - 1\right]$

$=$ ₹ 1,25,000$\left[\frac{132651}{125000} - 1\right]$

$=$ ₹ 1,25,000$\left[\frac{132651 - 125000}{125000}\right]$

$=$ ₹ 7651

35. Here, both pipes are opened at 6 AM and tank is full at 8 PM

$\therefore$ Time = From 6 AM to 8 PM

= 12 + 2 = 14 hours

Let B be closed after x hours

Then, part filled by A in 14 hours – part emptied by B in $(14 - x)$ hours = 1

$\Rightarrow \frac{14}{12} - \frac{14 - x}{18} = 1$

$\Rightarrow \frac{7}{6} - \frac{14 - x}{18} = 1$

$\Rightarrow \frac{21 - (14 - x)}{18} = 1$

$\Rightarrow \frac{21 - 14 + x}{18} = 1$

$\Rightarrow 7 + x = 18$

$\Rightarrow x = 18 - 7 = 11$ hrs.

$\therefore$ The pipe B is closed at 6 AM + $(14 - x)$ hr

= 6 AM + (14 – 11) hr

= 6 AM + 3 hr = 9 AM

Hence, the pipe B is closed at 9 AM

36. Distance = 300 km

Let, speed = x km/h

Then, $\frac{300}{x} - \frac{300}{x+10} = 1$ hour

$\Rightarrow 300\left[\frac{1}{x} - \frac{1}{x+10}\right] = 1$

$\Rightarrow 300\left[\frac{x+10-x}{x(x+10)}\right] = 1$

$\Rightarrow \frac{10}{x(x+10)} = \frac{1}{300}$

$\Rightarrow x(x + 10) = 3000$

$\Rightarrow x^2 + 10x - 3000 = 0$

$\Rightarrow x^2 + 60x - 50x - 3000 = 0$

$\Rightarrow x(x + 60) - 50(x + 60) = 0$

$\Rightarrow (x + 60)(x - 50) = 0$

either, $x + 60 = 0$ or $x - 50 = 0$

$\therefore \quad x = -60$ or $x = 50$

[–60 is ignoring]

The speed of the car = 50 km/hr

37. Relative speed of the train = (25 + 30) m/s

= 55 m/sec

and, distance = (300 + 250) m = 550 m

The time taken by the train to cross each other

$= \frac{550 \text{ m}}{55 \text{ m/s}} \quad \left[\text{time} = \frac{\text{Distance}}{\text{time}}\right]$

= 10 sec

38. By options

(*a*) 81 → 8 + 1 = 9, 81 – 27 = 54

(*b*) 72 → 7 + 2 = 9, 72 – 27 = 45

(*c*) 36 → 3 + 6 = 9, 36 – 27 = 9

(*d*) 63 → 6 + 3 = 9, 63 – 27 = 36

Here, the number = 63

The sum of digits = 6 + 3 = 9

and, 63 – 27 = 36

36 is reverse of 63

39. The total number of wheels = 120

Let the number of six-wheelers = x

Then, the number of four-wheelers = $\frac{3}{2}x$

Therefore,

$$6x + 4\left(\frac{3}{2}x\right) = 120$$

$\Rightarrow 6x + 6x = 120$

$\Rightarrow \quad 12x = 120$

$\Rightarrow \quad x = 10$

Hence, the number of six-wheelers in the garage = 10.

42. Given, The bisect of ∠A and ∠B meet at P

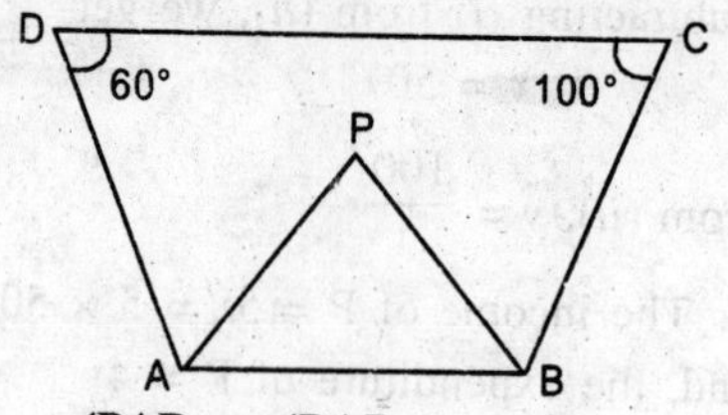

∴ ∠PAD = ∠PAB

and ∠PBC = ∠PBA

if DC ∥ AB

then, ∠D + ∠A = 180°

⇒ 60° + ∠A = 180°

⇒ ∠A = 180 – 60 = 120°

⇒ ∠A = ∠PAD + ∠PAB = 120°

⇒ ∠PAB + ∠PAB = 120°

⇒ 2∠PAB = 120°

∴ ∠PAB = 60°

and ∠C + ∠B = 180°

⇒ 100° + ∠B = 180°

⇒ ∠B = 180 – 100 = 80°

∠PBC + ∠PBA = 80°

⇒ ∠PBA + ∠PBA = 80°

⇒ 2∠PBA = 80°

⇒ ∠PBA = 40°

Now, In ΔAPB

∠APB + ∠ABP + ∠PAB = 180°

⇒ ∠APB + 40° + 60° = 180°

⇒ ∠APB = 180° – 100 = 80°

Hence, ∠APB = 80°

43. Given, perimeter of a square = 40 cm

$\Rightarrow \quad 4x = 40$ m

$\Rightarrow \quad x = 10$ m (x = side of a square)

and, perimeter of a rectangle = 40 m

$\Rightarrow 2(l + b) = 40$ m

$\Rightarrow l + b = 20$ m ...(i)

Now, Area (square) – area (rectangle) = 9 m^2

$x^2 - lb = 9$ [x = 10 m]

$\Rightarrow 10^2 - lb = 9$

$\Rightarrow \quad lb = 100 - 9 = 91$

$\because (l - b)^2 = (l + b)^2 - 4lb$

$\therefore (l - b)^2 = (20)^2 - 4(91)$

$\Rightarrow (l - b)^2 = 400 - 364 = 36$

$\Rightarrow (l - b)^2 = 6^2$

$\Rightarrow \quad l - b = 6$ m ...(ii)

Adding (i) and (ii), we get

$2l = 26 \Rightarrow l = 13$ m

from (i), $b = 20 - l = 20 - 13 = 7$ m

Hence, the possible dimensions of the rectangle is

$l = 13$ m, $b = 7$ m

44. Given, In a ∥gm ABCD

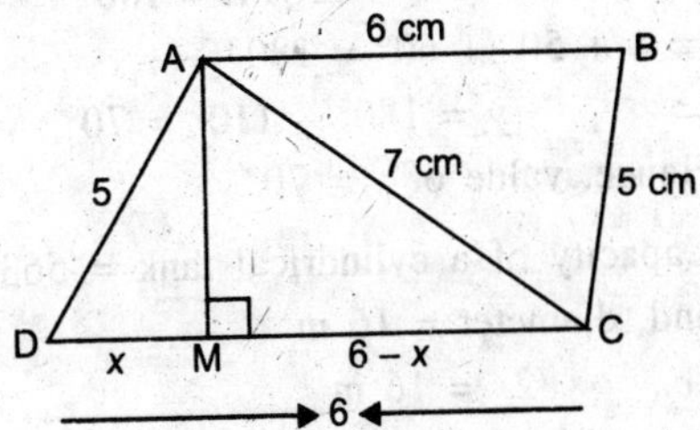

AB = 6 cm, BC = 5 cm

and AC = 7 cm

$\therefore$ CD = 6 cm, AD = 5 cm

Let AM be the perpendicular distance between $\overline{AB}$ and $\overline{CD}$

and MD = x cm

$\therefore$ MC = 6 – x cm

In ΔAMD

$AD^2 = AM^2 + MD^2$

$\Rightarrow AM^2 = AD^2 - MD^2$

$= 5^2 - x^2 = 25 - x^2$ cm ...(i)

and, In ΔAMC

$AC^2 = AM^2 + MC^2$

$\Rightarrow AM^2 = AC^2 - MC^2$

$= 7^2 - (6 - x)^2$

$= 49 - (6^2 + x^2 - 12x)$

$= 49 - 36 - x^2 + 12x$

$= 13 - x^2 + 12x$

$\Rightarrow AM^2 = 13 - x^2 + 12x$ ...(ii)

From (i) and (ii), we get

$25 - x^2 = 13 - x^2 + 12x$

$\Rightarrow 25 - x^2 - 13 + x^2 - 12x = 0$

$\Rightarrow 12 - 12x = 0$

$\Rightarrow \quad 12x = 12 \Rightarrow x = 1$ cm

$\therefore$ from (i), $AM^2 = 25 - x^2 = 25 - 1 = 24$ cm

$\Rightarrow \quad AM = \sqrt{24} = \sqrt{4 \times 6} = 2\sqrt{6}$ cm

Hence, the perpendicular distance

$= AM = 2\sqrt{6}$ cm

45. A well, depth = h = 16 m, r = 3.5 m = $\frac{7}{2}$ m

$\therefore$ Volume of a well (cylinder) = $\pi r^2 h$

$$= \frac{22}{7} \times \left(\frac{7}{2}\right)^2 \times 16 \text{ m}^3$$

Now, amount of earth = Volume of a well

= Volume of a rectangular platform

$$\therefore 25 \text{ m} \times 16 \text{ m} \times h = \frac{22}{7} \times \left(\frac{7}{2}\right)^2 \times 16 \text{ m}^3$$

$$\Rightarrow \quad h = \frac{22}{7} \times \frac{7}{2} \times \frac{7}{2} \times \frac{1}{25}$$

$$= \frac{77}{50} \text{ m} = 1.54 \text{ m}$$

Hence, the height of the platform = h = 1.54 m

46. Given, r = 10 cm

Total surface area of a cylinder = $2\pi rh + 2\pi r^2$

and, curved surface area of a cylinder = $2\pi h$

$\therefore$ Difference = $2\pi rh + 2\pi r^2 - 2\pi rh$

$= 2\pi r^2$

$= 2\pi \times 10^2$ cm²

$= 200\pi$ cm²

47. The mean of six number = 15

Sum of six number = 6 × 15 = 90

Given, 2 is taken away from every number

$\therefore$ new number = 90 − 2 × 6

= 90 − 12 = 78

New mean = $\frac{78}{6} = 13$

48. Let a triangle ABC in which AB = 45 cm

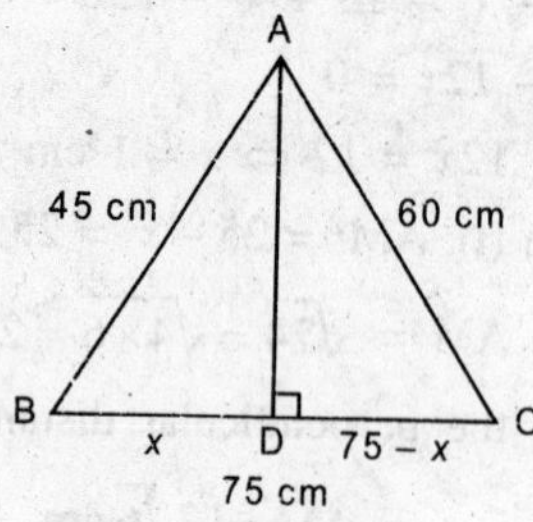

AC = 60 cm

and BC = 75 cm

Let, AD be the length drawn to the longest side (BC) from vertex A(AD ⊥ BC)

BD = x $\therefore$ DC = 75 − x

Then,

$AD^2 = AB^2 - BD^2 = AC^2 - DC^2$

$\Rightarrow 45^2 - x^2 = 60^2 - (75 - x)^2$

$\Rightarrow 2025 - x^2 = 3600 - (75^2 + x^2 - 150x)$

$\Rightarrow 2025 - x^2 = 3600 - (5625 + x^2 - 150x)$

$\Rightarrow 2025 - x^2 = 3600 - 5625 - x^2 + 150x$

$\Rightarrow 2025 - x^2 = -2025 - x^2 + 150x$

$\Rightarrow 2025 + 2025 = 150x$

$\Rightarrow 150x = 4050 \Rightarrow x = \frac{4050}{150} = 27$

$\therefore AD^2 = AB^2 - BD^2 = 45^2 - 27^2$

$= 2025 - 729 = 1296$

$\therefore AD^2 = 1296 = (36)^2$

$\Rightarrow$ AD = 36 cm

49. In the figure

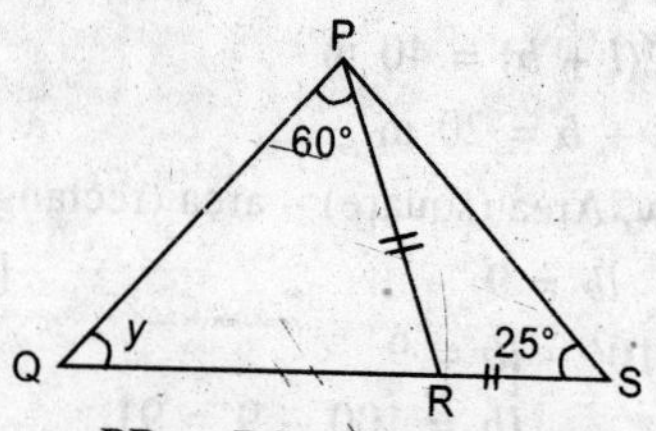

$\because$ PR = RS, ∠RSP = 25°

$\therefore$ ∠RSP = ∠RPS

$\therefore$ ∠RPS = 25°

In ΔPRS

$\therefore$ ∠PRS + ∠RSP + ∠RPS = 180°

$\Rightarrow$ ∠PRS + 25° + 25° = 180°

$\Rightarrow$ ∠PRS = 180° − 50° = 130°

$\Rightarrow$ ∠PRS = 130°

$\because$ ∠PRQ + ∠PRS = 180°

$\therefore$ ∠PRQ + 130° = 180°

$\therefore$ ∠PRQ = 180° − 130° = 50°

Now, In ΔPQR

∠PQR + ∠PRQ + ∠QPR = 180°

$\Rightarrow y + 50° + 60° = 180°$

$\Rightarrow y = 180° - 110° = 70°$

Hence, value of $y = 70°$

50. Capacity of a cylindrical tank = 5632 m^3

and, diameter = 16 m

i.e., $2r = 16$ m

$\therefore r = 8$ m

Volume of a cylindrical tank = 5632 m^3

$\pi r^2 h = 5632$

$\Rightarrow \frac{22}{7} \times 8^2 \times h = 5632$

$\Rightarrow h = \frac{5632 \times 7}{22 \times 8 \times 8}$

$= \frac{704 \times 7}{22 \times 8} = \frac{88 \times 7}{22} = 4 \times 7$ m

= 28 m

$\therefore$ Depth = h = 28 m

Previous Paper (Solved)

Sainik School Entrance Exam, 2019

(Class-IX)

PAPER-I : Maths, English, General Science & Social Studies

Subject : Mathematics

1. With the help of ruler and compass it is not possible to construct an angle of:
A. 22.5° B. 37.5°
C. 67.5° D. 40°

2. What time period is taken when interest is calculated half yearly?
A. twice as much as the number of given years
B. half as much as the number of given years
C. same as the number of given years
D. None of these

3. If a number is doubled then which of the following is a correct statement?
A. Its cube is two times the cube of the given number.
B. Its cube is three times the cube of the given number.
C. Its cube is six times the cube of the given number.
D. Its cube is eight times the cube of the given number.

4. Which of the following is the cube root of $\frac{-64}{243}$?
A. $\frac{7}{4}$ B. $\frac{-7}{4}$
C. $\frac{4}{7}$ D. $\frac{-4}{7}$

5. $\left[\left(\frac{1}{2}\right)^{-1}+\left(\frac{2}{3}\right)^{2}-\left(\frac{3}{4}\right)^{0}\right]^{-2}$ is equal to:
A. $\frac{81}{484}$ B. $\frac{81}{169}$
C. $\frac{169}{81}$ D. $\frac{16}{81}$

6. Which of the following is equal to $x^3 - 225x$?
A. $x(1 - 15x)(1 + 15x)$
B. $x(x - 15)(x + 15)$
C. $x(1 - 15x)(1 - 15x)$
D. $x(1 + 15x)(1 - 15x)$

7. The points (–3, 2) and (2, –3) represent:
A. different points
B. same point
C. the origin
D. None of these

8. If the dimensions of a room are l, b and h, ($\because l \rightarrow$ length, $b \rightarrow$ breadth and $h \rightarrow$ height) them which of the following is the area of its four walls?
A. $2h(l + b)$
B. $2h(l + h)$
C. $2l(h + h)$
D. $2h + l + b$

9. If [1X 2Y 6Z] is a number divisible by 9, then the least value of X + Y + Z is:
A. 0 B. 1
C. 6 D. 9

10. Which of the following is the Multiplicative identity for rational numbers?
A. 1
B. –1
C. 0
D. None of these

11. The mid value of a class interval is 42. If the class size is 10, then the upper and lower limits of the class are:
A. 37.5 and 47.5
B. 47 and 37
C. 37 and 47
D. 47.5 and 37.5

12. The speed of a car is $54\frac{1}{2}$ km/hr. The distance travelled by it in $\frac{7}{2}$ hours $\frac{35}{2}$ minutes is:
A. $\frac{999}{48}$ km
B. $\frac{9929}{48}$ km
C. $\frac{9919}{48}$ km
D. $\frac{9919}{28}$ km

13. The ages of A and B are in the ratio of 5 : 7. Four years from now the ratio of their ages will be 3 : 4. The present age of B is:
A. 20 years
B. 28 years
C. 15 years
D. 21 years

14. 36 is divided into parts such that 5 times the first part added to 3 times the second part makes 142. The two parts are:
A. 10 and 26
B. 12 and 24
C. 15 and 21
D. 17 and 19

15. Divide ₹ 1500 into two parts so that 10% of the larger part exceeds 8% of smaller part by ₹ 60. The value of larger and smaller parts are:
A. ₹ 1200 and ₹ 300
B. ₹ 850 and ₹ 650
C. ₹ 900 and ₹ 600
D. ₹ 1000 and ₹ 500

16. The value of $x + y + z$ in the adjoining figure is:

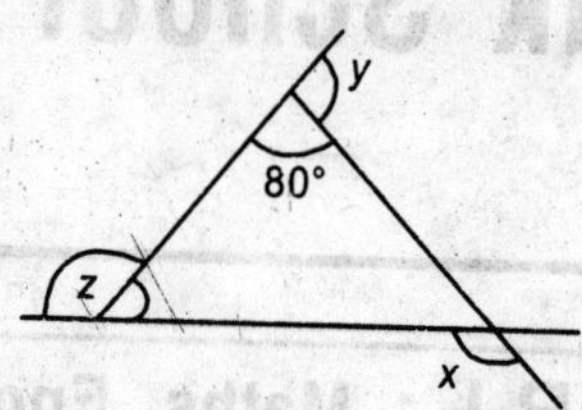

A. 180°
B. 270°
C. 360°
D. 720°

17. If an exterior angle of a regular polygon is of measure 12°, then the number of its sides is:
A. 12
B. 18
C. 22
D. 30

18. The smallest whole number by which 44 should be multiplied so as to make it a perfect square is:
A. 4
B. 11
C. 6
D. 5

19. There are 12321 workers in a factory. They stand in such a way that the number of workers in each row is equal to the number of rows. How many workers stand in each row?
A. 111
B. 121
C. 131
D. 141

20. Cubical boxes of volume 15625 cm^3 each are put in a cubical store of side 2.5 m. How many such boxes can be put in the store?
A. 100
B. 250
C. 500
D. 1000

21. If $a^2 + \frac{1}{a^2} = 27$, then the value of $a - \frac{1}{a}$ is:
A. ± 4
B. ± 3
C. ± 6
D. ± 5

22. If the sum of the lengths of bases of a trapezium is 12 cm and area is 14.1 cm^2, then its altitude will be:
A. 2.35 cm
B. 4.70 cm
C. 9.40 cm
D. 1 cm

23. If the length, width and height of a cuboid are 4.2 m, 3 m and 1.1 m, then its capacity in litres will be:
A. 12860 litres
B. 13860 litres
C. 14860 litres
D. 15860 litres

24. A road roller is 350 cm long and its diameter is 84 cm. It takes 500 complete revolutions to travel the road. The area covered by it in m^2 will be:
A. 4620 B. 6420
C. 2460 D. 4260

25. A solid cuboidal piece of wood measures 3 m × 2.5 m × 8 cm. Find the weight of the piece if 1 cubic cm of wood weighs 9 grams.
A. 4500 kg B. 5000 kg
C. 5400 kg D. 5600 kg

26. A well was dug with 14 m inner diameter and was 8 m deep. The earth dug out of it was evenly spread out on a rectangular plot of size 10 m × 8 m. Find the raise in the height of the plot.
A. 15.6 m B. 15.4 m
C. 15 m D. 15.5 m

27. If $5^{3x+4} = 25 \times 5^{4x-1}$ then the value of x is:
A. –3 B. –5
C. 5 D. 3

28. Sum of the digits of a two-digit number is 9. If 9 is subtracted from the number, the digits interchange their places. The original number is:
A. 81 B. 54
C. 72 D. 45

29. You are given the multiplication of two numbers as below:

$$\begin{array}{rrrrr} & & 5 & A & 3 \\ & & \times & B & 2 \\ \hline & 1 & C & 4 & 6 \\ + & 2 & D & 9 & 2 \\ E & 1 & F & G & 6 \\ \hline \end{array}$$

The values of the letters A, B, C, D, E, F and G are:
A. A = 2, B = 4, C = 0, D = 0, E = 2, F = 9, G = 6
B. A = 7, B = 4, C = 1, D = 0, E = 2, F = 0, G = 6
C. A = 2, B = 4, C = 1, D = 0, E = 2, F = 0, G = 6
D. A = 7, B = 4, C = 0, D = 9, E = 2, F = 9, G = 6

30. From a pack of 52 playing cards, one card is drawn at random. The probability of the drawn card being a black ten or a king is:
A. $\frac{5}{26}$ B. $\frac{3}{26}$
C. $\frac{3}{13}$ D. $\frac{2}{13}$

31. A spider is climbing a wall. It climbs up 5 cm, falls back 3 cm, climbs up another 4 cm, falls back 6 cm and climbs up another 5 cm. How far the spider has climbed from its starting point?
A. 5 cm B. 6 cm
C. 4 cm D. 23 cm

32. What will be the amount and compound interest on ₹ 5000 in 3 years if the rate of interest is 4% for the first year, 3% for the second year and 2% for the third year.
A. ₹ 5436.12 and ₹ 436.12
B. ₹ 5563.12 and ₹ 563.12
C. ₹ 5063.12 and ₹ 63.12
D. ₹ 5463.12 and ₹ 463.12

33. The smallest square number which is divisible by each one of the numbers 8, 9, 10 is:
A. 2600 B. 3600
C. 2900 D. 3900

34. If 25% of a number is less than 18% of 650 by 19, then find the number:
A. 293 B. 329
C. 239 D. 392

35. If the cost price is 25% of selling price then the profit percentage is:
A. 300% B. 305%
C. 350% D. 355%

36. Area of a rectangle whose length is $4ab$ and breadth is $6b^2$ is:

A. $24ab$ B. $24ab^2$
C. $24ab^3$ D. $24ab^4$

37. The total surface area of a cone having its slant height 9 dm and diameter of its base as 24 dm is:

A. 792 sq. dm B. 729 sq. dm
C. 279 sq. dm D. 297 sq. dm

38. A Cube of side 4 cm contains a sphere touching its side. Then the Volume of the gap in between is:

A. 30 cu.cm B. 30.48 cu.cm
C. 30.84 cu.cm D. 31 cu.cm

39. A chord of a circle is of length 6 cm and it is at a distance of 4 cm from the centre. Find the radius of the circle:

A. 3 cm B. 4 cm
C. 5 cm D. 6 cm

40. The mean of 40 observations was 160. It was detected on rechecking that the value of 165 was wrongly copied as 125 for computation of mean. Find the correct mean:

A. 161 B. 159
C. 166 D. 111

41. If $x + y = 12$ and $xy = 27$ then the value of $x^3 + y^3$:

A. 756 B. 765
C. 567 D. 576

42. In what time will a sum of money double itself at $6\frac{1}{4}\%$ p.a. on simple interest.

A. 13 years B. 14 years
C. 15 years D. 16 years

43. In a triangle ABC, E is the midpoint of median AD. Then the area of Δ BED is:

A. Area of Δ ABC
B. 0
C. $\frac{1}{2}$(area of Δ ABC)
D. $\frac{1}{4}$ (area of Δ ABC)

44. The radius of a spherical balloon increases from 7 cm to 14 cm as air is being pumped into it. Find the ratio of surface areas of the balloon in the two cases:

A. 1 : 4 B. 1 : 2
C. 4 : 1 D. 2 : 1

45. Two isosceles triangles have equal vertical angles and their areas in the ratio 25 : 36. Find the ratio of their corresponding heights.

A. 4 : 5 B. 5 : 6
C. 6 : 7 D. 5 : 7

46. The face value of each share is ₹ 10. If dividend is 16% then what will be the income from 600 shares?

A. ₹ 900 B. ₹ 960
C. ₹ 860 D. ₹ 800

47. A solid gold ball of radius 7 cm was melted and then drawn into a wire of diameter 0.2 cm. Find the length of the wire.

A. 457.33 m
B. 475.33 m
C. 547.33 m
D. 745.33 m

48. A horse is tethered for grazing inside a rectangular field 70 m by 52 m and is tethered to one corner by a rope 21 m long. How much area can it graze?

A. 346.5 sq. m B. 340 sq. m
C. 349.5 sq. m D. 348.5 sq. m

49. A race boat covers a distance of 66 km downstream in 110 minutes. It covers the same distance upstream in 120 minutes. The speed of the boat in still water is 34.5 km/hr. The speed of the stream will be:

A. 1.5 km/hr
B. 2 km/hr
C. 2.5 km/hr
D. 3 km/hr

50. The value of 10001^2:

A. 1002001
B. 100201
C. 100020001
D. 1000201

English Language

51. The correctly punctuated sentence is:
A. Mina said, wheres' Kishore?
B. Mina said where's Kishore!
C. Mina said, 'Where's Kishore?'
D. Mina said, 'Wheres' kishore!'

52. 'TO LET THE CAT OUT OF THE BAG' means:
A. To jump out of a problem
B. Have a pet animal
C. To feel extremely happy
D. Reveal something that was kept a secret before

53. Choose the correct order to make the sentence below meaningful:

Month / while / Mumbai / Last / it / in /
1 2 3 4 5 6
happened / living / I was
7 8 9

A. 1 8 9 2 7 5 6 3 4
B. 1 2 3 4 5 6 7 8 9
C. 5 7 8 9 2 4 3 6 1
D. 5 7 2 9 8 6 3 4 1

54. The adjective form of 'ADVANTAGE' is:
A. advantageous
B. advantagly
C. advantage
D. advantagement

55. The active voice of—"He had not been invited by us" is:
A. We had been invited by us.
B. We had invited by him.
C. We had not invited him.
D. We had not invited by us.

56. Identify the tense in the sentence given below:

When I arrived Ram had just left.
A. Present Perfect
B. Present Continuous
C. Past Perfect
D. Past Continuous

57. The synonym of the word 'SPLENDID' is:
A. Shortage B. Insignificant
C. impressive D. excess

58. The word 'brittle' means:
A. not easily breakable
B. easily breakable
C. easily understandable
D. easily portable

Directions (Qs. No. 59 and 60): *Find out the part containing error in the given statement.*

59. He is one of the talented student in our class.
A. He is one of the
B. talented student
C. in our class
D. no error

60. The thief was taken to the nearby police station.
A. The thief was
B. taken to the
C. nearby police station
D. no error

Directions (Qs. No. 61 and 62): *Fill in the blank by choosing the appropriate preposition from the given options.*

61. They have gone ______ an excursion.
A. to B. for
C. with D. on

62. The team rebelled ______ the captain.
A. upon B. over
C. with D. against

Directions (Qs. No. 63 and 64): *Choose the correct option if the given statements are changed into comparative degree.*

63. Silver is one of the most useful metals.
A. Silver is useful to any other metal.
B. Silver is useful than any other metal.
C. Silver is more useful than all other metals.
D. Silver is more useful than most of the metals.

64. Learning Italian is not as difficult as learning Japanese.

A. Learning Japanese is more difficult to learning Italian.

B. Learning Italian is not difficult than learning Japanese.

C. Learning Japanese is more difficult than learning in Italian.

D. Learning Japanese is more difficult than learning Italian.

65. The adjective form of 'apathy' is:

A. apathetically B. apathical
C. apathetic D. pathetic

66. The noun form of 'Proud' is:

A. proudy
B. pride
C. proudly
D. proudliness

Directions (Qs. No. 67 and 68): *Read the following passage and answer the questions that follow.*

Books are by far, the most lasting product of human effort. Temples crumble into ruins. Pictures and statues decay, but books survive. Time does not destroy the great thoughts which are as fresh today as when they first passed through the author's mind ages ago. The only effect of time has been to throw out the bad products, for nothing in literature can survive long unless it is really good and of lasting value. Books introduce us to the best society; they bring us into the presence of the greatest minds that have ever lived, we hear what they said and did; we see them as if they were really alive, we sympathize with them, enjoy with them and grieve with them.

67. According to the passage, books live forever because:

A. They have productive value.
B. Time does not destroy great thoughts.
C. They are in printed form.
D. They have the power to influence people.

68. According to the passage, temples, pictures and statues belong to the same category because:

A. All of them are beautiful.
B. All of them are substantial.
C. All of them are likely to decay.
D. All of them are fashioned by men.

69. Books introduce us into the best society as:

A. They give us a glimpse of the greatest minds.
B. They take us to the world of imagination.
C. They instill in us the qualities of the greatest minds.
D. They introduce us to elite class of the society.

70. Radha, "I won't buy a new car". (Choose the correct word to fill in the blank.)

Radha said that she ____ buy a new car.

A. won't B. will
C. wouldn't D. would

71. They will ask you a lot of questions at the interview. The sentence, when converted into the passive voice, would read as:

A. You are asked a lot of questions at the interview.
B. You were being asked a lot of questions at the interview.
C. You will be asked a lot of questions at the interview.
D. You are being asked a lot of questions at the interview.

72. The phrase *in cold blood* means:

A. Indifferently B. cruelly
C. thoughtlessly D. deliberately

73. The workers went out of the factory _____ to hold a protest rally. (Choose the correct word to fill in the blank.)

A. en masse B. en route
C. impasse D. de facto

74. *To put up with* means:

A. to close B. to prolong
C. to tolerate D. to forget

75. Fill in the blank with a possessive pronoun chosen from those given below.

Mani declared that the book was not _____.

A. our B. her
C. your D. hers

Subject: General Science

76. Rhizobium bacteria:
A. Help in digestion
B. Help in nitrogen fixation
C. Cause diseases
D. All of the above

77. The metal which is stored in kerosene?
A. Phosphorus
B. Magnesium
C. Sodium
D. Calcium

78. Poor conductors are:
A. Plastics B. Clothes
C. Wood D. All of these

79. There are following zones of a flame:
A. Two B. Three
C. Four D. No any zone

80. Force of friction always acts on moving objects and its direction shall be:
A. On any direction
B. Along the direction of motion
C. Perpendicular to the direction of motion
D. Opposite to the direction of motion

81. The stage of the embryo in which all the body parts can be identified is:
A. Fetus B. Zygote
C. Infant D. None of these

82. Diabetes is due to the malfunctioning of:
A. Adrenal gland B. Pituitary gland
C. Heart D. Pancreas

83. Naphthalene balls are obtained from:
A. Carbon B. Coke
C. Coal tar D. Coal gas

84. John accidentally placed his hand over a flame and immediately pulled it back. He felt the sensation of heat and reacted due to the action of:
A. Nerve cells
B. Blood cells
C. Skin surface
D. Nucleus of cells

85. A purple coloured nonmetal forms a brown solution in alcohol which is applied on wounds as an antiseptic. Name of the non-metal is:
A. Phosphorous
B. Carbon
C. Sulphur
D. Iodine

86. Given below are the harmful effects of weeds on crop plants. Choose the correct combination of statements.
(*i*) They interfere in harvesting.
(*ii*) They help crop plants to grow healthy
(*iii*) They compete with crop plants for water, nutrients, space and light.
(*iv*) They affect plant growth.
A. (*i*), (*iii*), (*iv*)
B. (*iii*), (*iv*)
C. (*iii*) only
D. (*i*), (*ii*), (*iii*), (*iv*)

87. Which of the following groups contain all synthetic substances?
A. Nylon, Terylene, Wool
B. PVC, Polythene, Bakelite
C. Cotton, Polycot, Rayon
D. Acrylic, Silk, Wool

88. Which of the following statement is true about endemic species?
A. They are found exclusively in a specific habitat
B. Endemic species can never become endangered
C. They are only found in zoos and botanical gardens
D. They are not affected by the destruction of their habitat

89. Identify the correct statement about cells.
A. All the cells have nucleus
B. Cells of an organ have similar structure
C. Cells of a tissue have similar structure
D. Shape of all types of cells is round

90. Aquatic animals in which fertilization occurs in water are said to be:
A. Viviparous without fertilization
B. Oviparous with external fertilization
C. Viviparous with internal fertilization
D. Oviparous with internal fertilization

91. The light from sun takes 500 s to reach the earth. Assuming that the speed of light is 3,00,000 kms^{-1}, calculate the distance between the sun and the earth.
A. 100 million km
B. 150 million km
C. 1500 million km
D. 15 million km

92. Which of the following is not an application of chemical effect of electric current?
A. Electroplating of metals
B. Purification of metals
C. Decomposition of elements
D. Decomposition of compounds

93. An earthquake of magnitude '6' on Richter scale has:
A. Ten times more destructive energy than an earthquake of magnitude '4'.
B. Hundred times more destructive energy than an earthquake of magnitude '4'.
C. Thousand times more destructive energy than an earthquake of magnitude '4'.
D. One and half times more destructive energy than an earthquake of magnitude '4'.

94. Which of the following statements is correct regarding rods and cones in the human eye?
A. Cones are sensitive to dim light
B. Cones are sensitive to bright light
C. Rods are sensitive to bright light
D. Rods can sense colour

95. Suppose a new planet is discovered between Uranus and Neptune, its time period of revolution around the sun would be:
A. Less than that of Neptune
B. More than that of Neptune
C. Equal to that of Neptune of Uranus
D. Less than that of Uranus

96. Ramesh was cooking potato curry on a chulha. To his surprise he observed that the copper vessel was getting blackened from outside. It may be due to:
A. Proper combustion of fuel
B. Improper cooking of potato curry
C. Improper combustion of the fuel
D. Burning of copper vessel

97. When a Copper vessel is exposed to moist air for long, it acquires a dull green coating. The green material is a mixture of:
A. Copper oxide and Copper carbonate
B. Copper hydroxide and Copper carbonate
C. Copper oxide and Copper nitrate
D. Copper hydroxide and Copper nitrate

98. The places meant for conservation of biodiversity in their natural habitat are:
(*i*) Zoological garden
(*ii*) Botanical garden
(*iii*) Sanctuary
(*iv*) National park
A. (*i*) and (*ii*)
B. (*ii*) and (*iii*)
C. (*iii*) and (*iv*)
D. (*i*) and (*iv*)

99. The same force 'F' acts on four different objects having the areas given below, one by one. In which case the pressure exerted will be the maximum?
A. 20 m^2
B. 50 m^2
C. 100 m^2
D. 10 m^2

100. Before playing the orchestra in a musical concert, a sitarist tries to adjust the tension and pluck the strings suitably. By doing so he is adjusting.
A. Intensity of sound only
B. Amplitude of sound only
C. Frequency of the sitar string with the frequency of other musical instruments
D. Loudness of sound

Subject: Social Science

101. The Chairman of the Drafting Committee of Indian Constitution was:
A. Sardar Patel
B. Dr. B.R. Ambedkar
C. Dr. Rajendra Prasad
D. J.L. Nehru

102. By the late of 18th Century East India Company was trying to expand the cultivation of:
A. Opium B. Indigo
C. Cotton D. Tea

103. EVMs were used for the first time in the _____ general elections.
A. 2001 B. 2002
C. 2003 D. 2004

104. There are _____ elected members in Rajya Sabha.
A. 543 B. 272
C. 233 D. 260

105. Minerals that lie at shallow depths are taken out by removing the surface layer, this is known as:
A. Open-cast mining
B. Shaft mining
C. Drilling
D. All of the above

106. The complainant has a _____ right to get a free copy of the FIR from the Police.
A. Fundamental B. Legal
C. Political D. Economic

107. Which article of the constitution states that untouchability has been abolished?
A. Article 14 B. Article 15
C. Article 16 D. Article 17

108. The Marathi newspaper *Kesari* was edited by:
A. Bipin Chandrapal
B. Bal Gangadhar Tilak
C. Sarojini Naidu
D. Lala Lajpat Rai

109. The difference between the birth rate and the death rate is called the:
A. Natural growth rate
B. Normal growth rate
C. Actual growth rate
D. None of the above

110. Dandi March was against the:
A. Salt Tax
B. Purna Swaraj
C. Non co-operation movement
D. Simon Commission

111. The British East India Company got a charter from Queen Elizabeth-I in:
A. 1600 AD B. 1599 AD
C. 1601 AD D. 1700 AD

112. Delhi Renaissance refers to the period from:
A. 1830 - 1857 AD B. 1857 - 1885 AD
C. 1825 - 1857 AD D. None of these

113. Woods Dispatch of 1854 refers to:
A. Educational Reform
B. Financial Reform
C. Forest Reform
D. None of these

114. The leader of the ruling party in Lok Sabha is:
A. The Prime Minister
B. The President
C. The Vice President
D. The Leader of Opposition

115. As per which article of the Indian Constitution every arrested person is guaranteed Fundamental Rights:
A. Article 20 B. Article 21
C. Article 23 D. Article 22

116. Which of the following gas was released in Bhopal Gas Tragedy?
A. Methyl Isocyanite
B. Ethyl Isocyanate
C. Methyl Alcohol
D. Ethyl Alcohol

117. Which one of the following is a leading producer of Copper in the world?

A. Bolivia
B. Chile
C. Ghana
D. Zimbabwe

118. Identify the state with "Lowest literacy" as per census 2011.

A. Bihar
B. Haryana
C. Rajasthan
D. Gujarat

119. The total number of Anglo Indians nominated to the Lok Sabha is:

A. 8
B. 6
C. 4
D. 2

120. Which one of the following countries has the highest percentage of forest land?

A. Australia
B. India
C. France
D. Japan

121. Who was the founder of the 'Brahmo Sabha'?

A. Annie Besant
B. Bal Gangadhar Tilak
C. Raja Ram Mohan Roy
D. Ishwar Chandra Vidyasagar

122. Child marriage restraint Act was passed in the year ____

A. 1929
B. 1909
C. 1919
D. 1853

123. What is a population pyramid?

A. A graphical presentation of the age, sex composition of a population.
B. When the population density of an area is so high that people live in tall buildings.
C. Pattern of population distribution in large urban areas.
D. Pattern of population distribution in rural areas.

124. Which age group of India is guaranteed free education by the Constitution?

A. 6-14 years
B. 5-13 years
C. 7-14 years
D. 6-12 years

125. Who wrote the book *'Poverty and Un-British Rule in India'*?

A. Dadabhai Naoroji
B. Badruddin Tyabji
C. Pherojshah Mehta
D. Bipin Chandrapal

PAPER-II

Intelligence Test

Directions (Qs. No. 126-128): *Choose the letters group that best represents a relationship similar to the one expressed in the original pair of letters group.*

126. MONKEY : XDJMNL : : TIGER : ?

A. QDFHS
B. SDFHS
C. SHFDQ
D. UJHFS

127. MAD is to JXA as RUN is to:

A. ORX
B. OSQ
C. PRJ
D. UXQ

128. Kilometer is to Distance as Poundal is to:

A. Density
B. Acceleration
C. Momentum
D. Force

Directions (Qs. No. 129-131): *Which number complete the second pair in the same way as the first pair.*

129. 20 : 11 : : 102 : ?

A. 49
B. 52
C. 61
D. 98

130. 13 : 25 : : 48 : ?

A. 95
B. 97
C. 109
D. 105

131. Tiff is to Battle as Frugal is to:

A. Sprint
B. Vague
C. Miserly
D. Vital

132. A is 40 m South-West of B. C is 40 m South-East of B. Then C is in which direction of A?

A. East B. West
C. North-East D. South

133. Choose the figure, which is different from others.

A	E	Z	N
1	2	3	4

A. 1 B. 2
C. 3 D. 4

134. If ENGLAND is written as 1234526 and FRANCE is written as 785291. How is GREECE coded?

A. 381191 B. 831191
C. 832252 D. 835545

135. Which word can't be formed by using the letters of the INTELLIGENCE word? Find that word.

A. TILLAGE B. INCITE
C. GENTLE D. NEGLECT

136. If + means divide, divide means –, – means ×, × means ÷ then 12 + 6/3 – 2 × 8 = ?

A. 2 B. 4
C. 8 D. 5

137. Select the figure from the answer set that would come in place of the question mark (?).

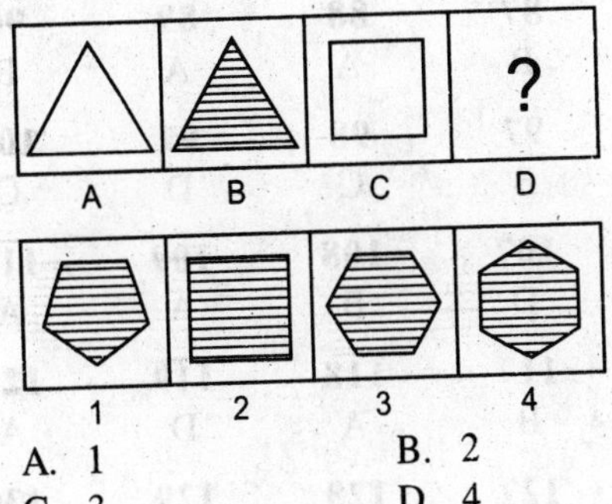

A. 1 B. 2
C. 3 D. 4

138. A Cube painted blue on all the faces is cut into 125 cubes of equal size. Then, how many cubes are not painted on any face?

A. 8 B. 16
C. 27 D. 54

139. If 1st October is Sunday, than 1st November will be:

A. Tuesday B. Friday
C. Wednesday D. Thursday

140. Find the missing number in the box.

0	3	8
15	24	35
48	?	80

A. 64 B. 63
C. 66 D. 84

141. Which one set of letters when sequentially placed at the gaps in the given letter series shall complete it?

ac_cab_baca_aba_aca_

A. acbcc B. aacbc
C. babbb D. bcbba

Directions (Qs. No. 142-145): *In each of the following questions. Find the word which cannot be made from the letters of the given word.*

142. REPUBLICAN

A. CLIP B. PURE
C. ANKLE D. BANE

143. ESTRANGE

A. GENERATE B. SERGEANT
C. REAGENTS D. GREAT

144. ADMINISTRATOR

A. ADMIT B. NEST
C. MANTA D. ROAD

145. SOCIALISATION

A. SCOUT B. CLASS
C. LIAISON D. ASSOCIATION

Directions (Qs. No. 146 and 147): *Choose the letters group that best represents a relationship similar to the one expressed in the original pair of letters groups.*

146. If LONDON is coded as MPOEPO. What code is needed for DELHI?

A. DEHLI B. EFIMJ
C. HLDEI D. EFMIJ

147. PNS : OOT : : DBH : ?

A. PPI B. BBI
C. CCI D. DDB

Directions (Qs. No. 148-150): *In the given series, find the next/missing term/number.*

148. MNOABCPQRDEFST??

A. GK
B. UV
C. GH
D. UG

149. AZ, CX, EV, ?

A. HT
B. HU
C. GS
D. GT

150. YX, UTS, ONML, ?

A. FEDCB
B. GFEDC
C. IHGFE
D. HGFED

ANSWERS

1	2	3	4	5	6	7	8	9	10
D	A	D	D	B	B	A	A	A	A
11	**12**	**13**	**14**	**15**	**16**	**17**	**18**	**19**	**20**
C	C	B	D	D	C	D	B	A	D
21	**22**	**23**	**24**	**25**	**26**	**27**	**28**	**29**	**30**
D	A	B	A	C	B	D	B	A	B
31	**32**	**33**	**34**	**35**	**36**	**37**	**38**	**39**	**40**
A	D	B	D	A	C	A	B	C	A
41	**42**	**43**	**44**	**45**	**46**	**47**	**48**	**49**	**50**
A	D	D	A	B	B	A	A	A	A
51	**52**	**53**	**54**	**55**	**56**	**57**	**58**	**59**	**60**
C	D	D	A	C	C	C	B	B	D
61	**62**	**63**	**64**	**65**	**66**	**67**	**68**	**69**	**70**
D	D	D	D	C	B	B	C	A	C
71	**72**	**73**	**74**	**75**	**76**	**77**	**78**	**79**	**80**
C	B	A	C	D	B	C	D	B	D
81	**82**	**83**	**84**	**85**	**86**	**87**	**88**	**89**	**90**
A	D	C	A	D	A	B	A	A	B
91	**92**	**93**	**94**	**95**	**96**	**97**	**98**	**99**	**100**
B	C	B	B	A	C	B	C	D	C
101	**102**	**103**	**104**	**105**	**106**	**107**	**108**	**109**	**110**
B	A,B	D	C	A	B	D	B	A	A
111	**112**	**113**	**114**	**115**	**116**	**117**	**118**	**119**	**120**
A	A	A	A	D	A	B	A	D	A
121	**122**	**123**	**124**	**125**	**126**	**127**	**128**	**129**	**130**
C	A	A	A	A	A	*	D	B	A
131	**132**	**133**	**134**	**135**	**136**	**137**	**138**	**139**	**140**
C	A	B	A	A	B	B	C	C	B
141	**142**	**143**	**144**	**145**	**146**	**147**	**148**	**149**	**150**
B	C	A	B	A	D	C	D	D	B

EXPLANATORY ANSWERS

3. Let the number is x,

Cube of the number $= x^3$

Now, the number $= 2x$

Cube of the number $= (2x)^3 = 8x^3$

Become 8 times of the given number.

4. $$\sqrt[3]{-\frac{64}{243}} = \sqrt[3]{\frac{(-4)\times(-4)\times(-4)}{7\times7\times7}}$$

$$= -\frac{4}{7}.$$

5. $$\left[\left(\frac{1}{2}\right)^{-1} + \left(\frac{2}{3}\right)^{2} - \left(\frac{3}{4}\right)^{0}\right]^{-2}$$

$$= \left[2+\frac{4}{9}-1\right]^{-2}$$

$$= \left[\frac{13}{9}\right]^{-2} \qquad \left[\because \left(\frac{b}{a}\right)^{-1} = \frac{a}{b}\right]$$

$$= \left[\frac{9}{13}\right]^{2} = \frac{9\times9}{13\times13} = \frac{81}{169}.$$

6. $x^3 - 225x$

$= x(x^2 - 225)$

$= x(x^2 - (15)^2)$

$[\because a^2 - b^2 = (a - b)(a + b)]$

$= x(x - 15)(x + 15).$

7.

So, points (–3, 2) and (2, 3) are different points.

8. Area of four walls of a room $= 2(l + b)h$.

9. A number is divisible by 9 if the sum of digit is divisible by 9

$$\therefore \frac{1+X+2+Y+6+Z}{9} = \frac{(X+Y+Z)+9}{9}$$

$\therefore$ least value of $X + Y + Z = 0$

$$\because \frac{0+9}{9} = 1.$$

10. 1 is the multiplicative identity for rational numbers.

11. Let the upper and lower limits of the class are x and y then,

$$\frac{x+y}{2} = 42$$

$x + y = 84$ ...(*i*)

$x - y = 10$ ...(*ii*)

Equation (*i*) + equation (*ii*), we get,

$2x = 94$

$x = 47$

From equation, (*i*)

$47 + y = 84$

$y = 37$

$\therefore$ Class interval are 37 and 47.

12. We have,

$$\text{Speed of a car} = 54\frac{1}{2}\text{ km} = \frac{109}{2}\text{ km}$$

$$\text{Time} = \frac{7}{2}\text{h}\frac{35}{2}\text{m}$$

$$= \frac{7}{2}\text{h} + \frac{35}{2}\times\frac{1}{60}\text{h}$$

$$= \frac{7}{2}+\frac{7}{24} = \frac{84+7}{24}$$

$$= \frac{91}{24}\text{h}$$

Distance = speed × time

$$= \frac{109}{2} \times \frac{91}{24}$$

$$= \frac{9919}{48} \text{ km.}$$

13. Let the present age of A and B are $5x$ and $7x$ respectively.

Then, After 4 years

$$\frac{5x+4}{7x+4} = \frac{3}{4}$$

$$20x + 16 = 21x + 12$$

$$21x - 20x = 16 - 12$$

$$x = 4$$

∴ Present age of B

$$= 7x$$

$$= 7 \times 4 = 28 \text{ years}$$

14. Let the first part = x

Then, second part = $36 - x$

According to question,

$$5x + 3(36 - x) = 142$$

$$5x + 108 - 3x = 142$$

$$2x = 34$$

$$x = 17$$

∴ First part = $x = 17$

Second part = $36 - x = 36 - 17 = 19$.

15. Let the smaller part = x

Then, larger part = $1500 - x$

According to question,

$$10\%(1500 - x) - 8\%x = 60$$

$$10(1500 - x) - 8x = 6000$$

$$15000 - 10x - 8x = 6000$$

$$18x = 15000 - 6000$$

$$18x = 9000$$

$$x = 500$$

∴ Smaller part = $x = 500$

Larger part = $1500 - x$

$$= 1500 - 500$$

$$= 1000.$$

16. In ΔABC,

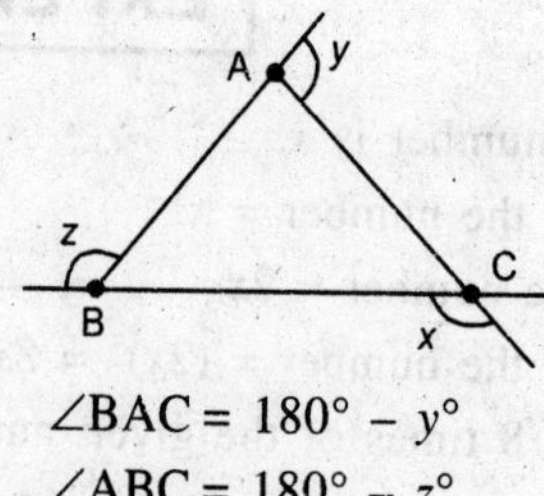

$$\angle BAC = 180° - y°$$

$$\angle ABC = 180° - z°$$

$$\angle ACB = 180° - x°$$

In a triangle, the sum of three angle is 180°

$$\therefore \quad \angle BAC + \angle ABC + \angle ACB = 180°$$

$$180 - y° + 180 - z° + 180 - x° = 180°$$

$$540 - (x° + y° + z°) = 180°$$

$$x° + y° + z° = 540 - 180$$

$$x° + y° + z° = 360°.$$

17. ∵ In a polygon

$$\text{Exterior angle} = \frac{360}{n}$$

$$\therefore \quad \frac{360}{n} = 12$$

$$n = \frac{360}{12}$$

$$n = 30.$$

18.

2	44
2	22
	11

$$\therefore \quad 44 = 2 \times 2 \times 11$$

∴ 11 will be the smallest number to make 44 perfect square.

19. Let, Number of workers in each row = x

∴ Number of rows = x

∴ Total work = $x \times x = x^2$

$$x^2 = 12321$$

	111
1	12321
	1
21	23
1	21
221	221
1	221
	×

$$x = \sqrt{12321}$$

$$x = 11$$

$\therefore$ 111 workers stand in each row.

20. Let n small cubical box are put in cubical store

$\therefore$ volume of cubical store

$= n \times$ volume of cubical boxes

$\because$ side of cubical store = 2.5 m = 250 cm

$\therefore \quad 250 \times 250 \times 250 = n \times 15625$

$$\therefore \quad n = \frac{250 \times 250 \times 250}{15625}$$

$$= \frac{15625000}{15625}$$

$$\therefore \quad n = 1000.$$

21. $$a^2 + \frac{1}{a^2} = 27$$

Substract 2 from both side, we get

$$a^2 + \frac{1}{a^2} - 2 = 27 - 2$$

$$a^2 + \frac{1}{a^2} - 2 = 25$$

$$a^2 + \frac{1}{a^2} - 2.a.\frac{1}{a} = 25$$

$$\left(a - \frac{1}{a}\right)^2 = 25$$

$$a - \frac{1}{a} = \sqrt{25}$$

$$a - \frac{1}{a} = \pm 5.$$

22. Area of trapezium

$= \frac{1}{2}$ (Sum of the length of base $\times$ Altitude)

$$\frac{1}{2} \times (12) \times h = 14.1$$

$$6h = 14.1$$

$$h = 2.35 \text{ cm.}$$

23. Volume of cuboid $= l \times b \times h$

$= 4.2 \times 3 \times 1.1 = 13.86 \text{ m}^3$

$\because \quad 1 \text{ m}^3 = 1000$ litre

$\therefore$ Capacity of cuboid (in litre)

$= 13.86 \times 1000$

$= 13860$ litres.

24. $\therefore$ Area covered in one revolutions $= 2\pi rh$

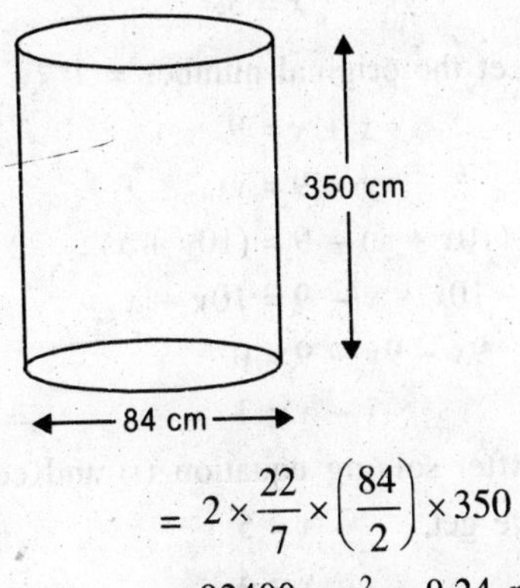

$$= 2 \times \frac{22}{7} \times \left(\frac{84}{2}\right) \times 350$$

$$= 92400 \text{ cm}^2 = 9.24 \text{ m}^2$$

$\because$ [1 m^2 = 10000 cm^2]

$\therefore$ Area covered in 500 complete revolution

$= 500 \times 9.24 = 4620 \text{ m}^2$.

25. Volume of cuboidal piece of wood

$= l \times b \times h$

$= (3 \times 100) \times (2.5 \times 100) \times 8$

$= 600000 \text{ cm}^3$

$\because$ weight of 1 cm^3 = 9 grams [given]

weight of 600000 cm^3 = 5400000 gm

= 5400 kg

[$\because$ 1 kg = 1000 gm]

26. Let the raise in the height of the plot $= h$ m

Volume of the earth dug out

= volume of earth spread out on the rectangular plot

$$\pi r^2 h' = l \times b \times h$$

$$\frac{22}{7} \times \left(\frac{14}{2}\right)^2 \times 8 = 10 \times 8 \times h$$

$$22 \times 7 \times 8 = 10 \times 8 \times h$$

$$h = \frac{154}{10} = 15.4 \text{ m.}$$

27. $5^{3x+4} = 25 \times 5^{4x-1}$

$5^{3x+4} = 5^2 \times 5^{4x-1}$

$5^{3x+4} = 5^{4x-1+2}$

$5^{3x+4} = 5^{4x+1}$

After comparing power of both side, we get,

$3x + 4 = 4x + 1$

$x = 3.$

28. Let the original number = 1 xy

$x + y = 9$ ...(*i*)

$xy - 9 = yx$

$(10x + y) - 9 = (10y + x)$

$10x + y - 9 = 10y + x$

$9x - 9y - 9 = 0$

$x - y = 1$ ...(*ii*)

After solving equation (*i*) and equation (*ii*) we get, $x = 5$,

$y = 4$

∴ the original number = 54.

29. Check from the options

(A) A = 2, B = 4

```
        5 (2) 3
      ×   (4) 2
   ------------
      1 (0) 4 6
  2 (0) 9 2 ×
   ------------
  (2) 1 (9) (6) 6
```

∴ C = 0, D = 0, E = 2, F = 9, G = 6

Hence, option (A) is the correct answer.

30. Number of black ten in the playing card = 2

Number of king in the playing card = 4

Total card = 52

$$\therefore \text{Required Probability} = \frac{2}{52} + \frac{4}{52}$$

$$= \frac{1}{26} + \frac{2}{26}$$

$$= \frac{1+2}{26} = \frac{3}{26}.$$

31. Spider climbed from the starting point

↑ ↓ ↑ ↓ ↑

$= (5 - 3) + (4 - 6) + 5$

$= 2 - 2 + 5$

$= 5$ cm.

32. Required Amount

$$= 5000\left(1+\frac{4}{100}\right)\left(1+\frac{3}{100}\right)\left(1+\frac{2}{100}\right)$$

$$= 5000 \times \frac{104}{100} \times \frac{103}{100} \times \frac{102}{100}$$

= ₹ 5463.12

Compound Interest

= 5463.12 − 5000

= 463.12.

33. The smallest number which is divisible by 8, 9 and 10

2	8,	9,	10
2	4,	9,	5
2	2,	9,	5
3	1,	9,	5
3	1,	3,	5
5	1,	1,	5
	1	1	1

= LCM (8, 9, 10)

$= 2 \times 2 \times 2 \times 3 \times 3 \times 5$

= 360

∵ $360 = 2 \times 2 \times 2 \times 3 \times 3 \times 5$

To make 360 perfect square we have to multiply by 2×5

2	360
2	180
2	90
3	45
3	15
5	5
	1

∴ Required smallest number

$= 360 \times 2 \times 5$

$= 3600.$

34. Let the number is x,

18% of 650 – 25% of $x = 19$

$$\frac{18 \times 650}{100} - \frac{25 \times x}{100} = 19$$

$$117 - \frac{x}{4} = 19$$

$$\frac{x}{4} = 98$$

$$x = 392.$$

35. Let selling price $= 2x$

Then, cost price = 25% of $x = \frac{x}{4}$

$$\% \text{ profit} = \frac{\text{SP} - \text{CP}}{\text{CP}} \times 100$$

$$= \frac{x - \frac{x}{4}}{\frac{x}{4}} \times 100$$

$$= \frac{3x}{x} \times 100 = 300\%.$$

36. We have,

Length $(l) = 4ab$

Breadth $(b) = 6b^2$

Area of Rectangular $= l \times b$

$= 4ab \times 6b^2$

$= 24ab^3.$

37. Total surface area of cone $= \pi r\,(r + l)$

$$= \frac{22}{7} \times \left(\frac{24}{2}\right)\left(\frac{24}{2} + 9\right)$$

$$= \frac{22}{7} \times 12 \times 21$$

$= 792$ sq. dm.

38. Diameter of sphere = side of cube = 4 cm

∴ radius of sphere = 2 cm

Volume of the gap

= Volume of cube – Volume of sphere

$$= a^3 - \frac{4}{3}\pi r^3$$

$$= (4)^3 - \frac{4}{3} \times \frac{22}{7} \times (2)^3$$

$= 64 - 33.52 = 30.48$ cm^3.

39. In ΔOMB,

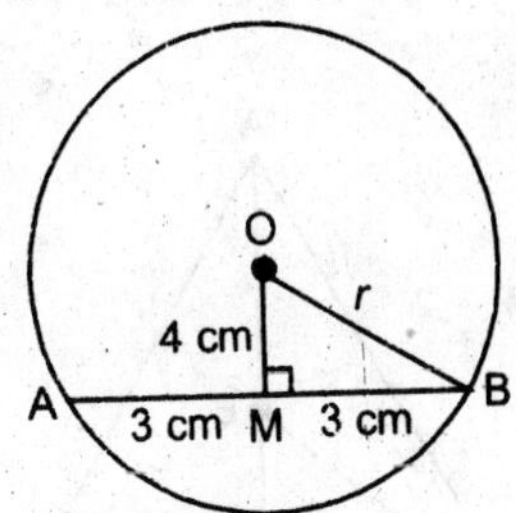

By Pythagorus theorem

$$r^2 = \text{OM}^2 + \text{MB}^2$$

$$r^2 = (4)^2 + (3)^2$$

$$r^2 = 16 + 9$$

$$r^2 = 25$$

$r = 5$ cm.

40. Correct mean $= 160 + \frac{165 - 125}{40}$

$$= 160 + \frac{40}{40}$$

$= 160 + 1 = 161.$

41. $x + y = 12$ and $xy = 27$

After taking square both side

$$x^2 + y^2 + 2xy = 144$$

$$x^2 + y^2 + 2 \times 27 = 144$$

$$x^2 + y^2 = 90$$

$$x^3 + y^3 = (x + y)\,(x^2 + y^2 - xy)$$

$= 12.(90 - 27)$

$= 12 \times 63$

$= 756.$

42. Let the sum of money = x

$$SI = 2x - x = x$$

$$SI = \frac{P \times r \times t}{100}$$

$$x = \frac{x \times \frac{25}{4} \times t}{100}$$

$$t = \frac{400}{25} = 16 \text{ years.}$$

43. Median divide the triangle into two equal part

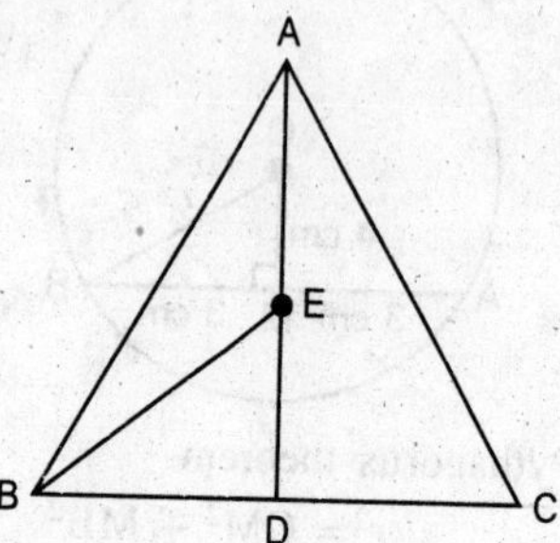

$\therefore$ Ar (ΔABD) = Ar (ΔADC)

Ar (ΔABE) = Ar (ΔBED)

$$\text{Ar}(\Delta BED) = \frac{1}{4}\text{Ar}(\Delta ABC).$$

44. Surface area of sphere = $4\pi r^2$

$$\therefore \text{ Required ratio} = \frac{4\pi r_1^2}{4\pi r_2^2}$$

$$= \left(\frac{r_1}{r_2}\right)^2 = \left(\frac{7}{14}\right)^2$$

$$= 1 : 4.$$

45. $\because$ ΔABC ~ ΔDEF (SAS)

$$\frac{\text{Ar}(\Delta ABC)}{\text{Ar}(\Delta DEF)} = \frac{AB^2}{DE^2} = \frac{AC^2}{DF^2}$$

$$= \frac{BC^2}{DE^2} = \frac{h_1^2}{h_2^2}$$

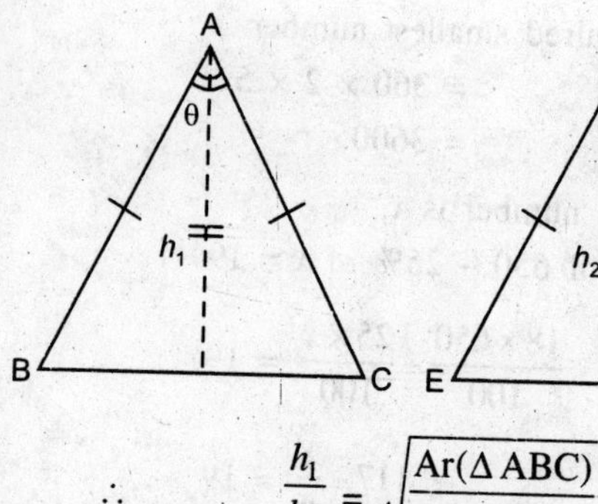

$$\therefore \quad \frac{h_1}{h_2} = \sqrt{\frac{\text{Ar}(\Delta ABC)}{\text{Ar}(\Delta DEF)}}$$

$$\frac{h_1}{h_2} = \sqrt{\frac{25}{36}} = \frac{5}{6}.$$

46. Face value of the 600 shares

= 600 × 10

= 6000

Annual Income = 6000 × 16%

= 960.

47. Let the length of the wire = x cm

Volume of ball = Volume of the wire

$$\pi(0.1)^2 \times x = \frac{4}{3}\pi(7)^3$$

$$x = \frac{4 \times 7 \times 7 \times 7}{3 \times 0.1 \times 0.1}$$

$$x = 45733 \text{ cm}$$

$$= 457.33 \text{ m}$$

[$\because$ 1 m = 100 cm]

48. Area grazing by Horse

= Area of Sector PBQ

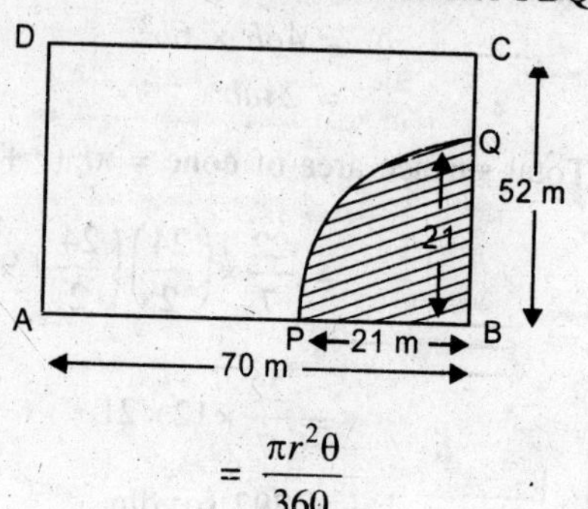

$$= \frac{\pi r^2 \theta}{360}$$

$$= \frac{\pi(21)^2 \times 90}{360}$$

$$= \frac{22}{7} \times \frac{21 \times 21}{4}$$

$= 346.5\ m^2$.

49. Let the speed of stream = x km/hr

Then, Boat upstream speed

= $(34.5 - x)$

Boat downstream speed = $(34.5 + x)$

According to question,

$$\frac{66}{34.5+x} = \frac{110}{60}$$

$345 + 10x = 360$

$10x = 15$

$x = 1.5$ km/h.

50. $(1001)^2$

We can written this as,

$(1000 + 1)^2$

$= (1000)^2 + (1)^2 + 2 \times (1000) \times (1)$

$= 1000000 + 1 + 2000$

$[\because (a + b)^2 = a^2 + b^2 + 2ab]$

$= 1002001.$

126. As,

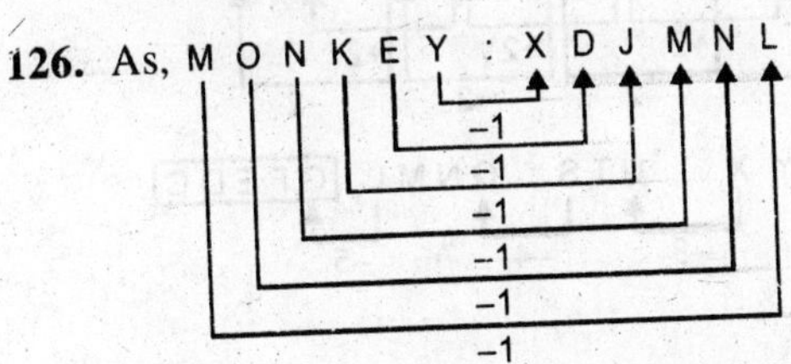

Similarly,

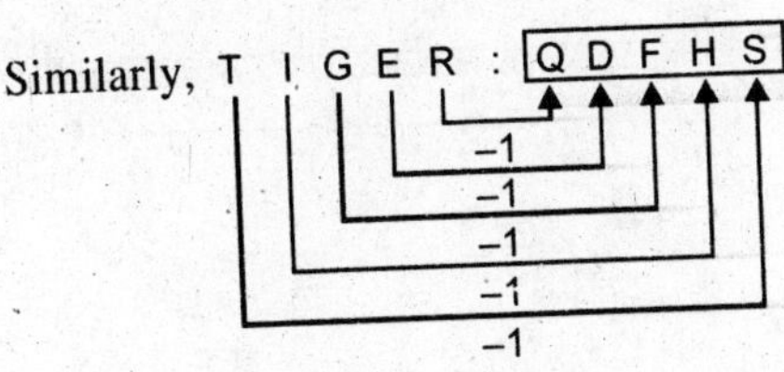

128. As Kilometer is the unit of Distance. Similarly Poundal is the unit of Force.

129. 20 : 11 :: 102 : 52

÷2 + 1   ÷2 + 1

130. 13 : 25 :: 48 : 95

×2 – 1   ×2 – 1

131. As Tiff and Battle are synonym word similarly Frugal and Miserly are also synonym word.

132.

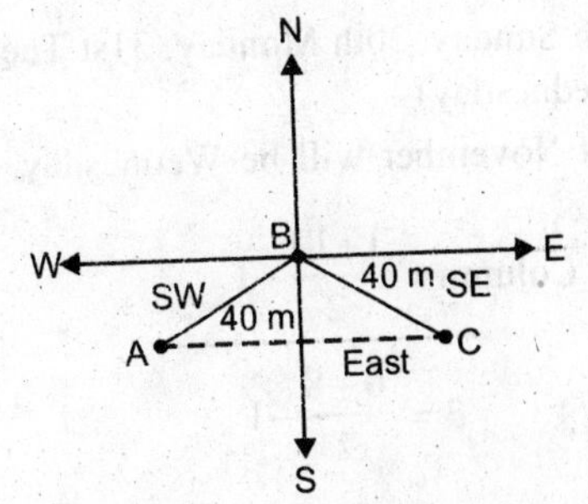

C is in East direction of A.

133. E is different from other, 'E' is a prime number place letter in the English alphabet.

134. As,

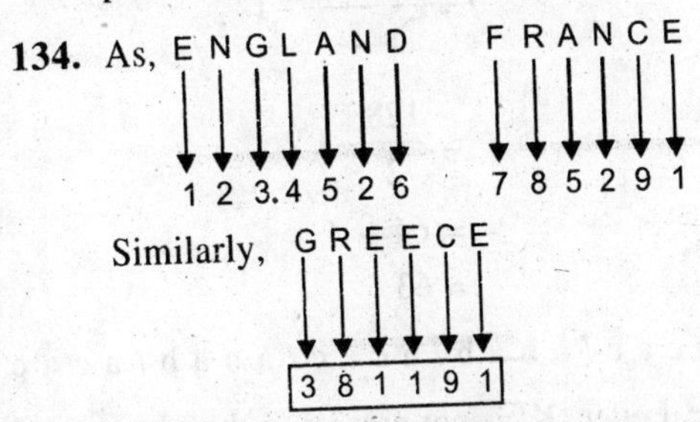

135. $\because$ Letter 'A' is present in the given word.

So, we can not formed (A) TILLAGE.

136. Given that,

$= 12 + 6/3 - 2 \times 8$

$= 12/6 - 3 \times 2 + 8$

According to BODMAS Rule,

$= 2 - 3 \times 2 + 8$

$= 2 - 6 + 8$

$= 2 + 2 = 4.$

138. $$n = \frac{\sqrt[3]{125}}{\sqrt[3]{1}} = \frac{5}{1} = 5$$

$\because$ Number of cube which are not painted

$= (n - 2)^3$

$= (5 - 2)^3$

$= (3)^3 = 27.$

139. Total number of days from 1st October to 1st November

= 32 days

= 4 week + 4 days

∵ 4 Extra day

= (29th Sunday, 30th Monday, 31st Tuesday, 1st Wednesday)

So, 1st November will be Wednesday.

140. $\text{IInd Column} = \frac{\text{I}+\text{III}}{2} - 1$

$$3 = \frac{0+8}{2} - 1$$

$$24 = \frac{15+35}{2} - 1$$

$$? = \frac{48+80}{2} - 1$$

$$= \frac{128}{2} - 1$$

$$= 64 - 1$$

$$= 63.$$

141. a c a c / a b a b / a c a c / a b a b / a c a c

142. ∵ Letter 'K' is not present in the given word so, ANKLE can not be formed.

143. ∵ Letter 'E' is only two times present in the given word so GENERATE word can not be formed

144. ∵ Letter 'E' is not present in the given word, so we can not formed NEST word.

145. ∵ Letter 'U' is not present in the given word, so we can not formed 'SCOUT' word.

146. As, L O N D O N

+1 +1 +1 +1 +1 +1

M P O E P O

Similarly, D E L H I

+1 +1 +1 +1 +1

E F M I J

147.

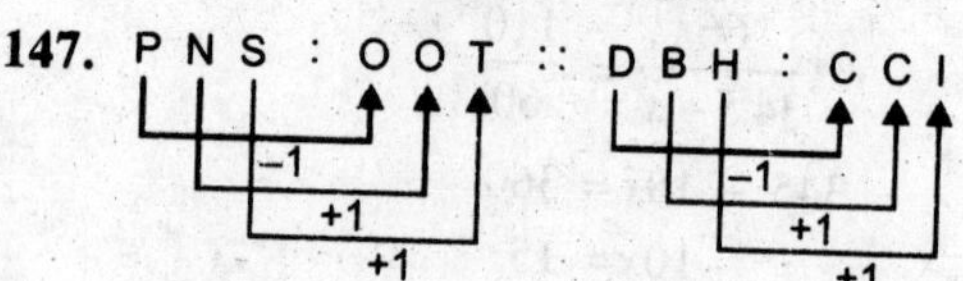

148. MNO ABC PQR DEF STU G

This is an alternate continue series of three letter

MNO PQR STU

ABC DEF GHU

Next term will be UG.

149.

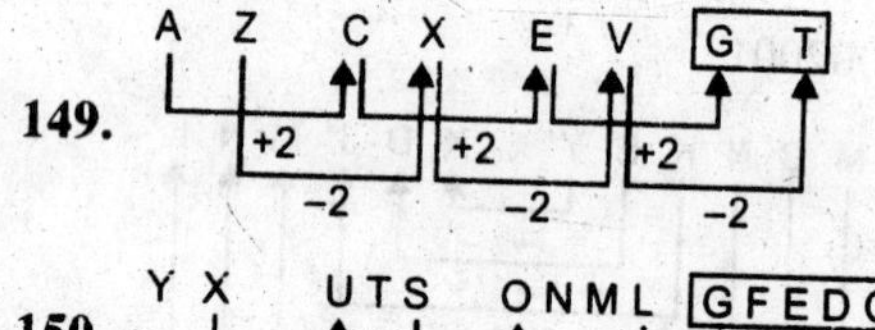

150. Y X UTS ONML GFEDC

−3 −4 −5

Previous Paper (Solved)

Sainik School Entrance Exam, 2018*

(Class-IX)

PAPER-I : Maths, English, General Science & Social Studies

Subject : Mathematics

1. If a number 573 xy is divisible by 90, then what is the value of $x + y$?
A. 6 B. 9
C. 3 D. 8

2. Which of the following numbers is in standard form?
A. $\frac{-24}{52}$ B. $\frac{-49}{71}$
C. $\frac{-27}{48}$ D. $\frac{28}{-105}$

3. What should be added to $\frac{-5}{7}$ to get $\frac{-2}{3}$?
A. $\frac{-29}{21}$ B. $\frac{29}{21}$
C. $\frac{1}{21}$ D. $\frac{-1}{21}$

4. The ages of A and B are in the ratio 5 : 7. Four years from now the ratio of their ages will be 3 : 4. Then the present age of B is:
A. 20 years
B. 28 years
C. 15 years
D. 21 years

5. Two consecutive even numbers are such that half of the larger number exceeds one-fourth of the smaller number by 5. Then the larger number is:
A. 16 B. 18
C. 32 D. 34

6. If 0.25 $(4f - 3)$ = 0.05 $(10f - 9)$, then f is equal to:
A. 0.6 B. 0.8
C. 0.5 D. 0.4

7. A number consists of two digits. The digit in the tens place exceeds the digit in the units place by 4. The sum of the digit is $\frac{1}{7}$ of the number. The number is:
A. 27 B. 72
C. 48 D. 84

8. How many sides does a regular polygon have, wherein, whose interior angle is eight times its exterior angle?
A. 16 B. 24
C. 18 D. 20

9. ABCD is a rectangle with ∠BAC = 48°. Then ∠DBC is equal to:
A. 38° B. 42°
C. 48° D. 132°

10. The angles A, B, C, D of a quadrilateral ABCD taken in order are in the ratio 3 : 7 : 6 : 4, then ABCD is a:
A. Rhombus
B. Parallelogram
C. Trapezium
D. Kite

* Held on 07/01/2018

11. A data set of n observations has mean $2\overline{X}$. While another data set of $2n$ observations has mean $\overline{X}$. Then the mean of the combined data set of $3n$ observations will be:

A. $\overline{X}$ B. $\frac{3}{2}\overline{X}$

C. $\frac{2}{3}\overline{X}$ D. $\frac{4}{3}\overline{X}$

12. In a class of 17 students, six boys failed in a test. Those who passed scored 12, 15, 17, 15, 16, 15, 19, 17, 18, 18 and 19 marks. The median score of 17 students in the class is:

A. 15 B. 16

C. 17 D. 18

13. The mean age of a class is 16 years. If the class teacher aged 40 years old is also included, the mean age increases to 17 years. The number of students in the class is:

A. 23 B. 33

C. 44 D. 16

14. From a well-shuffled deck of 52 cards, one card is drawn at random. What is the probability that the drawn card is a queen?

A. $\frac{1}{4}$ B. $\frac{1}{52}$

C. $\frac{1}{13}$ D. $\frac{1}{26}$

15. Which of the following numbers is not a perfect square?

A. 3600

B. 6400

C. 81000

D. 2500

16. Which least number must be subtracted from 176 to make it a perfect square?

A. 16 B. 7

C. 10 D. 4

17. $\frac{\sqrt{288}}{\sqrt{128}}$ is equal to:

A. $\frac{3}{2}$ B. 1.49

C. $\frac{\sqrt{3}}{2}$ D. $\frac{3}{\sqrt{2}}$

18. The volume of a cubical box is 32.768 cubic metres. Then the length of a side of the box is:

A. 32 m B. 320 m

C. 768 m D. 3.2 m

19. By what least number should 648 be multiplied to get a perfect cube?

A. 3 B. 6

C. 9 D. 18

20. Given that 3048625 = 3375 × 729. Then what is the cube root of 3048625?

A. 155

B. 135

C. 45

D. None of these

21. I borrowed ₹ 12000 from Jamshed at 6% per annum simple interest for 2 years. Had I borrowed this sum at 6% per annum compound interest, what extra amount would I have to pay?

A. ₹ 144 B. ₹ 1440

C. ₹ 72 D. ₹ 43.20

22. During a sale, a shop offered a discount of 10% on the marked price of all the items. What would a customer have to pay for a pair of jeans marked at ₹ 1450 and two shirts marked at ₹ 850 each?

A. ₹ 2835

B. ₹ 3150

C. ₹ 2300

D. None of these

23. If the cost price of 10 greeting cards is equal to the selling price of 8 greeting cards, then the gain or loss % is:

A. Loss of 25%

B. Loss of 20%

C. Gain of 25%

D. Gain of 20%

24. 'A' can do a piece of work in 20 days which 'B' alone can do in 12 days. 'B' worked at it for 9 days then 'A' can finish the remaining work in:

A. 3 days B. 5 days
C. 7 days D. 11 days

25. A car takes 2 hours to reach a destination by travelling at 60 km/hr. How long will it take while travelling at 80 km/hr?

A. 1 hr 30 mins
B. 1 hr 40 mins
C. 2 hrs 40 mins
D. None of these

26. If $x+\frac{1}{x}=5$ then $x^2+\frac{1}{x^2}=?$

A. 25 B. 27
C. 23 D. $25\frac{1}{25}$

27. $(a + 1)(a - 1)(a^2 + 1)$ is equal to:

A. $(a^4 - 2a^2 - 1)$ B. $(a^4 - a^2 - 1)$
C. $(a^4 + 1)$ D. $(a^4 - 1)$

28. $(82)^2 - 18^2$ is equal to:

A. 8218 B. 6418
C. 6400 D. 7204

29. How many edges does a square prism have?

A. 9 B. 12
C. 16 D. 8

30. Three cubes of iron whose edges are 6 cm, 8 cm and 10 cm respectively are melted and formed into a single cube. The edge of the new cube formed is:

A. 12 cm B. 14 cm
C. 16 cm D. 24 cm

31. If the capacity of a cylindrical tank is 1848 m^3 and the diameter of its base is 14 m, the depth of the tank is:

A. 8 m B. 12 m
C. 16 m D. 18 m

32. The edges of a cuboid are in the ratio 1 : 2 : 3 and its surface area is 88 cm^2. The volume of the cuboid is:

A. 64 cm^3 B. 96 cm^3
C. 120 cm^3 D. 48 cm^3

33. The parallel sides of a trapezium are in the ratio 4 : 3 and the perpendicular distance between them is 12 cm. If the area of the trapezium is 630 cm^2, then its shorter of the parallel side is:

A. 45 cm B. 42 cm
C. 60 cm D. 36 cm

34. The base of a triangle is four times its height and its area is 50 m^2. The length of its base is:

A. 10 m B. 15 m
C. 20 m D. 25 m

35. $\frac{3^n.3^{2n+1}}{9^n.3^{n-1}}$ is equal to:

A. 1 B. 9
C. 3 D. 3^n

36. $4^{3.5} : 2^5$ is the same as:

A. 4 : 1 B. 2 : 1
C. 7 : 5 D. 7 : 10

37. If $a = b^{2/3}$, and $b = c^{-2}$, then what is the value of a in terms of c?

A. $\frac{4}{c^3}$ B. $\sqrt[3]{c^4}$
C. $\frac{1}{\sqrt[3]{c^4}}$ D. $\sqrt[4]{c^3}$

Refer the following graph for Q. Nos. 38 to 42.

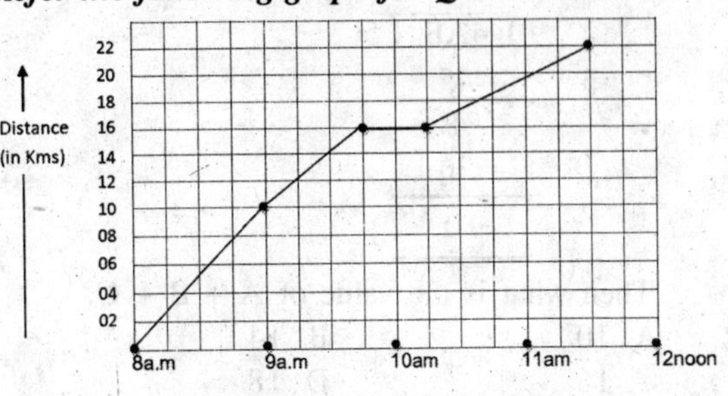

A courier–person cycles from a town to a neighbouring suburban area to deliver a parcel to a merchant. His distance from the town at different times is shown by the above graph?

38. What is the scale taken for the time axis?
A. 2 units = 1 hour
B. 1 unit = 2 hours
C. 1 unit = 4 hours
D. 4 units = 1 hours

39. How much time did the person take for the travel?

A. 2 hours B. $2\frac{1}{2}$ hours

C. $3\frac{1}{2}$ hours D. 4 hours

40. How far is the place of the merchant from town?
A. 11 km
B. 22 km
C. 13 km
D. 26 km

41. When did the person stop on the way?
A. between 8 am and 9 am
B. between 9 am and 10 am
C. between 10 am and 10.30 am
D. between 10.30 am and 11.30 am

42. During which period did he ride the fatest?
A. between 8 am and 9 am
B. between 9 am and 10 am
C. between 10 am and 10.30 am
D. between 10.30 am and 11.30 am

43. Find the values of A, B, C in the following:

```
9 ) 4AB ( 5C
  - 45
  ----
    3B
  - 36
  ----
     0
  ----
```

Then what is the value of A + B + C?
A. 10 B. 14
C. 16 D. 18

44. If y denotes the digit at hundreds place of the number $67y$ 19, such that the number is divisible by 11. The value of y is:
A. 3 B. 5
C. 4 D. 7

45. Find three whole numbers a, b and c such that $a + b + c = a \times b \times c$, then what is the value of $a^2 + b^2 + c^2$?
A. 14 B. 15
C. 16 D. 17

46. $3 + 23y - 8y^2$ is equal to:
A. $(1 - 8y)(3 + y)$
B. $(1 + 8y)(3 - y)$
C. $(1 - 8y)(y - 3)$
D. $(8y - 1)(y + 3)$

47. A motor car starts with a speed of 70 km/hr with its speed increasing every 2 hrs by 10 km/hr. In how many hours will it cover 345 km?

A. $2\frac{1}{4}$ hours

B. 4 hours 5 minutes

C. $4\frac{1}{2}$ hours

D. 3 hours

48. $\left(\frac{1}{4}x^2 - \frac{1}{2}x - 12\right) \div \left(\frac{1}{2}x - 4\right)$ is equal to:

A. $\left(x + \frac{3}{2}\right)$ B. $\left(\frac{1}{2}x - 3\right)$

C. $(2x + 3)$ D. $\left(\frac{1}{2}x + 3\right)$

49. 1200 soldiers in a fort had enough food for 28 days. After 4 days, some soldiers were transferred to another fort and thus the food lasted now for 32 more days. How many soldiers left the fort?
A. 300 B. 400
C. 200 D. 100

50. If the perimeter of an isosceles right triangle is $\left(6 + 3\sqrt{2}\right)$m, then the area of the triangle is:
A. 5.4 m^2
B. 81 m^2
C. 9 m^2
D. 4.5 m^2

English Language

51. The correctly punctuated sentence is:

A. He asked me, "whether I had done my work".

B. He asked me, "whether I had done my work"?

C. He asked me whether I had done my work?

D. He asked me whether I had done my work.

52. Which of the following will be the correct indirect speech if the statement given below is changed into it?

He said, "I shall leave these papers here."

A. He said that he would leave those papers there.

B. He said that he should leave those papers there.

C. He said that he would leave these papers there.

D. He said that he would leave those papers here.

53. The correct passive form of the following sentence is:

They asked me my name.

A. My name was asked me by them.

B. I was asked my name.

C. Me was asked my name by them.

D. My name was asked from them.

54. The correct meaning of the word 'calamity' is:

A. disaster
B. scourge
C. harm
D. injury

55. 'Red Letter Day' means:

A. a dangerous day

B. a rosy day

C. an important day

D. a bloody day

56. The correct antonym of the word 'assets' is:

A. liabilities

B. estate

C. responsibilities

D. hindrances

57. The plural form of 'alumnus' is:

A. alumnuses
B. alumna
C. alumnae
D. alumni

58. 'Alma Mater' is the place where one:

A. studied
B. married
C. died
D. was born

59. Identify the part which contains an error in the following sentence.

Ten miles are not a long distance.

A. ten miles

B. are not

C. a long distance

D. no error

60. Choose the correct order to make the sentence below meaningful.

(1) History of India/(2) than/(3) was there a/ (4) Mahatma Gandhi/(5) never in the/ (6) greater man.

A. 124356
B. 634521
C. 513126
D. 513624

61. Fill in the blank with a suitable Phrase Preposition.

He accepted the car .... his claim for ₹ 3,25,000.

A. on account of

B. by dint of

C. in lieu of

D. because of

62. The suitable prefix for the word "bitter" is:

A. im
B. in
C. un
D. em

63. Fill in the blank with a suitable Conjunction.

He is slow, ... he is sure.

A. and
B. for
C. but
D. or

64. Complete the following maxim.

Genius without education is like silver in the ....

A. shop B. mine
C. Well D. pit

65. Select the word that is opposite in meaning to the underlined word.

My first lecture in the classroom was a fiasco.

A. success B. joy
C. fun D. disaster

66. The right suffix for the word 'just' to make it an abstract noun is:

A. - ly B. - ify
C. - ice D. - ing

67. Select the word that is similar in meaning to the underlined word.

The requisite energy is derived from the battery.

A. insignificant
B. necessary
C. different
D. special

68. Select the word that is similar in meaning to the underlined word.

His candid opinion has won him many friends.

A. kind
B. courteous
C. generous
D. frank

69. Select the word that is opposite in meaning to the underlined word.

Everyone agreed that it was a piece of meticulous research.

A. careless
B. careful
C. cautious
D. scrupulous

70. The word 'avert' means:

A. avoid B. fall
C. hatred D. degenerate

71. The adjective form of 'boast' is:

A. boastful
B. boastly
C. boasty
D. boastile

Direction: *Read the following passage and answer the questions that follow.*

Vehicles do not move about the roads for mysterious reasons of their own. They move only because people want them to move in connection with the activities which the people are engaged in. Traffic is therefore a 'function of activities', and because, in towns, activities mainly take place in buildings, traffic in towns is a 'function of buildings'. The implications of this line of reasoning are inescapable.

72. Line 1 of the passage means that the vehicles move on the roads:

A. for reasons difficult to explain.
B. to serve specific purposes of people.
C. in a haphazard fashion.
D. in ways beyond our control.

73. The author says that traffic is a 'function of activities'. He means that:

A. human activities are taking place.
B. human activities are dependent on traffic.
C. traffic is not dependent on human activities.
D. traffic is connected with human activities.

74. The author suggests by his argument that:

A. to regulate traffic, more policemen have to be employed.
B. to regulate activities, traffic has to be controlled.
C. to regulate traffic, buildings have to be taken into consideration.
D. to understand the traffic problem, we must examine the social context in which it is found.

75. By 'this line of reasoning', the author means:

A. idea contained in this line.
B. idea contained in any one line of his argument.
C. the manner of arguing.
D. this row of printed characters.

Subject: General Science

76. Tungsten (a transition element) being a metal exhibits the following properties:

I. It is sonorous
II. It possesses high tensile strength
III. It possesses high melting point
IV. It has high density

Which of the above property/properties of Tungsten made it a suitable material for the filament of an electric bulb?

A. I, II and III
B. II and III
C. Only III
D. II, III and IV

77. Hepatitis-B is caused due to:

A. Virus
B. Protozoa
C. Bacteria
D. Fungi

78. The production of an exact copy of an animal by asexual reproduction is known as:

A. Cloning
B. Mating
C. Budding
D. Hatching

79. The device which can be used to detect very small current following in an electric circuit is:

A. LEAD
B. MCB
C. LED
D. None of these

80. Which of these unicellular organisms has no definite shape?

A. Amoeba
B. Paramecium
C. Euglena
D. Bacteria

81. Which is a thermosetting plastic?

A. Polythene
B. Melamine
C. PVC
D. Nylon

82. Solution of which of the following oxides in water will change the colour of blue litmus to red?

A. Sulphur dioxide
B. Magnesium oxide
C. Iron oxide
D. Copper oxide

83. In India, PCRA advises how to save petrol/diesel while driving. For this, PCRA gave several tips. Here, PCRA stands for:

A. Pollution Control Research Association
B. Petroleum Conservation Research Association
C. Petroleum Collection and Reserve Association
D. None of the above

84. An electrolyte is:

A. a metal
B. a solution
C. a liquid that conducts current
D. All of the above

85. As the angle between two plane mirrors is decreasing gradually, the number of images of an object placed between them:

A. first increases then decreases
B. first decreases then increases
C. increases
D. decreases

86. Purest form of carbon is:

A. Coal
B. Charcoal
C. Coke
D. All of these

87. Value of one light year in S.I unit is:

A. 1.5×10^{11} m
B. 9.46×10^{15} m
C. 1.5×10^{15} m
D. 9.46×10^{12} m

88. Which of the following liquids does not conduct electricity?

I. Lemon juice
II. Sugar solution
III. Distilled water
IV. Dilute Hydrochloric acid

A. I, II, and IV
B. Only III
C. Only IV
D. III and IV

89. I- Fungi, II- Bacteria

Consider the following statements and find the correct one:

A. II are small prokaryotes while I are large celled eukaryotes with defined mitochondria and other organelles.

B. I have a sexual reproduction through conjugation and transformation but II through genetic recombination.

C. II have a sexual reproduction through conjugation and transformation but I through genetic recombination.

D. All of the above

90. When the applied force is doubled and the object is still at rest, friction becomes:

A. doubled

B. halved

C. quadrupled

D. zero

91. Oxides of which element(s) is/are present in acid rain?

I. Carbon

II. Nitrogen

III. Sulphur

A. I and II
B. II and III
C. I and III
D. I, II and III

92. Which of the following tools would a farmer use to remove weeds from the field?

A. Hoe
B. Plough
C. Axe
D. Cultivator

93. .... are the smallest micro-organisms which can develop only inside the cell of the .... Organism. They do not respire, feed, grow, excrete or move on their own but they cannot .... When they are outside the .... cell, they behave as ....

Choose the correct order to fill in the blanks:

A. Bacteria, Host, Multiply, Animal, Living

B. Virus, Bacteria , Reproduce, Living, Non-living

C. Virus, Host, Exchange gases, Living, Non-living

D. Virus, Host, Reproduce, Living, Non-living

94. In the process of vulcanisation, Natural rubber is treated with an element X to improve its properties.

The element X can be:

A. Carbon
B. Nitrogen
C. Sulphur
D. Phosphorus

95. The standard value of atmospheric pressure is:

A. 78 cm of Hg

B. 76 mm of Hg

C. 45 cm of Hg

D. 0.76 cm of Hg

96. The sound from a mosquito is produced when it vibrates its wings at an average rate of 500 vibrations per second. What is the time period of vibration?

A. 2 s
B. 0.002 s
C. 0.02 s
D. 0.2 s

97. The change in focal length of an eye lens to focus the image of objects at varying distances is done by the action of:

A. Pupil
B. Iris
C. Retina
D. Ciliary muscles

98. Which cell organelle is called the Power House of a cell?

A. Lysosomes
B. Golgi bodies
C. Mitochondria
D. Ribosomes

99. The dramatic changes in body features associated with puberty are mainly because of the secretions of:

I. Thyroxine

II. Estrogen

III. Adrenalin

IV. Testosterone

A. I and II
B. II and III
C. I and III
D. II and IV

100. The earth rotates around its axis. The sun appears to rise in the east. Venus rotates in the opposite direction of Earth. We can therefore assume that on Venus, the sun sets in the:

A. East
B. West
C. North
D. South

Subject: Social Science

101. Who became the Nawab of Bengal after the death of Alivardi Khan?
A. Murshid Quli Khan
B. Mir Jafar
C. Sirajuddaulah
D. Mir Qasim

102. FIR means:
A. Final Information Report
B. First Information Report
C. Full Information Report
D. First Investigation Report

103. How many MPs are elected to the Rajya Sabha?
A. 272
B. 250
C. 245
D. 233

104. What is the meaning of 'media sets the agenda'?
A. Media supports the government
B. Media directs the people to agitate
C. Media shapes our thoughts by giving more importance to some issues
D. Media criticizes the government

105. The process in which different crops are grown in alternate rows is known as:
A. Crop rotation
B. Intercropping
C. Terrace farming
D. Contour cropping

106. Which of the following statements is/are correct?
1. 'Diwani' is the right to collect revenue
2. 'Faujdari adalat' refers to a civil court
3. Richard Wellesley implemented the Subsidiary Alliance

Select the correct answer using the codes given below:
A. 1 only
B. 1, 2 and 3
C. 1 and 3 only
D. 2 and 3 only

107. Which type of farming is practised to meet the needs of a farmer's family?
A. Subsistence Farming
B. Organic Farming
C. Commercial Farming
D. Mixed Farming

108. Biotic resources are:
A. made by human beings
B. derived from living things
C. derived from non-living things
D. None of the above

109. Separation of religion from the state means:
A. Communalism
B. Democracy
C. Secularism
D. All of the above

110. Arrange the following events of the Indian Freedom Movement in correct sequence beginning from the earliest:
1. The Non-Cooperation Movement
2. Quit India Movement
3. The Rowlatt Satyagraha
4. The March to Dandi

Select the correct answer using the code given below:
A. 3-1-4-2
B. 1-2-3-4
C. 3-1-2-4
D. 1-3-2-4

111. The Young Bengal Movement was led by:
A. Swami Vivekananda
B. Keshab Chandra Sen
C. William Jones
D. Henry Louis Vivian Derozio

112. .... refers to the court declaring that a person is not guilty of the crime which he/she was tried for by the court.

A. Appeal
B. Acquit
C. Accuse
D. None of these

113. Which of the following pairs is NOT correctly matched?

1. Nana Saheb — Kanpur
2. Rani Lakshmibai — Jhansi
3. Kunwar Singh — Lucknow
4. Bakht Khan — Delhi

Select the correct answer using the codes given below:
A. 1 and 3
B. 3 only
C. 4 only
D. 2 and 3

114. Which one of the following is a leading producer of copper in the world?
A. Bolivia
B. Ghana
C. Peru
D. Zimbabwe

115. AMUL stands for:
A. Anand Milk Union Limited
B. Anand Milk United Limited
C. Anand Mazdoor Union Limited
D. Ahmedabad Milk Union Limited

116. How many permanent members are there in the UN Security Council?
A. Three
B. Four
C. Five
D. Six

117. Cultivation on planter's own land was referred to as:
A. Ryoti
B. Mahalwari
C. Batai
D. Nij

118. Which of the following is a secondary activity?
A. Transport
B. Farming
C. Obtaining sugar from sugarcane
D. Bee keeping

119. Which one of the following is not a factor of soil formation?
A. Topography
B. Soil texture
C. Climate
D. Time

120. Viceroy .... partitioned Bengal in 1905.
A. Curzon
B. Minto
C. Irwin
D. Mountbatten

121. The leaders of the Khilafat agitation were:
A. Sayyid brothers
B. Ali brothers
C. Both A and B
D. None of these

122. Which of the following is not a fundamental right of citizens of India?
A. Right to equality
B. Right to education
C. Right to property
D. Right to freedom

123. To complain about the problem of hygiene & sanitation, a person living in a big city should go to:
A. Municipal Corporation
B. Municipal Committee
C. Nagar Panchayat
D. Zila Parishad

124. The Supreme Court was established on:
A. 26 January, 1950
B. 15 August, 1947
C. 26 November, 1949
D. 15 August, 1950

125. Which one of the following refers to the tomb of a Sufi Saint?
A. Idgah
B. Khanqah
C. Dargah
D. None of these

PAPER-II

Intelligence Test

Directions: *Choose the letters group that best represents a relationship similar to the one expressed in the original pair of letters groups.*

126. WINTER : IWTNRE :: LACSAP : ?
A. PASCAL B. SPLACA
C. ALSCPA D. LACSPA

127. GDLM : IBNK :: XSOH : ?
A. ZQQF B. WTMO
C. APQF D. ZQLF

128. TQW is to MJP as ZHN is to:
A. SAG B. GSA
C. YGM D. TEG

129. WEIGHT is related to KILOGRAM in the same way as DISTANCE is related to:
A. GRAM
B. POUND
C. LENGTH
D. KILOMETER

Directions: *Which number completes the second pair in the same way as the first pair?*

130. 26 : 5 :: 65 : ?
A. 6 B. 7
C. 8 D. 9

131. 16 : 56 :: 36 : ?
A. 96 B. 112
C. 118 D. 128

Directions: *In the given series, find the next/missing term.*

132. AT, BS, CR, DQ, ?
A. EP B. FP
C. ED D. EN

133. 4, 9, 16, 25, ?, 49
A. 50 B. 36
C. 64 D. 39

134. 0, 1, ?, 27, 64
A. 16 B. 32
C. 4 D. 8

135. A 5, C 10, E 15, G 20, ?
A. H 30 B. I 30
C. I 25 D. H 25

136. Insert a letter which completes both the words given below:

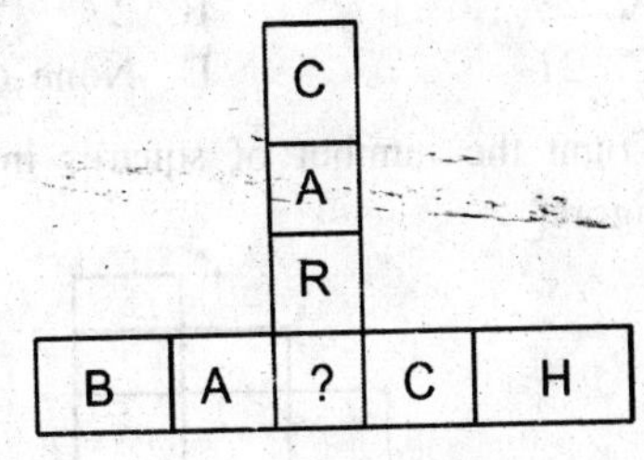

A. T B. K
C. V D. L

137. Insert the missing terms in the figure, so that the word formed is the name of a country when read clockwise direction.

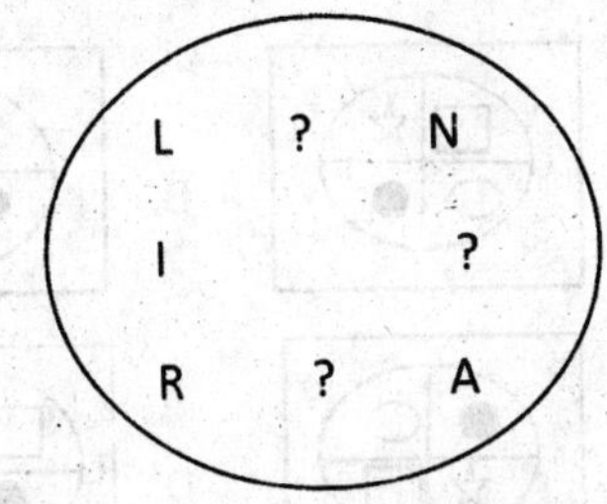

A. SAA B. SAK
C. APR D. PLC

138. Find the number that replaces the question mark.

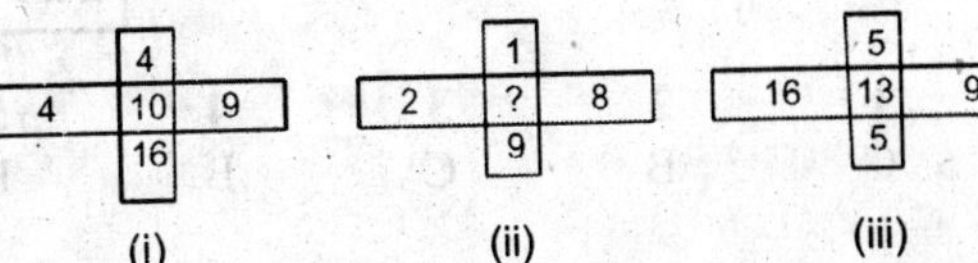

A. 12 B. 6
C. 5 D. 7

139. In a class of 30 students, Swati's rank is 11th from the top, what is her rank from the bottom?
A. 19th B. 20th
C. 22nd D. 21st

140. Ritu walks 50 m towards East, then turns to her right and walks 50 m, now she turns left and walks another 50 m, now again she turns left and walks another 50 m. In which direction is she from the starting point?
A. East B. North
C. North-East D. South-West

141. Find the fourth proportional to 3, 7 and 9.
A. 23 B. 27
C. 21 D. None of these

142. Count the number of squares in the given figure:

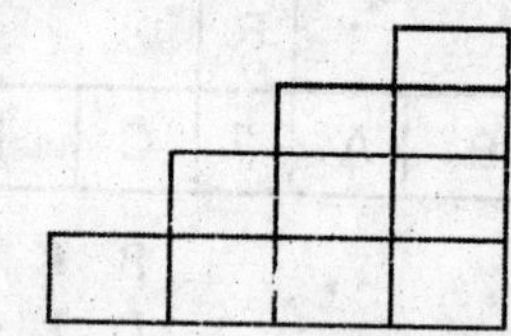

A. 14 B. 13
C. 10 D. None of these

143. Choose the figure, which is different from others.

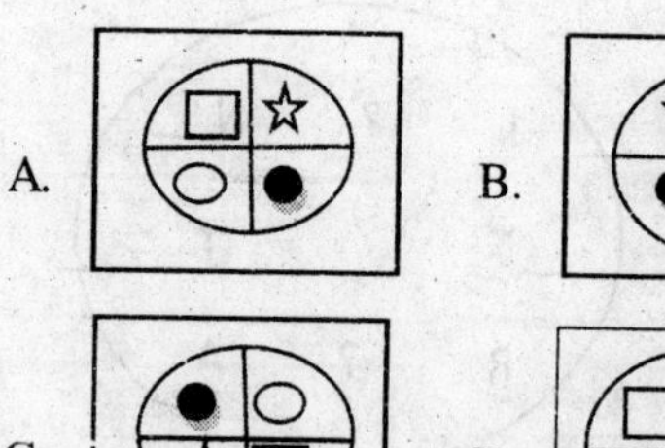

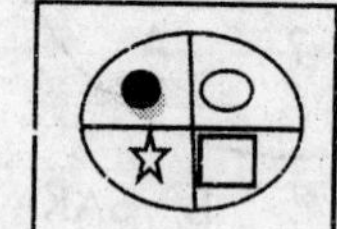

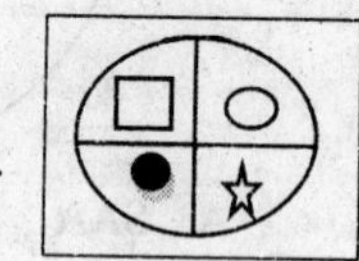

144. What is the sequence of the following when arranged in a dictionary?
A. Telegraph B. Telephone
C. Teleprinter D. Telemetry

145. CLOCK is 42145, LEAN is 2068.
CARE is 4690, then NECKLACE is
A. 80546240
B. 6054842
C. 80452640
D. 50842604

146. Which among the following year is a leap year?
A. 2500 B. 2800
C. 2600 D. 2700

Directions: *In each of the following questions, find the word which can not be made from the letters of the given word.*

147. CARPENTER
A. NECTAR B. CARPET
C. PAINTER D. REPENT

148. REASONABLE
A. BRAIN B. BONES
C. NOBLE D. ARSON

149. If '÷' stands for '×', '×' stands for '+', '+' stands for '–', then what is the value of $7 \div 21 \times 81 + 9 - 3 \times 14$?
A. 21 B. 24
C. 27 D. 28

150. Determine the term that would replace the question mark.

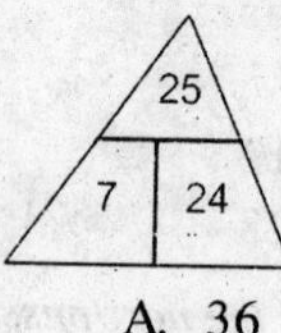

5
3 4

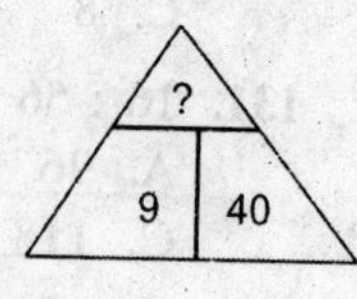

A. 36 B. 41
C. 35 D. 45

ANSWERS

1	2	3	4	5	6	7	8	9	10
C	B	C	B	B	A	D	C	B	C

11	12	13	14	15	16	17	18	19	20
D	A	A	C	C	B	A	D	C	B
21	22	23	24	25	26	27	28	29	30
D	A	C	B	A	C	D	C	B	A
31	32	33	34	35	36	37	38	39	40
B	D	A	C	B	A	C	D	C	B
41	42	43	44	45	46	47	48	49	50
C	A	D	C	A	B	C	D	A	D
51	52	53	54	55	56	57	58	59	60
D	A	B	A	C	A	D	A	B	D
61	62	63	64	65	66	67	68	69	70
C	D	C	B	A	C	B	D	A	A
71	72	73	74	75	76	77	78	79	80
A	B	D	D	C	C	A	A	C	A
81	82	83	84	85	86	87	88	89	90
B	A	B	B	C	C	B	B	A	A
91	92	93	94	95	96	97	98	99	100
D	A	D	C	B	B	D	C	D	A
101	102	103	104	105	106	107	108	109	110
C	B	D	C	B	C	A	B	C	A
111	112	113	114	115	116	117	118	119	120
D	B	B	C	A	C	D	C	B	A
121	122	123	124	125	126	127	128	129	130
B	C	A	A	C	C	A	A	D	C
131	132	133	134	135	136	137	138	139	140
B	A	B	D	C	A	B	C	B	A
141	142	143	144	145	146	147	148	149	150
C	B	D	C	C	B	C	A	C	B

EXPLANATORY ANSWERS

1. 57330 is divisible by 90

$5 + 7 + 3 + 3 = 18$ which is divisible by 9

$\therefore x = 3, y = 0$

Hence, $x + y = 3 + 0 = 3$

2. $\frac{-49}{71}$ is in standard form because it is in the lowest term.

3. $\frac{-5}{7} + x = -\frac{2}{3}$

$$\Rightarrow \quad x = -\frac{2}{3} + \frac{5}{7}$$

$$= \frac{-14+15}{21}$$

$$= \frac{1}{21}.$$

4. Let present age of A be $5x$ and present age of B be $7x$

After 4 years,

$$\frac{5x+4}{7x+4} = \frac{3}{4}$$

$\Rightarrow \quad 21x + 12 = 20x + 16$

$\Rightarrow \quad x = 4$

$\therefore$ Present age of B = 7 × 4 = 28 years.

5. Let two consecutive even numbers be x and $x + 2$

According to the question,

$$\frac{1}{2}(x+2) = \frac{1}{4}x+5$$

$\Rightarrow \quad \frac{x+2}{2} = \frac{x+20}{4}$

$\Rightarrow \quad 4x + 8 = 2x + 40$

$\Rightarrow \quad 2x = 32$

$\Rightarrow \quad x = 16$

$x + 2 = 16 + 2$

$= 18$

$\therefore$ Larger number = 18.

6. $0.25(4f - 3) = 0.5(10f - 9)$

$\Rightarrow \quad \frac{25}{100}(4f-3) = \frac{5}{100}(10f-9)$

$\Rightarrow \quad 5(4f - 3) = 10f - 9$

$\Rightarrow \quad 20f - 15 = 10f - 9$

$\Rightarrow \quad 10f = 6$

$\Rightarrow \quad f = \frac{6}{10}$

$= 0.6.$

7. Let ten's place digit number be x and unit's place digit number be y

$\therefore$ Number = $10x + y$

$x = y + 4$

$\Rightarrow \quad x - y = 4 \quad ...(i)$

$\Rightarrow \quad x + y = \frac{1}{7}(10x + y)$

$\Rightarrow \quad 7x + 7y = 10x + y$

$\Rightarrow \quad 3x - 6y = 0 \quad ...(ii)$

From (*i*) and (*ii*),

$x - y = 4 \;]\times 3$

$3x - 6y = 0 \;]\times 1$

$3x - 3y = 12$

$3x - 6y = 0$

$- \quad + \quad -$

$3y = 12$

$\Rightarrow \quad y = 12$

$\because \quad x - y = 4$

$x - 4 = 4$

$\Rightarrow \quad x = 8$

$\therefore$ Number = $10x + y$ = 84.

9.

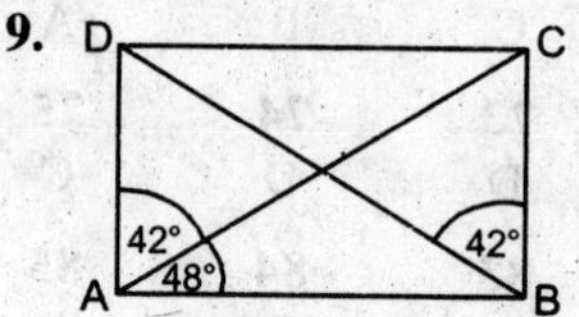

$\because$ ABCD is a rectangle

$\because \quad \angle BAC = 48°$

$\therefore \quad \angle DBC = 42°.$

10.

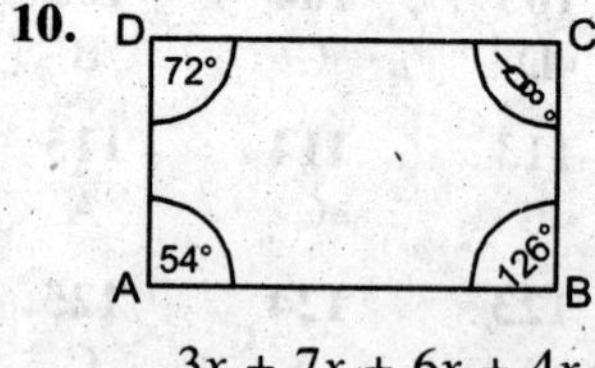

$3x + 7x + 6x + 4x = 360°$

$\Rightarrow \quad 20x = 360°$

$\Rightarrow \quad x = 18°$

A = 54°, B = 126°, C = 108°, D = 72°

$\because$ AB || CD but AD ∦ CD

$\therefore$ ABCD is trapezium.

12. Total students = 17 which is odd number

$\therefore$ Median = $\left(\frac{n+1}{2}\right)$th term = 9th term

$\because$ 6 boys failed who got less than 12

Marks written in increasing order

12, 15, 15, 15, 16, 17, 17, 18, 18, 19, 19

Hence, median = 9th term = 15.

13. Let number of students in the class be x

Total age of x students = $16x$

According to the question,

$17(x + 1) - 16x = 40$

$\Rightarrow 17x + 17 - 16x = 40$

$\Rightarrow x = 40 - 17$

$= 23$

$\therefore$ Number of the students = 23.

14. Required probability $= \dfrac{4}{52} = \dfrac{1}{13}$.

15. The number 81000 is not a perfect square.

$\sqrt{3600} = 60, \ \sqrt{6400} = 80, \ \sqrt{2500} = 50$.

16.

1	176	13
	1	
23	×76	
	69	
26	×7	

Hence, the required least no. = 7

If 7 is subtracted from 176, then it becomes a perfect square.

17. $\dfrac{\sqrt{288}}{\sqrt{128}} = \dfrac{12\sqrt{2}}{8\sqrt{2}} = \dfrac{3}{2}$.

18. Length of a side of the box

$= \sqrt[3]{32.768}$

$= \sqrt[3]{\dfrac{32768}{1000}}$

$= \dfrac{32}{10}$

$= 3.2$ m.

19. $648 = \underline{2 \times 2 \times 2} \times \underline{3 \times 3 \times 3} \times 3$

If we multiply 648 by 9 then it becomes a perfect cube.

Hence, least no. = 9.

20. $\because 3048625 = 3375 \times 729$

$= 5 \times 5 \times 5 \times 3 \times 3 \times 3 \times 9 \times 9 \times 9$

$\therefore \sqrt[3]{3048625}$

$= \sqrt[3]{5 \times 5 \times 5 \times 3 \times 3 \times 3 \times 9 \times 9 \times 9}$

$= 5 \times 3 \times 9$

$= 135$

Hence, cube root of 3048625 = 135.

21. S.I. $= \dfrac{12000 \times 6 \times 2}{100} =$ ₹ 1440

$A = p\left(1 + \dfrac{r}{100}\right)^t$

$= 12000\left(1 + \dfrac{6}{100}\right)^2$

$= 12000 \times \dfrac{53}{50} \times \dfrac{53}{50}$

$= \dfrac{67416}{5}$

$= 13483.20$

$\therefore$ C.I. = 13483.20 − 12000 = 1483.20

$\therefore$ C.I. − S.I. = 1483.20 − 1440 = 43.20

Required extra amount paid = ₹ 43.20.

22. 1450 + (2 × 850) = 1450 + 1700 = ₹ 3150

Discount $= \dfrac{10}{100} \times 3150 =$ ₹ 315

Amount paid = 3150 − 315 = ₹ 2835.

23. 10 − 8 = 2

Profit % $= \dfrac{2}{8} \times 100 = 25\%$.

24. A's 1 day work $= \dfrac{1}{20}$

B's 1 day work $= \dfrac{1}{12}$

B's 9 days work $= \dfrac{1}{12} \times 9 = \dfrac{3}{4}$ part

Remaining work $= 1 - \dfrac{3}{4} = \dfrac{1}{4}$ part

$\because \dfrac{1}{20}$ part A can do in 1 day

$\therefore \frac{1}{4}$ part A can do in $20 \times \frac{1}{4} = 5$ days

Hence, A can finish the remaining work in 5 days.

25. Distance covered by car in 2 hours

$= 60 \times 2$

$= 120$ km.

Time taken $= \frac{120}{80}$

$= \frac{3}{2}$ hrs.

$= 1\frac{1}{2}$ hrs.

$= 1$ hr 30 minutes.

26. $x^2 + \frac{1}{x^2} = \left(x + \frac{1}{x}\right)^2 - 2x\frac{1}{x}$

$= (5)^2 - 2$

$= 25 - 2 = 23$

Hence, the value of $x^2 + \frac{1}{x^2} = 23$.

27. $(a + 1)(a - 1)(a^2 + 1)$

$= (a^2 - 1)(a^2 + 1)$

$= a^4 - 1$.

28. $(82)^2 - (18)^2 = (82 + 18)(82 - 18)$

$= 100 \times 64$

$= 6400$.

30. Total volume of three iron cubes

$= 6^3 + 8^3 + 10^3$

$= 216 + 512 + 1000$

$= 1728$ cm^3

Now, volume of new cube $= 1728$

$\therefore$ Side of new cube $= \sqrt[3]{1728}$

$= \sqrt[3]{12 \times 12 \times 12}$

$= 12$ cm.

Hence, the edge of the new cube $= 12$ cm.

31. Volume of cylinder $= \pi r^2 h$

$\Rightarrow \quad 1848 = \frac{22}{7} \times 7 \times 7 \times h$

$\Rightarrow \quad h = \frac{1848}{22 \times 7}$

$= 12$ m.

Hence, depth of the tank $= 12$ m.

32. Suppose, $l = 1x$, $b = 2x$ and $h = 3x$

Surface area of cuboid $= 2(lb + bh + hl)$

$\Rightarrow \quad 2(2x^2 + 6x^2 + 3x^2) = 88$

$\Rightarrow \quad 22x^2 = 88$

$\Rightarrow \quad x^2 = 4$

$\Rightarrow \quad x = 2$

$\therefore l = 2$ cm, $b = 4$ cm and $h = 6$ cm.

Volume of cuboid $= l \times b \times h$

$= 2 \times 4 \times 6 = 48$ cm^3.

33.

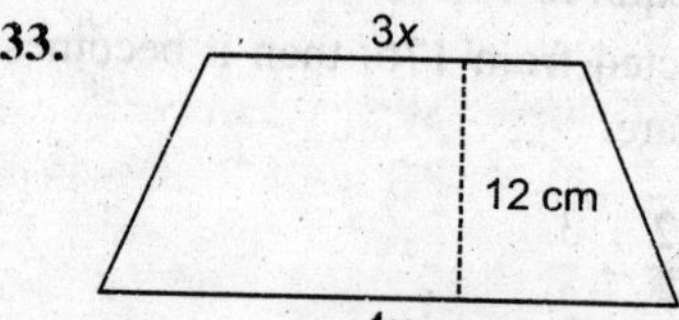

Area $= \frac{1}{2}(3x + 4x) \times 12$

$\Rightarrow \quad 630 = 7x \times 6$

$\Rightarrow \quad x = \frac{630}{7 \times 6}$

$= 15$

$3x = 3 \times 15$

$= 45$ cm

$4x = 4 \times 15$

$= 60$ cm

Hence, the shorter of the parallel side = 45 cm.

34. Suppose, the height of triangle $= x$ m.

$\therefore$ Base of the triangle $= 4x$ m

Area $= \frac{1}{2} \times 4x \times x$

$\Rightarrow \quad 50 = 2x^2$

$\Rightarrow \qquad x^2 = 25$

$\Rightarrow \qquad x = 5$

Hence, base of the triangle = $4x$

$= 4 \times 5 = 20$ cm.

35. $\dfrac{3^n . 3^{2n+1}}{9^n . 3^{n-1}} = \dfrac{3^{2n+1+n}}{(3^2)^n . 3^{n-1}}$

$= \dfrac{3^{3n+1}}{3^{2n+n-1}}$

$= \dfrac{3^{3n+1}}{3^{3n-1}}$

$= 3^{3n+1-3n+1}$

$= 3^2$

$= 9.$

36. $4^{3.5} : 2^5 = (2^2)^{3.5} : 2^5$

$= 2^7 : 2^5$

$= 2^{7-5}$

$= 2^2$

$= 4.$

$= 4 : 1.$

37. $\because \qquad a = b^{2/3}$

$= \left(\dfrac{1}{c^2}\right)^{2/3}$

$= \dfrac{1}{c^{4/3}}$

$= \dfrac{1}{\sqrt[3]{c^4}}$

Hence, the value of a in terms of $c = \dfrac{1}{\sqrt[3]{c^4}}$

43. Clearly,

A = 8 [$\because$ A – 5 = 3 $\because$ A = 8]

B = 6 [$\because$ B – 6 = 0 $\Rightarrow$ B = 6]

C = 4 [9 × C = 36 $\Rightarrow$ C = 4]

$\therefore$ A + B + C = 8 + 6 + 4 = 18.

44. 67 y 19

$\because$ The given number is divisible by 11

$\therefore$ Put $y = 4$

$6 + 4 + 9 = 19$

$7 + 1 = 8$

$19 - 8 = 11$

Which is multiple of 11.

Hence, the value of $y = 4$.

45. $\because \qquad a + b + c = a \times b \times c$

$\Rightarrow \qquad 1 + 2 + 3 = 1 \times 2 \times 3$

$\therefore \qquad a^2 + b^2 + c^2 = (1)^2 + (2)^2 + (3)^2$

$= 1 + 4 + 9$

$= 14$

Hence, the value of $a^2 + b^2 + c^2 = 14$.

46. $-8y^2 + 23y + 3$

$= -8y^2 + 24y - y + 3$

$= -8y(y - 3) - 1(y - 3)$

$= (y - 3)(-8y - 1)$

$= (1 + 8y)(3 - y)$

47.

Distance	Time
70 × 2 = 140 km	2 hrs.
80 × 2 = 160 km	2 hrs.
$90 \times \dfrac{1}{2} = 45$ km	$\dfrac{1}{2}$ hrs.

Total distance = 345 km, time = $4\dfrac{1}{2}$ hrs.

Hence, total distance 345 km covered in $4\dfrac{1}{2}$ hrs.

48. $\dfrac{1}{2}x - 4 \overline{\Big) \dfrac{1}{4}x^2 - \dfrac{1}{2}x - 12 \Big(} \dfrac{1}{2}x + 3$

$\dfrac{1}{4}x^2 - 2x$

$- \quad +$

$\dfrac{3}{2}x - 12$

$\dfrac{3}{2}x - 12$

$- \quad +$

Hence, required answer = $\left(\dfrac{1}{2}x + 3\right)$.

49. 28 days – 4 days = 24 days

In 24 days food lasted by 1200 soldiers

In 1 day food lasted by 1200 × 24 soldiers

In 32 days food lasted by $\frac{1200 \times 24}{32}$ soldiers

= 900 soldiers

No. of soldiers who left the fort

= 1200 – 900 = 300.

50.

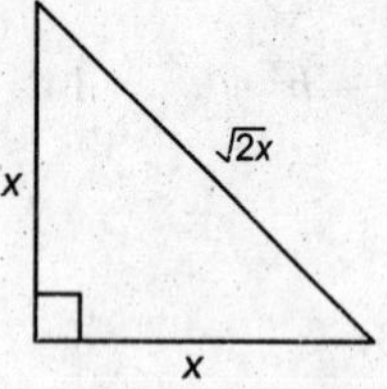

$$x + x + \sqrt{2}x = 6 + 3\sqrt{2}$$

$$\Rightarrow \quad 2x + \sqrt{2}x = 6 + 3\sqrt{2}$$

$$\Rightarrow \quad x(2 + \sqrt{2}) = 3(2 + \sqrt{2})$$

$$\Rightarrow \quad x = 3\left(\frac{2 + \sqrt{2}}{2 + \sqrt{2}}\right)$$

$$= 3$$

Area of triangle $= \frac{1}{2} \times b \times h$

$$= \frac{1}{2} \times 3 \times 3$$

$$= \frac{9}{2} \text{ m}^2$$

$$= 4.5 \text{ m}^2.$$

126. Given

WI NT ER : IW TN RE

There are three sets of letters, *i.e.*, WI, NT and ER, where each first and second letter is changing place mutually.

Similarly,

LA CS AP : AL SC PA

In LA, CS and AP the letters are changing place mutually.

127. Given

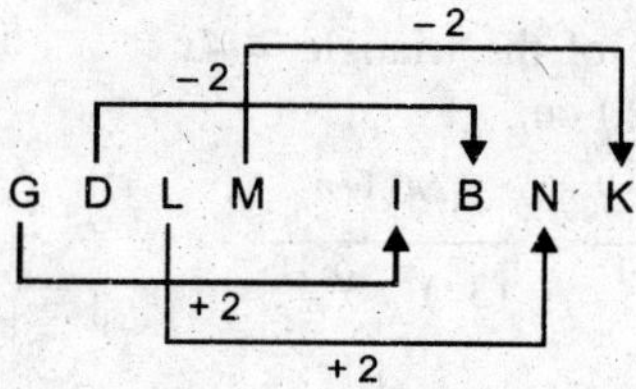

Similarly,

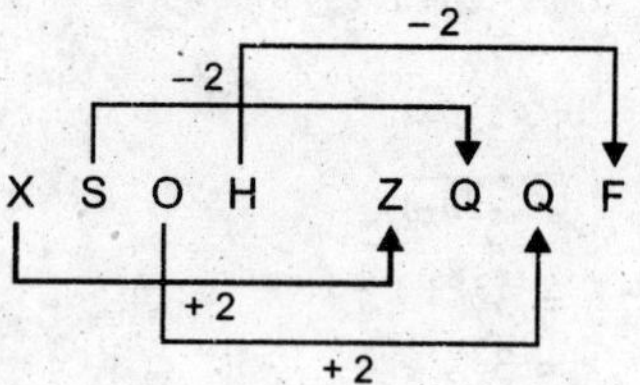

128. Given

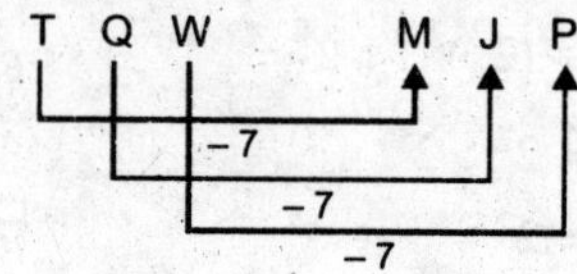

Similarly,

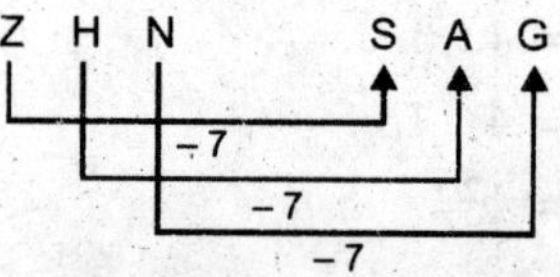

129. WEIGHT is related to KILOGRAM in the same way as DISTANCE is related to KILOMETER.

130. 26 : 5 :: 65 : 8

26 ↓ $5^2 + 1$; 65 ↓ $8^2 + 1$

131. 16 : 56 :: 36 : 112

132.

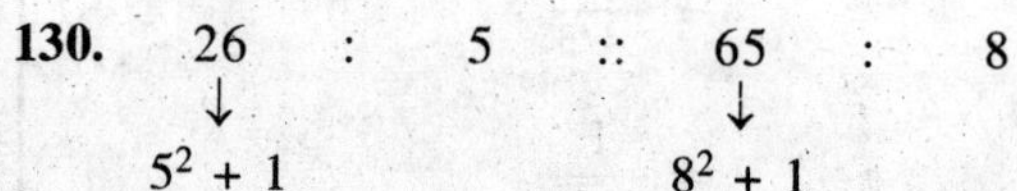

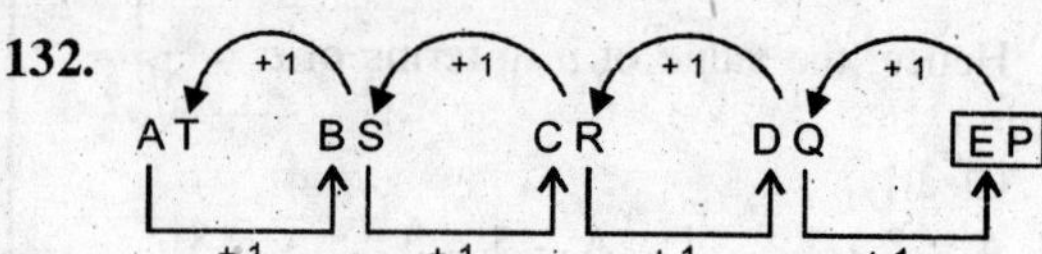

133.

4	9	16	25	36	49
↓	↓	↓	↓	↓	↓
2^2	3^2	4^2	5^2	6^2	7^2

Hence, 36 will come at the place of question mark.

134.

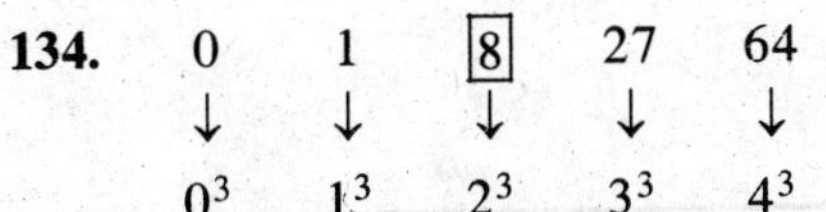

Hence, 8 will come at the place of question mark.

135.

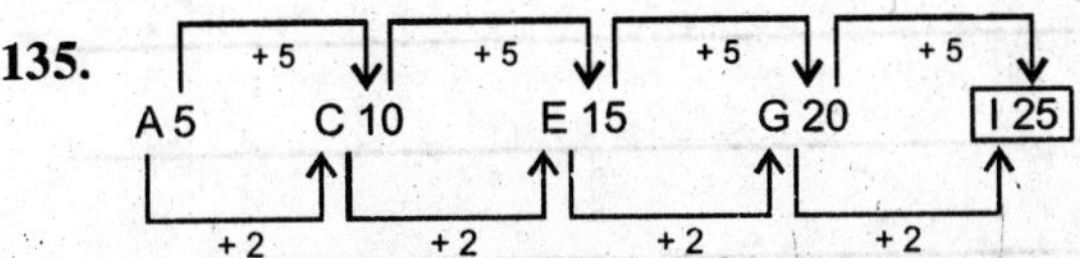

Hence, I 25 will come at the place of question mark.

136.

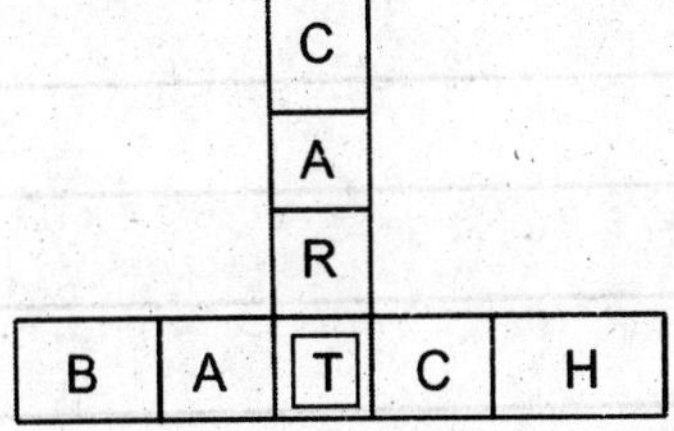

Hence, T will come at the place of question mark.

138.

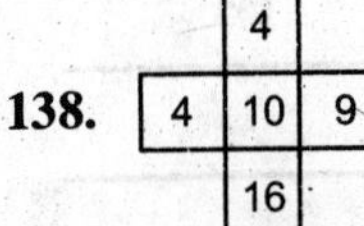

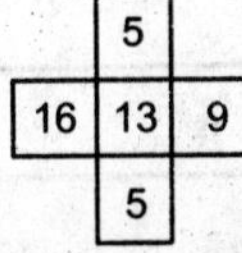

5
16 13 9
5

$16 \times 4 + 9 \times 4$
$= 64 + 36$
$= 100 = 10^2$

$2 \times 8 + 9 \times 1$
$= 16 + 9$
$= 25 = 5^2$

$16 \times 9 + 5 \times 5$
$= 144 + 25$
$= 169 = 13^2$

Hence, 5 will come at the place of question mark.

139.

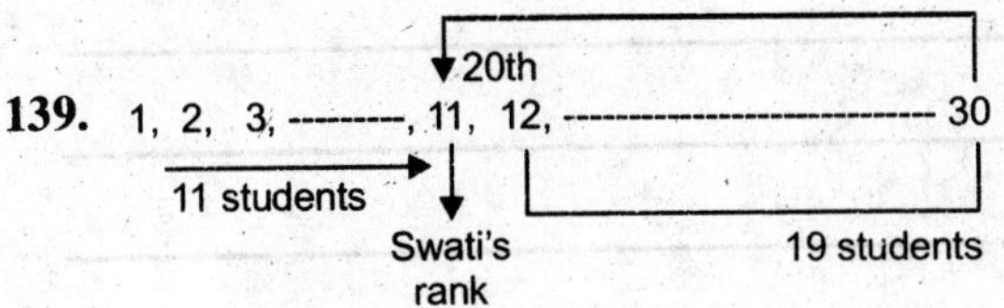

∵ Swati's rank = 11th from the top

∴ Swati's rank = 20th from the bottom.

140.

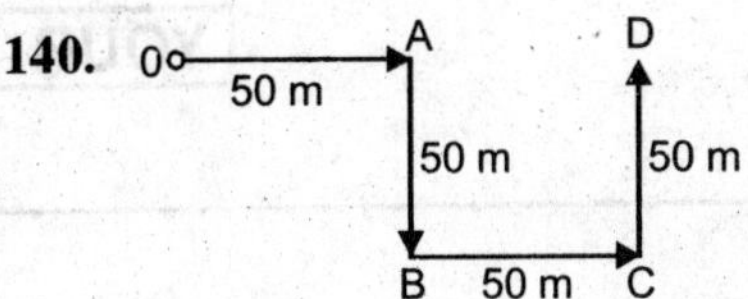

Now, she is in the East direction from the starting point.

141. Suppose the fourth proportional = x

∵ 3, 7, 9 and x are in proportional.

$$\therefore \quad \frac{3}{7} = \frac{9}{x}$$

$$\Rightarrow \quad 3x = 7 \times 9$$

$$\Rightarrow \quad x = \frac{7 \times 9}{3} = 21$$

Hence, the fourth proportional = 21.

145.

C L O C K → 4 2 1 4 5

L E A N → 2 0 6 8

C A R E → 4 6 9 0

Then,

N E C K L A C E → 8 0 4 5 2 6 4 0

146. The year 2800 is a leap year because it is divided by 400.

147. CARPENTER

The word PAINTER can not be made from the given word because the letter 'I' is not in the given word CARPENTER.

148. BRAIN can not be made from the given word REASONABLE because the letter 'I' is not in the given word REASONABLE.

150.

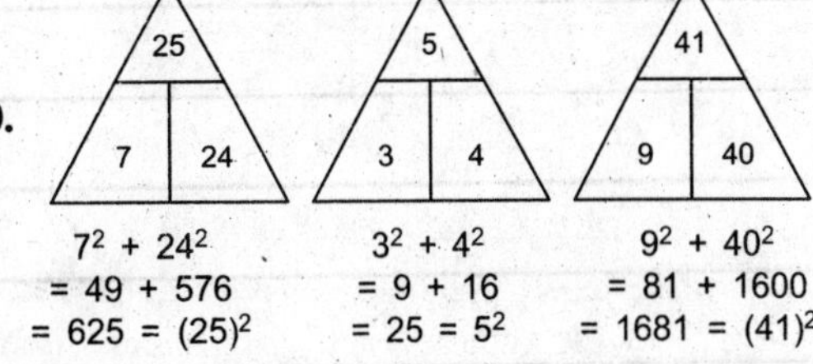

$7^2 + 24^2$
$= 49 + 576$
$= 625 = (25)^2$

$3^2 + 4^2$
$= 9 + 16$
$= 25 = 5^2$

$9^2 + 40^2$
$= 81 + 1600$
$= 1681 = (41)^2$

Hence, 41 will come at the place of question mark.

YOUR SPACE

Previous Paper (Solved)

Sainik School Entrance Exam, 2017

(Class-IX)

PAPER-I

Part–A : Mathematics

SECTION–I

1. Find the product of $(a^2) \times (2a^{22}) \times (4a^{26})$.
2. Using Euler's formula find the number of faces of polyhedron having 6 vertices & 12 edges.
3. Calculate the value of $100 \times 8 + 10 \times 1 + 7$.
4. What is the point of intersection of x-axis and y-axis called?
5. Find the value of x if $\frac{x-8}{5} = \frac{x-12}{9}$.
6. Eleven bags of wheat flour, each marked 5 kg, actually contained the following weights of flour (in kg) 4.97, 5.05, 5.08, 5.00, 5.06, 5.08, 4.98, 5.04, 5.07, 5.00. what is the probability that any of these bags chosen at contains more than 5 kg of flour?
7. If $X = \left[\left(\frac{56}{28}\right)^0 \div \left(\frac{2}{5}\right)^3\right] \times \left(\frac{16}{25}\right)$, then find the value of x.
8. Find cube root of 175616 by factorization method.
9. How many sides does a regular polygon have, if the measure of an exterior angle is 12°?
10. Evaluate $\left[\left(\frac{1}{3}\right)^{-1} - \left(\frac{1}{4}\right)^{-1}\right]^{-1}$.
11. 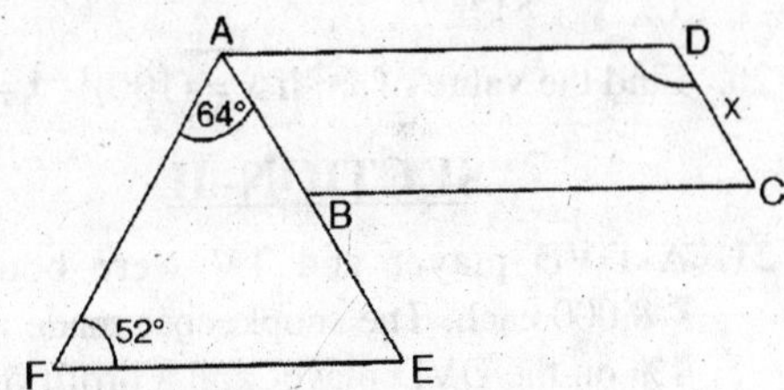

AD ∥ BC ∥ EF and AE ∥ DC

∠AFE = 52°   ∠EAF = 64°.

∠x = ...

12. If a spinning wheel has 3 Green sectors, 1 Blue and 2 Red sectors. What is the probability of getting a Green sector?
13. 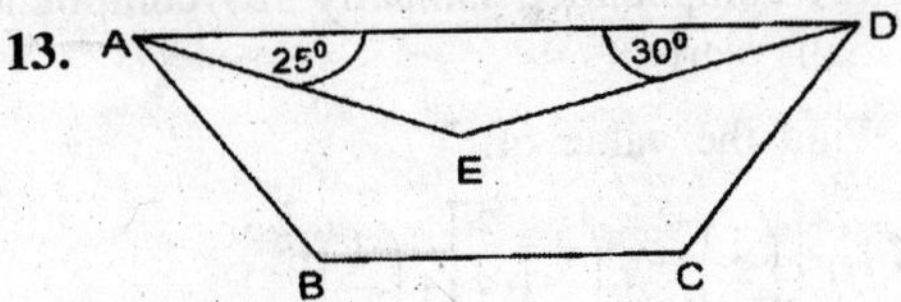

In trapezium

AE and DE bisect ∠CDA and ∠DAB.

Find ∠ABC and ∠DCB.

14. Two equal sides of an isosceles are each 3 m more than 3 times of third side. Find length of sides, if perimeter is 34 m.
15. The area of a circle is given as $\pi x^2 + 10\pi x + 25\pi$. Find the radius as an algebraic expression.
16. Three numbers are in ratio 1 : 2 : 3 and sum of their cubes is 4500. Find numbers.

17. Find

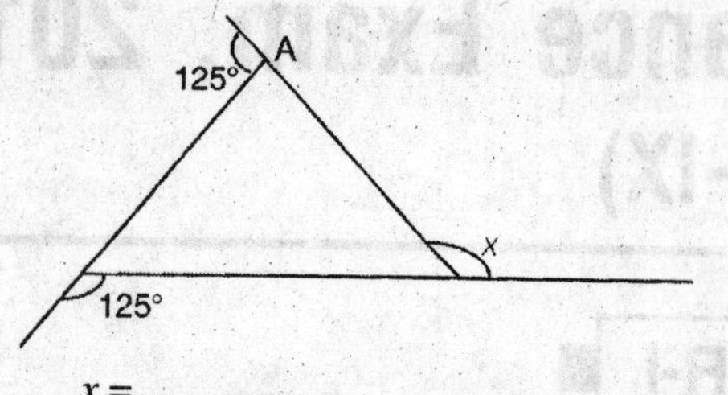

$x =$ ....

18. A coin is tossed 2 times. What are the total number of possible outcomes?

19. What is the range of data 30, 61, 55, 25, 2, 12, 17, 81?

20. Find the value of x^{-2} if $x = (100)^{1-4} \div (100)^0$.

SECTION–II

21. A DVD player and TV were bought for ₹ 8,000 each. The shopkeeper made a loss of 4% on the DVD player and a profit of 8% on the TV. Find the gain or loss per cent on the whole transaction.

21. Arif took a loan of ₹ 80,000 from a bank. If the rate of interest is 10% per annum, find the difference in amounts he would be paying after 1½ years, if the interest is (*a*) compounded annually (*b*) compounded half yearly.

23. Find the value of:

(*i*) $\left[\left(\frac{1}{2}\right)^{-2} + \left(\frac{1}{3}\right)^{-2}\right] + \left(\frac{1}{4}\right)^{-2}$

(*ii*) $(3^0 + 4^{-1}) \times 2^2$

24. What least number must be subtracted from 7250 to get a perfect square? Also, find the square root of this perfect square.

25. If $\left(y^2 + \frac{1}{y^2}\right) = 83$. Find $y^3 - \frac{1}{y^3}$.

26. A motor boat covers a certain distance downstream in a river in 5 hours. It covers the same distance upstream in 6 hours. The speed of water is 2 km/hr, find the speed of the boat in still water.

27. A dealer buys an article for ₹ 380. At what price must he mark it so that after allowing a discount of 5%, he still makes a profit of 25%?

28. The population of village is 20000. If the birth rate is 5% p.a. and death rate is 3% p.a., find the population after 2 years.

29. The distance between two stations is 550 km. Two trains start at the same time from the two stations on parallel tracks to cross one another. The speed of one train is 10 km/hr more than the other. If after 3 hours, the trains are 40 km apart, find their respective speed.

30. Simplify: $\frac{(5)^3 \times (10)^{-5} \times 3^{-5}}{5^{-7} \times 6^{-5}}$.

31. Show that $\left(\frac{4}{3} - \frac{3}{4y}\right)^2 + 2xy = \frac{16}{9x^2} + \frac{9}{16y^2}$.

32. The ratio between interior and exterior angle of a regular polygon is 8 : 1. Find the number of sides of the polygon.

33. Find the area of trapezium.

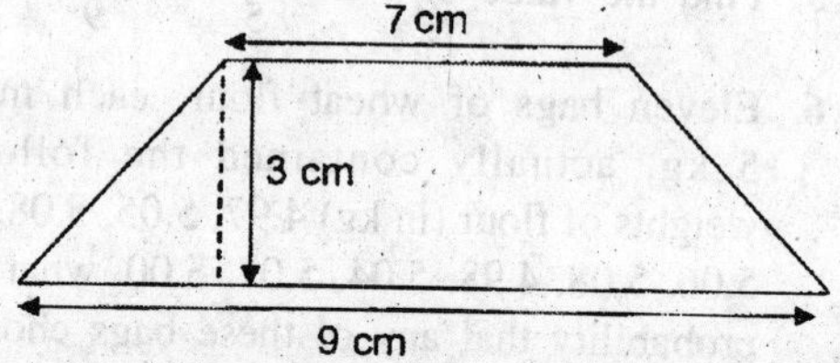

34. Find the height of cuboid whose base area is 360 cm^2 and volume is 1800 cm^3.

35. Represent $-\frac{3}{7}$, $-\frac{1}{7}$ and $\frac{2}{7}$ on a number line.

36. Find the length of longest pole that can be kept in a room of 12 m × 4 m × 3 m.

37. The diameter of base of a cylinder is 140 cm and volume is 1.54 m^2. Find its height.

38. Express 21^2 as sum of two consecutive integers.

39. If 21*y*5 is a multiple of 9, where *y* is a digit, what is the value of *y*?

40. Divide: $7(x^3y^2z^2 + x^2y^3z^2 + x^2y^2z^3)$ by $4(x^2y^2z^2)$

SECTION–III

41. The hour hand of a circular clock is 10 cm long. How much distance will it cover in 2 days or 48 hours?

42. A collage is made up of 400 rhombus shaped pieces and 200 trapezium. The diagonals of the rhombus are 6 cm and 4 cm long. Lengths of the parallel sides of the trapezium are 4 cm and 8 cm and the height is 10 cm. Find the area of the collage and also the cost of painting it at the rate of ₹ 250 per m^2.

43. The rainwater falling on a roof 40 m × 25 m is collected in a cylindrical tank with diameter 7 m and height 10 m. If the tank is completely filled, find the height of the rainwater on the roof.

44. MNOPQ is a regular pentagon. The bisector of angle M meets side OP at K. Find measure of ∠MKO.

45. How many wooden blocks of size 22 cm × 10 cm × 7 cm are required to make a wooden partition of 11 m × 3.5 m × 40 cm, if the glue and filling material used occupies one tenth of the wooden partition?

46. The sides of a swimming pool are 7 m, 6 m, and 15 m. If 8400 litres of water is pumped out, what is the decrease in water level?

47. Ajit bought 150 kg sugar at ₹ 50 per kg. He sold 70% of sugar at ₹ 70 per kg and balance at ₹ 40 per kg. Find overall profit/loss on the whole deal.

48. The following table gives the marks scored by 100 students in an Entrance Examination.

Marks	0-10	10-20	20-30	30-40	40-50	50-60	60-70	70-80
No. of Students	4	10	16	22	20	18	8	2

Represent this data in the form of a histogram.

49. Find the number of coins, 1.5 cm in diameter and 0.2 cm thick, to be melted to form a right circular cylinder of height 10 cm and diameter 4.5 cm.

50. In the adjoining figure, the bisectors of A & B meet at a point P.

If C = 96° and D = 30°, find APB.

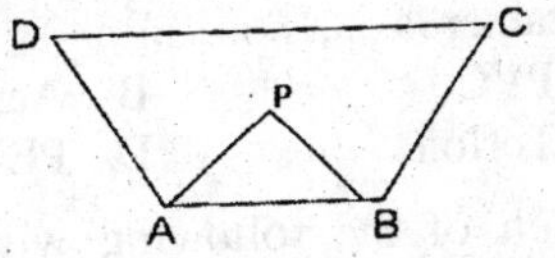

Part–B : Science

Select the correct answer of the following questions.

1. The synthetic fibre that appears to resemble wool is:
A. PET B. acrylon
C. rayon D. nylon

2. A prominent constellation looking like a distorted form of the letter W or M, is the:
A. Cassiopeia B. Big dipper
C. Orion D. Ursa minor

3. An example of a plastic which cannot be remoulded again by simple heating is;
A. Polythene B. PVC
C. Polystyrene D. Bakelite

4. Cellulose is made up of a large number of .... units.
A. amide B. amino
C. glucose D. sucrose

5. Relationship between a biotic community and an abiotic environment is called:
A. Biodiversity B. Ecosystem
C. Symbiosis D. Survival

6. Lactobacillus bacteria help to make:
A. Bread B. Pastries
C. Cake D. Curd

7. World Water day is observed on:
A. 24 March B. 23 March
C. 21 March D. 22 March

8. The place meant for conservation of biodiversity in their natural habitat are:
(*i*) Zoological gardens
(*ii*) Botanical gardens
(*iii*) Wildlife sanctuary
(*iv*) National Park
A. (*i*) and (*ii*) B. (*ii*) and (*iii*)
C. (*iii*) and (*iv*) D. (*i*) and (*iv*)

9. Which of the following is considered a clean fuel?
A. Cowdung cake B. Petrol
C. Kerosene D. Hydrogen

10. Which one of the following metals does not react with dilute HCl?
A. Magnesium B. Aluminium
C. Iron D. Copper

11. Solution of which of the following oxides in water will change the colour of Blue litmus to Red?
A. Sulphur dioxide B. Magnesium oxide
C. Iron oxide D. Copper oxide

12. The material used for making kitchen container is ....
A. PVC B. Acrylic
C. Teflon D. PET

13. Which of the following will not conduct electricity?
A. Lemon juice B. Vinegar
C. Tap water D. Vegetable oil

14. Which of the following is not part of solar system?
A. Asteroid B. Satellite
C. Constellation D. Comet

15. The phenomenon of 'Marble Cancer' is due to:
A. Soot particles B. CFCs
C. Log D. Acid rain

Write answers of the following questions.

16. Why a crackling sound is heard while taking off a sweater during winters?

17. Differentiate between "Spontaneous and Explosive combustion".

18. Calorific value of wood is 1800 kJ/kg. How much wood is required to produce heat energy of 144,000 kJ?

19. A force of 150 N is applied to an object of area 5 m^2. Calculate the pressure.

20. How reproduction of Hydra differs from that of Amoeba?

21. Explain why sliding friction is less than static friction.

22. How do vaccines work?

23. Hens and frogs are both oviparous exhibiting different types of fertilization. Explain.

24. What is meant by Water table?

25. Distinguish between 'Speedometer' and 'Odometer'.

26. What is freezing mixture? How common salt helps to clean pavements covered with snow?

27. Mention the effect of iodine in water on the growth of tadpoles.

28. Write short note on Adam's apple.

29. Eyes of nocturnal birds have large cornea and large pupil. How does it help them?

30. Explain how will you make a tester for testing electric current using a magnetic compass and empty matchbox, a battery of two cells and connecting wire.

31. Make sketch of human nerve cell. What functions nerve cell performs?

32. A block is kept in two different ways on a table as shown in figure. Explain in which positions the pressure exerted by the block on the table will be maximum.

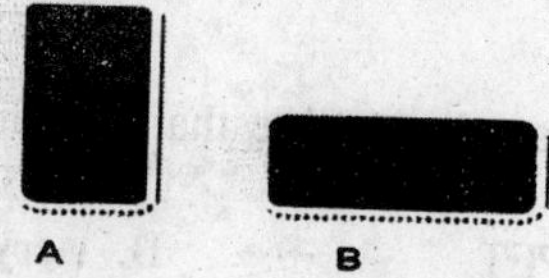

33. Do all the stars in sky move? Explain.

34. Explain the process which enables us to perceive motion in a cartoon film.

35. Why CFCs are considered pollutants?

36. Explain '**SOIL PROFILE**' using a neat and labelled diagram.

37. Distinguish between metals and non-metals. What are metalloids? Give any two examples of metalloids.

EXPLANATORY ANSWERS

Part–A : Mathematics

1. $(a^2) \times (2a^{22}) \times (4a^{26})$

$= 8a^{2+22+26} = 8a^{50}$.

2. From Euler's formula

$F + V - E = 2$

Here, F, Number of faces = ?

V, Number of vertices = 6

E, Number of edges = 12

$\therefore$ $F + 6 - 12 = 2$

$F - 6 = 2$

$F = 8$.

3. $100 \times 8 + 10 \times 1 + 7$

$= 800 + 10 + 7 = 817$.

4. Point of intersection of x-axis & y-axis is called origin.

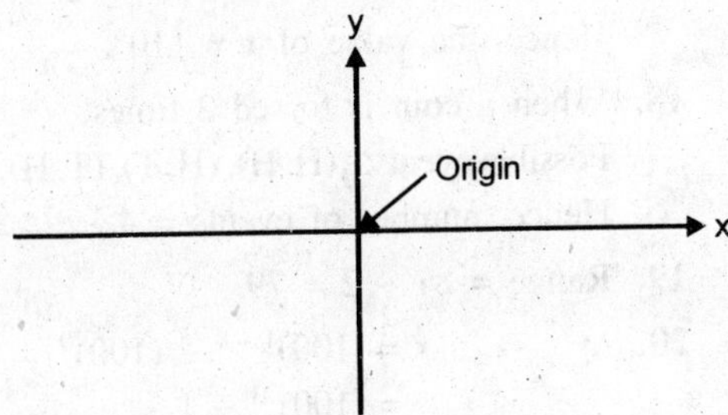

5. $\because \quad \frac{x-8}{5} = \frac{x-12}{9}$

$\Rightarrow \quad 9x - 72 = 8x - 60$

$\Rightarrow \quad x = 72 - 60 = 12$

Hence, the value of $x = 12$.

6. Required proabiliy $= \frac{6}{11}$.

7. $\because \quad x = \left[\left(\frac{56}{28}\right)^{\circ} \div \left(\frac{2}{5}\right)^{3}\right] \times \frac{16}{25}$

$= \left[1 \div \frac{8}{125}\right] \times \frac{16}{25}$

$= 1 \times \frac{125}{8} \times \frac{16}{25} = 10$

Hence, the value of $x = 10$.

8.

2	175616
2	87808
2	43904
2	21952
2	10976
2	5488
2	2744
2	1372
2	686
7	343
7	49
7	7
	1

$\therefore$ Cube root of $175616 = 2 \times 2 \times 2 \times 7$

$= 56$.

9. No. of sides of a regular polygon

$= \frac{360°}{12} = 30$.

10. $\left[\left(\frac{1}{3}\right)^{-1} - \left(\frac{1}{4}\right)^{-1}\right]^{-1}$

$= \left[\frac{3}{1} - \frac{4}{1}\right]^{-1} = [-1]^{-1} = -1$.

11.

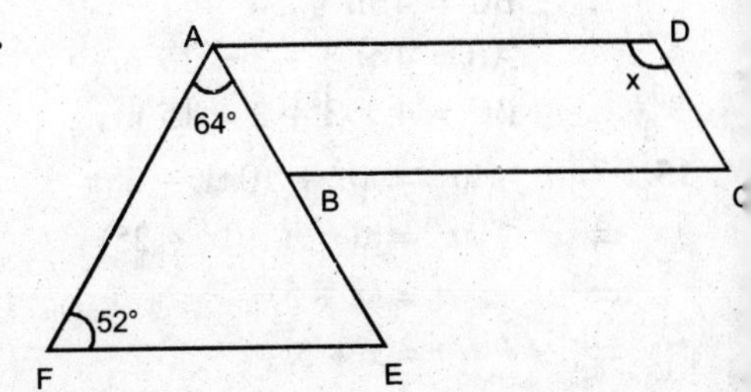

$\angle ADC = \angle x$

In $\Delta AEF, \angle AEF = 180° - \angle EAF - \angle AFE$

$= 180° - 64° - 52° = 64°$

From ||gm ABCD,

$\angle x + 64° = 180°$

$\angle x = 180° - 64° = 116°$.

12. Required probability $= \frac{3}{6} = \frac{1}{2}$.

13.

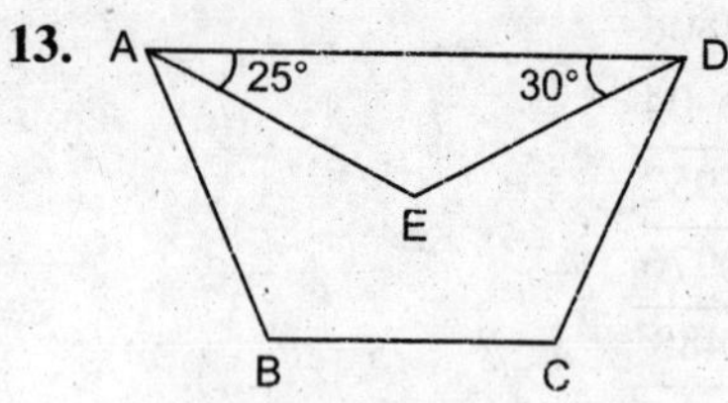

$\because$ ABCD is a trapezium in which AD || BC.

AE and DE are bisectors of $\angle BAD$ and $\angle ADC$.

$\therefore \quad \angle BAD = 50°$ and $\angle ADC = 60°$

$\therefore \quad \angle ABC = 180° - 50° = 130°$

and, $\angle DCB = 180° - 60° = 120°$.

14.

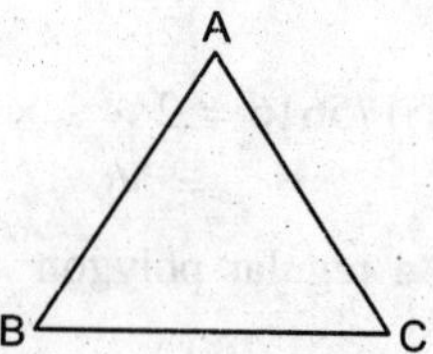

In ΔABC, AB = AC

Let, BC = x m

$\therefore \quad AB = (3x + 3)$m and $AC = (3x + 3)$m

According to the question,

$x + 3x + 3 + 3x + 3 = 34$

$\Rightarrow \quad 7x = 34 - 6 = 28$

$\Rightarrow \quad x = 4$

$\therefore \quad BC = 4$ m

$AB = 4 \times 3 + 3 = 15$ m

$BC = 4 \times 3 + 3 = 15$ m.

15. $\pi r^2 = \pi r^2 + 10\pi x + 25\pi$

$\Rightarrow \quad \pi r^2 = \pi(x^2 + 10x + 25)$

$\Rightarrow \quad r^2 = (x + 5)^2$

$\Rightarrow \quad r = x + 5$.

16. Let, the numbers are $1x$, $2x$ and $3x$.

According to the question,

$(1x)^3 + (2x)^3 + (3x)^3 = 4500$

$\Rightarrow \quad x^3 + 8x^3 + 27x^3 = 4500$

$\Rightarrow \quad 36x^3 = 4500$

$\Rightarrow \quad x^3 = \frac{4500}{36} = \frac{500}{4} = 125$

$\Rightarrow \quad x = 5$.

$\therefore$ Numbers are 5, 10 and 15.

17.

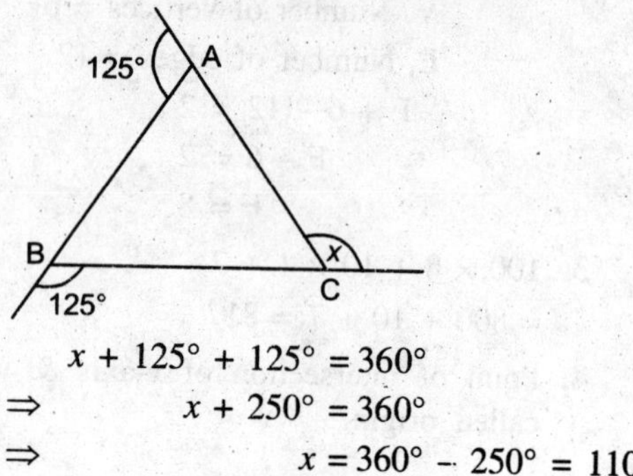

$x + 125° + 125° = 360°$

$\Rightarrow \quad x + 250° = 360°$

$\Rightarrow \quad x = 360° - 250° = 110°$

Hence, the value of $x = 110°$.

18. When a coin is tossed 2 times,

Possible events: {(H, H), (H, T), (T, H), (T, T)}.

Hence, number of events = 4.

19. Range = 81 − 2 = 79.

20. $\because \quad x = (100)^{1-4} \div (100)^0$

$= (100)^{-3} \div 1$

$= \left(\frac{1}{100}\right)^3$

$\therefore \quad x^{-2} = \frac{1}{x^2} = \left[\left(\frac{1}{100}\right)^3\right]^2 = \left(\frac{1}{100}\right)^6$

$= (100)^{-6}$.

21. Total CP = 8000 + 8000 = ₹ 16000

Total SP $= \frac{96}{100} \times 8000 + \frac{108}{100} \times 8000$

= 7680 + 8640 = ₹ 16320

SP > CP

$\therefore$ Profit = 16320 − 16000 = ₹ 320

Profit % $= \frac{320}{1600} \times 100 = 2\%$.

22. (*i*) P = ₹ 80000

$r = 10\%$

$t = 1\frac{1}{2}$ years

Simple interest for 1 year

$= \frac{80000 \times 10 \times 1}{100} = ₹\ 8000$

Amount = 80000 + 8000 = ₹ 88000

Simple interest for $\frac{1}{2}$ years

$= \frac{88000 \times 10 \times 1}{100 \times 2} = ₹\ 4400$

Amount = 88000 + 4400 = ₹ 92400

(*ii*) P = ₹ 80000

$r = 5\%$

$t = 3$ years

$$A = P\left(1+\frac{r}{100}\right)^t$$

$$= 80000\left(1+\frac{5}{100}\right)^3$$

$$= 80000\left(\frac{21}{20}\times\frac{21}{20}\times\frac{21}{20}\right)$$

= 10 × 9261 = ₹ 92610.

23. (*i*) $\left[\left(\frac{1}{2}\right)^{-2}+\left(\frac{1}{3}\right)^{-2}\right]+\left(\frac{1}{4}\right)^{-2}$

$= \left[(2)^2+(3)^2\right]+(4)^2$

$= [4 + 9] + 16$

$= 13 + 16 = 29.$

(*ii*) $(3^0 + 4^{-1}) \times 2^2$

$= \left(1+\frac{1}{4}\right)\times 4 = \frac{5}{4} \times 4 = 5.$

24.

8	7250 64	84
164	× 850 656	
	194	

∴ 7250 – 194 = 7056 which is perfect square

∴ Least number = 194

$\sqrt{7056} = 84.$

25. ∵ $y^2 + \frac{1}{y^2} = 83$

$y^2 + \frac{1}{y^2} - 2 = 83 - 2$

⇒ $\left(y-\frac{1}{y}\right)^2 = 81$

∴ $y-\frac{1}{y} = 9$

$y^3 - \frac{1}{y^3} = \left(y-\frac{1}{y}\right)^3 + 3.y.\frac{1}{y}\left(y-\frac{1}{y}\right)$

$= (9)^3 + 3(9)$

$= 729 + 27 = 756.$

26. Let, the speed of the boat = x km/hr

$\frac{d}{x-2} = 6$

⇒ $d = 6x - 12$ ...(*i*)

$\frac{d}{x+2} = 5$

⇒ $d = 5x + 10$ ...(*ii*)

From (*i*) and (*ii*)

$6x - 12 = 5x + 10$

⇒ $x = 22$

∴ Speed of the boat = 22 km/hr.

27. SP of the article = $380 \times \frac{125}{100}$

= 95 × 5 = ₹ 475

M.P. of $\frac{95}{100} = 475$

⇒ M.P. = $\frac{100 \times 475}{95} = 100 \times 5$

= ₹ 500.

28. Population after 2 years

$$A = P\left(1+\frac{r}{100}\right)^t$$

$$= 20000\left(1+\frac{2}{100}\right)^2$$

$$= 20000 \times \frac{51}{50} \times \frac{51}{50}$$

$$= 8 \times 2601 = 20808$$

Hence, population after two years = 20808.

29. A——550 km——B

Let, speed of one train = x km/hr

and, speed of other train = $(x + 10)$ km/hr

Distance covered in 3 hrs by first train

$= 3x$ km.

Distance covered in 3 hrs by other train

$= 3(x + 10)$ km

According to the question,

$$550 - (3x + 3x + 30) = 40$$

$$\Rightarrow \quad 550 - 6x - 30 = 40$$

$$\Rightarrow \quad 520 - 40 = 6x$$

$$\Rightarrow \quad 480 = 6x$$

$$\Rightarrow \quad x = 80$$

∴ Speed of first train = 80 km/hr

and Speed of other train = 90 km/hr

30. $\dfrac{(5)^3 \times (10)^{-5} \times 3^{-5}}{5^7 \times 6^{-5}}$

$$= \frac{5^3 \times (2\times 5)^{-5} \times 3^{-5}}{5^7 \times (2\times 3)^{-5}}$$

$$= \frac{5^3 \times 2^{-5} \times 5^{-5} \times 3^{-5}}{5^7 \times 2^{-5} \times 3^{-5}}$$

$$= \frac{5^{-2}}{5^7} = 5^{-9} = \left(\frac{1}{5}\right)^9.$$

31. $\left(\frac{4}{3}x - \frac{3}{4}y\right)^2 + 2xy$

$$= \left(\frac{4}{3}x\right)^2 + \left(\frac{3}{4}y\right)^2 - 2\left(\frac{4}{3}x\right) + \left(\frac{3}{4}y\right) + 2xy$$

$$= \frac{16}{9}x^2 + \frac{9}{16}y^2 - 2xy + 2xy$$

$$= \frac{16}{9}x^2 + \frac{9}{16}y^2$$

32. Let, the number of sides of the polygon is n.

Interior angle I : $\dfrac{2(n-2)\times 90°}{n}$

Exterier angle E : $\dfrac{360°}{n}$

From question, $\dfrac{\frac{2(n-2)\times 90°}{n}}{\frac{360°}{n}} = \dfrac{8}{1}$

$$\frac{(n-2)}{2} = 8$$

$$n - 2 = 16$$

$$n = 18.$$

33. Area of the trapezium

$$= \frac{1}{2} \times 3 \times (9 + 7)$$

$$= \frac{1}{2} \times 3 \times 16 = 24 \text{ cm}^2.$$

34. Height of cuboid $= \dfrac{\text{Volume}}{\text{Base area}}$

$$= \frac{1800}{360} = 5 \text{ cm}.$$

35. A —— $-\frac{7}{7}$, $-\frac{6}{7}$, $-\frac{5}{7}$, $-\frac{4}{7}$, $-\frac{3}{7}$, $-\frac{2}{7}$, $-\frac{1}{7}$, O, $\frac{1}{7}$, $\frac{2}{7}$, $\frac{3}{7}$, $\frac{4}{7}$, $\frac{5}{7}$, $\frac{6}{7}$, $\frac{7}{7}$ —— B

36. Length of the longest pole $= \sqrt{l^2 + b^2 + h^2}$

$$= \sqrt{(12)^2 + (4)^2 + (3)^2}$$

$$= \sqrt{144 + 16 + 9}$$

$$= \sqrt{169} = 13 \text{ m}.$$

37. Radius of the cylinder = 70 cm = 0.7 m.

Volume of cylinder $= \pi r^2 h$

$$\Rightarrow \quad 1.54 = \frac{22}{7} \times .7 \times .7 \times h$$

$$h = \frac{7 \times 1.54}{22 \times .49} = \frac{7 \times 154}{22 \times 49} = 1 \text{ m}.$$

Hence, height of the cylinder = 1 m.

38. $x + (x + 1) = 21^2$

$\Rightarrow \quad x + x + 1 = 441$

$\Rightarrow \quad 2x = 440 \Rightarrow x = 220$

and $\quad x + 1 = 220 + 1 = 221$

$\therefore \quad 220 + 221 = 441.$

39. 21y5 is a multiple of 9

$\therefore$ 2 + 1 + 1 + 5 = 9 which is divisible by 9.

$\therefore$ Value of y = 1.

40. $$\frac{7}{4}\left[\frac{x^3y^2z^2}{x^2y^2z^2}+\frac{x^2y^3z^2}{x^2y^2z^2}+\frac{x^2y^2z^3}{x^2y^2z^2}\right]$$

$$= \frac{7}{4}[x+y+z].$$

41. $C = 2\pi r$

$$= 2\times\frac{22}{7}\times 10 = \frac{440}{7} \text{ cm}$$

In 12 hours the hour hand moves 1 time.
In 48 hours the hour hand moves 4 times.
Hence, distance covered by hour hand in 48 hours.

$$= \frac{440}{7}\times 4 = \frac{1760}{7} \text{ cm}$$

$= 251.428$ cm

$\cong 251.43$ cm.

42. Area of the rhombus

$$= \frac{1}{2} \times \text{product of diagonals.}$$

$$= \frac{1}{2}\times 6 \times 4 = 12 \text{ cm}^2.$$

Area of 400 rhombus = 400 × 12
= 4800 cm².

Area of the trapezium

$$= \frac{1}{2}\times \text{height} \times \text{(sum of parallel sides)}$$

$$= \frac{1}{2} \times 10 \times (4 + 8) = 60 \text{ cm}^2.$$

Area of 200 trapezium = 200 × 60
= 12000 cm².

Total area of the collage = 4800 + 12000
= 16800 cm²

$\therefore$ Total Area = 1.68 m².

Cost of painting = 1.68 × 200
= ₹ 336.

43. Volume of cylinder

$= \pi r^2 h$

$$= \frac{22}{7}\times\frac{7}{2}\times\frac{7}{2}\times 10$$

$= 385 \text{ m}^3$

According to the question,

$40 \times 25 \times h = 385$

$$\Rightarrow \quad h = \frac{385}{40\times 25} = \frac{77}{200} \text{ m}$$

$$= \frac{77}{200} \times 100 \text{ cm}$$

$$= \frac{77}{2} \text{ cm} = 38.5 \text{ cm.}$$

44.

P, K, Q, O, 108°, M, N

For a regular polygon of n sides, interior angle

$$I = \frac{2(n-2)\times 90°}{n}$$

Here, $n = 5$

$$I = \frac{2(5-2)\times 90°}{5} = 108°$$

$$\therefore \angle KMN = \frac{108°}{2} = 54°.$$

In □ MNOK,

$54° + 108° + 108° + \angle MKO = 360°$

$270° + \angle MKO = 360°$

$\angle MKO = 90°.$

45. Wooden portion in the wooden Partition

$$= 11 \times 3.5 \times 0.4 \times \frac{9}{10}$$

$= 11 \times 3.5 \times 0.4 \times 0.9$

Number of wooden blocks required

$$= \frac{11 \times 3.5 \times 0.4 \times 0.9}{0.22 \times 0.10 \times 0.07}$$

$= 9000.$

46. Volume of swimming pool

$= 700 \times 600 \times 1500 \text{ cm}^3$

$= 63000000 \text{ cm}^3$

$1 l = 1000 \text{ cm}^3$

$8400 l = 8400000 \text{ cm}^3$

Required height $= \frac{630000000}{8400000} = 75$ cm.

47. CP = ₹ 150 × 50

= ₹ 7500

SP = ₹ $\frac{70}{100}(150) \times 70$ + ₹ 45 × 40

= 105 × 70 + 1800

= 7350 + 1800 = ₹ 9150

Profit = 9150 − 7500

= ₹ 1650

Profit % = $\frac{1650}{7500} \times 100$

= 22%.

48.

49. No. of coins $= \dfrac{\pi \times \frac{4.5}{2} \times \frac{4.5}{2} \times 10}{\pi \times \frac{1.5}{2} \times \frac{1.5}{2} \times 0.2}$

$= 450$

50.

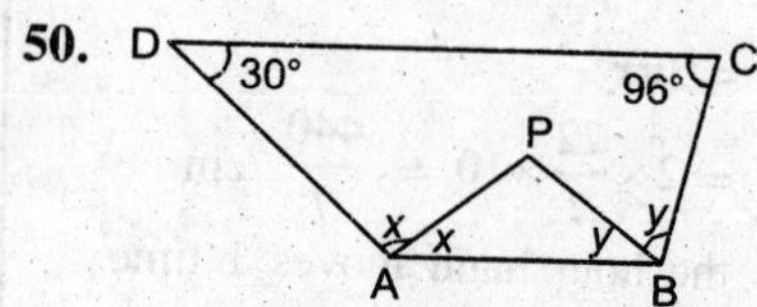

∵ ABCD is trapezium in which AB||CD, AP and BP are bisectors of ∠A and ∠B.

∵ $2x + 30° = 180° \Rightarrow 2x = 150° \Rightarrow x = 75°$

and $2y + 96° = 180° \Rightarrow 2y = 84° \Rightarrow y = 42°$

In ΔAPB, $x = 75°$, $y = 42°$

∴ ∠APB = 180° − (75 + 42)

= 180° − 117° = 63°.

Part–B : Science

1. B **2.** A **3.** D **4.** C **5.** B
6. D **7.** D **8.** C **9.** D **10.** D
11. A **12.** D **13.** D **14.** C **15.** D

16. A cracking sound is heard while taking off sweater made of synthetic fibre during winters especially when the weather is dry, because, since there is some humidity also present in the atmosphere and synthetic fibre gets charged and due to attraction forces acting between charged particles they oppose there detachment and create a crackling sound.

17.

Spontaneous combustion	**Explosion**
The combustion in which substance suddenly burst into flames, without the application of any apparent cause is called **spontaneous combustion.**	The combustion in which sudden reactions take place on ignition of some substances to produce heat, light, and sound is called **explosion.**
For example, sodium and phosphorus burn spontaneously in air, even when no external heat is provided to them.	For example, fireworks on ignition produce heat, light, and sound.

18. Required wood $= \frac{144000}{1800} = 80$ kg.

19. Pressure $= \frac{\text{Force}}{\text{Area}} = \frac{150 \text{ N}}{5 \text{ m}^2} = \frac{30 \text{ N}}{\text{m}^2}$.

20. Budding is a form of asexual reproduction in which a new organism develops from an outgrowth or bud due to cell division at one particular site. The new organism remains attached as it grows, separating from the parent organism only when it is mature, leaving behind scar tissue. Since the reproduction is asexual, the newly created organism is a clone and is genetically identical to the parent organism. Organisms such as hydra use regenerative cells for reproduction in the process of budding. In hydra, a bud develops as an outgrowth due to repeated cell division at one specific site. These buds develop into tiny individuals and when fully mature, detach from the parent body and become new independent individuals.

Binary fission is the mode of production in amoeba. Amoeba divides after it has reached its full size. The cell body and the nucleus divides into two parts. By this two daughter cells are formed.

21. Friction comes into play when irregularities present in the surfaces of two objects in contact get interlocked with each other. In sliding, the time given for interlocking is very small. Hence, interlocking is not strong. Therefore, less force is required to overcome this interlocking. Because of this reason, sliding friction is less than static friction.

22. Vaccines work by mimicking disease agents and stimulating the immune system to build up defenses against them.

Vaccines are like a training course for the immune system. They prepare the body to fight disease without exposing it to disease symptoms. When foreign invaders such as bacteria or viruses enter the body, immune cells called lymphocytes respond by producing antibodies, which are protein molecules.

23. Hen and frog both produce eggs. However, in case of hen, the fertilization takes place inside the body and is known as internal fertilisation while in case of frogs, the fertilisation takes place out the body known as external fertilisation.

24. Water table, also called Groundwater Table, upper level of an underground surface in which the soil or rocks are permanently saturated with water. The water table separates the groundwater zone that lies below it from the capillary fringe, or zone of aeration, that lies above it. The water table fluctuates both with the seasons and from year to year because it is affected by climatic variations and by the amount of precipitation used by vegetation. It also is affected by withdrawing excessive amounts of water from wells or by recharging them artificially.

25. Odometer measures the total distance covered by a vehicle. The reading of an odometer always increases. Suppose your car was showing 2150 km in its odometer. You travel to a nearby town and observe that the new reading is 2250 km. The distance you covered to reach the town is (2250 – 2150) = 100 km & the total distance your car has travelled from the day you bought it is 2250 km.

Speedometer measures the speed of the vehicle at any instant. When your car is not moving the speedometer will show 0 km/hr. When it begins to move it may show 10 km/hr. You put it in 3rd gear and after some time you may see 50 km/hr, If you apply brakes you will observe that the pointer of the speedometer is moving towards the zero. Reading of a speedometer always fluctuates or changes depending on the way you drive the car. It may momentarily show a constant speed if you drive with a constant speed.

26. **Freezing Mixture :** A mixture of two or more substances (*e.g.* ice water and salt, or dry ice and alcohol) which can be used to produce temperatures below the freezing point of water.

The actual reason that the application of salt causes ice to melt is that a solution of water and dissolved salt has a lower freezing point than pure water. When added to ice, salt first dissolves in the film of liquid water that is always present on the surface, thereby lowering its freezing point below the ice's temperature. Ice in contact with salty water therefore melts, creating more liquid water, which dissolves more salt, thereby causing more ice to melt, and so on. The higher the concentration of dissolved salt, the lower its overall freezing point. There is a limit, however, to the amount of salt that can be dissolved in water. Water containing a maximum amount of dissolved salt has a freezing point of about zero degrees Fahrenheit. Therefore, the application of salt will not melt the ice on a sidewalk if the temperature is below zero degrees F.

27. The growth and development of the animals like tadpole is controlled by the hormone called thyroxine produced by the thyroid gland. The proper function of thyroid gland and production of thyroxine needs iodine. Thus, if the water in which tadpole is living is deficient in iodine, it retards its growth.

28. In human males, the larynx grows larger during puberty and can be seen as a protruding part of the throat. This protrusion is known as the Adam's apple. In boys, under the influence of sex hormones, the larynx becomes prominent. As a result the vocal cords become longer and thicker, causing the voice to become hoarse. However, in females, the larynx is of a small size and is hardly visible. Therefore, girls have a high pitched voice, while the voice of boys is low pitched.

29. Eyes of nocturnal animals like owl has large cornea and a large pupil, these features increase their field of vision and an increase retinal surface and help them to collect more ambient light during night.

30. The circuit formed is as shown below:

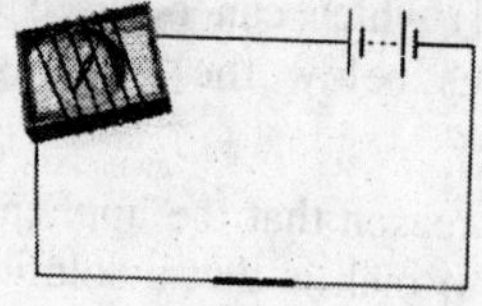

Circuit

The connecting wire is wrapped around the match box that contains the magetic compass. When the current from battery is passing, there is a magnetic field of current that is formed, which interacts with the magnetic compass and it shows deflection.

31.

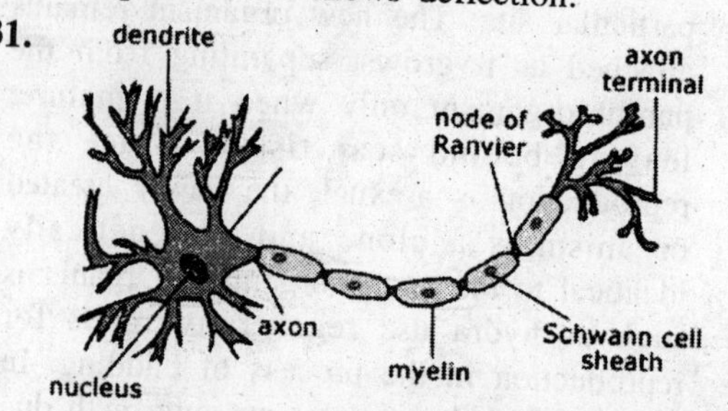

The function of a nerve cell is to transmit messages to the brain and also to take away messages from the brain to the receptor organs.

32. $$\text{Pressure (P)} = \frac{\text{Force (F)}}{\text{Area (A)}}$$

As the contact area in fig (A) is less then in fig (B).

Hence, Pressure exerted by block (A) is greater than B.

33. No. The Earth rotates from West to East on its axis. Hence, all stars in the sky (except the Pole star) appear to move from East to West. With reference to the Earth, the Pole star does not appear to move in the sky because it is located above the axis of rotation of the Earth in the north direction. It appears to remain stationary at a point in the sky.

34. Persistence of vision is the process which enables us to perceive motion in a cartoon film. Persistence of vision is the phenomenon in which the image of the object is retained on the retina for a very short period of time *i.e.* 1/16 of a second even after the object is removed.

35. CFCs are widely used as coolants in refrigeration and air conditioners, as solvents in cleaners, particularly for electronic circuit boards, as a blowing agents in the production of foam (for example; fire extinguishers), and as propellants in aerosols. Indeed, much of the modern lifestyle of the second half of the 20th century had been made possible by the use of CFCs.

Man-made CFCs however, are the main cause of stratospheric ozone depletion. CFCs have a lifetime in the atmosphere of about 20 to 100 years, and consequently one free chlorine atom from a CFC molecule can do a lot of damage, destroying ozone molecules for a long time. Although emissions of CFCs around the developed world have largely ceased due to international control agreements, the damage to the stratospheric ozone layer will continue well into the 21st century.

36. **Soil Profile:** If one could dig a massive trench (hole), about 50-100 ft vertically downwards into the ground, you will notice that you would have cut through various layers of soil types.

This cross section view is called a Soil Profile. The profile is made up of layers, running parallel to the surface, called Soil Horizons.

Each horizon may be slightly or very different from the other above or below it. Each horizon tells a story about the makeup, age, texture and characteristics of that layer.

Most soils have three major horizons. These are A Horizon, B Horizon and C Horizon. Aside these three, there are also the O, E and R horizons.

- **The O-Horizon:** The O horizon is very common in many surfaces with lots of vegetative cover. It is the layer made up of organic materials such as dead leaves and surface organisms, twigs and fallen trees. It has about 20% organic matter.
- **The A-Horizon:** The A horizon may be seen in the absence of the O horizon, usually known as the topsoil. It is the top layer soils for many grasslands and agricultural lands. Typically, they are made of sand, silt and clay with high amounts of organic matter. This layer is most vulnerable to wind and water erosion. It is also known as the root zone.
- **The E-Horizon:** The E horizon is usually lighter in colour, often below the O and A horizons. It is often rich in nutrients that are leached from the top A and O horizons. It has a lower clay content and are common in forested lands or areas with high quality O and A horizons.

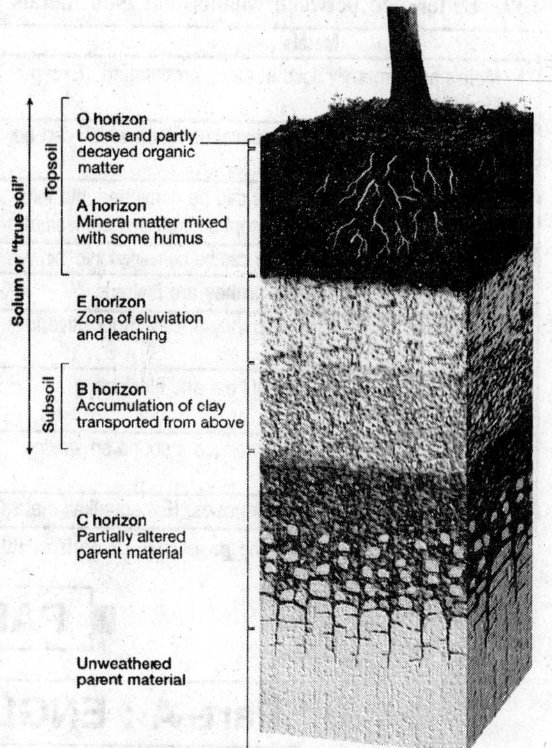

- **The B-Horizon:** The B-horizon has some similarities with the E-horizon. This horizon is formed below the O, A and E horizons and may contain high concentrations of silicate clay, iron, aluminum and carbonates. It is also called the illuviation zone because of the accumulation of minerals. It is the layer in which the roots of big trees end.
- **The C-Horizon:** The C horizon lacks all the properties of the layers above it. It is mainly made up of broken bedrock and no organic material. It has cemented sediment and geologic material. There is little activity here although additions and losses of soluble materials may occur. The C horizon is also known as saprolite.
- **The R-Horizon:** The R horizon is bedrock, material, compacted and cemented by the weight of the overlying horizons. It is the unweathered parent material. Rock types found here include granite, basalt and limestone.

37. Difference between Metals and Non-metals on the basis of their physical properties:

Metals	Non-metals
1. Metals are generally solid at room temperature. (Except Mercury)	1. Non-metals exist in all the three states *i.e.,* solid, liquid and gas.
2. Metals are generally hard. (except sodium which can be cut using a knife)	2. Non-metals are generally soft. (Except diamond which is the hardest substance on the earth)
3. Metals are Malleable; means can be converted into thin sheets using a hammer. (Except sodium and potassium)	3. Non-metals are generally brittle. Will broke down into pieces when beaten by a hammer.
4. Metals are ductile, means they can be converted into thin wires.	4. Non-metals are non-ductile.
5. Metals have shiny surface or they are lustrous.	5. They are non-lustrous. (Except iodine)
6. Metals can lose electrons so they are electropositive in nature.	6. Non-metals gain electrons so they are electronegative in nature.
7. Metals are good conductors of heat and electricity.	7. Non-metals are bad conductors of heat and electricity. (Except graphite)
8. Metals are sonorous. They produce a sound on striking with a hard surface.	8. They do not do so as they are not sonorous.
9. Metals generally have high densities. (Except alkali metals)	9. Non-metals generally have low densities.

The materials which have the properties of both metals and non-metals are called metalloids *e.g.,* silicon, boron.

PAPER-II

Part–A : ENGLISH LANGUAGE

1. Read the following passage and answer the questions that follow.

Prafulla Chandra Ray was born on 2 August 1861 in the district of Jessore, now in Bangladesh, close to the birth place of Madhusudan Dutt, widely regarded as the Milton of Bengal. It was the best of times and the worst. The British had by now perfected their role as masters and British values permeated the Indian upper classes to the very last detail like table manners. That of course, was not the worst of the British influence, there were several. What was far more demeaning to the educated Indians was the fact that senior Government positions were closed to them. Being forfeited of one's right in one's land of birth would become the rallying point for the Indian intelligentsia in the years to come.

Ray's father Harish Chandra Ray, a man of learning and taste, was closely associated with the cultural and intellectual leaders of the time and exerted great influence on his son. Ray had his early schooling in the village school founded by his father but soon his father shifted to Calcutta and at the age of nine, little Prafulla set eyes for the first time, on the bustling city that would be his home for many years to come. He was filled with wonder at ever-charging sights and sounds - the city seemed to change moods ever so often! His formal schooling was interrupted due to illness but that did not affect his education.

(*a*) How did the British perfect their role as masters?

(*b*) Educated Indians felt insulted because ....

(*c*) Prafulla was greatly influenced by his father because ....

(*d*) Prafulla's illness could not stop his learning because ....

(*e*) Intelligentsia in the paragraph means ....

2. Write a paragraph in about 100 words on *any one* of the following.

(*a*) Scene at the Railway Station

(*b*) A Day with my Grandparents

3. You are Abhinav a resident of House No. 99, Swachh Street, Sector-9, Bhopal. You feel concerned to see the modern children spending most of their time on the computer and mobile phones and indulging less in physical activities. You decide to write a letter to the Editor of 'The Times of India', Fort, Mumbai-400001 expressing your concern about the negative aspects of computer and mobile phones. Write the letter in about 150 words.

4. Fill in the blanks with appropriate prepositions or adverbs given in the brackets.

(*a*) The boy was walking .... (in/along/ at) the road when he saw an old man standing .... (beside/besides/into) a tree.

(*b*) When the police searched .... (for, from, No prepositions) the house, they found the smuggled items were looking .... (up/for/with) hidden in the kitchen.

(*c*) Mohan's brother caught him .... (from/by/at) the neck when Mohan tried to run away .... home (across, to, from).

(*d*) He spoke .... (at, in, to) Marathi.

(*e*) .... (At, In, For) the evening, the old man looked out of his window at the children walking one .... (after/on/ behind) the other.

5. Complete the following sentences by choosing the correct phrases from the brackets.

By leaps and bounds, touch down, heart and soul, bring the thieves to book, mend one's way

(*a*) The aeroplane will .... at 2 o' clock.

(*b*) The profits of his company are increasing ....

(*c*) It took several weeks for the police to ....

(*d*) She devoted herself .... to the pursuit of music.

(*e*) Parents' advice always helps one to ....

6. Change the following sentences into Passive or Active Voice as the case may be.

(*a*) Did you waste money?

(*b*) I was telling you a story.

(*c*) She dropped her son at the school.

(*d*) Flowers are plucked by Mary.

(*e*) The problem was solved.

7. The following sentences are incorrect. Find out the error and write the sentences correctly.

(*a*) I went to Goa the last year.

(*b*) Is she agree with us?

(*c*) I'm not very good for cooking.

(*d*) More you read less you understand.

(*e*) She dances good.

8. Write one word for the following group of words.

(*a*) An animal living both on land and in water.

(*b*) The crime of killing a king.

(*c*) A building where animals are killed for meat.

(*d*) A great lover of books.

(*e*) An unmarried woman.

9. Frame meaningful sentences by using each word.

(*a*) Site
Cite

(*b*) Incite
Insight

(*c*) Alter
Altar

(*d*) Need
Knead

(*e*) Navel
Naval

10. You are Ajeet. You feel quite distressed to see that man has been cutting trees indiscriminately for centuries to fulfil his selfish interest. Increasingly urbanization, rapid industrialization and growing population are leading to depletion of natural resources, hence, threatening the survival of mankind. You decide to write an article for your school magazine highlighting your views on the need to conserve nature. Using your own ideas, write the article in about 100-150 words on the topic 'Nature Conservation'.

Part–B : SOCIAL STUDIES

1. State True/False.

(*a*) Viveka Vardhini magazine was started by Kandukuri Veeresalingam.

(*b*) The partition of Bengal was ordered by Lord Cornwallis.

(*c*) The Vice-President is elected by only the elected members of the Lok Sabha and Rajya Sabha.

(*d*) Sikhs form the largest single minority community in India.

(*e*) Animal husbandry is the main production activity in the villages of India.

(*f*) Sariska Tiger Reserve is situated in Alwar, Rajasthan?

(*g*) The rubber plantation vegetation belongs to Tropical Evergreen forest.

(*h*) Death rate is also known as mortality rate.

(*i*) The prosecution is the legal party which an individual accused of breaking of law.

(*j*) Ruhr region of Germany is famous for rich deposits of coal.

(*k*) Protection of Women from Domestic Violence Act, 2000 is an act of the Parliament of India.

(*l*) Mother Dairy is the cooperative which has brought about the white revolution in the country.

(*m*) BPL stands for Behind Poverty Level.

(*n*) Every person has a Fundamental Right to be defended by a lawyer under the Article 22.

(*o*) Rowlatt Acts (February 1919), empowered the British to put Indian people in jail without a trial.

2. Fill in the blanks.

(*a*) The first Deputy Prime Minister of Independent India was ....

(*b*) The .... shepherds of Himachal Pradesh is a nomadic community.

(*c*) The author who described the revolt of 1857 as "the first war of independence" was ....

(*d*) The game of badminton originated in ....

(*e*) The highest mountain peak in the Karakoram Range is ....

(*f*) Narrow valleys between Shivalik and Himachal are known as ....

(*g*) .... is the largest coffee-producing nation in the world.

(*h*) Hampi is located within the ruins of Vijayanagara, beside the river ....

(*i*) In Lok Sabha there are .... seats.

(*j*) Emperor Ashoka belonged to .... dynasty.

(*k*) .... is a weather phenomenon caused when warm water from the Western Pacific Ocean flows eastward.

(*l*) The Delhi Police is under .... government.

(*m*) In India, Forest Research Institute is situated in ....

(*n*) The Battle of Buxar was fought in .... year.

(*o*) Governor of RBI is ....

(*p*) The river which joins Chenab in Pakistan is ....

3. Write the full form of the following abbreviations:

(*a*) LBW	(*b*) IMHO
(*c*) FBI	(*d*) EPABX
(*e*) GAIL	(*f*) UNESCO
(*g*) PIN	(*h*) SPCA
(*i*) SPICMACAY	(*j*) PVSM

4. Match the following:

(*a*) Lord Dalhousie	(*i*) 1914
(*b*) Osaka	(*ii*) Bauxite
(*c*) Criminal Tribe Act	(*iii*) Criminal Court
(*d*) First World War	(*iv*) Manchester of Japan
(*e*) Jet stream	(*v*) Chairman of the Drafting committee

(*f*) Odisha (*vi*) 1984

(*g*) Dr BR Ambedkar (*vii*) Chief Judge

(*h*) Qazi (*viii*) Doctrine of Lapse

(*i*) Bhopal Gas Tragedy (*ix*) High altitude westernly winds

(*j*) Faujdari adalat (*x*) 1871

5. Write short notes on any *five* of the following topic (limit 50 words)

(*a*) National Food Security Bill

(*b*) Public Interest Litigation

(*c*) Describe the life style of Gujjar Bakarwals

(*d*) India is a secular state

(*e*) River disputes in India

(*f*) Doctrine of Lapse

(*g*) Jan Lokpal Bill

EXPLANATORY ANSWERS

Part–A : English Language

1. (*a*) British perfected this role as masters by making Indians thin slaves and imposing their rule over India.

(*b*) they were denied senior government positions in their own country.

(*c*) his father was closely associated with the cultural and intellectual leaders of the time.

(*d*) he learnt many things under the influence of his father and Calcutta city as well.

(*e*) intellectuals or highly educated people regarded as possessing culture and political influence.

2. Scene at the Railway Station

Last Sunday, I went to the Railway station. I had to go to Delhi. I went to the booking window to buy a ticket. There was a long queue there. I stood in the queue. When my turn came, I bought the ticket and reached the platform. The train was late by half an hour. I sat on a bench at the platform. I saw the vendors crying for their wares. Some people were taking snacks with tea. Others were having cold drinks. Some were reading some newspaper or magazine. Others were just talking. Some were discussing politics. After some time, it was announced that the train was coming. People got up from the benches. As the train reached the platform, people rushed towards the train. Many coolies were seen carrying big bundles of luggage. I was able to board the train without much difficulty. Soon the signal was green. The guard whistled, waved the green flag and the train started. The platform became deserted now.

3.

House No. 99,
Swachh Street,
Sector-9, Bhopal
Date: 18/11/20......

The Editor
The Times of India,
Fort,
Mumbai-400001

Subject: Concern about modern children

Sir,

It is a matter of grave concern to see the modern children spending most of their time on the computer and mobile phones and indulging less in physical activities.

No doubt computer and mobile phone have big importance in the modern world but they should be used only when required and not for wasting much of one's time. Nowadays children keep chatting with friends or playing games. They are hardly seen doing any physical activity like outdoor games, yoga or exercise.

As a result they not only waste their time but they also lose the health and stamina. They often have weak eye sights, weak limbs, loss of appetite and constipation. This all makes them vulnerable to many diseases and disabilities.

Such children can neither be good students nor in future good citizens of India.

Yours truly,

Abhinav

4. (*a*) along, beside
   (*b*) No prepositions, for
   (*c*) by, from
   (*d*) in
   (*e*) in, behind

5. (*a*) touch down
   (*b*) by leaps and bounds
   (*c*) bring the thieves to book
   (*d*) heart and soul
   (*e*) mind one's way

6. (*a*) Was the money wasted by you?
   (*b*) You were being told a story by me.
   (*c*) Her son was dropped at the school by her.
   (*d*) Mary plucks flowers.
   (*e*) I solved the problem.

7. (*a*) I went to Goa last year.
   (*b*) Does she agree with us?
   (*c*) I'm not very good at cooking.
   (*d*) The more you read the less you understand.
   (*e*) She is a good dancer.

8. (*a*) Amphibian (*b*) Regicide
   (*c*) Slaughterhouse (*d*) Bibliophile
   (*e*) Spinster

9. (*a*) Everyone rushed to the site of accident. Can you cite a better example?
   (*b*) He was guilty of inciting violence. Bose was a man of deep insight.
   (*c*) You cannot alter the fact. She looked at the altar in the church.
   (*d*) You need not go there. Mother kneaded the flour to make dough.
   (*e*) A navel is considered centre of the human body. My father is a naval officer.

10. **Nature Conservation**

Since ages man is related with the environment. He resides in the surroundings alongwith different plants, trees and animals. Long ago he lived with the environment without disturbing its components. But now man has started extensively changing the surroundings, thus transforming the environment and consequently affecting the delicate balance of the ecosystem which is so essential for life on this planet, due to his ever expanding needs. People need food, water and space to live, air to breathe and energy to drive their machines. Increase in number of people, thus increase in consumption of food, water and space, leaves less and less space for other animals and plants which means that many environmental problems have been caused by people. Global warming, acid rain and holes in the ozone layer are just three such examples.

Protection of natural wealth and conservation of nature and life in all forms is a matter of great concern. Checking environmental degradation is a crying need. While degradation is affecting the entire planet and conservation has the attention of all countries, each person has personal responsibilities in this. Some measures must be taken by each one of us for survival of life on earth.

Part-B : Social Studies

1. (*a*) True (*b*) False (*c*) False
   (*d*) False (*e*) False (*f*) True
   (*g*) True (*h*) True (*i*) True
   (*j*) True (*k*) True (*l*) True
   (*m*) False (*n*) True (*o*) True

2. (*a*) Sardar Vallabhbhai Patel
   (*b*) Gaddi (*c*) V.D. Savarkar
   (*d*) England (*e*) K_2
   (*f*) Duns (*g*) Brazil
   (*h*) Tungabhadra (*i*) 552

(*j*) Mauryan (*k*) El Nino
(*l*) Central (*m*) Dehradun
(*n*) 1764 (*o*) Urjit Patel
(*p*) Jhelum

3. (*a*) LBW : Leg Before Wicket
(*b*) IMHO : International Medical Health Organisation
(*c*) FBI : Federal Bureau of Investigation
(*d*) EPABX : Electronic Private Automatic Branch Exchange
(*e*) GAIL : Gas Authority of India Limited
(*f*) UNESCO : United Nations Educational, Scientific and Cultural Organisation
(*g*) PIN : Postal Index Number
(*h*) SPCA : Society for the Prevention of Cruelty to Animals
(*i*) SPICMACAY : The Society for the Promotion of Indian Classical Music and Culture Amongst Youth
(*j*) PVSM : Param Vishist Seva Medal

4. (*a*) – (*viii*) (*b*) – (*iv*) (*c*) – (*x*)
(*d*) – (*i*) (*e*) – (*ix*) (*f*) – (*ii*)
(*g*) – (*v*) (*h*) – (*vii*) (*i*) – (*vi*)
(*j*) – (*iii*)

5. (*a*) National Food Security Act

The **National Food Security Act, 2013** (also **Right to Food Act**) is an Act of the Parliament of India which aims to provide subsidized food grains to approximately two thirds of India's 1.2 billion people. It was signed into law on 12 September 2013, retroactive to 5 July 2013.

The National Food Security Act, 2013 converts into legal entitlements for existing food security programmes of the Government of India. It includes the Midday Meal Scheme, Integrated Child Development Services scheme and the Public Distribution System. Further, the NFSA 2013 recognizes maternity entitlements. The Midday Meal Scheme and the Integrated Child Development Services Scheme are universal in nature whereas the PDS will reach about two-thirds of the population (75% in rural areas and 50% in urban areas).

(*b*) Public Interest Litigation

Public Interest Litigation is litigation for the protection of the public interest. In Indian law, Article 32 of the Indian constitution contains a tool which directly joins the public with judiciary. A PIL may be introduced in a court of law by the court itself (*suo motu*), rather than the aggrieved party or another third party. For the exercise of the court's jurisdiction, it is not necessary for the victim of the violation of his or her rights to personally approach the court. In a PIL, the right to file suit is given to a member of the public through judicial activism. The member of the public may be a non-governmental organization (NGO), an institution or an individual. The Supreme Court of India, rejecting the criticism of judicial activism, has stated that the judiciary has stepped in to give direction because due to executive inaction, the laws enacted by Parliament and the state legislatures for the poor since independence have not been properly implemented.

(*c*) Describe the life style of Gujjar Bakarwals:

The Gujjar Bakarwals of Jammu Kashmir were great herders of goat and sheep. Some of them migrated to Jammu in search of good pastures for their animals. They estabilished themselves in the area, and moved annually between their summer and winter grazing grounds.

In winter, when the high mountains were covered with snow, they with their herds in the low hills of the Shivalik range. With the onset of the summer, the snow melted and mountainsides were lush green. The variety of grasses that sprouted provided rich nutritious forage for their animal herds.

(*d*) India is a secular state

Secular state is one where people have freedom to make independent choices, which is very much present in India. India is a country of religions where exists diverse religious groups but, in spite of this the constitution stands for secular state of India and declares India as a "Sovereign, Socialist, Secular, Democratic, Republic." Many fundamental rights outlaw discrimination on the ground of religion and guarantees a freedom of worship and religion. As per the great Indian leaders like Gandhi and Nehru declared India as a secular state, a common home of the Hindus, Muslims, Sikhs, Christians, and all other citizens. The secularism has resulted in opening all posts to members of all communities.

(*e*) River disputes in India

Most rivers of India are plagued with interstate disputes. Almost all the major rivers of the country are inter-state rivers and their waters are shared by two or more than two states.

After independence, demand for water had been increasing at an accelerated rate due to rapid growth of population, agricultural development, urbanisation, industrialisation, etc. These developments have led to several inter-state disputes about sharing of water of these rivers.

Following interstate river water disputes are worth mentioning.

(*i*) Cauvery water dispute between Tamil Nadu, Karnataka and Kerala.

(*ii*) The Krishna water dispute between Maharashtra, Karnataka and Andhra Pradesh.

(*iii*) The Godavari river water dispute between Andhra Pradesh, Madhya Pradesh, Chhattisgarh, Odisha and Karnataka.

(*iv*) The Narmada water dispute between Gujarat, Maharashtra, Madhya Pradesh and Rajasthan.

(*f*) Doctrine of lapse

Doctrine of lapse was the policy of Dalhousie, the then Governor General, to annex the independent Indian States in 1848 A.D.

This doctrine was based on the idea that in case a ruler of dependent state died childless, the right of ruling over the State reverted or 'lapsed' to the sovereign.

This position, however, was complicated by adoption. Hindus, including Hindu rulers, attached great importance to the performance of their funeral rites by their sons and if they died without a male issue, they resorted to adoption. An adopted son was allowed to inherit private property but the political rights of ruling a State were different.

(*g*) Jan Lokpal Bill: The Jan Lokpal Bill (Citizen's Ombudsman Bill) is a draft anti-corruption bill drawn up by prominent civil society activists seeking the appointment of a Jan Lokpal, an independent body that would investigate corruption cases, complete the investigation within a year and envisages trial in the case getting over in the next one year.

Drafted by Justice Santosh Hegde (former Supreme Court Judge and former Lokayukta of Karnataka), Prashant Bhushan (Supreme Court Lawyer) and Arvind Kejriwal (RTI activist), the draft Bill envisages a system where a corrupt person found guilty would go to jail within two years of the complaint being made and his ill-gotten wealth being confiscated. It also seeks power to the Jan Lokpal to prosecute politicians and bureaucrats without government permission.

Previous Paper (Solved)

Sainik School Entrance Exam, 2016

(Class-IX)

PAPER-I

Part–A : Mathematics

SECTION–I

1. Solve : $\left(\frac{3}{7}\right)+\left(-\frac{6}{11}\right)+\left(-\frac{8}{11}\right)+\left(\frac{5}{11}\right)$.

2. Find any three rational numbers between 3 and 4.

3. Two numbers are in the ratio 5 : 3. If they differ by 18, what are the numbers?

4. Convert the following ratios to percentages.
(*i*) 2 : 3 (*ii*) 3 : 4

5. Find the number of sides of a regular polygon whose each exterior angle has a measure of 45°.

6. State whether True or False.
(*i*) All rhombuses are parallelograms.
(*ii*) All parallelograms are trapeziums.
(*iii*) All squares are not parallelograms.
(*iv*) All squares are trapeziums.

7. The list price of a frock is ₹ 220. A discount of 20% is announced on sales. What is the amount of discount on it and its sale price?

8. How many numbers lie between the squares of the following numbers?
(*i*) 25 and 26
(*ii*) 99 and 100

9. Find the square root of 6400 through prime factorisation method.

10. A dice is thrown then, find the probability of getting prime number.

11. Shyam bought an air cooler for ₹ 3300 including a tax of 10%. Find the price of the air cooler before VAT was added.

12. How many diagonals does each of the following have:
(*a*) Convex Quadrilateral
(*b*) A Regular Hexagon

13. Factorise : $x^2 - 7x + 12$.

14. Simplify the expression :
$3y\,(2y - 7) - 3\,(y - 4) - 63$ for $y = -2$.

15. Using the Identity (I), find $(2x + 3y)^2$.

16. Find the area of the quadrilateral PQRS shown in the figure.

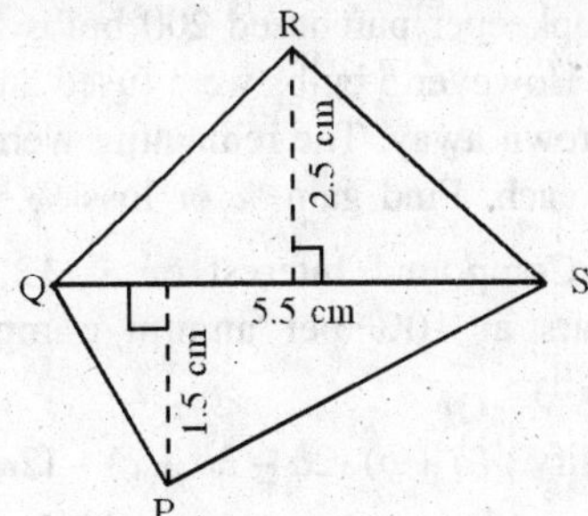

17. Find the height of a cylinder whose radius is 7 cm and the total surface area is 968 cm^2.

18. Evaluate $\frac{8^{-1} \times 5^3}{2^{-4}}$ using law of exponents and powers.

19. Six pipes are required to fill a tank in 1 hour 20 minutes. How long will it take if only five pipes of the same type are used?

20. Solve : $\frac{x}{4}+\frac{x}{6}=x-7.$

SECTION–II

21. The difference between two whole numbers is 66. The ratio of the two numbers is 2 : 5. What are the two numbers?

22. In the figure, BEST is a parallelogram. Find the values of angles *x*, *y* and *z*.

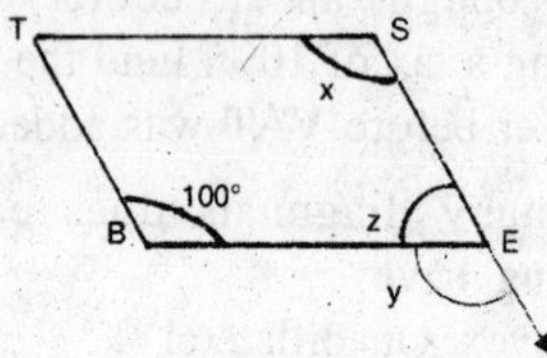

23. A bag has 4 red balls and 2 yellow balls. The balls are identical in all respects other than colour. A ball is drawn from the bag without looking into the bag. What is the probability of getting a red ball? Is it more or less than getting a yellow ball?

24. Write a Pythagorean triplet whose smallest number is 8.

25. A shopkeeper purchased 200 bulbs for ₹ 10 each. However 5 bulbs were fused and had to be thrown away. The remaining were sold at ₹ 12 each. Find gain % or loss %.

26. Find Compound Interest on ₹ 12,600 for 2 years at 10% per annum compounded annually.

27. Simplify : $(a + b)(2a - 3b + c) - (2a - 3b)c$.

28. For the given solid, draw the top view, front view and side view.

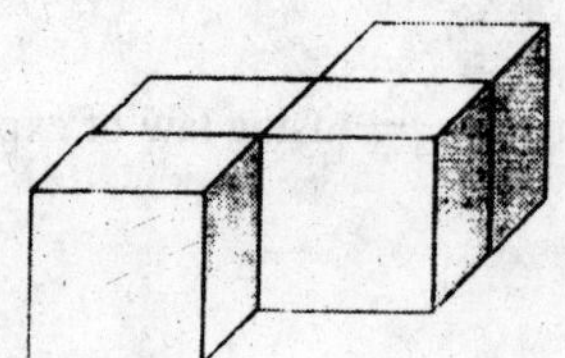

29. (*a*) How are prisms and cylinders alike?
(*b*) How are pyramids and cones alike?
(*c*) Is a square prism same as a cube?

30. A godown is in the form of a cuboid of measure 60 m × 40 m × 30 m. How many cuboid boxes can be stored if the volume of one box is 0.8 m^3?

31. A rectangular piece of paper 11 cm × 4 cm is folded without overlapping to make a cylinder of height 4 cm. Find the volume of the cylinder.

32. Simply : $\left\{\left(\frac{1}{3}\right)^{-2}-\left(\frac{1}{2}\right)^{-3}\right\}\div\left(\frac{1}{4}\right)^{-2}$.

33. If the three digit number 24*x* is divisible by 9, what is the value of *x*?

34. The four angles of a quadrilateral are in the ratio 2 : 3 : 5 : 8. Find the angles.

35. Sum of two numbers is 74. One of the numbers is 10 more than the other what are the numbers?

36. The perimeter of a rectangle is 13 cm and its width is $2\frac{3}{4}$ cm. Find its length.

37. CERI is a rhombus as shown in figure. Find *x, y, z*.

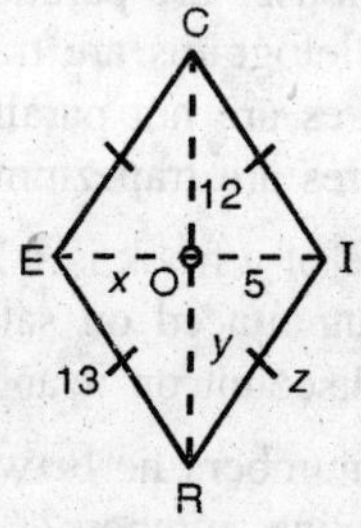

38. A sum of ₹ 10000 is borrowed at a rate of interest of 15% per annum for 2 years. Find the simple interest on this sum and the amount to be paid at the end of two years.

39. The population of a city was 20,000 in the year 2007. It increased at the rate of 5% per annum. Find the population at the end of year 2010.

40. If each edge of a cube is doubled

(*i*) How many times will its surface area increase?

(*ii*) How many times will its volume increase?

SECTION–III

41. Karan has a total of ₹ 590 as currency notes in the denominations of ₹ 50, ₹ 20 and ₹ 10. The ratio of number of ₹ 50 notes and ₹ 20 notes is 3 : 5. If he has a total of 25 notes, how many notes of each denomination does he have?

42. On a particular day, the sales (in rupees) of different items of a baker's shop are given below. Draw a pie-chart for this data.

(*a*) Ordinary Bread	:	320
(*b*) Fruit Bread	:	80
(*c*) Cakes and Pastries	:	160
(*d*) Biscuits	:	120
(*e*) other	:	40

43. A picnic is being planned in a school for class VIII. Girls are 60% of the total number of students and are 18 in number. The picnic site is 55 km from the school and the transport company is charging at the rate of ₹ 12 per km. The total cost of refreshments will be ₹ 4280. Find out the following :

(*a*) The ratio of the number of girls to the number of boys in the class.

(*b*) The cost per head if two teachers are also going with the class.

(*c*) If their first stop is at a place 22 km from the school, what per cent of the total distance of 55 km is this? What per cent of distance is left to be covered?

44. Total cost of 5 metres of a particular quality of cloth is ₹ 210. Tabulate the cost of 2, 4, 10 and 13 metres of cloth of same type using proportions.

45. Observe the histogram on figure and answer the questions given below:

(*i*) What information is being given by the histogram?

(*ii*) What group contains maximum girls?

(*iii*) How many girls have a length of more than 145 cm?

(*iv*) If we divide the girls into the following categories, how many would there be in each?

150 cm and more	– Group A
140 to less than 150 cm	– Group B
Less than 140 cm	– Group C

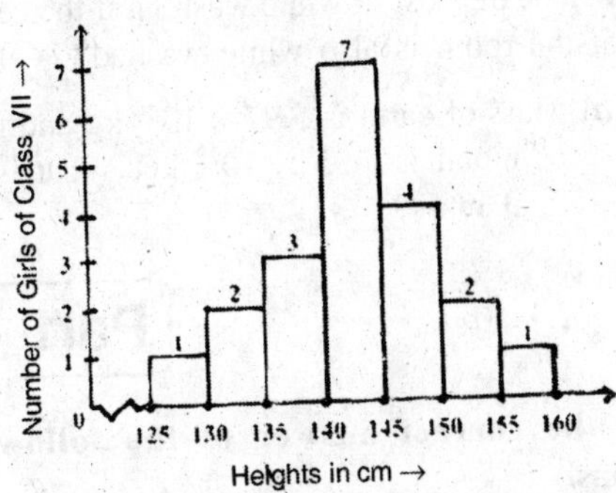

46. (*a*) Is 2352 a perfect square? If not, find the smallest multiple of 2352 which is a perfect square. Find the square root of the new number.

(*b*) Find smallest number by which 9408 must be divided so that the quotient is a perfect square. Find the square root of the quotient.

47. The rectangular park in figure is of length 30 m and width 20 m. Having understood the figure answers the following questions.

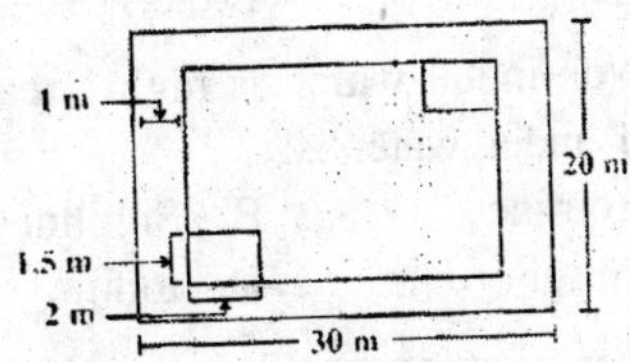

(*a*) What is the total length of the fence surrounding it?

(*b*) How much land is occupied by the park?

(*c*) There is a path of one metre width running inside along the perimeter of the park that has to be cemented. If 1 bag cement is required to cement 4 m^2 area, how many bags of cement will be required to construct the cemented path?

(*d*) There are two rectangular flower beds of size 1.5 m × 2 m each in the park as shown in the diagram and the rest has grass in it. Find the area covered by grass.

48. The internal measures of a cuboidal room are 12 m × 8 m × 4 m. Find the total cost of white washing all the four walls of the room, if the cost of white washing is ₹ 5 per m^2. What will be the cost of white washing if the ceiling of the room is also white washed?

49. (*a*) Mass of earth is 5.97×10^{24} kg and mass of moon is 7.35×10^{22} kg. What is the total mass?

(*b*) The distance between sun and earth is 1.496×10^{11} m and the distance between earth and moon is 3.84×10^{8} m. During solar eclipse moon comes between earth and sun. At that time what is the distance between moon and sun?

50. Define the following :

(*a*) A Bar Graph

(*b*) A Pie-chart

(*c*) A Histogram

(*d*) Frequency

(*e*) A Pictograph

Part–B : Science

Select the correct answer of the following questions.

1. Penicillin is a drug that can:

A. Interfere in the biological pathway of bacteria.

B. An antibiotic that can kill bacteria

C. Both A & B

D. None of the above

2. To hear a distinct echo the time interval between the original sound and the reflected sound must be:

A. 0.2 S B. 1 S

C. 2 S D. 0.1 S

3. The Non-metal which is highly reactive and stored under water is:

A. Bromine B. Sulphur

C. Phosphorus D. Iodine

4. Nitrogen fixation can be done by:

A. Industries

B. Rhizobium

C. Lightning

D. All of the above

5. The device used to measure the Purity of milk is:

A. Hydrometer B. Lactometer

C. Hygometer D. Maltometer

6. The Crops which are grown in the rainy season are called:

A. Rabi Crops B. Kharif Crops

C. Rainy Crops D. None of these

7. The number of nuclei present in a Zygote is:

A. one B. two

C. four D. None

8. Rayon is different from synthetic fibres because:

A. It has a silk like appearance

B. It is obtained from wood pulp

C. Its fibres can also be woven like of natural fibres

D. None of these

9. Choose the correct arrangement of the forces due to rolling, static and sliding friction in a decreasing order:

A. rolling, static, sliding

B. rolling, sliding, static

C. static, sliding, rolling

D. sliding, static rolling

10. The process of transferring of charge from a charged body to earth is called:

A. Discharging

B. Charging

C. Earthing

D. None of these

11. That part of the eye which gives a distinct colour to the eye is:
A. Iris B. Pupil
C. Cornea D. Lens

12. Green house gases are:
A. CO_2 B. CH_4
C. CFC D. All of the above

13. Hottest part of the candle flame is:
A. Innermost B. Outermost
C. Middle Zone D. Luminous

14. Those species of plants which are found in a particular area are called:
A. Species
B. Endemic species
C. Endangered species
D. None of these

15. A tadpole develops into an adult by the process of:
A. Fertilization
B. Metamorphosis
C. Embedding
D. Budding

Write answers of the following questions.

16. What is a constellation? Name any two constellations.

17. What is lateral inversion? Name the mirror in which image formed undergoes lateral Inversion.

18. What are chemical effects of electric current, give one use of such effect?

19. Write the difference between audible and inaudible sound.

20. Why objects moving in fluids must have special shapes?

21. Name of the type of force acting:
(*i*) A straw rubbed with paper attracts another straw.
(*ii*) A ball rolling along the ground.

22. What is insulin, where is it produced in the body?

23. Petroleum is called black gold, Why?

24. What do you mean by polymer, give one example of natural polymer?

25. What is the relation between loudness and amplitude. In which unit is loudness expressed. If the amplitude of the wave becomes thrice, what change will you observe in loudness?

Write answers of the following questions.

26. What are antibiotics? Give two examples.

27. What are weeds, how do they affect the growth of plants?

28. What is potable water and how is water purified?

29. What is cloning? Who performed it for the first time. Write the name of first mammal that was cloned?

30. What is deforestation? Write its causes.

31. LPG is better domestic fuel than wood, why?

32. What is refining. Write the fractions of petroleum refining?

33. Explain the difference between thermosetting plastics and thermoplastics. Give two examples of each.

34. Write three commercial uses of micro-organisms.

35. Differentiate between prokaryotes and eukaryotes with one example each.

36. Draw a diagram for Animal cell and Label the following:
(*a*) Cell membrane
(*b*) Vacuole
(*c*) Nucleus
(*d*) Cytoplasm

37. (*a*) Define force, give two examples of situations in which applied force causes a change in the shape of an object?
(*b*) In an experiment 4.5 kg of fuel was completely burnt, the heat produced was measured to be 90000 KJ, calculate the calorific value of fuel.

EXPLANATORY ANSWERS

Part–A : Mathematics

1. $\frac{3}{7}-\frac{6}{11}-\frac{8}{11}+\frac{5}{11}$

$= \frac{3}{7}-\frac{9}{11}$

$= \frac{33-63}{77} = \frac{-30}{77}.$

2. First rational number between 3 and 4

$= \frac{1}{2}(3+4) = \frac{7}{2}.$

2nd rational number between 3 and $\frac{7}{2}$

$= \frac{1}{2}\left(\frac{7}{2}+3\right) = \frac{1}{2}\left(\frac{7+6}{2}\right) = \frac{13}{4}$

3rd rational number between $\frac{7}{2}$ and 4

$= \frac{1}{2}\left(\frac{7}{2}+4\right) = \frac{1}{2}\left(\frac{7+8}{2}\right) = \frac{15}{4}.$

3. Let, numbers are $5x$ and $3x$

According to the question,

$5x - 3x = 18$

$\Rightarrow \quad 2x = 18$

$\Rightarrow \quad x = 9$

$\therefore$ Numbers are 45 and 27.

4. (*i*) $2 : 3 = \frac{2}{3}\times 100 = \frac{200}{3}\%$

$= 66.66\%$

(*ii*) $3 : 4 = \frac{3}{4}\times 100$

$= 75\%.$

5. No. of exterior angles $= \frac{360}{45} = 8$

Hence, polygon has 8 sides.

6. (*i*) All rhombuses are parallelograms **True**

(*ii*) All parallelograms are trapezium **True**

(*iii*) All squares are not parallelograms **False**

(*iv*) All squares are trapeziums **True**

7. Discount = 20% of ₹ 220

$= \frac{20}{100}\times 220 = ₹\ 44$

$\therefore$ S.P. of the frock = 220 − 44 = ₹ 176.

8. (*i*) Required no. = (25 + 26) − 1 = 50

(*ii*) Required no. = (99 + 100) −1 = 198

9. $6400 = 2\times 2\times 2\times 2\times 5\times 2\times 2\times 2\times 2\times 5$

$\therefore \quad \sqrt{6400} = \sqrt{2^8\times 5^2}$

$= 2^4 \times 5 = 16 \times 5 = 80.$

10. 1, 2, 3, 4, 5 and 6 numbers are in a dice

Total number = 6

Prime numbers = 2, 3, 5 = 3

$\therefore$ Probability of getting prime number

$= \frac{3}{6} = \frac{1}{2}.$

11. 100 + 10 = 110

Price of air cooler with tax ₹ 110 then price without tax = ₹ 100

Price of air cooler with tax ₹ 3300 then price without tax $= \frac{100}{110}\times 3300 = ₹\ 3000$

Hence, price of the air cooler before Vat = ₹ 3000.

12. (*a*) No. of diagonals in a convex quadrilateral

$= \frac{n(n-3)}{2} = \frac{4(4-3)}{2} = 2$

(*b*) No. of diagonals in a regular hexagon

$= \frac{6(6-3)}{2} = \frac{6\times 3}{2} = 9.$

13. $x^2 - 7x + 12 = x^2 - 4x - 3x + 12$
$= x(x-4) - 3(x-4)$
$= (x-4)(x-3)$

14. $3y(2y-7) - 3(y-4) - 63$
$= 6y^2 - 21y - 3y + 12 - 63$
$= 6y^2 - 24y - 51$
$= 6(-2)^2 - 24(-2) - 51 \quad [\because y = -2]$
$= 24 + 24 \times 2 - 51$
$= 24 + 48 - 51$
$= 72 - 51 = 21.$

15. $(2x + 3y)^2 = (2x)^2 + 2(2x)(3y) + (3y)^2$
$= 4x^2 + 12xy + 9y^2.$

16.

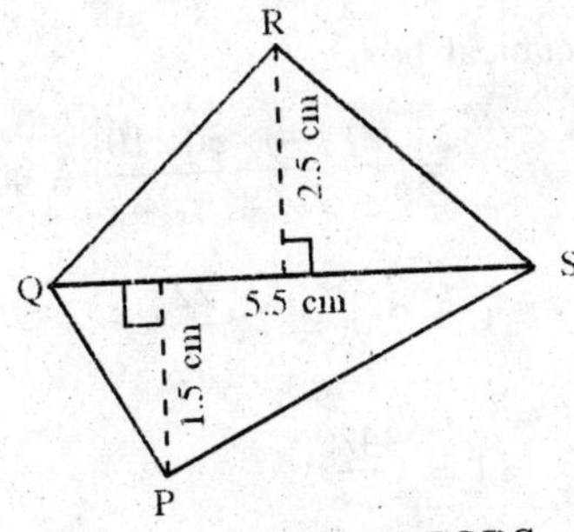

Area of quadrilateral PQRS

$= \frac{1}{2} \times \text{diagonal } (h_1 + h_2)$

$= \frac{1}{2} \times 5.5(2.5 + 1.5)$

$= \frac{1}{2} \times 5.5 \times 4$

$= 5.5 \times 2 = 11 \text{ cm}^2.$

17. Total surface area of cylinder $= 2\pi r(h + r)$

$\Rightarrow \quad 968 = 2 \times \frac{22}{7} \times 7 \times (h+7)$

$\Rightarrow \quad 968 = 2 \times 22 \times (h+7)$

$\Rightarrow \quad (h+7) = \frac{968}{2 \times 22} = \frac{88}{2 \times 2} = 22 \text{ cm}$

Hence, height of the cylinder
$= 22 \text{ cm} - 7 \text{ cm}$
$= 15 \text{ cm}.$

18. $\frac{8^{-1} \times 5^3}{2^{-4}} = \frac{1}{8} \times 5^3 \times 2^4$

$= \frac{1 \times 5^3 \times 2^4}{2^3} = 5^3 \times 2^1$

$= 125 \times 2 = 250.$

19. $\because$ 6 pipes can fill a tank in 80 minutes
$\therefore$ 1 pipe can fill that tank in 6×80 min.
$\therefore$ 5 pipes can fill that tank in

$= \frac{6 \times 80}{5}$ min $= 96$ min.

$= 1$ hour 36 minutes.

20. $\frac{x}{4} + \frac{x}{6} = x - 7$

$\Rightarrow \quad \frac{3x + 2x}{12} = x - 7$

$\Rightarrow \quad 5x = 12x - 84$

$\Rightarrow \quad 7x = 84 \therefore x = 12.$

21. Let, numbers are $2x$ and $5x$
According to the question,
$5x - 2x = 66$
$\Rightarrow \quad 3x = 66$
$\Rightarrow \quad x = 22$
$\therefore$ Numbers are 44 and 110.

22.

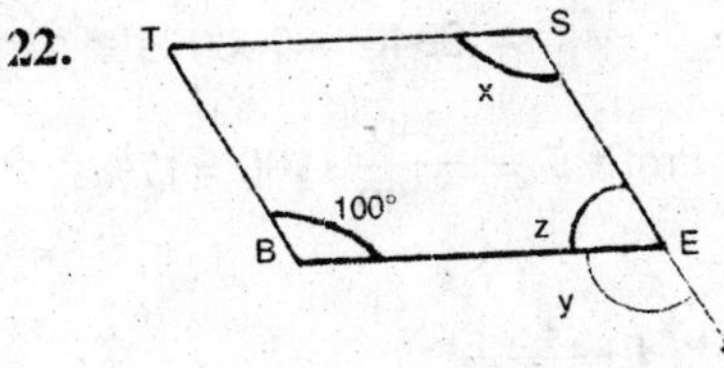

$\because$ BEST is a parallelogram.
$\therefore \quad \angle B = \angle S = 100°$
(opp. angles are equal)
$\therefore \quad x = 100°$
$\angle B + \angle E = 180°$
(Sum of adjacent angles = 180°)
$100 + \angle E = 180$

$\Rightarrow \quad \angle E = 80°$

$\therefore \quad z = 80°$

$\angle z + \angle y = 180°$ (Straight angle)

$80° + \angle y = 180°$

$\therefore \quad \angle y = 100°$

23. Total balls = 4 red + 2 yellow = 6 balls

Probability of getting a red ball

$$= \frac{4}{6} = \frac{2}{3}$$

Probability of getting a yellow ball

$$= \frac{2}{6} = \frac{1}{3}$$

Hence, probability of getting a red ball is more than getting a yellow ball.

24. We can get a pythagorean triplet

$2m, m^2 - 1, m^2 + 1$

Let, $\quad 2m = 8$

$\Rightarrow \quad m = 4$

$m^2 - 1 = (4)^2 - 1 = 15$

$m^2 + 1 = (4)^2 + 1 = 17$

Hence, 8, 15, 17 is a pythagorean triplet whose smallest number is 8.

25. C.P. of 200 bulbs = 200 × 10 = ₹ 2000

200 − 5 = 195

S.P. of 195 bulbs = 195 × 12 = ₹ 2340

Profit = SP − CP

= 2340 − 2000 = ₹ 340

$$\text{Profit } \% = \frac{340}{2000} \times 100 = 17\%.$$

26.

$$A = P\left(1 + \frac{r}{100}\right)^t$$

$$= 12600\left(1 + \frac{10}{100}\right)^2$$

$$= 12600 \times \frac{11}{10} \times \frac{11}{10}$$

= 126 × 121 = ₹ 15246

∴ C.I. = A − P = 15246 − 12600 = ₹ 2646.

27. $(a + b)(2a - 3b + c) - (2a - 3b)c$

$= 2a^2 - 3ab + ac + 2ab - 3b^2 + bc - 2ac + 3bc$

$= 2a^2 - ab + 4bc - ac - 3b^2.$

28.

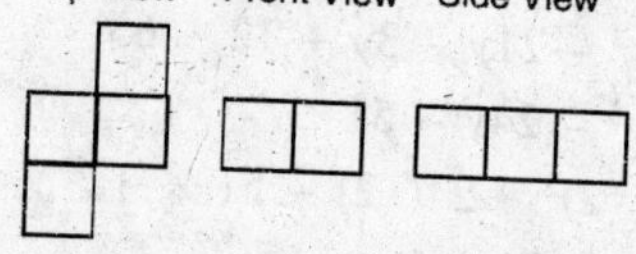

29. (*a*) A prism becomes like a cylinder when number of sides of base increases.

(*b*) A piramid becomes like a cone when the number of sides of base increases.

(*c*) No. It can be cuboid also.

30. No. of cubical boxes

$$= \frac{60 \times 40 \times 30 \times 10}{8} = 90000.$$

31.

$$C = 2\pi r = 2 \times \frac{22}{7} \times r$$

$$\Rightarrow \quad 11 = \frac{44r}{7}$$

$$\Rightarrow \quad r = \frac{11 \times 7}{44} = \frac{7}{4} \text{ cm.}$$

Volume of cylinder

$$= \pi r^2 h = \frac{22}{7} \times \frac{7}{4} \times \frac{7}{4} \times 4$$

$$= \frac{77}{2} = 38.5 \text{ cm}^3.$$

32.

$$\left\{\left(\frac{1}{3}\right)^{-2} - \left(\frac{1}{2}\right)^{-3}\right\} \div \left(\frac{1}{4}\right)^{-2}$$

$$= \left\{\left(\frac{3}{1}\right)^2 - \left(\frac{2}{1}\right)^3\right\} \div \left(\frac{4}{1}\right)^2$$

$= (9 - 8) \div 16$

$$= 1 \div 16 = \frac{1}{16}.$$

33. $9\overline{)24x}(27$

$\underline{18}$

$6x$

if $x = 3$

then 63

$\underline{63}$

$\times$

Hence, the value of $x = 3$.

34. Let, $\angle A = 2x°, \angle B = 3x°, \angle C = 5x°, \angle D = 8x°$

$\angle A + \angle B + \angle C + \angle D = 360°$

$\Rightarrow 2x + 3x + 5x + 8x = 360°$

$\Rightarrow 18x = 360°$

$\Rightarrow x = 20°$

$\therefore \angle A = 40°$

$\angle B = 60°,$

$\angle C = 100°$

$\angle D = 160°.$

35. Let, other number $= x$

$\therefore$ one number $= x + 10$

According to the question,

$x + 10 + x = 74$

$\Rightarrow 2x = 64$

$\Rightarrow x = 32$

$\therefore$ Numbers are 32 and 42.

36. Let, length of rectangle $= x$ cm

Perimeter $= 2(l + b)$

$$\Rightarrow 13 = 2\left(x + \frac{11}{4}\right)$$

$$\Rightarrow 13 = 2x + \frac{11}{2}$$

$$\Rightarrow 13 - \frac{11}{2} = 2x$$

$$\Rightarrow \frac{26-11}{2} = 2x \quad \Rightarrow \frac{15}{2} = 2x$$

$$\Rightarrow 4x = 15 \quad \Rightarrow x = \frac{15}{4} = 3\frac{3}{4}$$

Hence, length of rectangle $= 3\frac{3}{4}$ cm.

37.

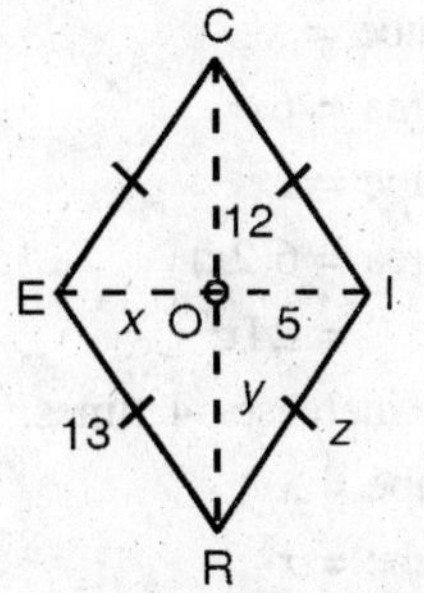

C, E, I, R, O, x, 5, 12, y, 13, z

In Δ COI,

$$CI = \sqrt{(12)^2 + (5)^2} = \sqrt{144+25} = \sqrt{169}$$

$= 13$ cm

$\because$ EO = OI = 5 cm

(diagonals bisect each other)

$\therefore x = 5$ cm

CO = OR = 12 cm

$\therefore y = 12$ cm

CI = RI = z = 13 cm

(All sides are equal).

38.
$$\text{S.I.} = \frac{P \times r \times t}{100}$$

$$= \frac{10000 \times 15 \times 2}{100} = 3000$$

Amount = P + SI

$= 10000 + 3000 =$ ₹ 13000.

39.
$$A = P\left(1 + \frac{r}{100}\right)^t$$

$$= 20000\left(1 + \frac{5}{100}\right)^3$$

$$= 20000 \times \frac{21}{20} \times \frac{21}{20} \times \frac{21}{20}$$

$$= \frac{441 \times 105}{2} = \frac{46305}{2}$$

$= 23152.5 = 23153$

Hence, population at the end of year 2010 = 23153.

40. Let, side of each cube = x

(*i*) Surface area = $6x^2$

Now, Side of cube = $2x$

$\therefore$ Surface area = $6(2x)^2$

$= 24x^2$

Hence, surface area increases 4 times.

(*ii*) Each side of cube = x

Volume of cube = x^3

Now, Side of cube = $2x$

Volume of cube = $(2x)^3$

$= 8x^3$

Hence, volume increases 8 times.

41. Let, number of notes of ₹ 50 and ₹ 20 are $3x$ and $5x$.

$\therefore$ No. of notes of ₹ 10 = $25 - (3x + 5x)$

$= 25 - 8x$

According to the question,

$3x \times 50 + 5x \times 20 + (25 - 8x) \times 10 = 590$

$\Rightarrow \quad 150x + 100x + 250x - 80x = 590$

$\Rightarrow \quad 250x - 80x = 590 - 250$

$\Rightarrow \quad 170x = 340$

$\Rightarrow \quad x = 2$

No. of notes of ₹ 50 = $3x = 3 \times 2 = 6$

No. of notes of ₹ 20 = $5x = 5 \times 2 = 10$

No. of notes of ₹ 10 = $25 - 8x$

$= 25 - 8 \times 2$

$= 25 - 16 = 9.$

42.

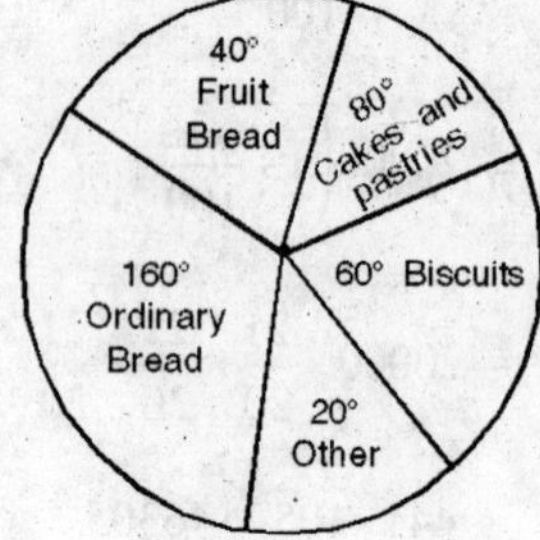

(*a*) $\dfrac{320 \times 360}{720} = 160°$

(*b*) $\dfrac{80 \times 360}{720} = 40°$

(*c*) $\dfrac{160 \times 360}{720} = 80°$

(*d*) $\dfrac{120 \times 360}{720} = 60°$

(*e*) $\dfrac{40 \times 360}{720} = 20°$

43. Let, total no. of students = x

According to the question,

60% of x = 18

$\Rightarrow \quad \dfrac{60}{100} \times x = 18$

$\Rightarrow \quad x = 30$

$\therefore$ Total no. of students = 30

No. of girls = 18

$\therefore$ No. of boys = 30 − 18

= 12.

(*a*) Girls : Boys $= \dfrac{18}{12} = \dfrac{3}{2} = 3:2$

(*b*) Total cost of transport charging

$= (55 \times 2) \times 12$

= ₹ 1320

Total cost with refreshment

$= 1320 + 4280$

$= 5600$

Cost per head $= \dfrac{5600}{32}$

= ₹ 175

(*c*) % Distance covered $= \dfrac{22}{55} \times 100$

= 40%

% of distance left = (100 − 40)%

= 60%.

44. Let, Length of the cloth = x m

and cost (in rupees) = y

x	2	4	5	10	13
y	y_2	y_3	210	y_4	y_5

We use the relation,

$$\frac{x_1}{y_1} = \frac{x_2}{y_2}$$

(*i*) Here, $x_1 = 5$

$y_1 = 210$ and $x_2 = 2$

Hence, $\frac{x_1}{y_1} = \frac{x_2}{y_2}$

$$\Rightarrow \frac{5}{210} = \frac{2}{y_2}$$

$$\Rightarrow y_2 = \frac{2\times 210}{5}$$

$$= 84$$

(*ii*) If $x_3 = 4$, then

$$\frac{5}{210} = \frac{4}{y_3}$$

$$\Rightarrow y_3 = \frac{4\times 210}{5} = 168.$$

(*iii*) If $x_4 = 10$, then

$$\frac{5}{210} = \frac{10}{y_4}$$

$$\Rightarrow y_4 = \frac{10\times 210}{5} = 420$$

(*iv*) If $x_5 = 13$, then

$$\frac{5}{210} = \frac{13}{y_5}$$

$$\Rightarrow y_5 = \frac{13\times 210}{5} = 546.$$

45. (*i*) Height and no. of the girls of class VII is represented by the histogram.

(*ii*) 145–150 groups contains maximum girls.

(*iii*) There are (4 + 2 + 1) girls have a length of more than 145 cm.

(*iv*) Group A – 3 girls.

Group B – 11 girls

Group C – 6 girls

46. (*a*)

2	2352
2	1176
2	588
2	294
3	147
7	49
7	7
	1

Hence, 2352 is not a perfect square. If we multiply 2352 by 3 then it becomes a perfect square.

$2352 \times 3 = 7056$

$\therefore \sqrt{7056} = 2 \times 2 \times 3 \times 7 = 84.$

(*b*)

2	9408
2	4704
2	2352
2	1176
2	588
2	294
3	147
7	49
7	7
	1

$\therefore$ The smallest number = 3.

If we divide 9408 by 3 then it becomes a perfect square.

$9408 \div 3 = 3136$

$\therefore \sqrt{3136} = 2 \times 2 \times 2 \times 7 = 56.$

47. (*a*) Perimeter of the rectangular park

$= 2(l + b) = 2(30 + 20) = 100$ m

(*b*) Area of the rectangular park

$= l \times b = 30 \times 20 = 600 \text{ m}^2$

(*c*) Area of the path

= Area with path – area without path

$= 600 - (30 - 2)(20 - 2)$

$= 600 - 28 \times 18$

$= 600 - 504 = 96\ m^2$

No. of bags of cement

$= \frac{96}{4} = 24.$

(*d*) Area of 2 flower beds

$= 2\left(1 \times \frac{3}{2}\right) = 3\ m^2$

$\therefore$ Area covered by grass

$= 504 - 3 = 501\ m^2.$

48. Area of the four walls $= 2(l + b) \times h$

$= 2(12 + 8) \times 4$

$= 160\ m^2$

Cost of white washing of the four walls

$= 160 \times 5$

$=$ ₹ 800

Area of the ceiling $= l \times b$

$= 12 \times 8$

$= 96\ m^2$

Cost of white washing of the ceiling

$= 96 \times 5 =$ ₹ 480

Hence, total cost of white washing

$= 800 + 480$

$=$ ₹ 1280.

49. (*a*) Total mass of Earth and Moon

$= 5.97 \times 10^{24}$ kg $+ 7.35 \times 10^{22}$ kg

$= \frac{597}{100} \times 10^{24}\ \text{kg} + 7.35 \times 10^{22}\ \text{kg}$

$= (597 \times 10^{22} + 7.35 \times 10^{22})$ kg

$= 604.35 \times 10^{22}$ kg.

(*b*) Distance between Sun and Earth

$= 1.496 \times 10^{11}$ m

and distance between Moon and Earth

$= 3.84 \times 10^{8}$ m

During Solar eclipes Moon comes between Earth and Sun.

Hence, the distance between Moon and Sun

$= 1.496 \times 10^{11} - 3.84 \times 10^{8}$

$= \frac{1496}{1000} \times 10^{11} - 3.84 \times 10^{8}$

$= 1496 \times 10^{8} - 3.84 \times 10^{8}$

$= (1496 - 3.84)10^{8}$

$= 1492.16 \times 10^{8}$ m.

50. (*a*) **A Bar Graph :** Bars of uniform width can be drawn horizontally or vertically with equal spacing between them and then the length of each bar represents the given number. Such method of representing data is called a bar diagram or bar graph.

(*b*) **A Pie-Chart :** The Pie-chart or a Pie-graph is a method of representing a given numerical data in the form of sectors of a circle. The sectors of the circle are constructed in such a way that the area of each sector is proportional to the corresponding value of the component of the data.

Central angle

$= \frac{\text{Value of the component}}{\text{Total value}} \times 360°.$

(*c*) **Histogram :** A histogram is a graphical representation of a frequency distribution in the form of rectangles with class intervals as bases and heights proportional to corresponding frequencies, such that there is no gap between any two successive rectangles. A histogram is a two dimensional diagram.

(*d*) **Frequency :** The number of times an observation occurs in the given data, is called the frequency of the observation. The number of observations correspon-ding to particular class is said to be the frequency of that class, e.g., frequency of the interval 5–10 is 6. It means 6 persons have got 5 or more articles but less than 10.

(*e*) **A Pictograph :** A pictograph represents data through pictures of objects. It helps answer the questions on the data at a glance.

Part–B : Science

1. C 2. D 3. C 4. D 5. B
6. B 7. B 8. B 9. C 10. C
11. A 12. D 13. B 14. B 15. B

16. A group of stars forming a recognizable pattern that is traditionally named after its apparent form or identified with a mythological figure, is known as constellation.

    The two constellations are named as– Andromeda and Antlia.

17. "Lateral inversion" means the apparent reversal of the mirror image's left and right when compared with the object. Image formed by plane mirror undergoes lateral inversion. Consider your own mirror image. The front-back reversal changes left and right in your image. That's because left and right depend on where your front and top are. If you move your right hand, the "mirror hand" that moves is still on your right side. There's no reversal in that sense. However, your right hand is perceived as the left hand of your image. That perceived reversal is what "lateral inversion" means.

18. When electric current is passed through a conducting solution, some chemical reaction takes place, for example, when electric current is passed through water, water dissociates into hydrogen and oxygen. Hydrogen is deposited over negative pole and oxygen is deposited over positive pole. Deposition of hydrogen and oxygen at different poles is visible in the form of bubbles. Chemical effects of electric current is used in electroplating.

19. Audible sound is the sound which is between 20 Hertz to 20000 Hertz and can be heard by human beings, whereas Inaudiable sound may be below 20 Hertz or above 20000 Hertz and this can't be heard by human beings.

20. When a body moves through a fluid, it experiences an opposing force which tries to oppose its motion through the fluid. This opposing force is known as the drag force. This frictional force depends on the shape of the body. By giving objects a special shape, the force of friction acting on it can be minimised. The streamlined shape encounters less resistance while moving through a fluid. This is not true for other shapes. So, objects moving in the fluids must have special shapes like boat or fish.

21. (*i*) A straw is said to have acquired a electrostatic charge after it has been rubbed with a sheet of paper. So, straw is a charged body.

    When you rubbed the straw on the straw paper (or shirt), you pulled off billions of tiny, invisible electrons from the paper and added them to the straw. Electrons have a negative charge and electrostatic force is responsible for attracting another straw.

    (*ii*) When a ball rolls, its kinetic energy has two parts; that due to its forward directed motion and that of its rolling rotation. The slowing of the ball's directed motion is due to the friction force between the ball and the ground.

22. Insulin is a hormone produced by the pancreas that allows human body to use sugar (glucose) from carbohydrates in the food that is eaten for energy or to store glucose for future use. It is produced in the body (Pancreas).

23. Petroleum is called black gold because it is the prime source of energy. It is black in colour and it is expensive like gold. Its bi-products are very valuable. It provides us kerosene, wax, plastic and other lubrication. It also acts like raw material in synthetic textiles, fertilizers and chemical industry.

24. A substance which has a molecular structure built up chiefly or completely from a large number of similar units bonded together, is

known as polymer. Example of natural polymer : silk, wool, DNA, cellulose and proteins.

25. Sound is a mechanical wave. This means it needs a material medium to travel through. The loudness *i.e.* the intensity of sound is directly proportional to the square of the amplitude. As the sound wave passes through, due to elasticity of the medium the energy will be lost and so the amplitude gets decreased. So at far distance the sound intensity will be very feeble.

When amplitude of the wave becomes trice, its loudness becomes nine times.

The phon is a unit of loudness level for pure tones. Its purpose is to compensate for the effect of frequency on the perceived loudness of tones.

26. Antibiotics are a type of antimicrobial used in the treatment and prevention of bacterial infection. Some antibiotics are also effective against fungi and protozoans.

Amikin (Amikacin) and Garamycin (Gentamicin) are the two examples of antibiotics. They are effective against Aerobic bacteria.

27. A valueless plant growing wild, especially one that grows on cultivated ground to the exclusion or injury of the desired crop, is known as weed.

Weeds reduce farm and forest productivity, they invade crops and in some cases harm livestock. They aggressively compete for water, nutrients and sunlight resulting in reduced crop yield and poor crop quality. They grow faster than native plants and reduce natural diversity.

28. Potable water is the water which is fit for consumption by humans and other animals. It is also known as drinking water in a reference to its intended use. Water purification is the removal of contaminants from raw water. Water is purified through five different methods:

(*i*) Boiling water.

(*ii*) Creating a purifying system in the wilderness.

(*iii*) Making a solar still.

(*iv*) Using a water purifier.

(*v*) Using purification tablets.

29. In biology, cloning is the process of producing similar populations of genetically identical individuals that occur in nature. Ian Wilmut, Keith Campbell and colleagues performed it for the first time. The first mammal that was cloned was a female domestic sheep (Dolly).

30. Deforestation is the process of clearing of virgin forests, or intentional destruction or removal of trees and other vegetation for agriculture, commercial, housing or firewood use without replanting and without allowing time for the forest to regenerate itself. Causes of deforestation are numerous:

(*i*) Expansion of cities to accomodate more people in the city.

(*ii*) Construction of roads are undertaken for smooth transportation.

(*iii*) Wood is used as fuel both directly and indirectly.

(*iv*) Due to overgrowing demand for food products, huge amount of trees are fell down to grow crops and for cattle grazing. Consequently, deforestation leads to several imbalances ecologically and environmentally.

31. It is true that LPG is better domestic fuel than wood. Burning of woods creates many air pollutants which can turn into respiratory problems. Moreover incomplete oxidation during burning of wood creates carbon monoxide, a poisonous gas. But in other hand, LPG is much better because it burns without giving smoke. It produces lesser amount of air pollutants. The most important thing is complete oxidation during burning of LPG does not lead to carbon monoxide production.

32. **Refining** is the process of purification of a substance or a form. The term is usually used of a natural resource that is almost in a usable form, but which is more useful in its pure form.

The primary end-products produced in petroleum refining may be grouped into four categories: light distillates, middle distillates, heavy distillates and others.

Light distillates

Liquid petroleum gas (LPG)

Gasoline (also known as petrol)

Heavy Naphtha

Light Naphtha

Middle distillates

Kerosene

Automotive and rail-road diesel fuels

Residential heating fuel

Other light fuel oils

Heavy distillates

Heavy fuel oils.

33. Thermoplastics is a material, usually a plastic polymer which becomes soft when heated and hard when cooled. Whereas thermo-setting plastics are polymer materials which are liquid or malleable at low temperatures but which change irreversibly to become hard at high temperatures. Examples of Thermoplastics–Polyethylene and poly-propylene (Bottle caps, Egg cartoons). However, the examples of Thermosetting plastics–Adhesives, semiconductor.

34. Three commercial uses of micro-organisms are in production of wine, alcohol and vinegar (acetic acid).
In broad sense these are used in: (*i*) Medicine, (*ii*) Soil fertility, (*iii*) Vaccine.

35. A prokaryote is a single-celled organism that lacks a membrane-bound nucleus (Karyon), mitochondria or any other membrane-bound organelles. Examples: Bacteria and Algae.

An eukaryote is any organism whose cells contain a nucleus and other organelles enclosed within membranes. Examples: Animal cells and Fungi.

36.

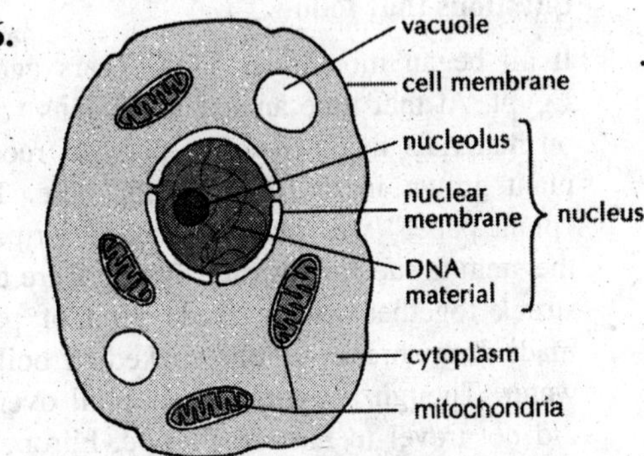

37. (*a*) A force is a push or pull upon an object resulting from the object's interaction with another object.

Two examples of push force are as follows:

A heavy box at rest is pushed to move it from one room to another. This changes the state of motion of the box.

A player pushes a football using his foot. This changes the state of motion of the ball.

Two examples of pull force are as follows:

Rope is pulled to draw water from a well. This changes the state of motion of the water bucket.

A drawer is pulled to open it. This changes the state of motion of the drawer.

(*b*) The calorific value of a fuel is expressed in kilojoules per kilogram (kJ/kg).

Calorific value of the fuel = 90000/4.5

= 20000 kJ/kg.

PAPER-II

Part–A : ENGLISH LANGUAGE

1. Read the following passage and answer the questions that follow.

It all began more than 5,000 years ago in Egypt. At that time ancient Egyptians wrote on materials made from the papyrus reed, a plant grown in the delta of the Nile. This "plant paper" was made by laying strips of the stem tissue side by side. These were then struck together with a crude kind of paste made from bread crumbs soaked in boiling water. Though papyrus travelled all over, it did not travel to Eastern Europe. Europeans had started using animal skins as their writing paper. This material was called parchment and although it was expensive, it had several advantages over the humble papyrus. First, the parchment could be folded over without it cracking unlike papyrus, which had to be rolled up into a scroll, making it cumbersome for a reader to handle. Second, as both sides of the parchment could be used for writing, no space was wasted. The material we use for writing today was invented over 1000 years earlier in China. A Chinese official named Tsai Loon made his paper in 105 A.D from a motley assortment of strange ingredients including mulberry and bamboo fibres, fishnets and rags. The Emperor Ho Ti was pleased with the invention. Tsai Loon was made an important man in his court. With success going to his head Loon got involved in dangerous business. Unable to face public exposure he committed suicide. The Chinese jealously guarded the secret of papermaking for more than 1,000 years. Unfortunately for the Chinese, the Moors learned it and it was brought to Spain and Sicily. From there it spread throughout Europe and by the 1200s paper mills had mushroomed in Italy and elsewhere. Paper got a big boost when Johannes Gutenberg, a German craftsman, invented the first practical mechanical printing press in 1455. The next 50 years saw thousands of books being printed all over Europe and the demand for paper grew. At present USA is the world's leading paper producer.

(*a*) What material was used by Egyptians to write on and how?

(*b*) How parchment was more easy to use than papyrus?

(*c*) Tsai Loon committed suicide because?

(*d*) How paper got a big boost after the year 1455?

(*e*) Pick out the words from the given passage which mean

(*i*) Unrefined

(*ii*) A collection of different things

(*iii*) Component.

2. Write a paragraph in about 100 words on *any one* of the following topics.

Mobile Phones—A Boon or A Bane

(OR)

Cleanliness is next to Godliness

3. Write a letter in about 120 words to the editor of a leading newspaper expressing your views on "Brain Drain".

4. Fill in the blanks with appropriate prepositions or adverbs given in the brackets.

(*a*) Summer has begun to set .... (out/in/by).

(*b*) The baby takes .... (down/after/up) her mother.

(*c*) Translate this passage from English .... (into/in/to) Telugu.

(*d*) When I parted .... (from/with/of) my mother, there were tears in my eyes.

(*e*) You are advised to learn this lesson word .... (by/to/for) word.

5. Complete the sentences given below by choosing the correct phrase from the brackets.

wild goose chase, cut a sorry figure, lion's share, through thick and thin, gift of the gab

(*a*) If you develop friendships with an individual, you must stand by him ....

(*b*) The Punjab wants a .... in the Beas river water.

(*c*) It was only through his .... that he managed to win the election.

(*d*) His efforts to go abroad for studies is a ....

(*e*) She .... when she could not speak correct English in front of her teachers.

6. Following sentences are INCORRECT. Find out the error and rewrite the following sentences correctly.

(*a*) He ran very fastly.

(*b*) The woodcutter fell three trees.

(*c*) If I will reach late, I shall be punished.

(*d*) No other man in the town is more wiser than Mr Sathi.

(*e*) The jury was divided on the issue.

7. Write one word for the following group of words.

(*a*) One who plays a game for pleasure and not professionally.

(*b*) A substance that kills germs.

(*c*) A place where young plants are reared.

(*d*) A speech made without preparation.

(*e*) A person who can neither read nor write.

8. Frame a meaningful sentence by using each word.

(*a*) Adapt
Adept

(*b*) Accept
Except

(*c*) Desert
Dessert

(*d*) Patrol
Petrol

(*e*) Team
Teem

9. Change the following DIRECT sentences into INDIRECT.

(*a*) Anil said to his sister, "How did you fare in the interview?"

(*b*) "Do you really want work?" said the merchant to the boy.

(*c*) He said to them, "Let us cast our votes sincerely."

(*d*) He said to me, "May you be happy!"

(*e*) The General said to his soldiers, "Bravo! You fought bravely."

10. Look at the picture critically, think of a suitable theme and write a story (in approx. 100 words)

Part–B : SOCIAL STUDIES

1. State True/False.

(*a*) James Mill divided Indian history into three periods–Hindu, Muslim and British.

(*b*) The Champaran movement was against Indigo plantation.

(*c*) In Meerut, an old Zamindar, Kunwar Singh, joined the rebel sepoys and battled with the British.

(*d*) Dharavi in Bombay is one of the world's largest slums.

(e) Swami Dayanand Saraswati founded the Arya Samaj in 1775.

(f) The largest state in India in terms of area is Rajasthan.

(g) Lake superior of North America is the smallest of five lakes.

(h) Shifting cultivation is known by the name of Jhumming in North-East India.

(i) Switzerland has no known mineral deposit in it.

(j) On the basis of their development and use, resources can be grouped as actual resources and local resources.

(k) There are 543 elected members in Lok Sabha.

(l) The Protection of women from Domestic Violence Act came into effect in 2010.

(m) Article 15 of the constitution states that untouchability has been abolished in India.

(n) The thinner most layer of the Earth is Core.

(o) Kolar gold mines are located in Andhra Pradesh.

2. Fill in the blanks.

(a) Warren Hastings became the first Governor-General of India in ....

(b) Haider Ali and Tipu Sultan were the rulers of........................ .

(c) A field left uncultivated for a while so that the soil recovers fertility is called ....

(d) ....is the closest celestial body to our earth.

(e) Coal and the petroleum are the examples of ....resources.

(f) A temporary alliance of groups or parties is called ....

(g) .... is our Defence Minister.

(h) The act of being fair or just and not favouring one side over another is being ....

(i) A non-government organisation which has been working to address the problem of sanitation ....

(j) .... is the 29th state of our country.

(k) The city known as Manchester of Japan ....

(l) .... is the leading producer of coffee in the world.

(m) The ores of metallic minerals are found in .... and metamorphic rocks.

(n) Method to check soil erosion on steep slopes is called ....

(o) Silicon Valley is located in ....

3. Write the full form of the following abbreviations:

(a) BHEL

(b) CTBT

(c) FIR

(d) ICBM

(e) INSAT

(f) NTPC

(g) KYC

(h) RAM

(i) PSLV

(j) NCERT

4. Match the following:

(a) Breeding of fish	(i) Viticulture
(b) Cultivation of grapes	(ii) Sachin Tendulkar
(c) Prarthana Samaj founded in	(iii) village
(d) The Veda Samaj founded in	(iv) Nelson Mandela
(e) Tomb of Sufi Saint	(v) 1864
(f) An open prayer place of Muslims	(vi) pisciculture
(g) ryot	(vii) 1867
(h) mahal	(viii) Dargah
(i) 'Playing it my Way' is a book written by	(ix) peasant

(j) 'Long Walk to Freedom' is a book written by

(x) Idgah

5. Write short notes on any five of the following topics (limit 50 words).

(a) FDI

(b) Independent Judiciary

(c) Mangalyaan

(d) The Battle of Buxar

(e) Conservation of Energy

(f) Information Technology

(g) Crime against Women

EXPLANATORY ANSWERS

Part–A : English Language

1. (a) The material used by Egyptians for writing purpose was made from the papyrus reed, a plant grown in the delta of the Nile. This 'plant paper' was made by laying strips of the stem tissue, which were then struck together with a crude kind of paste made from bread crumbs soaked in boiling water.

(b) Due to following reasons parchment was more easy to use than papyrus: Parchment could be folded over without it cracking unlike papyrus, both sides of the parchment could be used for writing and hence unlike papyrus, no space was wasted.

(c) Tsai Loon, a Chinese official, became an important person in the court of the emperor Ho Ti due to invention of his paper. With success going to his head Loon got involved in dangerous business and he was unable to face public exposure. Thus, he committed suicide.

(d) Paper got a big boot after the year 1455. The reason was that Johannes Gutenberg, a German craftsman invented the first practical mechanical printing press in 1455. Consequently, use of paper in the form of demand increased. That caused a big boost.

(e) (i) crude

(ii) motley

(iii) ingredients.

2. Mobile Phones – A Boon or A Bane

Mobile phones not only helps us keep in touch with our loved ones but also do a thousand other things. The most amazing thing about mobile phones, are it is suited for people of all ages. Be it a little kid who enjoys playing angry bird, to the grandma who loves listening to morning prayers on the smart phone. It is a device which has something of value for all ages.

But lately most of us have become addicted to mobile phones. This addiction is defined as spending more than seven hours a day using the phone and experiencing symptoms such as anxiety, insomnia and depression when cut off from the device. Such is the addiction in our nation that 49% of the citizens are willing to give up their television set for their smart phone. According to the recent study, kids spend seven hours a day on mobile phones, televisions and gaming consoles.

3.

G-10
Evergreen Apartment
Airoli, Navi Mumbai
12th Jan' 2016

To
The Editor
Times of India
Mumbai

Dear Sir/Madam,

Through the columns of your esteemed newspaper, I would like to voice my concern about the brain drain problem. Undoubtedly, the problem can be attributed to the craze among the talented youth to go abroad for better prospects.

Political corruption, nepotism and other ulterior considerations play a vital role when filling up the technical posts while merit takes a backseat. It leads to frustration among the talented youth who seek job opportunities abroad.

It is high time we recognise talent and provide our talented youth better job opportunities, so that they work for the good and prosperity of their motherland.

Moreover, there should be more emphasis on research and development, exclusively managed by scientists without the political interference.

Sincerely,

Vaibhav Praneet

4. (*a*) in

(*b*) after

(*c*) into

(*d*) with

(*e*) for

5. (*a*) through thick and thin

(*b*) lion's share

(*c*) gift of the gab

(*d*) wild goose chase.

(*e*) cut a sorry figure

6. (*a*) He ran very fast.

(*b*) The woodcutter felled the trees.

(*c*) If I reach late, I shall be punished.

(*d*) No other man in the town is wiser than Mr. Sathi.

(*e*) The jury were divided on the issue.

7. (*a*) Amateur

(*b*) Germicide

(*c*) Nursery

(*d*) Extempore

(*e*) Illiterate

8. (*a*) **Adapt** : He adapted this story for kids.

Adept : Dhoni is an adept cricket player.

(*b*) **Accept** : She accepted the gift with a big smile.

Except : Two children are identical except for their eye's colour.

(*c*) **Desert** : She was deserted by his friends.

Dessert : Aastha loves dessert.

(*d*) **Patrol** : My high speed was spotted by patrol car.

Petrol : Petrol is an inflammable substance.

(*e*) **Team** : A good leader always makes a good team.

Teem : Public bathrooms teem with bacteria.

9. (*a*) Anil asked his sister if she had fared in the interview.

(*b*) The merchant asked the boy whether he really wanted work.

(*c*) He advised them to cast their votes sincerely.

(*d*) He wished me that I might be happy.

(*e*) The General exclaimed with joy that soldiers fought bravely.

10. Ajay is an army officer. Once he was returning from his post with his colleague. They were passing through a lonely stretch of land. Suddenly they were surrounded by enemy soldiers in large numbers. As they were only two in number and the enemy was in large strength, they decided to move fast towards a safe place. The enemy followed them. They kept throwing tear gas shells on the enemy and created almost a wall of smoke. As they kept moving, they reached a safe and high place. Now they started firing on the enemy and killed most of them. His intelligence, quick-decision and bravery made him a hero.

Part-B : Social Studies

1. (*a*) True (*b*) True (*c*) True
(*d*) True (*e*) False (*f*) False
(*g*) False (*h*) True (*i*) True
(*j*) False (*k*) True (*l*) False
(*m*) False (*n*) False (*o*) False

2. (*a*) 1772
(*b*) Mysore
(*c*) Fallow land
(*d*) The Moon
(*e*) minerals
(*f*) Coalition
(*g*) Manohar Parrikar
(*h*) impartial
(*i*) Sulabh International
(*j*) Telangana
(*k*) is Osaka
(*l*) Brazil
(*m*) Ingeous rocks
(*n*) Terrace cultivation
(*o*) Northern California, U.S.

3. **BHEL** : Bharat Heavy Electrical Limited
CTBT : Comprehensive Test Ban Treaty
FIR : First Information Report
ICBM : Inter Continental Ballistic Missile
INSAT : Indian National Satellite
NTPC : National Thermal Power Corporation
KYC : Know Your Customer
RAM : Random Access Memory
PSLV : Polar Satellite Launch Vehicle
NCERT : National Council of Educational Research and Training

4. (*a*) – (*vi*) (*b*) – (*i*) (*c*) – (*vii*)
(*d*) – (*v*) (*e*) – (*viii*) (*f*) – (*x*)
(*g*) – (*ix*) (*h*) – (*iii*) (*i*) – (*ii*)
(*j*) – (*iv*)

5. (*a*) **FDI**

FDI refers to Foreign Direct Investment. It means direct investment of foreign countries in the field of commerce. In India, a large number of organised retailing has been developing in the past decade. As a result of which large private sectors also lured to indulge in it. Not only they but also foreign companies have also become a part of this. Due to this, India has become a main centre for foreigners to invest in different sectors for trade and it may lead India towards a great economic zone and ultimately as a super power.

(*b*) **Independent Judiciary**

It is well-said that an independent judiciary is the pillar of Democracy. So, the success of a working democracy is dependent upon an independent judiciary. Indian constitution provides for a constitutional democracy in which power is divided on geographical and functional basis. On functional basis it is divided among legislature, executive and judiciary. On practical grounds, judiciary in India has been kept separate from legislature and executive. The need of independent judiciary was necessitated on the following grounds. Interpretation of Constitution, to strengthen federal nature of Indian polity, and guardian of Fundamental Rights.

Arrangements are made for Independent Judiciary:

(*i*) A judge cannot be dismissed from service (Exception–through impeachment only) (*ii*) No salary deduction of Judges by Parliament

(*iii*) Judgements are immune from criticism.

(*c*) Mangalyaan

India make a mark in space on September 24, 2014 successfully entering Mars orbit with its Mangalyaan. India is the first nation to successfully put spacecraft in Mars orbit in maiden attempt with world's cheapest interplanetary mission costing just ₹ 450 crore. ISRO's PSLV C25 launched Mars orbiter mission from Sriharikota, Andhra Pradesh on November 5, 2013. Indian Scientists used an unusual 'Slingshot' method for this voyage. Ten pictures were sent by the orbiters of the Red Planet. The first picutre was received by the Indian Space Data Centre at Byalalu village, 40 kms away from Bengaluru. ISRO officials confirmed that pictures were of good quality. There are few questions on which scientists will work: How Martian weather system work and what happened to the water believed to have once existed on the Red Planet? The expected life of the craft is six months.

(*d*) The Battle of Buxar

The Battle of Buxar was fought on 22nd October 1764 between the forces under the command of the British East India Company led by Hector Munro and the combined army of Mir Qasim, the Nawab of Bengal. The battle fought at Buxar, then within the territory of Bengal. It was a closely contested battle in which the losses of English people numbered approx. 847 killed and wounded while on the other side of the Indian powers, more than 2000 officers and soldiers were killed. Consequently, Mir Qasim lost the battle and this battle brought Oudh and Delhi under the British control. The battle of Buxar mark one more turning point in the history of India, and said to have brought about the third revolution in Bengal.

(*e*) Conservation of Energy

Conservation of energy refers to reducing energy consumption through using less of an energy service. All energy produced and used has an impact on the environment. Even energy from natural sources impact the earth. On a global level, conserving energy is important, the reasons are : (*i*) Fossil fuel consumption, (*ii*) Environmental Protection. Conservation of energy can be done in home appliances, reduce, reuse and recycle of waste products, through home improvements, purchasing energy saver bulbs, use of less hot water by installing jacket etc. Conservation of energy is beneficial for us, our society, our country and for whole world.

Because:

(*i*) It improves the economy, saves money.

(*ii*) It is environmental friendly.

(*iii*) It improves national security and upgrades quality of life.

(*iv*) It also improves indoor air quality.

Thus, we may come into this conclusion that "Save Energy, Save World".

(*f*) Information Technology

The basic concept of Information Technology can be traced to the World War II alliance of the military and industry in the development of electronics, computers and information theory. But the term "Information Technology (IT) was coined by Jim Domsic of Michigan in November 1981. As far as its application is concerned, it is the application of computers and telecommunications equipment to store, retrieve, transmit and manipulate data, often in the context of a business or other enterprise. IT increases production and saves times. It improves communication through communication technology. It has a key role in improving data storage and file management. But on the other hand, several problems are also coming up through Information Technology, e.g., job elimination, implementation expenses and security breaches.

(g) Crime against Women

Act of violence is known as crime and in law crime is well-associated with punishment. Violence strikes women from all kinds of backgrounds and of all ages. It can happen at work, on the street or at home. There are many types of violence: Dating, Domestic, emotional abuse, human trafficking, sexual assault and abuse etc. In male dominant society, women have to face much more problems like inequality, tolerance etc. These problems turn into violence off and on and consequently crime emerges. However, to confront with this situation there are several laws in favour of women.

(*i*) The Immoral Traffic (Prevention) Act, 1956.

(*ii*) The Dowry Prohibition Act, 1961

(*iii*) Protection of Women from Domestic Violence Act, 2005.

(*iv*) The Sexual Harassment of Women at Workplace (Prevention, prohibition and redressal) Act, 2013.

But all are in vain if they will not be aware of such laws. Society has to go with women for every genuine matter.

YOUR SPACE

Previous Paper (Solved)

Sainik School Entrance Exam, 2015

(Class-IX)

PAPER—I

PART–A : Mathematics

Directions (Qs. 1 to 20): *Bear 2 marks each.*

1. Find two rational numbers between 1/4 and 3/8 and represent them in number line.

2. Simplify: $\frac{3^{-5} \times 10^{-5} \times 125}{5^{-7} \times 6^{-5}}$

3. Fifteen years from now Mohan's age will be four times his present age. What is Mohan's age after five years from now.

4. Find the least number of three digits which is greater than 100 and a perfect square.

5. Find the value of $x^3 - \frac{1}{x^3}$, given $x - \frac{1}{x} = 7$.

6. Resolve into factors : $17 - 32y - 4y^2$.

7. Find the cube root of 91125.

8. There are certain number of rows of trees in a garden. The number of trees in each row is twice the number of rows. If the number of trees in the garden is 1250, then the number of rows in the garden is ....

9. The marked price of an item is ₹ 1200. Find the discount percentage allowed on the item if it is sold for ₹ 1050.

10. A man borrowed ₹ 16000 at 10% per annum interest compounded half yearly. Find the amount repayable after one year.

11. The four angles of a quadrilateral are in the ratio 1 : 2 : 3 : 4. Find the measures of the angles.

12. What must be added to $4x^2 - 12x + 7$ to make it a whole square.

13. $(129^8)^9$ is equal to

(*a*) 129^{17} (*b*) 129^2

(*c*) 129^{72} (*d*) 129^0

14. The mean of the first ten natural numbers is:

(*a*) 5.10 (*b*) 5.5

(*c*) 5 (*d*) 6.2

15. Divide a sum of ₹ 10 between two persons A and B such that A gets Re 1 more than B.

16. The sum of two numbers is 45 and their ratio is 7 : 8. Find the numbers.

17. If 56 men can do a piece of work in 42 days, how many men will do it in 14 days?

18.

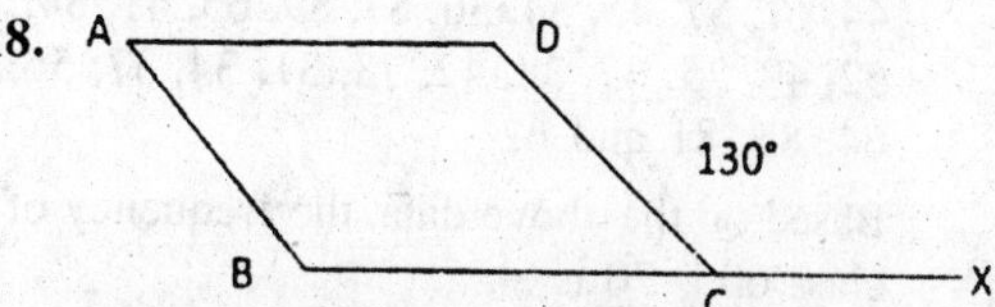

In the above figure, ABCD is a parallelogram, find all the angles of the parallelogram if measure of angle DCX = 130°.

19. A man loses 20% of his money. After spending 25% of the remainder, he has ₹ 480.00 left. How much money did he originally have?

20. By selling a towel for ₹ 126.90 a shopkeeper loses 6%. For how much should he sell the towel to gain 4%.

Directions (Qs. 21 to 40): *Bear 3 marks each.*

21. The digits of a two digit number are such that one is twice the other. When the digits are interchanged, the new number obtained is greater than the original number by 27. Find the number.

22. Solve: $\frac{2x-1}{6}-\frac{3x+2}{3}=\frac{1}{3}$.

23. Evaluate: $\left[\left\{\frac{\left(-\frac{1}{3}\right)^4}{\left(-\frac{1}{3}\right)^8}\right\}\times\left(-\frac{1}{3}\right)^5\right]$.

24. If $a^2+\frac{1}{a^2}=27$, then find the value of $a-\frac{1}{a}$.

25. A well is dug 20 m deep and has a diameter 7m. The earth which is so dug out is spread even on a rectangular plot 22 m long and 14 m broad. What is the height of the platform formed?

26. Find the area in sq cm of a rhombus whose side is 17 cm and one of its diagonals is 30 cm.

27. The marks obtained by 40 students in Mathematics are given below:

69, 59, 49, 39, 84, 68, 77, 48, 47, 57, 46, 41, 44, 67, 57, 45, 34, 36, 87, 89, 65, 41, 84, 78, 52, 49, 75, 37, 38, 42, 73, 31, 34, 37, 56, 59, 64, 85, 81 and 62.

Based on the above data, the frequency of the class 60 – 70 is ....

28. An article with a marked price of ₹ 600 is available at a discount of 18%. Find the discount given and also the price at which the article is available for sale.

29. If $5^{3x+4}=25\times5^{4x-1}$ find the value of x.

30. Walking at 4 km an hour, a person reaches his office 5 minutes late. If he walks at 5 km an hour, he will be 4 minutes too early. Then the distance of his office from his residence is ....

31. The internal measures of a cuboidal room are 12 m × 8 m × 4 m. Find the total cost of whitewashing all four walls of the room, if the cost of whitewashing is ₹ 5 per square metre. What will be the cost of whitewashing if the ceiling of the room is also whitewashed?

32. What least number must be subtracted from 2200 so as to get a perfect square?

33. A garrison of 2000 men has a provision for 15 weeks. How many men must leave so that the same provision may last for 20 weeks?

34. Multiply $(a^2+b^2+c^2-ab-bc-ca)$ by $(a+b+c)$.

35. Construct a histogram for the frequency distribution below:

Class Interval	Frequency
20-30	5
30-40	8
40-50	3
50-60	6
60-70	7

36. Solve $\left[\frac{\left(\frac{56}{28}\right)^0}{\left(\frac{2}{5}\right)^3}\right]\times\left(\frac{16}{25}\right)$.

37. Pipe A can fill a tank in 14 minutes, pipe B can fill it in 7minutes and pipe C can empty the full tank in 28 minutes. If all of them are opened simultaneously, find the time taken to fill the empty tank.

38. Four pipes 5 cm each in diameter are to be replaced by a single pipe discharging the same quantity of water. If the speed of water remains same in both the case, find the diameter of the single pipe.

39. Reduce the following expression into lowest term $\frac{a^2-b^2-2bc-c^2}{a^2+2ab+b^2-c^2}$

40. Simplify: $\frac{3x^2y^2}{2x^{-1}\times4yx^2}$.

Directions (Qs. 41 to 50): *Bear 10 marks each.*

41. A village, having a population of 4000. requires 150 litres of water per head per day. It has a tank which is 20 m long, 15 m broad and 6 m high. For how many days will the water of this tank last? Given 1 m^3 = 1000 litres.

42. The sum of the ages of a father and his son is 50 years. 5 years ago father's age was 7 times the son's age. Find their present ages.

43. (*a*) Solve the linear equation

$x - 0.3 + 0.05x = 2 - 1 - 4x$

(*b*) The sum of the digits of a certain two digits number is 7. Reversing its digits increases the number by 9. What is the number?

44. Construct a trapezium ABCD in which AB & DC are parallel, AB = 6 cm, DC = 3.5 cm $\angle A = 55°$, AD = 3.5 cm.

45. Parikshit made a cuboid of plasticine having dimensions 2 cm, 5 cm, 5 cm. What is the minimum number of such cuboid required to make a cube?

46. A horse is tethered in a corner of a rectangular plot 40 m by 36 m with a rope 14 m long. Find the area over which it can graze.

47. The pie chart below shows how Mr. Davis distributes his monthly income into different household expenses. See the pie chart to answer the following questions.

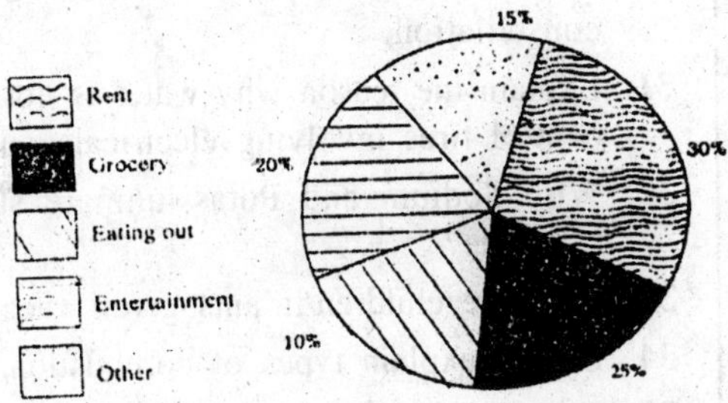

(*a*) In which of the above categories does Mr. Davis spend the greatest portion of his income?

(*i*) Grocery (*ii*) Entertainment
(*iii*) Eating out (*iv*) Rent

(*b*) What portion of the monthly income does Mr. Davis spend on entertainment?

(*i*) 10% (*ii*) 20%
(*iii*) 30% (*iv*) 25%

(*c*) What fraction of the monthly income does Mr. Davis spend on groceries?

(*i*) $\frac{1}{4}$ (*ii*) $\frac{1}{2}$
(*iii*) $\frac{1}{10}$ (*iv*) $\frac{3}{4}$

(*d*) If Mr. Davis earns ₹ 2,000/- per month, how much does he spend on groceries?

(*i*) ₹ 1,000 (*ii*) ₹ 250
(*iii*) ₹ 500 (*iv*) ₹ 700

(*e*) What is the ratio of expenditure between entertainment and grocery?

(*i*) 3:4 (*ii*) 4:5
(*iii*) 3:5 (*iv*) none of these

48. A man bought a TV and washing machine for ₹ 8000 each. He then sold the TV at a loss of 4% and the washing machine at a profit of ₹ 8%. Find the overall gain or loss percent in the whole transaction.

49. Factorise the following:

(*a*) $m^2 + n - mn - m$

(*b*) $x^4 + 12x^2 + 64$

50. (*a*) Solve: $(4x^2 + 7x^3y^2) - (-6x^2 - 7x^3y^2 - 4x) - (10x + 9x^2)$

(*b*) Using the identity:

$(x + a)(x + b) = x^2 + (a + b)x + ab$

Solve: 107×108

PART–B : Science

Note: *Part 'B' contains 37 questions, bearing 75 marks. Question No. 1 to 15 are multiple choice questions carrying 1 mark each, Question No. 16 to 25 carry 2 marks each, Question No. 26 to 35 carry 3 marks each, Question No. 36 & 37 carry 5 marks each.*

Fill in the blanks.

1. Blue green algae fix .... directly from air to enhance fertility of soil.

2. Species found only in a particular area is known as ....

3. Synthetic fibres are synthesized from raw material called ....

4. Phosphorus is a very .... non metal.

5. Process of separation of different constituents from petroleum is called ....

Select the Correct Answer.

6. The most common carrier of communicable diseases is
(*a*) Ant (*b*) Housefly
(*c*) Dragonfly (*d*) Spider

7. Which of the following can be beaten into thin sheets
(*a*) Zinc (*b*) Phosphorus
(*c*) Sulphur (*d*) Oxygen

8. Unwanted sound is called as
(*a*) Music (*b*) Pitch
(*c*) Noise (*d*) Shrill

9. The process of depositing a layer of any desired metal on another material by means of electricity is called
(*a*) Mixing (*b*) Electrolyting
(*c*) Electroding (*d*) Electroplating

10. Which of the following is **NOT** a planet of the sun?
(*a*) Sirius (*b*) Mercury
(*c*) Saturn (*d*) Earth

Mark 'T' if the statement is True and 'F' if it is False.

11. Generally, non metals react with acids. ( )

12. Coke is almost pure form of carbon. ( )

13. Kerosene is not a fossil fuel. ( )

14. Unicellular organisms have one celled body. ( )

15. An embryo is made up of a single cell. ( )

Write answers within the space provided under the questions:

16. Does pure water conduct electricity? If not what can we do to make it conductive.

17. Explain why sliding friction is less than static friction.

18. A pendulum oscillates 40 times in 4 seconds. Find its time period and frequency.

19. Define:
(*a*) Force of Gravity
(*b*) Pressure

20. Define adolescence.

21. Give two difference between Zygote and foetus.

22. Nylon is used for making parachutes, car se belts and ropes for rock climbing. Why?

23. List condition under which combustion ca take place.

24. List two advantages of using CNG & LPG a fuels.

25. What is malleability? Give two examples o malleable metals.

Write answers within the space provided unde each questions:

26. What is Marble Cancer? Write the ai pollutants that are affecting the beauty o Tajmahal.

27. Why is the distance between stars i expressed in light years? What do yo understand by the statement that a star is eight light years away from the earth?

28. Explain why plastic containers are favoured for storing food?

29. What are the major groups of micro organisms?

30. What is constellation? Name any two constellation.

31. Explain the reason why water is not used to control fires involving electrical equipment?

32. Why Sodium and Potassium are stored in kerosene?

33. Why are children/infants given vaccination?

34. Briefly explain types of combustion.

35. Draw labeled diagrams of plant cell and animal cell.

36. Write short notes on
(*a*) Cytoplasm (*b*) Nucleus of a Cell

37. Briefly answer the following questions.
(*a*) Why porters place a round piece of cloth on their head when they have to carry a heavy load?
(*b*) An inflated balloon was pressed against a wall after it had been rubbed with a piece of synthetic cloth. It was found that, the balloon sticks to the walls. What force might be responsible for attraction between the balloon and the wall?

EXPLANATORY ANSWERS

PART-A : Mathematics

1. First rational number between $\frac{1}{4}$ and $\frac{3}{8}$

$$= \frac{1}{2}\left(\frac{1}{4}+\frac{3}{8}\right) = \frac{1}{2}\left(\frac{2+3}{8}\right) = \frac{5}{16}$$

Second rational number between $\frac{1}{4}$ and $\frac{5}{16}$

$$= \frac{1}{2}\left(\frac{1}{4}+\frac{5}{16}\right) = \frac{1}{2}\left(\frac{4+5}{16}\right) = \frac{9}{32}.$$

$\frac{1}{4}$ $\frac{9}{32}$ $\frac{5}{16}$ $\frac{3}{8}$

2. Simplify : $\frac{3^{-5}\times 10^{-5}\times 125}{5^{-7}\times 6^{-5}}$

$$= \frac{3^{-5}\times 2^{-5}\times 5^{-5}\times 5^3}{5^{-7}\times 3^{-5}\times 2^{-5}}$$

$$= \frac{5^{-2}}{5^{-7}} = \frac{5^7}{5^2} = 5^5 = 3125.$$

3. Let Mohan's present age = x years

After 15 years Mohan's age

$= x + 15$

According to the question, $x + 15 = 4x$

$\Rightarrow \quad 3x = 15 \quad \Rightarrow \quad x = 5$

After 5 years Mohan's age

$= x + 5$

$= 5 + 5 = 10$ years.

4. Required number = 121.

5. $\because \quad x - \frac{1}{x} = 7$

$$\therefore \quad x^3 + \frac{1}{x^3} = \left(x - \frac{1}{x}\right)^3 + 3(x)\left(\frac{1}{x}\right)\left(x - \frac{1}{x}\right)$$

$= (7)^3 - 3 \times 7$

$= 343 - 21 = 322.$

6. $-4y^2 - 32y + 17$

$= -4y^2 - 34y + 2y + 17$

$= -2y\,(2y + 17) + 1\,(2y + 17)$

$= (2y + 17)\,(-2y + 1)$

$= (1 - 2y)(2y + 17).$

7.

3	91125
3	30375
3	10125
3	3375
3	1125
3	375
5	125
5	25
5	5
	1

$\therefore \quad \sqrt[3]{91125} = 3 \times 3 \times 5 = 45.$

8. Let number of rows = x and number of trees in each row = $2x$

According to the question,

$x \times 3x = 1250$

$\Rightarrow \quad x^2 = 625$

$\Rightarrow \quad x = 25$

$\therefore$ Number of rows in the garden = 25.

9. Discount = Marked price – Selling price

$= 1200 - 1050 =$ ₹ 150

Discount per cent $= \frac{150}{1200}\times 100$

$= \frac{25}{2}\% = 12\frac{1}{2}\%.$

10. P = ₹ 16000

$r = 10\%$ for half yearly $r = 5\%$

$t = 2$ years

$$A = P\left(1+\frac{r}{100}\right)^t$$

$$= 16000\left(1+\frac{5}{100}\right)^2$$

$$= 16000\times\frac{21}{20}\times\frac{21}{20}$$

$= 40 \times 441 = ₹\ 17640.$

11. Let $\angle A = 1x°$

$\angle B = 2x°$

$\angle C = 3x°$

$\angle D = 4x°$

$\because \angle A + \angle B + \angle C + \angle D = 360°$

$\Rightarrow x + 2x + 3x + 4x = 360°$

$\Rightarrow 10x = 360°$

$\Rightarrow x = 36°$

Hence, $\angle A = 36°$

$\angle B = 2 \times 36° = 72°$

$\angle C = 3 \times 36° = 108°$

$\angle D = 4 \times 36° = 144°$

12. $4x^2 - 12x + 7 + 2$

$= (2x)^2 - 2(2x)(3) + (3)^2$

$= (2x - 3)^2$

Hence, if we add 2 in the given expression, then it become a whole square.

13. $(128^8)^9 = (128)^{72} = 128^{72}$.

14. First-ten natural numbers are

1, 2, 3, 4, 5, 6, 7, 8, 9, 10

$$\text{Mean} = \frac{1+2+3+4+5+6+7+8+9+10}{10}$$

$$= \frac{55}{10} = 5.5.$$

15. Let B gets = ₹ x

$\therefore$ A gets = ₹ $(x + 1)$

$x + (x + 1) = 10$

$\Rightarrow 2x + 1 = 10$

$\Rightarrow 2x = 9$

$\Rightarrow x = \frac{9}{2} = 4.5$

Hence, B gets = ₹ 4.5

and A gets = ₹ 5.5.

16. Let the numbers are $7x$ amd $8x$

According to the question,

$7x + 8x = 45$

$\Rightarrow 15x = 45 \Rightarrow x = 3$

$7x = 7 \times 3 = 21$

$8x = 8 \times 3 = 24$

Hence, numbers are 21 and 24.

17. $m_1 \times d_1 = m_2 \times d_2$

$56 \times 42 = m_2 \times 14$

$$\therefore m_2 = \frac{56\times42}{14} = 4 \times 42 = 168$$

Hence, 168 men can complete that work in 14 days.

18.

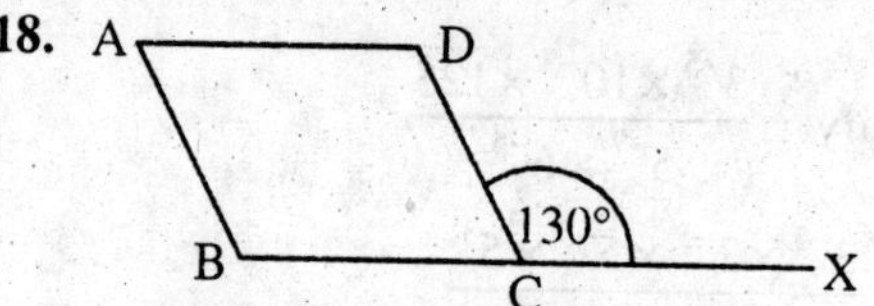

$\because$ ABCD is a parallelogram

$\because \angle DCX = 130°$

$\therefore \angle DCB = 180° - 130° = 50°$

$\angle A = \angle C = 50°$ (opp. angles of llgm)

$\angle B = \angle D = 130$

Hence, $\angle A = 50°$, $\angle B = 130°$, $\angle C = 50°$ and $\angle D = 130°$.

19. Let man had ₹ x

According to the question,

$$x - \frac{20}{100}\times x = x - \frac{x}{5} = \frac{4x}{5}$$

$$\frac{4x}{5} - \frac{25}{100}\times\frac{4x}{5} = 480$$

$$\Rightarrow \frac{3x}{5} = 480$$

$$\Rightarrow x = \frac{5\times480}{3} = 800$$

Hence, man had ₹ 800.

20. $100 - 6 = 94$

When SP is ₹ 94 then CP = ₹ 100

When SP is ₹ 126.90 then CP $= \frac{100}{94} \times 126.90$

$= \frac{100 \times 12690}{94 \times 100}$

$\therefore$ CP = ₹ 135

$100 + 4 = 104$

When CP is ₹ 100 then SP = ₹ 104

When CP is ₹ 135 then SP $= \frac{104}{100} \times 135$

$= \frac{52 \times 27}{10} = 140.40$

Hence, he should sell the towel for ₹ 140.40 to gain 4%.

21. Let ten's place digit number $= x$ and one's place digit number $= y$

$\therefore$ number $= 10x + y$

$y = 2x$

$10x + y + 27 = 10y + x$

$9x - 9y = -27$

$x - y = -3$

$x - 2x = -3$

$\Rightarrow x = 3$

$\therefore y = 2 \times 3 = 6$

Hence, number = 36.

22. $\frac{2x-1}{6} - \frac{3x+2}{3} = \frac{1}{3}$

$\Rightarrow \frac{2x-1-2(3x+2)}{6} = \frac{1}{3}$

$\Rightarrow \frac{2x-1-6x-4}{6} = \frac{1}{3}$

$\Rightarrow -4x - 5 = 2$

$\Rightarrow -4x = 7 \Rightarrow x = -\frac{7}{4}$.

23. $\left[\left\{\frac{\left(-\frac{1}{3}\right)^4}{\left(-\frac{1}{3}\right)^8}\right\} \times \left(-\frac{1}{3}\right)^5\right] = \left[\left(-\frac{1}{3}\right)^{-4} \times \left(-\frac{1}{3}\right)^5\right]$

$= \left(-\frac{1}{3}\right)^{-4+5} = \left(-\frac{1}{3}\right)^1 = \left(-\frac{1}{3}\right)$.

24. $\because a^2 + \frac{1}{a^2} = 27$

$\Rightarrow a^2 + \frac{1}{a^2} - 2 \cdot a \cdot \frac{1}{a} = 27 - 2$

$\Rightarrow \left(a - \frac{1}{a}\right)^2 = 25$

$\therefore a - \frac{1}{a} = 5.$

25. Volume of earth dug out $= \pi r^2 h$

$= \frac{22}{7} \times \frac{7}{2} \times \frac{7}{2} \times 20$

$= 22 \times 7 \times 5 \text{ m}^3$

Required height of the plateform

$= \frac{22 \times 7 \times 5}{22 \times 14} = \frac{5}{2} \text{ m} = 2.5 \text{ m}.$

26.

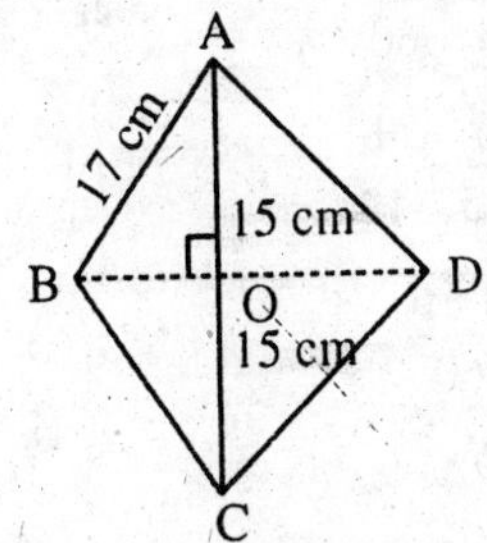

In ΔAOB,

$(OB)^2 = (17)^2 - (15)^2$

$= 289 - 225 = 64$

$\therefore$ OB = 8 cm

$\therefore$ BD = 8 × 2 = 16 cm

Area of rhombus $= \frac{1}{2} \times d_1 \times d_2$

$= \frac{1}{2} \times 16 \times 30 = 240 \text{ cm}^2.$

27.

C.I.	Frequency
30–40	8
40–50	10
50–60	6
60–70	6
70–80	4
80–90	6

Hence, frequency of the class 60–70 = 6.

28. M.P. = ₹ 600

Discount = 18% of 600

$= \frac{18}{100} \times 600 = ₹\ 108$

$\therefore$ S.P. = 600 − 108 = ₹ 492.

29. $\because \quad 5^{3x+4} = 25 \times 5^{4x-1}$

$\Rightarrow \quad 5^{3x+4} = 5^2 \times 5^{4x-1}$

$\Rightarrow \quad 5^{3x+4} = 5^{4x-1+2}$

$\Rightarrow \quad 5^{3x+4} = 5^{4x+1}$

$\Rightarrow \quad 3x + 4 = 4x + 1$

$\Rightarrow \quad x = 3$

30. Let the distance of his office from his residence is x km.

According to the question,

$$\frac{x}{4} - \frac{5}{60} = \frac{x}{5} + \frac{4}{60}$$

$$\Rightarrow \quad \frac{x}{4} - \frac{x}{5} = \frac{1}{15} + \frac{1}{12}$$

$$\Rightarrow \quad \frac{5x-4x}{20} = \frac{4+5}{60}$$

$$\Rightarrow \quad \frac{x}{20} = \frac{9}{60}$$

$$\Rightarrow \quad x = 3$$

$\therefore$ Required distance = 3 km.

31. Area of four walls

$= 2(lb + bh + hl)$

$= 2(12 \times 8 + 8 \times 4 + 4 \times 12)$

$= 2(96 + 32 + 48)$

$= 2 \times 176 = 352\ m^2$

Cost of whitewashing of four walls

= 352 × 5 = ₹ 1760

Area of the ceiling of the room

$= l \times b = 12 \times 8 = 96\ m^2$

Cost of whitewashing of ceiling of the room

= 96 × 5 = ₹ 480

Hence, total cost of whitewashing of four walls and ceiling of the room

= ₹ 1760 + ₹ 480

= ₹ 2240.

32.

```
 4 | 2200 | 46
   | 16   |
---+------
86 | 600
   | 516
   +-----
     84
```

2200 − 84 = 2116 which is perfect square

$\therefore$ Required least no = 84

33. For 15 weeks a provision last by 2000 men

For 1 week the same provision last by 15 × 2000 men

For 20 weeks the same provision last by

$\frac{15 \times 2000}{20}$ men = 1500 men

Hence, required no. of men to leave the garrison

= 2000 − 1500 = 500.

34. $(a + b + c)(a^2 + b^2 + c^2 - ab - bc - ca)$

$= a^3 + ab^2 + ac^2 - a^2b - abc - a^2c$
$\quad + a^2b + b^3 + bc^2 - ab^2 - b^2c - abc$
$\quad + a^2c + b^2c + c^3 - abc - bc^2 - ac^2$

$= a^3 + b^3 + c^3 - 3abc.$

35.

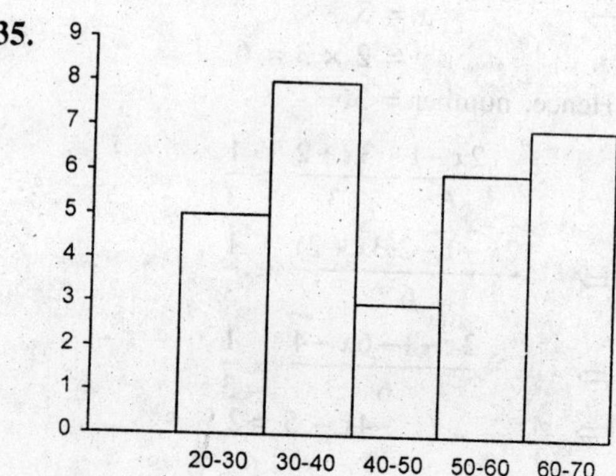

36. $$\left[\frac{\left(\frac{56}{28}\right)^0}{\left(\frac{2}{5}\right)^3}\right] \times \left(\frac{16}{25}\right) = \frac{1}{\frac{8}{125}} \times \frac{16}{25}$$

$$= \frac{125}{8} \times \frac{16}{25} = 10.$$

37. Net part filled in 1 minute

$$= \left(\frac{1}{14}+\frac{1}{7}-\frac{1}{28}\right)$$

$$= \left(\frac{2+4-1}{28}\right) = \frac{5}{28}$$

$\therefore$ The tank will be full in $\frac{28}{5}$ minutes

$$= 5\frac{3}{5} \text{ minutes.}$$

38. According to the question,

$$4\pi r^2 h = \pi R^2 h$$

$$\Rightarrow \quad 4\left(\frac{5}{2}\right)^2 = R^2$$

$$\Rightarrow \quad 4 \times \frac{25}{4} = R^2 \Rightarrow R^2 = 25$$

$$\Rightarrow \quad R = 5$$

$$\therefore \quad D = 5 \times 2 = 10 \text{ cm}$$

Hence, diameter of the single pipe = 10 cm.

39. $$\frac{a^2-b^2-2bc-c^2}{a^2+2ab+b^2-c^2} = \frac{a^2-(b^2+2bc+c^2)}{a^2+2ab+b^2-c^2}$$

$$\frac{a^2-(b+c)^2}{(a+b)^2-c^2} = \frac{(a+b+c)(a-b-c)}{(a+b+c)(a+b-c)}$$

$$= \frac{a-b-c}{a+b-c}.$$

40. $$\frac{3x^2y^2}{\frac{2}{x}\times 4yx^2} = \frac{3x^2y^2}{8yx} = \frac{3xy}{8}.$$

41. Total population of the village = 4000

Per head water requires = 150 litres

Per day water requires for the all population

= 4000 × 150 = 600000 litres

Volume of the tank = 20 m × 15 m × 6 m

= 1800 m³

$\because$ 1 m³ = 1000 litres

$\therefore$ 1800 m³ = 1800 × 1000

= 1800000 litres

$\therefore$ 600000 litres water requires for 1 day

$\therefore$ 1 litre water requires for $\frac{1}{600000}$ day

$\therefore$ 1800000 litres water requires for

$$\frac{1}{600000} \times 1800000 = 3 \text{ days}$$

Hence, the water of this tank will last in 3 days.

42. Let present age of father be x years and present age of son be y years

According to the question,

$x + y = 50$ ...(*i*)

5 years ago father's age = $(x - 5)$ years

5 years ago son's age = $(y - 5)$ years

$x - 5 = 7(y - 5)$

$\Rightarrow \quad x - 7y = -30$ ...(*ii*)

Solving (*i*) and (*ii*) then we get

$x = 40$ and $y = 10$

Hence, father's age = 40 years

and Son's age = 10 years.

43. (*a*) $x - 0.3 + 0.05x = 2 - 1 - 4x$

$\Rightarrow \quad x + 0.05x + 4x = 1 + 0.3$

$\Rightarrow \quad x(1 + 0.05 + 4) = 1.3$

$\Rightarrow \quad 5.05x = 1.3$

$$\Rightarrow \quad x = \frac{1.3}{5.05} = \frac{\frac{13}{10}}{\frac{505}{100}}$$

$$= \frac{13}{10} \times \frac{100}{505}$$

$$\therefore \quad x = \frac{26}{101}.$$

(*b*) Let ten's place digit numbers = x and one's place digit number = y

$\therefore$ number = $10x + y$

$x + y = 7$ ...(*i*)

$10x + y = 10y + x - 9$

$\Rightarrow \quad 9x - 9y = -9$

$\Rightarrow \quad x - y = -1$ ...(*ii*)

Solving (*i*) and (*ii*) then we get

$x = 3$ and $y = 4$

$\therefore$ number = 34.

44.

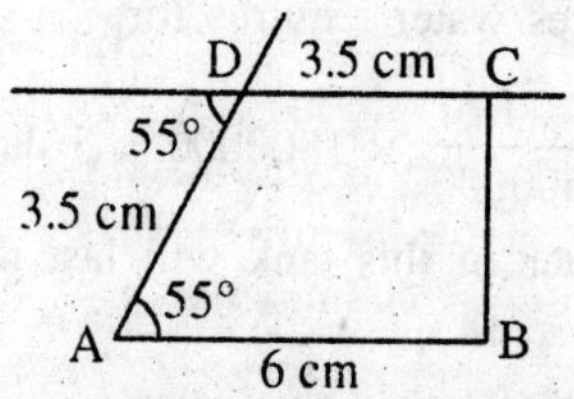

Hence, ABCD is a required trapezium.

45. Volume of each cuboid = $2 \times 5 \times 5 = 50 \text{ cm}^3$

Volume of 20 cuboid = $50 \times 20 = 1000 \text{ cm}^3$

$\therefore$ Required no. of cuboid to make a cube = 20.

46.

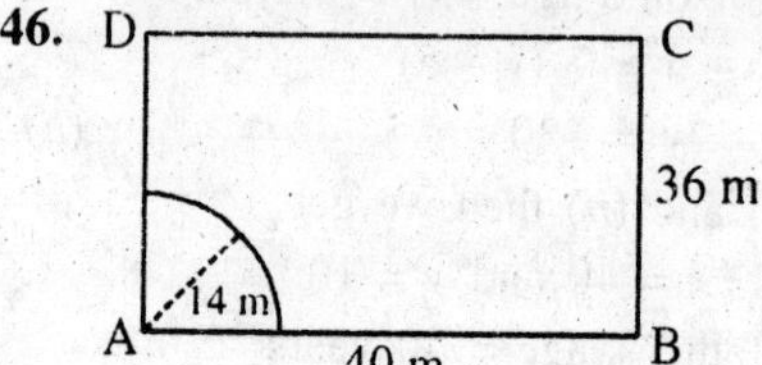

$$\text{Area of sector} = \frac{\theta}{360}\pi r^2$$

$$= \frac{90}{360} \times \frac{22}{7} \times 14 \times 14$$

$$= 154 \text{ m}^2$$

$\therefore$ The area over which the horse can graze $= 154 \text{ m}^2$.

47. (*a*) Mr. Davis spends the greatest portion of his income in Rent (30%).

(*b*) Mr. Davis spends 20% of the monthly income on entertainment.

(*c*) Required fraction = $25\% = \frac{25}{100} = \frac{1}{4}$.

(*d*) Mr. Davis spends on groceries

= 25% of ₹ 2000

$= \frac{25}{100} \times 2000 =$ ₹ 500.

(*e*) Required ratio $= \frac{20\%}{25\%} = \frac{4}{5} = 4 : 5$.

48. TV

CP = ₹ 8000

Loss = 4%

$\therefore$ SP $= \frac{94}{100} \times 8000$

= ₹ 7520

Washing Machine

CP = ₹ 8000

Profit = 8%

SP $= \frac{108}{100} \times 8000$

= ₹ 8640

Total CP = 8000 + 8000 = ₹ 16000

Total SP = 7520 + 8640 = ₹ 16160

Profit = 16160 – 16000 = ₹ 160

$$\text{Profit \%} = \frac{160}{16000} \times 100 = 1\%.$$

49. (*a*) $m^2 + n - mn - m$

$= m^2 - mn + n - m$

$= m(m - n) - 1\,(m - n)$

$= (m - n)(m - 1)$.

(*b*) $x^4 + 12x^2 + 64$

$= (x^2)^2 + (8)^2 + 2(x^2)(8) + 12x^2 - 16x^2$

$= (x^2 + 8)^2 - 4x^2$

$= (x^2 + 8)^2 - (2x)^2$

$= (x^2 + 8 + 2x)(x^2 + 8 - 2x)$

$= (x^2 + 2x + 8)(x^2 - 2x + 8)$.

50. (*a*) $4x^2 + 7x^3y^2 + 6x^2 + 7x^3y^2 + 4x - 10x - 9x^2$

$= 14x^3y^2 + x^2 - 6x$.

(*b*) 107×108

$= (100 + 7)(100 + 8)$

$= (100)^2 + (7 + 8)100 + 7 \times 8$

$= 10000 + 1500 + 56$

$= 11556$.

PART-B : Science

1. Nitrogen
2. Endemic species
3. Petrochemicals
4. Reactive
5. Refining

6	7	8	9	10
B	A	C	D	A

11. F **12.** T **13.** F **14.** T **15.** T

16. There is no salts contain in pure or distilled water. Therefore, it is a poor conductor of electricity. We may add (e.g. table salt) to make it conducting.

17. Sliding friction is always less than static friction. The reason is that two sliding objects find less time to get interlocked against each other's irregularities of surfaces as a result of which they do less friction.

18. The number of oscillations per second is called the frequency of oscillation.

The frequency (F) of oscillating pendulum

= The number of oscillations/ Time taken in seconds

= 40/4 Hz = 10 Hz

As we know, the Time period (T) is the total time taken for making one complete oscillation

∴ Time Period of oscillating pendulum

= 1/10 seconds = 0.1 second

19. (*a*) **Force of gravity:** It is the force exerted by the gravitational field of a massive object on any body within the vicinity of its surface.

(*b*) **Pressure:** It is the force applied perpendicular to the surface of an object per unit area over which that force is distributed.

20. The transitional period between puberty and adulthood in human development or in other words, the process or state of growing to maturity is known as adolescence.

21. (*i*) The product of fusion of the nuclei of the sperm and egg is termed as zygote where as the stage of the embryo which resembles a human being is foetus.

(*ii*) Zygote is a unicellular structure but foetus is a multicellular structure.

22. Nylon fibre is strong, elastic and light. Its thread is stronger than a steel wire. So, we use many articles made from nylon such as ropes and car seat belts, etc. Nylon is also used for making parachutes and ropes for rock climbing.

23. Conditions under which combustion take places :

1. The requirement of some fuel is necessary for combustion. During combustion a fuel substance reacts with oxygen to give off heat. The fuel may be in solid, liquid or gas form.
2. Combustion cannot take place in the absence of air (oxygen). Therefore, Oxygen in air is essential for combustion.
3. For combustion, an inflammable substance must be heated to its ignition temperature. Ignition temperature is the lowest temperature at which a combustible substance catches fire.

24. Advantages of using CNG and LPG as fuels:

(*i*) They are more efficient and can be easily transported; either in cylinders or through pipelines.

(*ii*) They are less polluting than other fossil fuels.

25. Malleability is the ability of a metal to be hammered into thin sheets. Gold and silver are highly malleable. When a piece of hot iron is hammered, it takes the shape of a sheet. Two examples of malleable metals are iron and silver.

26. Statues and structures whcih are made up of marble and limestone are slowly corroded as the contaminated rain water containing the acids (acid rain) fall on them. Both sulphuric acid and nitric acid present in rain water dissolve marble to form salts. Acid rain corrodes the marble of the monument and this phenomenon is also known as marble cancer.

Dust and carbon particles that are airborne are causing discoloration on the marble dome and minarets of the Tajmahal, turning the white color of the Indian landmark to brown. That's why the beauty of Tajmahal is in danger.

27. A light year is simply the distance that light travels in a year. It is not a measure of time, but of distance. It is also a unit of distance.

So, the light from this star takes 8 years to reach the earth once it is emitted from the star, the speed of light = 3×10^5 km/s

the length of a year in seconds

= 365.25 days × 24 hr/d × 60 min/hr × 60 s/min

= 3.156×10^8 s/yr

therefore, 1 light year is equivalent to

= 3×10^5 km/s × 3.156×10^8 s/yr

= 9.47×10^{12} km/yr.

28. Plastic containers are favoured for storing food for the below mentioned reasons:

1. Plastic containers are light weight so they are easy to handle.
2. The price of plastic containers is very less as compared to other containers.
3. They are durable having good strength.

29. Microorganisms can be divided into six major **groups:** bacteria, archaea, protozoa, algae, fungi, and viruses. Each type has a characteristic cellular composition, morphology, mean of locomotion, and reproduction.

30. **Constellations:** The word 'constellation' has been derived from the Latin name *Stella* means 'Star' and 'together'. So, 'constellation' means a group of stars. The group of stars, as seen from the Earth, appears to form a particular figure like a bear/a question mark etc.

About 88 constellations have been identified till now. Some of them are easily identifiable, e.g., Ursa Major, Ursa Minor, Cassiopeia, etc.

Ursa Major (Great Bear): 'Ursus' (a Latin word) means a bear. Ursa is the feminine gender of ursus. It is the third largest constellation in the sky.

This constellation known as *Saptarishi Mandal* in India, is visible in the northern sky in summer months from April to September in India.

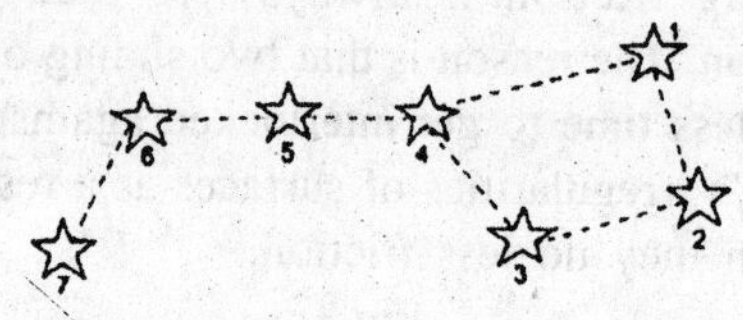

Fig. *Ursa major*

31. Pure water that does not contain any salt is a bad conductor of electricity but normal water which contains many salts is a good conductor of electricity. Trying to douse fires; involving electrical equipment; with water can result in electric shock. Due to this, water is not used to control fires involving electrical equipment.

32. Sodium & potassium are highly reactive metals and they reacts easily with H_2O (water or moisture). They burn violently as there is moisture in air. To prevent their burning they are stored in kerosene as moisture cannot enter in it.

33. Children are given vaccinations to develop antibodies against various diseases in their bodies so that they are less likely to become serious. Many diseases have been eradicated (stopped) through the decades of vaccinations of babies and young children. However, when parents didn't have their

babies and toddlers vaccinated, many of these awful and deadly diseases may be re-appeared.

34. Types of Combustion: Combustion can be divided into three types - rapid combustion, spontaneous combustion and explosion.

(*i*) **Rapid Combustion:** Combustion in which a substance burns rapidly and produces heat and flame is known as rapid combustion. For example, combustion of natural gas, LPG, petrol etc.

(*ii*) **Spontaneous Combustion:** When a substance suddenly starts burning into a flame; without supply of any external cause such as heating; the combustion is called spontaneous combustion. Phosphorous and sulphur start burning instantaneously at room temperature.

(*iii*) **Explosion:** When combustion is accompanied by sudden production of heat, sound and large amount of gas, it is called explosion. Firecrackers and bombs are substances which show explosion.

35.

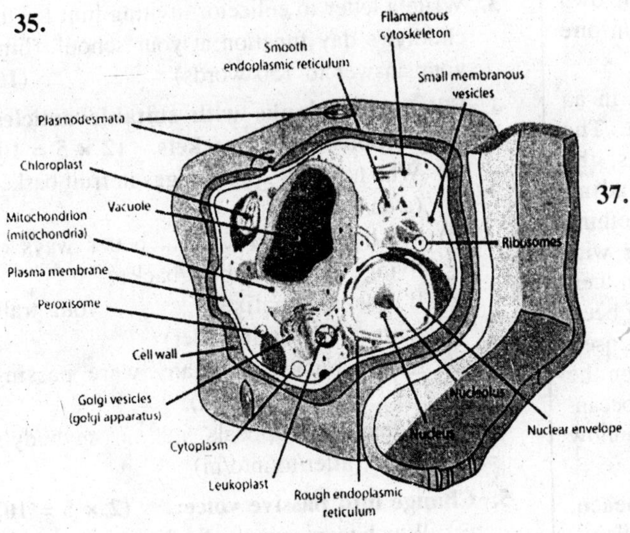

Fig. *Plant cell*

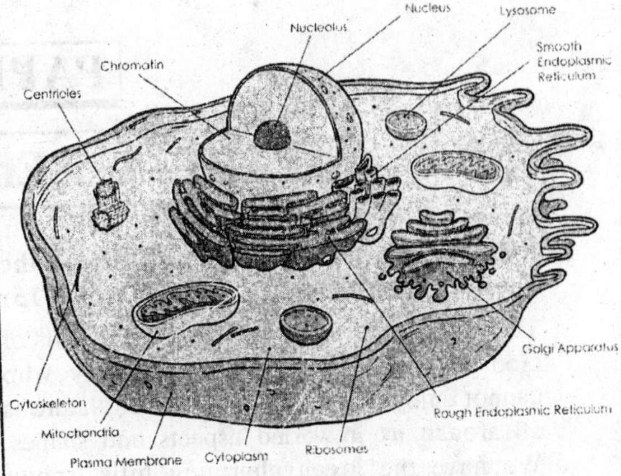

Fig. *Animal cell*

36. (*a*) The jelly-like substance between the nucleus and the cell membrane is called cytoplasm. Various cell organelles like ribosomes, mitochondria etc. are suspended inside cytoplasm. It helps exchange and storage of substances among cell-organelles.

(*b*) It is generally spherical and situated in the centre of the cell. It can be seen with the help of a microscope. Nucleus is separated from the cytoplasm by a membrane called the nuclear membrane. It also contains thread-like structures called chromosomes which carry genes and help in inheritance or transfer of characters from the parents to the offspring.

37. (*a*) Potters place a round cloth on their head as their heads are round. If they have to carry all the load on their bear heads, all the pressure will be forced upon the tip of the head and they feel too heavy. That is why they use a round cloth, to distribute the pressure equally an their head. As result of which the load seem lighter.

(*b*) Electrostatic force is acting between the charged balloon and the wall. So, it responsible for the attraction between the two.

PAPER—II

PART–A : English Language

1. Read the following passage and answer the questions that follow. **(3 × 5 = 15)**

The beauties of nature are the greatest gifts of God to man. How unlucky are they who cannot enjoy and appreciate nature. Nature is all around us in varied aspects and shapes. We have the green charming hills, snow-capped mountains, and the rising and setting sun in its varied and unforgettable glory. The dew drops on the blades of grass look like iridescent pearls. The silvery moon and the twinkling stars bedeck the sky. The roaring waves in the vast ocean and the lakes which look like sheets of water add to the glorious treasure. Even the violent aspects of nature like the thundering clouds with dazzling flashes fighting, the torrential rain, and the all-powerful storm are some of the aspects of nature which Tennyson termed as nature "red in tooth and claw". But they have their own charms which captivate man and even inspire in his heart.

One can enjoy the beauties of nature in an abundant measure at a hill station. The floating clouds, the dancing springs, the winding rivulets, the all pervading multicolour flowers, emitting sweet, soothing smell, the trees standing like sentinels with birds singing sweet harmonious songs in their branches. the cool breeze, the humming bees, the delicious fruits- all cater to human senses. Beauty lies in the eyes of the beholder on the earth, in the air, in the sky and in the ocean. His heart leaps up when he beholds a rainbow in the sky.

Nature teaches man the lesson of peace, innocence, purity, love, harmony, simplicity, hope and faith in the glory of God. Wordsworth believes that nature is the greatest store-house of wisdom, apart from being a source of eternal happiness:

(*a*) What is termed by Tennyson as "Red in tooth and Claw"?

(*b*) What are the captivating beauties of Hills?

(*c*) What lessons do nature teach humans?

(*d*) Write synonyms for the following words which means in above passage:

(*i*) Dazzling ....

(*ii*) Capped ....

(*iii*) Soothing ....

(*e*) Pick out words opposite to following words from the passage:

(*i*) Calm ....

(*ii*) Faded ....

(*iii*) Limited ....

2. Write a para in about 100 words on ONE of the following given topics. **(10)**

(*a*) Hazards of Polythene

(*b*) Role of Media

3. Write a letter to collector inviting him for the children's day function at your school. (limit your answer to 150 words) **(15)**

4. Fill in the blanks with suitable articles/ prepositions in the brackets. **(2 × 5 = 10)**

(*a*) Who has kept .... eggs in fruit basket. (a/an/the)

(*b*) We have turned .... better ways of living. (towards/about/back)

(*c*) It was i who fixed .... your train journey. (at/up/in/under)

(*d*) In the busy road many were passing .... (out/by/off/on)

(*e*) Indian food appeals .... anybody's taste. (after/to/into/in)

5. Change into passive voice: **(2 × 5 = 10)**

(*a*) Which team won the final match last year?

(*b*) We have sold all the tickets of the show.

(*c*) One should do one's duty.

(*d*) We do not accept ATM cards.

(*e*) We will sell all kinds of clothes here.

6. **Following sentences are INCORRECT. Find out the error and rewrite the following sentences correctly.** **(2 × 5 = 10)**
   (*a*) He gave me some advices.
   (*b*) Will you tell me the reason of an earthquake?
   (*c*) One should work hard if he wants to pass the exam.
   (*d*) All but I were present in class.
   (*e*) The flower pot is placed in the centre.

7. **Write one word for the following group of words.** **(1 × 5 = 5)**
   (*a*) One who is all powerful
   (*b*) A study of body
   (*c*) An animal who preys on other animal
   (*d*) That through which light cannot pass
   (*e*) One who looks at the dark side of things

8. **Frame a meaningful sentence by using each word.** **(2 × 5 = 10)**
   (*a*) Ode, Owed (*b*) Ceiling, Sealing
   (*c*) Mist, Missed (*d*) Chord, Cord
   (*e*) Cite, Sight

9. **Change the following DIRECT sentences into INDIRECT sentence.** **(1 × 5 = 5)**
   (*a*) Ruby said, "Raj, how is your knee today?"
   (*b*) Raman said, "Let us decide on the place."
   (*c*) She said, "Wow! How lovely the house is."
   (*d*) I said, "Did you call at my house last night?"
   (*e*) He said, "Please lend me your umbrella".

10. **Look at the picture critically, think of a suitable theme and write a story. (in approx. 100 words)** **(10)**

PART–B : Social Studies

1. **State True or False.** **(1 × 15 = 15)**
   (*a*) James Mill glorified India and its culture in his book "A HISTORY OF BRITISH INDIA".
   (*b*) The Maratha power was crushed in the third Anglo - Maratha war.
   (*c*) The mughal emperor appointed the company as the diwan of the provinces of Bengal in the year 1700.
   (*d*) The tribal chiefs lost their authority under the British rule.
   (*e*) Birsa Munda was convicted on the charges of rioting.
   (*f*) After the revolt of 1857 the Governor-general of India was given the title of Admiral General.
   (*g*) The Tata iron and steel company began to produce steel after the First World War.
   (*h*) Raja Ram Mohan Roy founded the Aryasamaj in 1875.
   (*i*) The Simon commission had two Indian representatives.
   (*j*) The Jalianwalabagh massacre occurred in Amritsar on Baishakhi day.
   (*k*) All natural resources of energy are renewable.
   (*l*) Chile and Peru are leading producers of copper.
   (*m*) Bauxite is the ore of aluminum.
   (*n*) Our constitution guarantees rights of minorities against the majority.
   (*o*) The total membership of the Loksabha is 500.

2. **Fill in the blanks.** **(1 × 15 = 15)**
   (*a*) The court language of Mughals was ....
   (*b*) The coin of Rupia was first issued by ....
   (*c*) The first Europeans to come to India were ....

(*d*) The title of Governor General changed to that of Viceroy in the year ....

(*e*) Delhi became the capital of India in ....

(*f*) Type of party system that has evolved in India is ....

(*g*) The first General Election in India was held in ....

(*h*) Panchayati Raj was first introduced in the state of ....

(*i*) The last Moughal Emperor was ....

(*j*) The third research centre of India in Antarctica is ....

(*k*) .... is the latest established High Court in India.

(*l*) .... is often referred to as 'Manchester of India'.

(*m*) The President of the constituent assembly was ....

(*n*) .... allowed the company to use the vast revenue resources of Bengal.

(*o*) .... was the capital of British India before Delhi.

3. Expand the abbreviations. (1 × 10 = 10)

(*a*) RTI (*b*) SAARC
(*c*) ISRO (*d*) NDA
(*e*) BARC (*f*) NATO
(*g*) UNO (*h*) IPL
(*i*) TISCO (*j*) UNICEF

4. Match the following columns. (1 × 10 = 10)

(*a*) Rocks and minerals — (*i*) Bangalore
(*b*) Tiger of Mysore — (*ii*) productive use of land
(*c*) Kunwar Singh — (*iii*) a waterborne disease
(*d*) Humus — (*iv*) Bihar
(*e*) William Jones — (*v*) a biotic resources
(*f*) The arms act — (*vi*) South Africa
(*g*) Simon commission — (*vii*) a linguist
(*h*) Cholera — (*viii*) 1878
(*i*) Diamond mines — (*ix*) 1927
(*j*) Silicon Valley — (*x*) Tipu sultan

5. Write short notes on ANY FIVE of the following topics (limit 50 words) (5 × 5 = 25)

(*a*) Women Empowerment.

(*b*) Revolt of 1857.

(*c*) Methods of Soil Conservation.

(*d*) Green Earth

(*e*) Cultural Diversity

(*f*) Conventional and non-conventional sources of energy.

(*g*) Panchayati Raj.

(*h*) Battle of Plassey.

EXPLANATORY ANSWERS

PART-A : English Language

1. (*a*) The violent aspects of nature like thundering clouds with lighthings the torrential rain, and the powerful storm are termed by Tennyson as "Red in tooth and Claw".

(*b*) The floating clouds, the dancing springs, the winding rivulets, the multicolour flowers, trees, birds, cool breeze, humming bees, fruits are the captivating beauties of hills.

(*c*) The nature teaches man the lesson of peace, innocence, purity, love, harmony, simplicity, hope and faith in the glory of God.

(*d*) (*i*) Glittering (*ii*) Covered (*iii*) Calming

(*e*) (*i*) Violent (*ii*) Dazzling (*iii*) Abundant

2. (*b*) Role of Media

Media plays a great role in today's world. It brings us news, views, entertainment and information. Media has immense potential in shaping the modern society. What we see and learn through media directly affects our mind and actions. This helps us form our views on various issues and affects our response to various situation in our lives. We get to know about the current affairs of our own city, country and the world through the news and other programmes in media. We get entertained through films, music, serials, stories and jokes viewed or lead in media. All this help make us nature and creative.

3.
Examination Hall
ABC School
Dated : ....

The Collector
XYZ City
Respected Sir,

Subject : *Invitation for children's day function*

I am writing this letter on behalf of ABC School, XYZ City. Our school is organising the children's day function on 14 November. We celebrate this day with great enthusiasm every year. Every year we invite an honourable dignitary as honourable chief guest.

This year the school committee has decided to invite your goodself in this occasion. Hope you will spare two hours from your busy schedule to grace the occasion.

The function will start at 10 am with prayers, followed by a cultural programme and fancy dress competition, a painting competition and will conclude at 12.00 noon with prize distribution to the winners of various competitions and to meritorious students.

There will be an arrangement of light refreshment for all present.

I sincerely hope you to accept this invitation and bless and inspire the students of our school. A line of confirmation in return will be highly appreciated.

Thank you

Yours Sincerely

4. (*a*) the (*b*) towards
(*c*) up (*d*) by
(*e*) to

5. (*a*) The final match was won by which team last year?
(*b*) All the tickets of the show have been sold.
(*c*) Duty ought to be done.
(*d*) ATM cards are not accepted.
(*e*) All kinds of clothes shall be sold (here).

6. (*a*) He advised me.
or
He gave me some pieces of advice.
(*b*) Can you tell me the cause of an earthquake.
(*c*) One must work hard to pass the exam.
(*d*) All except I were present in the class.
(*e*) The vase is kept at the centre.
or
The flower pot is placed in the middle.

7. (*a*) Almighty (*b*) Physiology
(*c*) Predator (*d*) Opaque
(*e*) Pessimist

8. (*a*) **Ode:** The poem is an ode to the king.
Owed: He owed his life to his master.
(*b*) **Ceiling:** There is a crack in the ceiling.
Sealing: The officer ordered the sealing of shops.
(*c*) **Mist:** The mist was cleared as the sun rose.
Missed: He missed his parents a lot.
(*d*) **Chord:** There was a small chord drawn on circle.
Cord: The charger has a short cord.
(*e*) **Cite:** He cited many examples in support.
Sight: There was a beautiful sight of hills.

9. (*a*) Ruby asked Raj how was his knee that day.
(*b*) Raman proposed to decide the place.
(*c*) She exclaimed how lovely was the house.
(*d*) I enquired whether he/she had called at my house the previous night.
(*e*) He requested to borrow my umbrella.

10. One day I along with my parents visited the sea beach in Goa. While I was playing with my sister making castles in the sand, we saw a snail. It was very small in size but carrying a big load on its back. It was moving very slowly but didnot stop for rest despite the load on its back. We kept on looking at it closely. Many thoughts came to my mind about it. It was such a tiny creature but taught me to carry our load ourselves. It also taught me of moving ahead with patience and perseverance.

PART-B : Social Studies

1. (*a*) False (*b*) True (*c*) False
   (*d*) True (*e*) True (*f*) False
   (*g*) False (*h*) False (*i*) False
   (*j*) True (*k*) False (*l*) True
   (*m*) True (*n*) False (*o*) False

2. (*a*) Persian (*b*) Shershah
   (*c*) Portuguese (*d*) 1858
   (*e*) 1912 (*f*) Multi party system
   (*g*) 1952 (*h*) Rajasthan
   (*i*) Bahadur Shah II (*j*) Bharati
   (*k*) Tripura (*l*) Ahmedabad
   (*m*) Dr. Rajendra Prasad (*n*) Shah Alam II
   (*o*) Calcutta

3. (*a*) Right to Information
   (*b*) South Asian Association for Regional Cooperation
   (*c*) Indian Space Research Organisation
   (*d*) National Defence Academy
   (*e*) Bhabha Atomic Research Centre
   (*f*) North Atlantic Treaty Organisation
   (*g*) United Nations Organisation
   (*h*) Indian Premier League
   (*i*) Tata Iron and Steel Company
   (*j*) United Nations International Children's Emergency Fund

4. (*a*) – (*ii*) (*b*) – (*x*) (*c*) – (*iv*)
   (*d*) – (*v*) (*e*) – (*vii*) (*f*) – (*viii*)
   (*g*) – (*ix*) (*h*) – (*iii*) (*i*) – (*vi*)
   (*j*) – (*i*)

5. (*b*) **Revolt of 1857**

   The revolt of 1857 was the most widespread challenge to the British rule, at that time. It brought together people of various sections, regions, religions and occupations with one objective of overthrowing the British empire. The reasons were different — political, economic, social, religious and military but there was a common ground.

   The growing resentment against the foreign rule came out in the open in the 1857 revolt. The immediate reason was the British government's decision to introduce a new type of rifle in the army. To load the cartridge, its paper covering smeared with grease had to be bitten off. The soldiers believed that the grease was made from the fat of a cow or a pig. The use of cartridges offended the religious sentiments of both Hindu and Muslim soldiers. They refused to touch these cartridges but their British officers insisted on its use. The Mutiny sparked off on May 10, 1857 in Meerut when Indian soldiers were convicted and imprisoned for their refusal to use these cartridges. About two months earlier, Mangal Pandey had rebelled in Barrackpore on the same issue and had wounded two Englishmen. The colleagues of the convicted soldiers in Meerut attacked the jail and set them free. The Meerut soldiers, on arrival in Delhi, were joined by local infantry. They proclaimed Bahadur Shah as Emperor of India, who became the rallying point of the opponents of British rule. Uprisings were there in Assam, Orissa, Uttar Pradesh, Bihar, Sindh, Rajasthan, Punjab, Maharashtra, Hyderabad, and Bengal. At many places, the people revolted even before the soldiers did or even when army regiments were present. Even where the people did not revolt, they showed strong sympathy for rebels.

   The suppression of the revolt was accompanied and followed by inhuman atrocities by the British troops on rebel leaders and the common civilian population. The revolt was neither a war of independence nor a mere military uprising. It proved to be a turning point in Indian history, the Company's rule coming to an end and British government taking the reins of administration directly in its hands. The army was thoroughly reorganised, with increase in European soldiers. In the administration, all essential services were placed under the charge of Europeans. Indian states lost their independence, recognising the paramountcy of the British crown. The indirect effects of the revolt were growth of extremism in Indian politics and the use of "divide and rule" policy on religious ground by the British government.

(c) Methods of Soil Conservation

Soil conservation is a set of management strategies for prevention of soil being eroded from the Earth's surface or becoming chemically altered by overuse, acidification, salinization or other chemical soil contamination. It is a component of environmental soil science. Several Methods of Soil conservation have been adopted in India. More than 40 million hectares of land in India have been reclaimed from water erosion, wind erosion and gully erosion. Raindrop erosion has been checked by creating grassland cover.

- By afforestation soil erosion may be checked as the trees keep the soil tight with their roots. Unplanned cutting of trees has been checked.
- Special attention has been given on the reservation of specific places used for grazing cattle's.
- Scientific methods of cultivation have been implemented in a number of areas to check soil erosion by unscientific cultivation. Contour faring is also introduced.
- To check soil erosion by Jhum cultivation, a programme of educating the tribal people has been taken by the govt. of India.
- To check wind erosion planting of trees in the opposite direction of the wind has been taken into consideration. This is an important method of Soil Conservation planned in India.

(f) Conventional and Non-Conventional Sources of Energy

Conventional energy, such as thermal powers (from coal, petroleum, and natural gas), hydel power (from high velocity of running water) are tapped and used abundantly at present. Their uses are practiced for a long time. But, in contrast to conventional sources of energy, non-conventional sources of energy (solar energy, tidal energy, geo-thermal energy, wind energy etc) are not used frequently and in large scale (commercially). Their uses are comparatively more recent. Except hydel power, the sources of thermal power i.e., other conventional energies are non renewable in nature. But the sources of non-conventional energy are flow-resources. There is no anxiety for their exhaustion.

Except hydel power, the generation of other conventional energy produces air pollution. But the generation of non-conventional energy does not produce air pollution.

Except hydel power, the other conventional energy is costly. But comparatively, the non-conventional energy is much cheaper.

(g) Panchayati Raj

Since time immemorial, Panchayats have existed in India at the village levels. They have looked after the welfare of the villagers, planned the developmental work and even carried out the judicial work. Though our Constitution did not prescribe any particular structure for democratic institutions at lower levels, the directive principles did include this as one of the aim. A three tier set up was formed by the Government, with the Village Panchayats at the lowest level and Zila Parishads at the districts level. However, some states adopted two-tier structure. Moreover, it was observed that the state Governments were reluctant to share power with the lower level democratic institutions. So, these bodies were deprived of financial resources, elections were not held regularly and no attempt was made to facilitate their smooth working.

In order to provide statutory backing to the Panchayati Raj Institutions and given them more powers and responsibilities, a Constitutional Amendment Bill was introduced in the Parliament in 1989. It was adopted in the Lok Sabha but fell through in the Rajya Sabha. In 1992, the bill was introduced again and this time it was approved by both the houses.

The bill stipulates setting up of three level Panchayati Raj institutions in all the states. The elections after five years have been made mandatory. Those institutions have been provided with adequate financial sources and administrative support. Their responsibility has been outlined and local developmental work has been given to them. In addition, these bodies play an important role in the planning process. The bodies are called Gram Panchayat, Panchayat Samiti and Zila Parishad.

A bill to provide statutory backing to these Urban Local Government has also been approved. In the cities and bigger towns, corporations are set up. In smaller towns, Municipal Committees or Councils are set up. In even smaller towns, Town Area Committees and Notified Area Committees are set up.

(*h*) Battle of Plassey

The battle took place on June 23, 1757. After Mir Madan's death in the field, Siraj suspended the fight for the day on Mir Jafar's treacherous advice. The withdrawal caused disaster. The troops of the three traitors retreated without having fired a single shot during the whole day. Clive's sharp attack broke up the nawab's battle lines. Siraj had already fled away, and there was no commander left to conduct an orderly retreat. The English casualty numbered 23 killed (7 Europeans, 16 sepoys) and 49 wounded (13 Europeans, 36 sepoys). On the nawab's side about 500 men were killed and a due proportion (including Mohan Lal) wounded. All his artillery, baggage, camp equipage, stores and cattle fell into the victor's hands.

Consequences of Plassey: Sir Jadunath Sarkar says: "On 23 June 1757 the Middle Ages of India ended and her Modern Age began. In the space of less than one generation, in the twenty years from Plassey (1757-76), the land began to recover from the blight of medieval theocratic rule". This is a retrospective reading of the consequences of the battle of Plassey. Luke Scrafton, who served as the Company's Resident at the nawab's *durbar* after Plassey, wrote: "The general idea at this time entertained by the servants of the Company was that the battle of Plassey did only restore us to the same situation we were in before the capture of Calcutta (by Siraj-ud-daula); the *subah* (subahdar) was conceived to be independent as ever, and the English returned into their commercial character..." This statement ignores the fact that substantial restraints on the nawab's independence had been imposed by Mir Jafar's pre-Plassey treaty (June 5, 1757) with the English. Legally, however, the English did not become political masters of Bengal in 1757. A few years later the Supreme Court of Calcutta held that only the inhabitants of Calcutta and not those of other English factory areas were British subjects. Theoretically, therefore, the English retained their "commercial character" even after Plassey.

Plassey gave the English certain immediate advantages in military and commercial and created a field for the establishment of their political influence in "three provinces abounding in the most valuable production of nature and art". The exclusion of the French from Bengal strengthened their position of South Indian struggle. Success strengthened their self confidence. As early as 1759 Clive suggested to Pitt the Elder, a leading member of the King's government in London, the advisability of establishment of direct control of the crown over the Company's possessions in Bengal.

Previous Paper (Solved)

Sainik School Entrance Exam, 2014

(Class-IX)

PAPER—I

PART–A : Mathematics

Directions (Qs. 1 to 20): *Bear 2 marks each.*

1. Represent 4/8 and –7/4 on the number line.

2. Simplify: $\frac{3}{17} \div \frac{8}{17} \times \frac{2}{3} + \left(-\frac{2}{7}\right) \times \frac{35}{33} \div \left(-\frac{7}{11}\right)$.

3. The sum of two numbers is 15 and the sum of their squares is 113. Find the numbers.

4. Multiply: $(a + 7)$ by $(a^2 + 3a + 5)$.

5. If $x + \frac{1}{x} = 3$, find the value of $\left(x^2 + \frac{1}{x^2}\right)$.

6. Factorise: $25a^2 - 4b^2 + 28bc - 49c^2$.

7. Solve: $\frac{2p - \frac{3}{4}}{9p + \frac{4}{7}} = \frac{1}{4}$.

8. Find the square root of 128881 by the division method.

9. Arun bought a pair of Skates at a sale where the discount given was 20%. If the amount he pays is ₹ 1600, find the marked price.

10. Find the Compound interest on ₹ 12600 for 2 yrs at 10% per annum Compounded annually.

11. Two adjacent angles of a Parallelogram have equal measures. Find the measure of each of the angles of the Parallelogram.

12. An Unbiased Die is thrown. What is the Probability of getting an even number greater than 5?

13. Find the ratio of the circumferences of two concentric circles of radii 2 m and 3 m.

14. The median of the given data is:
133, 73, 89, 108, 94, 140, 94, 85, 100, 120.
(*a*) 97 (*b*) 79
(*c*) 94 (*d*) None of these

15. Two numbers are in the ratio 5:3. If they differ by 18, then the numbers are:
(*a*) 36 and 54 (*b*) 36 and 18
(*c*) 45 and 27 (*d*) 63 and 45

16. The point (0, 6) lies on:
(*a*) X-axis (*b*) Y-axis
(*c*) Origin (*d*) None of these

17. The smallest natural number by which 392 must be multiplied so as to get a Perfect Cube is:
(*a*) 2 (*b*) 7
(*c*) 4 (*d*) 5

18. The diagonals of a rhombus are 64 cm and 48 cm. The height of the rhombus is:
(*a*) 30.5 cm (*b*) 36.5 cm
(*c*) 38.4 cm (*d*) 58.6 cm

19. In the figure given below, find the value of x.

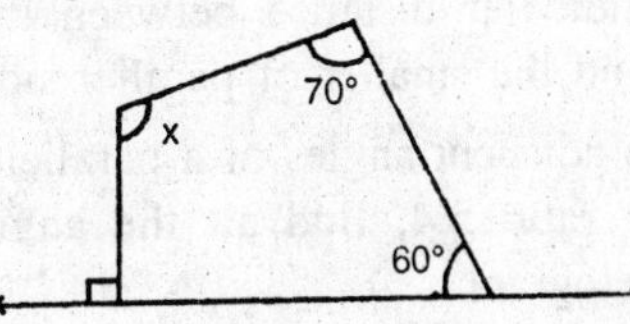

20. The sum of three consecutive odd numbers is 105. Find the numbers.

Directions (Qs. 21 to 40): *Bear 3 marks each.*

21. A number consisting of two digits becomes $\frac{5}{6}$ of itself, if its digits are interchanged. If

the difference of the digits is 1, find the number.

22. Solve: $\dfrac{3x^2-8}{5x^2+2}=\dfrac{4}{7}$.

23. Find: $-\dfrac{2}{3}\times\dfrac{3}{5}+\dfrac{5}{2}-\dfrac{3}{5}\times\dfrac{1}{6}$.

24. Find the value of: $8\left(x^3-\dfrac{1}{x^3}\right)$ if $2x-\dfrac{2}{x}=3$.

25. If $(x + y + z) = 9$ and $(xy + yz + zx) = 23$, then find the value of $(x^3 + y^3 + z^3 - 3xyz)$.

26. Find the area of a rhombus whose side is 6 cm and whose altitude is 4 cm.

27. Evaluate: $\dfrac{8^{-1}\times5^3}{2^{-4}}$.

28. An article was sold at ₹ 18000 at a discount of 10%. Find the marked price of the article and the amount of discount allowed.

29. Find k, $(3/7)^{-5} \times (7/3)^{11} = (3/7)^{8k}$.

30. Divide:

$(x^{3/2} - xy^{1/2} + x^{1/2}y - y^{3/2})$ by $(x^{1/2} - y^{1/2})$

31. There are 100 students in a hostel. Food provision for them is for 20 days. How long will these Provision last, if 25 more students join the group?

32. The area of a trapezium is 384 cm^2. If its parallel sides are in the ratio 3:5 and the perpendicular distance between them is 12 cm, find the smaller of parallel sides.

33. If two adjacent angles of a parallelogram are in the ratio 5:4, find all the angles of the parallelogram.

34. Find the least number that must be added to 1300 so as to get a Perfect Square.

35. Simplify: $(a + b)(c - d) + (a - b)(c + d) + 2(ac + bd)$.

36. Find the height of a Cylinder whose radius is 7 cm and the total Surface area is 968 cm^2.

$\left(\text{Use } \pi = \dfrac{22}{7}\right)$

37. Construct a frequency distribution table for the data on weights (in kg) of 20 students of a class using the intervals 30 – 35, 30 – 35 and so on.

40, 38, 33, 48, 60, 53, 31, 46, 34, 36, 49, 41, 55, 49, 65, 42, 44, 47, 38, 39.

38. ₹ 1400 is divided among A, B, C so that A receives half as much as B and B receives half as much as C. How much will each of them get?

39. Examine if 117912 is a perfect cube or not. If not, find the smallest positive integer by which it must be multiplied so that the product is a perfect cube.

40. A well with 14 m inside diameter is dug 8 m deep. The Earth taken out of it has been evenly spread all around it to a width of 21 m to form an embankment. Find the height of the embankment.

Directions (Qs. 41 to 50): *Bear 10 marks each.*

41. Arjun is twice as old as Shriya. Five years ago his age was three times Shriya's age. Find their present ages.

42. The adjacent figure HOPE is a parallelogram. Find the angles measures x, y and z.

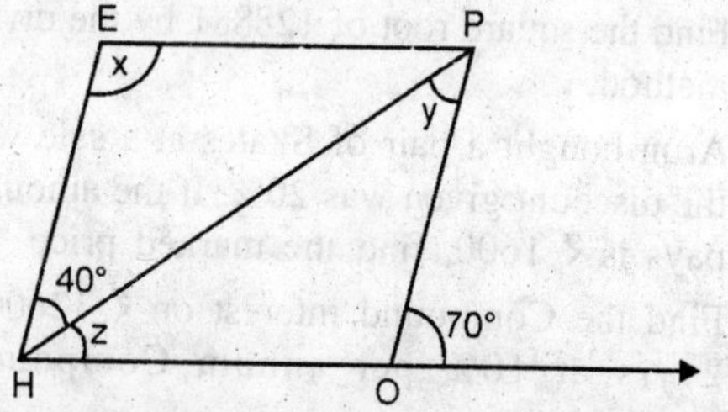

43. A sum of money at compound interest amounts to thrice in 3 years. In how many years will it be 9 times itself at the same rate of interest?

44. (*a*) Factorise: $x^2 + 6x - 16$.

(*b*) If $a + b = 14$ and $ab = 20$, find the value of $a^2 + b^2$.

45. A road roller takes 750 complete revolutions to move once over to level a road. Find the area of the road if the diameter of a road roller is 85 cm and length is 1 m.

46. The shape of a garden is rectangular in the middle and semi-circular ends. Total length of the garden including the semi-circular ends is 20 m and its breadth is 7 m. Find the perimeter and area of the garden.

47. The denominator of a rational number is greater than its numerator by 8. If the numerator is increased by 17 and the denominator is decreased by 1, the number obtained is 3/2. Find the rational number.

48. During a Sale, a shop offered a discount of 10% on the marked prices of all the items. What would a customer have to pay for a pair of jeans marked at ₹ 1450 and two shirts marked at ₹ 850 each?

49. Factorise and then Simplify the expression, $12xy\,(9x^2 - 16y^2) \div 4xy\,(3x + 4y)$.

50. A cow is tied to a pole fixed at one corner of a square field of grass of side 40 m by means of a rope 20 m long. Taking $\pi = 3.14$

(*i*) find the maximum area of the part of the field in which the cow can graze.

(*ii*) find the area of the remaining part of the field.

(*iii*) find the length of the rope, if the cow grazes 1256 m^2 of the field.

PART–B : Science

Note: *Part 'B' bearing 75 marks, contains 37 questions. Q.Nos. 1 to 15 carry one mark each, Q.Nos. 16 to 25 carry two marks each, Q.Nos. 26 to 35 carry three marks each, Q.Nos. 36 and 37 carry five marks each.*

1. Malaria is caused by:

(*a*) Virus (*b*) Protozoa

(*c*) Bacteria (*d*) Fungi

2. The next nearest star to earth other than the Sun is:

(*a*) Aurora Australis (*b*) Aurora Barialis

(*c*) Alpha Centauri (*d*) Proxima Centauri

3. The only non-metal which is liquid in state at room temperature is:

(*a*) Bromine (*b*) Boron

(*c*) Iodine (*d*) Indium

4. A cubical wooden block has the dimension 30 cm × 20 cm × 10 cm, placed on a flat surface. In which of the following cases the pressure applied is maximum?

When it is placed on surface area

(*a*) 30 cm × 20 cm (*b*) 20 cm × 10 cm

(*c*) 30 cm × 10 cm (*d*) None of the above

5. What is the time taken by the moon to complete one revolution around the Sun?

(*a*) 29 days

(*b*) 15 days

(*c*) 365 days (approx.)

(*d*) 183 days (approx.)

6. Which one of the following is not a communicable disease?

(*a*) Cholera (*b*) Tuberculosis

(*c*) Common cold (*d*) Polio

7. Which is correct order of Agricultural practices?

(*i*) Tilling

(*ii*) Irrigation

(*iii*) Sowing

(*iv*) Adding manure and fertilizer

(*v*) Harvesting

(*a*) (*i*), (*iv*), (*iii*), (*ii*), (*v*)

(*b*) (*i*), (*iii*), (*iv*), (*ii*), (*v*)

(*c*) (*ii*), (*i*), (*iv*), (*v*), (*iii*)

(*d*) (*i*), (*iii*), (*ii*), (*v*), (*iv*)

8. When disease carrying microbe enters our body, the body produces

(*a*) Antigen (*b*) Antidote

(*c*) Antibody (*d*) Antioxidant

9. The gland known as 'Master gland' in our body is:

(*a*) Sweat gland (*b*) Pituitary gland

(*c*) Salivary gland (*d*) Sebaceous gland

10. If a ray of light incident on a plane mirror along the normal then the measure of the angle of incidence (in degree)

(*a*) 90
(*b*) 45
(*c*) 0
(*d*) Depends on which direction the ray is reflected

11. The instrument used to detect the charge in a body is
(*a*) Electrometer (*b*) Electroscope
(*c*) Voltmeter (*d*) Barometer

12. For a male child the pair of chromosomes should be
(*a*) XX (*b*) XY
(*c*) YX (*d*) YY

13. The waves produced by earthquake on the surface of earth is known as
(*a*) Seismic wave (*b*) Shock wave
(*c*) Mechanical wave (*d*) Matter wave

14. The axis of the Earth inclined to its orbital plane at an angle of
(*a*) 23.5 degree (*b*) 53.6 degree
(*c*) 66.5 degree (*d*) 90 degree

15. If you stand between two parallel mirrors the number of image/images that you observe is/are
(*a*) One (*b*) Two
(*c*) Eight (*d*) Infinite

16. Write two suitable examples where friction is increased for our benefit.

17. When a copper vessel is exposed to moist air for long it acquires a dull green coating. Why?

18. Why fossil fuels are exhaustible natural resources?

19. What are Endemic and Endangered Species? Give one example of each?

20. A force of 60 N is applied towards east direction.

What is the magnitude and direction of the force so that:
(*a*) The net force is zero
(*b*) The net force is 110 N towards East?

21. What are chromosomes? What are their function?

22. What is Global warming? Why it is a major concern for us?

23. Why are the oily food stuffs such as chips and kurkures are kept in sealed packet and flushed with nitrogen?

24. Why ornaments are generally made with Gold and Silver?

25. Paper by itself catches fire easily whereas a piece of paper wrapped around an aluminum pipe does not—Give reason.

26. What is Acid rain? What are its consequences?

27.

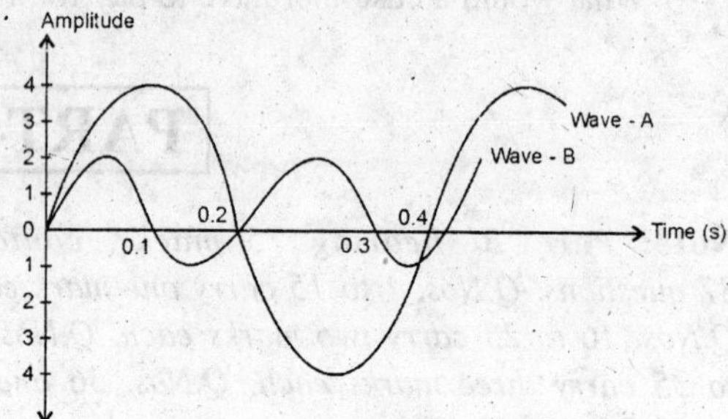

(*a*) Which sound wave is of more pitch?
(*b*) Which one is more loud sound?

28. How do amoeba reproduce? Explain in brief with suitable diagram.

29. Write the differences between a plant cell and animal cell.

30. Current is passed through Copper sulphate (blue colour) solution kept in a beaker by two copper rods connected with a battery.
(*a*) What changes do you notice in the solution and why?
(*b*) On which electrode a brown deposition is seen?
(*c*) Mark the two electrodes as anode and cathode.

31. What are Geostationary Satellites? What are their uses?

32. As a member of your society what would you do to reduce air pollution?

33. What are Hormones? Why adrenalin is known as Stress hormone? From where Insulin and Thyroxin hormones are produced?

34. Why lightning occurs between two clouds?

35. How do we hear any sound?

36. Two beakers marked 'A' and 'B' contains aqueous solution of copper sulphate ($CuSO_4$) and Ferrous sulphate ($FeSO_4$) respectively. An Iron rod is placed in beaker A and a copper rod in beaker B. What changes do you observe after some time in the two beakers? If there is any change explain it with proper chemical equation.

37. (*a*) Draw a diagram of human eye and label

(*i*) Retina (*iv*) Cilliary muscles

(*ii*) Optic nerve (*v*) Eye lens

(*iii*) Cornea (*vi*) Iris

(*b*) How our eye adjusts automatically with the varying intensity of light?

EXPLANATORY ANSWERS

PART-A : Mathematics

1. 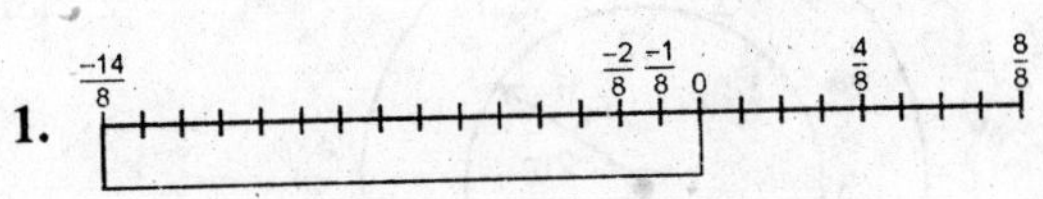

2. $\frac{3}{17} \div \frac{8}{17} \times \frac{2}{3} + \left(-\frac{2}{7}\right) \times \frac{35}{33} \div \left(-\frac{7}{11}\right)$

$= \frac{3}{17} \times \frac{17}{8} \times \frac{2}{3} - \frac{2}{7} \times \frac{35}{33} \times \left(-\frac{11}{7}\right)$

$= \frac{1}{4} + \frac{10}{21} = \frac{21+40}{84} = \frac{61}{84}.$

3. Let the numbers are a and b

$a + b = 15$ ...(*i*)

$a^2 + b^2 = 113$

$(a + b)^2 = a^2 + b^2 + 2ab$

$\Rightarrow (15)^2 = 113 + 2ab$

$\Rightarrow 225 = 113 + 2ab$

$\Rightarrow 2ab = 225 - 113 = 112$

$\Rightarrow ab = \frac{112}{2} = 56$

Now $(a - b)^2 = (a + b)^2 - 4ab$

$= 225 - 4 \times 56$

$= 225 - 224 = 1$

$\therefore a - b = 1$ ...(*ii*)

Solving (*i*) and (*ii*), we get

$a = 8$ and $b = 7$

$\therefore$ numbers are 8 and 7.

4. $(a + 7)(a^2 + 3a + 5)$

$= a^3 + 3a^2 + 5a + 7a^2 + 21a + 35$

$= a^3 + 10a^2 + 26a + 35.$

5. $\because \left(x + \frac{1}{x}\right) = 3$

$\therefore x^2 + \frac{1}{x^2} = \left(x + \frac{1}{x}\right)^2 - 2x \cdot \frac{1}{x}$

$= (3)^2 - 2$

$= 9 - 2 = 7$

Hence, the value of $x^2 + \frac{1}{x^2} = 7.$

6. $25a^2 - 4b^2 + 28bc - 49c^2$

$= 25a^2 - (4b^2 - 28bc + 49c^2)$

$= (5a)^2 - (2b - 7c)^2$

$= (5a + 2b - 7c)(5a - 2b + 7c).$

7. $\frac{2p - \frac{3}{4}}{9p + \frac{4}{7}} = \frac{1}{4}$

$\Rightarrow \frac{\frac{8p-3}{4}}{\frac{63p+4}{7}} = \frac{1}{4}$

$\Rightarrow \frac{(8p-3)}{4} \times \frac{7}{(63p+4)} = \frac{1}{4}$

$\Rightarrow \quad 56p - 21 = 63p + 4$

$\Rightarrow \quad 56p - 63p = 4 + 21$

$\Rightarrow \quad -7p = 25$

$\Rightarrow \quad p = -\frac{25}{7}.$

8.

3	128881	359
	9	
65	388	
	325	
709	6381	
	6381	
718	×	

$\therefore \sqrt{128881} = 359.$

9. 100 – 20 = 80

When amount pays ₹ 80 then MP = ₹ 100

When amount pays ₹ 1600 then MP

$= \frac{100}{80} \times 1600$

$\therefore$ MP = ₹ 2000.

10. Here, P = ₹ 12600, r = 10%, t = 2 years.

$$A = P\left(1 + \frac{r}{100}\right)^t$$

$$= 12600\left(1 + \frac{10}{100}\right)^2$$

$$= 12600 \times \frac{11 \times 11}{10 \times 10} = 126 \times 121$$

= ₹ 15246

$\therefore$ C.I. = A – P = 15246 – 12600

= ₹ 2646.

11.

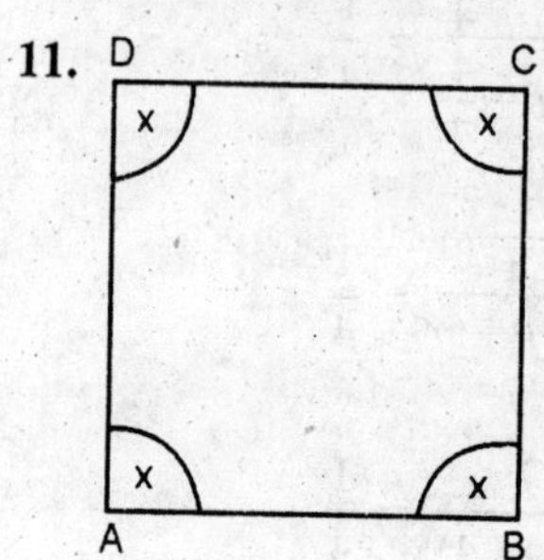

$\because$ ABCD is a parallelogram

$\therefore \angle A + \angle B + \angle C + \angle D = 360°$

$\Rightarrow \quad x + x + x + x = 360°$

$\Rightarrow \quad 4x = 360°$

$\Rightarrow \quad x = \frac{360}{4} = 90°$

Hence, the measure of each angles = 90°.

12. A die has 1, 2, 3, 4, 5, 6 numbers.

Even number greater than 5 = 1

$\therefore$ Required probability $= \frac{1}{6}$.

13.

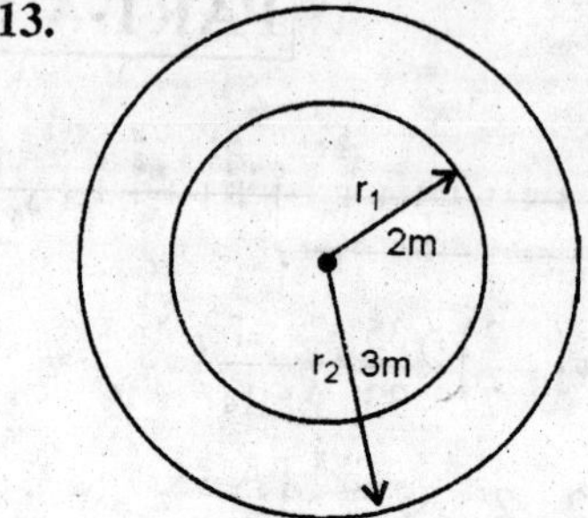

$$\frac{C_1}{C_2} = \frac{2\pi r_1}{2\pi r_2} = \frac{2}{3}$$

$\therefore \quad C_1 : C_2 = 2 : 3$

Hence, required ratio = 2 : 3.

14. 73, 85, 89, 94, 94, 100, 108, 120, 133, 140

Here $\quad n$ = 10 which is even number

$$\therefore \quad \text{Median} = \frac{\frac{n}{2}\text{th term + next term}}{2}$$

$$= \frac{\text{5th term + 6th term}}{2}$$

$$= \frac{94 + 100}{2} = \frac{194}{2} = 97$$

Hence, required median = 97.

15. Let the numbers are $5x$ and $3x$

According to the question,

$5x - 3x = 18$

$\Rightarrow \quad 2x = 18$

$\Rightarrow \quad x = 9$

$$5x = 5 \times 9 = 45$$
$$3x = 3 \times 9 = 27$$

Hence, numbers are 45 and 27.

16. The point (0, 6) lies on Y-axis.

17.

2	392
2	196
2	98
7	49
7	7
	1

$392 = 2 \times 2 \times 2 \times 7 \times 7$

If 392 multiplied by 7 then it becomes a perfect cube.

Hence, the required number = 7.

18.

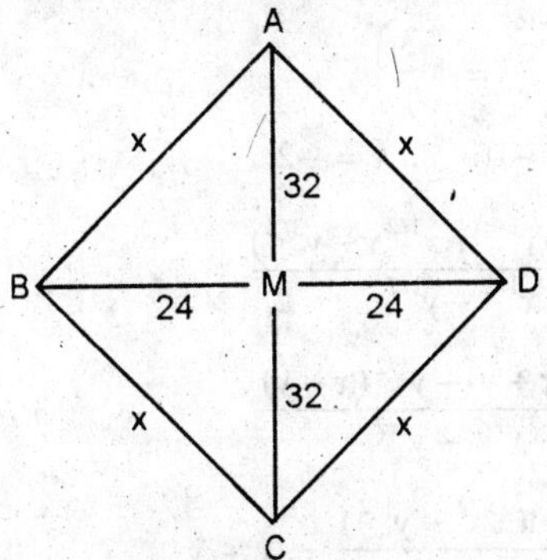

In ΔABM,

$$x^2 = (32)^2 + (24)^2$$
$$= 1024 + 576$$
$$\Rightarrow \quad x^2 = 1600$$
$$\Rightarrow \quad x = 40$$

$\therefore$ Side of rhombus = 40 cm

$$\text{Area of rhombus} = \frac{1}{2} \times d_1 \times d_2$$
$$= \frac{1}{2} \times 48 \times 64$$
$$= 48 \times 32 = 1536 \text{ cm}^2$$

Rhombus is also a parallelogram

$\therefore$ Area of ||gm = $b \times h$

$$\Rightarrow \quad 1536 = 40 \times h$$
$$\Rightarrow \quad h = \frac{1536}{40} = \frac{384}{10}$$
$$= 38.4 \text{ cm}$$

$\therefore$ Required height = 38.4 cm.

19.

ABCD is a quadrilateral

$\angle DAB = 180 - 90 = 90°$ (linear pair)

$$\angle A + \angle B + \angle C + \angle D = 360°$$
$$90° + 60° + 70° + x = 360°$$
$$\Rightarrow \quad x + 220° = 360°$$
$$\Rightarrow \quad x = 360° - 220°$$
$$= 140°.$$

20. Let three consecutive odd numbers are x, $x + 2$ and $x + 4$

According to the question,

$$x + x + 2 + x + 4 = 105$$
$$\Rightarrow \quad 3x + 6 = 105$$
$$\Rightarrow \quad 3x = 99$$
$$\Rightarrow \quad x = 33$$

$\therefore$ numbers are 33, 35 and 37.

21. Let ten's place digit number = x and unit's place digit number = y

$\therefore$ number = $10x + y$

According to the question,

$\because \quad x - y = 1 \Rightarrow x = 1 + y$

and $\quad 10y + x = \frac{5}{6}(10x + y)$

$$\Rightarrow \quad 6(10y + x) = 5(10x + y)$$
$$\Rightarrow \quad 60y + 6x = 50x + 5y$$
$$\Rightarrow \quad 55y = 44x$$
$$\Rightarrow \quad 5y = 4x$$
$$\Rightarrow \quad 5y = 4(1 + y)$$

$\Rightarrow \quad 5y = 4 + 4y$

$\Rightarrow \quad 5y - 4y = 4 \Rightarrow y = 4$

$\therefore \quad x = 1 + y = 1 + 4 = 5$

number = 54.

22. $\dfrac{3x^2-8}{5x^2+2} = \dfrac{4}{7}$

$\Rightarrow 21x^2 - 56 = 20x^2 + 8$

$\Rightarrow x^2 = 64 \Rightarrow x = \pm 8.$

23. $-\dfrac{2}{3}\times\dfrac{3}{5}+\dfrac{5}{2}-\dfrac{3}{5}\times\dfrac{1}{6}$

$= -\dfrac{2}{5}+\dfrac{5}{2}-\dfrac{1}{10} = \dfrac{-4+25-1}{10}$

$= \dfrac{20}{10} = 2.$

24. $8\left(x^3 - \dfrac{1}{x^3}\right)$

$= 8x^3 - \dfrac{8}{x^3} = (2x)^3 - \left(\dfrac{2}{x}\right)^3$

$= \left(2x - \dfrac{2}{x}\right)^3 + 3(2x)\left(\dfrac{2}{x}\right)\left(2x - \dfrac{2}{x}\right)$

$= (3)^3 + 12(3) \qquad \left[\because 2x - \dfrac{2}{x} = 3 \text{ given}\right]$

$= 27 + 36 = 63.$

25. $\because x + y + z = 9$

and $xy + yz + zx = 23$

$\because x^3 + y^3 + z^3 - 3xyz$

$= (x + y + z)\{(x + y + z)^2 - 3(xy + yz + zx)\}$

$= 9\{(9)^2 - 3(23)\}$

$= 9\{81 - 69\} = 9 \times 12 = 108.$

26. Area of rhombus = base × height

$= 6 \times 4 = 24 \text{ cm}^2$

27. $\dfrac{8^{-1}\times 5^3}{2^{-4}} = \dfrac{(2^3)^{-1}\times 5^3}{2^{-4}}$

$= 2^{-3} \times 2^4 \times 5^3$

$= 2 \times 125 = 250.$

28. $100 - 10 = 90$

When SP ₹ 90, then MP = ₹ 100

When SP ₹ 18000, then MP

$= \dfrac{100}{90}\times 18000 = 20000$

$\therefore \quad$ MP = ₹ 20000

Discount = MP − SP

= 20000 − 18000

= ₹ 2000.

29. $\left(\dfrac{3}{7}\right)^{-5} \times \left(\dfrac{7}{3}\right)^{11} = \left(\dfrac{3}{7}\right)^{8k}$

$\Rightarrow \left(\dfrac{3}{7}\right)^{-5} \times \left(\dfrac{3}{7}\right)^{-11} = \left(\dfrac{3}{7}\right)^{8k}$

$\Rightarrow \left(\dfrac{3}{7}\right)^{-16} = \left(\dfrac{3}{7}\right)^{8k}$

$\Rightarrow 8k = -16 \quad \therefore k = -2.$

30. $\dfrac{(x^{3/2} - xy^{1/2} + x^{1/2}y - y^{3/2})}{x^{1/2} - y^{1/2}}$

$= \dfrac{x^{1/2}(x+y) - y^{1/2}(x+y)}{x^{1/2} - y^{1/2}}$

$= \dfrac{(x+y)(x^{1/2} - y^{1/2})}{(x^{1/2} - y^{1/2})} = x + y.$

31. 100 + 25 = 125 students

$\because$ 100 students can eat the food in 20 days

$\therefore$ 1 student can eat the food in 20 × 100 days

$\therefore$ 125 students can eat the food in $\dfrac{20\times 100}{125}$

= 16 days.

32. Area of trapezium = $\dfrac{1}{2}\times h(b_1 + b_2)$

$\Rightarrow \quad 384 = \dfrac{1}{2}\times 12(3x + 5x)$

$\Rightarrow \quad 384 = 6 \times 8x$

$\Rightarrow \quad x = \dfrac{384}{6\times 8} = 8$

$\therefore \quad 3x = 3 \times 8 = 24$ cm

$5x = 5 \times 8 = 40$ cm

$\therefore$ Smaller of parallel side = 24 cm.

33.

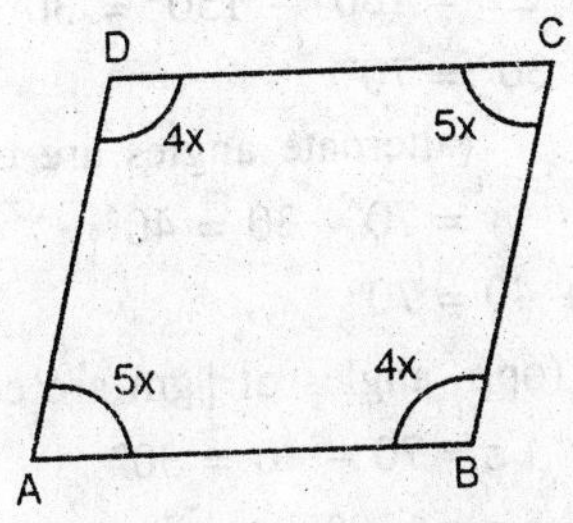

Let ABCD is a parallelogram in which

$\angle A = 5x°$ and $\angle B = 4x°$

$\therefore \quad \angle C = 5x$ and $\angle D = 4x$

$\angle A + \angle B + \angle C + \angle D = 360°$

$\Rightarrow \quad 5x + 4x + 5x + 4x = 360°$

$\Rightarrow \quad 18x = 360° \Rightarrow x = \frac{360°}{18} = 20°$

$\therefore \angle A = 5 \times 20 = 100°, \angle B = 4 \times 20 = 80°$

$\angle C = 5 \times 20 = 100°, \angle D = 4 \times 20 = 80°$

34.

3	1300	36
	9	
66	400	
	396	
	4	

$\therefore \quad (37)^2 = 1369$

$\therefore \quad 1369 - 1300 = 69$

$\therefore$ required number = 69.

35. $(a + b)(c - d) + (a - b)(c + d) + 2(ac + bd)$

$= ac - ad + bc - bd + ac + ad - bc - bd + 2ac + 2bd$

$= 2ac - 2bd + 2ac + 2bd$

$= 4ac.$

36. Total surface area of cylinder $= 2\pi r (h + r)$

$\Rightarrow \quad 968 = 2 \times \frac{22}{7} \times 7(h + 7)$

$\Rightarrow \quad 968 = 44(h + 7)$

$\Rightarrow \quad (h + 7) = \frac{968}{44} = 22$

$\Rightarrow \quad h = 22 - 7 = 15$ cm.

Hence, height of the cylinder = 15 cm

37.

C.I.	Frequency
30 – 35	3
35 – 40	4
40 – 45	4
45 – 50	5
50 – 55	1
55 – 60	1
60 – 65	1
65 – 70	1
	Total = 20

38. Let C's share = ₹ x

$\therefore$ B's share = ₹ $\frac{x}{2}$

A's share = $\frac{1}{2}$ of B's share

$= \frac{1}{2} \times \frac{x}{2} =$ ₹ $\frac{x}{4}$

According to the question,

$\frac{x}{4} + \frac{x}{2} + x =$ ₹ 1400

$\frac{x + 2x + 4x}{4} = 1400$

$\Rightarrow \quad 7x = 1400 \times 4$

$\Rightarrow \quad x = \frac{1400 \times 4}{7}$

$= 200 \times 4 =$ ₹ 800

$\therefore$ A's share = $\frac{x}{4} = \frac{800}{4} =$ ₹ 200

B's share = $\frac{x}{2} = \frac{800}{2} =$ ₹ 400

C's share = x = ₹ 800

39.

2	117912
2	58956
2	29478
3	14739
17	4913
17	289
17	17
	1

Clarly the given number is not a perfect cube.

$\underline{2 \times 2 \times 2} \times \underline{17 \times 17 \times 17} \times 3 \times (3 \times 3)$

If we multiply the given number by 9 then it will become a perfect cube.

Hence, required number = 9.

40. Let height of the embankment = x m

According to the question,

$\Rightarrow \quad \pi(R^2 - r^2)x = \pi r^2 h$

$\Rightarrow \quad (28^2 - 7^2)x = 7 \times 7 \times 8$

$\Rightarrow \quad (28 + 7)(28 - 7)x = 7 \times 7 \times 8$

$\Rightarrow \quad 35 \times 21 \times x = 7 \times 7 \times 8$

$\Rightarrow \quad x = \frac{7 \times 7 \times 8}{35 \times 21} = \frac{8}{15}$ m

$= 0.53$ m

Hence, height of the embankment = 0.53 m.

41. Let Shriya's present age = x years

$\therefore$ Arjun's present age = $2x$ years

Five years ago Shriya's age = $(x - 5)$ years

Five years ago Arjun's age = $(2x - 5)$ years

According to the question,

$2x - 5 = 3(x - 5)$

$\Rightarrow \quad 2x - 5 = 3x - 15$

$\Rightarrow \quad 2x - 3x = -15 + 5$

$\Rightarrow \quad -x = -10$

$\therefore \quad x = 10$

Hence, Shriya's present age = 10 years

and Arjun's present age = 20 years.

42.

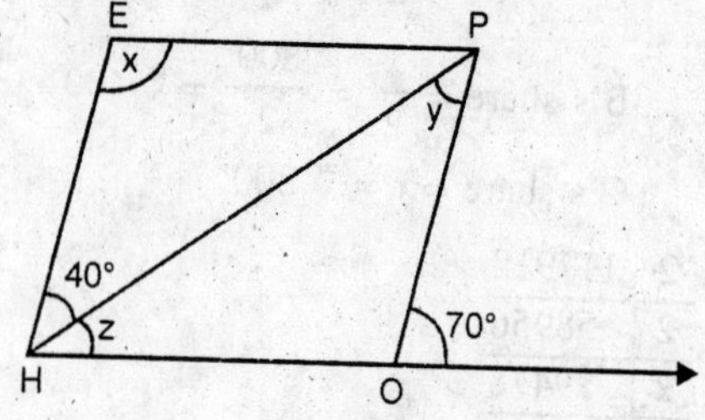

$\because$ HOPE is a parallelogram

$\therefore \quad \angle POH = 180° - 70° = 110°$ (linear pair)

$\therefore \quad \angle HEP = 110°$ (opp. angles of ||gm)

$\therefore \quad x = 110°$

In ΔHEP,

$x + 40 + \angle P = 180°$

$110° + 40 + \angle P = 180°$

$\Rightarrow \quad \angle P = 180° - 150° = 30°$

$y + 30° = 70°$

(alternate angles are equal)

$\therefore \quad y = 70 - 30 = 40°$

$z + 40 = 70°$

(opp. angles of ||gm are equal)

$\therefore \quad z = 70 - 40 = 30°$

Hence, $x = 110°$

$y = 40°$

and $z = 30°$.

43. Let P = ₹ 100

Amount = ₹ 300, t = 3 years

$$A = P\left(1 + \frac{r}{100}\right)^t$$

$\Rightarrow \quad 300 = 100\left(1 + \frac{r}{100}\right)^3$

$\Rightarrow \quad \frac{300}{100} = \left(1 + \frac{r}{100}\right)^3$

$\Rightarrow \quad 3 = \left(1 + \frac{r}{100}\right)^3$

Squaring both sides

$$(3)^2 = \left[\left(1 + \frac{r}{100}\right)^3\right]^2$$

$\Rightarrow \quad 9 = \left(1 + \frac{r}{100}\right)^6$

$\therefore$ time = 6 years.

44. (*a*) $x^2 + 6x - 16$

$= x^2 + 8x - 2x - 16$

$= x(x + 8) - 2(x + 8)$

$= (x + 8)(x - 2)$

(*b*) $\because \quad a + b = 14, ab = 20$

$a^2 + b^2 = (a + b)^2 - 2ab$

$= (14)^2 - 2(20)$

$= 196 - 40 = 156.$

45. Area of the road = $2\pi rh \times 750$

$$= 2\times\frac{22}{7}\times\frac{42}{100}\times 1\times 750$$

$$= 132 \times 15 = 1980 \text{ m}^2.$$

46.

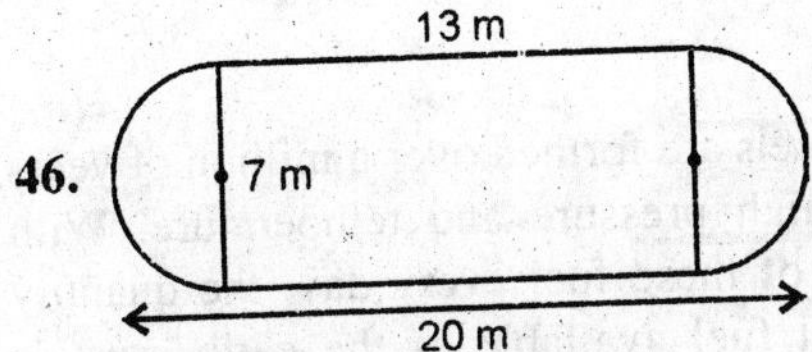

Perimeter of the garden

$= 2\pi r + 2(l + b)$

$$= 2\times\frac{22}{7}\times\frac{7}{2}+2(13+7)$$

$= 22 + 40 = 62$ m

Area of the garden

= Area of circle + Area of rectangle

$= \pi r^2 + l \times b$

$$= \frac{22}{7}\times\frac{7}{2}\times\frac{7}{2}+13\times 7$$

$$= \frac{77}{2}+91$$

$= 38.5 + 91 = 129.5 \text{ m}^2.$

47. Let numerator = x

denominator = $x + 8$

$\therefore$ fraction = $\frac{x}{x+8}$

According to the question,

$$\frac{x+17}{x+8-1} = \frac{3}{2}$$

$$\Rightarrow \frac{x+17}{x+7} = \frac{3}{2}$$

$\Rightarrow$ $3x + 21 = 2x + 34$

$\Rightarrow$ $x = 13$

$x + 8 = 13 + 8 = 21$

$\therefore$ fraction = $\frac{13}{21}$.

48. Discount = 10%

Value of total MP = 1450 + 1700

= ₹ 3150

Discount = 10% of ₹ 3150

$$= \frac{10}{100}\times 3150 = ₹\ 315$$

Amount payed by the customer

= ₹ 3150 − 315

= ₹ 2835

49. $12xy\,(9x^2 - 16y^2) \div 4xy\,(3x + 4y)$

$$= \frac{12xy(3x+4y)(3x-4y)}{4xy(3x+4y)}$$

$= 3(3x - 4y)$

$= 9x - 12y.$

50. (*i*) The area which can cow graze

$$= \frac{1}{4}\pi r^2$$

$$= \frac{1}{4}\times 3.14\times 20\times 20$$

$$= \frac{1}{4}\times\frac{314}{100}\times 400 = 314 \text{ m}^2$$

(*ii*) Area of the field = $(40)^2$

$= 40 \times 40 = 1600 \text{ m}^2$

Area of the remaining part

$= 1600 - 314 = 1286 \text{ m}^2$

Now area grazed by the cow = 1256 m^2

(*iii*) Area = $\frac{1}{4}\pi r^2$

$$1256 = \frac{1}{4}\times\frac{314}{100}\times r^2$$

$$\Rightarrow r^2 = \frac{1256\times 4\times 100}{314}$$

$\Rightarrow$ $r^2 = 4 \times 4 \times 10 \times 10$

$\Rightarrow$ $r = 4 \times 10$

$= 40$ m

$\therefore$ Length of the rope = 40 m

PART-B : Science

1	2	3	4	5	6	7	8	9	10
B	D	A	A	A	A	B	C	B	C
11	12	13	14	15					
B	B	A	C	D					

1. Malaria is transmitted through the bite of infected female anopheles mosquito caused by the plasmodium (unicellular organism).

2. After sun, the near most star is proxima centauri at a distance 4.22 light year from the earth.

3. Bromine is the only liquid non-metallic element.

4. A body exert maximum pressure when contact area is maximum.
Here maximum area of contact comes with 30 cm × 20 cm = 600 cm^2.

7. Correct order of agricultural practices: tilling, sowing, adding manure and fertilizer, irrigation, harvesting.

10. As the incident ray is

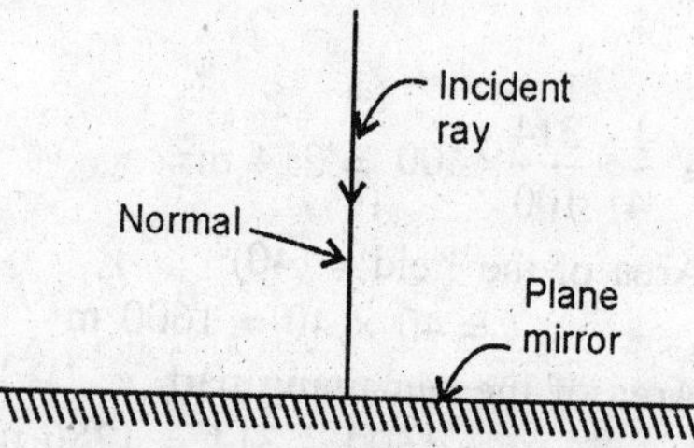

16. It enables us to walk without slipping. The breakers and tiers of our cars and bicycles depend on friction to function properly.

17. When a copper vessel is exposed to moist air for long, it acquires a dull green coating. The green material is a mixture of copper hydroxide ($Cu(OH)_2$) and copper carbonate ($CuCO_3$). The following is the reaction

$$2Cu \xrightarrow[\text{moist air}]{+H_2O + CO_2 +} O_2 \rightarrow Cu(OH)_2 + CuCO_3$$

So, copper also get rusted, a greenish deposit on the surface of copper vessels is a mixture of copper hydroxide and copper carbonate.

18. Fossil fuels are formed over a million of years under high pressure and temperature. With the use of these fuel every day, the quantity of fossil fuel available in the earth crust is slowly depleting. Since they can not be formed artificially and quickly in any industry we have to depend on the natural process for its formation. Further the process takes million of years. With its extraction/removal from earth crust in the same rate it is likely to get exhausted in a few hundred years. Therefore it is essential for us to exploit these natural resources carefully to minimise the wastage and conserve for the future generation.

19. An endemic species is one whose habitat is restricted to a particular area. The term could refer to an animal, a plant, a fungus, or even a microorganism. The definition differs from "indigenous", or "native", species in that the latter, although it occurs naturally in an area, is also found in other areas. Endemic species are often endangered, and particular examples may become a focus point for campaigns to protect **biodiversity** in a given environment. Some have become national, or regional, emblems.

The endangered species are those living organisms which are almost on the verge of extinction. Thousands of species of plants and animals are endangered and the number increases each year.

Asian Elephant and **Blue whale** are two species endangers.

20. (*a*) 60 N ← [ ] → 60 N

Net force is zero when equal force of 10 N applied towards west direction.

(*b*) Net force is 110 N towards east

so, $110 = 60 + R$

$\therefore$ $R = 110 - 60$

$= 50$ N towards east.

21. Chromosomes are thread-like structures located inside the nucleus of animal and plant cells. Each chromosome is made of protein and a single molecule of deoxyribonucleic acid (DNA). Passed from parents to offspring, DNA contains the specific instructions that make each type of living creature unique.

For an organism to grow and function properly, cells must constantly divide to produce new cells to replace old, worn-out cells. During cell division, it is essential that DNA remains intact and evenly distributed among cells. Chromosomes are a key part of the process that ensures DNA is accurately copied and distributed in the vast majority of cell divisions. Still, mistakes do occur on rare occasions.

22. Global Warming is the increase of Earth's average surface temperature due to effect of greenhouse gases, such as carbon dioxide emissions from burning fossil fuels or from deforestation, which trap heat that would otherwise escape from Earth. This is a type of *greenhouse effect.*

Earth's climate is mostly influenced by the first 6 miles or so of the atmosphere which contains most of the matter making up the atmosphere. This is really a very thin layer if you think about it. In the book **The End of Nature,** author Bill McKibbin tells of walking three miles to from his cabin in the Adirondack's to buy food. Afterwards, he realized that on this short journey he had travelled a distance equal to that of the layer of the atmosphere where almost all the action of our climate is contained. In fact, if you were to view Earth from space, the principle part of the atmosphere would only be about as thick as the skin on an onion! Realizing this makes it more plausible to suppose that human beings can change the climate. A look at the amount of greenhouse gases we are spewing into the atmosphere, makes it even more plausible.

23. The most effective way to prevent oxygen damage is to remove and replace the oxygen with an inert gas. All those clear cello-packs of potato or corn chips, pretzels or popcorn that display their contents of salt and greasy calories so effectively on supermarket shelves are inflated with nitrogen gas. Punch a small hole in one and squeeze the gas inside onto a burning match. The flame will go out.

To store grain and dry goods for years, keep them in plastic bags filled with nitrogen and sealed inside plastic tubs or metal cans.

24. Gold and silver are used to make ornaments because they are lustrous, malleable, and do not corrode in water as gold also effects on our skin an make it more clear and give it extra glow, that why princess, princes, kings and mostly queens used to where more gold ornaments, so that they look more beautiful. So, gold and silver are used to make ornaments.

This is simple,

1. silver and gold are very soft metals and can be moulded into different shapes
2. they are very pure forms of metals so there are very little impurities
3. they are not very reactive in open atmosphere, i.e., almost inert metals.

25. Because for burning or combustion, a substance must me heated to its ignition temperature. Paper wrapped around an aluminium pipe does not catch fire as on heating, it is unable to attain the ignition temperature due to transfer of heat to aluminium pipe which is good conductor of heat.

26. Acidification of rain-water is identified as one of the most serious environmental problems of transboundary nature. Acid rain is mainly a mixture of sulphuric and nitric acids depending upon the relative quantities of oxides of sulphur and nitrogen emissions.

Due to the interaction of these acids with other constituents of the atmosphere, protons are released causing increase in the soil acidity. Lowering of soil pH mobilizes and leaches away nutrient cations and increases availability of toxic heavy metals. Such changes in the soil chemical characteristics reduce the soil fertility which ultimately causes the negative impact on growth and productivity of forest trees and crop plants. Acidification of water bodies causes large scale negative impact on aquatic organisms including fishes. Acidification has some indirect effects on human health also. Acid rain affects each and every components of ecosystem. Acid rain also damages man-made materials and structures. By reducing the emission of the precursors of acid rain and to some extent by liming, the problem of acidification of terrestrial and aquatic ecosystem has been reduced during last two decades.

27. (*a*) The higher the frequency, the higher the pitch of the sound. Hence, sound B has more pitch.

(*b*) Sound A is more loud, because it has greater amplitude.

28. The reproduction of amoebas is called binary fission. This is when the amoeba splits itself in half, creating two new amoebas. Amoebas are single celled organisms like protists.

A sexuality (reproduction by binary fission) is often thought to be a defining characteristic of amoebae. However, analysis of 71 isolates of amoeba from the same geographical area along a river indicated that sex must be occurring in that particular lineage. Recently, Lahr *et al.* proposed that the majority of amoeboid lineages are, contrary to popular belief, at least anciently sexual, and that most current asexual groups have arisen recently and independently. In addition, recent evidence also indicates that several other single-celled eukaryotes that were previously regarded as asexual are, or were in the past, capable of sexual reproduction. These findings have led to the idea that sex was present in the earliest common ancestor of all eukaryotes.

REPRODUCTION IN AMOEBA

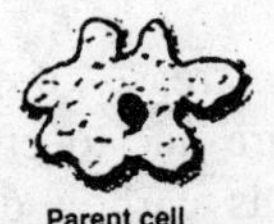

Parent cell

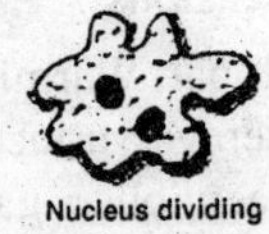

Nucleus dividing

Cytoplasm divides

Two daughter cells

29.

	Animal Cell	Plant Cell
Cell wall	Absent	Present (formed of cellulose)
Shape	Round (irregular shape)	Rectangular (fixed shape)
Vacuole	One or more small vacuoles (much smaller than plant cells).	One, large central vacuole taking up 90% of cell volume.
Centrioles	Present in all animal cells	Only present in lower plant forms.
Chloroplast	Animal cells don't have chloroplasts	Plant cells have chloroplasts because they make their own food
Cytoplasm	Present	Present
Endoplasmic Reticulum (Smooth and Rough)	Present	Present
Ribosomes	Present	Present

Mitochondria	Present	Present
Plastids	Absent	Present
Golgi Apparatus	Present	Present
Plasma Membrane	Only cell membrane	Cell wall and a cell membrane
Microtubules/ Microfilaments	Present	Present
Flagella	May be found in some cells	May be found in some cells
Lysosomes	Lysosomes occur in cytoplasm	Lysosomes usually not evident
Nucleus	Present	Present
Cilia	Present	It is very rare

30. Electrolysis of $CuSO_4$ Using Active Electrodes (e.g., copper)

Ions Present: Cu^{2+}, H^+, OH^- and SO_4^{2-}

Reaction at Anode

- Both SO_4^{2-} and OH^- gets attracted here but not discharged. Instead, the copper anode discharged by losing electrons to form Cu^{2+}. So, the electrode size decreases.
- $Cu\ (s) \rightarrow Cu^{2+}\ (aq) + 2e^-$

Reaction at Cathode

- Cu^{2+} produced from anode gains electrons at cathode to become Cu atoms becoming copper. Hence, the copper is deposited here and the electrode grows.
- $Cu^{2+}\ (aq) + 2e^- \rightarrow Cu(s)$

Overall Change

- There is no change in solution contents as for every lost of Cu^{2+} ions at cathode is replaced by Cu^{2+} ions released by dissolving anode.
- Only the cathode increases size by gaining copper and anode decreases size by losing copper.
- We can use this method to create pure copper on cathode by using pure copper on cathode and impure copper on anode.
- Impurities of anode falls under it.

31. A geostationary satellite is an earth-orbiting *satellite*, placed at an altitude of approximately 35,800 kilometers (22,300 miles) directly over the equator, that revolves in the same direction the earth rotates (west to east). At this altitude, one orbit takes 24 hours, the same length of time as the earth requires to rotate once on its axis. The term geostationary comes from the fact that such a satellite appears nearly stationary in the sky as seen by a ground-based observer. *BGAN*, the new global mobile communications network, uses geostationary satellites.

These satellites have revolutionized global *communications, television broadcasting* and *weather forecasting*, and have a number of important *defense* and *intelligence* applications.

32. Air pollution, including that of ozone, is mainly the result of human activities. The small things you do every day can help reduce air pollution and hence improve the protection of the environment as well as human health.

Here are some tips on what you can do, on a day-to-day basis, to help prevent air pollution:

Take public transport or carpool!

A good solution for longer journeys may be public transport or carpooling, since more people can be transported in a single vehicle. If you choose to take the car rather than the train or bus, for instance, you will generate several times more ozone pollution and up to 30 times more CO_2 emissions.

Walk or use the bike!

45% of the ozone precursors and 38% of the particulate matter emitted in Europe comes from transport. On average, one out of three journeys we do by car is only to go as far as 2 km. Replacing a car ride by walking or using the bicycle not only helps reduce traffic but also emissions.

Go for local produce!

Transporting goods from one side of the world to the other generates a lot more air pollution than transporting them short distances. Try to buy locally produced goods and eat local foods that are in season: transporting and producing them doesn't generate as much air pollution.

Save electricity!

Don't leave your electronic devices—TV sets, computers, DVD's—on stand-by mode. Switch them off completely and you will save about 10% of your electricity bill. Buy energy-saving light bulbs and "A"-labelled household appliances. Less electricity consumed means less power produced and fewer pollutants into the air from burning of fossil fuels.

33. Hormones is a regulatory substance produced in an organism and transported in tissue fluids such as blood or sap to stimulate specific cells or tissues into action.

Adrenalin is often referred to as 'emergency hormones' because they are released when a person feels excited. Thus it is this hormone that often give people the strength to do otherwise—impossible deeds and prevent emergencies.

34. Lighting occurs due to an accumulation of charge, electrons if you like, in the air. As a storm grows, electrical charges build up in the clouds. At the same time, oppositely charged particles are growing in number on the earth's surface. As you know opposite charges attract and due to the large number of charges this attraction grows quickly. At some point the attraction becomes large enough to overcome air's resistance to electrical flow, in this case the flow of charges between the ground and the clouds. These particles move toward each other at incredible speeds and when they meet they complete an electrical circuit. Charge from the ground then surges upward at nearly one-third the speed of light and we see a bright flash of lightning.

35. Sound is created when an object vibrates. This causes the air around it to vibrate. These vibrations in the air, known as sound waves, are collected by the outer ear, travel down the ear canal and strike the eardrum. From here they pass to the small bones of the middle ear, which transmit them to the auditory nerve in the inner ear. The auditory nerve connects directly to the brain. At this age, children need to know simply that sound travels through the air and we hear it when it reaches our ears.

36. **For Beaker A**

$Fe + CuSO_4 \rightarrow FeSO_4 + Cu$

For Beaker B

$2Al + 3\ FeSO_4 \rightarrow Al_2\ (SO_4)_3 + 3Fe$

37.

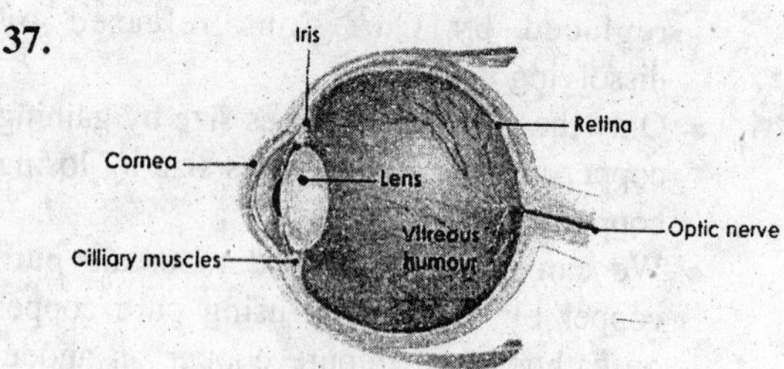

PAPER—II

PART–A : English Language

1. Read the following passage and answer the questions that follow. (3 × 5 = 15)

Rain in countryside attracts the lovers of nature. It is pleasant and helpful. But rain in city creates a different kind of sight. For some people the heavy downpour may have a Chilling effect, but it has its charm with the roar of thunder and the flash of lightening. On a rainy day the lanes and the streets look like rivulets, and the entire city becomes magically converted into Venice. The street wears a deserted look. Occasionally a man tries to plod his way. His clothes are tucked up and he holds the umbrella in one hand and his bag in the other. A sudden gush of wind tilts his umbrella and he gets drenched. If a vehicle passes speedily by splashing muddy water on him, he looks a pitiable creature. Sometimes the streets become water-logged and traffic comes to a halt.

The men who dwell in comfortable houses sit in their cosy rooms and look out of the window to catch a glimpse of some unusual sight. The howl of the wind and the patters of the rain constitute a symphony for them and some of them feel a poetic fervour in their hearts. The poor persons however, suffer a lot. Leaky roofs, rain-soaked floors and chocked up-drains fill them with despair. The street hawkers cannot carry on their trade. The busy house-wife wears a worry face as her oven does not burn.

Many people come out of their houses and wait for the town buses because they have the urgency of going to their work. As the town buses do not come in time they feel irritated. Sometimes they are disappointed. Boys and girls do not go to school because of rain. Life is painful when it rains in torrents.

When the rain stops, the sight becomes more interesting. Small children come out to the flooded streets and float paper boats. They like to splash water. Buses and cars begin moving on the streets. Life seems to begin normal activity as if a patient recovers from illness.

(*a*) How 'Rain is pleasant and helpful'?

(*b*) How does rain bring happiness to rich while misery to poor section of the society?

(*c*) How does rain affect the daily life of the people?

(*d*) How does the life normalize after the rain subsides?

(*e*) Pick out the words from the given passage which mean

(*i*) Wet (para 1)

(*ii*) Live (para 2)

(*iii*) Comfortable (para 2)

2. Write a paragraph in about 100 words on any one of the given topics. (10)

(*a*) Plan a picnic for your class.

or

(*b*) Harmful effects of junk and fast food.

3. You are Himanshu, a resident of Benaras Chowk, Ambikapur. Write a letter to the Chairman Municipality expressing your deep concern over the poor condition of roads and the inconvenience faced by the people of your locality.

(Maximum 150 words) **(15)**

4. Fill in the blanks with appropriate prepositions or adverbs given in the brackets. (2 × 5 = 10)

(*a*) My mother ran .... (up/out of/into) milk yesterday and I went to buy some.

(*b*) Could you turn .... (out/off/up) the music while I am talking?

(*c*) Geetanjali's car broke .... (up/off/down) on her way to office.

(*d*) Fazia's boss called .... (down/out/off) the meeting till tomorrow.
(*e*) That problem is actually quite simple to figure .... (up/out/down).

5. Complete these sentence by choosing the correct phrases from the brackets.

[poke his nose into, white collar, once in a blue moon, got the green signal, apple of their eyes] (2 × 5 = 10)

(*a*) Swati's parents stopped at nothing for her wedding; clearly she is the ....
(*b*) Nishant .... for his radical project.
(*c*) Why does he always have to .... other people's affairs?
(*d*) Though my gardener is uneducated and poor, he is saving to send his son to a good school since he wants the boy to get a .... job.
(*e*) After joining the coaching classes I .... get chance to play cricket with my friends.

6. Following sentences are INCORRECT. Find out the error and rewrite the following sentences correctly. (2 × 5 = 10)

(*a*) Money begets money, Don't they?
(*b*) He, I and you were asked to write the details.
(*c*) They had no manner.
(*d*) No other boy of the class is more taller than Ram.
(*e*) No sooner had he reached the station when the train left.

7. Write one word for the following group of words. (1 × 5 = 5)

(*a*) One who eats human flesh?
(*b*) A person's first speech.
(*c*) One who draws maps and charts.
(*d*) A group of angry people.
(*e*) One who dies for country?

8. Frame a meaningful sentence by using each word. (2 × 5 = 10)

(*a*) Accede, Exceed
(*b*) Morning, Mourning
(*c*) Hoist, Host
(*d*) Temper, Tamper
(*e*) Differ, Defer

9. Change the following DIRECT sentences into INDIRECT. (1 × 5 = 5)

(*a*) The student said to his teacher, "Do you teach my brother"?
(*b*) The cricketers said, "Hurrah! The ICC T20 World Cup is ours".
(*c*) The father said to his son, "Don't walk so fast else you may fall".
(*d*) The clerk said to the officer, "Why do you not accept a bribe?"
(*e*) He said, "Let us go out for a picnic in this lovely weather."

10. Look at the picture critically, think of a suitable theme and write a story. (in approx. 100 words) (10)

PART–B : Social Studies

1. State True/False. (1 × 15 = 15)

(*a*) The Battle of Seringapatam was fought between East India Company and Tipu Sultan in 1799.
(*b*) Captain Alexander Read introduced the Ryotwari system in India.
(*c*) Kunwar Singh was a leader of the rebel sepoys in Lucknow at the time of the Revolt of 1857.
(*d*) Dargah means the tomb of a Sufi Saint.
(*e*) The last Viceroy of British India was Lord Canning.

(*f*) Emigrants are people who arrive in a country.

(*g*) Information Technology Industry is known as Sunrise Industry.

(*h*) Cotton is also known as the 'Golden Fibre'.

(*i*) Viticulture means cultivation of grapes.

(*j*) Kalpakkam nuclear power station is in Karnataka.

(*k*) Resources that are found everywhere like the air we breathe, are called localised resources.

(*l*) Sardar Vallabhbhai Patel was the first Deputy Prime Minister of India.

(*m*) Bhopal Gas Tragedy took place on 02 December, 1986.

(*n*) There are 233 elected members in the Rajya Sabha.

(*o*) Right to Life is a Fundamental Right Under Article 21 of the Indian Constitution.

2. Fill in the blanks. **(1 × 15 = 15)**

(*a*) In 1875, the Arya Samaj was founded by .... in Bombay.

(*b*) C.V. Raman was given the Nobel Prize for his work in Physics in ....

(*c*) .... was the British Military Officer at the time of Jallianwala Bagh Massacre.

(*d*) Silicon used in the computer industry is obtained from ....

(*e*) .... is the largest producer of bauxite in the world.

(*f*) Petroleum and its derivatives are called .... as they are very valuable.

(*g*) Silicon Valley is located in ....

(*h*) The Supreme Court of India was established in the year ....

(*i*) In India, Lok Sabha is presided over by the ....

(*j*) The .... of India is the Supreme Law-making institution.

(*k*) New Delhi was constructed as a 10-square-mile city on .... Hill.

(*l*) Mala Irular is a tribal group of people who belong to the state of ....

(*m*) Gol Gumbaz, the largest dome in India is located in the state of ....

(*n*) India's first satellite 'Arya-bhatta' was launched in ....

(*o*) 'Long Walk to Freedom' is a book written by ....

3. Expand the abbreviations. **(1 × 10 = 10)**

(*a*) PIL

(*b*) EVM

(*c*) ASEAN

(*d*) DRDO

(*e*) FDI

(*f*) GSI

(*g*) NHRC

(*h*) IRBM

(*i*) ILO

(*j*) TELCO

4. Match the following columns. **(1 × 10 = 10)**

(*a*) Battle of Plassey	(*i*) 1856
(*b*) Battle of Buxar	(*ii*) 1757
(*c*) Annexation of Awadh	(*iii*) 1764
(*d*) Annexation of Sindh	(*iv*) 1849
(*e*) Annexation of Punjab	(*v*) 1843
(*f*) Bhangi	(*vi*) Gujarat
(*g*) Pabhi	(*vii*) Andhra Pradesh
(*h*) Sikkaliar	(*viii*) Tamil Nadu
(*i*) Manash National Park	(*ix*) New Delhi
(*j*) Supreme Court of India	(*x*) Assam

5. Write short notes on any five of the following topics (limit 50 words) **(5 × 5 = 25)**

(*a*) Indian women in Olympic Games.

(*b*) Key features of Indian Constitution.

(*c*) Right to Education.

(*d*) The "Blue Rebellion".

(*e*) The Battle of Plassey.

(*f*) Fossil Fuel.

(*g*) Conservation of Water Resources.

(*h*) Renewable sources of Energy.

EXPLANATORY ANSWERS

PART-A : English Language

1. (*a*) The rain is pleasant and helpful as it brings the Chilling effect and attracts lovers of nature to the countryside. It also helps crops and often vegetation grow. The environment becomes cool and greener.

   (*b*) The rich sit in their cosy homes and enjoy the rain time looking out of the windows while the poor suffer with their leaky roofs, rain-soaked floors and choked up-drains. They are unable to move out to earn and find it difficult to burn their ovens to cook food.

   (*c*) The daily life of people is greatly affected by rain as streets and roads are water-logged and slippery. There are traffic-jams and problems in commuting. It is difficult to keep clothes dry and reach to work places in time. Hawkers are out lesser, hence, scarcity of things is also imminent.

   (*d*) Life normalizes slowly after the rain subsides. Children come out to float paper boat and splash water. Traffic starts moving gradually. In all normalizes in the manner a patient recovers from illness.

   (*e*) (*i*) Drenched

   (*ii*) Dwell

   (*iii*) Cosy

2. (*b*) **Harmful effects of junk and fast food**

Every living being has to eat to continue living. We should eat only fresh, well-washed and well-cooked food articles which are free from dust and flies. Fried foods and foods containing excess of fat, spices and chillis are harmful. Roadside eating should be avoided. Therefore, it is of paramount importance to eat good and useful things and eat them at the proper time and in the best way. It is essential that we take a balanced diet. We must take our meals at the fixed hours. We must take our food in the right quantity. Under-eating can cause us weakness and chronic under-eating can lead to under-nourishment and cause tuberculosis, asthma or other diseases by reducing our immunity. It should be seen particularly in children that they eat the required quantity of food, since because of excessive exertion, they lose many of their calories. Also for growing purposes and brain and nerve development, they need extra protein and fats. We should not over-eat. Chronic over-eating can cause several diseases like those of stomach, heart of liver. We should take our food along with other members of the family at the table. We should take the last meal two or three hours before going to bed. There should be a good time gap between two meals, so that the food gets digested in our stomach.

3.

Benaras Chowk,
Ambikapur,
Dated ....

The Chairman,
Municipal Corporation,
Ambikapur.

Respected Sir,

The road connecting our colony with the main road has been in a pathetic condition for the past six months. The surface has been broken at several places. It is full of pot-holes which are deep enough to trap the wheels of light vehicles. The road is almost impassable now.

Driving on this road would mean breaking one's bones. It is highly dangerous during the rainy season. When the water covers the road, it is impossible to see the pot-holes. A driver who drives on it unawares will certainly wreck his body and vehicle by falling into these holes. Several accidents have occurred on this road due to its bad condition.

Hired vehicles' drivers refuse to come to our colony through this road. They fear damage to their vehicles. Therefore, most of the time we have to walk 1 km. to reach our colony.

We have made several complaints earlier to get this road repaired but no action has been taken on our request so far. You are requested to look into the matter personally and take an early action.

Yours truly

Himanshu

4. (*a*) out of (*b*) off
(*c*) down (*d*) off
(*e*) out

5. (*a*) apple of their eyes
(*b*) got the green signal
(*c*) poke his nose into
(*d*) white collar
(*e*) once in a blue moon

6. (*a*) Money begets money. Doesn't it?
(*b*) I, you and he were asked to write the details.
(*c*) They have no manners.
(*d*) Ram is the tallest boy in the class.
(*e*) No sooner did he reach the station then the train left.

7. (*a*) Cannibal (*b*) Maiden
(*c*) Cartographer (*d*) Mob
(*e*) Martyr

8. (*a*) **Accede:** The teacher acceeded to the student's request.
Exceed: His expenditure exceeds his income.
(*b*) **Morning:** He gets up early in the morning.
Mourning: The nation was mourning the death of the leader.
(*c*) **Hoist:** National flag was hoisted on the building.
Host: He hosted a grand party.
(*d*) **Temper:** He has a hot temper.
Tamper: Do not tamper with the seal of meter.
(*e*) **Differ:** I differ with your opinion.
Defer: The meeting was deferred.

9. (*a*) The student asked his teacher whether he taught his brother.
(*b*) The cricketers exclaimed with joy that the ICC T20 World Cup was their.
(*c*) The father advised his son not to walk that fast else he might fall.
(*d*) The clerk asked the officer why he did not accept a bribe.
(*e*) He proposed to go out for a picnic in that lovely weather.

10. Environmental Pollution

The earth is a wonderful planet. But, unfortunately, man is making a criminal misuse of it by polluting it through his wanton activities. At present, the earth has become a highly polluted planet. There is most deleterious pollution in the air, in water, in the soil and even in space. Many big cities like Delhi and Kolkata in India and Karachi in Pakistan are no longer worth-living. One feels suffocated in these cities. The petrol and diesel fumes from automobiles and smoke from the chimneys of mills and chemical plants spread highly toxic gases in the air. The thoughtless felling down of trees and forest wealth is depleting the ratio of oxygen in the air. The use of refrigerators and airconditioners is leading to the thinning of ozone layer in the atmosphere. The rivers are getting stuffed with toxic effluents from the factories. The excessive use of pesticides and insecticides is also playing havoc with the soil and underground water. The toxic elements from factories reach the sea through streams and destroy the fishes and sea plants. The innumerable space ships revolving in space spread dangerous debris there which ultimately falls on the earth. There is also the highly pernicious noise pollution as a result of high pitch of T.V. sets, radios, jugging automobiles, horns, buzzers, mikes, etc. It harms sensitive human nerves. Let us take care to make our earth pollution free.

PART-B : Social Studies

1. (*a*) False (*b*) False
(*c*) False (*d*) True
(*e*) False (*f*) False
(*g*) True (*h*) True
(*i*) True (*j*) False
(*k*) False (*l*) True
(*m*) False (*n*) True
(*o*) True

2. (*a*) Dayanand Saraswati
(*b*) 1930
(*c*) General O'Dyer
(*d*) Sand
(*e*) Australia
(*f*) Medicinal material
(*g*) USA
(*h*) 1950
(*i*) Speaker
(*j*) Parliament
(*k*) Raisina
(*l*) Tamil Nadu
(*m*) Karnataka
(*n*) 1975
(*o*) Nelson Mandela

3. (*a*) Public Interest Litigation
(*b*) Electronic Voting Machine
(*c*) Association of South-East Asian Nations
(*d*) Defence Research & Development Organisation
(*e*) Foreign Direct Investment
(*f*) Geological Survey of India
(*g*) National Human Rights Commission
(*h*) Intermediate Range Ballistic Missile
(*i*) International Labour Organisation
(*j*) Tata Engineering and Locomotive Company

4. (*a*) – (*ii*) (*b*) – (*iii*) (*c*) – (*i*)
(*d*) – (*v*) (*e*) – (*iv*) (*f*) – (*vii*)
(*g*) – (*vi*) (*h*) – (*viii*) (*i*) – (*x*)
(*j*) – (*ix*)

5. (*b*) Key Features of Indian Constitution

- It is the longest written Constitution in the world consisting of 26 Chapters, over 450 Articles and 12 Schedules.
- Proclaims India a Sovereign Democratic Republic.
- Fundamental Rights are guaranteed to all citizens of India.
- Directive Principles of State Policy have been incorporated into the Constitution.
- It established the Parliamentary System of Government (the President of the Union is the constitutional head, the Council of Ministers or the Union Cabinet is the real Executive and is responsible to the Lok Sabha).
- It is federal in form (in normal times) but unitary in spirit (during emergencies).
- It is neither too rigid (some provisions can be amended by a simple majority) nor too (some previsions require special majority for amendment).
- It declares India to be a Secular State.
- It guarantees single citizenship to all citizens.
- It guarantees adult franchise (every adult above 18 years has the right to vote; before 1989 the age limit was 21 years) and the system of joint electorates.
- It provides for an independent judiciary; the Supreme Court acts as a guardian of the Constitution.

(*c*) **Right to Education**

Article 21A declares that the State shall provide free and compulsory education to all children of the age of six to fourteen years in such a manner as the State may determine. Thus, this provision makes only elementary education a Fundamental Right and not higher or professional education.

This provision was added by the 86th Constitutional Amendment Act of 2002. This amendment is a major milestone in the country's aim to achieve 'Education for All'. The government described this step as 'the dawn of the second revolution in the chapter of citizens' rights'.

Even before this amendment, the Constitution contained a provision for free and compulsory education for children under Article 45 in Part IV. However, being a directive principle, it was not enforceable by the courts. Now, there is scope for judicial intervention in this regard.

This amendment changed the subject matter of Article 45 in directive principles. It now reads—'The state shall endeavour to provide early childhood care and education for all children until they complete the age of six years.' It also added a new fundamental duty under Article 51A that reads—'It shall be the duty of every citizen of India to provide opportunities for education to his child or ward between the age of six and fourteen years'.

In 1993 itself, the Supreme Court recognised a Fundamental Right to primary education in the right to life under Article 21. It held that every child or citizen of this country has a right to free education until he completes the age of 14 years. Thereafter, his right to education is subject to the limits of economic capacity and development of the state. In this judgement, the Court overruled its earlier judgement (1992) which declared that there was a fundamental right to education up to any level including professional education like medicine and engineering.

(e) The Battle of Plassey

- The Mughal farman was mis interpreted by the British, and they misused the *dastaks* or free passes.
- The British fortified Calcutta against the Nawab's orders.
- Siraj-ud-daula was young and energetic; however, being inex perienced and hasty he lost the battle.
- The battle paved the way for the British mastery of Bengal.
- The victory boosted the prestige of the British and made them a major contender for the Indian empire.
- It enabled the Company and its servants to amass untold wealth.
- This marked the beginning of the 'drain of wealth' from India to Britain.

(f) Fossil Fuel

Fossil fuels are hydrocarbons, primarily coal, fuel oil or natural gas, formed from the remains of dead plants and animals.

The utilization of fossil fuels has enabled large-scale industrial development and largely supplanted water-driven mills, as well as the combustion of wood or peat for heat.

Fossil fuel is a general term for buried combustible geologic deposits of organic materials, formed from decayed plants and animals that have been converted to crude oil, coal, natural gas, or heavy oils by exposure to heat and pressure in the earth's crust over hundreds of millions of years.

The burning of fossil fuels by humans is the largest source of emissions of carbon dioxide, which is one of the greenhouse gases that allows radiative forcing and contributes to global warming.

(h) Renewable Sources of Energy

Renewable energy is energy generated from natural resources—such as sunlight—which are renewable (naturally replenished). Renewable energy technologies include:

- Biofuels
- Biomass
- Geothermal
- Hydro power
- Solar power
- Tidal power
- Wave power
- Wind power

YOUR SPACE

Previous Paper (Solved)

Sainik School Exam, 2013

(Class-IX)

PAPER—I

PART–A : Mathematics

Directions (Qs. 1 to 20) : *Bear 2 marks each. Tick (✓) on the correct choice.*

1. The circumference of a circle of diameter d is :
A. πd B. $2\pi d$
C. $1/2\pi d$ D. πd^2

2. The number of edges in a Cube is :
A. 12 B. 8
C. 6 D. 24

3. The value of $x^2 - 3$ at $x = -1$ is :
A. –2 B. –1
C. –4 D. –5

4. The solution of the equation $4x + 5 = 21$ is :
A. 2 B. 4
C. 6 D. 10

5. Which of the following forms a Pythagoram Triplet?
A. 3, 4, 5 B. 5, 6, 7
C. 8, 9, 10 D. 5, 10, 15

6. The point (5, 0) lies on :
A. X-axis
B. Y-axis
C. Origin
D. Equal distant from X and Y-axis

7. The common factor of $14x^2y$ and $21xy^2$ is :
A. 7 B. xy
C. $7xy$ D. $7x^2y^2$

8. $x^m \div x^n$ is expressed as :
A. x^{m-n} B. $x^{m/n}$
C. x^{mn} D. x^{-mn}

9. The diagonal of squares is $\sqrt{2}$ m. Its area will be :
A. 4 m^2 B. 2 m^2
C. 1 m^2 D. 16 m^2

10. The area of rhombus is :
A. $\frac{1}{2}$ × product of diagonals
B. Product of diagonals
C. 2 × product of diagonals
D. Side × Diagonal

11. The coefficient of z in $(-5xyz)$ is :
A. –5 B. $-5xy$
C. 5 D. –1

12. 20% of an hour is :
A. 20 minutes B. 12 minutes
C. 15 minutes D. 10 minutes

13. The Ratio of 5 metres to 10 km is :
A. 1:20 B. 1:2
C. 2:1 D. 1:2000

14. The probability of getting a Head when a coin tossed is :
A. –1 B. 0.5
C. +1 D. Zero

15. The mid-value of a class called the :
A. Frequency B. Class-mark
C. Tally mark D. Range

16. The sum of first n odd numbers is :
A. n^2 B. $n^2 - 1$
C. $2n^2$ D. $n^2 + 1$

17. The cube of 0.01 is :
A. 0.001 B. 0.003
C. 0.0003 D. 0.000001

18. Three angles of a quadrilateral are 105°, 120° and 75° respectively. What will be the measure of its fourth angle?
A. 50° B. 60°
C. 70° D. 75°

19. Sum of two numbers is 95. If one exceeds the other by 15, find the numbers?

A. 40, 55 B. 35, 60
C. 45, 50 D. 65, 30

20. Which one of the following is not a perfect square?

A. 729 B. 121
C. 361 D. 524

Directions (Qs. 21 to 40) : *Bear 3 marks each.*

21. Find five rational numbers between $\frac{-3}{2}$ and $\frac{5}{3}$

22. Factorise : $16(x + y)^2 - 25(x - y)^2$

23. Find : $\frac{2}{5}\times\left(\frac{-3}{7}\right)-\frac{1}{6}\times\frac{3}{2}+\frac{1}{14}\times\frac{2}{5}$

24. Find the value of : $x^3-\frac{1}{x^3}$ if $x-\frac{1}{x}=5$

25. Find the value of : $a^2 + b^2 + c^2$ if $a + b + c = 13$ and $ab + bc + ca = 27$.

26. Each exterior angle of a regular polygon is 40°. Find the number of its sides.

27. The perimeter of a rhombus is 100 cm and one of its diagonal is 40 cm long. Find the length of the other diagonal.

28. The average of three numbers is 39. If the first number is twice the second and the second is four times the third, find the numbers.

29. The difference between two selling prices of a shirt at profits of 4% and 5% is ₹ 6. Find cost price of the shirt.

30. Evaluate: $\left(2-3x^2+x-x^3+x^4\right)\div\left(x^2+2-3x\right)$

31. If 8 men can reap 80 hectares in 24 days, how many hectares can 36 men reap in 30 days?

32. The perimeter of a parallelogram is 150 cm. One of its sides is greater than other by 25 cm. Find the lengths of all the sides of the parallelogram.

33. The dimensions of a cuboid are in the ratio 2:3:4 and its total surface area is 5200 cm^2. Find the volume of the cuboid.

34. A Physical Training Teacher wants to arrange maximum possible number of 6000 students in a big sports field such that the number of rows is equal to the number of columns. Find the number of rows, if 71 students were left out after the arrangements.

35. Simplify : $(p - q + r)^2 - (p - q - r)^2$

36. The radius and height of the cylinder are in the ratio of 5 : 7 and its volume is 550 cm^3. Find its radius.

37. The difference between two positive integers is 36. The quotient, when one integer is divided by the other is 4. Find the two integers.

38. Three partners A, B and C invest ₹ 1600, ₹ 1800 and ₹ 2300 respectively in business. How should they divide a profit of ₹ 1938?

39. A fort had provision for 150 men for 45 days. After 10 days 25 men left the fort. How long will the food last at the same rate?

40. Water is pouring into a cuboidal reservoir at the rate of 60 litres per minute. If the volume of the reservoir is 108 m^3, find the number of hours it will take to fill the reservoir.

Directions (Qs. 41 to 50) : *Bear 10 marks each.*

41. What must be subtracted from $8x^4 + 14x^3 - 15x^2 + x - 8$ so that resulting polynomial is exactly divisible by $x^2 + 3x - 2$.

42. The ages of Ravi and Hema are in the ration 5 : 7. Four years later, their ages will be in the ratio 3 : 4. Find their ages.

43. Factorise : $x^4 - (y + z)^4$.

44. A circular pond has a 90 cm wide foot path along its edge. A man walks around the outer edge of the foot path with 66 cm long steps. In 400 steps, he makes a full round. What is the radius of the pond?

45. The population of a place increased to 133100 in 2011 at a rate of 10% per annum. Find the population in 2008.

46. A suitcase with measures 80 cm × 48 cm × 24 cm is to be covered with a tarpaulin cloth.

How many metres of tarpaulin of width 96 cm is required to cover 100 such suitcases?

47. A square lawn, each side measuring 24m, has a 2m path around the outside three sides only. Find the area of path.

48. Find the value of 'm' if (*a*) $11^m \div 11^{-3} = 11^{11}$
(*b*) $m^4 = 7^{-2} \div 7^{-14}$

49. A Copper rod of diameter 1 cm and length 8 cm is drawn into make a wire of length 32 m with uniform thickness. Find the thickness of the wire.

50. A 275 m long train is running at a speed of 72 km/hr. In how much time will it cross a platform of length 725 m. Also find the distance travelled in 20 seconds?

PART–B : Science

Note: *Part 'B' bearing 75 marks, contains 37 questions. Q.No. 1 to 15 carry one mark each, Q.No. 16 to 25 carry two marks each, Q.No. 26 to 35 carry three marks each, Q.No. 36 & 37 carry five marks each.*

1. Fluid friction can be reduced by :
A. Lubricants B. Streamlining
C. Ball bearing D. Oiling

2. The main constituent of the air is :
A. CO_2 B. O_2
C. N_2 D. H_2

3. Splitting of light into its component colours is called :
A. Dispersion B. Refraction
C. Reflection D. Deviation

4. The filament of an electric bulb must have :
A. High melting point and low resistance
B. Low melting point and low resistance
C. High melting point and high resistance
D. Low melting point and high resistance

5. It is difficult to walk on ice because :
A. Friction is low
B. Ice melts one to pressure
C. Small area of contact
D. Friction is high

6. Wool and silk are polymers of :
A. Cellulose B. Proteins
C. Monomers D. Elastomers

7. When Zinc is added to HCl :
A. CO_2 gas is released
B. Zn becomes yellow
C. H_2 gas is released
D. Chlorine gas is released

8. The good quality of Coal is :
A. Anthracite B. Bituminous
C. Peat D. Lignite

9. $MgO + H_2O \rightarrow$
A. $MgO_2 + H_2$ B. $Mg(OH)_2$
C. $Mg_2 + 2OH_2$ D. $MgH + O_2$

10. An electrolyte is a :
A. Solid that conducts electricity
B. Liquid that conducts electricity and breaks up chemically
C. Solid that does not conduct electricity
D. Liquid that conducts electricity and does not breaks up chemically

11. The bacteria in curd is called :
A. Curd Bacteria B. Streptococcus
C. Lactobacillus D. Rhizobium

12. In an animal cell which of the following is present :
A. Cell wall B. Plastid
C. Large vacuoles D. Mitochondria

13. In a human body Hormones are secreted by :
A. Endocrine glands B. Liver
C. Bile D. Salivary glands

14. Release of egg from ovary is called :
A. Menarche B. Menstruation
C. Ovulation D. Fertilization

15. World Water day is observed on :
A. 24 March B. 23 March
C. 22 March D. 21 March

16. A man is walking at uniform speed of 5 km/hr. How much distance he will cover in 10 minutes?

17. Define Force. Give one example of force.

18. What is Myopia? How it is corrected?

19. List out any four by-products of Petroleum.

20. What is Stainless Steel? Give two advantages of Stainless Steel.

21. Draw a labelled diagram of 'Dry Cell'. Explanation is NOT required.

22. Why do living organisms need food?

23. By which process do bacteria reproduce? Name the process.

24. List four harmful effects of micro-organisms.

25. How does Tsunami occur?

26. Sound is reflected by a mountain and it is heard after 4 seconds at the point of source. If the velocity of sound is 320 m/s, calculate the distance of the mountain from the source.

27. Why is Venus the hottest planet even though Mercury is closest to the Sun?

28. Give the names and compositions of alloys that are used for the following:
   A. Making bodies of ships
   B. Making bodies of aircraft
   C. Making outdoor statues

29. Write short answers for each of the following:
   A. Ignition temperature.
   B. Producer Gas
   C. Water Gas.

30. Explain with the help of diagram how silver can be electroplated on an iron spoon?

31. Define internal and external fertilization and give one example of each.

32. State any three differences between manures and fertilizers.

33. State the harmful effects of deforestation?

34. List out the various agricultural tasks (practices) a farmer has to perform on his field to cultivate crop plants.

35. What is Green house effect? Name two gases that cause Green house effect.

36. A. Draw and label different zones of a flame.
   B. Give the principle involved in Soda Acid fire extinguisher with chemical equation.

37. A. Write the differences in properties between synthetic and natural fibres with reference to (*i*) tensile strength (*ii*) long-lasting quality (*iii*) drip-dry quality.
   B. Write the materials required for the preparation of the following fibres.
   (*i*) Nylon   (*ii*) Terylene

EXPLANATORY ANSWERS

PART-A : Mathematics

1. Circumference of a circle of diametered $= \pi \times d$

2. The number of edges in a cube is 12.

3. The value of $x^2 - 3$ at $x = -1$

   $x^2 - 3 = (-1)^2 - 3 = 1 - 3 = -2$

4. $4x + 5 = 21$

   $\Rightarrow 4x = 16 \Rightarrow x = 4$

5. 3, 4, 5

   $(5)^2 = 25$

   $(3)^2 + (4)^2 = 9 + 16 = 25$

   $\therefore$ 3, 4, 5 forms a pythagoram triplet.

6. The point (5, 0) lies on X-axis

7. The common factor of $14x^2y$ and $21xy^2$ is $7xy$.

8. $x^m \div x^n = x^{m-n}$

9. $a^2 + a^2 = (\sqrt{2})^2 \Rightarrow 2a^2 = 2$

   $a^2 = 1$

   $a = 1$

   $\sqrt{2}$ a a

   $\therefore$ Area of square $= a^2 = 1$ m^2.

10. The area of rhombus

   $= \frac{1}{2} \times$ Product of diagonals.

11. The co-efficient of z in $(-5xyz)$ is $-5xy$.

12. 20% of an hour $= \frac{20}{100} \times 60$ minutes

$= 12$ minutes.

13. The ratio of 5 m to 10 km

$= \frac{5}{10 \times 1000} = 1 : 2000$

14. The probability of getting a head when a coin tossed $= \frac{1}{2} = 0.5$

15. The mid-value of a class is called the class-mark.

16. The sum of first n odd numbers is n^2.

17. The cube of 0.01 $= \frac{1}{100} \times \frac{1}{100} \times \frac{1}{100}$

$= \frac{1}{1000000} = 0.000001$

18. Let fourth angle be $x°$

$105 + 120 + 75 + x = 360°$

$\Rightarrow x + 300 = 360 \Rightarrow x = 60°$

19. Let one number $= x$ and other number $= 95 - x$

$x + 15 = 95 - x$

$\Rightarrow 2x = 95 - 15 = 80$

$\Rightarrow x = 40$

$95 - 40 = 55$

$\therefore$ numbers are 40, 55.

20.

2	524
2	262
	131

$\therefore$ 524 is not a perfect square.

21. First rational number between $\frac{-3}{2}$ and $\frac{5}{3}$

$= \frac{1}{2}\left(\frac{-3}{2} + \frac{5}{3}\right) = \frac{1}{2}\left(\frac{-9+10}{6}\right) = \frac{1}{12}$

2nd rational no between $\frac{-3}{2}$ and $\frac{1}{12}$

$= \frac{1}{2}\left(\frac{-18+1}{12}\right) = \frac{-17}{24}$

3rd rational number between $\frac{1}{12}$ and $\frac{5}{3}$

$= \frac{1}{2}\left(\frac{1+20}{12}\right) = \frac{21}{24} = \frac{7}{8}$

4th rational number between $\frac{7}{8}$ and $\frac{5}{3}$

$= \frac{1}{2}\left(\frac{40+21}{24}\right) = \frac{61}{48}$

5th rational number between $\frac{61}{48}$ and $\frac{5}{3}$

$= \frac{1}{2}\left(\frac{61+80}{48}\right) = \frac{141}{96}$.

22. $16(x + y)^2 - 25(x - y)^2$

$= \{4(x+y)\}^2 - \{5(x-y)\}^2$

$= [4(x+y)+5(x-y)][4(x+y)-5(x-y)]$

$= (4x + 4y + 5x - 5y)(4x + 4y - 5x + 5y)$

$= (9x - y)(-x + 9y)$

23. $\frac{2}{5} \times \left(\frac{-3}{7}\right) - \frac{1}{6} \times \frac{3}{2} + \frac{1}{14} \times \frac{2}{5} = \frac{-6}{35} - \frac{1}{4} + \frac{1}{35}$

$= \frac{-5}{35} - \frac{1}{4} = \frac{-1}{7} - \frac{1}{4} = \frac{-4-7}{28} = \frac{-11}{28}$.

24. $\because \quad x - \frac{1}{x} = 5$

$\therefore \quad x^3 - \frac{1}{x^3} = \left(x - \frac{1}{x}\right)^3 + 3 \cdot x \cdot \frac{1}{x}\left(x - \frac{1}{x}\right)$

$= (5)^3 + 3(5) = 125 + 15 = 140.$

25. $a + b + c = 13$ and $ab + bc + ca = 27$

$(a + b + c)^2 = a^2 + b^2 + c^2 + 2(ab + bc + ca)$

$(13)^2 - 2(27) = a^2 + b^2 + c^2$

$169 - 54 = a^2 + b^2 + c^2$

$115 = a^2 + b^2 + c^2$

26. Each exterior angle of polygon $= \frac{360°}{n}$

$40° = \frac{360°}{n}$

$n = \frac{360}{40} = 9$

27. Perimeter of Rhombus = 100 cm

Side of Rhombus $= \frac{100}{4} = 25$ cm

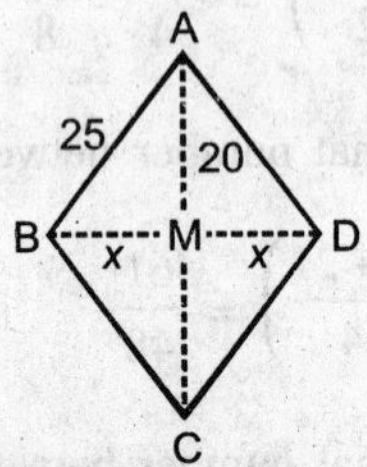

In ΔABM,

$$x^2 = (25)^2 - (20)^2$$
$$= 625 - 400 = 225$$
$$x = 15 \text{ cm}$$

$\therefore$ Length of other diagonal is 30 cm.

28. Let third number be x

second number $= 4x$

first number $= 8x$

Total number $= 39 \times 3 = 117$

$x + 4x + 8x = 117$

$\Rightarrow \quad 13x = 117 \Rightarrow x = 9$

Here the numbers are 72, 36, 9.

29. Let CP $= x$

$$\text{Profit \%} = \frac{\text{Profit}}{\text{CP}} \times 100$$

$$\frac{4x}{100} = \text{Profit}$$

$$\text{SP} = \frac{x}{25} + x = \frac{26x}{25}$$

$$\frac{5x}{100} = \text{Profit}$$

$$\frac{x}{20} + x = \frac{21x}{20}$$

$$\frac{21x}{20} - \frac{26x}{25} = 6$$

$$\frac{105x - 104x}{100} = 6$$

$$x = 600$$

$\therefore$ Cost price = ₹ 600

30. $x^2 - 3x + 2 \overline{) x^4 - x^3 - 3x^2 + x + 2} (x^2 + 2x + 1$

$x^4 - 3x^3 + 2x^2$

$- \quad + \quad -$

$2x^3 - 5x^2 + x + 2$

$2x^3 - 6x^2 + 4x$

$- \quad + \quad -$

$x^2 - 3x + 2$

$x^2 - 3x + 2$

$- \quad + \quad -$

$= x^2 + 2x + 1.$

31. 8 men working 24 days can reap 80 hectare

1 man working 1 day can reap $\frac{80}{8 \times 24}$ hectare

36 men working 30 days can reap $\frac{80 \times 30 \times 36}{8 \times 24} = 450$ hectare.

32.

D x C
x + 25 x + 25
A B

$x + x + (x + 25) + (x + 25) = 150$

$4x + 50 = 150$

$4x = 100$

$x = 25$

AB = CD = 25 cm

BC = AD = 25 + 25 = 50 cm.

33. Let length $= 2x$ cm, breadth $= 3x$ cm, height $= 4x$ cm

Total surface area of cuboil $= 2(lb + bh + hl)$

$2(lb + bh + hl) = 5200$

$2(2x \times 3x + 3x \times 4x + 4x \times 2x) = 5200$

$6x^2 + 12x^2 + 8x^2 = 2600$

$26x^2 = 2600 \Rightarrow x^2 = 100 \Rightarrow x = 10$

$l = 10 \times 2 = 20$ cm, $b = 3 \times 10 = 30$ cm

$h = 10 \times 4 = 40$ cm

Volume $= 20 \times 30 \times 40 = 24000$ cm^3.

34. $6000 - 71 = 5929$

$\sqrt{5929} = 77$

$\therefore$ number of rows = 77

35. $(p-q+r)^2-(p-q-r)^2$
$= (p^2+q^2+r^2-2pq-2qr+2pr)-(p^2+q^2+r^2-2pq+2qr-2pr)$
$= p^2+q^2+r^2-2pq-2qr+2pr-p^2-q^2-r^2+2pq-2qr+2pr$
$= 4pr-4qr.$

36. Let radius and height of cylinder are $5x$ and $7x$ respectively.
Volume of cylinder $= \pi r^2 h$

$$550 = \frac{22}{7}\times(5x)^2\times 7x$$

$$550\times 7 = 22\times 25x^2\times 7x$$

$$\Rightarrow \quad x^3 = \frac{550\times 7}{22\times 25\times 7} = 1$$

$$\Rightarrow \quad x = 1$$

$\therefore$ radius of cylinder $= 5\times 1 = 5$ cm.

37. Let first integer $= x$ and
2nd integer $= x-36$
According to the question,

$$\frac{x}{x-36} = 4 \quad\Rightarrow\quad 4x-144 = x$$

$$\Rightarrow \quad 3x = 144 \quad\Rightarrow\quad x = 48$$

$$x-36 = 48-36 = 12$$

$\therefore$ Integers are 48 and 12

38. A, B, C invested ₹ 1600, ₹ 1800, ₹ 2300 their ratios are 16 : 18 : 23

$$\text{A's share} = \frac{16}{16+18+23}\times 1938$$

$$= \frac{16}{57}\times 1938 = 16\times 34 = ₹\ 544$$

$$\text{B's share} = \frac{18}{57}\times 1938 = 18\times 34 = ₹\ 612$$

$$\text{C's share} = \frac{23}{57}\times 1938 = 23\times 34 = ₹\ 782$$

39. $150-25 = 125$ men
45 days $-$ 10 days $=$ 35 days.
For 150 men food last in 35 days

For 125 men food last in $\frac{150\times 35}{125} = 6\times 7$
$= 42$ days.

40. 1 litre $= 1000$ ml $= 1000$ cm^3

$$= \frac{1000}{100\times 100\times 100}\text{ m}^3 = \frac{1}{1000}\text{ m}^3$$

$$60 \text{ litre} = \frac{60}{1000}\text{ m}^3 = \frac{6}{100}\text{ m}^3$$

$\frac{6}{100}$ m^3 can fill in 1 minute.

108 m^3 can fill in $\frac{1\times 100\times 108}{6\times 60}$ hrs $= 30$ hrs.

41.

$$\begin{array}{r|l} & \quad 8x^2-10x+31 \\ x^2+3x-2 & 8x^4+14x^3-15x^2+x-8 \\ & 8x^4+24x^3-16x^2 \\ & \quad - \quad - \quad + \\ \hline & -10x^3+x^2+x-8 \\ & -10x^3-30x^2+20x \\ & + \quad + \quad - \\ \hline & 31x^2-19x-8 \\ & 31x^2+93x-62 \\ & - \quad - \quad + \\ \hline \end{array}$$

If we subtract $-112x+54$ from $8x^4+14x^3-15x^2+x-8$ then it is exctly divisible by x^2+3x-2.

42. Let Ravi's age $= 5x$ years and Hema's age $= 7x$ years

$$\frac{5x+4}{7x+4} = \frac{3}{4}$$

$$\Rightarrow 21x+12 = 20x+16$$

$$\Rightarrow x = 4$$

Ravi's age $= 4\times 5 = 20$ years
Hema's age $= 4\times 7 = 28$ years

43. $x^4-(y+z)^4 = \left(x^2\right)^2-\left[(y+z)^2\right]^2$

$$\left[x^2+(y+z)^2\right]\left[x^2-(y+z)^2\right]$$

$$= \left[x^2+(y+z)^2\right]\left[(x+y+z)(x-y-z)\right]$$

44. C $= 66\times 400$ cm $\quad$ [$\because$ 1 Step $= 66$ cm $\therefore$ 400 steps $= 66\times 400$ cm]

$$66\times 400 = 2\times\frac{22}{7}\times r$$

$$r = \frac{66\times 400\times 7}{22\times 2} = 4200 \text{ cm} = 42 \text{ m}$$

45. Let 100 population in 2008

$$A = 100\left(1+\frac{10}{100}\right)^3$$

$$= 100\times\frac{11}{10}\times\frac{11}{10}\times\frac{11}{10} = \frac{1331}{10}$$

In 2011 population is $\frac{1331}{10}$ then in 2008 population was 100

when 133100 then $\frac{100\times10\times133100}{1331}$

= 100000

46. Surface area of suitcase
= 2(80 × 48 + 24 × 48 + 80 × 24)
= 2(6912) = 13824 cm^2.
Surface area of 100 suitcase
= 13824 × 100 = 1382400 cm^2
Required length of tarpauline

$$= \frac{1382400}{96} = 14400 \text{ cm} = 144 \text{ m}.$$

47.

52m²
52m²
48m²

Area of square without path = 24 × 24 = 576 m^2
Area of square with path = 28 × 28 = 784 m^2
But road only three side
∴ Area of one side = 28 × 2 = 56 m^2
∴ Area of with path = 784 – 56 = 728 m^2
∴ Area of path = 728 – 576 = 152 m^2.

48. (*a*) $11^m \div 11^{-3} = 11^{11}$

$11^{m+3} = 11^{11} \Rightarrow m + 3 = 11 \Rightarrow m = 8$

(*b*) $m^4 = 7^{12} \Rightarrow m^4 = \left(7^3\right)^4$

$\Rightarrow m = 7^3 = 343$

49. 32*m* = 32 × 100 cm

$\pi r^2 \times 32 \times 100 = \pi \times 1 \times 8$

$$r^2 = \frac{1}{400}$$

$$r = \frac{1}{20} \text{ cm} = 0.05 \text{ cm}$$

50. 275 m + 725 m = 1000 m = 1 km
72 km = 60 min

$$1 \text{ km} = \frac{60}{72} \text{ min} = \frac{5}{6}\times60 = 50 \text{ seconds}$$

∵ 50 seconds = 1000 m

$$20 \text{ seconds} = \frac{1000}{50}\times20 = 400 \text{ m}$$

∴ Distance travelled in 20 seconds = 400 m.

PART-B : Science

1	2	3	4	5	6	7	8	9	10
B	C	A	C	A	A	C	A	B	B
11	**12**	**13**	**14**	**15**					
C	D	A	C	C					

16. Speed in m/min.

$$= \frac{5\times1000}{60} = 83.33 \text{ m/min.}$$

Hence, Distance travelled in 10 minutes
= 83.33 × 10 = 833.33 metres.
or, = 0.833 km

17. Force is any influence that tends to change the state of rest or the uniform motion in a straightline of a body. The action of an unbalanced or resultant force results in the acceleration of the body. Force is a vector quantity, its SI unit is Newton (N).

Example: A block kept on table, here table exert force on block to hold it.

18. The person suffering from myopia can not be able to see the far flung object but easily see the near most object.

Remedial measure: The myopia affected person uses concave lens of suitable focal length so that image starts to form at retina.

19. By petroleum substances like petrol, kerosene, oil, various hydrocarbons, ether, natural gases etc. are extracted. These components are extracted by the method of fractional distillation and appropriate refining.

20. Stainless steel is a varieties of iron. In ordinary iron steel, only iron and carbon are composed, but if in small amount metals like chromium, manganese, nickel etc. are present then it is called stainless steel. There are two advantages of stainless steel are as follows :

(*i*) It is not affected from air, water, moisture etc.

(*ii*) It remains free from rusting.

21.

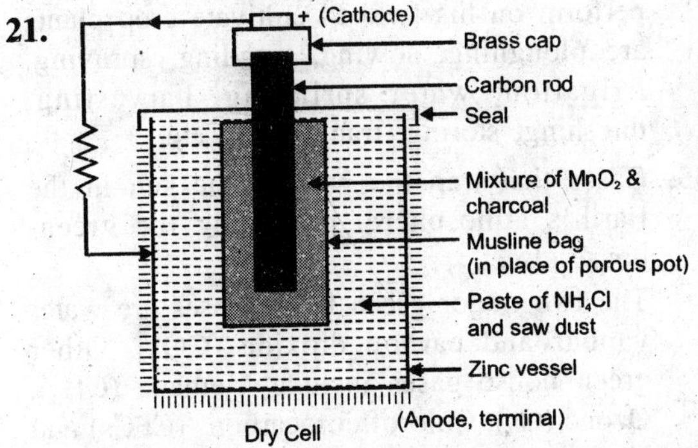

Dry Cell

22. The purpose of taking food by living organisms is to supply nutrients to the cells. The food we eat is made up of complex molecules. These molecules are first broken down by digestive enzymes into simpler molecules. The simpler molecules are then absorbed in the intestine and they reach the blood stream. Blood carries them to the cells, which take them in according to their needs.

23. In bacteria reproduction, there are two process take place :

(*i*) **Asexual reproduction :** This is a simple process of cell division, in which one bacterium splits into new ones. Asexual reproduction in bacteria are done by conidia and endospore.

(*ii*) **Sexual reproduction :** Some bacteria also exhibits the reproduction by sexual method and members of such bacterial species contain a virus like agent called fertility or 'F' factor.

24. They are causes for diseases in human being, so they called pathogens.

Harmful effects of micro-organism

1. Human diseases
2. Animal and plant diseases
3. Food poisoning
4. Denitrification

25. A tsunami is a series of waves travelling across the ocean due to a sudden displacement of a large body of water. This displacement can be caused by events such as undersea earthquakes, undersea landslides, land sliding into the ocean, volcanic eruptions or even asteroid impact.

26. Let the distance of mountain from the stationary source is d m

To hear the reflection sound, it travel distance $2d$

$$2d = \text{Velocity of sound} \times \text{Time}$$
$$= 320 \times 4$$
$$d = \frac{320 \times 4}{2} = 640 \text{ m.}$$

27. Venus planet is composed from 97% CO_2 and in the rest 3% nitrogen, water vapour, some other elements are found. There is condensed cloud of sulphuric acid from its surface upto 80 km height. These clouds reflect most of the sun rays incident on this and cause in increase in atmospheric pressure more than 90 times than on earth. This makes the planet extremely hot and like a blast furnace.

28. (A) Bodies of ships

Alloy : Magnelium

Composition : 95% Al, 5% Mg.

(B) Bodies of aircraft

Alloy : Duralumin

Composition : 95% Al, 4% Cu, 0.5% Mg, 0.5% Mn.

(C) Statues

Alloy : Brass

Composition : 90% Cu, 10% Sn.

29. (A) The minimum temperature at which any substance starts to burn, is called ignition temperature.

(B) When air is passed over red not coke producer gas is formed ($CO + N_2$) (1 : 2).

Mainly CO acts as fuel. It gives 1100 – 1700 Kcal/kg. It is used in the manufacture of glass & steel. It is also used on a substitute for petrol.

(C) When steam is passed over red not coke, water gas is formed ($CO + H_2$) (1 : 1) used an gaseous fuel. It provides 2500 – 3000 Kcal/kg. It is used in furnaces for welding in the manufacture of H_2 (Bosch process). NH_3 & alcohol as catalyst.

30. 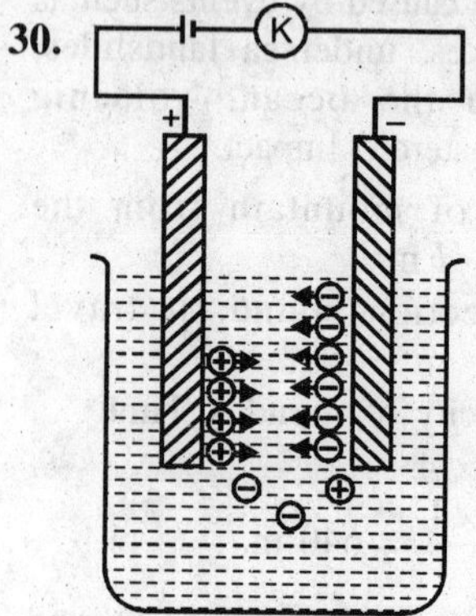

Electrolysis process

Electroplating is a process of depositing one metal (generally a superior metal) over another metal (generally a basal metal) through the process of electrolysis. Electroplating may be carried out for preservation or decoration.

31. Internal fertilization: Sexual reproduction begins with fertilization, which is the process of union of two different gametes. The process of fusion of two gametes takes place inside the human body is called internal fertilization. Fertilization in human being is an example of internal fertilization.

External fertilization: Fertilization usually takes place outside the body is called external fertilization. In fishes and amphibia fertilization takes place externally.

32. Manure consists of organic substances obtained from the decomposition of animal wastes, dead plants and animals by the action of microbes. When microbes grow with garbage and organic wastes, they eat and split these wastes. It results in the production of organic manure that is superior to chemical fertilizers in many ways.

Fertilizers are inorganic chemicals synthesised in industries. They contain essential plant nutrients like nitrogen, potassium or phosphorus. They are prepared in a concentrated form and easy to transport.

33. With increasing population of the world there has been an increasing pressure on forest for obtaining agricultural land as well as various forest products such as timber and firewood. As a result, the area under all types of forests is declining rapidly. In addition, the density of trees in the existing forest in most of the tropical regions is decreasing.

34. The various agricultural taskes a farmer has to perform on his field to cultivate crop plants are ploughing, sowing, weeding, spraying, irrigation, water sprinking, harvesting, threshing, storing, transporting etc.

35. Gases that trap the heat of the sun in the Earth's atmosphere, producing the green-house effect.

The two major green house gases are water vapour and carbon dioxide (CO_2). Other green house gases include Methane (CH_4), Ozone (O_3), Chlorofluorocarbons (CFCs) and Nitrous oxide (N_2O).

36. (A)

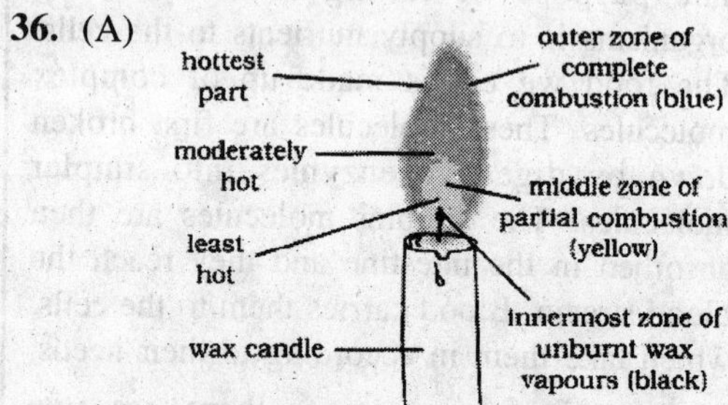

(B) Fire requires oxygen and fuel in order to burn. Fire extinguishers remove or displace the surrounding oxygen, smothering the flames. A soda acid fire extinguisher is an emergency fire protection device that can extinguish or control small fires. Often crafted from highly polished brass or copper, the soda acid fire extinguisher is activated by turning the unit upside down, thereby dumping the baking soda into acid water (similar to the effect achieved by placing baking soda in vinegar). The combined baking soda and acid produce carbon dioxide gas to project the enclosed liquid toward the flames. A soda acid fire extinguisher will discharge water under the pressure created by the production of carbon dioxide gas. The creation of the carbon dioxide is due to the chemical reaction of acid an soda mixing.

$$2NaHCO_3(aq.) + H_2SO_4(l) \rightarrow Na_2SO_4(eq.) + 2H_2O(l) + 2CO_2(g)$$

37. (A)

Natural Fibers	***Synthetic Fibers***
1. Fibers are found in staple or filament form.	1. It is found in filament form but sometimes it could be converted into staple or cut length.
2. No spinning process is needed for filament production.	2. Melt, Wet or Dry spinning process is needed for filament production.
3. No need of chemical solution for yarn production.	3. Chemical solution is essential for yarn production.
4. Most of the fibers are hydrophilic in nature.	4. Most of the times, they are hydrophobic.
5. It needs to scouring and bleaching process before wet processing.	5. Scouring and bleaching is done in very few cases.
6. It is easy to dye the fiber.	6. Coloration is not so easy as natural fiber.
7. Most of the cases it becomes ash after burning.	7. It becomes melt in burning.
8. Natural fiber is called environment friendly.	8. Synthetic fibers are not environment friendly. Some fibers are harmful for the environment like: Polypropylene.
9. Comparatively less durable than synthetic fiber.	9. Synthetic fibers are more durable than natural fiber.

(B) (*i*) **Nylon:** Nylon is made of repeating units linked by amid bonds frequently referred to as polyamide. Chemical elements include carbon, hydrogen, nitrogen, and oxygen.

(*ii*) **Terylene:** These fibers do not absorb any water hence after washing cloths they dry up very fast. It is used to prepare shirts, sarees and in the preparation of cloth for other garments, water pipes and in the preparation of soils for boats.

PAPER—II

PART–A : English Language

1. Read the following passage and answer the questions below it.

Abraham Lincoln is one of those great men whose life story is also the history of the nation to which they belong. The famous phrase 'from log cabin to White House' sums up his career. However, Lincoln's greatness does not lie in fulfillment of his personal ambition but in his work for his country and humanity. It is to him, as to no other individual, that the USA owes its present position as one of the greatest world powers. It was Lincoln who laid the foundation of freedom and unity. Yet having accomplished all this, he had the humility to say, "I have done nothing to make any human being remembered that I have lived."

(*a*) Who was Abraham Lincoln?

(*b*) What was his achievement?

(*c*) What makes him really great?

(*d*) In your view, what was his main contribution to USA?

(*e*) What quality/trait of Lincoln is revealed in his comment about himself?

2. Write a paragraph about 100 words on *one* of the following topics :

(*a*) Relevance of Newspapers

(*b*) The National leader I like the most

3. Write a letter advising your cousin who has the habit of watching TV for long hours.

4. Change into passive voice.
   (*a*) He is holding an exhibition of his paintings.
   (*b*) You ought to respect your elders.
   (*c*) This box contains nine balls.
   (*d*) Who won the final match yesterday?
   (*e*) I do not know their cousin.

5. Use the correct form of the verbs in brackets:
   (*a*) If her brother (arrive) in time, we shall go for shopping.
   (*b*) When they reached the railway station, the train (leave) already.
   (*c*) I (earn) my pocket money since I left school.
   (*d*) This is the best book I ever (read).
   (*e*) By next year he (finish) writing his autobiography.

6. Fill in the blanks with a suitable word out of three below each sentence
   (*a*) When the robbers had put all the money in the bag, they ______.
      (*i*) fleed
      (*ii*) fled
      (*iii*) flee
   (*b*) As soon as we arrived in the Hostel, we ______ our pullovers.
      (*i*) hang
      (*ii*) hanged
      (*iii*) hung
   (*c*) An educationist __________ down the foundation of this institute.
      (*i*) lay
      (*ii*) laid
      (*iii*) lie
   (*d*) Colour TV ______ us ₹ 15,000 last year.
      (*i*) cost
      (*ii*) costed
      (*iii*) has costed
   (*e*) The bridge ______ up by the enemy.
      (*i*) blowed
      (*ii*) was blown
      (*iii*) was blowed

7. Fill in the blanks with suitable prepositions:
   (*a*) They agreed ________ all our proposals.
   (*b*) She failed to act ________ her father's advice.
   (*c*) Beware ________ dogs lest you should be bitten.
   (*d*) Trust ________ God and do the right.
   (*e*) We should not laugh ________ the poor.

8. Change the following DIRECT sentences into INDIRECT.
   (*a*) The teacher said to the boys, "Water boils at 100°C."
   (*b*) Ram said to me "Have you finished your work?"
   (*c*) She said to him, "Did you attend the party yesterday?"
   (*d*) The old man said to the boy, "Please help me."
   (*e*) My mother will say, "You're always late."

9. Give one word for each of the following groups of words:
   (*a*) A substance used as a medicine ________
   (*b*) A financial gain ________
   (*c*) A person who can treat teeth and gums ________
   (*d*) The call of a bird __________
   (*e*) A bridge that carries a road over other roads ___________

10. What do the following idiomatic expressions mean? Tick the correct choice.
   (*a*) To win laurels
      (*i*) to win a lottery
      (*ii*) to win an honour
      (*iii*) to win a victory
      (*iv*) to fulfil an ambition
   (*b*) To cut a sorry figure
      (*i*) to look untidy
      (*ii*) to make a bad drawing
      (*iii*) to behave rudely
      (*iv*) to turn out a bad performance
   (*c*) To smell a rat
      (*i*) to experience bad smell
      (*ii*) to misunderstand
      (*iii*) to see a hidden meaning
      (*iv*) to suspect a trick
   (*d*) To keep one's head
      (*i*) to be proud

(ii) to be self-respecting
(iii) to concentrate
(iv) to remain cool

(e) To read between the lines
(i) to misunderstand
(ii) to read too much meaning into
(iii) to understand the writer's hidden meaning
(iv) not to be able to read clearly

PART–B : Social Studies

1. State TRUE/FALSE

(i) Queen Victoria was the Empress of England at the time of establishment of the East India Company.

(ii) Siraj ud Daula became the Nawab of Bengal after the death of Alivardi Khan.

(iii) Doctrine of Lapse was introduced by Lord Wellesley.

(iv) Nij and Ryoti were the two main types of Indigo Cultivation.

(v) Tantia Tope was a close associate of Rani Laxmi Bai during the revolt of 1857.

(vi) Biogas is essentially a mixture of Methane and Carbon Dioxide.

(vii) The number of live birth per one hundred people is called birth rate.

(viii) In the Federal System of Govt. there is only one level of Govt.

(ix) Introduction of The Greased cartridges was the immediate cause of the revolt of 1857.

(x) Tarapur Nuclear Power Station is in Maharashtra.

(xi) Jute is also called the Golden Fibre.

(xii) President can nominate Twenty members to the Lok Sabha.

(xiii) Battle of Buxar was fought in the year 1764.

(xiv) Agriculture and fishing are the good examples of Primary Activity.

(xv) Cultivation of Grapes is called Horticulture.

2. Fill in the blanks.

(i) ______ and ______ were the main architects of New Delhi.

(ii) Hyber Ali and Tipu Sultan were the rulers of ______.

(iii) ______ was the first Governor General of India.

(iv) ______ was the main leader of the rebels in Bihar during the revolt of 1857.

(v) Article ______ of the Indian constitution abolishes untouchability.

(vi) Thorium is found in large quantities in the ______ sands of Kerala.

(vii) The revolt of 1857 started at ______ on 10 May 1857.

(viii) ______ is the largest producer of Copper in the world.

(ix) Natural Resources which are found everywhere are called ______ resources.

(x) The ore of Aluminium is called ______.

3. Expand the following abbreviations.

(i) LCA	(ii) ASI
(iii) LPG	(iv) JPC
(v) NSG	(vi) IAEA
(vii) IPCC	(viii) CITES
(ix) TISCO	(x) ISRO

4. Match the following columns :

(i) Gomastha	(a) 1849
(ii) Permanent settlement of revenue	(b) California
(iii) Diwani	(c) Right to equality
(iv) Lord Wellesley	(d) Leader of Rebels
(v) Annexation of Punjab	(e) Right to vote
(vi) Universal Adult Franchise	(f) Right to collect revenue
(vii) Article 14	(g) Subsidiary Alliance

(*viii*) Birsa Munda (*h*) Lord Cornwallis
(*ix*) Silicon Valley (*i*) Assam
(*x*) Kaziranga National Park (*j*) Agents of Planters

5. Write brief notes on any *six* of the following. Each question carries five marks.

(*i*) Fundamental Rights
(*ii*) Tidal Energy
(*iii*) Causes of the revolt of 1857
(*iv*) Lokpal Bill
(*v*) Renewable resources of Energy
(*vi*) Importance of the battle of Plassey
(*vii*) Natural disasters

EXPLANATORY ANSWERS

PART-A : English Language

1. (*a*) Abraham Lincoln was the president of USA.

(*b*) He laid the formation of freedom and unity in USA.

(*c*) Lincoln's work for his country and humanity makes his really great.

(*d*) The credit of USA being one of the greatest world powers mainly goes to him for his contribution to it.

(*e*) The quality of humility and humbleness is revealed in his comment about himself.

2. (*a*) **Relevance of Newspapers**

Newspapers are rightly called the fourth estate. They are a powerful part of the media which forms and moulds the public opinion. It is imperative that the newspapers should not be biased or prejudiced. They must express their opinions in an objective and impartial manner. Newspapers give us news, views and reviews. They also express the views of the readers in the Readers' column. Often they have separate columns for women, children, sports, business, stock exchange, health, science, literature, sports, etc. They cater to the needs of all kinds of readers. They highlight public opinion and criticise government policies. They can be very helpful in fighting anti-social institutions like dowry system, black marketing, terrorism, etc. Newspapers also have columns for classified advertisements which are sub-divided into services, jobs, courses, property, matrimonials, education, health, training, kennel, poultry, automobiles, lost and found, etc. Reading a newspaper in the morning is as important as having a morning cup of tea. We can't think of life without them.

3. 50, Gagan Vihar
Delhi-110051
12th Feb., 2013

My dearest Shruti,

I hope you are in perfect health. I have received a letter from your mom in which she has expressed her concern about your habit of watching T.V. for long hours. After reading her letter. I am also worried about you as you are my dearest cousin.

Like all scientific inventions, the television is a good servant but a bad master. It is extremely useful in several ways if we make the proper use of it, but can prove very harmful if it is not properly used. Accordingly, it is also known as the small or silver screen and the idiot box.

There are several instructive as well as entertaining T.V. serials besides regular films. We have university and teaching programmes which add to our knowledge. But an over-indulgence to T.V. can be equally harmful. Excessive indulgence to T.V. can impair both our eyes and mind. Its moderate viewing can be useful to our mind and act as relief from boredom.

Some programmes in the T.V. are good. But some are just boring and unimaginative. In certain parts of the world T.V. is being condemned. In Europe people are tired of it as it causes T.V. addiction among adolescents.

I believe, after going through this letter you will restrain your habit of excessively watching T.V. and utilise your time in your studies and other useful works.

Yours loving cousin,
Kriti

4. (*a*) An exhibition of his paintings is being held.
(*b*) Your elders ought to be respected.
(*c*) Nine balls are contained in the box.
(*d*) By whom was the final match won yesterday?
(*e*) Their cousin is not known to me.

5. (*a*) If her brother arrives in time, we shall go for shopping.
(*b*) When they reached the railway station, the train had already left.
(*c*) I have been earning my pocket money since I left school.
(*d*) This is the best book I have ever read.
(*e*) By next year he would have finished writing his autobiography.

6. (*a*) fled (*b*) hung
(*c*) laid (*d*) costed
(*e*) was blown

7. (*a*) to (*b*) on
(*c*) of (*d*) in
(*e*) at

8. (*a*) The teacher told the boys that water boils at 100°C.
(*b*) Ram asked me if I had finished my work.
(*c*) She asked him if he had attended the party the previous day.
(*d*) The old man requested the boy to help him.
(*e*) My mother will say that I am always late.

9. (*a*) Drug (*b*) Profit
(*c*) Dentist (*d*) Chirping
(*e*) Over bridge

10. (*a*) (*ii*) to win an honour
(*b*) (*iv*) to turn out a bad performance
(*c*) (*iv*) to suspect a trick
(*d*) (*iv*) to remain cool
(*e*) (*iii*) to understand the writer's hidden meaning

PART-B : Social Studies

1. True—(*ii*), (*iv*), (*v*), (*vi*), (*ix*), (*x*), (*xi*), (*xiii*), (*xiv*)
False—(*i*), (*iii*), (*vii*), (*viii*), (*xii*), (*xv*)

2. (*i*) Edwin Lutyens, Herbert Baker
(*ii*) Mysore
(*iii*) Lord William Bentick
(*iv*) Kunwar Singh
(*v*) 17
(*vi*) Monozite
(*vii*) Meerut
(*viii*) Chile
(*ix*) Ubiquitous
(*x*) Bauxite

3. (*i*) Light Combat Aircraft
(*ii*) Archaeological Survey of India
(*iii*) Liquefied Petroleum Gas
(*iv*) Joint Parliamentary Committee
(*v*) National Security Guard
(*vi*) International Atomic Energy Agency
(*vii*) Intergovernmental Panel on Climate Change
(*viii*) Convention on International Trade in Endangered Species
(*ix*) Tata Iron and Steel Company
(*x*) Indian Space Research Organisation

4. (*i*) – (*j*) (*ii*) – (*h*)
(*iii*) – (*f*) (*iv*) – (*g*)
(*v*) – (*a*) (*vi*) – (*e*)
(*vii*) – (*c*) (*viii*) – (*d*)
(*ix*) – (*b*) (*x*) – (*i*)

5. (*a*) **Fundamental Rights:** The Constitution of India defines fundamental rights in Part-III that guarantees every citizen with some rights irrespective of race, place of birth, religion, caste, creed or gender. These are the essential rights which a person born along with.

The Fundamental Rights are essential for the development of the personality of an individual and to preserve dignity of a human. Any person can move to court if anyone challenges his fundamental right.

These Fundamental Rights not only protects individuals from any arbitrary state actions but also prevents violation of human rights. Some Fundamental Rights apply for both the Indian citizen as well as persons of other nationality whereas others are available only to Indian citizens.

***(b)* Tidal Energy:** Tides are the waves caused due to the gravitational pull of the moon and also sun (though its pull is very low). The rise is called high tide and fall is called low tide. This building up and receding of waves happens twice a day and causes enormous movement of water. It is so powerful that it has caused many mishaps and resulted in sinking of ships. Thus tidal energy forms a large source of energy and can be harnessed in some of the coastal areas of the world. Tidal dams are built near shores for this purpose. During high tide, the water flows into the dam and during low tide, water flows out which result in turning the turbine.

***(c)* Causes of the revolt of 1857:** The immediate cause of the revolt was the use of grease in the rifle cartridges which was derived from beef and pork which offended the religious sentiments of Hindu and Muslim sepoys.

***(d)* Lokpal Bill:** The word Lokpal has been derived from the Sanskrit words "Lok" meaning People and "pal" meaning caretaker. Therefore, the word Lokpal means "caretaker of people".

Mr. Shanti Bhushan proposed the first Lokpal Bill in 1968 and got it passed in 4th Loksabha but failed in Rajya Sabha in the year 1969. Thereafter, Lokpal Bill was introduced in 1971, 1977, 1985, 1989, 1996, 1998, 2001 and 2005 and in 2008 but was never passed and is still pending in Parliament.

Under the Lokpal Bill there is a provision for filing complaints with the Ombudsman against the Prime minister, other ministers and Member of Parliament. This was for removing the sense of injustice from the minds of citizens and to install public confidence in the efficiency of the administrative machinery by completing the investigations regarding corruption within a year.

***(e)* Renewable resources of Energy:** Renewable energy is energy that comes from natural resources such as sunlight, wind, rain, tides, waves and geothermal heat, which are renewable because they are naturally replenished at a constant rate.

Renewable energy is a natural source of energy available in large quantity and is sustainable.

***(f)* Importance of the battle of Plassey:** The Battle of Plassey, fought between Nawab of Bengal, Siraj Ud Daulah and British East India Company is judged as one the pivotal battles. The battle took place on June 23, 1757 at Plassey (Palashi), India.

The Battle of Plassey is an important landmark in the history of India. It marked the establishment of British rule in India. The British got a foothold in India from where they were able to conquer the whole India.

***(g)* Natural disasters:** A natural disaster is a major adverse event resulting from natural processes of, or effecting, the Earth; examples include floods, severe weather, volcanic eruptions, earthquakes, and other geologic processes. A natural disaster can cause loss of life or property damage, and typically leaves some economic damage in its wake, the severity of which depends on the affected population's resilience, or ability to recover.

Previous Paper (Solved)

Sainik School Exam, 2012

(Class-IX)

PAPER—I

PART–A : Mathematics

Directions (Qs. 1 to 20) : *Bear 2 marks each.*

1. Find the value of $(8^2 + 15^2)^{1/2}$.

2. If area of a square is 1600 m^2. Find each side of the square.

3. Find the cube root of 46656.

4. A cycle is sold at a gain of 15%. Had it been sold for ₹ 150 more, the gain would have been 20%, find the Cost Price of the cycle.

5. Divide $12x^3 - 8x^2 - 6x + 10$ by $3x - 2$. Also verify the result.

Dividend = Divisor × Quotient + Remainder.

Also write the degrees of Divisor, Dividend and Quotient.

6. Factorize $x^2 + 9x + 20$.

7. Solve the equation $\frac{2x-3}{3x+2} = \frac{-2}{3}$

8. If sum of two numbers is 45 and their ratio is 7 : 8 then, find the numbers.

9. A die is thrown once. What is the probability of getting a prime number?

10. The ratio of ages of Gulshan and Pankaj is 10 : 9. If Gulshan's age after 6 years be 26 years then what is the present age of Pankaj?

11. Find the area of a rhombus whose side is 6.5 cm and whose altitude is 4 cm.

12. Find the area of an equilateral triangle of sides 20 cm each.

13. If 17 is added to 8 times of a number, the result is 209. What is the number?

A. 23 B. 27
C. 24 D. 29

14. Find the smallest number by which 675 must be multiplied so that it becomes a perfect square.

A. 2 B. $\frac{3}{5}$
C. 4 D. 3

15. The factorization of $x^2 - 9x + 20$ is:

A. $(x - 2)(x - 10)$ B. $(x + 4)(x + 5)$
C. $(x - 4)(x + 5)$ D. $(x - 4)(x - 5)$

16. The ratio of sides of two squares is 3 : 4. What is the ratio of their perimeters?

A. 3 : 4 B. 2 : 5
C. 4 : 5 D. 3 : 7

17. A box contains 3 blue balls, 2 white balls and 4 red balls. If a ball is taken out at random from the box. What is the probability that it will be a white one?

A. $\frac{2}{9}$ B. $\frac{1}{9}$
C. $\frac{7}{9}$ D. $\frac{5}{9}$

18. If 8 is added in square root of a number, the result is 34. What is the number?

A. 566 B. 872
C. 766 D. 676

19. $\frac{40 \times 15 + 25}{26 + 4 \div 4 - 2} = ?$

20. A gardener grows 5625 trees in the garden. If he grows trees in such a way that number of trees in a row is equal to the number of rows. What is the number of rows?

Directions (Qs. 21 to 40) : *Bear 3 marks each.*

21. What is the least number which is subtracted from 1026 so that the remainder is a perfect square?

22. What sum will produce compound interest ₹ 496.50 in 3 years at 10% per annum?

23. If an article is sold at a gain of 10% instead of a loss of 10% then difference in selling price is ₹ 55. What is the cost price of the article?

24. Average age of A, B and C is 36 years. If average age of B and C is 30 years and age of B is 22 years then what is the sum of the ages of A and C?

25. Find the value of $3\frac{1}{2}+2\frac{1}{3}-3\frac{1}{4}$.

26. If $x+\frac{1}{x}=4$, then find the value of $x^3+\frac{1}{x^3}$.

27. If $a+b+c=15$ and $a^2+b^2+c^2=77$ then what will be the value of $ab+bc+ca$?

28. Find the value of $\left(\frac{256}{6561}\right)^{3/8}\times\left(\frac{81}{16}\right)^{3/4}$.

29. Find the smallest number by which 5184 is to be multiplied to make a perfect cube. Also find the smallest number by which 5184 is to be divided to make a perfect cube. Find cube root in both the cases.

30. A rectangular park is of length 50 m and breadth 42 m, outside the park there is a path of breadth 2 m which runs around the park. Find the area of the path. Also find the cost of cementing the path at a rate of ₹ 7.50 per square metre.

31. Pipe *A* can fill a tank in 45 hours and pipe *B* can fill it in 36 hours. If both the pipes are opened in the empty tank. In how many hours will it be full?

32. Divide $6x^4-5x^3+7x^2+13x-5$ by $2x^2-3x+5$. Also find the remainder.

33. What is the total surface area of hemisphere in cm^2 whose radius is 10 cm?

34. Find the smallest number that must be subtracted from 62580 to obtain a perfect square is—

35. Meenu bought two fans for ₹ 1200 each. She sold one at a loss of 5% and other at a profit of 10%. Find the selling price of each. Also find out the total profit or loss.

36. If 3 men or 6 boys can complete a work in 16 days, then in how many days 12 men and 8 boys will complete the same work?

37. Population of a town increases by 4% annually. What will be the population after 3 years if the present population of the town is 31250?

38. Sum of the digits of a two digit number is 12. The given number exceeds the number obtained by interchanging the digits by 36. Find the number.

39. Simplify $4\times81^{1/2}\times(81^{1/2}+81^{3/2})$

40. Curved surface area of a right circular cylinder is 4.4 m^2. If the radius of the base of the cylinder is 0.7 m, find its height.

Directions (Qs. 41 to 50): *Bear 10 marks each.*

41. Sita goes to school from her house. If she travels 10 km/hr she is late by 20 minutes and when she travels 15 km/hr she reaches 10 minutes early. What will the distance between her house and school?

42. Find the value of

$$\frac{(a-b)^2}{(b-c)(c-a)}+\frac{(b-c)^2}{(a-b)(c-a)}+\frac{(c-a)^2}{(a-b)(b-c)}$$

43. The area of a triangle is equal to the area of a square which is 60 cm long. Then, find the side of a triangle which is 120 cm away from the vertical point of the triangle.

44. A shopkeeper marks his goods 20% above cost price. He offers 10% discount to his customers. What is his gain per cent?

45. If ₹ 9000 is divided among three workers in the ratio $\frac{1}{3}:\frac{1}{4}:\frac{1}{6}$ respectively, then what is the share of the third worker?

46. The area of two similar triangles ABC and PQR are 64 cm² and 121 cm² respectively. If QR = 15.4 cm then, find BC.

47. Find the length of the longest rod that can be placed in a room of which length, breadth and height are 12 m, 9 m and 8 m respectively.

48. First factorize then simplify the given expression $\frac{x^2+7x+12}{x+3}$.

49. Find the value of $\frac{27^{3n+1}}{9^{n+5}} \times \frac{81^{-n}}{3^{3n-7}}$.

50. Three spherical balls whose radii are 6 cm, 8 cm and x cm respectively are melted and recast into a single sphere whose radius is 12 cm. Then, find the value of x.

PART–B : Science

Note: *Part 'B' bearing 75 marks, contains 37 questions. Q.No.1 to 15 carry one mark each, Q.No. 16 to 25 carry two marks each, Q.No. 26 to 35 carry three marks each, Q.No. 36 and 37 carry five marks each.*

1. The light year is the unit of :
A. distance B. time
C. intensity of light D. mass

2. The vaseline is extracted through the :
A. plant gum B. coaltar
C. pern wax D. petroleum

3. The chemical name of tear gas is :
A. acetophenon
B. benzophenon
C. α-bromo acetophenon
D. α-chloro acetophenon

4. Which of the following disease occurs due to the bacteria?
A. Tuberculosis B. Jaundice
C. Small pox D. Mumps

5. Which of the following gas pollutes the most of the air?
A. Carbon dioxide B. Carbon monoxide
C. Sulphur dioxide D. Hydrocarbon

6. Which of the following pairs is wrong?
A. Conical root — onion
B. Furiform root — radish
C. Napiform root — turnip
D. Pneumatophores — mangrove plant

7. Atom bomb is based upon the principle of :
A. Nuclear fusion B. Nuclear fission
C. Both of them D. None of these

8. The food poisoning occurs due to :
A. Clostrideam Teteni
B. Clostrideam Boutulium
C. Salmonela Toyphosis
D. Baslils Anthresis

9. The first scientist who synthesized the gene or chromosome in the laboratory :
A. Mendel B. Darwin
C. Watson & Crick D. Khorana

10. The largest source of conventional energy in our biosphere is :
A. Sun B. Wind
C. Ocean Water D. Any of these

11. The edible part of cauliflower is :
A. Fruit B. Bud
C. Flower D. Thalmus

12. Who was the inventor of dynamite?
A. Otto Han B. Rutherford
C. Edison D. Alfred Nobel

13. The Bernoulli's theorem is :
A. Energy conservation
B. Mass conservation
C. Both of these
D. None of these

14. Which of the following is negatively charged?

A. α-rays B. β-rays
C. γ-rays D. x-rays

15. For shaving which type of mirror is used:
A. Concave mirror
B. Plane mirror
C. Convex mirror
D. None of these

16. Define the relative velocity.

17. Write the two advantages of frictional force.

18. What is the uses of glucose?

19. In the rainy season the siren of train are listened upto a far distances sharply than summer season, why?

20. How the carbon fibres are formed and what are the uses of carbon fibres?

21. What is Horticulture?

22. What is Standard Atmospheric Pressure?

23. What is compound?

24. What is the functions of Lysosomes?

25. What is the reason of twinkling of stars?

26. Differentiate the temporary magnet and permanent magnet.

27. What is the cause, symptoms and preventive measures of Influenza?

28. What is controlled chain reaction? Write its use.

29. What is difference between mortar and concrete?

30. Write the working function of human ear.

31. What is the main cause of temporary hardness a of water and how it can be removed?

32. What is Ammeter?

33. What is difference between blood and plasma?

34. Write the uses of sulphur?

35. Differentiate the plant cell and the animal cell.

36. Write the main functions of protein.

37. What is myopia? Write its cause and remedial measures.

EXPLANATORY ANSWERS

PART-A : Mathematics

1. $\sqrt{8^2+15^2} = \sqrt{64+225} = \sqrt{289} = 17.$

2. Each side of square = $\sqrt{1600}$ = 40 m.

3. $46656 = \overline{2\times2\times2}\times\overline{2\times2\times2}\times\overline{3\times3\times3}\times\overline{3\times3\times3}$

∴ Cube root of 46656 = 2 × 2 × 3 × 3 = 36.

4. Let the cost price of the cycle be ₹ 100.

∴ S.P. at the gain of 15% = ₹ 115

and S.P. at the gain of 20% = ₹ 120

∵ difference of two S.Ps. = 120 – 115
= ₹ 5

When difference is ₹ 5 then C.P.
= ₹ 100

∴ When difference is ₹ 150 then C.P.

$$= \frac{100\times150}{5} = ₹\ 3000.$$

5. $3x - 2)\ 12x^3 - 8x^2 - 6x + 10\ (4x^2 - 2$

$12x^3 - 8x^2$
$-\quad +$
____
$-6x + 10$
$-6x + 4$
$+\quad -$
____
$+6$

Dividend = Divisor × Quotient + Remainder

$12x^3 - 8x^2 - 6x + 10 = (3x-2)(4x^2-2) + 6$
$= 12x^3 - 6x - 8x^2 + 4 + 6$
$= 12x^3 - 8x^2 - 6x + 10$

Now, Degree of Divisor = 1, of Divident = 3, Degree of quotient = 2.

6. $x^2 + 9x + 20 = x^2 + 5x + 4x + 20$
$= x(x + 5) + 4(x + 5)$
$= (x + 4)(x + 5).$

7. $\frac{2x-3}{3x+2} = \frac{-2}{3} \Rightarrow 3(2x - 3) = -2(3x + 2)$
$\Rightarrow 6x - 9 = -6x - 4$
$\Rightarrow 12x = 5 \quad \Rightarrow x = \frac{5}{12}.$

8. Let numbers are $7x$ and $8x$
$7x + 8x = 45 \Rightarrow 15x = 45 \Rightarrow x = 3$
Hence, the numbers are 21 and 24.

9. Total number = 1, 2, 3, 4, 5, 6 = 6
Number of prime numbers = 2, 3, 5 = 3
$P(\text{Prime}) = \frac{3}{6} = \frac{1}{2}.$

10. Let present ages of Gulshan and Pankaj be $10x$ and $9x$.
According to the question,
After 6 years Gulshan's age = 26 years
$\therefore 10x + 6 = 26 \Rightarrow 10x = 26 - 6 = 20$
$\Rightarrow x = \frac{20}{10} = 2$
$\therefore$ Pankaj's present age = $9 \times 2 = 18$ years.

11. Area of rhombus = side × altitude
$= 6.5 \times 4 = 26 \text{ cm}^2.$

12. Area of an equilateral triangle
$= \frac{\sqrt{3}}{4} \times (\text{side})^2 = \frac{\sqrt{3}}{4} \times (20)^2$
$= 100\sqrt{3} \text{ cm}^2.$

13. C: Let the number be x
According to the question,
$x \times 8 + 17 = 209$
$8x = 209 - 17 = 192$
$x = \frac{192}{8} = 24$
$\therefore$ Number = 24.

14. D: $\because \quad 675 = 3 \times 3 \times 3 \times 5 \times 5$
$= 3 \times (3)^2 \times (5)^2$

It is clear that 675×3 gives $(3)^2 \times (3)^2 \times (5)^2$ which is perfect square.
$\therefore$ required smallest number = 3.

15. D: $x^2 - 5x - 4x + 20 = x(x - 5) - 4(x - 5)$
$= (x - 4)(x - 5).$

16. A: Let sides of the squares be $3x$ and $4x$ respectively.
$\therefore$ Perimeter of 1st square = $4 \times 3x = 12x$
Permeter of 2nd square = $4 \times 4x = 16x$
$\therefore$ Ratio of perimeters = $12x : 16x$
$= 3 : 4.$

17. A: Total number of balls = 9
Number of white balls = 2
$\therefore$ Required probability = $\frac{2}{9}.$

18. D: Let the number be x
According to the question,
Square root of number = $\sqrt{x}$
$\therefore \sqrt{x} + 8 = 34$
$\Rightarrow \sqrt{x} = 34 - 8 = 26$
$\Rightarrow x = 26 \times 26 = 676$
$\therefore$ Number = 676.

19. $\because \frac{40 \times 15 + 25}{26 + 4 \div 4 - 2} = ?$
$\Rightarrow \frac{600 + 25}{26 + \frac{4}{4} - 2} = ?$
$\Rightarrow \frac{625}{26 + 1 - 2} = ? \quad \frac{625}{26 + 1 - 2} = ?$
$\Rightarrow 25 = ?$

20. $\because$ Number of rows in the garden will be square root of 5625.

```
        75
    7 | 5625
      | 49
  145 |  725
      |  725
      |   ×
```

Square root of 5625 = $\sqrt{5625} = 75$
$\therefore$ Number of rows = 75.

21.

$$\begin{array}{r|l} & 32 \\ 3 & 1026 \\ & 9 \\ \hline 62 & 126 \\ & 124 \\ \hline & 2 \end{array}$$

So, it is clear that we have to subtract 2 from 1026 to get a remainder 1024 which is a perfect square of 32.

22. Compound Interest

$$= \text{Principal}\left[\left(1+\frac{\text{Rate}}{100}\right)^{\text{Time}}-1\right]$$

$$496.50 = \text{Principal}\left[\left(1+\frac{10}{100}\right)^3-1\right]$$

$$496.50 = \text{Principal}\left[\left(\frac{11}{10}\right)^3-1\right]$$

$$= \text{Principal} \times \frac{331}{1000}$$

$$\therefore \text{Principal} = \frac{496.50 \times 1000}{331} = ₹\ 1500$$

∴ Required sum = ₹ 1500.

23. Let C.P. = ₹ 100,

Loss = 10%

∴ S.P. = 100 − 10 = ₹ 90

Profit = 10%

∴ S.P. = 100 + 10 = ₹ 110

Difference in SP = 110 − 90 = ₹ 20

When difference ₹ 20 then

CP = ₹ 100

When difference ₹ 55 then

$$\text{CP} = ₹\ \frac{100}{20} \times 55$$

= ₹ 275

∴ CP = ₹ 275

24. Average age of A, B and C = 36 years

Total age of A, B and C = 36 × 3

= 108 years

Average age of B and C = 30 years

Total age of B and C = 30 × 2 = 60 years

∴ Age of A = 108 − 60 = 48 years

Age of B = 22 years (Given)

∴ Age of C = 60 − 22 = 38 years

∴ Total age of A and C = 48 + 38 = 86 years.

25. $3\frac{1}{2}+2\frac{1}{3}-3\frac{1}{4}$

$$= \left(3+2-3+\frac{1}{2}+\frac{1}{3}-\frac{1}{4}\right)$$

$$= 2+\left(\frac{6+4-3}{12}\right) = 2+\frac{7}{12} = 2\frac{7}{12}.$$

26. $x^3+\frac{1}{x^3} = \left(x+\frac{1}{x}\right)^3 - 3\cdot x\cdot\frac{1}{x}\left(x+\frac{1}{x}\right)$

= 64 − 3(4)

= 64 − 12 = 52.

27. ∵ $(a + b + c)^2$

$= a^2 + b^2 + c^2 + 2(ab + bc + ca)$

∴ $ab + bc + ca$

$$= \frac{(a+b+c)^2-(a^2+b^2+c^2)}{2}$$

$$= \frac{(15)^2-77}{2} = \frac{225-77}{2} = \frac{148}{2}$$

= 74.

28. $\left(\frac{256}{6561}\right)^{3/8} \times \left(\frac{81}{16}\right)^{3/4}$

$$= \left[\left(\frac{2}{3}\right)^8\right]^{3/8} \times \left[\left(\frac{3}{2}\right)^4\right]^{3/4}$$

$$= \left(\frac{2}{3}\right)^3 \times \left(\frac{3}{2}\right)^3$$

$$= \left(\frac{2}{3}\times\frac{3}{2}\right)^3 = (1)^3 = 1.$$

29.

2	5184
2	2592
2	1296
2	648
2	324
2	162
3	81
3	27
3	9
	3

$\therefore \quad 5184 = \overline{2\times2\times2} \times \overline{2\times2\times2} \times \overline{3\times3\times3} \times \overline{3}$

$\therefore$ The number by which to be multiplied to make a perfect cube $= 3 \times 3 = 9$

and the number by which to be divided to make a perfect cube $= 3$

Cube root in I case $= 36$

and cube root in II case $= 12$.

30. $\because$ Area of rectangle ABCD

$= 50 \times 42 = 2100 \text{ m}^2$

Area of rectangle PQRS

$= 54 \times 46 = 2484 \text{ m}^2$

$\therefore$ Area of the path $= 2484 - 2100$

$= 384 \text{ m}^2$

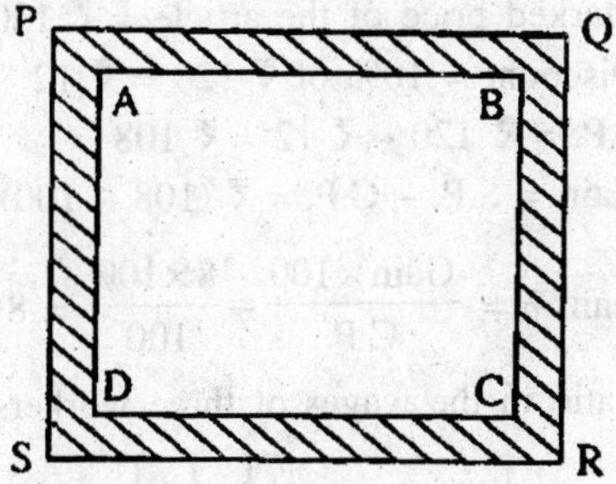

And cost of cementing the path

$= 384 \times ₹\ 7.50$

$= ₹\ 2880.00.$

31. Pipe A filled in 1 hour $= \dfrac{1}{45}$

Pipe B filled in 1 hour $= \dfrac{1}{36}$

Pipe $(A + B)$ filled together in 1 hour $= \dfrac{1}{45} + \dfrac{1}{36}$

$= \dfrac{4+5}{180} = \dfrac{9}{180} = \dfrac{1}{20}$

Hence, the tank will be filled in 20 hours.

32. $2x^2 - 3x + 5)6x^4 - 5x^3 + 7x^2 + 13x - 5(3x^2 + 2x - 1$

$6x^4 - 9x^3 + 15x^2$

$(-) \quad (+) \quad (-)$

$4x^3 - 8x^2 + 13x - 5$

$4x^3 - 6x^2 + 10x$

$(-) \quad (+) \quad (-)$

$-2x^2 + 3x - 5$

$-2x^2 + 3x - 5$

$(+) \quad (-) \quad (+)$

$\times$

$\therefore$ Remainder = 0.

33. T.S. of a hemisphere $= 3\pi r^2$

$= 3\pi \times (10)^2$

$= 300\pi \text{ cm}^2.$

34. $62580 = 62500 + 80$

$= (250)^2 + 80$

$\therefore$ Reqd. number = 80.

35. S.P. of Ist fan $= 1200 \times \dfrac{95}{100}$

$= ₹\ 1140$

and S.P. of IInd fan $= 1200 \times \dfrac{110}{100}$

$= ₹\ 1320$

and Total profit = Total (S.P. – C.P.)

$= (1320 + 1140) - (1200 + 1200)$

$= 2460 - 2400$

$= ₹\ 60.$

36. $\because$ Work of 3 Men = Work of 6 Boys

$\therefore$ Work of 12 Men $= 2 \times 12 = 24$ Boys

$\therefore$ 12 Men + 8 boys $= 24 + 8 = 32$ Boys

$\because$ 6 boys can complete the work in 16 days

$\therefore$ 32 Boys will complete the work in $\dfrac{16\times6}{32}$

$= 3$ days.

37. $P = 31250$

$r = 4\%$

And $n = 3$

Population after three years

$$= 31250\left(1+\frac{4}{100}\right)^3$$

$$= 31250 \times \frac{26}{25}\times\frac{26}{25}\times\frac{26}{25}$$

$= 35152.$

38. Let the number be $(10x + y)$

$\therefore \quad x + y = 12 \quad ...(1)$

and $(10x + y) - (10y + x) = 36$

$\Rightarrow \quad 9x - 9y = 36$

$\Rightarrow \quad x - y = 4 \quad ...(2)$

$x + y = 12$

and $x - y = 4$

$\therefore \quad 2x = 16$

$\therefore \quad x = 8$ and $y = 4$

$\therefore$ The required number is 84.

39. $4\times81^{1/2}\times\left[(81^{1/2}+81^{3/2})\right]$

$= 4 \times 9\ [9 + 9 \times 9 \times 9] = 36[9 + 729]$

$= 36 \times 738 = 26568.$

40. Here, $2\pi rh = 4.4\ \text{m}^2$

$\Rightarrow 2\times\frac{22}{7}\times0.7\times h = 4.4$

$\therefore \quad h = \frac{4.4\times7}{2\times22\times0.7} = 1\text{m}.$

41. 20 minutes $= \frac{20}{60}\text{hr} = \frac{1}{3}\text{hr}$

10 minutes $= \frac{10}{60}\text{hr} = \frac{1}{6}\text{hr}$

Let distance between house and school = x km.

According to the question,

$$\frac{x}{10}-\frac{x}{15} = \frac{1}{3}+\frac{1}{6}$$

$$\Rightarrow \frac{3x-2x}{30} = \frac{2+1}{6}$$

$$\Rightarrow \frac{x}{30} = \frac{1}{2} \Rightarrow 2x = 30 \Rightarrow x = 15$$

$\therefore$ Distance between Sita's house and school = 15 km.

42. According to the question,

$$\frac{(a-b)^3}{(a-b)(b-c)(c-a)}+\frac{(b-c)^3}{(a-b)(b-c)(c-a)}+\frac{(c-a)^3}{(a-b)(b-c)(c-a)}$$

$$= \frac{(a-b)^3+(b-c)^3+(c-a)^3}{(a-b)(b-c)(c-a)}$$

$\because \ (a - b) + (b - c) + (c - a) = 0$

$\therefore (a - b)^3 + (b - c)^3 + (c - a)^3 = 3(a - b)(b - c)(c - a)$

$$\therefore \quad \frac{3(a-b)(b-c)(c-a)}{(a-b)(b-c)(c-a)} = 3.$$

43. Area of square = $(\text{side})^2 = (60)^2 = 3600\ \text{cm}^2$

Area of triangle = Area of square

$\therefore$ Area of triangle = $3600\ \text{cm}^2$

$$\frac{1}{2}\times b\times h = 3600$$

$$b = \frac{2\times3600}{120} = 60\ \text{cm}.$$

$\therefore$ Side of the triangle = 60 cm.

44. Let C.P. of the article = ₹ 100

Marked price of the article = ₹ 120

Discount = 10% of ₹ 120 = ₹ 12

S.P. = ₹ 120 – ₹ 12 = ₹ 108

Gain = S.P. – C.P. = ₹ (108 – 100) = ₹ 8

$$\text{Gain\%} = \frac{\text{Gain}\times100}{\text{C.P.}} = \frac{8\times100}{100} = 8\%.$$

45. Ratio in the wages of three workers

$$= \frac{1}{3}:\frac{1}{4}:\frac{1}{6} = 4 : 3 : 2$$

Sum of the ratios = 4 + 3 + 2 = 9

Share of third worker $= \frac{2}{9}\times9000$ = ₹ 2000.

46. $\because \Delta ABC \sim \Delta PQR$

$$\therefore \quad \frac{BC}{QR} = \frac{AD}{PS}$$

$$\frac{\text{area of }\Delta ABC}{\text{area of }\Delta PQR} = \frac{64}{121}$$

$$\frac{\text{area of }\Delta ABC}{\text{area of }\Delta PQR} = \frac{BC^2}{QR^2}$$

$$\frac{64}{121} = \left(\frac{BC}{QR}\right)^2$$

$$\Rightarrow \quad \left(\frac{8}{11}\right)^2 = \left(\frac{BC}{15.4}\right)^2$$

$$\Rightarrow \quad \frac{8}{11} = \frac{BC}{15.4}$$

$$\Rightarrow \quad BC = \frac{8\times 15.4}{11} = 11.2 \text{ cm.}$$

47. The longest rod that can be placed in the room is the length of its diagonal

$\therefore$ Length of the longest rod $= \sqrt{l^2+b^2+h^2}$

$$= \sqrt{(12)^2+(9)^2+(8)^2}$$

$$= \sqrt{144+81+64}$$

$$= \sqrt{289} = 17 \text{ m.}$$

48. $$\frac{x^2+7x+12}{x+3} = \frac{x^2+4x+3x+12}{x+3} = \frac{x(x+4)+3(x+4)}{x+3} = \frac{(x+4)(x+3)}{(x+3)} = (x+4).$$

49. $$\frac{27^{3n+1}\cdot 81^{-n}}{9^{n+5}\cdot 3^{3n-7}} = \frac{(3^3)^{3n+1}\cdot[(3)^4]^{-n}}{(3^2)^{n+5}\cdot 3^{3n-7}} = \frac{3^{9n+3}\cdot 3^{-4n}}{3^{2n+10}\cdot 3^{3n-7}} = \frac{3^{5n+3}}{3^{5n+3}} = 1.$$

50. $V_1 = \frac{4}{3}\pi\, 6^3$, $V_2 = \frac{4}{3}\pi\,(8)^3$, $V_3 = \frac{4}{3}\pi\,(x)^3$

According to the question,

$$\frac{4}{3}\pi(216+512+x^3) = \frac{4}{3}\pi(12)^3$$

$$728 + x^3 = 1728$$

$$x^3 = 1000 \quad \Rightarrow \quad x = 10$$

$\therefore$ Radius of third sphere = 10 cm.

PART-B : Science

1	2	3	4	5	6	7	8	9	10
A	D	D	A	B	A	B	B	C	A
11	**12**	**13**	**14**	**15**					
D	D	A	A	A					

16. The relative velocity of one body with respect to the another is the rate of change of displacement of one body relative to another and vice-versa.

17. The advantages of frictional force is as follow:

(*i*) If the force of friction doesn't exist on the road where vehicles run then wheels would start to slip and ultimately vehicles would derail.

(*ii*) Due to the forces of friction man stands and moves.

18. Glucose is used in making different types of wine, in sweets and preservetors of fruits juices, medicines like gluconate etc.

19. The density of dry air is more than that of moist air. Thus in moist air the speed of sound is more than dry air. This is the reason why in rainy season the siren of the train are listened up to a far distances sharply then summer season.

20. Carbon fibres are made from long chains of carbon atoms and the incident of corrosion doesn't take place. When the synthetic fibres are heated in the absence of oxygen then fibres start to decompose and carbon fibres are formed. Carbon fibres are used in making parts of space vehicles and sports items.

21. The branch of science under which the development and the cultivating techniques of temperate, sub-tropical and tropical fruits, vegetables, ornamental and medicinal plants, species and plantation crops etc are studied is called Horticulture.

22. The Standard Atmospheric pressure is the pressure required of 76 cm of *Hg* column or 760 mm of *Hg* column, which is equivalent to 1 atm.

23. The compound is that pure substance which is formed by the chemical combination of two or more elements composed in a definite ratio. Also the physical and chemical properties of the formed compound are different than that of its constituents or component elements.

24. The functions of Lysosome are as follow:

(*i*) Lysosome destroys every foreign substance like bacteria etc inside the cell.

(*ii*) Lysosome replaces old and weak cellulor organelles, so that new cellulor organelles be originate in the cell.

(*iii*) If there is need to destroy or replace completely damaged or dead cells then Lysosome breaks its membranes and releases its fluid entirely at a time. Also as Lysosome destroyes itself in such process so it is also called *suicide vesicle (bag) of the cell.*

25. Atmospheric air has various layers of various densities. Whenever light ray coming from stars incident on air surface (layer) then it refracts from various layers and since air layers are not static, thus we realise that stars are twinkling due to different position in different time intervals.

26. Differences between temporary magnet and permanent magnet are as follow:

(*i*) **Temporary Magnet:** Temporary magnets are those in which magnetic substance magnetises easily and demagnetises quickly. That's why these magnets are also called electromagnets. Usually for constructing temporary magnet soft irons are utilised.

Electromagnets (temporary magnets) are used frequently in the electric alarm, in the core of transformer, in the dynamo in which soft irons are magnetised.

(*ii*) **Permanent Magnet:** Permanent magnets are those in which magnetic substance magnetises by slowly and steadily in the long span of time and demagnetises also not easily, so stainless steel is utilised for its construction and to obtain good quality of permanent magnet.

In loudspeaker, needle indicator, Galvanometer etc permanent magnet of steel are attached.

27. Influenza is an acute viral infection, usually epidemic in occurrence and transmits through the air borne droplets in the respiratory tract. This disease is also called Flu. The common symptoms of the influenza are inflammation in respiratory with fever, chill and muscular aches etc. The preventive measures of it are to use attenuated live virus vaccines like teramycine, tetracycline antibiotics. Also by doing the mouth wash through the solution of potassium permanganate the patient of the influenza get relaxed.

28. A fission chain reaction which proceeds slowly and in balanced way without any explosion and in which the energy released can be controlled is called controlled chain reaction.

Nuclear reactors operate on this principle, which are the main sources of the nuclear power and in which controlled nuclear chain reaction takes place. In a nuclear reactor the energy released through fission is used to generate electricity. Several nuclear power plants for the generation of electricity are operating in India and in the various countries of the world.

29. If along with cement some sand (silica) be mixed then this specific mixture is called mortar which is used in the building construction, bridge construction etc.

But if along with cement and sand some little stone particles are mixed up then this mixture is called concrete which is a main component of the building construction.

30. The human ear has two types of working function—to hear and to maintain balance. The working function of the hearing is performed by cochlea present in the inner ear while the maintainance of the balance is

performed by the various organelle components like ampula, by sensory of limbs utreculus and sacculus etc.

31. The existence of the temporary hardness of the water due to the bicarbonates of calcium and magnesium salts. The temporary hardness of water is removed by boiling it. If sodium carbonate is mixed into the water and boiled then permanent and temporary both types of hardness can be removed.

32. Ammeter is a current measuring device and can measure high current. Basically it is a low resistance moving coil galvanometer. It is always connected in series in the electrical circuit in which the current is to be measured. An ideal ammeter should have zero resistance. In fact ammeter of low resistance is more accurate although it is less sensitive.

33. Blood and Plasm: Blood is a red, sticky fluid with a salty taste and its colour varies from a bright scarlet to a bluish red. In the adult's body the blood is nearly 5-6 litres. Through the electron microscope we can see that the blood is composed of a watery fluid called plasma. The plasma is composed through a number of fluid elements or cells like red blood cells (erythrocytes), white blood cells (leucocytes) and platelets (thermobocytes) etc. Thus plasma is a clear yellow watery fluid serves as a vehicle for the transportation of red blood cells, white blood cells, platelets and the various necessary substances for the vital functioning of the body cells. Plasma also acts in the blood clotting by releasing a straw-coloured fluid and in the defence of the body against the various diseases.

34. Sulphur is used today in Beauty parlours to provide a specific touch of hair style, it is also used in the production of SO_2, H_2SO_4, CS_2 etc., in the manufacturing of matches, explosive etc. It is also used in making ointments of sulphurs as the medicine of skin diseases, in the production of sulpha drugs, calcium and magnesium bisulphides are used as bleaching agent. Sulphur is also utilised in dyes, colour industries, in destroying germs, insects and as fungicide.

35. Differences between plant cell and animal cell as follow:

Plant cell	Animal cell
In plant cell a trilayered cell wall is found which is made from cellulose.	There is no any cell wall in animal cell but the cell is covered by plasma membrane.
In almost plants cell except some like Fungi, Bacteria, chlorophyll is found.	No any chlorophyll is found in animals cell.
Centrosome doesn't occur in plant cell.	In animal cell near the nucleus, centrosome occurs which takes part in the cell division.
Lysosome usually doesn't occur in plant cell.	But lysosome occurs in animal cell.
Vacuole occurs in almost plant cell.	But vacuole doesn't occur in animal cell.
In almost plant cells centriols do not exist.	But in almost animal cells centriols exist.

36. Main functions of protein as follow:

(*i*) It is necessary for the physiological growth of the body and due to lack of it bodily growth is disrupted.

(*ii*) It takes part in the synthesis of cells, protoplasm and tissues culturing etc.

(*iii*) The proteins act like bio catalyst and biotic regulator.

(*iv*) It helps in the development of genetical characteristics and in controlling the hereditary activities.

(*v*) In emergency it also provides instantaneous energy.

(*vi*) It helps in the movement and transportational activities.

37. If a person can not be able to see the far flung object but easily see the near most object.

In this case: This type of eye's defect is called myopia or short sightedness

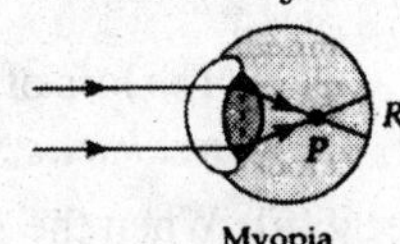

Myopia

(*a*) The sphericity of the eye lens is increased.

(*b*) The focal length of the lens decreases.

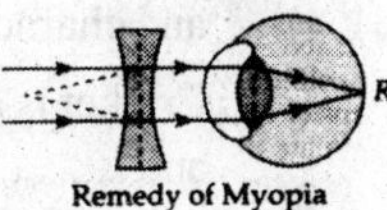

Remedy of Myopia

(*c*) Power of the eye lens increases, thus here image doesn't form on the retina but at the front of it.

The myopia affacted person uses concave lens of suitable focal length so that now image starts to form at retina.

PAPER—II

PART–A : English Language

1. *Read the given passage and answer the questions that follow:*

But we do not judge a cricketer so much by the runs he gets as by the way he gets them. "In literature as in finance", says Washington Irwin, "much paper and much poverty may co-exist". In cricket too many runs and much dullness may be associated. If cricket is menaced with creeping paralysis, it is because it is losing the spirit of joyous adventure and becoming a mere instrument for compiling tables of averages. There are dull, mechanical fellows who turn out runs with as little emotion as a machine churns out pins. There is no colour, no enthusiasm and no character in their play. Cricket is not an adventure to them; it is a business.

Some players display astonishing technical perfection; but the soul of the game is missing in them. There is no sunshine in their play, no swift surprise or splendid unselfishness. Without these things, without gaiety, daring and the spirit of sacrifice, cricket is a dead thing.

(*a*) Which words/lines in the passage tell us that the writer considers 'style' too important in scoring? **(3 Marks)**

(*b*) On the basis of your reading of the passage, complete the following sentences. **(2 × 6 = 12 Marks)**

(*i*) The loss of .... is making cricket a .... game.

(*ii*) When the game lacks colour, enthusiasm and character, it becomes a ....

(*iii*) Cricket is a dead thing without .... and ....

(*c*) Explain : "These are dull mechanical fellows" **(5 Marks)**

2. Give one word for the following: **(2 × 5 = 10 Marks)**

(*a*) A person who does not believe in God.

(*b*) Life history of a person written by another.

(*c*) A disease which spreads by contact.

(*d*) One who collects stamps.

(*e*) Medical study of the skin and its diseases.

3. Rewrite the following sentences after necessary correction. **(2 × 5 = 10 Marks)**

(*a*) They have practiced a lot to get the level.

(*b*) Why do you loose temper at minor issues?

(*c*) Ram as well as Mohan have been found guilty.

(*d*) Munshi Premchand is one of the best Hindi Writer.

(*e*) Are you afraid from him?

4. Distinguish the following words with the help of sentence formation: **(4 × 5 = 20 Marks)**

(*a*) Accept, Except

(*b*) Access, Excess

(*c*) Beside, Besides

(*d*) Device, Devise

(*e*) Loose, Lose.

5. Look at the words and phrases below. Rearrange them to form meaningful sentence: **(3 × 5 = 15 Marks)**

(*a*) pan/take/three/of water/in/cups/a

(*b*) till/the water/put/heat/on the/pan/the/boils/stove/and

(*c*) of/tea leaves/the heat/to lower/the water/add/tea spoons/two/of

(*d*) for/let/simmer/two minutes/the water/more

(*e*) into/sugar and milk/now/the tea/three cups/pour/add/and

6. You are concerned about our excessive dependence on machines, resulting in our becoming unhealthy and asocial. Write a letter to the editor of a newspaper giving vent to your concern, making some suggestions in this regard.

(Word limit-250 words) **(25 Marks)**

PART–B : Social Studies

1. *State True/False:* **(15 × 1 = 15 Marks)**

(*a*) Tipu Sultan was popularly known as Tiger of India. **[True/False]**

(*b*) India shares its boundary with six foreign countries. **[True/False]**

(*c*) India won the gold medal in recent Olympic in wrestling discipline. **[True/False]**

(*d*) The next commonwealth games will be held in New Delhi. **[True/False]**

(*e*) Emigrants are those who arrive in a country and Immigrants are people who leave a country. **[True/False]**

(*f*) Reserve Bank of India is the central bank of Govt of India. **[True/False]**

(*g*) There are 24 Sainik Schools in India. **[True/False]**

(*h*) Mir Quasim became the Nawab of Bengal after the Battle of Plassey. **[True/False]**

(*i*) The Swadeshi movement was started by Gandhiji in 1905. **[True/False]**

(*j*) There are six official languages of United Nations. **[True/False]**

(*k*) Our fundamental rights are not based on Human Rights. **[True/False]**

(*l*) Apartheid is the best form of racialism. **[True/False]**

(*m*) IAEA stands for Indian Atomic Energy Agence. **[True/False]**

(*n*) Rajya Sabha is also known as the lower house of Parliament. **[True/False]**

(*o*) Taj Mahal was made by Emperor Shahajahan. **[True/False]**

2. *Fill in the blanks:* **(15 × 1= 15 Marks)**

(*a*) The present Secretary General of UN is ....

(*b*) Human Rights Day is celebrated throughout the world on ....

(*c*) .... is measured on Richter Scale.

(*d*) In a Secular State, there is .... discrimination against any religion.

(*e*) The East India Company was formed by ....

(*f*) "SEPOY MUTINY" against British Rule in India broke out in the year ....

(*g*) The first Governor General of India was ....

(*h*) General Dyer was responsible for .... massacre.

(*i*) The battle of Buxer was fought in .... AD.

(*j*) First five year plan came into effect in the year ....

(*k*) The rank of the Chief of the Air Staff is ....

(*l*) Babri Masjid is located in ....

(*m*) Highest Court of India is known as ....

(*n*) National Anthem was composed by ....

(*o*) Devanagari is the script of ....

3. *Give full form of following abbreviations:* **(1 × 10 = 10 Marks)**

(*a*) SAARC (*b*) PIN
(*c*) ONGC (*d*) BARC
(*e*) UFO (*f*) LTTE
(*g*) LPG (*h*) UNICEF
(*i*) DRDO (*j*) GMT

4. *Match the following and write the corresponding alphabets of your answer in the box :* **(10 × 1 = 10)**

(*a*) Unification of Germany	(1) 1974
(*b*) Gandhiji was assassinated on	(2) 1991
(*c*) First President of India	(3) 1990
(*d*) Disintegration of USSR	(4) President
(*e*) First Commonwealth Games	(5) 30 January, 1948
(*f*) Champions of first 20-20 Cricket Tournament	(6) 1952

(*g*) First battle of Panipat (7) India
(*h*) Supreme Commander of Indian Armed Forces (8) Dr Rajendra Prasad
(*i*) Indian National Congress (9) 1526
(*j*) First Nuclear test by India (10) 1885

5. *Write short notes on any five. (word limit 50)*
(5 × 5 = 25 Marks)

(*a*) Globalisation
(*b*) Green Revolution
(*c*) HiFi
(*d*) Water Harvesting
(*e*) Commonwealth Games
(*f*) Quit India Movement
(*g*) RTI Act

EXPLANATORY ANSWERS

PART-A : English Language

1. (*a*) But we do not judge a cricketer so much by the runs he gets as by the way he gets them.

(*b*) (*i*) spirit, dull

(*ii*) business

(*iii*) gaiety, daring; spirit of sacrifice

(*c*) Dull mechanical fellows means the cricketers are playing in a monotonous boring way without taking risks and doing variations in their play.

2. (*a*) Theist (*b*) Biography

(*c*) Contagious (*d*) Philatelist

(*e*) Dermatology

3. (*a*) They have practised a lot to reach this level.

(*b*) Why do you lose temper over minor issues?

(*c*) Ram as well as Mohan has been found guilty.

(*d*) Munshi Premchand was one of the best Hindi writers.

(*e*) Are you afraid of him?

4. (*a*) They accepted my proposal easily.
Except Rohan all were present.

(*b*) I was granted access to the system.
The expenses were in excess to his income.

(*c*) I sat beside him on the bed.
Besides reading, I can write French.

(*d*) This is a very useful device.
They devised new ways to solve the problem.

(*e*) His belt was loose.
Do not lose time in idle things.

5. (*a*) Take three cups of water in a pan.

(*b*) Put the pan on the stove and heat till the water boils.

(*c*) Add two tea spoons of tea leaves to lower the heat of the water.

(*d*) Let the water simmer for two minutes more.

(*e*) Add sugar and milk now and pour the tea into three cups.

6. G-3/701,
Sector-5
Vaishali,
11th Sept., 2012
The Editor
The Times of India.
New Delhi.

Subject: ***About the excessive dependence on machines***

Dear Sir,

Through the columns of your esteemed daily I want to highlight my views about the excessive dependence on machines.

Machines were invented to help the humans in doing difficult jobs easily, increasing productivity and efficiency but the excessive dependence on these machines is now resulting in our becoming unhealthy and asocial. In our daily life we now depend so much on machines that we do not want to do any work ourself. Anything we do, we need a machine to help us. Nobody wants to use their mind and body for any work. We do not use our mind because we now use calculators and computers, we do not play outdoors healthy games because we have television, music systems, videogames and electronic gadgets to keep us busy indoors. We do not walk and run anymore because we have motorbikes and cars. All this is making our mind and body dull and unhealthy and at the same time making us asocial. We chat with friends on mobiles and internet but donot want to go out and meet anyone personally and discuss social issues.

This excessive dependence on machines is taking its toll on our health and the society. People now do not enjoy good health, they are either obese or poor body structures, poor stamina, sleeplessness and loss of appetite etc.

People have become asocial also as they keep themselves shut behind doors most of times busy with televisions or computers. They have become so recluse that they are hardly aware of their neighbours names or happenings in the neighbourhood. They hardly attend any social meeting. These are not healthy signs for a society. We must limit our dependence on machines so as to have healthy bodies, minds and to become social again to form a healthy society and healthy India.

Yours sincerely,
R.K. Gupta

PART-B : Social Studies

1. True—(*f*), (*g*), (*h*), (*j*), (*l*), (*o*)

False—(*a*), (*b*), (*c*), (*d*), (*e*), (*i*), (*k*), (*m*), (*n*)

2. (*a*) Ban ki-Moon (*b*) 10th December
(*c*) Earthquake (*d*) no
(*e*) a group of merchants
(*f*) 1857 (*g*) Warren Hastings
(*h*) Jallianwala Bagh (*i*) 1764
(*j*) 1951 (*k*) Air Chief Marshal
(*l*) Ayodhya (*m*) Supreme Court
(*n*) Rabindranath Tagore
(*o*) Hindi Language

3. (*a*) SAARC – South Asian Association for Regional Cooperation
(*b*) PIN – Postal Index Number
(*c*) ONGC – Oil and Natural Gas Corporation
(*d*) BARC – Bhabha Atomic Research Centre
(*e*) UFO – Unidentified Flying Object
(*f*) LTTE – Liberation Tigers of Tamil Eelam
(*g*) LPG – Liquefied Petroleum Gas
(*h*) UNICEF – United Nations International Children's Emergency Fund
(*i*) DRDO – Defence Research and Development Organisation
(*j*) GMT – Greenwich Mean Time

4. (*a*) – (3) (*b*) – (5) (*c*) – (8)
(*d* – (2) (*e*) – (6) (*f*) – (7)
(*g*) – (9) (*h*) – (4) (*i*) – (10)
(*j*) – (1)

5. **(*a*) Globalisation:** Globalisation means integrating the domestic economy with the world economy. It is a process which draws countries out of their insulation and makes them join rest of the world in its march towards a new world economic order.

It involves increasing interaction among national economic system, more integrated financial markets, economies of trade, higher factor mobility, free flow of technology and spread of knowledge throughout the world.

(*b*) Green Revolution: Green revolution refers to the development and use of such HYV seeds during the decade of 1960 which led to phenomenal increase in the output of food crops. In India, the green revolution denotes a positive change in agriculture brought about by the substitution of traditional techniques and methods of cultivation by modern ones.

(c) HiFi: High fidelity — or hi-fi or hifi — reproduction is a term used by home stereo listeners and home audio enthusiasts to refer to high-quality reproduction of sound to distinguish it from the power quality sound produced by inexpensive audio equipment, or the inferior quality or sound reproduction characteristic of recordings made until the late 1940s. Ideally, high-fidelity equipment has minimal amounts of noise and distortion and an accurate frequency response.

(d) Water Harvesting: Water harvesting in its broadest sense will be defined as the "collection of runoff for its productive use." Runoff may be harvested from roofs and ground surfaces as well as from intermittent or ephemeral watercourses.

Water harvesting techniques which harvest runoff from roofs or ground surfaces fall under the term :

1. Rainwater Harvesting
2. Floodwater Harvesting

(e) Commonwealth Games: The Commonwealth Games is an international, multi-sport event involving athletes from the Commonwealth of Nations. The event was first held in 1930 and takes place every four years. The Games are described as the third largest multi-sport event in the world after the Olympic Games and the Asian Games.

It was initially known as the British Empire Games and was renamed to the British Empire and Commonwealth Games in 1954 and the British Commonwealth Games in 1970, before finally gaining its current title for the 1978 edition. The Games are overseen by the Commonwealth Games Federation (CGF), which also controls the sporting programme and selects the host cities.

(f) Quit India Movement: The Quit India Movement also called the August Movement of India was a civil disobedience movement that was launched in the month of August, in the year 1942. The Quit India Movement was a call by Mahatma Gandhi for the country's immediate independence.

The main factor which led to the launch of the Quit India Movement was Gandhi's protest against the return of Sir Stafford Cripps. On 14th July, 1942, the Congress Working Committee adopted the 'Quit India' resolution and on 8th August, 1942, the resolution was accepted by the All India Congress Committee after some modifications. These two dates are very significant in the Indian history of independence movements.

(g) RTI Act: The Government of India has enacted the Right to Information Act, 2005 which has come into effect from October 12, 2005. The Right to Information under this Act is meant to give to the citizens of India access to information under control of public authorities to promote transparency and accountability in these organisations. The Act, under Sections 8 and 9, provides for certain categories of information to be exempt from disclosure. The Act also provides for appointment of a Chief Public Information Officer to deal with requests for information.

Previous Paper (Solved)

Sainik School Exam, 2011

(Class-IX)

PAPER—I

PART–A : Mathematics

Directions (Qs. 1 to 20) : *Bear 2 marks each.*

1. Represent $\frac{5}{3}$ and $\frac{-5}{3}$ on the number line.

2. Evaluate the following:

$$\left\{(24^2+7^2)^{\frac{1}{2}}\right\}^3$$

3. Three numbers are to one another 2 : 3 : 4. The sum of their cubes is 33967. Find the numbers.

4. Multiply:
$(2x^2 - 4x + 5)$ by $(x^2 + 3x - 7)$

5. If $x + \frac{1}{x} = 4$, find the value of $x^2 + \frac{1}{x^2}$.

6. Factorise $4x^2 - 4xy + y^2 - 9z^2$

7. Solve $\frac{x+2}{3} - \frac{x+1}{5} = \frac{x-3}{4} - 1$.

8. Rahim's income is 25% more than that of Raman. What per cent is Raman's income less than Rahim's income?

9. After allowing a discount of 12% on the market price of an article, it is sold for ₹ 880. Find its market price.

10. Find the compound interest on ₹ 12,000 for 3 years at 10% per annum compounded annually.

11. One angle of a quadrilateral is 108° and the remaining three angles are equal. Find the three equal angles.

12. An unbiased Die is thrown. What is the probability of getting an even number?

13. The multiplicative inverse of $-2\frac{5}{3}$ is :

A. $\frac{11}{3}$ B. $\frac{3}{11}$

C. $\frac{-3}{11}$ D. $\frac{-11}{3}$

14. Two positive numbers are in the ratio of 3 : 5. If they differ by 18, then the numbers are :

A. 27 & 45 B. 36 & 54

C. 18 & 36 D. 45 & 63

15. A bag contains 8 black balls, 10 red balls and 12 blue balls. A ball is drawn from the bag without looking into the bag. The probability of getting neither a blue ball nor a black ball is :

A. $\frac{11}{15}$ B. 1

C. $\frac{2}{3}$ D. $\frac{1}{3}$

16. The smallest number by which 72 must be multiplied so as to get a perfect cube is :

A. 2 B. 3

C. 4 D. 5

17. The factors of $x^2 - 6x - 16$ are :

A. $(x-8)$ & $(x-2)$ B. $(x+8)$ & $(x+2)$

C. $(x+8)$ & $(x-2)$ D. $(x-8)$ & $(x+2)$

18. The diagonals of a rhombus are 8.5 cm and 14 cm respectively. Its area (in cm^2) is :

A. 59.5 B. 119

C. 29.75 D. 22.5

19. In the Figure given below, find the value of x

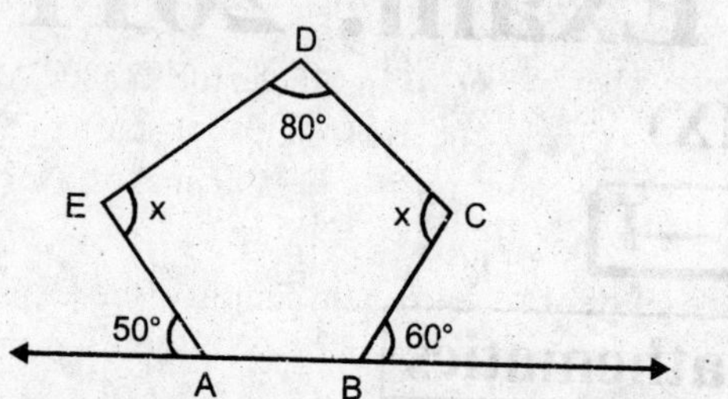

20. Find the greatest 4-digit number which is a perfect square.

Directions (Qs. 21 to 40) : *Bear 3 marks each.*

21. Find 5 rational numbers between $\frac{3}{5}$ and $\frac{3}{4}$.

22. Factorise: $(ax + by)^2 + (ay - bx)^2$.

23. Find : $\frac{2}{5} \times \frac{-3}{7} - \frac{1}{14} - \frac{3}{7} \times \frac{3}{5}$.

24. If $x + \frac{1}{x} = 3$, find the value of $x^3 + \frac{1}{x^3}$.

25. If $a + b + c = 13$ and $a^2 + b^2 + c^2 = 69$ evaluate $ab + bc + ca$.

26. If the area of a rhombus is 120 cm^2 and one of its diagonals be 10 cm. Find its perimeter.

27. Evaluate : $\frac{8^{\frac{1}{3}} \times 16^{\frac{1}{3}}}{32^{-\frac{1}{3}}}$

28. By selling 144 hens a person lost the Selling Price of 6 hens. Find the loss in percentage.

29. Evaluate : $\left(\frac{729}{216}\right)^{\frac{1}{3}} \times \frac{6}{9}$

30. Divide: $x^{3m} - y^{3n}$ by $x^m - y^n$.

31. If 15 workers can build a wall in 48 hours, how many workers will be required to do the same work in 30 hours?

32. If the perimeter of a trapezium be 52 cm, its non-parallel sides are equal to 10 cm each and its altitude is 8 cm, find the area of the trapezium?

33. The area of the parallelogram with base 42 m is same as that of the triangle with base 63 m and height of the triangle is 36 m. Find the height of the parallelogram?

34. Find the least number which must be added to 893304 to obtain a perfect square?

35. Simplify $(x + 2y)(1 + 3x + 4y) - 6y(x - y)$.

36. Find the height of a cylinder whose volume is 1.54 m^3 and diameter of the base is 140 cm (use $\pi = \frac{22}{7}$).

37. Divide 34 into two parts in such a way that $\frac{4}{7}^{th}$ of one part is equal to $\frac{2}{5}^{th}$ of the other.

38. ₹ 3500 is to be shared among three people so that the first person gets 50% of the second, who in turn gets 50% of the third. How much will each of them get?

39. Six typists working 5 hours a day can type the manuscript of a book in 16 days. How many days will four typists take to do the same job each working 6 hours a day?

40. A well with 10 m inside diameter is dug 14 m deep. Earth taken out of it is spread all around the well to a width of 5 m to form an embankment. Find the height of embankment?

Directions (Qs. 41 to 50): *Bear 10 marks each.*

41. Ram is thrice as old as Raju. 5 years ago Ram's age was 4 times Raju's age. Find their present ages.

42. In the following Fig., PQRS is a parallelogram. RL ⊥ PQ, RM ⊥ PS. If ∠QRL = 30°, find the values of angles: x, y, z.

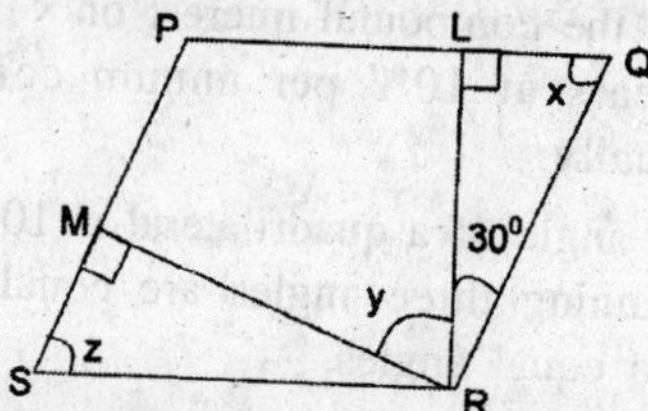

43. Rajesh purchased a hairdryer for ₹ 5400 including 8% VAT (Value Added Tax). Find the price before VAT was included.

44. Simplify $\left(\frac{3x}{2}+5\right)^2-\left(\frac{3x}{2}-5\right)^2$.

45. The radius of a road roller is 49 cm and its length is 125 cm. How much area (in m^2) of a play ground will be levelled in 400 revolutions moving once over the ground?

(use $\pi = \frac{22}{7}$)

46. A building 16 m tall casts a shadow of 6.4 m. Find the height of a building which casts a shadow of 1.6 m at the same time.

47. Half of the herd of deer are grazing in the field and three-fourth of the remaining are playing nearby. The rest of the 9 are drinking water from the pond. Find the number of deer in the herd.

48. A dealer buys an article for ₹ 380. At what price must he mark on it so that after allowing a discount of 5%, he still makes a profit of 25%?

49. Factorise and then simplify the expression

$$\frac{39y^3(50y^2-98)}{26y^2(5y+7)}$$

50. Sunil is painting the wall and the ceiling of a cuboidal hall with length, breadth and height of 15 m, 10 m and 7 m respectively. From each can of paint 100 m^2 of area is painted. How many cans of paint will be needed to paint the room?

PART–B : Science

Note: *Part 'B' bearing 75 marks, contains 37 questions. Q.No.1 to 15 carry one mark each, Q.No. 16 to 25 carry two marks each, Q.No. 26 to 35 carry three marks each, Q.No. 36 and 37 carry five marks each.*

1. Yeast helps in the production of :
A. Sugar B. Alcohol
C. Oxygen D. Carbon di-oxide

2. Glowing of an Electric lamp is not combustion because :
A. Heat produced is not enough
B. Light produced is too much
C. It is a physical change
D. It is not a chemical reaction

3. Carbon exists in amorphous form as :
A. Diamond
B. Graphite
C. Charcoal
D. Carbon mono-oxide

4. Out of the different types of fuels the one which is excellent is :
A. Solid fuel B. Liquid fuel
C. The Gaseous Fuel D. None of these

5. Pasteurization of milk destroys its :
A. Fat content
B. Vitamins
C. Pathogenic bacteria
D. Sugar content

6. The allotrope of carbon which is a good conductor of heat and is used as lubricant is :
A. Lampblack
B. Finely powered charcoal
C. Graphite
D. None of these

7. Petrol or Gasoline is obtained by distillation of Petroleum at temperatures, between :
A. 150° – 300°C
B. above 300°C
C. 70° – 90°C
D. above 400°C

8. In a flame the un-burnt carbon particles are present in the :
A. Dark inner Zone
B. Luminous Zone
C. Non-luminous Zone
D. Blue Zone

9. The host of malaria causing protozoa is :
A. Anopheles mosquito
B. The cow
C. The earthworm
D. Air

10. Desert Plants are more likely to have :
A. Large flat leaves
B. Short root system
C. Reduced leaves
D. A large number of stomata

11. The process of heating ore in the absence of air below its melting point is called :
A. Smelting B. Roasting
C. Calcinations D. Decomposition

12. Hypermetropia is corrected by using :
A. Concave lens B. Convex lens
C. Bi-focal lens D. Plano-convex lens

13. Magnified virtual Image is produced by :
A. Concave Mirror
B. Convex Mirror
C. Plane Mirror
D. Plano-convex Mirror

14. Which of the following is NOT a planet of the sun?
A. Sirius B. Mercury
C. Saturn D. Earth

15. Phases of the moon occur because :
A. We can see only that part of the moon which reflects light towards us.
B. Our distance from the moon keeps changing.
C. The shadow of the Earth covers only a part of the moon's surface.
D. The thickness of the moon's atmosphere is not constant.

16. Write one difference between regular and diffused reflection of light.

17. How earthquake occurs? Write the name of the instrument which can measure the earthquake.

18. What do you mean by force? Write one example where force is used to change the shape of an object.

19. Write two differences between manure and fertilizers.

20. Explain why plastic containers are favoured for storing food?

21. What is irrigation? What are the main sources of irrigation?

22. What is the angle of incidence of a ray if the reflected ray is at an angle of 90° to the incident ray? Draw Ray Diagram.

23. A pendulum oscillates 40 times in 4 seconds. Find out its time period and frequency.

24. Which Microbial diseases are called as communicable diseases?

25. What are the advantages of using CNG and LPG as fuels?

26. Explain how soil gets affected by the continuous plantation of crops in a field.

27. Explain the mechanism of Nitrogen fixation by bacteria and blue green algae.

28. Describe how coal is formed from dead vegetation. What is this process called?

29. Explain how CO_2 is able to control fires.

30. What are vaccines? Name two diseases caused by virus.

31. What is balanced diet? What are the main components of balanced diet?

32. A. What do you mean by Electroplating?
B. Write any two application of Electroplating.
C. What you will add to the pure water so that it will conduct Electricity?

33. What are artificial satellites? Write one of its uses. Name two artificial satellites India had built and launched.

34. A. What will happen to the net force when two different forces are acting on an object opposite to each other?
B. Write one example of a contact force.
C. Name two factors on which the pressure acted on any object depends.

35. What is noise pollution? Write any two harmful effects of noise pollution.

36. Explain why objects moving in fluids must have special shape?

37. Define the term Biosphere Reserve. What are National Park and Sanctuary? What is Red Data Book?

EXPLANATORY ANSWERS

PART-A : Mathematics

1.

−5		−5/3	0	5/3		5
Q	D	C	O	A	B	P

2. $\left\{(24^2+7^2)^{\frac{1}{2}}\right\}^3 = [(576+49)]^{\frac{3}{2}}$

$= (625)^{\frac{3}{2}} = (25^2)^{\frac{3}{2}} = (25)^3$

$= 15625.$

3. Let the numbers are $2x$, $3x$ and $4x$

$(2x)^3 + (3x)^3 + (4x)^3 = 33957$

$8x^3 + 27x^3 + 64x^3 = 33957$

$99x^3 = 33957$

$\Rightarrow \quad x^3 = \frac{33957}{99} = 343$

$\Rightarrow \quad x = 7$

∴ Numbers are 14, 21 and 28.

4. $(2x^2 - 4x + 5)(x^2 + 3x - 7)$

$= 2x^4 + 6x^3 - 14x^2 - 4x^3 - 12x^2 + 28x + 5x^2 + 15x - 35$

$= 2x^4 + 2x^3 - 21x^2 + 43x - 35.$

5. $x^2 + \frac{1}{x^2} = \left(x+\frac{1}{x}\right)^2 - 2(x)\left(\frac{1}{x}\right)$

$= (4)^2 - 2 = 16 - 2 = 14.$

6. $4x^2 - 4xy + y^2 - 9z^2$

$= (2x - y)^2 - (3z)^2$

$= (2x - y + 3z)(2x - y - 3z).$

7. $\frac{x+2}{3} - \frac{x+1}{5} = \frac{x-3}{4} - 1$

$\frac{5(x+2)-3(x+1)}{15} = \frac{x-3-4}{4}$

$\Rightarrow \frac{5x+10-3x-3}{15} = \frac{x-7}{4}$

$\Rightarrow \frac{2x+7}{15} = \frac{x-7}{4} \Rightarrow 15x - 105 = 8x + 28$

$\Rightarrow 7x = 133$

$x = 19.$

8. Let Raman's income ₹ 100

∴ Rahim's income = ₹ 125

Percentage less in Raman's income in respect of Rahim's income $= \frac{125-100}{125} \times 100$

$= 20\%.$

9. $100 - 12 = 88$

When SP ₹ 88 then MP = ₹ 100

When SP ₹ 880 then MP = ₹ $\frac{100}{88} \times 880$

MP = ₹ 1000.

10. $A = P\left(1+\frac{r}{100}\right)^t = 12000\left(1+\frac{10}{100}\right)^3$

$= 12000 \times \frac{11\times11\times11}{10\times10\times10}$

A = 1331 × 12 = ₹ 15972

CI = 15972 − 12000 = ₹ 3972.

11. Let three equal angles be x

$x + x + x + 108 = 360°$

$3x = 360 - 108 = 252°$

$x = 84°.$

12. Total number = 1, 2, 3, 4, 5, 6 = 6

Even number = 2, 4, 6 = 3

Probability (even) $= \frac{3}{6} = \frac{1}{2}.$

13. (C)

14. (A) Let numbers are $3x$ and $5x$

$5x - 3x = 18$

$2x = 18$

$x = 9.$

∴ Numbers are 27 and 45.

15. (D) Total number of balls = 10 + 8 + 12 = 30

Number of red balls = 10

∴ Probability (red balls) $= \frac{10}{30} = \frac{1}{3}.$

16. (B)

2	72
2	36
2	18
3	9
3	3
	1

$72 = 2 \times 2 \times 2 \times 3 \times 3$

72×3 becomes a perfect cube

Hence, required number = 3.

17. (D) $x^2 - 8x + 2x - 16$

$x(x - 8) + 2(x - 8)$

$(x - 8)(x + 2)$.

18. (A) Area of rhombus $= \frac{1}{2} d_1 \times d_2 = \frac{1}{2} \times 8.5 \times 14$

$= 8.5 \times 7 = 59.5 \text{ cm}^2$.

19. $120° + x° + 80° + x° + 130° = 540°$

$2x + 330° = 540°$

$2x = 210°$

$x = 105°$.

20.

```
  9| 9999 |99
   | 81   |
189| 1899
   | 1701
     198
```

$\therefore$ Required number $= 9999 - 198$

$= 9801$

21. I rational number $= \frac{1}{2}\left(\frac{3}{5} + \frac{3}{4}\right)$

$= \frac{1}{2}\left(\frac{12+15}{20}\right) = \frac{27}{40}$

II rational number $= \frac{1}{2}\left(\frac{3}{5} + \frac{27}{40}\right)$

$= \frac{1}{2}\left(\frac{24+27}{40}\right) = \frac{51}{80}$

III rational number $= \frac{1}{2}\left(\frac{3}{4} + \frac{27}{40}\right)$

$= \frac{1}{2}\left(\frac{30+27}{40}\right) = \frac{57}{80}$

IV rational number $= \frac{1}{2}\left(\frac{27}{40} + \frac{51}{80}\right)$

$= \frac{1}{2}\left(\frac{54+51}{80}\right) = \frac{105}{160} = \frac{21}{32}$

V rational number $= \frac{1}{2}\left(\frac{57}{80} + \frac{105}{160}\right)$

$= \frac{1}{2}\left(\frac{114+105}{160}\right) = \frac{219}{320}$.

22. $a^2x^2 + b^2y^2 + 2axby + a^2y^2 + b^2x^2 - 2abxy$

$a^2(x^2 + y^2) + b^2(x^2 + y^2) = (x^2 + y^2)(a^2 + b^2)$.

23. $\frac{2}{5} \times \frac{-3}{7} - \frac{1}{14} - \frac{3}{7} \times \frac{3}{5}$

$\frac{-6}{35} - \frac{1}{14} - \frac{9}{35} = \frac{-12-5-18}{70} = \frac{-35}{70} = \frac{-1}{2}$.

24. $\because \quad x + \frac{1}{x} = 3$

$\therefore x^3 + \frac{1}{x^3} = \left(x + \frac{1}{x}\right)^3 - 3(x)\left(\frac{1}{x}\right)\left(x + \frac{1}{x}\right)$

$= 27 - 3(3)$

$= 27 - 9 = 18$.

25. $(a + b + c)^2 = a^2 + b^2 + c^2 + 2(ab + bc + ca)$

$169 = 69 + 2(ab + bc + ca)$

$100 = 2(ab + bc + ca)$

$\therefore \; ab + bc + ca = 50$.

26. $\frac{1}{2} d_1 \times d_2 = 120$

$10d_2 = 240$

$d_2 = 24$ cm

In ΔABO

$AB^2 = 144 + 25 = 169$

$AB = 13$

Perimeter $= 13 \times 4 = 52$ cm.

27. $\frac{8^{\frac{1}{3}} \times 16^{\frac{1}{3}}}{32^{\frac{1}{3}}} = \left(\frac{128}{32}\right)^{\frac{1}{3}}$

$= 4^{\frac{1}{3}}$.

28. SP of 144 hens = CP of 144 hens – SP of 6 hens

$\Rightarrow$ SP of 150 hens = CP of 144 hens

$$\text{loss \%} = \frac{150-144}{144}\times 100$$

$$= \frac{6}{144}\times 100 = \frac{25}{6} = 4\frac{1}{6}\%.$$

29. $$\left(\frac{729}{216}\right)^{\frac{1}{3}}\times\frac{6}{9} = \left[\left(\frac{9}{6}\right)^{3}\right]^{\frac{1}{3}}\times\frac{6}{9}$$

$$= \frac{9}{6}\times\frac{6}{9} = 1.$$

30. $$\frac{(x^m)^3-(y^n)^3}{x^m-y^n} = \frac{(x^m-y^n)(x^{2m}+x^m y^n+y^{2n})}{(x^m-y^n)}$$

$$= x^{2m} + x^m y^n + y^{2n}$$

31. To complete a wall in 48 hrs requires 15 workers

To complete same wall in 30 hrs requires

$$\frac{15\times 48}{30} = 24 \text{ workers}$$

32.

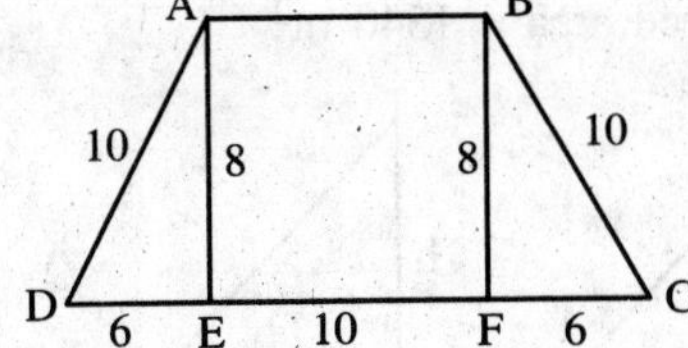

$$\text{Area of trapezium} = \frac{1}{2}\times h(b_1+b_2)$$

$$= \frac{1}{2}\times 8(10+22)$$

$$= 4\times 32 = 128 \text{ cm}^2.$$

33. $$\text{Area of triangle} = \frac{1}{2}\times 63\times 36$$

$$= 63\times 18 = 1134 \text{ m}^2.$$

Area of parallelogram = $b \times h$

$$h = \frac{\text{Area}}{b} = \frac{1134}{42} = 27$$

$\therefore$ Height of the parallelogram = 27 m.

34.

```
   9 | 893304 | 945
     | 81     |
-----+--------
 184 | 833
   4 | 736
-----+--------
1885 | 9704
   5 | 9425
-----+--------
     | 279
```

```
1886 | 9704
   6 | 11316
```

$\therefore$ 11316 – 9704 = 1612

If we add 1612 in 893304 then it becomes a perfect square.

35. $(x + 2y)(1 + 3x + 4y) - 6y(x - y)$

$x + 3x^2 + 4xy + 2y + 6xy + 8y^2 - 6xy + 6y^2$

$= 3x^2 + 14y^2 + 4xy + x + 2y$

36. Diameter = 140 cm

$\therefore$ Radius = 70 cm = 0.7 m

Volume of cylinder = $\pi r^2 h$

$$= \frac{22}{7}\times 0.7\times 0.7\times h$$

$\Rightarrow$ $1.54 \times 7 = 22 \times 0.49h$

$$h = \frac{154\times 7}{22\times 49} = 1\text{m}.$$

37. Let first part = x and other part = $34 - x$

According to the question,

$$\frac{4}{7}x = \frac{2}{5}(34-x)$$

$20x = 14(34 - x)$

$20x = 14 \times 34 - 14x$

$34x = 14 \times 34$

$x = 14$

First part = 14

2nd part = 34 – 14 = 20.

38. Let third share = ₹ x

$$\text{2nd share} = ₹\, x\times\frac{50}{100} = \frac{x}{2}$$

$$\text{First share} = \frac{x}{2}\times\frac{50}{100} = \frac{x}{4}$$

$$x+\frac{x}{2}+\frac{x}{4} = 3500$$

$$\Rightarrow \frac{4x+2x+x}{4} = 3500$$

$\Rightarrow$ $7x = 3500 \times 4 \Rightarrow x = 2000$

First share = 500

$$\text{2nd share} = \frac{2000}{2} = 1000.$$

39. Required days $= \dfrac{16\times5\times6}{4\times6} = 20$.

40. Diameter = 10 m

radius = 5 m

h = 14 m

Volume of earth taken out $= \pi r^2 h$

$= \dfrac{22}{7}\times5\times5\times14$

$= 1100\ m^3$

Now earth spread out of a hollow cylinder

External radius = 5 + 5 = 10 m

Inner radius = 5 m,

let h be the height

$\pi(R^2 - r^2)h = 1100$

$\dfrac{22}{7}(10^2 - 5^2)h = 1100$

$\dfrac{22}{7}\times75h = 1100$

$h = \dfrac{1100\times7}{22\times75} = \dfrac{14}{3} = 4\dfrac{2}{3}$ m

Hence, height of embankment = 4.66 m.

41. Let Raju's present age = x years

Ram's present age = $3x$ years

According to the question,

$3x - 5 = 4(x - 5)$

$3x - 5 = 4x - 20$

$\Rightarrow \quad x = 15$

Raju's present age = 15 years,

Ram's age = 45 years.

42. In ΔRQL,

$x + 30 + 90° = 180°$

$x = 180 - 120 = 60°$

$x = z = 60°$ (opp. angles are equal)

In ΔSMR,

$z + 90 + \angle R = 180°$

$60 + 90 + \angle R = 180°$

$150 + \angle R = 180° \qquad \therefore \angle R = 30°$

In parallelogram PQRS,

$\angle P = \angle R$

$\angle P + \angle S + \angle R + \angle Q = 360°$

$30 + 30 + y + 60 + 30 + 30 + y + 60 = 360°$

$2y + 240 = 360°$

$y = 60°$

$\therefore \ x = 60°, \ y = 60°, \ z = 60°.$

43. $100 + 8 = 108$

When with VAT the price = ₹ 108

then without VAT the price = ₹ 100

When with VAT the price = ₹ 5400

then without VAT the price

$= \dfrac{100}{108}\times5400$ = ₹ 5000

Required price = ₹ 5000.

44. $\left(\dfrac{9x^2}{4} + 15x + 25\right) - \left(\dfrac{9x^2}{4} - 15x + 25\right)$

$= \dfrac{9x^2}{4} + 15x + 25 - \dfrac{9x^2}{4} + 15x - 25$

$= 30x$

45. $r = 49$ cm $= \dfrac{49}{100}$ m, $h = \dfrac{125}{100}$ m $= \dfrac{5}{4}$ m

C.S.A. of roller $= 2\pi rh = 2\times\dfrac{22}{7}\times\dfrac{49}{100}\times\dfrac{5}{4}$

$= \dfrac{77}{20}\ m^2$

1 revolution $= \dfrac{77}{20}\ m^2$

400 revolutions $= \dfrac{77}{20}\times400 = 1540\ m^2$

$\therefore$ Required area $= 1540\ m^2$

46.

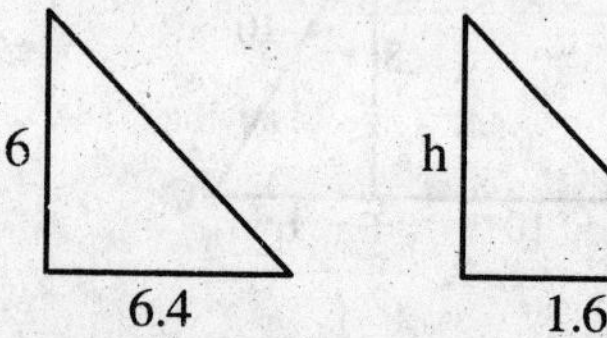

$\dfrac{16}{h} = \dfrac{6.4}{1.6} \Rightarrow h = \dfrac{16\times1.6}{6.4} = 4$ m

$\therefore$ Required height = 4 m.

47. Let number of deer = x

According to the question,

$\dfrac{x}{2} + \dfrac{3}{4}\left(\dfrac{x}{2}\right) + 9 = x$

$\Rightarrow \quad \dfrac{x}{2} + \dfrac{3x}{8} + 9 = x$

$\dfrac{4x + 3x + 72}{8} = x$

$\Rightarrow \quad 8x - 7x = 72$

$x = 72$

$\therefore$ Required number = 72.

48. Let MP = ₹ 100

Discount = $\frac{5}{100} \times 100$ = ₹ 5

SP = ₹ 100 – 5 = 95

Profit = 25%

CP = $95 \times \frac{100}{125} = 95 \times \frac{4}{5}$ = ₹ 76

When CP ₹ 76 then MP = ₹ 100

When CP ₹ 380 then MP = ₹ $\frac{100}{76} \times 380$

= ₹ 500

$\therefore$ Required MP = ₹ 500.

49. $\frac{39y^3(50y^2 - 98)}{26y^2(5y+7)}$

$= \frac{39y^3 \times 2(25y^2 - 49)}{26y^2(5y+7)}$

$= \frac{78y^3(5y+7)(5y-7)}{26y^2(5y+7)}$

$= 3y(5y - 7) = 15y^2 - 21y.$

50. Area of four walls = $2(l + b)h$

$= 2(15 + 10)7$

$= 50 \times 7 = 350 \text{ m}^2$

Area of ceiling = $15 \times 10 = 150 \text{ m}^2$

Total area = $350 + 150 = 500 \text{ m}^2$

Number of cans = $\frac{500}{100} = 5.$

PART-B : Science

1	2	3	4	5	6	7	8	9	10
B	D	C	C	C	C	C	B	A	C
11	**12**	**13**	**14**	**15**					
C	B	A	A	A					

16. When light rays fall on polished surface they change their direction in a well-defined manner. This is called regular reflection. Light falling on non-polished surfaces does not change the direction in a well-defined manner. This is called diffuse reflection.

17. Earthquakes occur by the displacement of tectonic plates of the earth over each other. Seismograph is used to measure earthquakes.

18. Force: Force is a push or pull that tends to change the momentum of object. In other words, force is the product of mass and acceleration.

The S.I. unit of force is newton (N). 1 newton force is that force which produces an acceleration of 1 metre/second^2 in a mass of 1 kg.

Force accelerates or decelerates the motion of a body. It also changes the direction of motion.

When force is applied to a piece of chalk, it is crushed and there occurs a change in its shape.

19.

Manure	Fertilizer
(*i*) It is obtained from decomposition of dead plants and animals waste.	(*i*) It is synthesized in factories from chemicals.
(*ii*) It restores the water retention ability of soil.	(*ii*) It does not help in water retention by the soil.
(*iii*) It is slowly absorbed by the plants.	(*iii*) It is readily absorbed by the plants.
(*iv*) It cannot be stored in a house.	(*iv*) It can be stored in a house.
(*v*) It is needed in large quantity.	(*v*) It is needed in less quantity.

20. Plastic containers are used for storing food as plastic surface does not corrode and reacts with food moisture also does not pass through plastic.

21. Watering the harvest is generally called irrigation. The main sources of irrigation are rainwater, river, canals and groundwater.

22.

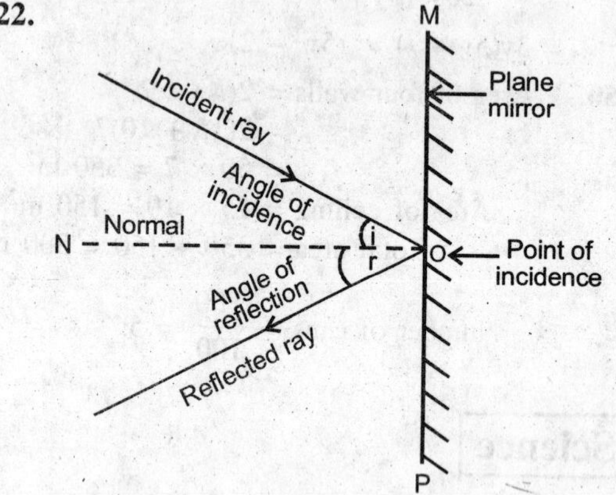

23. Frequency of oscillations is defined as the number of oscillations of a vibrating body per second. It is given by

$$\Rightarrow \text{Frequency} = \frac{\text{Number of oscillations}}{\text{Total time}}$$

$$= \frac{40}{4} = 10 \text{ Hz}$$

The time required to complete one oscillation is known as time period. It is given by the inverse of frequency.

$$\therefore \text{Time period} = \frac{1}{\text{Frequency of oscillation}}$$

$$= \frac{1}{10} = 0.15.$$

24. Cholera and Tuberculosis are two microbial communicable diseases.

25. The advantages of using LPG and CNG as fuels are—

- High calorific value
- No residue
- Minimal smoke and pollution
- Burns readily, preheating not required. This is because it has a low ignition temperature.

26. In a field, the soil get affected by the continuous plantation of crops as each crop absorbs and uses a large quantity of natural fertility factors of the soil such as chemical nutrients and macronutrients. To replenish the soil manures and fertilizers are added to the soil.

27. Blue-green algae like Nostoc and Anabaena are able to fix nitrogen in the form of nitrates and thus increase the fertility of soil.

Some bacteria like Rhizobium and Azotobacter absorb free nitrogen from the air and convert it into nitrogenous compounds.

28. Coal is formed as the result of high temperature and pressure on the logs of woods (trees) and the remains of animals which got buried under the earth, millions of years ago. This process is called carbonization.

29. Oxygen helps in burning and CO_2 on the contrary diminishes or resists burning. When a fire is surrounded by CO_2 it is controlled because of this property of CO_2.

30. Vaccination is a process of inoculation of a substance (vaccine) into a healthy person in order to develop immunity against a disease. Immunity is the ability of a body to recognise, destroy and eliminate external disease-causing agents. Vaccination helps a person to acquire immunity against a certain disease. The vaccine is a solution containing the disease-causing organisms in a diluted or weakened form.

Influencza and AIDS are caused by virus.

31. Balanced diet contains all essential components in the optimum proportion and quantity for maintaining the various body activities and development. 60% carbohydrates, 25% fats, 15% proteins and vitamins, minerals, roughage and water are various components of a balanced diet.

32. A. It is the process in which the more reactive metal surfaces are covered with less reactive metals using electric current.

B. It is done to prevent corrosion of metals. It gives shine and finishing to the metal surface.

C. Sodium chloride (NaCl).

33. An artificial satellite is a man-made system placed in a stationary orbit round the earth by means of a multistage rocket. The satellite is placed on the rocket which is launched from earth.

Applications of Artificial Satellites

1. It is used to study the atmosphere.
2. Information about the earth can be obtained.
3. Weather forecast can be done.
4. Radiation from the sun and outer space can be studied.
5. Distant telecasting, television service can be operated by geostationary satellites.
6. Meteorites can be studied.

Two name of Artificial satellites India had built and launched:

1. Aryabhatt, 2. Insat-2B.

34. A. There will be no change in the position of the object.

B. The brakes of a vehicle.

C. Area of object and magnitude of force.

35. Undesirable high pitch sounds of anything such as motor vehicles, machines, loud music or of airplanes are known as sound pollution. Sound pollution may cause irreparable damage to human ears and may also cause many psychological disorders in human beings.

36. The objects moving in fluids must have special shape so as to reduce or minimise the frictional force of viscosity of the fluid. The lesser the friction the smoother will be the movement. Objects should be pointed for this.

37. These are the areas for protection of natural habitat and maintenance of endangered and other important species by certain protected areas such as national parks, wildlife or bird sanctuaries. In India, there are 99 national parks, 515 sanctuaries and 17 biosphere reserves.

Biosphere Reserves : Biosphere reserves are multipurpose protected areas with following major objectives :

(*i*) to conserve diversity and integrity of plants, animals and micro-organisms.

(*ii*) to promote ecological conservation.

(*iii*) to educate, train and create awareness about environmental aspects and eco-friendly living.

Red Data Book: The Red Data Book is the State document established for documenting rare and endangered species of animals, plants and fungi as well as some local sub-species that exist within the territory of the state or country. This book provides central information for studies and monitoring programmes on rare and endangered species and their habitats.

PAPER—II

PART–A : English Language

1. *Read the given passage and answer the questions that follow:*

The group of tired dusty riders arrived at a fork in the road. Their leader immediately sprang to the ground after first throwing his rein to one of the others, and began to examine minutely the sandy track. The problem was simple; if the fleeing enemy had taken the left turning, there remained little hope of catching them, since he knew that is led back to a small settlement of native huts where they should be sheltered by the friendly inhabitants. If, on the other hand, they had branched to the right, they would have before them the open desert, not a flat expanse of sand such as they had just crossed, but a country broken by series, behind any of which a whole army could hide

He turned to his companions to see if he could read any solution in their faces. But they were too occupied by their aching limbs and several were taking a quick drink from the flasks which hung at their belts. He realised every minute's delay lessened their chances of overtaking their adversaries. So, with a rapid glance at the sun, he jumped once more into the saddle and with his whip indicated the way they were to go. **(3 × 3 = 9)**

(*a*) Answer the following questions briefly :

(*i*) What, if any was the difference in the nature of the terrain they had already traversed and the one lying ahead?

(*ii*) What difficulties did they expect if they took the branch to the right?

(*iii*) Where and why did they stop?

(*b*) On the basis of your reading of the passage complete the following : **(6 × 1 = 6)**

The group of ....(*i*) searching for their .... (*ii*). Their leader rode off the horse and examined the .... (*iii*) track. He wanted to overtake his enemy but his followers ware taking a quick .... (*iv*) finally with the rapid glance at the .... (*v*). He jumped again into the .... (*vi*).

(*c*) What was the possibility to catch the enemy by the riders? **(5 Marks)**

2. Write a short essay (not exceding 100 words) on **any one** of the following topics: **(10 Marks)**

(*a*) Naxalism: A Threat to Internal Security

(*b*) Word Cup Cricket-2011

3. Write a letter to the editor of a national daily giving your views about the rising number of terrorist activities, in the country. **(5 Marks)**

4. *Choose the correct option and write the same in blank space:* **(10 Marks)**

(*a*) The writing contains many .... ideas.

(*i*) vogue (*ii*) vague

(*b*) The coachman .... the horse with a whip.

(*i*) threshed (*ii*) thrashed

(*c*) As the child grew into a young man the .... of his shirt at the shoulders got a light strains.

(*i*) seam (*ii*) seem

(*d*) In the .... part of the year the company are often in a position to return the refunds or other dues.

(*i*) latter (*ii*) letter

(*e*) A group of burglars .... a pedestrian with rods.

(*i*) battered (*ii*) bettered

5. *Rearrange the following words to form meaningful sentence* **(3 × 5 = 15)**

(*a*) she/lunch/hosted/a/party/later

(*b*) care/is/aunt's/under/her/baby

(*c*) novel/hour/this/one/me/took

(*d*) is/wise/foolish/penny/pound/he.

(*e*) married/are/getting/not/today/they

6. *Fill appropriate preposition in the blanks.*

(*a*) I assured him .... my support.

(*b*) What are your reasons .... resigning?

(*c*) The sentry is armed .... a gun.

(*d*) The rod was cut .... two.

(*e*) I wish .... go home.

(*f*) His strength consists .... his honesty.

(*g*) Birds live .... trees.

(*h*) He insisted .... me to go there.

(*i*) He picks a quarrel every body.

(*j*) I cautioned you .... his tricks.

7. *Match words under* ***A*** *with their synonyms under* ***B.*** **(5 Marks)**

A	B
(*a*) Jolly	(*i*) Cruel
(*b*) Tame	(*ii*) Untrue
(*c*) Callous	(*iii*) Merry
(*d*) Liberty	(*iv*) Gentle
(*e*) False	(*v*) Freedom

8. *Give one word for the following:* **(10 Marks)**

(*a*) A child whose parents are dead.

(*b*) A list of books in a library.

(*c*) One who spends very little.

(*d*) Place where bees are kept.

(*e*) Living for ever.

9. *Make new words by using, dom, en, ary, ness, at the suffix of the following words:* **(5 Marks)**

(*a*) Blind ....

(*b*) Wis ....

(*c*) Sharp ....

(*d*) Honor ....

(*e*) Weak ....

PART–B : Social Studies

1. *State True/False:* **(15×1 = 15)**

(*i*) Bodh Gaya, the most sacred place of Buddhists is in Bihar. **[True/False]**

(*ii*) 'Satyameva Jayate' in the state emblem has been taken from Gita. **[True/False]**

(*iii*) The constitution of India was adopted on 26 January, 1950. **[True/False]**

(*iv*) Minimum age to quality for the President's post is 35 years. **[True/False]**

(*v*) Vikramaditya was the name given to Chandragupta Maurya. **[True/False]**

(*vi*) Sher Shah defeated Mughal king Babur. **[True/False]**

(*vii*) Din-I-lahi was launched by Akbar. **[True/False]**

(*viii*) Brahmo Samaj was founded by Dayanand Saraswati. **[True/False]**

(*ix*) Champaran movement was meant for solving the problems of Indian farmers. **[True/False]**

(*x*) Bhagat Singh was hanged in the year 1931. **[True/False]**

(*xi*) 'Liberty, Equality and Fraternity' was the slogan of Russian Revolution. **[True/False]**

(*xii*) Magna Carta is a charter of rights. **[True/False]**

(*xiii*) Silk was introduced by Chinese. **[True/False]**

(*xiv*) The 'Sati' tradition was abolished by Lord give. **[True/False]**

(*xv*) There is the great variations of vegetation in the Monsoon Region due to variation in the amount of rainfall in different places. **[True/False]**

2. *Fill in the blanks* **(15×1= 15)**

(*a*) 'Jog' the highest fall of India is located in ---------- (state)

(*b*) Dharival is the place associated with the industry of ----------

(*c*) ---------- is known as the land of Golden fleece.

(*d*) The north-south extent of India is --------

(*e*) Mahatma Gandhi Setu is built over the river ----------

(*f*) Indian Military Academy is located at ----------

(*g*) Chanakya is also known as ----------

(*h*) The bird that never makes its nest is ---------

(*i*) Santa Cruz International Air Port is located at ----------

(*j*) ---------- is the largest producer of mica. in the world.

(*k*) ---------- crop is sown in October and November and harvested in April.

(*l*) Vardhman Mahavir was the guru of ---------

(*m*) 'Dilli chalo' was the slogan of ---------

(*n*) Simon Commission came to India in ---------

(*o*) The Ramayana was written by ---------

3. *Expand the abbreviations:*

(*a*) WHO (*b*) SEZ

(*c*) UNO (*d*) CAG

(*e*) VAT (*f*) BHEL

(*g*) PSLV (*h*) NTPC

(*i*) ESRO (*j*) GMT

4. *Match the following by writing the correct alphabet from column A with column B in the answer column:*

A	B
(*i*) Kiel	(*a*) It was launched by Muhammad Ali and Shaukat Ali
(*ii*) Mixed Farming	(*b*) are heavenly bodies known for their tails
(*iii*) Isobar	(*c*) is the supreme commander of defence forces
(*iv*) Article 356	(*d*) is a fundamental right which can not be suspended even during emergency
(*v*) Indian National Army	(*e*) This canal links North sea with Baltic sea
(*vi*) Khilafal Movement	(*f*) It is the fibrous material present in plants and their products
(*vii*) President of India	(*g*) Line on the map connecting places with the same atmospheric pressure
(*viii*) Comets	(*h*) Deals with constitutional emergency
(*ix*) Right to live	(*i*) When farming and animal husbandry are practiced on the same farm
(*x*) Roughage	(*j*) It was setup by Rash Bihari Bose

5. *Write short notes on any five of the following topics:* **(5 × 5 = 25)**

(*a*) Green Revolution

(*b*) Jallianwala Bagh Tragedy

(*c*) India's Moon Mission

(*d*) Food Chain

(*e*) Right to Education

(*f*) Smt. Pratibha Patil

(*g*) Wildlife Conservation in India

EXPLANATORY ANSWERS

PART-A : English Language

1. (*a*)

(*i*) What they had crossed was a flat expanse of sand and what they lay ahead to the right was series of ridges of sand.

(*ii*) The difficulties were that ahead lay a country full of ridges of sand providing cover to the fleeing enemy.

(*iii*) They stopped at a fork in the road in order to decide whether they should turn left or right.

(*b*) (*i*) riders (*ii*) enemy

(*iii*) track (*iv*) drink

(*v*) sun (*vi*) saddle

(*c*) If the fleeing enemy had taken the left turning there remained little hope of catching then because it is led back to a small settlement of native huts where they should be sheltered by the friendly inhabitants. But if the had branced to right they would have before them the open desert.

2. (*a*)

As its historical evolution indicates, the naxal movement in India, in last few years shown the tendency of expanding its support base as well as intensification of violent activities. It has assumed regional and international orientation in view of the success of Maoist in the neighbouring Nepal. This has emboldened Naxal groups in India. They are at present well entrenched in worst affected areas of West Bengal, Chhattisgarh, Jharkhand, Andhra Pradesh and Odisha. Their guerrilla tactics has surprised the security forces. Besides, their wide support in rural and tribal areas of these states, they have generated certain amount of sympathy among certain urban educated and intellectual sections.

To counter the Naxal threat, military action is not enough alone. Work should be done on multi dimensional fronts. Surrender and resettlement schemes should be launched by the state governments in the affected areas, where naxals surrendering to the government are given financial incentives and facilities for their resettlement.

Naxal violence is not a law and order problem in India. It is serious security threat to India with international and regional dimensions. The need of the hour is to adopt both social and administrative measures to tackle the threat posed by the naxal groups. Besides, the better training of security forces, planning and coordination is must for the success of government measures.

(*b*) India after 28 years, has again become the King of World Cricket. On April 2, 2011, India defeated former champion Sri Lanka by six wickets, in the final match played at Vankhede Stadium, Mumbai.

Out of 14 teams, 8 teams reached the quarter finals of this World Cup. In these, from group A were Pakistan, Australia, New Zealand and Sri Lanka while from group B were West Indies, India, South Africa and England. In this, Pakistan had beaten West Indies, New Zealand beaten South Africa, India beaten Australia and Sri Lanka beaten England to enter the semi finals. In the first semi final on 29th March, Sri Lanka had beaten New Zealand with five wickets and secured its place in the World Cup final for the third time. The 1996 Champian, Sri Lanka reached the semi final in a row twice. The second semi-final was played on 30th March at Mohali. In this very exciting match, India downed Pakistan by 29 runs and crossed to the final.

The hero of this remarkable victory, Yuvraj Singh of Indian team in the World Cup, which was played from 18th February to 2nd April 2011, has been chosen the man of the tournament. He won the Asia Cup for India after a long gap of 15 years. He won the first T-20 World Cup, the Champion's league and finally the World Cup 2011.

3. Place..................

Date....................

To

The Editor-in-Chief

The Harold

Rajaji Marg

Lucknow-17

Sir,

Sub: *Rising Number of Terrorist Activities*

I would like to express my views on the rising number of terrorist activities in India. I hope these would find space in the columns of your esteemed daily (in section Readers' Thoughts, appearing every Sunday).

The incidents of Kaluchak, Doda, Srinagar and other areas of Jammu and Kashmir have put the Indian police and security forces on the state of maximum alert. Pakistan is perpetuating the reign of terrorism. She is also resorting to heavy shelling along the LoC in Punjab and Jammu and Kashmir. Under the cover of this shelling, the Pakistani army and the ISI send terrorists into the Indian territory. They indulge in the acts of bomb blasts, killing of innocent people and attacks on important buildings. Innocent Kashmiris and security forces are the hapless victims of these terrorist attacks.

A war against Pakistan would not put out the fire of terrorism. We must respond to this guerilla war with a guerilla war. Our must rise to the occasion and meet this challenge with courage. We are with the people of Jammu and Kashmir during this critical phase of time. We shall also give all types of moral and financial support to innocent Kashmiri brothers and sisters.

Your well wisher,

....

4. (*a*) latter (*b*) battered
(*c*) thrashed (*d*) vague
(*e*) seam

5. (*a*) Later she hosted a lunch party.
(*b*) Baby is under her aunt's care.
(*c*) This novel took me one hour.
(*d*) He is penny wise pound foolish.
(*e*) Are they not getting married today.

6. (*a*) of (*b*) for (*c*) with
(*d*) in (*e*) to (*f*) under
(*g*) in (*h*) upon (*i*) with
(*j*) against

7. (*a*) (*iii*) (*b*) (*iv*) (*c*) (*i*)
(*d*) (*v*) (*e*) (*ii*)

8. (*a*) orphan (*b*) catalogue/bibliograph
(*c*) miser (*d*) apiary
(*e*) immortal

9. (*a*) Blind <u>ly</u> (*b*) Wis <u>dom</u>
(*c*) Sharp <u>en</u> (*d*) Honor <u>ary</u>
(*e*) Weak <u>ness</u>

PART-B : Social Studies

1. True—(*a*), (*d*), (*g*), (*i*), (*j*), (*l*), (*m*), (*o*)
False—(*b*), (*c*), (*e*), (*f*), (*h*), (*k*), (*n*)

2. (*a*) Karnataka (*b*) Woollen goods
(*c*) Australia (*d*) 3200 (*e*) Ganga
(*f*) Dehradun (*g*) Kautilya (*h*) Cuckoo
(*i*) Mumbai (*j*) India (*k*) Rabi
(*l*) Jains (*m*) Subhash Chandra Bose
(*n*) 1928 (*o*) Valmiki

3. (*a*) WHO – World Health Organisation
(*b*) SEZ – Special Economic Zone

(*c*) UNO – United Nations Organisation

(*d*) CAG – Comptroller and Auditor General

(*e*) VAT – Value Added Tax

(*f*) BHEL – Bharat Heavy Electricals Ltd.

(*g*) PSLV – Polar Satellite Launch Vehicle

(*h*) NTPC – National Thermal Power Corporation

(*i*) ESRO – European Space Research Organisation

(*j*) GMT – Greenwich Mean Time

4. (*i*) – (*e*) (*ii*) – (*i*) (*iii*) – (*g*)
(*iv*) – (*h*) (*v*) – (*j*) (*vi*) – (*a*)
(*vii*) – (*c*) (*viii*) – (*b*) (*ix*) – (*d*)
(*x*) – (*f*)

5. (*a*)

Green Revolution: It is the phenomenon that led to great increase in production of foodgrain crops. The introduction of high-yielding varieties, coupled with proper irrigation and increased use of fertilizers, weedicides and pesticides resulted in record production of foodgrains. Improved soil practices and agricultural implements and bringing more land under cultivation also caused the change. The green revolution made country self-sufficient in foodgrains, improved the conditions of farmers and created a large demand for agricultural inputs and implements.

(*b*) **Jallianwala Bagh Tragedy:** On April 13, 1919, a public meeting was held in the Jallianwala Bagh of Amritsar to protest against the arrest of two nationalist leaders, Satya Pal and Dr. Saifuddin Kitchlew. However, a British military officer, General Dyer came there with his platoon. Without giving a warning, he ordered his troops to fire on the unarmed assembly. About a thousand people were killed and several thousand injured. The massacre aroused the fury of the Indian people which was replied with further brutalities by the government.

(*c*) **India's Moon Mission:** India's first mission to the moon Chandrayaan-I began on October 22, 2008 when Indian Moon rocket PSLV C11 blasted off at 6.22 a.m. and placed Chandrayaan into temporary orbit around earth in just 18 minutes. With this India becomes the 6th country to launch Moon Mission. In a major blow to India's maiden mission to the moon, the Indian Space Research Organisation (ISRO) abruptly lost contact with Chandrayaan-1 at 01.30 a.m. on August 29, 2009. This means no command can be given to the spacecraft and no data, including images of the moon's surface, are being received from it. The Chandrayaan-1 mission has come to an end in ten months instead of its slated life of two years. The spacecraft had completed 312 days in orbit, making more than 3,400 orbits around the moon and sent back more than 70,000 images of the lunar surface, which provided breathtaking views of lunar mountains and craters, especially craters in the permanently shadowed areas of the moon's polar region. It also collected data on the chemical and mineral content of the moon's soil. ISRO claimed that the mission had met most of its scientific objectives.

(*d*) **Food Chain:** The food (or energy) can be transferred from one organism to the other through food chains. Plants are the producers of food which is eaten up by a herbivores (animals consuming plants only) or an omnivores (animals consuming plants as well as animals). These animals may in turn by eaten up by a carnivores (animals eating meat only). Finally, a carnivore may be eaten up by a larger carnivore. This is how a food chain moves, representing unidirectional transfer of energy.

(*e*) **Right to Education:** The Government of India by Constitutional (86th Amendment) Act, 2002 had added a new Article 21 A, which provides that the state shall provide free and compulsory education to all children of the age 6 to 14 years as the state may by law determine." And further strengthened this Article 21A by adding clause (K) to Article 51-A which provides—"who is a parent or guardian to provide opportunities for education to his child or ward between the age 6 and 14 years." The government schools shall provide free education to all the children and the schools will be managed by school management committees. Private schools shall admit at least 25% of the children in their school without any fee. The National commission for elementary education shall be constituted to monitor all aspects of elementary education including quality.

The Bill seeks to make access to education more equitable. Vetting of students and parents, and demands for arbitrary capitation fees to secure admission to public schools will be prescribed under the legislation which obliges private schools to make a quarter of their places available to disadvantaged children on a non-fee paying basis. It mandates school management committees to take charge of neighbourhood schools. It also speaks of a common board that will do away with the differential educational standards in the country.

(*f*) **Smt. Pratibha Patil:** Smt. Pratibha Patil, the 13th President of India is the first woman and first Maharashtrian to hold this post.

She born on December 19, 1934 in Nadgaon and did her schooling from R.R. School Jalgaon. After getting the Post Graduate Degree in Arts from M.J. College Jalgaon, she obtained law degree from Government College Mumbai.

A trained lawyer, Pratibha Patil joined politics at the age of 27 and won her first election for MLA from Jalgaon in 1962. Later she handled the various portfolios in state government and also became the Deputy chairman of the Rajya Sabha from 1986-88. Finally she was swon in the President on July 25, 2007 and her tenure ended on July 25, 2012

(*g*) **Wildlife Conservation in India:** To the utter dismay of the entire world, the wildlife is being destroyed at a very quick pace. Two reasons can be cited for this destruction: (a) natural reasons; and (b) human reasons. Although both these types of reasons are responsible for the destruction of the wild life, yet natural reasons have proved to be less harmful than human reasons. In the present times (starting from the seventeenth century to date), nearly 120 species of mammals (who were birds) have become extinct. The list of those birds, who became extinct during the past 200 years, includes Dodo (of Mauritius), Sarcohayenkera (of Florida), Avetopickete (of South America), Migratorius (of the pigeon category) and Panthera Leo Melenochitus (of Florida).

According to a report by the UNO, nearly 10,000 species (of the total 1,30,000 species of all the wild animals of the world) are either extinct or on the verge of being extinct.

For protecting wildlife, the efforts of the government would have to be coupled with the process of enlightening all the sections of Indian society. We will have to protect the silent, harmless wild animals from nature and poachers.

Previous Paper (Solved)

Sainik School Exam, 2010

(Class-IX)

PAPER—I : Mathematics and Science

1. If $\sqrt{2401} = \sqrt{7^x}$, then find the value of x.
2. Solve $(-216 \times 729)^{1/3}$.
3. Find the value of $\left(x^{a-b}\right)^c \times \left(x^{b-c}\right)^a \times \left(x^{c-a}\right)^b$.
4. If $(x-y) = 6$ and $xy = 1$, then find the value of $x^3 - y^3$.
5. Divide $(38x - 8x^2 - 35)$ by $(4x - 5)$.
6. If $(x-1)$ is the HCF of (x^2-1) and $px^2 - q(x+1)$, then prove that $p = 2q$.
7. If a is prime number, then find the HCF of a and $(a+1)$.
8. Find the value of x, if $25x - 19 - [3 - (4x - 5)] = 3x - (6x - 5)$
9. The sum of two numbers is 11 and their product is 30, then find the numbers.
10. Two numbers are in the ratio 3 : 5. If 9 be subtracted from each, then they are in the ratio of 12 : 23. Find the second number.
11. If 11% of a number exceeds 7% of the same by 18, the number is
    A. 300 B. 450
    C. 350 D. 370
12. 50% of a% of b is 75% of b% of c. Find the value of c.
13. By selling sugar at ₹ 11.16 per kg, a man losses 7%. To gain 7%, it must be sold (per kg) at
    A. ₹ 11.24 B. ₹ 12.84
    C. ₹ 14.64 D. ₹ 13.24
14. The simple interest on ₹ 1300 at the rate of 5% per annum for 146 days is
    A. ₹ 38 B. ₹ 26
    C. ₹ 48 D. ₹ 39
15. Find the compound interest on ₹ 100000 compounded quarterly for 9 months at the rate of 4% per annum.
16. 15 boys earn ₹ 900 in 5 days, how much will 20 boys earn in 7 days?
17. Pipe A can fill a tank in 45 h and pipe B can fill it in 36 h. If both the pipes are opened in the empty tank. In how many hours will it be full?
18. A boat goes 40 km upstream in 8 h and a distance of 36 km downstream in 6 h. Find the speed of the boat in standing water (in km/h).
19. Find the value of 'a'

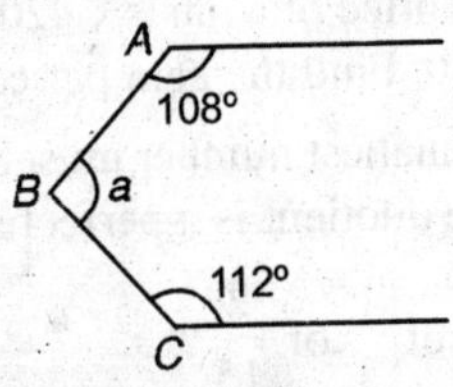

20. In figure, $AD \| EF \| BC$, if $EB = 2AE$ and $DF = 1$ cm, find the length of FC.

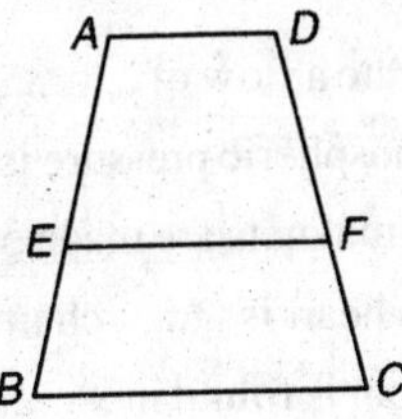

21. In the given figure, find the measure of all interior angle of triangle.

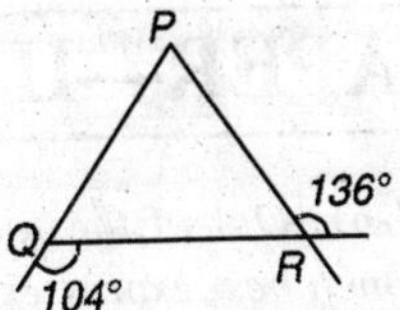

22. Find the area of an equilateral triangle having the length of side 10 cm.

23. Find the length of the diagonal of a rectangle whose sides are 12 cm and 5 cm.

24. $ABCD$ is a rhombus, if $\angle ADB = 50°$, find all angles of rhombus.

25. Find the value of $x°$ in the given figure.

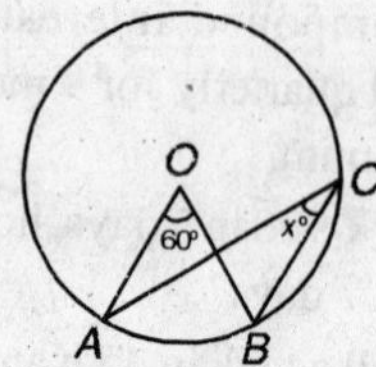

26. In a cyclic quadrilateral $ABCD$, if $\angle B - \angle D = 60°$, then the measure of the smaller of the two is
A. 60° B. 40°
C. 38° D. 30°

27. Find the median of the following data.
13, 15, 11, 9, 7, 16, 5, 8

28. If the cost price of a fan is ₹ 420 and its selling price ₹ 450. Find the gain per cent.

29. By what smallest number must 882 be divided so that the quotient is a perfect square?

0. What part of $\frac{1}{3}$ of $\frac{2}{15}$?

5. On joule is equal to .... arg.

32. The wave theory of light was propounded by ....

33. Current is rate a flow of ....

34. Unit of atmospheric pressure is ....

35. Permanent magnets are made of ....

36. The human heart is .... chambered.

37. Haemoglobin is found in ....

38. The main constituents of human skeleton is ....

39. The purest form of carbon is ....

40. Water gas is a mixture of ....

41. What type of force acts on a car moving round a curve?
A. Centifugal force B. Centripetal force
C. Cohesive force D. All of these

42. Two bulbs, 60 W and 120 W, are connected in series by AC main which bulb will glow brighter.
A. Bulb of 60 W B. Bulb of 120 W
C. Both equal D. None of these

43. Photochemical reactions takes place in presence of
A. heat B. light radiation
C. water D. air

44. The nucleus of hydrogen contains
A. one proton and one neutron
B. on proton and no neutron
C. two protons and one neutron
D. two protons and two neutrons

45. The largest gland in the human body is the
A. Liver B. Pancreas
C. Gastric D. Thyroid

46. It is easy to swim in the water of sea as compare to the water of a river.

47. What is the spectrum of light?

48. What is intensity of magnetic field?

49. Write a short note on Bio-gas.

50. What is glass-fibres?

51. Define the pesticides.

52. What are the thermosetting polymers?

53. What are the steps of cell divison?

54. Name the enzyme responsible for forming curd from milk?

55. What do you mean by balanced diet?

PAPER—II : Language and Social Studies

Directions (Q. 1-6): Out of the four alternatives, choose the one which best expresses the meaning of the given word.

1. DETRIMENTAL
A. deplorable B. fundamental
C. harmful D. disgraceful

2. COLOSSAL
A. gigantic B. colourful
C. beautiful D. fantastic

3. STUBBORN
A. timid B. arrogant
C. adamant D. angry

4. INVARIABLE
A. usual B. universal
C. constant D. similar

5. INDICTMENT
A. revelation B. acquittal
C. refusal D. accusation

6. DULCET
A. sweet B. dull
C. hard D. sour

Directions (Q. 7-12): Choose the word opposite in meaning to the given word.

7. EPHEMERAL
A. eternal B. transitory
C. mortal D. temporal

8. LATENT
A. unspoken B. later
C. implicit D. obvious

9. MONOTONOUS
A. disastrous B. terrifying
C. terrible D. interesting

10. OBSCENE
A. disobedient B. decent
C. dislocate D. cautious

11. FLOURISH
A. perish B. degenerate
C. decay D. dismiss

12. CONFORM
A. differ B. reject
C. question D. ignore

Directions (Q. 13-22): Sentences are given with blanks to be filled in with an appropriate and suitable word. Four alternatives are suggested for each question. Choose the correct alternative out of the four.

13. We warned her .... the danger.
A. from B. about
C. against D. of

14. We all laughed .... the affair.
A. over B. about
C. for D. on

15. The chairman, as well as the members .... to blame for this misfortune.
A. are B. were
C. is D. has

16. By .... united struggle, we may achieve success.
A. a B. an
C. the D. None of these

17. She feared that she ....
A. will fail B. may fail
C. might have fail D. would fail

18. He is the most generous man, I .... him for a long time.
A. knew B. have known
C. know D. had known

19. The sudden change in his behaviour came as a surprise to me, I began ....
A. to cut a sorry figure
B. to smell a rat
C. to turn a new leaf
D. to blow hot and cold

20. The streets are lighted .... electricity.
A. with B. by
C. on D. in

21. Homeopathic treatment, they say, cuts .... the need for operation and risk from surgery.
A. off B. out
C. down D. away

22. My friends fail to see why I should ride the .... horse just because I have won a prize.
A. great B. good
C. big D. high

Directions (Q. 23-28): Groups of four words are given. In each group, one word is wrongly spelt. Find the wrongly spelt word.

23. A. metaphor B. expletive
C. allegary D. parody

24. A. neurosurgeon B. homoeopath
C. bureaucrat D. veterinary

25. A. accumulate B. challenge
C. beginning D. tolerant

26. A. peruse B. persuade
C. persuit D. pursue

27. A. waitage B. baggage
C. luggage D. village

28. A. receive B. conceive
C. perceive D. decieve

Directions (Q. 29-34): In the following questions, choose that part of the sentence which has an error. If there is no error, choose (D).

29. She was running (A) / a very high fever (B) / and thus her mother takes (C) / her to the doctor. No error (D)

30. He talked on the phone (A) / for hours together (B) / who really irriated (C) / her to the doctor. No error (D)

31. Although his speech (A) / was not very clearly (B) / everyone understood the underlying meaning. (C) / No error (D)

32. Despite working (A) / very hard, he (B) / failed to achieve the desiring results. (C) / No error (D)

33. He was very excited (A) / about go to (B) / the park with (C)/his younger brother. No error (D)

34. Saddened by (A) / the sudden demise of (B) / his favourite pet, he decided not to go to the party. (C) / No error (D)

Directions (Q. 35-40) : Out of the four alternatives, choose the one which can be substituted for the given words/sentence.

35. A government by officials
A. Oligarchy B. Aristocracy
C. Plutocracy D. Bureaucracy

36. One who walks in sleep
A. Somniloquist B. Egoist
C. Somnambulist D. Altruist

37. Commencement of adjacent words with the same letter
A. Pun B. Alliteration
C. Transferred epithet D. Oxymoron

38. Careful in the spending of money, time etc
A. Punctual B. Economical
C. Miserly D. Calculative

39. Reproducing or memorizing word for word
A. Verbatim B. Verbose
C. Verbiage D. Verbalism

40. That which cannot be captured
A. Untakable B. Ungrippable
C. Impregnable D. Slippery

Directions (Q. 41-45): Read the following passage carefully and answer the questions given bewlo it.

"The beauty of the Japanese landscape is that it conveys philosophical messages through each feature. The use of curving pathways rather than straight lines, for instance. This feature springs from the belief that only evil travels in straight lines, good forces tend to wander. Then, odd numbers of plants on trees are used in these gardens because these numbers are considered auspicious. Even, the plants used are symbolic. For example, the Cyprus represents longevity and the bamboo symbolisms abundance", says Sadhana Roy Chaudhary.

In Japan, nature is said to be so closely intertwined with human life that parents actually plant a sapling in their garden when a child is born in the family, letting the growth of the child coincide with the growth of the plant.

41. They prefer curving pathways because
A. they are inauspicious
B. they can walk easily
C. they stumble over straight ones
D. good spirits walk on them

42. 'Abundance' means
A. long life B. happiness
C. plenty D. permanent

43. The Japanese parents plant a sapling at the time of birth of a child because
A. it is auspicious to plant a sapling
B. it is closely associated with the growth of the child
C. it gives longevity to the child
D. it gives happiness to the child

44. According to the passage, the Japanese are
A. superstitious
B. philosophical
C. lovers of nature
D. lovers of numerology

45. The Japanese pathways tend to be
A. symbolic B. beautiful
C. curved D. straight

Directions (Q. 46-50): Make meaningful sentences of the jumbled words for each of the following questions.

46. Saw, lion, he, away, and, he, a, fled.
47. Should, hard, to, you, work, achieve, goal, your.
48. The, disappeared, dog, sun, rose, and, the.
49. Yet, poor, is, trustworthy, he, is he.
50. Will, more, one, and, you, it, try, achieve.

Directions (Q. 51-55): Rewrite the following sentences as directed.

51. When I saw her, she was not singing a song. (Make Affirmative)
52. They were playing cards. (Make Interrogative)
53. I had not played a match. (Make Affirmative)
54. I had already visited Agra. (Make Interrogative)
55. She will wait for me. (Make Interrogative)

Directions (Q. 56-60): Change the following from direct to indirect speech.

56. They say to Ram, "We will go to Jaipur."
57. He said to Hina, "I like you."
58. He said to her, "What do you want?"
59. Ram said to me, "Have a glass of milk?"
60. She said to me, "Do come again."

Directions (Q. 61-65): Change the following sentences into passive voice.

61. She is helping the students.
62. Ram is making tea.
63. Is he writing a letter?
64. Why do you write a letter?
65. Please open the door.

66. Write a letter to the Health officer of your city complaining about the insanitary conditions in your locality.
67. Write an essay in about 250 words on 'Violence in Society.'
68. Vishnu Sharma wrote Panchtantra and ....
69. Amoghvarsha was a famous king of ....
70. Buddha belonged to small gana known as the .... gana.
71. Kalinga was conquered by Ashoka in ....
72. The fourth Buddhist council was held by ....
73. Upanishads are books on ....
74. .... veda is divided into 'white' and 'black' parts.
75. The large Shiva temple at Thanjaver was built by ....
76. Decimal system was introduced by ....
77. The phrase 'Light of Asia' is attributed to ....
78. The title 'Raja' was given to Ram Mohan Roy by ....
79. Akbar defeated Mewar's Rana Pratap Singh in the battle of Haldighati in ....
80. .... wrote a book 'Fatuhat Firozshahi.'
81. .... built the fortified city of 'Tughlaqabad' and made it his capital.
82. The festival of Nauroz was started by .... in Delhi sultanate.
83. .... died while playing chaugan.
84. Timur invaded India during the reign of ....
85. Rana Kumbha of Mewar built the famous 'Kirti Stambh' to commermorate his victory against ....
86. Al beruni came to India with ....
87. 'Adhai-Din-Ka-Jhonpara', built by Qutubuddin Aibak, is located in ....
88. 'Biwi Ka Maqbara' is the tomb of ....
89. Brahmo samaj was founded by .... in ....
90. Communist party was founded in 1921 by ....
91. The headquarters of Ghadar party was at ....

92. J.L. Nehru described .... as "we are provided with a car, all breaks and no engine."

93. In Bengal, the headquarters of East India Company was located at ....

94. Hyder Ali established his rule in Mysore by over throwing ....

95. The first Governer-General of India was appointed under the provisions of the Act of ....

96. .... prominently fought for and got widow remarriage legalized.

97. .... is called the 'Father of Indian Renaissance.'

98. Rani Lakshmi Bai died fighting the British in the battle of ....

99. .... gave the slogan 'Inquilab Zindabad.'

100. .... is also referred to as the 'Red planet.'

101. Brightest star outside our solar system is ....

102. Fastest revolution in solar system is of ....

103. .... rotates backward (clockwise) unlike other planets.

104. .... is the densest of all plants.

105. .... is the nearest position of earth to sun.

106. The Earth is divided into .... longitudinal zones.

107. The Earth's snape is very close to an ....

108. Water vapour present in the air is known as ....

109. .... solidified from magna and lava.

110. Carbon dioxide is largely responsible for the .... effect.

111. .... determines the angle of inclination of solar rays.

112. Air pressure is measured with the help of ....

113. The cool air, off the high plateaus and ice fields draining into the valley is called ....

114. .... is the longest highway of India.

115. .... is the biggest buyer of iron-ore from India accounting for about $\frac{3}{4}$th of India's total exports.

116. .... is the longest peninsular river of India.

117. .... is popularly known as the roof of the world.

118. .... is the highest Himalayan peak in India.

119. Indian constitution was completed on ....

120. In Emergency, fundamental rights are ....

121. Right to Constitutional Remedies makes Fundamental Rights ....

122. Constitution was passed by the Constituent Assembly of India on ....

123. .... is the leader of the Lok Sabha.

124. The Chairman and other members of the UPSC are appointed by the ....

125. The President nominates .... MPs to the Rajya Sabha.

126. .... decides whether a bill is an ordinary bill or a money bill.

127. A resolution seeking the removal of the Vice-President can originate only in ....

128. A judge of High Court continues his office till .... years of age.

129. The first high court to be established in India was ....

130. President's rule can be imposed under Art ..... .

131. .... is considered the Father of Indian Economic Reforms.

132. A broad gauge railway is .... metre wide.

133. The first train was flagged from .... to .... station in India.

134. Study of universe is called ....

135. 14th November is celebrated as ....

136. Fundamental Right is borrowed from .... constitution.

137. .... was the first woman to become Prime Minister of a country.

138. Arjun is the name given to ....

139. The first bank established in India was ....

140. The author in 'Indica' is ....

141. The first woman film star nominated to the Rajya Sabha was ....

142. Gandhi-Irwin pact resulted in the ending of ....

143. The government of India introduce new economic policy in ....

144. .... founded the All-India Harijan Sangh.

145. The full name of NCERT is ....

146. A period of 100 years is called ....

147. National Rural Development Institute is situated at ....

EXPLANATORY ANSWERS

PAPER—I : Mathematics & Science

1. $\sqrt{2401} = \sqrt{7^x}$

$\Rightarrow \quad 2401 = 7^x$

$\Rightarrow \quad 7^4 = 7^x$

$\therefore \quad x = 4.$

2. $(-216 \times 729)^{1/3}$

$= (-216)^{1/3} \times (729)^{1/3}$

$= (6 \times 6 \times 6)^{1/3} \times (\underline{3 \times 3 \times 3} \times \underline{3 \times 3 \times 3})^{1/3}$

$= 6 \times 3 \times 3$

$= 54.$

3. $(x^{a-b})^c \times (x^{b-c})^a \times (x^{c-a})^b$

$= x^{ac-bc} \times x^{ba-ca} \times x^{cb-ab}$

$= x^{ac-bc+ba-ca+cb-ab}$

$= x^0 = 1.$

4. $\because (x - y) = 6$

On squaring both sides, we get

$(x-y)^2 = 6^2$

$x^2 + y^2 - 2xy = 36 \quad$ (given $xy = 1$)

$x^2 + y^2 - 2 \times 1 = 36$

$x^2 + y^2 = 36 + 2 = 38$

$\because \quad x^3 - y^3 = (x-y)(x^2 + y^2 + xy)$

$= 6(38 + 1) = 6 \times 39 = 234.$

5.

$$\begin{array}{r|l} & -2x+7 \\ 4x-5 & -8x^2+38x-35 \\ & -8x^2+10x \\ & \;\;+ \quad\; - \\ \hline & 28x-35 \\ & 28x-35 \\ & - \quad + \\ \hline & \times \end{array}$$

Quotient $= -2x + 7$.

6. Since, $(x - 1)$ is the HCF of given expressions, so it will be

$\therefore p \times (1)^2 - q(1 + 1) = 0$

$p = 2q.$

7. Since, prime number has only two factors 1 and the number itself.

So, HCF $(a, a + 1) = 1$.

8. Given, $25x - 19 - [3 - (4x - 5)]$

$= 3x - (6x - 5)$

$\therefore \quad 25x - 19 + 4x - 8 = -3x + 5$

$\Rightarrow \quad 29x + 3x = 5 + 27$

$\Rightarrow \quad 32x = 32$

$\Rightarrow \quad x = 1.$

9. Let the numbers be x and $11 - x$.

Since, $\quad x(11 - x) = 30$ (given)

$\Rightarrow \quad x^2 - 11x + 30 = 0$

$\Rightarrow \quad (x-5)(x-6) = 0$

$\Rightarrow \quad x = 5,6.$

10. Let the numbers be $3x$ and $5x$.

Then, $\quad \dfrac{3x-9}{5x-9} = \dfrac{12}{23}$

$\Rightarrow \quad 23(3x - 9) = 12(5x - 9)$

$\Rightarrow \quad x = 11$

$\therefore$ Second number $= 5x = 5 \times 11 = 55.$

11. (B) According to question,

11% of x – 7% of x = 18

$\Rightarrow$ 4% of x = 18

$$x = \frac{18 \times 100}{4}$$

$x = 450.$

12. $\therefore \frac{50}{100} \times \frac{a}{100} \times b = \frac{75}{100} \times \frac{b}{100} \times c$

$$c = \frac{50}{75} a$$

$= 0.667a.$

13. (B) Let CP of sugar per kg be ₹x.

$\therefore$ 93% of $x = 11.16$

$\Rightarrow x = \frac{11.16 \times 100}{93} = 12$

So, CP = ₹12 per kg

SP = 107% of ₹12

$= \frac{107}{100} \times 12 =$ ₹12.84.

14. (B) SI $= \frac{1300 \times 5 \times 146}{365 \times 100} =$ ₹26.

15. $r = 4\%$ for quarterly, $r = \frac{4}{4} = 1\%$

$$t = \frac{9 \times 4}{12} = 3 \text{ years}$$

$$A = P\left(1 + \frac{r}{100}\right)^t = 100000\left(1 + \frac{1}{100}\right)^3$$

$= 100000 \times \frac{101}{100} \times \frac{101}{100} \times \frac{101}{100}$

$= 103030.1$

C.I. = A − P = 103030.1 − 100000

= ₹ 3030.1

16. Since, 15 boys earn in 5 days = ₹ 900

One boy earn in one day = ₹ $\frac{900}{15 \times 5}$

= ₹12

$\Rightarrow$ 20 boys earn in 7 days = ₹12 × 20 × 7

= ₹1680.

17. Pipe A filled in 1 h $= \frac{1}{45}$

Pipe B filed in 1 h $= \frac{1}{36}$

Pipe $(A + B)$ filled together in 1 h $= \frac{1}{45} + \frac{1}{36}$

$= \frac{1}{20}$

Hence, the tank will be fill in 20 h.

18. Speed of boat in upstream $= \frac{40}{8}$

= 5 km/h

Speed of boat in downstream $= \frac{36}{6}$

= 6 km/h

$\therefore$ Speed of boat in still water $= \frac{1}{2}(5+6)$

= 5.5 km/h.

19. Here, $\angle A + \angle C + a = 360°$

$\Rightarrow 108° + 112° + a = 360°$

$\Rightarrow a = 360° - 220°$

$\Rightarrow a = 140°.$

20. Since, $AD \parallel EF \parallel BC$ (given) and AB and DC are transversal lines.

$\therefore \frac{AE}{EB} = \frac{DF}{FC}$

[by using intercept property]

$\Rightarrow \frac{AE}{2AE} = \frac{1.5}{FC}$

$\Rightarrow \frac{1}{2} = \frac{1.5}{FC}$

$\Rightarrow FC = 3\text{cm}.$

21. Now, $\angle R = 180° - 136° = 44°$

$\angle Q = 180° - 104° = 76°$

$\angle P = 180° - (44° + 76°)$

$= 60°.$

22. Let ABC is an equilateral triangle with each side of length 10 cm.

Area of equilateral triangle $= \frac{\sqrt{3}}{4}(\text{side})^2$

$= \frac{\sqrt{3}}{4}(10\times10) = 25\sqrt{3}\text{ cm}^2$.

23. Length of diagonal $= \sqrt{12^2+5^2}$

$= \sqrt{144+25}$

$= \sqrt{169}$

$= 13$ cm.

24. In ΔABD

Now, $AD = AB$

$\angle ADB = \angle ABD = 50°$

and $\angle ABD + \angle ADB + \angle BAD = 180°$

$\Rightarrow \angle BAD = 180° - 100° = 80°$

$\angle A = \angle C = 80°$

(opposite angles of 11gm)

In BCD,

$x + x + 80 = 180°$

$\Rightarrow 2x = 100$

$\Rightarrow x = 50°$

$\therefore \angle CDB = \angle CBD = 50°$

and $\angle A = \angle C = 80°$

$\angle B = \angle D = 100°$

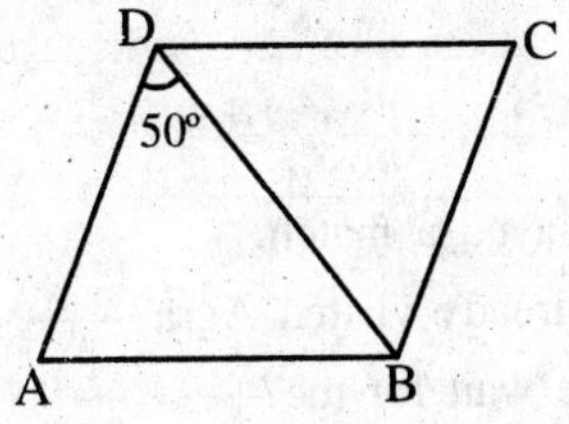

25. Here, $\angle AOB = 2(\angle ACB)$

Central angle = 2 × circumference angle by same are

$\Rightarrow 60° = 2x$

$\therefore x = 30°$.

26. (A) Since $\angle B + \angle D = 180°$ (*i*)

$\angle B - \angle D = 60°$ (*ii*)

From (*i*) and (*ii*)

$\Rightarrow \angle B = 120°$ and $\angle D = 60°$.

27. Arranging the given data in ascending order, we get

5, 7, 8, 9, 11, 13, 15, 16

Here, $n = 8$ which is even.

$\therefore$ Median = average of 4th and 5th values

$= \frac{9+11}{2} = 10$.

28. Total gain = Selling Price – Cost Price

$= 450 - 420$

$=$ ₹30

$\therefore$ Gain per cent $= \frac{30}{420}\times100$

$= 7\frac{1}{7}\%$.

29. LCM of 882 = 2 × 3 × 3 × 7 × 7

So, 882 is divided by 2, to make quotient a complete square.

30. Let x part of $\frac{1}{3}$ is $\frac{2}{15}$.

Then, $x\times\frac{1}{3} = \frac{2}{15}$

$\Rightarrow x = \frac{2}{15}\times3$

$\Rightarrow x = \frac{2}{5}$.

31. 10^7 **32.** Huygen

33. Charge **34.** Bar

35. Steel **36.** Four

37. Blood **38.** Calcium

39. Diamond **40.** CO, H_2

41. (B) **42.** (A)

43. (C) **44.** (B)

45. (A)

46. The density of sea water is greater than that to the river water, so less volume of water is replaces for swimming.

47. When a beam of white light is passed through a glass prism, the beam of several colours is formed on a white screen. It is called spectrum of white light.

48. The intensity of magnetic field is defined as the force experienced by a unit north pole placed at a point in the field. The unit H is Amp. term/metre. The direction of H is the same as the direction of B and is related as $B = \mu H$.

Where μ is called the magnetic permeability.

49. The gaseous mixture obtained by the degradation of animal and plant wastes by anaerobic micro-organisms in the presence of water is called bio-gas.

50. Glass drawn or blown into extremely fine fibres that retain the tensile strength of glass while yet being flexible. These fibres are called glass fibres.

51. These are the substances used to kill animals responsible for economic damage to crops and stored cereals.

52. The polymers which do not soften on heating and retain their original shape are known as thermosetting polymers. *eg,* bakelite.

53. The three steps of cell division are given below
(i) Replication of genome
(ii) Karyo kinesis (division of nucleus)
(iii) Cyto Kinesis (division of cytoplasm)

54. The name of enzyme responsible for forming curd from milk is rennin.

55. Balanced diet contains all essential components in the optimum proportion and quantity for maintaining the various body activities and development. 60% carbohydrates, 25% fats, 15% proteins and vitamins, minerals, roughage and water are various components of a balanced diet.

PAPER—II : Language and Social Studies

1	2	3	4	5	6	7	8	9	10
C	A	C	C	D	A	C	B	C	A
11	**12**	**13**	**14**	**15**	**16**	**17**	**18**	**19**	**20**
A	A	C	D	B	B	C	B	A	A
21	**22**	**23**	**24**	**25**	**26**	**27**	**28**	**29**	**30**
C	A	C	D	A	A	C	A	C	B
31	**32**	**33**	**34**	**35**	**36**	**37**	**38**	**39**	**40**
B	C	B	D	D	C	B	C	B	A
41	**42**	**43**	**44**	**45**					
B	C	C	D	D					

46. He saw a lion and the fled away.

47. You should work hard to achieve your goal.

48. The sun rose and the dog disappeared.

49. He is poor yet he is trustworthy.

50. One more try and you will achieve it.

51. When I saw her, she was singing a song.

52. Where they playing cards?

53. I had played a match.

54. Had I already visited Agra?

55. Will she wait for me?

56. They tell Ram that they will go to Jaipur.

57. He told Hina that he liked her.

58. He asked her what she wanted.

59. Ram asked her what she wanted.

60. She requested me to come again.

61. The students are being helped by her.

62. Tea is making made by Ram.

63. Is a letter being written by him?

64. Why is a letter written by you?

65. You are requested to open the door.

66. To,

The Health Officer,

Rampur.

June 15, 2010

Sir,

Reg. : Insanitary Conditions In Arera Colony I, on behalf of the residents of Arera Colony, would like to bring to your notice the insanitary conditions prevailing in our locality.

Once, a posh colony, now Arera Colony is a store-house of dirt and garbage. The heaps of rubbish are visible at every step. The drains are silted and overflow with foul smelling water. Even sewers are overflowing emitting foul smell. In the absence of dustbins, the residents throw the garbage and domestic rubbish on the roads. Even the educated residents are careless of the sanitary needs of the locality. The streets are often littered with domestic refuse.

The roads are in very bad conditions. During rainy season, they are source of potential danger for accidents. The manholes are without covers. The rain water collected in the depressions of the roads breed mosquitoes. There is every danger of breaking out of infectious diseases. One has to be wary of going out at night. Many accidents have taken place causing loss of life and limb.

We have brought these conditions to the notice of the Sanitary Inspector again and again. But, he has not taken even a single step. Sweepers are hardly to be seen on their duty. The absence of the sweepers add to the sufferings of the residents.

In view of the above, you are requested to visit the locality and take remedial steps to improve the sanitary conditions. Rainy season is likely to set in within this month. We shall be highly obliged if you could take early action in the matter.

Thanking you,

Your faithfully,

XYZ

67. Violence in Society

Violence in a civilized society is quite a common feature the world over. There is no denying the fact that the cause of all violence in civilized society is loss of faith in God and human values. This loss of faith has dehumanised man to such an extent that he is ready to injure, maim and kill anybody. There are many kinds of violence in the society. The violence is spreading widely in every area of society. There is violence in the form of civil war, bomb blasts, dacoity, rapes, murders, abduction etc.

Communal riots and ethnic violence have taken deep roots in Indian society. The whole nation is at the mercy of politicians for their selfish gains.

They take advantage of religious sentiments of people to build up their vote banks. The rallies are held by the leaders to show their strength and might to the nation. This has given rise to religious fundamentalism and militancy.

Today our society is facing a new form of menace. It arises from criminal politician nexus. It is hard to find a politician without a criminal link. This nexus has come to infect bureaucracy as well. In fact, bureaucrats are always at the service of the politicians to gain their own interest. As a result of this nexus among criminals, politicians and bureaucrats, the failure of police force in controlling crime and violence in Indian society is inevitable.

Worst of all, there has been a rise in the activities of the terrorists. The killing of the minorities in Kashmir is a daily news. The terrorists try to terrorize the people by indulging in bomb blasts, killings and using very powerful weapon sent by Pakistan and China.

Both Pakistan and China have formed a clandestine nexus to destroy the stability of the nation. It is high time, we should realise that peace is very important for the economic prosperity of the people. There is no dearth of laws to deal with such anti-social elements. In fact, there is a lack of political will and determination to eleminate such unlawful elements.

68. Gupta **69.** Rashtra Kutas
70. Sakhya **71.** 261 BC
72. Kanishka **73.** Philosophy
74. Yajur **75.** Rajraja Chola-I
76. Bhaskara **77.** Buddha
78. Akbar-II **79.** 1576
80. Firoz Shah Tughlaq
81. Ghiyas-ud-din Tughlaq
82. Balban **83.** Qutub-ud-din Aibak
84. Nasiruddin Mahmud
85. Malwa **86.** Mahmud Ghazni
87. Ajmer **88.** Aurangzeb's wife
89. Raja Ram Mohan Roy, 1828
90. MN Roy **91.** San Francisco
92. Government of India Act, 1935
93. Fort William **94.** Nanjaraj
95. 1833
96. Ishwar Chandra Vidyasagar
97. Raja Ram Mohan Roy
98. Kalpi **99.** Iqbal
100. Mars **101.** Sirius
102. Venus **103.** Venus
104. Earth **105.** Perihelion
106. 24 **107.** Oblate spheroid
108. Humidity **109.** Igneous rocks
110. Green house **111.** Latitude
112. Barometer **113.** Katabatic
114. NH-7 **115.** Japan
116. Godavary **117.** Pamir
118. Mt. Kanchenjunga
119. 26th November, 1949
120. Suspended **121.** Justiciable
122. November 26, 1949
123. Prime Minister **124.** President
125. 12 **126.** Speaker
127. Rajya Sabha **128.** 62
129. Allahabad High Court
130. 356 **131.** PV Narasimha Rao
132. 1,676 **133.** Bombay, Thane
134. Cosmology **135.** Children's day
136. USA Constitution
137. Sirimavo Bandaranaika
138. Tank
139. Punjab National Bank
140. Nicoloson
141. Meena Kumari
142. Civil disobedience
143. 1972
144. Dadabhai Naoroji
145. National Council of Educational Research and Training
146. Century **147.** Hyderabad

Previous Paper (Solved)

Sainik School Exam, 2009

(Class-IX)

PAPER—I : Mathematics and Science

1. As in the figure, O is the centre of the circle, with AB as diameter if $\angle AOC = 60^\circ$ then $\angle OCB$ is :

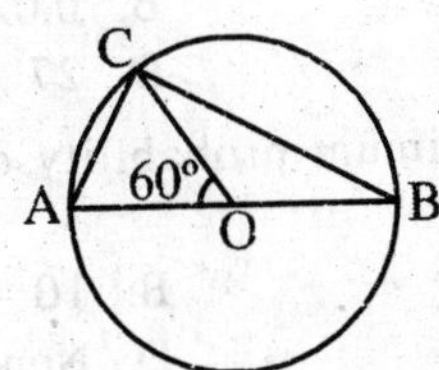

A. 50° B. 30°
C. 40° D. 60°

2. The angles of a quadrilateral are in the ratio 3 : 4 : 5 : 6, then one of the angles of the quadrilateral is :

A. 90° B. 105°
C. 100° D. None of these

3. The area of an equilateral triangle with one of its side 10 cm is :

A. $75\sqrt{3}$ B. $25\sqrt{3}$
C. $100\sqrt{3}$ D. $50\sqrt{3}$

4. One of the factors of the expression $3x^2 - 4x - 7$ is :

A. $x + 2$ B. $x - 2$
C. $x - 1$ D. $3x - 7$

5. Waheeda paid a sum of Rs. 3300 including VAT (Value Added Tax) of 10% for a cooler, price of cooler before VAT is :

A. Rs. 3000 B. Rs. 3600
C. Rs. 3630 D. Rs. 2700

6. The area of a trapezium with sum of parallel sides 24 cm and the distance between parallel sides, 9 cm is :

A. 182 B. 128
C. 108 D. 180

7. The quantity of milk in liters that can be stored in a cube with side 10 cm is :

A. 10 liters B. 20 liters
C. 1 liters D. None of these

8. When $7x^2 + 14xy + 21xy^2$ is divided by $7x$ then the remainder is :

A. $7x + 2xy + 3y^2$ B. $7x + 2y + 3y^2$
C. $x + 2y + 3y^2$ D. None of these

9. The mode of the data 3, 10, 4, 13, 4, 3, 12, 4, 6, 6, 3, 6, 4, 10 :

A. 3 B. 6
C. 4 D. None of these

10. The possible 'one's' digits of the square root of 998001 number is :

A. 3, 1 B. 2, 9
C. 1, 9 D. 1, 7

11. Area of a square with one side x is equal to the area of a triangle with base x. The altitude of the triangle is :

A. $2x$ B. x
C. $4x$ D. $\frac{x}{2}$

12. If $\left(\frac{-2}{3}\right)^3 \cdot \left(\frac{-2}{3}\right)^2 = \left(\frac{-2}{3}\right)^{2m-1}$ then the value of m is :

A. 3 B. 2
C. 1 D. 0

13. Expansion of $\left(2x - \frac{3}{x}\right)^2$ is :

A. $4x^2 - \frac{9}{x^2}$ B. $4x^2 + \frac{9}{x^2} - 6$
C. $4x^2 + \frac{9}{x^2} - 12$ D. None of these

14. Two numbers are in the ratio 5 : 3. If they differ by 18 then smaller number is :

A. 54 B. 27
C. 45 D. 35

15. The value of $\sqrt[3]{50653} - \sqrt{625}$ is :

A. 13 B. 27
C. 12 D. 15

16. The value of $x^3 - 8y^3 - 36xy - 216$, when $x = 2y + 6$ is :

A. 10 B. 1
C. 100 D. 0

17. Simplified form of $\left(\frac{x^6 y^{-5} z^{-3}}{x^{-6} y^5 z^{-3}}\right)^2$ is :

A. 1 B. $x^{22}y^{-20}z^{14}$
C. $x^{24}y^{-20}z^{12}$ D. $x^{26}y^{-20}z^{12}$

18. The volume of right circular cylinder of base diameter 6 cm and height 2.5 cm is : $\left(\text{use } \pi = \frac{22}{7}\right)$

A. $\frac{595}{7}$ cm^3 B. $\frac{395}{7}$ cm^3
C. $\frac{695}{7}$ cm^3 D. $\frac{495}{7}$ cm^3

19. The radius of base of a conical tent with volume 432π m^3 and height 9 m is :

A. 15 m B. 12 m
C. 18 m D. 14 m

20. Area of a rhombus whose diagonals are of lengths 10 cm and 8.2 cm is :

A. 82 cm^2 B. 48 cm^2
C. 44 cm^2 D. 41 cm^2

21. The simple interest for Rs. 9580.00 at 2.5% per annum for four years is :

A. 985 B. 958
C. 900 D. 980

22. Which of the following is a factor of $x^2 + 6x + 8$?

A. $x - 4$ B. $x - 2$
C. $x + 4$ D. None of these

23. For the expression $9x^2 + 18xy + 10y^2$, the term to be subtracted to make it a perfect square is:

A. $6y^2$ B. $2y^2$
C. y^2 D. None of these

24. The LCM of the expressions, $6x^3y^2, 3x^2y^3, 4x^2y^2$ and $12x^3y^3$, is :

A. $6x^3y^2$ B. $2x^2y^2$
C. $12x^3y^2$ D. None of these

25. The value of $(0.3)^3$:

A. 0.27 B. 0.027
C. 2.7 D. 27

26. The maximum probability of an event is always:

A. 100 B. 10
C. 1 D. None of these

27. Which of the following statement is false for a parallelogram?

A. Its opposite angles are equal
B. It has two pairs of opposite sides equal
C. Its diagonals bisect each other
D. None of these

28. The smallest number that must be subtracted from 62580 to obtain a perfect square is :

A. 180 B. 380
C. 170 D. 80

29. The compound interest on Rs. 12600 for 2 years at 10% per annum compounded annually is :

A. 1260 B. 2526
C. 2646 D. 1526

30. If $\frac{x+3}{2x+5} = \frac{4}{7}$ then the value of x is :

A. 2 B. –1
C. 1 D. –2

31. The value of $x^{5/7} \div x^{12/7}$ is :

A. $\frac{1}{x}$ B. $x^{1/17}$
C. x^{17} D. None of these

32. If $a + b + c = 0$, then the value of $a^3 + b^3 + c^3$ is:

A. $3(a + b + c)$ B. $3abc$
C. $3(ab + bc + ca)$ D. None of these

33. What is the total surface area of hemisphere in cm^2 whose radius is 10 cm ?

A. 300π B. 350π

C. 420 D. None of these

34. Which of the following number is a perfect cube?

A. 80000 B. 640000

C. 1000000 D. 12500

35. Which of the following is false ?

A. 0 is a rational number

B. 27, is a factor of 3

C. $\sqrt{225} = 15$

D. 7 is a factor of 56

36. If $p^2 - 6p + 7$ is divided by $(p - 1)$ the remainder will be :

A. Positive B. Zero

C. Negative D. None of these

37. A rectilinear figure is called closed when :

A. It has no free ends

B. It has all free ends

C. It has some free ends

D. None of these

38. The circumference of a circle is 3.14 m. Its area will be equal to :

A. 4π B. $\frac{\pi}{4}$

C. 314π D. None of these

39. The value of $(356)^2 - (355)^2$ is :

A. 1 B. 711

C. 611 D. 709

40. If $\frac{2x+3}{3x-2} = \frac{7}{4}$ then value of x is :

A. –2 B. 1

C. –1 D. 2

41. Divide $6x^4 - 5x^3 + 7x^2 + 13x - 5$ by $2x^2 - 3x + 5$. Also find the remainder.

42. Factorise the following :

(A) $a^4 + 2a^2b^2 + b^4 - 225$

(B) $4x^2 + 9y^2 + 25z^2 - 12xy + 30\,yz - 20zx$

43. Bansi has 3 times as many two-rupee coins as he has five-rupee coins. If he has in all a sum of Rs. 77, how many coins of each denomination does he have ?

44. Meenu bought two fans for Rs. 1200 each. She sold one at a loss of 5% and other at a profit of 10%. Find the selling price of each. Also find out the total profit or loss.

45. Kamla borrowed Rs. 26,400 from a Bank to buy a scooter at a rate of 15% p.a. compounded yearly. What amount will she pay at the end of 2 years and 4 months to clear the loan?

46. In a building there are 24 cylindrical pillars. The radius of each pillar is 28 cm and height is 4 m. Find the total cost of painting the curved surface area of all pillars at the rate of Rs. 8 per m^2.

47. A cuboid of length 44 cm, breadth 20 cm and height 10 cm is made up of modelling clay. A child reshapes it in the form of a cylinder with radius of base 20 cm. Find the height of the cylinder.

48. The marks of 30 students of class VIII, obtained in a test (out of 75), are given below—

42, 21, 50, 37, 42, 37, 38, 42, 49, 52, 38, 53, 57, 47, 29, 59, 51, 33, 17, 17, 39, 44, 42, 39, 14, 7, 27, 19, 54, 51.

Construct a grouped frequency table with class intervals of equal width. One of class interval being 30–40.

49. A closed box is made of thin sheet of metal. The dimensions of the box are 80 cm × 60 cm × 25 cm. ignoring the thickness of the metal sheet, find :

(i) the area of the sheet required to make the box in m^2.

(ii) the cost of metal sheet at the rate of Rs. 40 per m^2.

50. Simplify :

$(a + b)(2a - 3b + c) - (2a + 3b - c)(a - b)$.

51. A person is standing 5 m away in front of plain mirror. What will be the distance between him and the image?

52. Name two main defects of human eye.

53. What is electrolysis ? What are the components obtained after the electrolysis of water ?

54. List two places where oil refineries are located in our country.

55. What is acid rain?

56. Explain why Saucepan handles are made of thermosetting plastics?

57. What is the difference between Vector and Pathogen?

58. What are the roles of the following structures in human circulatory system?
(a) Pulmonary artery
(b) Aorta
(c) Pulmonary vein

59. What are differences between plant and animal cell?

60. What is Frictional Force? What are its advantages and disadvantages?

61. Describe Chemical properties of Metals and Non-metals, with reference to reaction with oxygen, water and acids.

62. What force is responsible for holding a satellite in its orbit around the earth?

63. Pitch of sound is determined by which factor of the vibrating body?

64. What is the nature of image formed by plain mirror?

65. Do all liqids conduct electricity?

66. What is the unit of pressure?

67. What is lightning of clouds ? List two precautions one must observe during Lightning.

68. What is Artificial Satellite? List some of its applications.

69. What are the different ways in which water gets contaminated?

70. What are the advantages of using CNG and LPG as fuels?

71. Choose the correct answer from the given options:
(a) The constituent of petroleum used for making ointments, candles, vaseline etc. is—
(i) Naptha
(ii) Bitumen
(iii) Gasoline
(iv) Paraffin wax
(b) Burning of fossil fuels is a major cause of—
(i) Water pollution (ii) Air pollution
(iii) Soil pollution (iv) Noise pollution
(c) Electric plugs and switches are made from .... plastics.
(i) Thermosetting (ii) Thermoplastics
(iii) Thermoelastic (iv) Thermodynamics
(d) Name the petroleum product used for surfacing of roads—
(i) Naptha
(ii) Bitumen
(iii) Gasoline
(iv) Paraffin wax
(e) A chemical process in which a substance reacts with oxygen to give off heat is—
(i) Smelting (ii) Combustion
(iii) Calcinations (iv) Explosion
(f) The following is an antibiotic—
(i) Sodium bicarbonate
(ii) Alcohol
(iii) Streptomycin
(iv) Yeast

72. Define Apiculture.

73. Define Endemic species.

74. Define Kharif crop with one example.

75. What is the full form of B.C.G. Vaccine?

76. Who discovered cell at first ?

77. What happens when Copper Sulphate reacts with Zinc ? Write chemical reaction in words.

78. What is the use of Insulin? Which disease is associated with it?

79. What are the differences between Viviparous and Oviparous with example?

80. What are the differences between Enzymes and Hormones?

81. What is Force ? What is SI Unit of Force? What are the effects of Force?

EXPLANATORY ANSWERS

1. (B) $\angle OCB = \angle OBC$ $[\because OB = OC]$
$= \angle ABC$
$= \frac{1}{2}\angle AOC$
$= \frac{1}{2}(60^\circ) = 30^\circ$

2. (C) Ratio in angles $= 3 : 4 : 5 : 6$
$\therefore$ Sum of ratios $= 3 + 4 + 5 + 6$
$= 18$
$\therefore$ I angle $= \frac{3}{18} \times 360$
$= 60^\circ$
II angle $= \frac{4}{18} \times 360$
$= 80^\circ$
III angle $= \frac{5}{18} \times 360$
$= 100^\circ$

3. (B) Area of equilateral $\Delta = \frac{\sqrt{3}}{4} \times (\text{side})^2$
$= \frac{\sqrt{3}}{4} \times 10 \times 10$
$= 25\sqrt{3}\ \text{cm}^2$

4. (D) $3x^2 - 4x - 7 = 3x^2 - (7 - 3)x - 7$
$= 3x^2 - 7x + 3x - 7$
$= x(3x - 7) + 1\,(3x - 7)$
$= (3x - 7)(x + 1)$

5. (A) $\because$ $100 + 10 = 110$
$\therefore$ Price of cooler before VAT
$= \frac{100}{110} \times 3300$
= Rs. 3000

6. (C) Area $= \frac{1}{2} \times 24 \times 9$
$= 12 \times 9 = 108\ \text{cm}^2$

7. (C) Quantity of milk $= 10 \times 10 \times 10\ \text{cm}^3$
$= 1000\ \text{cm}^3$
= 1 litre

8. (D) $\because$ Divident = Divisor × Quotient + Remainder
$\Rightarrow 7x^2 + 14xy + 21xy^2$
$= 7x \times (x + 2y + 3y^2) + 0$
$\therefore$ Reqd. Remainder = 0

9. (C)

x	Frequency
3	3
4	4
6	3
10	2
12	1
13	1

$\therefore$ Mode = 4

10. (C) $\because$ 'Ones' digit of the number 998001 = 1
$\therefore$ The possible one's digit of square root of the number = 1, 9

11. (A) $\because$ Area of square $= x^2$
$\therefore$ Altitude of the triangle $= 2 \times \frac{x^2}{x}$
$= 2x$

12. (A) $\because$ $\left(-\frac{2}{3}\right)^3 \times \left(-\frac{2}{3}\right)^2 = \left(-\frac{2}{3}\right)^{2m-1}$
$\Rightarrow \left(-\frac{2}{3}\right)^5 = \left(-\frac{2}{3}\right)^{2m-1}$
$\Rightarrow 2m - 1 = 5$
$\therefore m = 3$

13. (C) $\left(2x - \frac{3}{x}\right)^2 = 4x^2 + \frac{9}{x^2} - 2 \times 2x \times \frac{3}{x}$
$= 4x^2 + \frac{9}{x^2} - 12$

14. (B) Smaller number $= \dfrac{3 \times 18}{(5-3)}$

$= 27$

15. (C) $\sqrt[3]{50653} - \sqrt{625} = 37 - 25$

$= 12$

16. (D) $x^3 - 8y^3 - 36xy - 216$

$= (x)^3 - (2y)^3 - (6)^3 - 3\,(x)\,(2y)\,(6)$

$= (x - 2y - 6)\,(x^2 + 4y^2 + 36 + 2xy + 6x - 12xy)$

$= 0$ $[\because x - 2y - 6 = 0]$ because $x = 2y + 6$

17. (C) $\left(\dfrac{x^6 y^{-5} z^3}{x^{-6} y^5 z^{-3}}\right)^2$

$= (x^{12} y^{-10} z^6)^2$

$= x^{24} y^{-20} z^{12}$

18. (D) Volume of cylinder $= \dfrac{22}{7} \times 3 \times 3 \times 2.5$

$= \dfrac{495}{7}$ cm^3

19. (B) Let, the radius of conical tent be 'r'

$\because$ $\dfrac{1}{3}\pi \times r^2 \times 9 = 432\pi$

$\Rightarrow$ $r^2 = \dfrac{432\pi \times 3}{\pi \times 9} = 144$

$\therefore$ $r = 12$ m

20. (D) Area of the rhombus

$= \dfrac{1}{2}$ (Product of diagonals)

$= \dfrac{1}{2} \times 10 \times 8.2$

$= 41$ cm^2

21. (B) S.I. $= \dfrac{9580.00 \times 2.5 \times 4}{100}$

$= \dfrac{9580 \times 10}{100}$

$=$ Rs. 958

22. (C) $x^2 + 6x + 8 = x^2 + 4x + 2x + 8$

$= x\,(x + 4) + 2(x + 4)$

$= (x + 4)\,(x + 2)$

23. (C) $= 9x^2 + 18xy + 9y^2 = 9(x^2 + 2xy + y^2) + y^2$

$= 9(x + y)^2 + y^2$

$\therefore$ On subtracting y^2, the remainder will be perfect square.

24. (D) L.C.M. of $6x^3y^2$, $3x^2y^3$, $4x^2y^2$ and $12x^3y^3$

$= 12x^3y^3$

25. (B) $(0.3)^3 = 0.027$

26. (C) The maximum probability of an event is always $= 1$ (unity)

27. (D)

28. (D) $\because$ $62580 = 62500 + 80$

$= (250)^2 + 80$

$\therefore$ Reqd. number $= 80$

29. (C) C.I. $= 12600\left[\left(1 + \dfrac{10}{100}\right)^2 - 1\right]$

$= 12600\left(\dfrac{121}{100} - 1\right)$

$= 12600\dfrac{(121 - 100)}{100}$

$= 12600\left[\dfrac{21}{100}\right]$

$= \dfrac{12600 \times 21}{100}$

$=$ Rs. 2646

30. (C) $\because$ $\dfrac{x + 3}{2x + 5} = \dfrac{4}{7}$

$\Rightarrow$ $4(2x + 5) = 7(x + 3)$

$\Rightarrow$ $8x + 20 = 7x + 21$

$\Rightarrow$ $8x - 7x = 21 - 20$

$\Rightarrow$ $x = 1$

31. (A) $x^{5/7} \div x^{12/7} = x^{5/7 - 12/7}$

$= x^{\frac{(5-12)}{7}}$

$= x^{\frac{-7}{7}} = x^{-1}$

$= \dfrac{1}{x}$

32. (B) $\because \quad a + b + c = 0$

$\Rightarrow \quad a + b = -c \quad ...(i)$

$\Rightarrow \quad (a + b)^3 = (-c)^3$

$\Rightarrow \quad a^3 + b^3 + 3ab(a + b) = -c^3$

$\Rightarrow \quad a^3 + b^3 + 3ab(-c) = -c^3$

From equation (*i*)

$\therefore \quad a^3 + b^3 + c^3 = 3abc$

33. (A) T.SA. of a hemisphere $= 3\pi r^2$

$= 3\pi \times (10)^2$

$= 300\pi \text{ cm}^2$

34. (C) $1000000 = (100)^3$ = Perfect cube

35. (B) $\because$ 27 is a factor of 3 is a false statement.

36. (A) Remainder $= (1)^2 - 6(1) + 7$

$= 1 - 6 + 7 = 8 - 6$

$= 2 = +\text{ve}.$

37. (A)

38. (B) $\because$ Circumference

$= 2\pi r = 3.14$

$\Rightarrow \quad r = \dfrac{3.14}{2\pi}$

$\therefore \quad \text{Area} = \pi\left(\dfrac{3.14}{2\pi}\right)^2$

$= \dfrac{\pi \times 3.14 \times 3.14}{4\pi^2}$

$= \dfrac{\pi \times \pi \times \pi}{4\pi^2}$ (because $3.14 = \pi$)

$= \dfrac{\pi}{4} \text{ m}^2$

39. (B) $(356)^2 - (355)^2$

$\because \quad a^2 - b^2 = (a + b)(a - b)$

$= (356 + 355)(356 - 355)$

$= 711 \times 1$

$= 711$.

40. (D) $\because \quad \dfrac{2x+3}{3x-2} = \dfrac{7}{4}$

$\Rightarrow \quad 4(2x + 3) = 7(3x - 2)$

$\Rightarrow \quad 8x + 12 = 21x - 14$

$\Rightarrow \quad 21x - 8x = 12 + 14$

$\Rightarrow \quad 13x = 26$

$\therefore \quad x = 2$

41. $2x^2 - 3x + 5)6x^4 - 5x^3 + 7x^2 + 13x - 5(3x^2 + 2x - 1$

$6x^4 - 9x^3 + 15x^2$

$(-) \quad (+) \quad (-)$

$4x^3 - 8x^2 + 13x - 5$

$4x^3 - 6x^2 + 10x$

$(-) \quad (+) \quad (-)$

$-2x^2 + 3x - 5$

$-2x^2 + 3x - 5$

$(+) \quad (-) \quad (+)$

$\times$

$\therefore$ Remainder = 0

42. (a) Given Exp.

$= a^4 + 2a^2b^2 + b^4 - 225$

$= (a^2 + b^2)^2 - (15)^2$

$= (a^2 + b^2 + 15)(a^2 + b^2 - 15)$

(b) Given Exp.

$= 4x^2 + 9y^2 + 25z^2 - 12xy + 30yz - 20zx$

$= (4x^2 - 12xy + 9y^2) + 30yz - 20zx + 25z^2$

$= (2x - 3y)^2 - 10z(2x - 3y) + 25z^2$

$= (2x - 3y)^2 - 2 \times 5z(2x - 3y) + (5z)^2$

$= (2x - 3y - 5z)^2$

43. Let the number of five rupee coins be x

$\therefore$ No. of 2 rupee coins $= 3x$

$\because \quad x \times 5 + 3x \times 2 = 77$

$\Rightarrow \quad 11x = 77$

$\therefore \quad x = 7$

$\therefore$ No. of 5 rupee-coins = 7

and that of 2 rupee-coins = 21

44. S.P. of Ist fan $= 1200 \times \dfrac{95}{100}$

= Rs. 1140

and S.P. of IInd fan $= 1200 \times \dfrac{110}{100}$

= Rs. 1320

and Total profit = Total (S.P. – C.P.)

$= (1320 + 1140)$

$- (1200 + 1200)$

$= 2460 - 2400$
$= \text{Rs. } 60$

45. Amount

$$= 26,400\left[\left(1+\frac{15}{100}\right)^2 \cdot \left(1+\frac{15}{100}\times\frac{1}{3}\right)\right]$$

$$= 26,400 \times \frac{529}{400} \times \frac{21}{20} = \frac{33\times529\times21}{10}$$

$= \text{Rs. } 36,659.7$

46. Total cost of painting

$$= 24 \times 2 \times \frac{22}{7} \times \frac{28}{100} \times 4 \times 8$$

$$= \frac{24\times44\times16\times8}{100}$$

$= \text{Rs. } 1351.68$

47. $\because$ Volume of cylinder = Volume of cuboid

Let 'h' be the height

$$\frac{22}{7} \times 20 \times 20 \times h = 44 \times 20 \times 10$$

$$\therefore \quad h = \frac{44\times20\times10\times7}{22\times20\times20}$$

$= 7 \text{ cm}$

48.

S. No.	Class Interval	Tally Marks	Frequency
1.	0–10	I	1
2.	10–20	IIII	4
3.	20–30	III	3
4.	30–40	~~IIII~~ II	7
5.	40–50	~~IIII~~ II	7
6.	50–60	~~IIII~~ III	8
		Total	30

49. (i) Area of sheet

$$= 2\left(\frac{80}{100}\times\frac{60}{100}+\frac{60}{100}\times\frac{25}{100}+\frac{80}{100}\times\frac{25}{100}\right)$$

$= 2(0.48 + 0.15 + 0.20)$

$= 1.66 \text{ m}^2$

(ii) cost of sheet $= 1.66 \times 40$
$= \text{Rs. } 66.40$

50. Given Exp.

$= (a + b)(2a - 3b + c) - (2a + 3b - c)(a - b)$
$= (2a^2 - 3ab + ca + 2ab - 3b^2 + bc)$
$\quad - (2a^2 - 2ab + 3ab - 3b^2 - ca + bc)$
$= 2a^2 - 3ab + ca + 2ab - 3b^2 + bc - 2a^2 + 2ab$
$\quad - 3ab + 3b^2 + ca - bc$
$= -2ab + 2ca = 2a(c - b)$

51. The distance of image formed by a plane mirror is double the distance of object from the mirror. Therefore the distance is $5 + 5 = 10$ m.

52. Two main defects of human eye are—
1. Myopia (short sightedness)
2. Hypermetropia (long sightedness)

53. Electrolysis is the process of dissociation of substance in a solution into ions by an electric current.

Electrolysis of water will give hydrogen gas and oxygen gas at electrodes.

54. The two important oil refineries in India are—
1. Mathura Oil Refinery, Mathura (U.P.)
2. Digboi Oil Refinery, Digboi (Asom).

55. The air pollutants such as NO_2 and SO_2 react with H_2O (water) under the influence of thunder storm produce HNO_3 (nitric acid) and H_2SO_4 (sulphuric acid). These acids when comes down with rain then such a rain is called acid rain. The acid rain in harmful for living organism and soil.

56. Saucepan handles are made of thermosetting plastics because thermosetting plastics are good insulator. Therefore they are poor conductor of heat and electricity.

57. **Vector**—Vector is a career of Pathogen *e.g.* arthropod, that transmits a pathogen from an organism to host.

Pathogen—A pathogen, also called as infectious agent is a biological organism that causes disease or illness to its host.

58. (a) **Pulmonary artery**—The pulmonary arteries carry deoxygenated blood from heart to the lungs.

(b) **Aorta**—The aorta is the largest artery in the body, originating from the left ventricle of the heart. It carries oxygenated blood to all parts of the body in the systemic circulation.

(c) **Pulmonary vein**—The vein carries oxygenated blood from the lungs to the left atrium of the heart.

59.

S.N.	Plant cell	Animal cell
1.	Plant cells have difinite cell wall, made of cellulose.	1. Animal cells have no any cell wall.
2.	Vacuoles are prominent, one or more.	2. Vacuoles, if any, are small and temporary.
3.	Centrosome is absent.	3. Centrosome is present.
4.	Usually contains plastids.	4. Do not contain plastids.

60. Frictional Force—When a body slides over the surface of another body a frictional force parallel to the surfaces in contact is generated. The frictional force on each body is opposite to the direction of its motion relative to the other. Frictional force arises due to interaction between molecules of the two bodies is contact and exists between the surfaces even before the relative motion starts.

Friction is harmful in many ways but is also necessary. So it is said that **friction is necessary evil**.

Advantages

1. Brakes of vehicles will not work without friction.
2. The transfer of power from one part of a machine through the other part through belts will not be possible without friction.
3. Friction helps us driving a car on the road.
4. Friction helps us in walking. Without friction, when our foot press the ground it will slip.
5. Adhesive will not work without friction.
6. Nuts and bolts for holding the parts of machinery together will not work.

Disadvantages

1. Due to friction a large amount of energy is wasted and efficiency of a machine is reduced considerably.
2. Friction causes wear and tear of moving parts of machineries in contact.

61. Chemical properties of Metals and non-metals

	Reacting substances	Metal	Non-metal
1.	Hydroxides	Basic	Acidic
2.	Oxides	Basic	Acidic
3.	Oxidising or Reducing power	Metals are reducing agents	Non-metals are generally oxidizing agents.
4.	Electro-positive/ negative nature	form positive ions	form negative ions
5.	Electrolysis	They are liberated at cathode.	They are liberated at anode.
6.	Action of HCl or H_2SO_4	H_2 gas is liberated.	Do not liberate H_2 gas.

62. There are two forces responsible for holding the satellite in the orbit around the earth. These forces are centrifugal force and centripetal force. The centripetal force pull the satellite toward earth. The other force is centrifugal force which act against the gravitational force. The equilibrium between these two forces hold the satellite in its orbit.

63. Pitch of the sound is determined by the frequency of vibrating body.

64. Plane mirror forms the virtual, erect image of an object. The size of image is same as the object and image is formed at the same distance as that of object.

65. The liquid can conduct electricity only when it is ionised in positive and negative ions. Some liquids have the capability to ionised. Therefore, all liquids do not conduct electricity.

66. Unit of pressure is newton/metre^2 (N/m^2).

67. Clouds get charged due to friction in their movement. When the potential difference between two oppositely charged clouds becomes very high, insulation of air between them breaks and charge passes between them. It results in the production of large amount of heat. This produces flash of light which we call lightning. During this process air expands and nearby air rushes to fill its space. This produces violent sound. We call it thunder.

During rainy season when lightning generally occurs, we should take two precautions to escape being hit by it. We should remain inside a building and we should not take shelter under a tree.

68. An artificial satellite is a man-made system placed in a stationary orbit round the earth by means of a multistage rocket. The satellite is placed on the rocket which is launched from earth.

Applications of Artificial Satellites

1. It is used to study the atmosphere.
2. Information about the earth can be obtained.
3. Weather forecast can be done.
4. Radiation from the sun and outer space can be studied.
5. Distant telecasting, television service can be operated by geostationary satellites.
6. Meteorites can be studied.

69. Water gets contaminated through the following ways—

- Most of our water bodies as ponds, lakes, streams, rivers, etc., have become contaminated due to industrial waste, domestic waste and other man-made waste.
- Heavy flux of sewage, and agricultural wastes contaminate water.
- Water is polluted by pesticides used in the domestic and agriculture fields.

70. CNG compressed natural gas and LPG is liquified Petroleum gas.

The advantages of using LPG and CNG as fuels are—

- High calorific value
- No residue
- No smoke
- Burns readily, preheating not required. This is because it has a low ignition temperature.

71. (a) (iv) Paraffin wax
(b) (ii) Air pollution
(c) (i) Thermosetting
(d) (ii) Bitumen
(e) (ii) Combustion
(f) (iii) Streptomycin

72. Apiculture or beekeeping is the rearing, maintenance of bee for the production of honey.

73. Endemic species are found only at particular place on the earth. Its distribution is restricted to geographical, biological or climatic reasons.

74. The Kharif crop is the autumn harvest (also known as the summer or monsoon crop) in India. Kharif crops are usully sown in the beginning of the first rains in July. Example—Paddy, maize, etc.

75. The full form of BCG is **Bacille Calmette Guerin.**

76. **Robert Hooke** observed cork cells for the first time in 1665 using the newly invented compound microscope.

77. When a reactive metal Zinc reacts with copper sulphate ($CuSO_4$) solution, a red precipitate of copper and a blue colour of $ZnSO_4$ is obtained

$$CuCO_4 + Zn \rightarrow ZnSO_4 + Cu\downarrow$$

78. **Insulin** is a protein harmone, secreted by the ß cells of islet of Langerhans in the pancreas. Insulin regulates glucose level in the blood. Underproduction of insulin results in the accumulation of large amounts of glucose in the blood and its subsequent excretion in the urine. This condition is known as **diabetes mellitus.**

79. **Viviparous**—It is a form of reproduction in animals in which the developing embryo obtains its nourishment directly from the mother via a placenta.

It occurs in some insects and other arthropods, in certain fishes, amphibians and reptiles and in majority of mammals.

Oviparous—It is a kind of reproduction in which fertilized eggs are laid in animal and hatched by her to give birth of young one.

It occurs in most animals except marsupials and birds.

80.

Enzymes	Hormones
1. They act at a site where they produce.	1. They are produced at one site by blood and carried to another site of action.
2. They are not used up in their action.	2. They are used up in their action.
3. Enzyme control reactions are reversible.	3. Hormone controlled reactions are not reversible.
4. Enzymes are simple protein.	4. Hormones are peptids, amino acid, steroid and the in derivatives.

81. Force: Force is a push or pull that tends to change the momentum of object. In other words, force is the product of mass and acceleration.

The S.I. unit of force is newton (N). 1 newton force is that force which produces an accelleration of 1 metre/second^2 in a mass of 1 kg.

Force accelerates or decelerates the motion of a body. It also changes the direction of motion.

PAPER—II : Language and Social Studies

1. Write a short essay (100 words) on any of the following—

(A) The uses and abuses of Television

(B) Protection of Wild Life

2. Read the following passage and answer the questions that follow—

Japan's most famous dog

In front of the enormous Shibuya train station in Tokyo, there is a life-size bronze statue of a dog. Even though the statue is very small when compared to the huge neon signs flashing, it isn't difficult to find. It has been used as a meeting point since 1934 and today you will find hundreds of people waiting there for their friends to arrive.

Hachiko, an Akita dog, was born in 1923 and brought to Tokyo in 1924. His owner, Professor Eisaburo Uyeno and he were inseparable friends right from the start. Each day Hachiko would accompany his owner, a professor at the Imperial University, to Shibuya train station, when he left for work. When he came back, the professor would always find the dog patiently waiting for him. Sadly, the professor died suddenly at work in 1925 before he could return home.

Although Hachiko was still a young dog, the bond between him and his owner was very strong and he continued to wait at the station everyday. Sometimes, he would stay there for days at a time, though some believe that he kept returning because of the food he was given by street vendors. He became a familiar sight to commuters over time. In 1934, a statue of him was put outside the station. In 1935, Hachiko died at the place he last saw his friend alive.

(A) What is the importance of the statue of the dog?

(B) Who was the owner of Hachiko and what was he ?

(C) Where would Hachiko accompany his owner to ?

(D) How did Hachiko show his faithfulness to his owner?

(E) How do you know that the bond between Hachiko and his master was very strong?

3. Write a courteous letter to your neighbour who disturbs you in your studies by playing his music system at high volume.

4. Tick mark the right word or phrase, from the options below, which means the same as the italic word or phrase in the sentences—

(A) He *is running* his own business.

(i) proceeding (ii) moving

(iii) operating (iv) sprinting

(B) He needs to *check* his homework.

(i) ensure (ii) try out

(iii) examine (iv) invoice

(C) The girl *slipped out* of her dormitory.
 (i) sneaked out (ii) blurted out
 (iii) fell down (iv) skidded

(D) He *drives me to the edge* because he never stops talking!
 (i) irritates me (ii) steers me
 (iii) moves me (iv) frightens me

(E) We had been planning for months to go to the beach. Then, just last night, *out of the blue*, she informed me that she wasn't going to come along.
 (i) unsurprisingly (ii) suddenly
 (iii) expectedly (iv) outer space

5. Choose the correct option and write it in the blank—

(A) Things are not as they ......
 (i) seam (ii) seem

(B) A type of corn is called ......
 (i) maize (ii) maze

(C) On the .... he is a nice person.
 (i) whole (ii) hole

(D) He .... better but he did it anyway.
 (i) knew (ii) new

(E) Always try to buy low and .... high.
 (i) sell (ii) cell

6. Fill the appropriate preposition in the blanks—

(A) The teacher asked the class to do the exercise .... the bottom of page 24.

(B) He was always very good ...... Geography when he was at school.

(C) There was a lot of coughing .... the performance of the play.

(D) He's working on his homework .... the moment.

(E) They travelled to Delhi .... September 15th.

(F) The applications must reach .... the 30th November.

(G) The leaves fell .... the well due to storm.

(H) He ran .... the thief.

(I) Pravin is younger .... Nitin.

(J) The Ashram Express is running .... time.

7. Make new words by using *ive, en, ate, or ous,* at the end of the following words with necessary changes in the spelling—

bright	soft ....
active	fortune ....
expense	select ....
danger	mystery ....
wood	labour ....

8. Fill in the blanks in the following sentence with appropriate words from the box—

nag	onlooker	gènuine	minute
mended	marsh	palmtop	precise
applying	hollow		

(A) If something is very small, it is ....

(B) Ground near a lake, river or the sea that tends to flood and is always wet, is called a ......

(C) I've left my watch at the jeweller's to be ......

(D) To .... means to criticise or complain repeatedly and annoyingly, often as a way of trying to persuade someone to do something.

(E) An .... is someone who watches something that is happening in a public place but is not involved in it.

(F) Something which is exactly what it appears to be, real, not false is ....

(G) The dog found a .... in the ground and hid the bone there.

(H) The army is reported to be .... considerable resistance in some remote rural areas.

(I) Another word for exact and accurate is ....

(J) .... is the name for a computer, small enough to fit in your hand.

9. Write short notes on any five (words limit 50)—

(i) Socialism.

(ii) Democracy.

(iii) Human Rights.

(iv) Causes of environmental pollution.

(v) Tsunami.

(vi) Conservation of resources: Need & methods.

(vii) Non-conventional Sources of energy.

10. State True/False—

(i) Battle of Haldighati was fought between Rana Pratap and Akbar.

(ii) The right to vote is called Suffrage.

(iii) A free press is not a good asset for any country.

(iv) Bangalore is called as Silicon plateau / valley of India.

(v) Emigrants are those who arrive in a country and Immigrants are people who leave a country.

(vi) Human interference and changes of climate can maintain the ecosystem.

(vii) Akbar was friendly towards most Rajput rulers.

(viii) Guru Govind Singh was the 5th Sikh Guru.

(ix) Rajasthan is the most thickly populated state in India.

(x) Tata Iron & Steel Industry is private sector industry.

(xi) In the Western World, modern cities grew with industrialization.

(xii) Ozone layer protects us from harmful sun rays.

(xiii) As we go up the layers of atmosphere, the atmospheric pressure increases.

(xiv) Sri Lanka is located to the West of India.

(xv) General Dyer was responsible for massacre at Jalian Wala Bagh.

11. Match the following and write the corresponding alphabets of your answer in the box provided—

(i) Indian National Congress	(a) 1931	☐
(ii) Partition of Bengal	(b) 1929	☐
(iii) Formation of Muslim League	(c) 1927	☐
(iv) Non co-operation Movement	(d) 1942	☐
(v) First Battle of Panipat	(e) 1793	☐
(vi) Quit India Movement	(f) 1921	☐
(vii) Simon Commission	(g) 1906	☐
(viii) Permanent Settlement	(h) 1905	☐
(ix) Lahore session of Indian National Congress	(i) 1885	☐
(x) Civil Disobediance Movement	(j) 1526	☐
	(k) 1930	☐

12. Fill in the blanks—

(i) Dr. Rajendra Prasad was the first .... of India.

(ii) The .... is at top of the judicial system.

(iii) The mixture of minerals and organic matters make soil ....

(iv) Parliament is a legislature at Central level. It consist of .... and .... houses.

(v) The method of sowing in Jhum Cultivation is known as ....

(vi) The study of the remains of buildings, made of stones and bricks, paintings and sculpture is known as ....

(vii) .... is the process in which metals are extracted from their ores, by heating beyond the melting point.

(viii) The process/method of collecting rainwater from rooftops and directing it to an appropriate location and storing it for future use is called ....

(ix) It is said that rights and .... go together.

(x) .... is the example of regional party in Punjab.

(xi) The process of changing water drops into steam/water vapour is called ....

(xii) Delta is formed at .... of a river.

(xiii) .... was the adopted son of Peshwa Bajirao II.

(xiv) .... is popularly known as 'Tiger of Karnatka'.

(xv) Earthquake is measured on .... scale.

13. Give full form of following abbreviations—

(i) NGOs ....

(ii) ONGC ....

(iii) CNG ....
(iv) RTI ....
(v) FIR ....
(vi) ISRO ....
(vii) LPG ....
(viii) PM ....
(ix) UNESCO ....
(x) WHO ....

EXPLANATORY ANSWERS

1. **(A) The Uses and Abuses of Television:** Television, the most popular means of private and public—entertainment, knowledge and education, is a miraculous invention of science. Like every invention of science, it is both a blessing and a curse. If properly used, it brings latest news from every corner of the world with live pictures and events in motion. Some channels like Discovery, Wild Life and Astha give us not only interesting facts of life, but also enlighten us with moral and spiritual message. But at the same time, some foreign channels display highly immoral and sexul scene through half-naked heroes and heroines. Young generations fall in the trap of glamourous world and not only waste their time but also acquire low moral values and dirty habits. In this aspect Television is indeed a curse.

(B) Protection of Wild Life: A shelter and surrounding of wild animals can be called 'Wild Life', in which wild and ferocious animals live. Protection of wild life is important for two things:

(a) If jungles are not protected, wild animals can create havoc.

(b) Due to merciless killing of wild animals, there may be caused natural imbalance.

2. (A) It is a meeting place where hundreds of people wait for the arrival of their friends.

(B) The owner of Hachiko was Eisaburo Uyeno, who was a Professor at the Imperial University.

(C) Hachiko accompanied his owner everyday to Shibuya railway station from where his master boarded the train.

(D) Hachiko waited for his master every-day at the station and died at the spot where he last saw his master.

(E) Hachiko waited for his dead owner every day until death.

3.

F-9/10, Sector-10
Vikaspuri
New Delhi
Dated: 25.10.2009

Dear Nihal Ji,

With due respect, this letter is being sent to you for kind attention for the discomfort caused by you. I along with my family resides just in front of your quarter. I am a professor and I have three school-going children. So, we are connected to studies.

I would like to point out that your music system is being played at a very high volume which disturb us in our studies.

Please play your music system in a low tone. As I know you are a very sensible and reasonable person. So, kindly don't take it otherwise.

With Regards

Y.B. Sah

To
Sri Nihal Ranjan
F-9/10, Sector-10
Vikaspuri, New Delhi

4. (A) (iii) operating (B) (iii) examine
(C) (i) sneaked out (D) (i) irritates me
(E) (ii) suddenly

5. (A) (ii) seem (B) (i) maize
(C) (i) whole (D) (i) knew
(E) (i) sell

6. (A) at (B) at
(C) during (D) at
(E) on (F) by
(G) into (H) after
(I) to (J) on

7. brighten soften
activate fortunate
expensive selective
dangerous mysterious
wooden laborious

8. (A) minute (B) marsh
(C) mended (D) nag
(E) onlooker (F) genuine
(G) hollow (H) applying
(I) precise (J) Palmtop

9. **(i) Socialism**—Socialism refers to a socio-economic order, which promotes social equality among different classes and groups, collective and public ownership of resources and makes distribution equitable. It is against inequality. In political sphere it advocates people's participation. It emphasises foreign relations on equal base.

(ii) Democracy—Democracy is a rule by the people. In a democracy administrative works are controlled and regulated by people's representatives. Democracy emphasises people's welfare. In democracy personal liberty is dominant. Even the state can not succeed it.

(iii) Human rights—Human rights refers to basic rights and freedom to which all humans are entitled. Examples of rights and freedoms which have came to be thought of as human right include civil and political right, such as the right to life and liberty, freedom of expression, and equality before the law and economic, social and cultural rights.

(iv) Cause of environmental pollution—Our environment contains both biological and non-biological substances. Increasing amount of non-biological substance in atmosphere is called environment pollution. Industralisation, excess use of resources for increasing population, new product of transportation and consumers culture promote non-biological substances in atmosphere. It contaminates our environment.

(vii) **Non-conventional sources of Energy**—Demand of energy is increasing in our day to day life. Combustion of coal, oil and wood provides us energy but they are harmful to our environment. They produce CO_2 and other gases which destroy ozone layer and make the earth's layer hot. Due to higher demand of energy and pollution free environment non-conventional sources of energy are required. These sources are—wind, water, sun rays and sea tides.

10. (i) True (ii) True
(iii) False (iv) True
(v) False (vi) False
(vii) True (viii) False
(ix) False (x) True
(xi) True (xii) True
(xiii) True (xiv) False
(xv) True

11. (i) (i) (ii) (h)
(iii) (g) (iv) (f)
(v) (j) (vi) (d)
(vii) (c) (viii) (e)
(ix) (b) (x) (k)

12. (i) President (ii) Supreme Court
(iii) Fertile (iv) Lower, Upper
(v) Shifting agriculture
(vi) Archaeology (vii) Smelting
(viii) Rainwater Harvesting
(ix) Duties
(x) Shiromani Akali Dal
(xi) Evaporation (xii) The mouth
(xiii) Nana Sahib (xiv) Tipu Sultan
(xv) Richter

13. (i) Non Governmental Organisations
(ii) Oil and Natural Gas Commission
(iii) Compressed Natural Gas
(iv) Right to Information
(v) First Information Report
(vi) Indian Space Research Organisation
(vii) Liquified Petroleum Gas
(viii) Prime Minister
(ix) United Nations Educational, Scientific and Cultural Organisation
(x) World Health Organisation

Previous Paper (Solved)

Sainik School Exam, 2008

(Class-IX)

PAPER—I MATHEMATICS AND SCIENCE

PART–A : Mathematics

1. *(i)* What will be the square root of 8953.40 upto three decimal place?

(ii) How will $0.\overline{57}$ be written in the form of $\frac{p}{q}$?

2. *(i)* If $(56)^2 - (51)^2 = 5p$, then find the value of p.

(ii) What is value of $18 - |-7| + |11| - |-22|$?

(iii) If $a + b = 3$ and $ab = 2$, then find the value of $a^3 + b^3$.

(iv) What is the value of $(0.7) \times (0.5)^3 \times (0.3)^2$.

3 *(i)* Find the H.C.F of 70, 27 and 187.

(ii) Find the L.C.M of 18, 96 and 28.

4. Simplify the following :

(i) $\frac{0.0025 \times 1.4}{0.0175}$.

(ii) $(0.000064)^{5/6}$.

(iii) $\frac{(2.65)(2.65)-(1.65)(1.65)}{2.65+1.65}$

(iv) $\left(\frac{3xy}{9x^2y^2} \times \frac{x^2}{y}\right) \div \frac{18xy}{4x}$.

(v) $\frac{(48)^{-2} \times (64)^{1/2}}{(24)^{-1}}$.

5 *(i)* A cyclist covers a distance of 35 km in 5 hours. What is his average speed?

(ii) If x% of 800 = 100, then find the value of x.

(iii) If cost of 8 pens is Rs 72, then what will be cost of 13 such pens?

(iv) Perimeter of a square is 240 m, then what will be area of that square?

6 *(i)* On adding 7 to 25 times of y gives x. Write this statement in equation form.

(ii) Simplify : $11\frac{1}{4} \div 3\frac{3}{5} \times 6\frac{2}{3} + \frac{1}{6}$.

(iii) Write 2345.678 in scientific symbol.

(iv) In the given figure, O is the centre of the circle. Find $\angle x$ and $\angle y$.

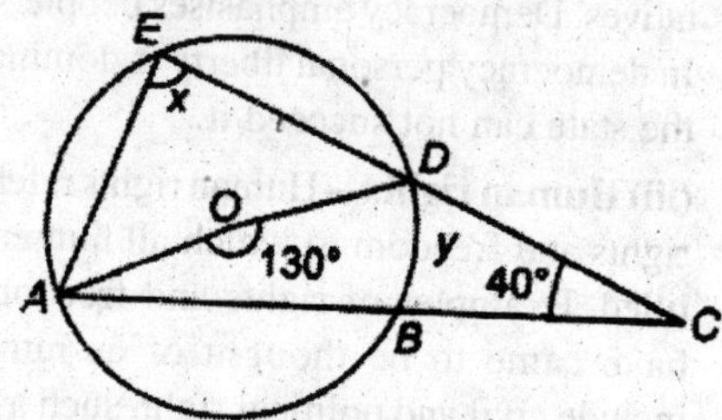

7 *(i)* Simplify : $\frac{7x^2 - 7y^2}{x - y}$.

(ii) Find the quotient of $\frac{x+y}{9xy} \div \frac{x^2-y^2}{4x^2y^2}$.

(iii) Find the value of $[(8)^{2/3}]^{-3/2}$.

(iv) Simplify : $\frac{0.538 \times 0.538 - 0.462 \times 0.462}{1 - 0.924}$.

8. How long will a man take to complete a double round of a circular garden having radius 70m with a speed of 4km/hour?

9. If 3 men or 6 boys can complete a work in 16 days, then in how many days 12 men and 8 boys will complete the same work?

10. Average speed of a car is 56 km/hour. How much distance it will cover in 45 minutes?

11. If selling price of a table is ₹ 784 and the profit is 12%, then what is its cost price?

12. A minute hand of a watch is 3.5 cm in length. How much area it will cover in 20 minutes?

13. Calculate the amount on a sum of ₹ 1600 for $1\frac{1}{2}$ years at a rate of 10% per annum compound interest, when interest is added half yearly.

14. Out of two complementary angles if one angle is 10° more than the other, then determine the other angles.

15. In the figure given below, *AB* is diameter of the circle, *APQ* and *RBQ* are two straight lines, then determine ∠*PRB*.

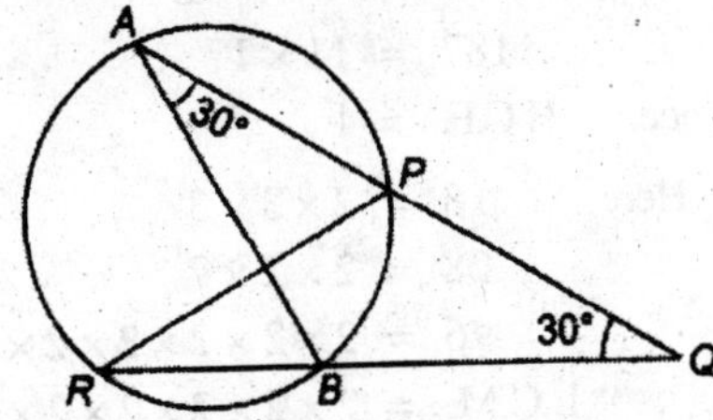

16 *(i)* A sewing machine is sold for ₹ 660 at a loss of 12%. What is its cost price?

(ii) What is square root of 0.00053361?

17. It height of a right circular cone is 1.02 m and the base radius is 28 cm, then find its volume.

18. A right angled triangle of sides 5 cm, 12 cm and 13 cm is rotated along the side 12 cm. Find the volume of solid made after rotation.

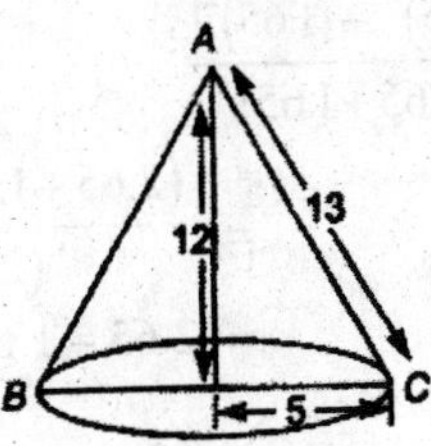

19. Diagonals of a rhombus are 5 cm and 3.4 cm, find its area.

20. In the given figure, *O* is the centre of the circle and *AOC* is the diameter. *B* is on the circumference and ∠*BOA* = 130°, *D* is on the circumference of the corresponding semi-circle and is also joined with *C* and *B*, then find the value of ∠*BDC*.

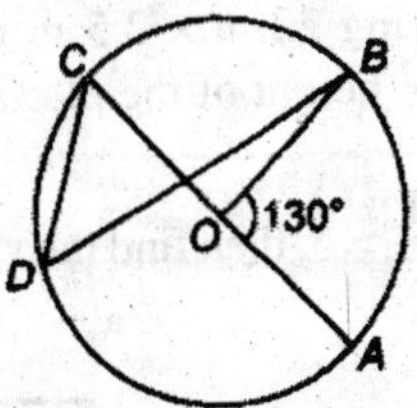

21 *(i)* On subtracting one-fourth of a number from one-third of the same number, the resultant is 12, then find the number.

(ii) Factorize the following : $\left(a^2 - 2 + \frac{1}{a^2}\right)$.

22. Below is given a page of entries of a saving account of a bank. If the rate of interest is 5% per annum, then what will be the interest at the last of the year? Interest is calculated on the least amount in each month after 10th.

Date 1999	Description	Credit (Rs)	Debit (Rs)	Balance	Initial
1 January	B.F.	—	2000.00	2000.00	
8 Jan.	Cash	—	200.00	2200.00	
10 Feb.	By cheque	500.00	—	1700.00	
24 Feb.	Cash		300.00	2000.00	
18 July	Cash		500.00	2500.00	
30 July	By cheque	700.00	—	1800.00	
6 Nov.	Cash		300.00	2100.00	
9 Dec.	Cash		100.00	2200.00	

23. A shopkeeper bought 288 oranges for ₹ 57.60. Out of them, he sold 150 oranges at the rate of ₹ 0.30 each and the remaining for ₹ 29.88. How much profit did he earn in the transaction?

24. Diameter of the moon is one-fourth of the diameter of the earth approximately. What part is volume of moon to the earth's volume?

25. The difference of compound interest and simple interest of a certain sum of money at the rate of 5% per annum for 2 years is Rs. 15. Find the sum of money.

26. Find the mean, mode and median of the following series
4, 5, 6, 7, 7, 8, 8, 9, 9, 10, 11, 12, 13.

27. A well 7 m in diameter and 40 m deep is dug and from the outcoming soil a platform measuring 22 m × 2.5 m is constructed, then find the height of the platform.

28. If $x - \frac{1}{x} = 5$, then find the value of $\left(x^3 - \frac{1}{x^3}\right)$.

29. Which stock is the most beneficial– stock at the rate of ₹ 80 or 6% stock at the rate of ₹ 104.

30. Population of a town increases by 4% annually. What will be the population after 3 years if the present population of the town is 31250?

EXPLANATORY ANSWERS

1 *(i)*

	94.622
9	8953.400000
+9	81
184	853
+4	736
1886	11740
+6	11316
18922	42400
+2	37844
189242	455600
+2	378484
	77116

∴ Required square root = 94.622

(ii) Let, $x = 0.\overline{57}$

$$= 0.575757...$$

$$\Rightarrow \quad 100x = 57.5757... = 57.\overline{57}$$

$$\Rightarrow \quad 99x = 57$$

$$\therefore \quad x = \frac{57}{99} = \frac{19}{33}$$

2 *(i)*

$$5p = (56)^2 - (51)^2$$
$$= (56 - 51)(56 + 51)$$
$$= 5 \times 107$$
$$\therefore \quad p = \frac{5 \times 107}{5} = 107$$

(ii) $18 - |-7| + |11| - |-22|$

$$= 18 - 7 + 11 - 22 = 29 - 29$$
$$= 0$$

(iii)

$$a^3 + b^3 = (a + b)^3 - 3ab(a + b)$$
$$= (3)^3 - 3 \times 2 \times 3$$
$$= 27 - 18 = 9$$

(iv) $(0.7) \times (0.5)^3 \times (0.3)^2$

$$= 0.7 \times 0.125 \times 0.09$$
$$= 0.007875$$

3 *(i)*

$$70 = 2 \times 5 \times 7$$
$$27 = 3 \times 3 \times 3$$
$$187 = 11 \times 17$$

Hence, H.C.F. = 1

(ii) Here,

$$18 = 2 \times 3 \times 3$$
$$28 = 2 \times 2 \times 7$$
$$96 = 2 \times 2 \times 2 \times 2 \times 2 \times 3$$
$$\therefore \quad \text{L.C.M.} = 2 \times 2 \times 2 \times 2 \times 2 \times 3 \times 3 \times 7$$
$$= 2016$$

4 *(i)*

$$\frac{0.0025 \times 1.4}{0.0175} = \frac{25 \times 14}{175 \times 10} = \frac{2}{10} = 0.2$$

(ii)

$$(0.000064)^{5/6} = [(0.2)^6]^{5/6}$$
$$= (0.2)^5$$
$$= 0.00032$$

(iii)

$$\frac{(2.65)^2 - (1.65)^2}{(2.65 + 1.65)}$$
$$= \frac{(2.65 + 1.65)(2.65 - 1.65)}{(2.65 + 1.65)}$$
$$= 2.65 - 1.65 = 1$$

(iv)

$$\left(\frac{3xy}{9x^2y^2} \times \frac{x^2}{y}\right) \div \frac{18xy}{4x}$$
$$= \frac{3xy}{9x^2y^2} \times \frac{x^2}{y} \times \frac{4x}{18xy}$$
$$= \frac{2x}{27y^3}$$

(v) $\frac{(48)^{-2} \times (64)^{1/2}}{(24)^{-1}} = \frac{1}{48 \times 48} \times \frac{8}{1} \times 24$

$= \frac{1}{12} = (12)^{-1}$

5 (i) Average speed $= \frac{\text{Distance}}{\text{Time}} = \frac{35}{5} = 7$ km/hour

(ii) Here,

$\frac{800 \times x}{100} = 100$

$\therefore \quad x = \frac{100}{8} = \frac{25}{2} = 12\frac{1}{2}\%$

(iii) $\because$ Cost of 8 pens = ₹ 72

$\therefore$ Cost of 1 pen $= \frac{72}{8} =$ ₹ 9

$\therefore$ Cost of 13 pens $= 13 \times 9 =$ ₹ 117

(iv) Side of square $= \frac{\text{Perimeter}}{4} = \frac{240}{4}$

$= 60$ m

$\therefore$ Area of square $= 60 \times 60$

$= 3600 \text{ m}^2$

6 (i) $25y + 7 = x$

(ii) $11\frac{1}{4} \div 3\frac{3}{5} \times 6\frac{2}{3} + \frac{1}{6}$

$= \frac{45}{4} \div \frac{18}{5} \times \frac{20}{3} + \frac{1}{6}$

$= \frac{45}{4} \times \frac{5}{18} \times \frac{20}{3} + \frac{1}{6}$

$= \frac{125}{6} + \frac{1}{6} = \frac{125+1}{6}$

$= \frac{126}{6} = 21$

(iii) $2345.678 = 2.345678 \times 10^3$

(iv) $\angle x = \frac{1}{2} \times 130 = 65°$ (The angle made on cicumference is half the angle made on the centre.)

$\therefore \angle DBC = 65°$ (From cyclic quadrilateral ABDE)

$\angle y = 180° - (65° + 40°)$

$= 180 - 105 = 75°$

7 (i) $\frac{7x^2 - 7y^2}{x - y} = \frac{7(x+y)(x-y)}{(x-y)} = 7(x+y)$

(ii) $\frac{x+y}{9xy} \div \frac{x^2 - y^2}{4x^2y^2}$

$= \frac{x+y}{9xy} \times \frac{4x^2y^2}{(x+y)(x-y)} = \frac{4xy}{9(x-y)}$

(iii) $[(8)^{2/3}]^{-3/2} = [\{(2)^3\}^{2/3}]^{-3/2}$

$= [(2)^2]^{-3/2} = 2^{-3}$

$= \frac{1}{8}$

(iv) $\frac{0.538 \times 0.538 - 0.462 \times 0.462}{1 - 0.924}$

$= \frac{(0.538 + 0.462)(0.538 - 0.462)}{0.076}$

$= \frac{1 \times 0.076}{0.076} = 1$

8. Circumference of the circular garden

$= 2 \times \frac{22}{7} \times 70 = 440$ m

Distance covered in two round of the garden

$= 2 \times 440 = 880$ m

$= \frac{880}{1000}$ km $= \frac{22}{25}$ km

$\therefore$ Required time $= \frac{22}{25 \times 4}$ hour

$= \frac{22}{25 \times 4} \times 60$ minutes

$= 13\frac{1}{5}$ minutes

$= 13$ minutes $\frac{1}{5} \times 60$ Sec.

$= 13$ minutes 12 Sec.

9. $\because$ Work of 3 Men = Work of 6 Boys

$\therefore$ Work of 12 Men = $2 \times 12 = 24$ Boys

$\therefore$ 12 Men + 8 boys = $24 + 8 = 32$ Boys

$\because$ 6 boys can complete the work in 16 days

$\therefore$ 32 Boys will complete the work in $\frac{16 \times 6}{32}$

= 3 days.

10. Time = 45 Minutes = $\frac{45}{60} = \frac{3}{4}$ Hour

Average speed = 56 km/hour

$\therefore$ Distance covered = $56 \times \frac{3}{4} = 42$ km

11. For a profit of 12%

$\because$ When selling price is ₹ 112, cost price

= Rs 100

$\therefore$ When selling price is ₹ 784, cost price

$= \frac{100}{112} \times 784 =$ ₹ 700

12. Area covered by minute hand is 20 minutes

$= \frac{20}{60} \times \frac{22}{7} \times (3.5)^2$

$= \frac{1}{3} \times \frac{22}{7} \times \frac{7}{2} \times \frac{7}{2}$

$= \frac{77}{6}$ cm^2

13. Principal = ₹ 1600

Time = $\frac{3}{2}$ Year = 3 Half years.

Rate = 10% Per annum

= 5% half year

Amount = $1600 \left(1 + \frac{5}{100}\right)^3$

$= 1600 \times \frac{21}{20} \times \frac{21}{20} \times \frac{21}{20}$

$= \frac{18522}{10}$

= Rs. 1852.20

14. Let, both angles be x and $x + 10$ respectively

Then, $x + x + 10 = 90°$

$\Rightarrow$ $2x = 80°$

$\therefore$ $x = 40°$

Now $x + 10 = 40° + 10°$

$= 50°$

Required angle will be 50° and 40° respectively.

15.

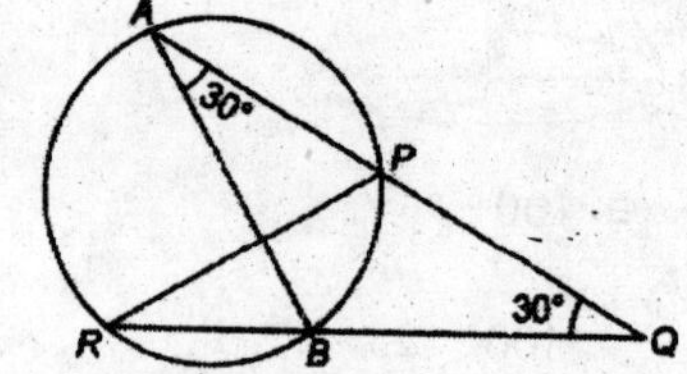

$\because$ $\angle PRB = \angle PAB$

(Because angles are made on the same arc)

$\therefore$ $\angle PRB = \angle PAB = 30°$

16 *(i)* For a loss of 12%

$\because$ When selling price is ₹ 88, then cost price

= ₹ 100

$\therefore$ When selling price is ₹ 660, then cost price

$= \frac{100}{88} \times 660 =$ ₹ 750

(ii)

	0.0 2 3 1
2	$0.00\ \overline{05}\ \overline{33}\ \overline{61}$
+2	4
43	133
+3	129
461	461
+1	461
	×

or $\sqrt{0.00053361} = 0.0231$

17. $h = 1.02$ m = 102 cm

and $r = 28$ cm

$\because$ Volume of the cone $= \frac{1}{3}\pi r^2 h$

$= \frac{1}{3} \times \frac{22}{7} \times 28 \times 28 \times 102$

$= 83776$ cm^3

18. The figure made after rotation of the right angled triangle along the side of 12 cm, will be required cone.

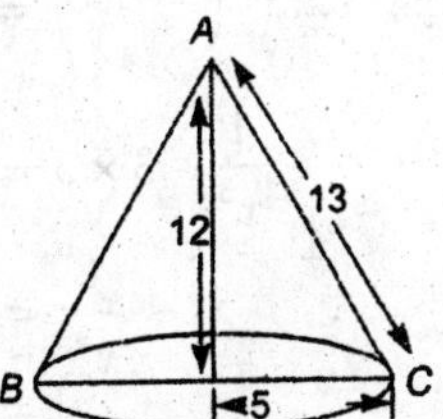

$\therefore$ Volume of required solid $= \frac{1}{3}\pi \times r^2 \times h$

$= \frac{1}{3} \times \frac{22}{7} \times 5 \times 5 \times 12 = \frac{2200}{7}$

$\simeq 314.29 \text{ cm}^3$

19. Area of Rhombus $= \frac{1}{2} \times$ Product of Diagonals

$= \frac{1}{2} \times 5 \times 3.4 = 8.5 \text{ cm}^2$

20.

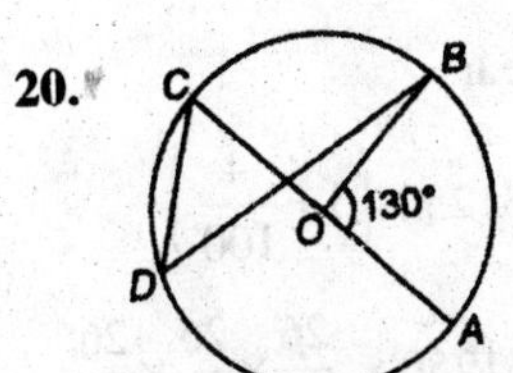

$\angle COB = 180° - \angle BOA = 180° - 130°$
$= 50°$

Now, $\angle CDB = \frac{1}{2}\angle COB$

$= \frac{1}{2} \times 50 = 25°$

21 *(i)* Let the number be x

A/q, $\frac{x}{3} - \frac{x}{4} = 12$

$\Rightarrow \frac{x}{12} = 12$

$\therefore x = 12 \times 12 = 144$

(ii) $a^2 - 2 + \frac{1}{a^2} = a^2 - 2.a.\frac{1}{a} + \left(\frac{1}{a}\right)^2 = \left(a - \frac{1}{a}\right)^2$

22. Calculation of Interest

Year 1999 Month	Amount on which interest is levied (₹)
January	2200
February	1700
March	2000
April	2000
May	2000
June	2000
July	1800
August	1800
September	1800
October	1800
November	2100
December	2200
	Total = 23400

Interest at the last of the year $= \frac{23400 \times 5 \times 1}{100 \times 12}$

$= \frac{585}{6} = ₹\,97.50$

23. Selling price of 288 Oranges

$= 150 \times 0.30 + 29.88$

$= 45 + 29.88$

$= ₹\,74.88$

$\therefore$ Profit $= 74.88 - 57.60 = ₹\,17.28$

24. Let the radius of the Moon and the Earth be x m and $4x$ m.

Then, $\frac{\text{Volume of Moon}}{\text{Volume of Earth}} = \frac{\frac{4}{3}\pi x^3}{4/3\ \pi(4x)^3}$

$= \frac{x^3}{64x^3} = \frac{1}{64}$

25. Here, the difference of compound interest and simple interest is ₹ 15, Hence, the simple interest on the amount of one year's simple interest will be ₹ 15 for one year.

S.I. for one year $= \frac{15 \times 100}{5 \times 1}$

$= ₹\,300$

$$\text{Principal} = \frac{300 \times 100}{5 \times 1} = ₹\ 6000$$

26. Sum of totat terms= 4 + 5 + 6 + 7 + 7 + 8 + 8 + 9 + 9 + 10 + 11 + 12 + 13 = 109

Now, $\text{Mean} = \frac{\text{Sum of total terms}}{\text{No. of terms}}$

$= \frac{109}{13} = 8.38$

$\text{Mode} = \text{Value of} \left(\frac{13+1}{2}\right) \text{th term}$

= Value of 7th term = 8

Median = 7, 8 and 9 because frequency of each is 2.

27. Let, the height of the platform = h m

Then, Volume of the platform

= Volume of soils dug from the well

$\Rightarrow 22 \times 14 \times h = \frac{22}{7} \times \left(\frac{7}{2}\right)^2 \times 20$

$\therefore h = \frac{770}{22 \times 14} = 2.5$ m

28. Here, $x - \frac{1}{x} = 5$

Then, $\left(x - \frac{1}{x}\right)^3 = (5)^3$

$\Rightarrow x^3 - \frac{1}{x^3} - 3.x.\frac{1}{x}\left(x - \frac{1}{x}\right) = 125$

$\Rightarrow x^3 - \frac{1}{x^3} - 3 \times 5 = 125$

$\therefore x^3 - \frac{1}{x^3} = 125 + 15$

$= 140$

29. Here, income on first stock on a cash of ₹ 100

$\frac{5 \times 100}{80} = ₹\ 6.25$

Income on second stock on a cash of ₹ 100

$\frac{6 \times 100}{104} = ₹\ 5.77$

Hence, first stock is more beneficial.

30. $P = 31250$

$r = 4\%$

And $n = 3$

Population after three years

$= 31250 \left(1 + \frac{4}{100}\right)^3$

$= 31250 \times \frac{26}{25} \times \frac{26}{25} \times \frac{26}{25}$

$= 35152$

PART 'B' : SCIENCE

Directions (Q. 1 to 10) : *Choose the correct answer from given alternatives.*

1. Pasturisation of milk destroys its :

A. Fatty element
B. Vitamine
C. Pathogenic Bacteria
D. Sugar

2. What controls the light to be entered into the eye?

A. Iris B. Cornea
C. Cone D. Pupil

3. Which one is NOT applicable for Coke?

A. On industrial level coke is used as fuels.
B. It is used in metallurgy.
C. It is used in laboratory.
D. It is used to make elecrode.

4. Lighting of electric-lamp is not called combustion, because

A. sufficient heat is not released
B. released light is maximum
C. it is a physical change
D. it is not a chemical reaction

5. The hardest allotrope of carbon is :

A. Coal B. Animal charcoal
C. Diamond D. None of the above

6. Which lens is used to correct hypermetropia?
A. Concave B. Convex
C. Plane-concave D. None of the above

7. Allotrope of carbon which is a good conductor of heat and is used as lubricant is :
A. Kajal
B. Fine powdery charcoal
C. Graphite
D. None of the above

8. Which of the following has the least ignition temperature?
A. Wood B. Wax
C. Gasoline D. Kerosene oil

9. Yeast is used in the production of :
A. Sugar B. Alcohol
C. Oxygen D. CO_2 gas

10. Which one is an example of Metamorphic rock?
A. Slate B. Granite
C. Rock D. Dolomite

Directions (Q. 11 to 20) : *Fill in the blanks :*

11. Formation of curd from milk is due to ....

12. The technique used to separate the constituents of petrolium is..........

13. If the area is doubled then the pressure on liquid surface becomes ....

14. The rod used as anode in a dry cell is made up of ....

15. In the absent of limit supply of air the process of heating the ore below the melting point is called ....

16. Substance whose atoms have only few free electrons are called ....

17. Chemical cell is first discovered by ....

18. The most reactive metal which is kept in kerosene oil is ....

19. The principle of buoyancy was given by ....

20. Entamoeba histolytica is a ....

Directions (Q. 21 to 37) : *Give answers in brief :*

21. What is antibiotics? Who discovered Penecillin?

22. What is Communicable diseases? Give some examples.

23. What do you get on burning of diamond?

24. Why is methane called Marsh Gas?

25. Why is rainbow formed in the sky?

26. What is Petrochemicals?

27. Why the bloods comout from the nose of mountaineers at heights?

28. Why are algae similar to plants?

29. Resistance of 2, 4 and 8 ohms are connected in parallel. What will be the effective resistance ?

30. What is the difference between prism and a glass block?

31. Draw a sketch of formation of image by a convex lense, when the object is kept between F_1 and $2F_1$.

32. How is CO_2 gas prepared in the laboratory? Give any two usage of it.

33. What do you know about amoebaisis? What will you do to prevent it?

34. With the help of a diagram show a path of rays passing through the prism. Define also the angle of deviation.

35. What is manure?

36. How does soap act upon dirt? Write two differences between soap and detergent.

36. What happens when (give equation) –
A. Zinc reacts with conc. sulphuric acid.
B. Aluminium reacts with conc. sulphuric acid.
C. Zinc reacts with conc. hydrochloric acid.
D. Aluminium reacts with conc. hydrochloric acid.
E. Sodium reacts with water.

ANSWERS WITH HINTS

1. (C) **2.** (A) **3.** (D) **4.** (C) **5.** (C)
6. (B) **7.** (C) **8.** (C) **9.** (B) **10.** (A)

11. Bacteria
12. Fractional distillation
13. Half
14. Carbon
15. Calcination
16. Semiconductors
17. Volta
18. Sodium

19. Archimedes

20. Protozoa

21. Antibiotics are chemical substances produced by micro-organism that inhibits the growth of another micro-organism, widely used as drugs to combat bacterial diseases.

22. Infectious pathogenic diseases may be trasmitted to one man to another man through toxic substances produced by infectious agents. e.g. AIDS, Diptheria, hepatitis, influenza, tuberculosis etc.

23. Diamond $\xrightarrow[\text{in vacuum}]{1500°C}$ No change.

Diamond $\xrightarrow[\text{in vacuum}]{1800°C}$ Graphite;

Diamong $\xrightarrow[\text{in vacuum}]{2000°C}$ Graphite (rapidly)

24. In marshy places methane is released by the decomposition of organic matter in the presence of bacteria. That is why methane is also called marsh gas.

25. Rainbow is a beautiful natural phenomenon based upon dispersion of light on a large scale. The spectrum of sunlight is formed by the rain-drops suspended in the air. The colours of the rainbow are similar to those which we get in the solar spectrum obtained by the glass prism. The rainbow so-called because it is in the form of a bow.

26. Petrochemicals are obtained by fractional distillation or by cracking of petroleum (Crude oil).

27. On the high altitude or mountain, the density of air becomes less. So, due to low air resistance in the surrounding environment our body exert bloods from nose mainly.

28. Like plants, chloroplasts and cell membrane both are found in algae. Cell wall provide protection and shape to the cell.

29. Here, $\frac{1}{R}=\frac{1}{2}+\frac{1}{4}+\frac{1}{8} = \frac{4+2+1}{8}=\frac{7}{8}$

$\therefore \quad R = \frac{8}{7}$ ohm

30. Prism deviate white rays on the Screen and divide it into several colours what it exist but block of glass has no such properties.

31.

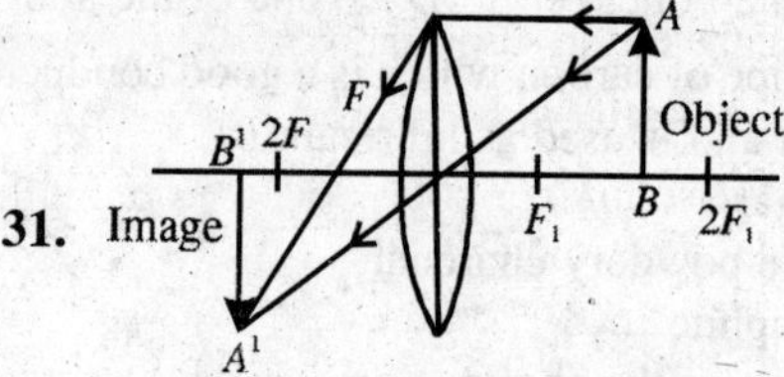

32. Laboratory method of CO_2 preparation : It is prepared by the decomposition of limestone/ marble with dil hydrochloric acid.

$CaCO_3 + 2HCl \rightarrow CaCl_2 + H_2O + CO_2\uparrow$

Uses of CO_2 gas

(i) It is used in formation of carbonated soft drinks like soda water and other carbonated drinks.

(ii) It is used as fire extinguisher.

33. Amoebiasis is a dysentery which is caused by *Entamoeba histolytica* characterised by discharge of mucous and blood along with stool. In acute condition, parasite may invade intestinal wall causing porosis and may come to other organs and infect them.

It may be prevented by proper sanitation and hygiene.

34.

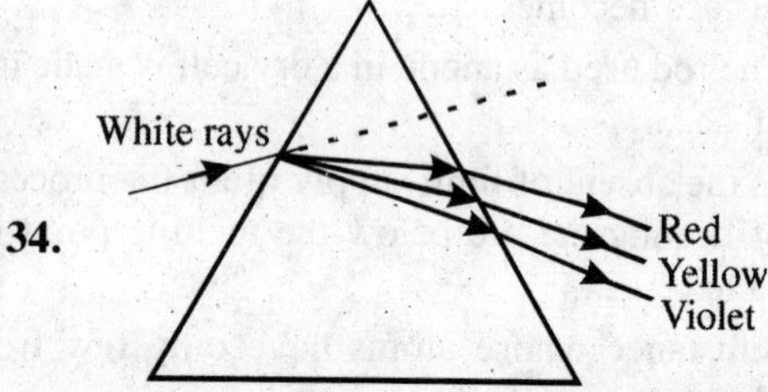

Angle of deviation is the angle between the direction of incidence rays & deviated rays.

35. Manure : Manures are materials which are mixed up with soil. They contain almost all the nutrients required by the plants. This results in the increase in the soil fertility alongwith crop productivity. Manures are of three types :

(i) Farm yard manures (ii) Composited manure

(ii) Green manure.

36. Soaps are sodium and potassium salts of higher carboxylic acids used as cleansing agents. In general soaps are biodegradable.

Detergents are water soluble, surface active agents, removing greasy and oily deposits and retaining the dirt in suspension of ease of rinsing.

Difference between soaps and detergents :

- Soap is the sodium or potassium salts of higher fatty acid. The ionic group in soap is $-COO^- Na^+$.
- Synthetic detergents are the sodium salts of long chain sulphonates. The ionic group is $-SO_3^- Na^+$ or $-SO_4^- Na^+$.

37. A. $Zn + H_2SO_4 \rightarrow ZnSO_4 + H_2\uparrow$

B. $2Al + 3H_2SO_4 \rightarrow Al_2(SO_4)_2 + 3H_2\uparrow$

C. $Zn + 2HCl \rightarrow ZnCl_2 + H_2\uparrow$

D. $2Al + 6HCl \rightarrow 2AlCl_3 + 3H_2\uparrow$

E. $2Na + 2H_2O \rightarrow 2NaOH + H_2\uparrow$

PAPER - II : LANGUAGE AND SOCIAL STUDY

PART - A : ENGLISH LANGUAGE

Directions : *Questions from 1 to 20 have four answers each. Select the correct answer and encircle its letter.*

1. He scored a ...... century in his first cricket match.
A. brilliant B. maiden
C. praiseworth D. slow

2. People took ...... a big procession against high prices.
A. out B. on
C. from D. inside

3. Mahatma Gandhi preached ..... thinking and simple living.
A. good B. ideal
C. high D. nobel

4. He was accused ...... smuggling.
A. in B. for
C. of D. about

5. If ...... is lost everything is lost.
A. character B. health
C. wealth D. book

6. .... were watching cricket match.
A. She, they and I B. They, I and she
C. She, I and they D. I, she and they

7. Police arrested the thief ..... a hotel.
A. from B. by
C. at D. over

8. Though he worked hard ...... he failed in the examination.
A. but B. and
C. still D. yet

9. A soldier is rewarded for ....
A. smartness B. bravery
C. good manners D. personality

10. Politics has become ...... these days.
A. cheap B. fashion
C. paying D. dirty

11. We read newspapers ...... getting knowledge.
A. with B. at
C. in D. for

12. Economy can be called ...... for goods and services.
A. storage B. basket
C. lockup D. godown

13. Essay writing is the ...... form of communication of ideas.
A. good B. fair
C. best D. better

14. ...... many cooks spoil the broth.
A. So B. Many
C. Too D. Not

15. His performance on stage won applause of ..... .
A. crowd B. meeting
C. audience D. viewers

16. Internet is latest marvel ...... science.
A. at B. with
C. of D. over

17. There was a big ...... for admission in the university.
A. gathering B. rush
C. assembly D. crowd

18. History tells us ...... past glories of our country.
A. in B. for

C. about D. since

19. By virtue of his nice manners Mohan became .... of eyes of his parents.

A. star B. gold

C. beloved D. apple

20. Jawahar Lal Nehru was a distinguished statesman ...... the world.

A. on B. for

C. of D. over

Directions (Q. 21-25) : *From the given words select the one which is ANTONYM (opposite in meaning) to the underlined words in the following sentences.*

21. The speaker asked the legislators to show <u>patience</u>.

A. discipline B. anger

C. impatience D. wisdom

22. People <u>scorn</u> blackmailers and corrupt persons.

A. ignore B. welcome

C. tolerate D. hate

23. My friend, this world is not <u>heaven</u>.

A. garden B. market

C. hell D. den

24. The governor <u>vetoed</u> the recommendations of the minister.

A. approved B. rejected

C. decided D. moulded

25. Shakespeare is famous for creating best <u>heroes</u> in his dramas.

A. villains B. clowns

C. warriors D. counter

Directions (Q. 26-30) : *Select the appropriate SYNONYM (which is nearest in meaning) to the underlined words in the following questions.*

26. <u>DELICIOUS</u>

A. sweet B. fine

C. tasty D. rare

27. <u>EMPHASIS</u>

A. repetition B. stress

C. choice D. favourable

28. <u>FOWL</u>

A. bird B. bad

C. irregular D. worth seeing

29. <u>CULPRIT</u>

A. villain B. non serious

C. fool D. wrong doer

30. <u>PERFECT</u>

A. ideal B. desirable

C. complete D. correct

Directions (Q. 31-35) : *Rewrite the following sentences as directed.*

31. Good teachers seldom differentiate ...... their students.
(Fill in suitable preposition)

32. ...... films and literature should be banned.
(Fill in adjective of ethics)

33. Though there was a lot of discussion ...... no decision was taken.
(Fill in suitable conjunction)

34. One should not use ...... means in examination.
(Fill in adjective of question)

35. ...... he failed in the entrance test.
(Fill in suitable adverb)

Directions (Q. 36-40) : *In the following questions some sentences have errors. Select the part in which the error lies and encircle its letter (A), (B) or (C). If there is no error, encircle the letter (D).*

36. Adolf Hitler (A), fascist dictator in Germany/(B), was responsible for second world war/(C). No error/(D).

37. The headquarters/(A), of international court of/(B) justice is on GENEVA/(C). No error/(D).

38. None of the players/(A) did not hear/(B) the decision of the referee/(C). No error/(D).

39. India was unlucky/(A) to make a bid/(B) for Hockey gold medal in Sydney/(C). No error/(D).

40. The crowd/(A) broke into the hall/(B) on back side/(C). No error/(D).

Directions (Q. 41-45) : *Encircle (A), (B), (C) for the correct spellings.*

41. A. Illustretion B. Illustration
C. Ellustration

42. A. Handicapped B. Handcupped
C. Hendicaped

43. A. Often B. Offen
C. Ofan

44. A. Tishew B. Techew
C. Tissue

45. A. Recorrence B. Recurrence
C. Recourans

Directions (Q. 46-50) : *Make meaningful sentences of the jumbled words for each of the following questions.*

46. could, due, in, the, he, not, compartment, to, enter, the, great, rush.

47. optician, was, Mohan, to, advised, good, consult.

48. given difficult, police, story, to, is, the, it, believe, by.

49. companions, best, our, books, are.

50. out, took, supporters, a, of, procession, the, candidate, winning.

Directions (Q. 51-55) : *Rewrite the following sentences as directed.*

51. Discipline and regularity always pay.
(Change into negative)

52. Political parties in our country do not endeavour to serve the country.
(Change into interrogative)

53. There is unity .... diversity.
(Put in suitable preposition)

54. Kashmir offers many ..... scenes of natural beauty.
(Fill in appropriate adjective of picture)

55. He asked "Where are you going, my friend?"
(Change into indirect)

Directions (Q. 56-60) : *Write a single word for each group of words given below.*

56. Large number of keys.

57. Speech delivered for the first time.

58. Group of players.

59. Dues to be paid by a company.

60. Market where share business is carried.

Directions (Q. 61-65) : *Read the following passage and answer the questions given below.*

The great defect of our civilization is that it does not know what to do with the knowledge. Science has given us powers yet we use them like small children. For example, we do not know how to manage our machines. Machines were made to be man's servants, yet he has grown so dependent on them that they in a fair way have become his masters. Already most men spend most of their lives looking after and waiting upon machines. But the machines are very stern masters. They must be fed with coal, given petrol to drink and oil to wash with and they must be kept at right temperature and handled by knowledgeable artisans. If they do not get their meals or not maintained properly they grow sulky, refuse to work or spread ruin and disaster. They may bring great losses and uneven competition. So we have to be very attentive and look after them properly.

61. What does the author tell us about civilization?
A. It is ignorant
B. Dependent on machines
C. Does not know what to do with knowledge
D. Does not have good managers

62. How do we use powers given by science?
A. In an efficient manner
B. Do not know about them
C. Like children
D. Misuse them

63. What do machines require?
A. Knowledge to use them
B. Power to control them
C. Fuel and maintenance
D. Skilled workers

64. What harm machines can cause?
A. Grow sulky and spread disaster
B. Stoppage of work
C. Spoil the products
D. Bring about wear and tear

65. What is true relationship between machine and man?
A. Of a friend B. Of a dependent
C. Equality D. Servant and master

66. Develop the following outlines into a short story.
A true story of Taimur the Lame ...... In early days he lost heart ...... disappointment due to defeats and betrayal of his soldiers and relatives. He thought to commit suicide .... throwing himself from mountain top. Rested for a while in a cave ...... saw an ant carrying morsel of grain on slipping wall ...... fell many times ...... but did not give up. Finally it reached her destination. Taimur was impressed by its perseverance ...... came out ...... collected army and recaptured his kingdom. Became famous ...... subdued many rulers ...... came to India also.

67. Write a paragraph in about 150 words about the Present System of Examination.

68. Write a letter to your father requesting him to allow you to join an educational tour.

EXPLANATORY ANSWERS

1. (B) **2.** (A) **3.** (C) **4.** (C) **5.** (A)
6. (A) **7.** (C) **8.** (D) **9.** (B) **10.** (C)
11. (D) **12.** (A) **13.** (C) **14.** (C) **15.** (C)
16. (C) **17.** (B) **18.** (C) **19.** (D) **20.** (C)
21. (C) **22.** (B) **23.** (C) **24.** (B) **25.** (A)
26. (C) **27.** (B) **28.** (A) **29.** (D) **30.** (A)

31. Between
32. Immoral or Unethical or obscence
33. Yet **34.** Questionable
35. Unfortunately.

36. (B) **37.** (C) **38.** (B) **39.** (B) **40.** (C)
41. (B) **42.** (A) **43.** (A) **44.** (C) **45.** (B)

46. He could not enter in the compartment due to the great rush.
47. Mohan was advised to consult good optician.
48. It is difficult to believe the story given by police.
49. Books are our best companions.
50. Supporters of the winning candidate took out a procession.
51. Indiscipline and irregularity never pay.
52. Do the political parties in our country endeavour to serve the country?
53. There is unity in diversity.
54. Kashmir offers many picturesque scenes of natural beauty.
55. He asked his friend where he was going.
56. Bunch of keys. **57.** Maiden speech.
58. Team of players. **59.** Liabilities.
60. Stock Exchange.

61. (C) **62.** (C) **63.** (A) **64.** (A) **65.** (D)

66. A true story of Taimur, the Lame is very inspiring. In early days he lost heart and felt great disappointment due to his defeats and betrayal by his soldiers and relatives. He thought to commit suicide by throwing himself from mountain top. Before doing so, he rested for a while in a cave. While resting there he saw an ant carrying a morsel of grain on a slipping wall. The ant fell many times from the wall but did not give up. Finally it reached its destination. Taimur was impressed by its perseverance and came out of the cave. He collected a huge army and recaptured his kingdom. He became famous as a warrior and subdued many rulers. Finally he came to India also.

67. Present System of Examination

Examinations are a necessary evil. It is quite understandable that whenever we put in hard work to make successful any venture, we wait for some time to see or guess the results that might have been achieved or might possibly be achieved. It is in this context that examinations become unavoidable, though methods and yardsticks employed may differ and that even widely.

A student studies the whole year and then needs to be examined. It is even in the interest of the student himself or herself to know where he or she stands and how far his or her efforts have borne fruit.

However, the examination system as we have today becomes a farce in essence. It is because of many reasons and factors. The most distressing among these factors is the menace of copying. The students who may be dullards but can manage to indulge in large-scale copying get high marks, whereas the really meritorious students who have worked hard get low marks.

Even otherwise, the prevalent examination system encourages cramming. Those who have a good memory or can indulge in cramming, steal a march over others who cannot do this. Then, it is extremely painful to all lovers of transparency that sometimes even the question papers are sold in the market a day or so before an examination.

Some efforts have been made to bring reforms in the examination such as the introduction of gradation system, the setting of a number of different question papers, objective questions, etc. But much still remains to be desired and done.

68.

Letter to father requesting him to allow you to join an educational tour.

Boys Hostel-II
39, New Convent School
Gwalior
July 21,........

My dear Father,

The tour of our school students is leaving next week for some prominent historical cities such as Agra, Mathura, Delhi, Panipat, Kurukshetra, Amritsar, etc.

It will be a twenty student tour for about ten days and will be led by Shri Prem Prakash, our teacher of history who is a renowned scholar. He will explain to us every significant thing which has some historical and educational value.

The tour will cost only Rs 500/- per student including boarding, lodging, transport and other expenses.

Dear father, it is a rare chance. Kindly allow me to join this tour and send me Rs 500/- at the earliest.

Convey my regards to mamma.

Yours affectiontely
(Krishna Gulati)

PART - B : SOCIAL STUDIES

Directions (Q. 1 to 20): *Fill in the blanks.*

1. The industry stablished, owned and managed by the Government and the allied private investors is called ....
2. The road joining President's House and India Gate is called ....
3. Capital of Malaysia is ....
4. The gulf which separates Sri Lanka from India is ....
5. Office of .... became the most powerful office of Maratha Kingdm.
6. National language of Pakistan is ....
7. The old name of Bangladesh is ....
8. The crack on the crust from which magma comes out on the earth surface, is called ....
9. The instrument used in mapping of seismic waves is called ....
10. Deposition of sedimentary soils in triangular shape at the mouth of the river is called ....
11. The largest continent of the world is ....
12. India's largest coastal line lies in the state of ....
13. The state which produces maximum sugarcane in India, is ....
14. The difference of birth rate and death rate is called ....
15. .... pass lies in Hindukush mountain.
16. .... is made due to deposition of sands or rocks (coarse sands) at sea coast.
17. The highest peak in India is ....
18. Meaning of Japanese word 'Nippon' is ....
19. The Himalayan range which lies in the north of Shiwalik is called ....
20. .... is the federal state and is capital of two states.

Directions (Q. 21 to 40): *State True/False.*

21. Cramp soils are made up of fine particles brought by rivers. (T/F)
22. In Basimer's process metals are separated from their ores by heating. (T/F)
23. The President is the head of the government. (T/F)
24. India is the largest country in population in the world. (T/F)
25. Jhelum, Chenab, Ravi, Beas and Satluj are the main tributaries of Yamuna. (T/F)
26. The process of shifting rocky materials and upper soil from the surface is called soil erosion. (T/F)
27. India's largest state in area is Maharashtra. (T/F)
28. The government formed by more than one party is called coalition government. (T/F)
29. The name given to untouchables by Mahatma Gandhi was Sudras. (T/F)
30. The headquarter of United Nations is situated in the city of Jeneva. (T/F)
31. India carried out her nuclear experiments at Pokharan. (T/F)
32. According to the ancient caste-system, the people associated with trade and commerce were called traders. (T/F)
33. The woman who burnt herself with her husband's dead body was called sati. (T/F)
34. The green colour of the National flag signifies sacrifices. (T/F)

35. S. Ramanujam is called the missile man of India. (T/F)
36. Vicc President administers the Oath of secrecy to the President of India. (T/F)
37. Production of goods in the factory with the help of machines were called industrial revolution. (T/F)
38. Banda Bahadur became the leader of Sikhs after the death of Guru Govind Singh. (T/F)
39. The first battle of Panipat was fought between Babar and Rana Sangram Singh. (T/F)
40. The Local government of villages is called Panchayata. (T/F)

Directions (Q. 41 to 55): *Give Answer in Brief—*

41. Write in brief about the electoral system in India.
42. Describe in short about the provision of President's Rule under Article 356.
43. What do you know about Bardoli Satyagraha?
44. What is crop rotation?
45. Write a short note on Sedimentary Rocks.
46. Write the main features of Government of India Act, 1935.
47. What are the main Organs of the United Nations? Write functions of the secretariat.
48. What is difference between poverty line and poor quality of life?
49. Write a short note on 'Panchsheel'.
50. Why should VAT replace Sales Tax?
51. How did the revolt of 1857 marked a turning point in the history of India?
52. What were the methods adopted by Mahatma Gandhi to mobilise masses for Swaraj?
53. How does cholesterol affect the body?
54. Define GDP.
55. Write a short note on Biodiversity?

EXPLANATORY ANSWERS

1. Joint venture
2. Raj Path
3. Kuala Lumpur
3. Gulf of Mannar
5. Peshwa
6. Urdu
7. Eastern Pakistan
8. Crack eruption
9. Richter Scale
10. Delta
11. Asia
12. Gujarat
13. Uttar Pradesh
14. Population Growth
15. Khaiber
16. Delta
17. K-2
18. Rising Sun
19. Middle Himalaya or Himachal
20. Chandigarh
21. True
22. True
23. True
24. False
25. False
26. True
27. False
28. True
29. False
30. False
31. True
32. False
33. True
34. False
35. False
36. False
37. True
38. True
39. False
40. True

41. Electroral system in India is based on adult franchise, i.e. every person who is a citizen of India and who is not less than 18 years of age shall be entitled to vote at the election provided. He is not disqualified by any provision of the constitution or of any law made by the appropriate Legislature on the ground of non-residence, unsoundness of mind, crime, or corrupt or illegal practice.

42. Under Article 356, if the President is satisfied either on the recommendation of the Governor or on his own that the Government of a particular state cannot be carried on it in accordance with the Constitution, he may declare emergency in the state.

43. Bardoli Satyagraha took place in 1928 in which Sardar Patel successfully led the Peasant's no-tax payment agitation against an increase in land revenue at Bardoli in Maharashtra.

44. When a number of crops are grown one after the other in a fixed rotation to maintain the fertility of the soil, it is called crop rotation. The rotation of crops may complete in a year in some of the areas while it may involve more than one year's time in others.

45. These rocks are formed from materials which have accumulated as a result of various processes, viz., by the build-up of particles derived from other rocks or from the remains of organically formed matter or from deposits created by chemical action. The rocks formed by the deposition of sediment in water are conglomerates. Peat, lignite, Gypsum, and limestone are examples of these rocks.

46. Its chief features were the establishment of (a) An All - India Federation consisting of British India and the Indian States; (b) Dyarchy at the centre; and (c) Autonomy in provinces. But the special powers granted to the Governor - General and the provincial Governors under this Act defeated the very object of this Act.

47. Main Organs of the United Nations are following : (i) General Assembly, (ii) Security Council, (iii) Economic and Social Council, (iv) Trusteeship Council (v) International Court of Justice, (vi) Secretariat.

Functions of the Secretariat : The Secretariat being the chief administrative office of the UNO, its functions are manifold. Its main function is to corrdinate and supervise the activities of UN organs.

48. **Poverty Line :** It is to be found at the level of income at which a person or a family barely subsists.

Poor Quality of Life : It exists when certain sections of people are not aware of how to utilise their resources to satisfy their basic needs in spita of high income levels.

49. There were the five principles enunciated by the Prime Ministers of India and China in 1954 as a basis of international cooperation. They were :

(i) mutual respect for each other's territorial integrity and sovereignty; (ii) nonagression; (iii) non-interference in each other's internal affairs; (iv) equal and mutual benefit and (v) peaceful co-existence.

50. VAT stands for Value-Added Tax, which is a direct tax at the source, while Sale Tax is an indirect tax imposed by the state Governments on trader on their sales. If VAT replaces Sales Tax, it will save lot of procedural formalities and harassment to the draders.

51. The revolt of 1857 marked a turning point in the history of India. The rule of the East India Company came to an end and the control passed to the British Crown. The British Government promised not to annex any more Indian States. The Indian States accepted the paramountcy of the British Government and become loyal allies of the British rule.

52. Mahatma Gandhi's mass movement included defiance of laws, peaceful demonstrations, boycott of courts, stoppage of work, boycott of educational institutions, picketing of shops selling liquor and foreign goods, non-payment of taxes and the closing of vital business.

53. Cholesterol is a white waxy sterol present in the tissues of the human body in which it performs a number of vital functions. It is an important contributor not the structure of cell membranes and an element in the production of certain essential hormones. Its excessive production in man leads to blockage of arteries and coronary heart disease.

54. The measure of the total flow goods and services produced by the economy of a country in a year. It is generally calculated at factor costs, i.e., cost of production of goods and services. When the taxes are also taken into account, the GDP is at market prices, i.e., the prices at which the buyers purchased.

55. It is the short form of biological diversity. It represents and means the whole range of ecosystems, living organisms and genetical materials that human beings co-inhabit the Earth with. Importantly, it includes within its ambit not only just what is traditionally known as wildlife (wild plants and animals) and natural habitats but also domesticated species (crops, livestocks, etc.), and genetic material like germ-plasm, seeds etc. Biological reserves are designed to preserve the genetic diversity in representative ecosystems.

Previous Paper (Solved)

Sainik School Exam, 2007

(Class-IX)

PAPER—I MATHEMATICS AND SCIENCE

PART–A : Mathematics

1. Find the value of $\left(\frac{256}{6561}\right)^{3/8} \times \left(\frac{81}{16}\right)^{3/4}$.

2. Find the value of $x^3 - \frac{1}{x^3}$, if $x - \frac{1}{x} = 7$.

3. Find 105 × 105, using algebraic identity.

4. Find the cube root of 46656.

5. Find the smallest number which must be subtracted from 2050 to get a perfect square number. Also find the square root of the number.

6. Find the square root of – 104.04.

7. State whether True or False :

(i) Two lines perpendicular to the same line intersect each other.

(ii) In a rectangle diagonals are equal and bisect each other at right angles.

(iii) In a circle, the line joining the center to the mid-point of a chord is perpendicular to the chord.

(iv) If a and b are integers such that $a^2 > b^2$ then $a^3 > b^3$.

(v) The radical form of $(a^{1/p})^{1/q} = \sqrt[pq]{a}$.

8. Fill in the blanks :

(i) If $x = 7$, then the value of $(x - 1)(x - 3)(x - 5)(x - 7)(x - 9)(x - 11) =$ ....

(ii) The quadrilateral whose four vertices lie on the circumference of a circle is called ....

(iii) The region enclosed by a polygon is known as .... of the polygon.

(iv) The line segment joining the vertex to the mid-point of opposite side of a triangle is ....

(v) The area of a rhombus is ....

9. ABCD is a cyclic quadrilateral. Diagonal AC and BD are joined. If ∠ BAC = 45° and ∠ BCA = 60° find :

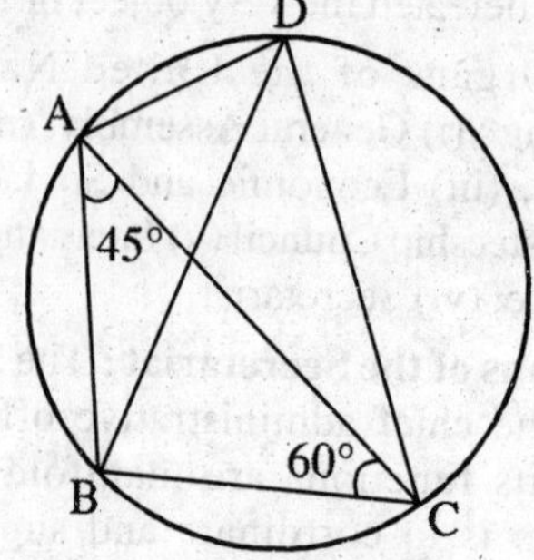

(i) ∠ BDC

(ii) ∠ ABC

(iii) ∠ ADC.

10. The angles P, Q, R and S of a quadrilateral PQRS are in the ratio 1 : 3 : 7 : 9. Find—

(i) All the angles.

(ii) What special name will you give it? State with reason.

11. Find the square root of $56\frac{569}{1225}$.

12. Find the cube root of $\frac{9261}{19683}$.

13. Find the value of $\left(\frac{390625}{42875}\right)^{1/8}$

14. A cycle is sold at a gain of 15%. Had it been

sold for ₹ 150 more, the gain would have been 20%, find the Cost Price of the cycle.

15. A sum of money amounts to ₹ 453690 in 2 years at 6.5% per annum compounded annually. Find the sum.

16. Find the value of $125a^3 - 27b^3$, if $5a - 3b = 13$ and $ab = 20$.

17. Solve the equation

$$\frac{\frac{x}{4}-\frac{3}{5}}{\frac{4}{3}-7x} = -\frac{3}{20}.$$

18. Find the area of the Trapezium whose parallel sides are 24 cms and 14.5 cms and non-parallel sides are 9.5 cms and 11 cms and whose altitude is 2.6 cms.

19. Find the volume of a right circular cylinder whose diameter is 5.6 cms and height is 8 cms.

20. Divide $12x^3 - 8x^2 - 6x + 10$ by $3x - 2$. Also verify the result.
Dividend = Divisor × Quotient + Remainder.
Also write the degrees of Divisor, Dividend and Quotient.

21. Mariam bought two fans for ₹ 3690. She sold one at a profit of 15% and other at a loss of 10%. If Mariam obtained the same amount for each fan, find the cost price of each fan. Also find the gain or loss per cent on the whole transaction.

22. A race boat covers a distance of 66 kms down-stream in 110 minutes. It covers this distance upstream in 2 hours. Find the speed of the boat in still water and also the speed of the stream.

23. A water tank of dimension 2 m × 1.5 m × 1m can be filled by pipe A in 4 hours, by pipe B in 6 hours and it can be emptied by pipe C in 3 hours. Find the time taken to fill the tank when all the three pipes are on at a time. Also find the capacity of the water tank.

24. The circumference of the base of a right circular cylinder is 176 cms. If its height is 0.5 m, find the curved surface area and total surface area, if both the ends are closed.

25. Sum of the digits of a two digit number is 12. The given number exceeds the number obtained by interchanging the digits by 36. Find the number.

26. Weekly savings in rupees of 30 students of Class VIII are 38, 42, 40, 35, 72, 27, 57, 62, 59, 80, 84, 73, 65, 40, 76, 40, 38, 60, 58, 38, 54, 39, 50, 44, 71, 83, 45, 38, 80 and 77. Construct group frequency table with class intervals equal to 5.

27. Read the following Histogram and answer the questions given below :

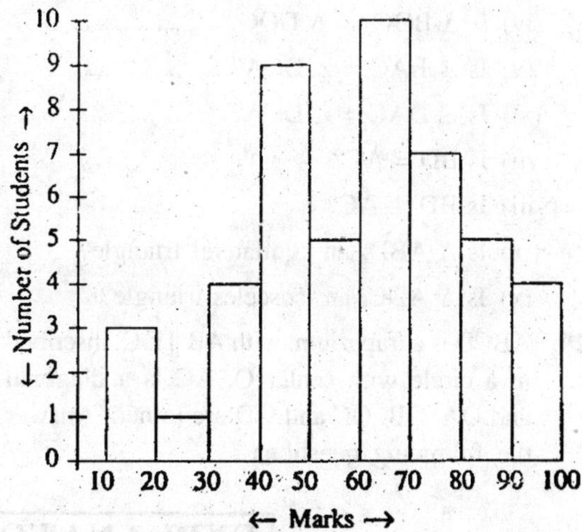

(i) What is the number of students in the lowest marks group?

(ii) How many students have scored more than 60 marks?

(iii) In which group(s) the number of students are same?

(iv) What is the size of each class?

(v) Write the number of students in the highest marks group.

28. ABCD is a rhombus and diagonals AC and BD intersecting each other at O. Answer the following questions in Yes or No.

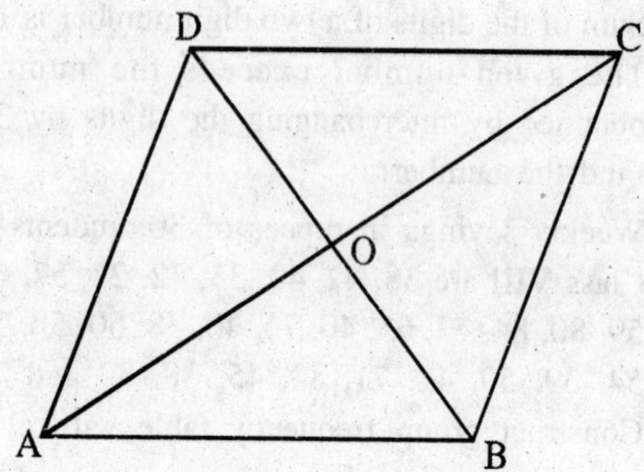

(i) Is OB = OD? ....

(ii) Is BC = DC? ....

(iii) Is ∠ BCO = ∠ DCO? ....

(iv) Is Δ BOC ≅ Δ DOC? ....

(v) Is ∠ BAC = ∠ DCA? ....

(vi) Is ∠ DAC = ∠ DCA? ....

(vii) Is BD = AC?

(viii) Is BD ⊥ AC?

(ix) Is Δ ABD, an equilateral triangle?

(x) Is Δ ADC, an isosceles triangle?

29. ABCD is a trapezium, with AB ∥ DC, inscribed in a circle with center O, AC is a diagonal and OA, OB, OC and OD are joined. Answer the following questions :

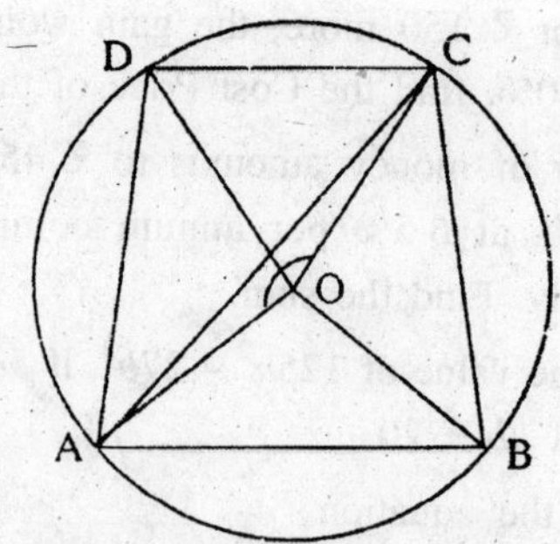

(i) Is ∠ BAC = ∠ DCA? Why?

(ii) Is ∠ BAC = $\frac{1}{2}$ ∠ BOC? Why?

(iii) Is ∠ BOC = ∠ DOA? Why?

(iv) If ∠ AOC = 140°, find ∠ OAC

(v) If ∠ DCA = 70°, find ∠ BOC.

30. Find the smallest number by which 5184 is to be multiplied to make a perfect cube. Also find the smallest number by which 5184 is to be divided to make a perfect cube. Find cube root in both the cases.

31. A cycle merchant allows 25% discount on the marked price of the cycles and still makes a profit of 20%. If he gains ₹ 360 over the sale of one cycle, find the marked price, cost price and selling price of the cycle.

32. A rectangular park is of length 50 m and breadth 42 m, outside the park there is a path of breadth 2 m which runs around the park. Find the area of the path. Also find the cost of cementing the path at a rate of ₹ 7.50 per square meter.

EXPLANATORY ANSWERS

1. $\left(\frac{256}{6561}\right)^{3/8} \times \left(\frac{81}{16}\right)^{3/4}$

$$= \left[\left(\frac{2}{3}\right)^8\right]^{3/8} \times \left[\left(\frac{3}{2}\right)^4\right]^{3/4}$$

$$= \left(\frac{2}{3}\right)^3 \times \left(\frac{3}{2}\right)^3$$

$$= \left(\frac{2}{3}\times\frac{3}{2}\right)^3 = (1)^3 = 1$$

2. ∵ $x - \frac{1}{x} = 7$

$\Rightarrow$ $\left(x-\frac{1}{x}\right)^3 = (7)^3$

$$\Rightarrow x^3 - \frac{1}{x^3} - 3\left(x - \frac{1}{x}\right) = 343$$

$$\Rightarrow x^3 - \frac{1}{x^3} - 3\times 7 = 343$$

$$\therefore x^3 - \frac{1}{x^3} = 343 + 21$$

$$= 364$$

3. 105×105

$= (100 + 5)(100 + 5)$

$= 100 \times 100 + 100 \times 5 + 100 \times 5 + 5 \times 5$

$= 10000 + 500 + 500 + 25$

$= 11025$

4. $46656 = \overline{2\times2\times2} \times \overline{2\times2\times2} \times \overline{3\times3\times3} \times \overline{3\times3\times3}$

$\therefore$ Cube root of $46656 = 2 \times 2 \times 3 \times 3$

$= 36$

5.

```
         45
    ----------
  4 | 20 50
    | 16
    ----------
 85 | 450
    | 425
    ----------
    | 25
```

$\therefore$ Reqd. number = 25

and square root = 45

6.

```
         10.2
    ----------
  1 | 104.04
    | 1
    ----------
202 | 0404
    | 404
    ----------
    | ×
```

Square root of 104.04 = 10.2

7. (i) False (ii) False

(iii) True (iv) True

(v) True

8. (i) Zero

(ii) Cyclic quadrilateral

(iii) Area.

(iv) Median

(v) $\frac{1}{2}\times$ One diagonal x second diagonal

9. (i) $\angle BDC = \angle BAC = 45°$

(Angles of the same segment)

(ii) $\angle ABC = 180° - (45° + 60°)$

$= 75°$

(iii) $\angle ADC = 180° - \angle ABC$

(Opposite angles of a cyclic □ are supplementary)

$= 180° - 75°$

$= 105°$

10. (i) $\because$ Ratio of angles P, Q, R and S

$= 1 : 3 : 7 : 9$

$\therefore$ Sum of ratios $= 1 + 3 + 7 + 9 = 20$

$\therefore \angle P = \frac{1\times360}{20} = 18°$

$\angle Q = \frac{3\times360}{20} = 54°$

$\angle R = \frac{7\times360}{20} = 126°$

and $\angle S = \frac{9\times360}{20} = 162°$

(ii) $\because \angle P + \angle S = 18° + 162° = 180°$

$\therefore$ PQ || RS

$\therefore$ The quadrilateral is trapazium.

11. $\because 56\frac{569}{1225} = \frac{69169}{1225} = \left(\frac{263}{35}\right)^2$

$\therefore$ Sq. root of $56\frac{569}{1225} = \sqrt{\left(\frac{263}{35}\right)^2} = \frac{263}{35}$

$= 7\frac{18}{35}$

12. $\frac{9261}{19683} = \frac{343\times27}{729\times27} = \frac{343}{729}$

$= \frac{7\times7\times7}{3\times3\times3\times3\times3\times3} = \left(\frac{7}{9}\right)^3$

$\therefore$ Cube root of $\frac{9261}{19683} = \sqrt{\left(\frac{7}{9}\right)^3}$

13. $\left(\frac{390625}{42875}\right)^{1/8} = \left[\frac{(5)^8}{5^3 \times 7^3}\right]^{1/8}$

$= \frac{5}{5^{3/8} \times 7^{3/8}}$

$= \frac{5^{5/8}}{7^{3/8}} = \left[\frac{5^5}{7^3}\right]^{1/8}$

14. Let the cost price of the cycle be ₹ 100.

$\therefore$ S.P. at the gain of 15% = ₹ 115

and S.P. at the gain of 20% = ₹ 120

$\because$ difference of two S.Ps. = 120 – 115

= ₹ 5

When difference is ₹ 5 then C.P.

= ₹ 100

$\therefore$ When difference is ₹ 150 then C.P.

$= \frac{100 \times 150}{5}$

= ₹ 3000

15. $\because$ We know that,

$A = P\left(1 + \frac{R}{100}\right)^n$

$\therefore \quad 453690 = P\left(1 + \frac{6.5}{100}\right)^2$

$= P\left(\frac{106.5 \times 106.5}{100 \times 100}\right)$

$\therefore \quad P = \frac{453690 \times 100 \times 100}{106.5 \times 106.5}$

= ₹ 400000

16. $125a^3 - 27b^3 = (5a - 3b)^3 + 45ab\,(5a - 3b)$

$= (13)^3 + 45 \times 20 \times 13$

$= 13\,[169 + 900]$

$= 13 \times 1069$

$= 13897$

17. $\frac{\frac{x}{4} - \frac{3}{5}}{\frac{4}{3} - 7x} = \frac{-3}{20}$

$\Rightarrow \frac{\frac{5x-12}{20}}{\frac{4-21x}{3}} = \frac{-3}{20}$

$\Rightarrow \frac{3(5x-12)}{20(4-21x)} = \frac{-3}{20}$

$\Rightarrow \frac{5x-12}{4-21x} = 1$

$\Rightarrow 5x - 12 = 21x - 4$

$\Rightarrow 16x = -8$

$\therefore \quad x = -\frac{1}{2}$

18. Area of a trapezium

$= \frac{1}{2} \times$ sum of parallel sides $\times$ altitude

$= \frac{1}{2} \times (24 + 14.5) \times 2.6$

$= 50.05 \text{ cm}^2$

19. Radius of the cylinder $= \frac{1}{2} \times 5.6$

= 2.8 cm

and height of the cylinder = 8 cm

$\therefore$ Volume of the cylinder $= \pi r^2 h$

$= \frac{22}{7} \times 2.8 \times 2.8 \times 8$

$= 197.12 \text{ cm}^3$

20. $3x - 2)\ 12x^3 - 8x^2 - 6x + 10\ (4x^2 - 2$

$12x^3 - 8x^2$

$-6x + 10$

$-6x + 4$

$+6$

Dividend = Divisor × Quotient + Remainder

$12x^3 - 8x^2 - 6x + 10$

$= (3x - 2)(4x^2 - 2) + 6$

$= 12x^3 - 6x - 8x^2 + 4 + 6$

$= 12x^3 - 8x^2 - 6x + 10$

Now, Degree of Divisor = 1

Degree of Dividend = 3

Degree of Quotient = 2

21. Let the C.P. of one fan be ₹ x.

$\therefore$ C.P. for the other fan

$= ₹\ (3690 - x)$

$\because \quad \frac{x \times 115}{100} = \frac{(3690 - x) \times 90}{100}$

$\Rightarrow \quad 115x = 332100 - 90x$

$\Rightarrow \quad 115x + 90x = 332100$

$\Rightarrow \quad 205x = 332100$

$\therefore \quad x = \frac{332100}{205} = 1620$

$\therefore$ C.P. of one fan = ₹ 1620

and C.P. of other fan

$= 3960 - 1620 =$ ₹ 2340

$\therefore$ S.P. of both fans together

$= \frac{1620 \times 115}{100} + \frac{2340 \times 90}{100}$

$= 1863 + 2106$

= ₹ 3969

$\therefore$ Total profit = 3969 − 3690 = ₹ 279

and gain % on whole transaction

$= \frac{279 \times 100}{3690}\%$

$= 7.56\%$

22. Let the speed of boat in still water be x km/hr and the speed of the stream be y km/hr

$\because \quad \frac{66}{x+y} = \frac{110}{60}$

$\Rightarrow \quad x + y = \frac{66 \times 60}{110} = 36 \quad ...(1)$

and $\quad \frac{66}{x-y} = 2$

$\therefore \quad x - y = \frac{66}{2} = 33 \quad ...(2)$

$\therefore \quad x + y = 36$

and $\quad x - y = 33$

$\Rightarrow \quad 2x = 69$

$\therefore \quad x = \frac{69}{2} = 34.5$ km/hr

and $\quad y = \frac{3}{2} = 1.5$ km/hr

$\therefore$ Speed of the boat in still water = 34.5 km/hr and the speed of the stream = 1.5 km/hr.

23. $\because$ The pipe A fills the tank in 4 hrs.

$\therefore$ In 1 hr. the pipe A will fill

$= \frac{1}{4}$ part of the tank

Similarly In 1 hr. the pipe B will fill

$= \frac{1}{6}$ part of the tank

and In 1 hr. the pipe C will empty

$= \frac{1}{3}$ part of the tank

$\therefore$ When all the pipes A, B and C are on, the part of tank will be filled

$= \frac{1}{4} + \frac{1}{6} - \frac{1}{3}$

$= \frac{3 + 2 - 4}{12}$

$= \frac{1}{12}$

Hence when all the three pipes A, B and C are on, the tank will be filled in 12 hours.

Capacity of the water tank

$= 2 \text{ m} \times 1.5 \text{ m} \times 1 \text{ m}$

= 3 cubic metre

24. $\because$ Circumference of the base of the cylinder

$= 2\pi r = 176$ cm

$\Rightarrow \quad 2 \times \frac{22}{7} \times r = 176$

$\therefore \quad r = \frac{176 \times 7}{2 \times 22} = 28$ cm and height (h) = 0.5 m

$= 50$ cm

$\therefore$ Curved surface area $= 2\pi rh$

$$= 2\times\frac{22}{7}\times 28\times 50$$

$$= 8800 \text{ cm}^2$$

and total surface area $= 2\pi rh + 2\pi r^2$

$$= 2\pi(28 \times 50 + 28 \times 28)$$

$$= 2\times\frac{22}{7}(1400 + 784)$$

$$= 13728 \text{ cm}^2$$

25. Let the number be $(10x + y)$

$\therefore$ $x + y = 12$ ...(1)

and $(10x + y) - (10y + x) = 36$

$\Rightarrow$ $9x - 9y = 36$

$\Rightarrow$ $x - y = 4$ ...(2)

$x + y = 12$

and $x - y = 4$

$\therefore$ $2x = 16$

$\therefore$ $x = 8$ and $y = 4$

$\therefore$ The required number is 84.

26.

C.I.	Tally marks	Frequency
25–30	|	1
30–35		0
35–40	𝍸 |	6
40–45	𝍸	5
45–50	|	1
50–55	||	2
55–60	|||	3
60–65	||	2
65–70	|	1
70–75	|||	3
75–80	||	2
80–85	||||	4
		30

27. (i) The number of students in the lowest marks group = 3.

(ii) No. of students who have scored more than 60 marks $= 10 + 7 + 5 + 4$
$= 26$

(iii) The number of students are same in (50 – 60) and (80 – 90) *i.e.,* 5 and, In group (30 – 40) and (90 – 100) *i.e.,* 4.

(iv) Size of each class is 10.

(v) No. of students in the highest marks group = 4.

28. (i) yes (ii) yes
(iii) yes (iv) yes
(v) yes (vi) yes
(vii) no (viii) yes
(ix) no (x) yes

29. (i) Yes, $\angle$ BAC = $\angle$ DCA
(because angles are alternate)

(ii) Yes, $\angle \text{BAC} = \frac{1}{2}\angle \text{BOC}$

(because on the same segment BC, the angle at the centre is twice of the angle at the circumference)

(iii) Yes, $\angle BOC = \angle DOA$

because $\angle BAC = \angle DCA$

and $\angle BOC = 2\angle BAC$

and $\angle DOA = 2\angle DCA$

$\therefore$ $\angle BOC = \angle DOA$

(iv) In Δ OAC

$\angle OAC + \angle OCA + \angle AOC = 180°$

and $\angle OAC = \angle OCA$

(because OA = OC radii of the same circle)

$\therefore$ $2\angle OAC + 140° = 180°$

$\Rightarrow$ $2\angle OAC = 180° - 140°$

$= 40°$

$\therefore$ $\angle OAC = \frac{40°}{2} = 20°$

(v) $\because$ $\angle DCA = 70° = \angle BAC$

and $\angle BOC = 2\angle BAC$

$\therefore$ $\angle BOC = 2 \times 70° = 140°$

30.

2	5184
2	2592
2	1296
2	648
2	324
2	162
3	81
3	27
3	9
	3

$\therefore \quad 5184 = \overline{2\times2\times2} \times \overline{2\times2\times2} \times \overline{3\times3\times3} \times \overline{3}$

$\therefore$ The number by which to be multiplied to make a perfect cube $= 3 \times 3 = 9$ and the number by which to be divided to make a perfect cube $= 3$

Cube root in I case = 36

and cube root in II case = 12

31. Let the M.P. of the cycle be ₹ x.

$\because$ S.P. of the cycle after discount

$$= x - \frac{25}{100}x$$

$$= ₹\ \frac{3x}{4}$$

Profit = 20%

$\therefore$ C.P. of the cycle $= \dfrac{\frac{3x}{4} \times 100}{(100+20)}$

$$= ₹\ \frac{5x}{8}$$

$\because \quad \dfrac{3x}{4} - \dfrac{5x}{8} = ₹\ 360$

$\Rightarrow \quad \dfrac{6x - 5x}{8} = 360$

$\therefore \quad x = 360 \times 8 = ₹\ 2880$

$\therefore$ Marked Price of the cycle = ₹ 2880

C.P. of the cycle $= \dfrac{5}{8} \times 2880 = ₹\ 1800$

and S.P. of the cycle $= \dfrac{3}{4} \times 2880 = ₹\ 2160$

32. $\because$ Area of rectangle ABCD $= 50 \times 42 = 2100\ m^2$

Area of rectangle PQRS $= 54 \times 46 = 2484\ m^2$

$\therefore$ Area of the path $= 2484 - 2100 = 384\ m^2$

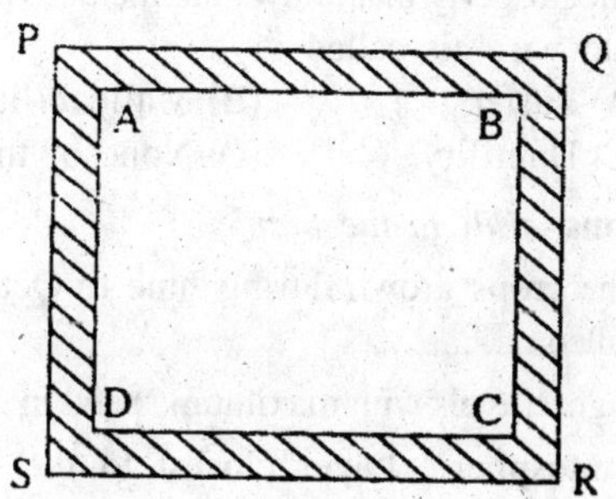

And cost of cementing the path $= 384 \times ₹\ 7.50 = ₹\ 2880.00$

PART 'B' : SCIENCE

Directions : *Choose the correct answer from given alternatives:*

1. Most abundant gas in air is :
(A) Oxygen (B) Nitrogen
(C) Carbon dioxide (D) Argon

2. Chemical name of Vinegar is :
(A) Hydrochloric acid
(B) Formic acid
(C) Benzoic acid
(D) Acetic acid

3. Steel is the alloy of :
(A) Iron and Copper (B) Iron and Carbon
(C) Iron and Tin (D) Iron and Nickel

4. Instrument used to measure air pressure is called :

(A) Hydrometer (B) Barometer
(C) Voltmeter (D) Air Pump

5. Ozone is the allotrope of :
(A) Oxygen (B) Carbon
(C) Argon (D) Nitrogen

6. Malaria is caused by :
(A) Bacillus bacteria
(B) Plasmodium parasite
(C) Virus
(D) Mycoplasma

7. Loss of electron in an atom gives rise to :
(A) Positive ion (B) Negative ion
(C) Ionic compound (D) Neutral atom

8. LPG consists mainly :
(A) Butane (B) Propane
(C) Ethane (D) All of these

9. Metals on combustion produce :
(A) Basic Oxide (B) Acidic Oxide
(C) Neutral Oxide (D) Ash

10. The property that allows the metal to be drawr into wires is called :
(A) Luster (B) Malleability
(C) Ductility (D) None of these

Directions—*Fill in the blanks :*

11. The crops grown during June to October are called ....

12. Light travels with maximum speed in ....

13. Atmospheric Layer closest to the Earth is called ....

14. A camera has a .... lens in it.

15. Electric generators work on the principle of .... to produce electricity.

16. Full form of CNG is ....

17. The distance between focus and optical center of a lens is called ....

18. Diamond is the allotrope of ....

19. Atoms of an element that have same atomic number but different mass number are called ....

20. Molecular formula of Methane is ....

Directions—*Give Answers in Brief :*

21. What do you understand by the term corrosion? How corrosion in iron can be prevented?

22. Describe Green House effect and its significance.

23. Draw a typical cell and label important organelles in it.

24. What do you understand by micro-organism? Describe its useful and harmful effects.

25. Describe about renewable and non-renewable sources of energy.

26. What is the difference between Voltaic Cell and Dry Cell?

27. Differentiate between Plant Cell and Animal Cell.

28. Carbon dioxide gas when passed through lime water, turns milky, why?

29. What is the difference in the structure of Diamond and Graphite?

30. What are fullerenes?

31. How can wind energy produce electricity?

32. Atomic Number and Mass Number of Sodium atom is 11 and 23 respectively. Calculate the number of Protons, Neutrons and Electrons present in Sodium atom.

33. What do you understand by Redox Reaction?

34. What are the factors responsible for the depletion of the Ozone Layer in the atmosphere?

35. Name the planets of the Solar System?

ANSWERS WITH HINTS

1. (B) 2 (D) 3. (B) 4. (B) 5. (A)
6. (B) 7. (A) 8. (B) 9. (A) 10. (C)

11. Kharif.

12. Vacuum.

13. Troposphere.

14. Convex.

15. Electro Magnetic Induction.

16. Condensed Natural Gas.

17. Focal Length.

18. Carbon.

19. Isotopes.

20. CH_4.

21. Reaction of a metal with air, moisture and other compounds leading to the formation of oxide, carbonate, hydroxide, etc. on its surface. Rusting of iron is a common example of corrosion. The simplest precaution consists of coating the metal with the protective layers of paint.

22. Carbon dioxide (CO_2), an important constituent of greenhouse gas, is also a natural constituent of the atmosphere. The spectral properties of CO_2 in the atmosphere are such that it tends to prevent the long wave radiations (*e.g.*, infra-red) from earth from escaping into outer space and deflect it back to earth. The latter has an increased amount of temperature at surface. This phenomenon is called **greenhouse effect**.

23.

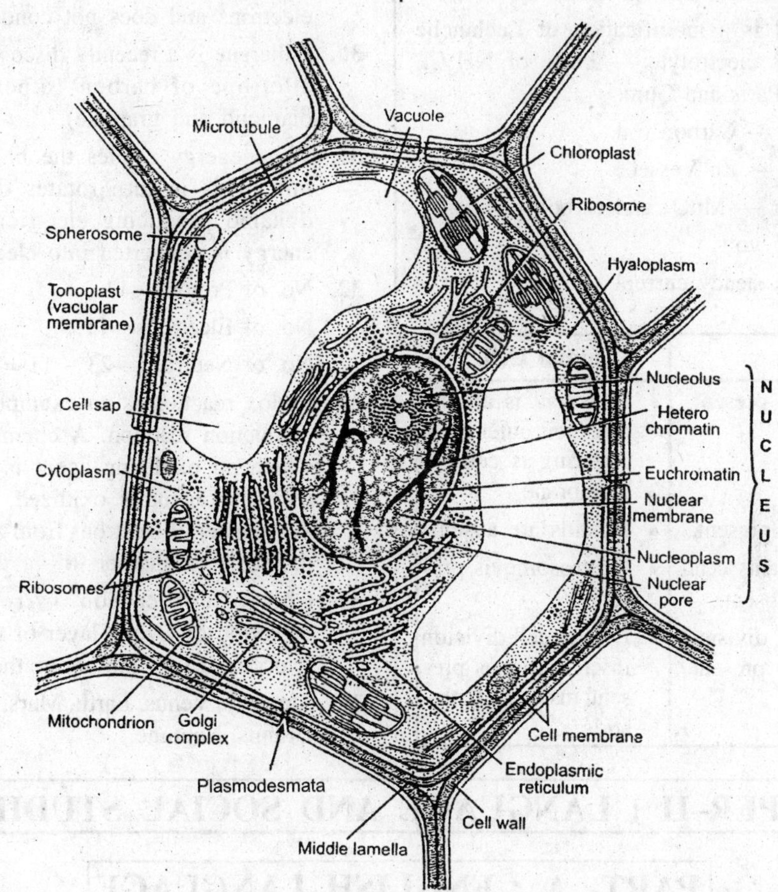

Fig: A Plant Cell Under Electron Microscope

24. Any organism that can be observed only with the add of a microscope is termed **micro-organism.** Microorganisms include bacteria, algae, viruses, protozoans and fungi. **Useful effect:** Certain bacteria are useful too nitrogen fixation (*e.g.* Azotobacter and Rhizobium), certain fungi like *Penicillium notatum* yields antibiotic Penicillin.

Harmful effect: Various bacteria cause human diseases (*e.g.*, Cholera caused by *Vibrio cholerae* and Diarrhoea caused by *Bacillus coli*), certain fungi cause plant diseases (*e.g.*, covered smut of oat is caused by *Ustilago kolleri* and Blight of paddy caused by *Xanthomonas Oryzae.*

26. Voltaic cell is a simple cell having Electrolyte-dil H_2SO_4

+ ve plate—Cu plate

– ve plate—Zn plate

Max EMF = 1.08 volt

It suffers from defects of local action and polarisation. It does not give constant current.

A dry cell is a modification of Leclanche cell. It has electrolyte — Paste of NH_4Cl, Plaster of Paris and Gum.

+ ve plate — Carbon rod.

– ve plate — Zn Vessel.

Depolariser — MnO_2 and carbon powder

EMF = 1.5 volt

It can give steady current.

27.

Plant Cell	Animal Cell
• Cell wall is present.	• Cell wall is absent and their outer most covering is cell membrane.
• Plastids are present.	• Plastids are absent.
• In higher plants centrosome is absent.	• Centrosome is present.
• During cell division cell plate is present.	• During cell division invagination is present instead of plastids.

28. Calcium carbonate ($CaCO_3$) is formed when carbon dioxide (CO_2) passes through lime water [$Ca(OH)_2$].

$Ca\ (OH)_2 + CO_2 \rightarrow CaCO_3 + H_2O$

Colour of $CaCO_3$ is white and it is insoluble in water. Hence, finally water appears white (milky).

29. Graphite contains free electrons and is a good conductor of electricity. Hence, it is used to make electrodes. Diamond does not have free electrons and does not conduct electricity.

30. Fullerene is a recently discovered crystalline allotrope of carbon (other forms being diamond and graphite).

31. Wind energy rotates the blades of a wind mill. This in turn rotates the armature of dynamo producing electricity. Thus wind energy is converted into electrical energy.

32. No. of Protons—11

No. of Electrons—11

No. of Neutrons—23 – 11 = 12

33. Redox reaction is an example of oxidation-reduction reaction. A chemical reaction in which an oxidizing agent is reduced and a reducing agent is oxidized, thus involving the transfer of electrons from one atom, ion or molecule to another.

34. Chlorofluorocarbon is responsible for depletion of Ozone layer of the atmosphere. It occurs 15-20 km above the earth surface.

35. Mercury, Venus, Earth, Mars, Jupiter, Saturn, Uranus, Neptune.

PAPER–II : LANGUAGE AND SOCIAL STUDIES

PART- A : ENGLISH LANGUAGE

Directions (Q. 1-15): *Each question is followed by three or four alternatives. Select the correct answer and encircle its letter. You are not required to write the choice in the blank.*

1. He ran .... the road and was run down by a car.

(A) along (B) across

(C) on (D) in

2. The car skidded and fell .... a ditch.

(A) on (B) in

(C) into (D) None of these

3. It is suggested that a ring road be .... to relieve the congestion.

(A) build (B) built

(C) had built (D) had been built

4. I often wonder how you .... getting along.
(A) were (B) are
(C) has been (D) had been

5. A large number of colleges are affiliated...... Delhi University.
(A) with (B) to
(C) from (D) by

6. He boasted .... his accomplishments.
(A) of (B) on
(C) about (D) into

7. A pair of trousers .... given to the servant.
(A) has been (B) have been
(C) had been (D) is given

8. If you render .... help I will succeed.
(A) a little (B) little
(C) very little (D) the little

9. The services are very punctual and the aeroplane will definitely land .... time.
(A) on (B) in
(C) over (D) for

10. At last he yielded ...., the temptation.
(A) for (B) to
(C) at (D) on

11. The government .... implementing the plan.
(A) is (B) are
(C) were (D) has

12. The government .... taken this decision unanimously.
(A) has (B) have
(C) has been (D) had been

13. As soon as he went, the cattle .... scattered.
(A) was (B) were
(C) are (D) None of these

14. I prefer tea .... coffee.
(A) than (B) to
(C) or (D) and

15. I saw the man taking rest .... the shade of the tree.
(A) in (B) on
(C) under (D) among

Directions (Q. 16-20): *Select the appropriate synonym which is nearest to the meaning to the given words.*

16. adequate:
(A) complete (B) substantial
(C) early (D) sufficient

17. emulate:
(A) study (B) admire
(C) follow (D) imitate

18. obsolete:
(A) boring (B) inaccessible
(C) out-of-date (D) unfashionable

19. uncouth:
(A) snobbish (B) unnatural
(C) unconventional (D) ungracious

20. nomadic:
(A) roving (B) barbarous
(C) brave (D) wild

Directions (Q. 21-25): *Select the appropriate antonym, which is nearly opposite in meaning to the word given.*

21. smart:
(A) lazy (B) active
(C) indecent (D) casual

22. ecstasy:
(A) grief (B) bereavement
(C) sorrow (D) agony

23. dilate:
(A) distend (B) contract
(C) blink (D) stretch

24. deteriorated:
(A) aggravated (B) improved
(C) worsened (D) changed

25. discarded:
(A) highlighted (B) forwarded
(C) elaborated (D) accepted

Directions (Q. 26-30): *Choose the correct spellings from the given choices and encircle the correct one.*

26. (A) trankil (B) tranquil
(C) trenquil (D) tranquill

27. (A) adeptation (B) adaptetion
(C) adaption (D) adaptation

28. (A) dispasionate (B) dispassionate
(C) despassionate (D) dispassionat

29. (A) meraculous (B) miracolous
(C) miraculous (D) maraculous

30. (A) imaculately (B) immaculately
(C) imeculately (D) emaculately

Directions (Q. 31-35): *Out of the given alternatives, choose the correct word which is very close to the definition.*

31. A person who can read the future with the help of numbers.
(A) Palmist
(B) Numerologist
(C) Astrologist
(D) Tarot

32. A person who tries to be what he is not.
(A) Liar (B) Hypocrite
(C) Crook (D) Pretender

33. A person who sells illicit liquor.
(A) Hawker (B) Grocer
(C) Druggist (D) Bootlegger

34. A person who loves mankind.
(A) Philanthropist (B) Atheist
(C) Ascetic (D) Agnostic

35. A person who sells buttons, zips, threads etc.
(A) Haberdasher (B) Grocer
(C) Tinker (D) Tailor

Directions (Q. 36-40): *The following sentences contain errors. Select the part with the error and encircle its letter (A), (B), (C). If there is no error, encircle (D).*

36. The picture (A) is the best (B) of the two. (C) No error. (D)

37. Those who are (A) excessively careful for their (B) health are generally healthy. (C) No error. (D)

38. The speaker advised (A) the youth to refrain (B) in indulging in vandalism. (C) No error. (D)

39. Most of the members at the meeting felt that (A) the group appointed for investigating the case (B) were not competent to do the job efficiently. (C) No error. (D)

40. It does not matter how you do it; what I want (A) is that you should finish (B) the work within a month. (C) No error. (D)

Directions (Q. 41-45): *Rearrange the following groups of words and make meaningful sentence in the space provided.*

41. nor a miracle / yoga is / neither magic.

42. personality cover a / and official life / for an adult / that includes / broader area / his personal.

43. and help him / can influence / at his best / yoga / one's personality / to be.

44. touches every phase / personality / is a / in the life / broad concept that / of a human being.

45. personality means / good physique / for a student / a good academic record / and a.

Directions (Q. 46-50): *Change the narration of the following sentences—*

46. The kidnappers said, "If you don't pay the ransom we will kill your daughter."

47. Tom refused to lend her any more money.

48. She exclaimed, "How beautifully the moon-light shines on the sleeping bank of the river!"

49. She asked him to go immediately and finish the work.

50. The prince said, "It gives me great pleasure to be here with you, this evening".

Directions (Q. 51-55): *Change the voice of the following.*

51. The wall is being built by the mason.

52. The sudden noise frightened the horse.

53. Why did your brother write such a letter?

54. He will finish the work in a fortnight.

55. Some boys were helping the wounded man..

Directions (Q. 56-60): *Rewrite the following as directed.*

56. We must eat to live. *(Turn into a compound sentence)*

57. He said he was innocent. *(Turn into a simple sentence)*

58. Nelson knew the value of obedience so well that he anticipated some censure for his act. *(Rewrite using 'too' for 'so')*

59. No other metal is as useful as iron. *(Turn the sentence into comparative degree)*

60. Some girls of the class are cleverer than Naomi. *(Turn into superlative degree)*

Directions (Q. 61-65): *Read the following passage carefully and answer the following questions—*

It has part of Nelson's prayer that the British fleet might be distinguished by humanity in the victory which he expected. Setting an example himself, he twice gave orders to cease firing upon the ship Redoubtable supposing that he had struck because her great guns were silent; for as she carried no flag, there was no means of instantly ascertaining the fact. From the ship which he had thus twice spared, he received his death. A ball fired from her mizzen—top which, in the then situation of the two vessels was not more than fifteen yards from the part of the deck where he was standing, struck the epaulette on the left shoulder. He fell upon his face on the spot which was covered with his poor secretary's blood. Hardy, who was a few steps from him turned round and saw three men raising him up. "My backbone is shot through!" Yet even now, for a moment losing his presence of mind he observed as they were carrying him down the ladder, that the tiller ropes which had been shot away, were not replaced and ordered that new ones should be roped immediately. Then that he might not be seen by the crew he took out his handkerchief, he covered his face and his stars. Had he concealed these badges of honour from the enemy, England, perhaps would not have had cause to receive with sorrow the news of the battle of Trafalgar. The cockpit was crowded with wounded and dying men. Nelson was laid on a pallet in the midshipmen's berth. It was soon perceived, upon examination that the wound was mortal. This, however, was concealed from all, except Captain Hardy, the Chaplain and the medical attendants. Nelson was certain that no human care would avail him. He insisted that the surgeon should leave him and attend to those to whom it might be useful.

Directions: *Answer the following questions.*

61. Find one synonymous word from the passage the meaning of which is 'to hide'.

62. What did Nelson want the British fleet to be?

63. What qualities of Nelson's character are revealed by this passage?

64. Why did Nelson suggest that the surgeon should leave him and attend to others?

65. How can Nelson be said to have been partly responsible for his own death?

66. Write a courteous letter to your neighbour whose dog annoys you by barking at night.

67. Write a readable story from the given outline. King Solomon was noted for his wisdom ...(1)... Queen of Sheba heard of his fame ...(2)... came to visit him ...(3)... impressed by his wealth and grandeur ...(4)... wanted to test his power of solving puzzles ...(5)... showed him two garlands of flowers, one in right hand and the other in left ...(6)... one real and the other artificial ...(7)... asks, "Which is which ?" ...(8)... courtiers puzzled ... (9)... both garlands looked the same ... (10)... Solomon silent ...(11)... Queen feels triumphant ...(12)... Solomon ordered windows to be opened ...(13)... bees flew in from garden ...(14)... buzzed about the Queen ...(15)... all settled in garland in her right hand ...(16)... Solomon said the flowers in right hand real, in left hand artificial ...(17)... Queen was impressed with his wisdom.

68. Write a passage in about 150 words on "Computers in Our Daily Life".

ANSWERS WITH EXPLANATIONS

1. (B) **2.** (C) **3.** (B) **4.** (B) **5.** (B)
6. (A) **7.** (A) **8.** (A) **9.** (B) **10.** (B)
11. (A) **12.** (A) **13.** (D) **14.** (B) **15.** (A)
16. (D) **17.** (D) **18.** (C) **19.** (D) **20.** (A)
21. (A) **22.** (D) **23.** (B) **24.** (B) **25.** (D)
26. (B) **27.** (D) **28.** (B) **29.** (C) **30.** (B)

31. (B) **32.** (B) **33.** (D) **34.** (A) **35.** (A)

36. (B) Change 'the best' to 'better' because comparision between two pictures.

37. (C) Change 'for' to 'about'.

38. (C) Change 'in' to 'from' because from is used after refrain.

39. (C) Change 'were' to 'was' because group is a collective noun.

40. (D) No error.

41. Yoga is neither magic nor a miracle.

42. For an adult personality covers a broader area that includes his personal and official life.

43. Yoga can influence one's personality and help him to be at his best

44. Personality is a broad concept that touches every phase in the life of a human being.

45. Personality means a good academic record and a good physique for a student.

46. The kidnappers threatened if he did not pay the ransom they would kill his daughter.

47. Tom said, "Not lend her any more money".

48. She exclaimed with joy that the moonlight shone beautifully on the sleeping bank of the river.

49. She cried, "Go immediately and finish the work."

50. The prince said that it gave him great pleasure to be there with him, that evening.

51. The mason is building the wall.

52. The horse was frightened of the sudden noise.

53. Why was such a letter written by your brother?

54. The work will be finished by him in a fortnight.

55. The wounded man was being helped by some boys.

56. We must eat so that we may live.

57. He claimed his innocence.

58. Nelson knew the value of obedience too well to anticipate some censure for his act.

59. Iron is more useful metal than any other metal.

60. Naomi is not the cleverest girl of the class.

61. Conceal.

62. Nelson wanted that the British fleet might be distinguished by humanity in the victory. Setting an example himself he twice gave orders to cease firing upon the ship.

63. Nelson shows humanity even in the war. When he knew that his death was imminent he insisted the attending surgeon not to care of him and take care of other wounded soldiers.

64. Nelson was certain that no human care would avail him. The service of surgeon might be useful to other wounded persons.

65. Nelson ordered to cease firing upon the ship. He had been struck from the ship which he had thus twice spared from which he received his death.

66. Dear Tripathiji,

Being your neighbour and maintaining the cordial and amiable relation. I hesitate to write the letter to apprise you of my annoyance due to your dog that barks uninterruptedly at night without any reason. By its regular barking, I and other residents of this locality suddenly wake up and then we can not sleep because of its barking. I hope you will well understand my problem, as I am your neighbour and it is the duty of a person to live peacefully and let live others too. I know that you are very humble and gracious man who has his own identity and recognition. I hope that you will not mind for this letter and think positively and do accordingly.

Thanks a lot and hoping for a favourable initiative.

Yours sincerely

XYZ

67. (1) when, (2) she, (3) and was, (4) but she, (5) she, (6) hand, (7) she, (8) the, (9) since, (10) in shape and size, (11) for a while, (12) then, (13) a large number of, (14) they, (15) and, (16) now, (17) the.

68. Charles Babbage has done a marvellous job for the service of mankind. He invented such a nice thing for which we shall he indebted to him for generations. Now, throughout the world, computers have a source as well as conduit of information. A computer is a device for automatically carrying out a program of instructions. It is a powerful general purpose machine because it can be programmed to do a wide variety of computations. Computers perform functions long familiar to people in other forms. Computers have shifted from file cabinet, adding machine and voice telephone to digital computers, telecommunications and software and have made such a big difference in our lives. Retrieval, copying, storage and transmission of information once digitally encored can be completely error free. Computers can perform operations with extraordinary speed and store incredibly large amount of information in a very small space. Thus, computer has made the life of a man very easy and has changed it radically.

PART–B : SOCIAL STUDIES

Directions (Q. 1-20): *Fill in the blanks.*

1. General Dyer was responsible for........ massacre.
2. .... cells convert sunlight directly into electricity.
3. The rank of the Chief of the Air Staff is ......
4. .... is the Supreme Commander of the Indian Armed Forces.
5. .... is measured on Richter Scale.
6. India is one of the .... members of the United Nations.
7. There can be no .... without disarmament.
8. Racialism is anti.....
9. Human Rights Day is celebrated throughout the world on ......
10. The most important source to know about the Earth's interior is ......
11. .... means wise use of resources.
12. The Russian Revolution took place in ......
13. The present Secretary General of UN is ......
14. The inner core of the Earth comprises iron and ....
15. The original rock is called ....
16. Terrorism is a tool to impose the minority decision over ....
17. The first Viceroy of India was......
18. Indian National Army was founded by ......
19. In a Republic, the head of the State is elected by ......
20. .... movement began in the modern age in Europe.

Directions (Q. 21-35): *State True/False.*

21. The most power and prominent Tamil militant group is the Liberation Tigers of Tamil Ealem. (T/F)
22. Bangladesh is a secular State. (T/F)
23. The Tashkent Declaration was signed in Moscow. (T/F)
24. India was not founder member of the United Nations. (T/F)
25. The Headquarters of the SAARC is at Delhi. (T/F)
26. Our fundamental rights are not based on Human Rights. (T/F)
27. Apartheid is the best form of racialism. (T/F)
28. IAEA stands for Indian Atomic Energy Agency. (T/F)
29. There are six official languages of the United Nations. (T/F)
30. Terrorist use violence to help the government. (T/F)
31. The Swadeshi movement was started by Gandhiji in 1905. (T/F)
32. Social reforms introduced by the British were readily accepted by the Indians. (T/F)
33. Delhi could not regain its prestige after its sack by Nadir Shah. (T/F)
34. The modern age came all of a sudden. (T/F)
35. Mir Qasim became the Nawab of Bengal after the Battle of Plassey. (T/F)

Directions (Q. 36-45): *Match the following and write the corresponding alphabets of your answer in the box provided—*

36. Hyder Ali	☐	(a)	First Nizam of Hyderabad
37. Chin Qilich Khan	☐	(b)	Was the ruler of Mysore
38. Battle of Buxar	☐	(c)	1773
39. Regulating Act	☐	(d)	1764

40. Disintegration of USSR ☐ (e) 1990

41. Unification of Germany ☐ (f) 1991

42. Formation of Indian National Congress ☐ (g) 1905

43. Gandhiji was assassinated on ☐ (h) 26 January, 1950

44. India becomes a Republic in ☐ (i) 30 January, 1948

45. Partition of Bengal ☐ (j) 1885

Directions (Q. 46-55): *Answer briefly.*

46. What is Recycling?

47. What is Globalisation?

48. What is the Green Revolution?

49. What is Capitalism?

50. What is Sustainable Development?

51. Define Per Capita Income.

52. What is Relief?

53. Define Droughts and Floods.

54. What do you understand by the term "Divide and Rule" ?

55. Distinguish between Natural and Human resources.

ANSWERS WITH EXPLANATIONS

1. Jalianwala Bagh **2.** Photoelectric
3. Air Chief Marshal **4.** President of India
5. Intensity of Earthquake
6. Founding **7.** Peace
8. Humanitarian **9.** 10th December
10. Seismic wave **11.** Energy
12. 1917 **13.** Ban-Ki-Moon
14. Nickel **15.** Metamorphic
16. Majority **17.** Canning
18. Captain Mohan Singh
19. People **20.** Communist
21. True **22.** False
23. False **24.** False
25. False **26.** False
27. True **28.** False
29. True **30.** False
31. False **32.** False
33. True **34.** False
35. False **36.** (b)
37. (a) **38.** (d)
39. (c) **40.** (f)
41. (e) **42.** (j)
43. (i) **44.** (h)
45. (g)

46. Recycling is the reprocessing of discarded or waste materials into new products. Recycling generally prevents the waste of potentially useful materials. It reduces the consumption of raw materials and reduces energy usage. Recycling is a key concept of modern waste management and is the third component of the waste hierarchy.

47. Globalisation is a process, by which the people of world are unified into single society. This process is a combination of economic, technological, socio-cultural and political process.

48. Due to application of ecologically sound principles of agriculture has resulted into green revolution, *i.e.,* increased agricultural production to feed the increasing population. In fact, the green revolution of the late 1960's was based on new genetic strains of rice and wheat, improved irrigation and better application of fertilizers and it has achieved a doubling and tripling of crop yields in many tropical countries. Consequently **Norman Borlaug** (Father of green revolution of the world) and **M. S. Swaminathan** (Father of green revolution of India) have provided certain solutions for agriculture extensions and intensifications and have suggested certain new nutritions food resources for humans.

49. Capitalism generally refers to an economic and social system, in which the means of production are predominantly privately owned and are operated for profit.

50. Sustainable development has been defined as balancing the fulfilment of human needs without harming of the natural environment so that these needs can be met not only in the present, but in the infinite future.

51. Per Capita Income means how much each individual receives in monetary terms of the yearly income that generated through productive activities in the country. In briefly it can be defined as the national income divided by the total population.

52. Relief is the shape of the earth's surface. High relief generally denotes large local differences in the height of the land, whereas low relief indicates little.

53. A drought is a long period of time during which no rain falls. Flood is the high discharge of a river, resulting from conditions such as heavy rain fall, intense melting of snow and ice, breaching of natural barriers, and the collapse of man made barrages.

54. Every imperialist country seeks to maintain its rule over the conquered people by dividing them. This is done by creating differences between two sections. In the revolt of 1857, Hindus and Muslims fought shoulder to shoulder against the British. After 1858, the British followed a systematic policy of dividing Hindus and Muslims. Britishers followed this policy till to 1947.

55. Natural resources are naturally occurring substances that are considered valuable in their relatively natural form. Natural resources are classified into renewable and non-renewable resources; whereas human resources is a term which many organizations describe the combination of traditionally administrative personnel functions with performance management employee relations and resource planning.

Previous Paper (Solved)

Sainik School Exam, 2006

(Class-IX)

PAPER-I—MATHEMATICS AND SCIENCE

PART–A : Mathematics

1. Sam's monthly salary is ₹ 10,100. His son's monthly salary is ₹ 8,200. How much should they save so that they are left with 85% of their income to expend?
2. If $3x + 4y = 6$, $6x + 8y = k$, then find the value of k.
3. The angles of triangle are $3x$, $(2x + 20)$ and $(5x - 40)$. Hence show that the triangle is equilateral.
4. Rahul can do a piece of a work in 25 days, which Hari can alone finish in 20 days. Both together work for 5 days and then Rahul leaves. How many days will Hari take to finish the remaining work?
5. If the digits of a two digit number are interchanged and the number then obtained is doubled, we get a number which is bigger than the original number by 41, what was the original number if its digit in the unit place is bigger than the digit in the ten's place by 1?
6. Solve the equation $x^4 - 25x^2 + 144 = 0$.
7. A number is 15 less than 3 times another number. If the sum of those two numbers is 17, what is the bigger number of the two?
8. By selling an article for ₹ 500, a man loses 25%. At what price he must sell in order to gain 20%?
9. How many small bobs of radius 2 cm can be made from a sphere of radius 4 cm?
10. If $3p + 2q = 12$, $pq = 6$, then what is the value of $27p^3 + 8q^3$?
11. Ram borrowed ₹ 1500 from his friend at 8% interest per annum. He returned the money after 10 months. How much did he pay to his friend?
12. A soap-cake has dimensions 7 cm × 5 cm × 2.5 cm. How many soap-cakes can be placed in a card-board whose length, breadth and height are 56 cm, 40 cm and 25 cm respectively?
13. There are 25 equal squares with one side equal to 14 cm. Find the area.
14. Rajdhani Express covers 441 km between New Delhi and Kanpur in 4 hours 30 minutes. Calculate its speed per hour.
15. A bicycle factory produces 82 bicycles a day. How many bicycles did the factory produce in a year, if there were 82 holidays in the year?
16. Rationalise the denominator of $\frac{3}{\sqrt{8}-\sqrt{5}}$.
17. State if the following statements are true or false:

    (i) Area of rhombus = $\frac{\text{Product of diagonals}}{2}$

    (ii) Angles made on the same chord at the same segment on the circumference of a circle are equal.
18. Find ∠D in the following parallelogram ABCD.

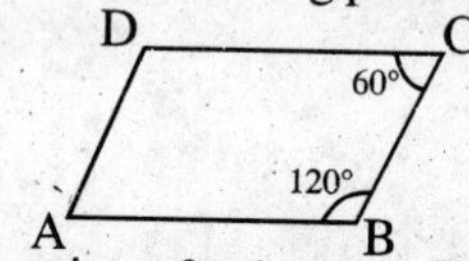

19. If selling price of a book is ₹ 59 and its cost price is ₹ 50, find the profit per cent.
20. A steamer travels 4375 km in 25 days. Find the average speed per day.
21. The cost of 10 chairs is the same as the cost of 6 tables. If the cost of a table is ₹ 400, find the total cost of 10 chairs and 3 tables.
22. What least number should be added to the least number of four digits, so that the resulting number is exactly divisible by 89?
23. (A) What per cent is 64 of 80?

    (B) What per cent is 25 of $12\frac{1}{2}$?

24. An article bought for ₹ 380 was sold at a loss of 5%. Find the loss and selling price.

25. The depth of a swimming pool is 344 cm, 278 cm, 198 cm, 147 cm and 233 cm at five different places.

(A) Find the average depth of the swimming pool.

(B) At how many places the depth is more than the average depth?

26. Which is the greatest four-digit number, which is exactly divisible by 88?

27. Find the volume of a cuboid whose length is 1m, breadth is 15 cm and height is 25 cm.

28. Construct a triangle DEF in which DE = EF = DF = 4.5 cm. Measure its each angle.

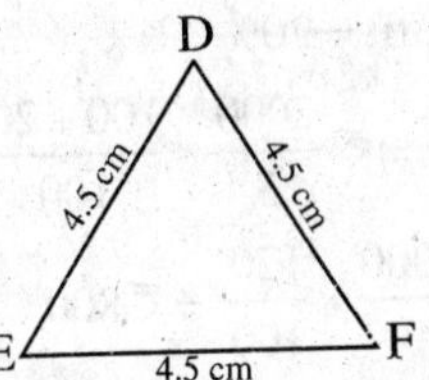

29. Mohan gets 120 marks out of 250 and Neeta got 140 out of 280. Whose score is higher?

30. One side of a square tile is 12 cm. How many tiles can you fix on a wall which is 8 m long and 4.5 m high?

EXPLANATORY ANSWERS

1. Here, total income = 10100 + 8200 = ₹ 18300

They save = 100 − 85 = 15%

Hence, saving = $18300 \times \frac{15}{100}$ = ₹ 2,745

2. Here, $3x + 4y = 6$

And also, $6x + 8y = k$

$\Rightarrow 2(3x + 4y) = k$

$\Rightarrow 2 \times 6 = k$

$\therefore\ k = 12$

3. Sum of angles of a triangle is 180°,

Then, $3x + (2x + 20) + (5x - 40) = 180$

$\Rightarrow 10x - 20 = 180$

$\Rightarrow 10x = 200$

$\therefore\ x = 20$

Hence, angles of triangle are 3 × 20°, 2 × 20° + 20°, 5 × 20° − 40

or, 60°, 60°, 60°

So, the triangle is an equilateral triangle.

4. Here, (Rahul + Hari)'s 5 days' work

$= 5\left(\frac{1}{25} + \frac{1}{20}\right) = 5\left(\frac{5+4}{100}\right) = 5 \times \frac{9}{100} = \frac{9}{20}$

Remaining work $= 1 - \frac{9}{20} = \frac{11}{20}$

But, 1/20 work is done by Hari in 1 day

Hence, $\frac{11}{20}$ work will be done by Hari in

$= \left(\frac{20 \times 11}{20}\right) = 11$ days.

5. Let digit at ten's position be x.

Hence, digit at unit's position = $x + 1$

Then, given two-digit number

$= 10x + (x + 1) = 11x + 1$

From the question,

$2[10(x + 1) + x] - (11x + 1) = 41$

$\Rightarrow 2(11x + 10) - (11x + 1) = 41$

$\Rightarrow 22x + 20 - 11x - 1 = 41$

$\Rightarrow 11x = 22$

$\therefore\ x = 2$

Hence, the original number is

$11x + 1 = 11 \times 2 + 1 = 23$

6. $x^4 - 25x^2 + 144 = 0$

$\Rightarrow x^4 - 16x^2 - 9x^2 + 144 = 0$

$\Rightarrow x^2(x^2 - 16) - 9(x^2 - 16) = 0$

$\Rightarrow (x^2 - 16)(x^2 - 9) = 0$

Either, $x^2 - 16 = 0$ or $x^2 - 9 = 0$

$\therefore\ x = \pm 4$ $\quad \therefore\ x = \pm 3$

7. Let the bigger number = x

then smaller number = $17 - x$

From the question,

$x = 3(17 - x) - 15$

$\Rightarrow x = 51 - 3x - 15$

$\Rightarrow 4x = 36$ or $x = 9$

Hence, the bigger number = 9

8. Here, S.P. of article = ₹ 500

Loss = 25%

Hence, C.P. of article = ₹ $500 \times \frac{100}{100 - 25}$

$= ₹\, 500 \times \frac{100}{75} = ₹\, \frac{2000}{3}$

Now, Profit = 20%

Then, S.P. $= ₹\, \frac{2000}{3} \times \frac{100+20}{100}$

$= ₹\, \frac{2000}{3} \times \frac{120}{100} = ₹\, 800$

9. Let n be the number of small bobs, then

$n \times \frac{4}{3}\pi(2)^3 = \frac{4}{3}\pi(4)^3$

$\therefore\ n = \frac{4 \times 4 \times 4}{2 \times 2 \times 2} = 8$

10. Here, $3p + 2q = 12$

Cubing both sides,

$(3p + 2q)^3 = (12)^3$

$\Rightarrow 27p^3 + 8q^3 + 3(3p)(2q)(3p + 2q) = 1728$

$\Rightarrow 27p^3 + 8q^3 + 18 \times 6 \times 12 = 1728$

$\therefore\ 27p^3 + 8q^3 = 1728 - 1296 = 432$

11. Given,

P = ₹ 1500, R = 8%

$T = \frac{10}{12} = \frac{5}{6}$ year

$\therefore$ Interest, $I = \frac{P \times R \times T}{100}$

$= \frac{1500 \times 8 \times 5}{100 \times 6} = ₹\, 100$

So, total money paid to his friend

= ₹ (1500 + 100) = ₹ 1600

12. Required number of soap-cakes

$= \frac{\text{Volume of card-board}}{\text{Volume of soap-cakes}}$

$= \frac{56 \times 40 \times 25}{7 \times 5 \times 2.5}$

$= 640$

13. Here, area of 1 square

$= (14 \times 14)\ cm^2 = 196\ cm^2$

Hence, area of 25 such squares

$= (196 \times 25)\ cm^2 = 4900\ cm^2$

14. Here, distance of the journey = 441 km

Time taken = 4 hr 30 min

$= 4\frac{1}{2}$ hr $= \frac{9}{2}$ hr

Then, speed of the train $= \frac{441}{9/2}$

$= 441 \times \frac{2}{9} = 98$ km/hr

15. Here, working days in a year

= 365 – 82 = 283 days

Hence, factory produces bicycles in a year

= 283 × 82 = 23206

16. $\frac{3}{\sqrt{8}-\sqrt{5}} = \frac{3}{\sqrt{8}-\sqrt{5}} \times \frac{\sqrt{8}+\sqrt{5}}{\sqrt{8}+\sqrt{5}}$

$= \frac{3(\sqrt{8}+\sqrt{5})}{8-5} = \frac{3(\sqrt{8}+\sqrt{5})}{3} = \sqrt{8}+\sqrt{5}$

17. *(i)* True; *(ii)* True

18. From the given figure,

$\angle D = \angle B$ (opposite angles) = 120°

19. Here, profit = ₹ 59 – ₹ 50 = ₹ 9

So, profit % $= \frac{9}{50} \times 100 = 18\%$

20. Average speed per day $= \frac{4375}{25} = 175$ km/day

21. Here, cost of 6 tables = ₹ 400 × 6 = ₹ 2400

But cost of 10 chairs = Cost of 6 tables

= ₹ 2400

Cost of 3 tables = ₹ 400 × 3 = ₹ 1200

Now, cost of 10 chairs + 3 tables

= ₹ (2400 + 1200) = ₹ 3600

22. Least number of four digits = 1000

$$\begin{array}{r} 11 \\ 89\overline{)1000} \\ \underline{89} \\ 110 \\ \underline{89} \\ 21 \end{array}$$

Hence, required number = 89 – 21 = 68

23. (A) The percentage of 64 of 80

$= \frac{64}{80} \times 100 = 80\%$

(B) The percentage of 25 of $12\frac{1}{2}$

$= 25 \times \frac{2}{25} \times 100 = 200\%$

24. C.P. of article = ₹ 380

Loss = 5%

(i) Loss = ₹ 380 × $\frac{5}{100}$ = ₹ 19

(ii) S.P. of article = C.P. – Loss

= 380 – 19 = ₹ 361

25. (A) Here, average depth

$$= \frac{344+278+198+147+233}{5} \text{ cm}$$

$$= \frac{1200}{5} \text{ cm} = 240 \text{ cm}$$

(B) It is clear that only at 2 places depths are more than the average depth.

26. The greatest four-digit number = 9999

```
      113
  88)9999
     88
     ---
     119
      88
     ---
     319
     264
     ---
      55
```

Hence, the required number

= 9999 – 55 = 9944

27. Here, length of cuboid = 1 m

Breadth of cuboid = 15 cm = 0.15 m

Height of the cuboid = 25 cm = 0.25 m

Hence, volume of cuboid

$= 1 \times 0.15 \times 0.25 \text{ m}^3$

$= 0.0375 \text{ m}^3$

28. *Steps of Construction :*

Take EF = 4.5 cm. Take E and F as centres and radius equal to 4.5 cm draw arcs to cut each other at D. Join DE and DF. Now DEF is the required triangle.

It is an equilateral triangle.

Hence, its angles are :

$\angle DEF = 60°, \angle EFD = 60°, \angle FDE = 60°$

29. Here, percentage of Mohan = $\frac{120}{250} \times 100 = 48\%$

Percentage of Neeta = $\frac{140}{280} \times 100 = 50\%$

So, Neeta's score is higher.

30. Required number of tiles = $\frac{\text{Area of the wall}}{\text{Area of the tiles}}$

$$= \frac{8 \times 4.5}{0.12 \times 0.12}$$

$$= \frac{8 \times 45 \times 1000}{12 \times 12}$$

$$= 2500$$

Part 'B' — Science

1. Which gas is filled inside an electric bulb?
2. What are carbon, diamond and graphite together called?
3. Name a gas which may suffocate a person in a closed room.
4. What is the effect on frequency when a ray of light is transmitted from air to glass?
5. Which energy is converted by an electric motor into mechanical energy?
6. Which chemical is widely used for purifying drinking water and why?
7. Why does the temperature of the earth increases due to global warming?
8. How much heat energy is given to heat 20 g of water to raise its temperature by 4°C?
9. Why is Na_2CO_3 used for identifying an acid solution?
10. What is Radar used for?
11. Who discovered the wave nature of light?
12. Write two essential differences between X-rays and radiation emitted by radioactive materials.
13. An element of group 14 has an atomic number 14. Examine if this element will have metallic properties or not.
14. Define electronegativity.
15. Write balanced equations for the following reactions and identify the type of reaction:
    (i) Zinc carbonate (s) → Zinc oxides (s) + Carbon dioxide (g)
    (ii) Magnesium (s) + Hydrochloric acid (aq) → Magnesium chloride (aq) + Hydrogen (g)

(iii) Potassium bromide (aq) + Barium iodide (aq) → Potassium iodides (aq) + Barium bromide (aq)

(iv) Hydrogen (g) + Chlorine (g) → Hydrogen chloride (g)

16. What is escape velocity from the earth's surface?
17. What is pitch of sound and on which factors does it depend?
18. One micron is equal to how many metres?
19. What does a light year represent?
20. Which energy is converted by dynamo into electrical energy?
21. Why is G called the universal gravitational constant?
22. How much work is done by a force of 10 N in moving an object through a distance of 1 m in the direction of the force?
23. Why is ice at 0°C more effective in cooling than water at 0°C?
24. What is acceleration? Write down the units of acceleration in C.G.S. and SI systems. Is it a scalar or vector quantitiy?
25. Why is Newton's first law of motion called law of inertia?

EXPLANATORY ANSWERS

1. Generally, inert gases are filled inside an electric bulb to prevent oxidation. Nitrogen is also used.
2. Allotrope is any of two or more physical states in which an element can exist.
3. Carbon monoxide reacts with haemoglobin permanently, which makes it incapable of carrying oxygen.
4. Speed of light in glass is less than that in vacuum. From air to glass frequency is unaltered but wave-length decreases.
5. Electric motor is converting electrical energy into mechanical energy.
6. Potassium permanganate is widely used because it has disinfectant quality.
7. In global warming, the heat received by the Sun is radiated into the atmosphere. But, the excessive carbon dioxide accumulating near the Earth's surface traps the heat and prevents it from escaping, which resulting in the warming up of the Earth.
8. $m = 20g = 20 \times 10^{-3}$ kg

   $c = 4.18 \times 10^3$ J/kg/°C $t = 4$°C

   We know, Q = m.c.t.

   $\therefore$ Q $= 20 \times 10^{-3} \times 4.18 \times 10^3 \times 4$

   = 334.4 joules
9. $Na_2CO_3 + H^+ \rightarrow CO_2$ (gas)
10. Radar is used for finding out the position and movement of solid objects, especially, aircraft and ships, which cannot be seen by sending out short radio waves which they reflect.
11. de-Broglie discovered the wave nature of light.
12. **X-rays**

    (i) After the cathode rays strike the spot they emit radiation.

    (ii) They have glow of light even if the source of fluorescence is removed.

    Radiations emitted by radioactive materials

    (i) The radiations emitted by radioactive materials have three α, β and γ rays.

    (ii) They do not depend on physical and chemical state of materials.
13. The electronic configuration of the element is 2, 8, 4. This is silicon. The last shell has four electrons. It has the characters of both metals and non-metals. So, the element does not have metallic properties.
14. The property of an atom in a molecule to attract the bonding pair of electrons towards itself is known as electro-negativity. In hydrogen chloride gas, the bonding pair of electrons lies more towards chlorine atom. So, the chlorine atom a slight negative charge and hydrogen, a slight positive charge.
15. *(i)* $ZnCO_3 (s) \rightarrow ZnO (s) + CO_2$

    Decomposition reaction.

    (ii) $Mg (s) + 2HCl (aq) \rightarrow MgCl_2 (aq) + H_2$

    Displacement reaction.

    (iii) $2KBr (aq) + BaI_2 (aq) \rightarrow 2KI + BaBr_2$

    Double displacement reaction.

    (iv) $H_2 (g) + Cl_2(g) \rightarrow 2HCl (g)$

    Combination reaction.
16. Escape Veclocity is a velocity with which a body should be projected then it never returns to the

gravitational field of earth. Its value is 11.2 km/sec from earth's surface.

17. Pitch of the sound is the sensation of vibration produced by a note. Which depends upon frequency.

18. 1 micron = 10^{-6} metre.

19. Light Year is a unit for measuring the distance of astronomical bodies and which is equal to distance travelled by light in one year.

20. A dynamo converts mechanical energy into electrical energy.

21. Because the value of G does not depend on the medium between the two bodies and not on the masses of the bodies or the distance between them.

22. Here, Force, F = 10 N, Distance, $s = 1$ m
$W = F \times s$
$= 10 \times 1$ J = 10 J.

23. During melting of ice it absorbs heat equal to its latent heat of fusion, 3.35×10^5 J/kg. Hence, ice can take away more heat than the same amount of water at 0°C. So, the ice cube at 0°C is more effective in cooling than the same mass of water at 0°C.

24. **Acceleration:** The rate of change of increased velocity is known as acceleration. Its units in C.G.S. and S.I. systems are cm/s^2 and m/s^2. It is also a vector quantity.

25. From Newton's first law of motion, no object can change its state of rest or of the uniform motion in a straight line by itself. An external force is to be applied to bring about the change in the state of rest or of motion of the object. Hence, Newton's first law gives a concept of inertia. So, that the first law of motion is also called law of inertia.

PAPER-II—LANGUAGE AND SOCIAL STUDIES

Part 'A' — English Language

Directions (Qs. 1 to 3): *Each sentence has one or two blanks, each blank indicating that something has been omitted. Beneath the sentence, there are four words or sets of words. Choose the word or set of words that best fits the meaning of the sentence as a whole.*

1. Life is a petty thing unless it is moved by the ____ urge to ____ its boundaries.
   A. unfalling _____ mark
   B. indomitable ____extend
   C. passionate ____ confine
   D. compulsive _____ define

2. If you want to succeed let there be no ____ in your effort.
   A. let up B. let off
   C. let on D. let by

3. After an initial depression, the young man ____ the sudden demise of his father
   A. got out B. got over
   C. got off D. got by

Directions (Qs. 4 to 11) : *Fill in the blank with correct word from the four given options.*

4. He is ____ honourable man.
   A. a B. an
   C. the D. some

5. Meena is ______ SDO.
   A. a B. an
   C. the D. some

6. He sat ____ a big stone.
   A. on B. upon
   C. in D. for

7. He was _____ himself with joy.
   A. beside B. besides
   C. in D. for

8. Distribute these apples ____ five children.
   A. between B. among
   C. for D. in

9. Yesterday the temperature was _______ the average.
   A. above B. over
   C. beyond D. below

10. I have been waiting _____ two hours.
    A. in B. over
    C. since D. for

11. Neem is famous all ____ the world.
    A. in B. over
    C. around D. beyond

Directions (Qs. 12 to 14) : *In the following questions, nor word in capital letter is followed by four words or phrases. Choose the word or phrase which is most nearly similar in meaning to the word in capital letters.*

12. ATTRIBUTE
A. Infer
B. Impute
C. Inhere
D. Inundate

13. DEXTERITY
A. Ability B. Skill
C. Intelligence D. Agility

14. ABJECT
A. Wretched B. Solid
C. Helpful D. Soft

Directions (Qs. 15 to 18) : *Questions are not complete sentences. One or more words are left out of each sentence. Under each sentence, you will see four words or phrases. Choose the one word or phrase that completes the sentence correctly.*

15. The troublesome tartar above the gumline _____ by careful toothbrushing.
A. can reduce
B. can be reduced significantly
C. reduced
D. is reduce

16. _______ in an electric typewriter is the ability to correct spelling errors.
A. There are many new features
B. New features
C. One of the new features
D. The new features

17. It is not easy for a casual observer to distinguish _______ genuine paintings and copies.
A. between B. in
C. to D. a

18. Generally speaking, every person ____ the potential to be a teacher, to some extent.
A. is having B. has
C. have D. to have

Directions (Qs. 19 & 20) : *Find out the antonym of the given word from the alternatives given below it.*

19. IRASCIBLE
A. picaresque B. angry
C. good-natured D. crack

20. PERNICIOUS
A. malicious B. salutary
C. harmful D. tedious

Directions (Qs. 21 & 22) : *Find out the synonym of the given word from the alternatives given under it.*

21. FRACTIOUS
A. bad-mouthed B. inadequate
C. incomplete D. bad-tempered

22. PHLEGMATIC
A. solid B. lively
C. pneumatic D. stolid

Directions (Qs. 23 to 25) : *Among the four sentences only one is correct. Choose correct one.*

23. A. He went to Kashmir few years ago.
B. He went to Kashmir five years back.
C. He went to Kashmir five years before.
D. He went to Kashmir five years past.

24. A. She is anxious of my health.
B. She is anxious for my health.
C. She is anxious to my health.
D. She is anxious with my health.

25. A. Your conduct admits no excuses.
B. Your conduct admit no excuses.
C. Your conduct is unexcusable.
D. Your conduct admit of no excuses.

Directions (Qs. 26 to 28) : *In the following question, a word in capital letter is followed by four words or phrases. Choose the word or phrase which is most nearly opposite in meaning to the word in capital letters.*

26. PHOBIA
A. Awe B. Disregard
C. Qualm D. reverence

27. WHEEDLE
A. Negotiate B. Wheels
C. Dragon D. Ladle

28. EXTENUATING
A. Aggravating B. Exotic
C. Expanding D. Abolishing

Directions (Qs. 29 to 32) : *Each of the following idioms are followed by four alternatives, choose the correct option.*

29. Between devil and the deep sea.
A. In a dilemna.
B. A drowning man.
C. Deep sea diver.
D. To be cool tempered.

30. To fight tooth and nail.
A. Making every effort to loose.
B. To fight cowardly.
C. To fight a loosing battle.
D. Making every effort to win.

31. Lions share.
A. The part of a lion.
B. Food of lion.
C. Major part.
D. Shares of good company.

32. To eat a humble pie
A. to eat slowly B. to have good dish
C. to appologise D. to eat good pie

Directions (Qs. 33 to 35) : *A part of each of the following sentences is given in italic. Pick the correct substitute from your options given.*

33. He has grown quite *feeble*.
A. poor B. week
C. weak D. strong

34. It takes time to *eradicate* poverty.
A. Finish B. Control
C. Uproot D. Minimise

35. Take the statement with a *grain* of salt.
A. Hope B. Senservation
C. Spirit D. Welcome

Directions (Qs. 36 to 40) : *Rearrange the following group of words and make meaningful sentences. Write your sentence in the space provided.*

36. a little, I, apple juice, market, brought/from/the
37. you, say, in, no truth, what, is, there
38. you, money, have, any, box, left, in, your
39. the whistle, blows, there, any, danger, is, if
40. from, the, shop, he, buy, didn't, anything.

Directions (Qs. 41 to 45): *In the following sentences some sentences have ERRORS. Select the part in which the error lies and encircle its letter A, B or C. If there is no error encircle D.*

41. (A) An unit is an abstract idea,/ (B) defined either by reference to/ (C) a randomly chosen material standard or to a natural phenomenon./ (D) No error.

42. (A) Microwaves are the principle carriers/ (B) of television, telephone and data transmissions/ (C) between stations on earth and between the earth and satellites./ (D) No error.

43. (A) Mahavira was an advocate of nonviolence and vegetarianism,/ (B) who revived and reorganized the Jain doctrine/ (C) and established rules for their monastic order./ (D) No error.

44. (A) Amit has been deceiving Mona/ (B) for many years but she/ (C) has not still tumbled to it./ (D) No error.

45. (A) A major contribution of Mathura sculptors/ (B) of that period were the creation and popularization/ (C) of the Buddha's image in human farm. / (D) No error.

Directions (Qs. 46 to 50): *Rewrite the following sentences by substituting the underlined words with one word, without changing the meaning:*

46. His handwriting is so bad that one cannot read it.

47. He received a letter that carried neither the writer's name nor his address.

48. His post was such as no remuneration was paid to him for this.

49. Finding the murdered man lying in the room, I was stunned with horror.

50. When the thief saw the policeman, he took to his heels.

Directions (Qs. 51 to 55): *Rewrite the following sentences after correcting errors :*

51. He has not sold his house till last week.
52. I am going to school by taxi everyday.
53. He went for riding.
54. Our school is built by bricks.
55. I shall explain them this.

Directions (Qs. 56 to 60): *Read the following passage carefully and answer the questions given below:*

Inactivity, I think, is the greatest cause of overweight at present. By and large, people are eating less than they did in the last century. But their physical activity has decreased much more rapidly than their food intake. Everything that has happened to our society in terms of labour saving devices, transport, etc., has contributed to this. Most of us have forgotten what man used to be like in the past age. For instance, it would be difficult to find a city dweller who spends as much energy as did an office-goer of the past. He was a clerk who did a lot of domestic work for an hour for all the six days in the week, walked one hour to work, toiled in the office for ten hours, and walked home in the evening. On Sundays he took his family out for a walk besides doing the regular domestic work. Modern society has pushed us more and more into the state of inactivity which naturally leads to overweight and causes many physical ailments such as high blood pressure and heart problems.

Answer the following–

56. Which of the two, eating much or inactivity, is the real cause of overweight in modern society?

57. What factors have contributed to our reduced activity?

58. What kind of physical work was done by an office goer on working days in the past?

59. What did he do on Sundays?

60. What is the real cause of modern ailments like high blood pressure and heart troubles?

Directions (Qs. 61 to 65): *Rewrite the following sentences as directed:*

61. Neeru is ______a fool and a knave.
(Fill in the blank with an appropriate connector).

62. Sushma is too tired to work.
(Rewrite the sentence using 'so.. that')

63. She said to me, 'Do not waste your time in idle gossip'.
(Rewrite in reported speech).

64. It is a very nice book.
(Rewrite changing into an exclamatory sentence).

65. Why are you wasting your time?
(Change the Voice)

66. Read the following passage carefully and make a precis is not more than 50 to 60 words.
There are few men who are not ambitious of distinguishing themselves in the society in which they live, and of going considerable among those within whom they converse. There is a kind of gramdeur and respect which the humblest part of mankind endeavour to obtain in the little circle of their friends and acquaintances. The poorest man, who lives upon common aims, gets his set of admirers and delights in the superiority which he enjoys over those who are in some respects beneath him. This ambition which is so natural to the soul of man, might I think, receive a very happy turn' and if rightly directed contributes to a persons advantage as it generally does to his uneasiness and disquiet.

67. Write a passage in about 100 words on 'Power of Knowledge'.

68. You are Anand Sharma, who has just shifted to a new house B-5/33, Shalimar Bagh, Kanpur from S-22, Preet Vihar, Kanpur. Write a letter to the Postmaster of your previous colony requesting him to redirect all your letters to your new address.

ANSWERS

1	**2**	**3**	**4**	**5**	**6**	**7**	**8**	**9**	**10**
D	A	B	B	B	A	B	B	D	D
11	**12**	**13**	**14**	**15**	**16**	**17**	**18**	**19**	**20**
B	B	B	A	B	C	A	B	C	B
21	**22**	**23**	**24**	**25**	**26**	**27**	**28**	**29**	**30**
D	A	A	B	C	D	A	A	A	D
31	**32**	**33**	**34**	**35**	**41**	**42**	**43**	**44**	**45**
C	C	C	A	C	A	D	C	D	B

SOME SELECTED EXPLANATORY ANSWERS

36. I brought a little apple juice from the market.

37. There is no truth in what you say.

38. Have you any money left in your box?

39. Is there any danger if the whistle blows?

40. He didn't buy anything from the shop.

46. His handwriting is illegible.

47. He received an anomymous letter.

48. His post was honorary.

49. Finding the murdered man lying in the room, I was horrified.

50. Spotting the policeman, the thief took to his heels.

51. He had not sold his house till last week.

52. I go to school by taxi everyday.

53. He went riding.

54. Our school is built of bricks.

55. I shall explain this to them.

57. Lack of physical activity, laboursaving devices and fast transportation have contributed to our reduced activity.

58. In the past, an office-goer used to do a lot of domestic work for an hour for all the six days in the week, walked one hour to work, toiled in the office for ten hours and also walked home in the evening.

59. He took his family out for a walk besides doing the regular domestic work on Sundays.

60. The real cause of modern ailments like high blood pressure and heart troubles has punched us more and more into the state of inactivity which naturally leads to overweight.

61. Neeru is both a fool and a knave.

62. Sushma is so tired that she cannot work.

63. She advised me not to waste my time in idle gossip.

64. What a nice book it is!

65. Why is your time being wasted (by you)?

56. Of the two, inactivity is the real cause of overweight in modern society.

68. B-5/33, Shalimar Bagh,
Kanpur,
Feb. 8, 2003

To
The Postmaster,
Shalimar Bagh Post Office,
Kanpur

Sub. : Change of Address

Dear Sir,

I am a resident of Shalimar Bagh. I recently shifted from my old address, S-22, Preet Vihar, Kanpur to B-5/33 Shalimar Bagh, Kanpur. I, therefore request you to redirect all my letters to my new address.

This is particularly urgent as I am expecting an official letter, which is more important for my entire career. So, I therefore, request you kindly to take immediate steps and instruct the postman in my previous area to redirect all letters to me at my new address.

Thanking you,

Yours faithfully,
(Anand Sharma)

66. Heading : Channelising Ambition

Precis : Ambition is natural to the soul of man. Each one of us, in whatever position he is placed in life, wants to distinguish himself and earn the admiration and respect of his peers. Ambition can be directed in the proper direction to a person's advantage and also enhance his self-worth, placing him in a superior position over others.

67. Due to knowledge a weak man becomes more powerful than an ignorant but physically strong fellow. With the help of power of knowledge he can keep the latter subservient to his will. As a priest he creates certain fears into the minds of the ignorant and makes them obey him. So, some kings with the help of spiritual leaders were able to keep large number of people in subjugation. But what ever knowledge clever people may have, a stage comes when they fail to cast hypnotising spell on the people. With the ferocity of a hungry lion, the people rise in revolt against authority. All knowledge and skill fails to help the so-called powerful to continue his way over the unlucky men with little knowledge. So had knowledge been really a powerful force in many parts of the country, there would have been no increase of the ignorant.

Part 'B' — Social Studies

SECTION-I (One Mark each)

1. The change of seasons is caused by the ______ of the earth.
2. ______ are the longest mountain ranges in the world.
3. 'Agni' is the name given to a class of _____ of the Indian Defence fources.
4. A 'taxidermist' is one who is a specialist in ______.
5. 'Bicameral legislature' refers to a legislative body having _______.
6. _______ was the capital city of the Mauryan kings.
7. Arya Bhatta is a well-known name in Indian History in the field of ______.
8. Mohammad Ghori defeated Prithvi Raj Chauhan at the Battle of _______.
9. The Indian National Congress was founded by ______.
10. The Congo River is now being called the _____ River.
11. The national song Vande Mataram in Sanskrit was composed by ______

12. The southern-most tip of mainland India is located at______.

13. Bhadohi and Mirzapur in Uttar Pradesh are well-known for their ______ industry.

14. The Election Commission consists of a Chairman and members. (Number to be indicated).

15. 'Rangali Bihu' is an important festival celebrated by the poeple of _____ State.

16. The 'William sisters' are top class _____ players.

17. 'Dhyan Chand Trophy' is awarded to the winners in the game of ______.

18. The Golden Boot award in FIFA World Cup Soccer, 2006 was awarded to _______.

19. When both sides make equal points in a game of Badminton/Tennis, it is called _______.

20. The sports award given by the Government of India to coaches for training outstanding sports persons is called_________.

21. The Constitution of India was formally adopted by the Constituent Assembly on _____. (Date)

22. At the Battle of Talikota, the Deccan Sultans defeated the forces of _______.

23. Pulakesin I and Pulakesin II were important rulers of the _______ dynasty.

24. ________ is known as the 'Playground of Europe'. (Give the name of country).

25. "Teacher's Day" is observed in the country every year on ________.

26. _______ is the name which the River Brahmaputra is known is Tibet.

27. Jute manufacturing industry is concentrated in the Indian State of _______.

28. The largest planet in the solar system is ______.

29. Relative humidity is usually measured by ______. (Name the instrument)

30. The meridian (longitude) adopted for determining the Indian Standard Time (IST) is _______.

31. ______ State is referred to as the "Tiger State of India".

32. The animal 'yak' is found in India in the higher mountain reaches of _______ State.

33. The joyous harvest festival celebrated annually in Tamil Nadu is called ______.

34. India's largest river island, named Majuli, is located in _______ State.

35. The frescoes of Ajanta and the Ellora cave temples, were the works of the _____ Kings.

36. The national game of Canada is ______.

37. The Marathon Race (in athletics) covers a distance of ______.

38. Tiger Woods is a professional _______ player.

39. The 17th Commonwealth Games were held in the year 2002 at _______.

40. The words 'Satyameva Jayate' in Devnagari script appearing in the Indian State Emblem means ______.

41. 'Leelavati' written by Bhaskaracharya, is a treatise on ______.

42. A belt of calms lying between the zones of trade winds and westerlies in the two hemispheres of earth is known as _______.

43. Sher Shah defeated ______ at the Battle of Khanwah to become the Emperor of Delhi. (Name of the defeated King to be stated).

44. The acceptance of the Mountbatten Plan by the Congress and Muslim League leaders led to the enactment of the _______ Act.

45. The practice of 'Sati' was abolished by law during the Viceroyalty of Lord ______.

SECTION-II (3 Marks each)

46. Where are the following located?
(a) August Kranti Maidan; (b) Brindavan Gardens; (c) Emperor Akbar's Tomb; (d) Wular Lake

47. Expand the abbreviations given below: (a) FIPB; (b) STQC; (c) PVSM; (d) SAPTA; (e) IREDA

48. What invention/discovery is associated with the following names?
(a) J.J. Thomson; (b) Max Plank; (c) J. Robert Oppenheimer; (d) W. Harvey; (e) Caxron.

49. Name the authors of the following books/works:
(a) Panch Tantra; (b) Anand Math; (c) Time Machine; (d) The Autobiography of an Unknown Indian; (e) Life of Pi.

50. What is 'fibre optics' and what its utility?

51. Mention the names of any two languages that were included in the 8th schedule of the Indian Constitution in the year 1992.

52. What are 'antioxidants'? How are they useful to humans?
53. Why are fighter airplanes generally flown at great heights?
54. If a metal is called as a 'noble metal' what does it signify?
55. Mention any two important uses to which the sugarcane begasse (fibrous residue left after juice extraction) can be put.

EXPLANATORY ANSWERS

1. revolution
2. Himalayas
3. Missile
4. The art of preparing and stuffing the skins of dead animals, birds and fishes so that they look like living ones.
5. Two houses, Upper House and Lower House.
6. Patliputra
7. Mathematics
8. Second Battle of Tarain in 1192
9. A.O. Hume
10. River Zaire
11. Bankim Chandra Chatterjee
12. Indira Point
13. Carpet
14. Two
15. Assam
16. Lawn Tennis
17. Hockey
18. Miroslav Klose (Germany)
19. Deuce
20. Dronacharya
21. November 26, 1949
22. Vijayanagar
23. Chalukya
24. Switzerland
25. 5th September
26. Tsangpo
27. West Bengal
28. Jupiter
29. Hygrometer
30. 81.5°
31. West Bengal
32. Himachal Pradesh and J&K
33. Pongal
34. Assam
35. Chandella
36. Ice-hockey
37. 26 miles
38. Golf
39. Manchester (England)
40. Truth always triumphs
41. Mathematics
42. Cancer belt of calm
43. Rana Sanga
44. Indian Independence Act
45. William Bentinck
46. *(a)* Mumbai; *(b)* Mysore; *(c)* Secundera; *(d)* Jammu & Kashmir.
47. (a) Foreign Investment Promotion Board; *(b)* Standardisation Testing and Quality Control; (c) Param Vishisht Seva Medal; *(d)* South Asian Preferential Trading Agreement; *(e)* Indian Renewable Energy Development Agency.
48. (a) Electron; (b) Quantum Theory; (c) Atomic Bomb; (d) Circulation of Blood; (e) First English Printing Press.
49. (a) Vishnu Sharma; (b) Bankim Chandra Chatterjee; (c) H.G. Wells; (d) Nirad C. Choudhary; (e) Yane Martel.
50. Fibre optics is a technique of transmitting light waves through very thin wires called optical fibres made of glass, transparent plastic, quartz, nylon or polystyrene.
51. Sindhi and Konkani
52. Antioxidants are the agents added to rubber, plastics, paint and oils etc. These are used to prevent the harmful effects to the materials of oxidation.
53. In order to avoid detection from the radar, the Fighter airplanes are generally flown at great heights.
54. Noble metals are silver, gold and platinum, they do not corrode or tarnish in air or water and are not easily attached by acids.
55. Sugarcane Bagasse is used as fuel and for making fibre-board etc.

Previous Paper (Solved)

Sainik School Exam, 2005

(Class-IX)

PAPER-I—MATHEMATICS AND SCIENCE

PART–A : Mathematics

1. Fill in the blanks :

A. Chords equidistant from the centre are .....

B. Area of a trapezium = ...

C. The curved surface which joins the two bases of right circular cylinder is called .....

D. The magnitude of the region occupied by a solid in space is called .....

E. Angle subtended by an arc at the centre is .... the angle subtended by it on the remaining part of the circle.

2. State True or False :

A. If p and q are perfect squares ($q \neq 0$), then

(i) $\sqrt{p \times q} = \sqrt{p} \times \sqrt{q}$

(ii) $\sqrt{\dfrac{p}{q}} = \dfrac{\sqrt{p}}{\sqrt{q}}$ (T/F)

B. The cube root of a negative perfect cube is positive (T/F)

C. A constant is a polynomial of degree zero (T/F)

D. Two lines which are parallel to the same line are not parallel to each other (T/F)

E. Opposite angles of a cyclic quadrilateral are not supplementary (T/F)

3. Evaluate 103×106 without directly multiplying the given numbers.

4. Find the value of $p^3 - 8y^3$ if $p - 2y = 2$ and $py = 8$.

5. Is expression $\sqrt{ax} + x^2 - x^3$ a polynomial? If yes, state reasons.

6. Prove that number 1058 is not a perfect square.

7. Find the smallest number by which the number 3087 must be multiplied so that the product has a cube root.

8. Find the value of $\left(\dfrac{625}{81}\right)^{\frac{1}{4}}$

9. Mr. Murali bought a watch at 20% discount on its marked price but sold it at the marked price. Find the gain % of Mr. Murali in this deal.

10. Arif got a loan of ₹ 8,000 from a bank. If the rate of interest is 10% per annum compounded annually, calculate the compound interest that Arif will have to pay after 3 years.

11. Find the area of a rhombus whose side is 6.5 cm and whose altitude is 4 cm.

12. Find the area of an equilateral triangle of sides 20 cm each.

13. The diameter of a cycle wheel is 70 cm. Find how many times the wheel will revolve in order to cover a distance of 110 cm.

14. Curved surface area of a right circular cylinder is 4.4 m^2. If the radius of the base of the cylinder is 0.7 m, find its height.

15. Find the value of x in $\dfrac{5x-7}{3x} = 2$.

16. Find the value of $\angle x$ and $\angle y$ in the following figure:

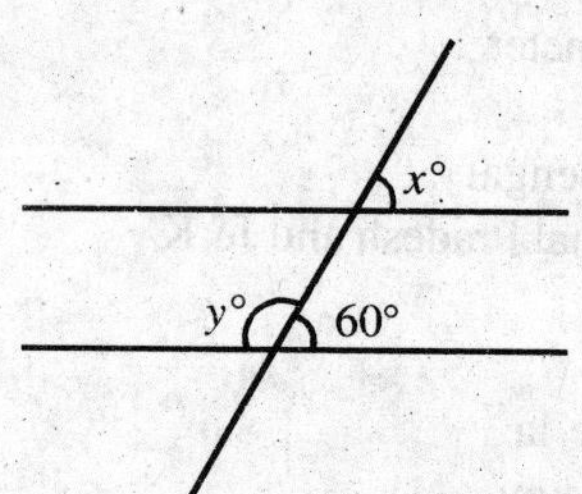

17. In the following figure PAQ || DE || BC, if AD = 3 cm, DB = 6 cm and EC = 8 cm, find AE.

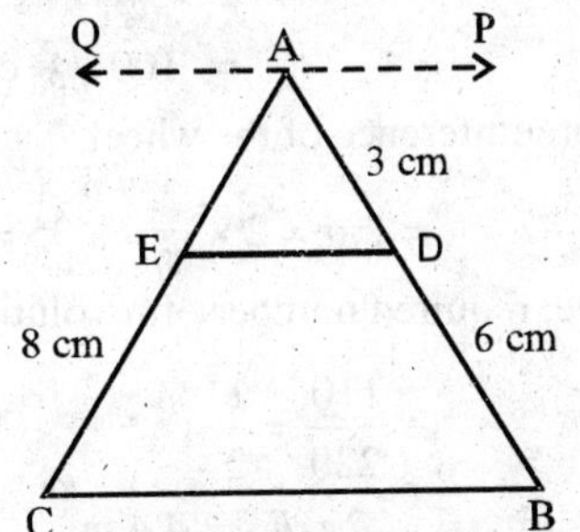

18. A chord of a circle is of length 6 cm and is at a distance of 4 cm from the centre. Find the radius.

19. In the fig., $\angle AOB = 90°$, $\angle BOC = 110°$ where O is the centre of circle, Find:

A. $\angle AOC$ B. $\angle ABC$

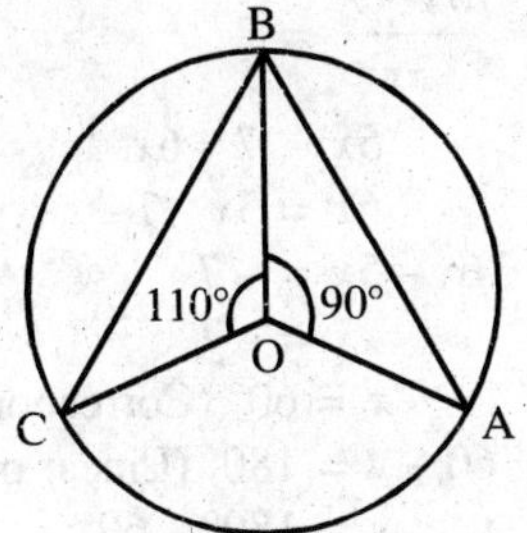

20. In the given figure find $\angle ADC$.

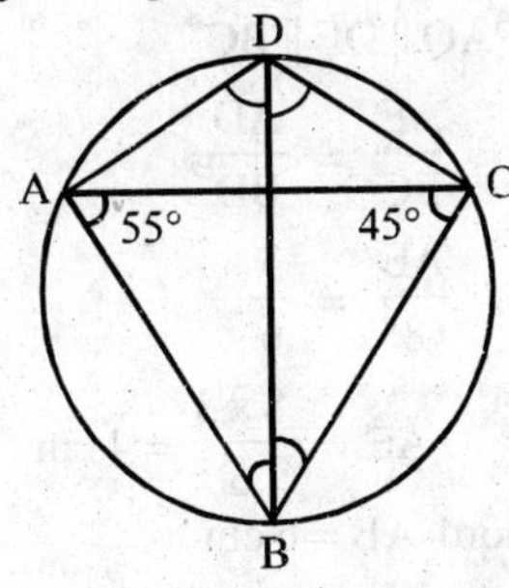

21. The difference between two positive integers is 36. The quotient, when one integer is divided by the other is 4. Find the two integers.

22. Two side of a parallelogram are 20 cm and 25 cm. If the altitude corresponding to the sides of length 25 cm is 10 cm, find the altitude corresponding to the other pair of sides.

23. Find the area of an isosceles right angled triangle of equal sides 40 cm each.

24. A crater falls near a village creating a circular pit of diameter 200 m. Find the affected area of land.

25. A motor boat goes downstream in a river and covers the distance between two coastal towns in five hours. It covers this distance upstream in six hours. If the speed of the stream is 2 km/h, find the speed of the boat in still water.

26. Two circles having the same centre have radii 350 m and 490 m. What is the difference in their circumferences.

27. Find the total surface area of a cone, if its slant height is 16 cm and diameter of its base is 24 cm.

28. The diameter of the Moon is approximately one fourth the diameter of the earth. What fraction is the volume of the Moon of the volume of the earth?

29. Find the square root of 0.008281.

30. Find the value of $\left(\frac{32}{243}\right)^{-\frac{4}{5}}$

31. A shopkeeper purchased 100 blankets at ₹ 2000 each. He found that 10 blankets were defective and he sold these at ₹ 1200 each. At what rate should he sell the remaining blankets so as to gain 14% on the whole?

32. The compound interest on ₹ 1800 at 10% per annum for a certain period of time is ₹ 378. Find the time in years.

EXPLANATORY ANSWERS

1. A. equal

B. $\frac{1}{2}$ (Sum of parallel side) × perpendicular distance between the parallel sides.

C. curved surface

D. volume

E. two times.

2. A. (i) True, (ii) True B. False

C. True D. False

E. False

3.
$$\begin{aligned} 103 \times 106 &= (100+3) \times (100+6) \\ &= 10000 + (3+6) \times 100 + 18 \\ &= 10000 + 900 + 18 \\ &= 10918 \end{aligned}$$

4. $p^3 - 8y^3 = (p-2y)^3 + 3 \times p \times 2y\,(p-2y)$
$= (p-2y)^3 + 6py\,(p-2y)$
$= (2)^3 + 6 \times 8 \times 2 = 8 + 96 = 104$

5. $\sqrt{ax} + x^2 - x^3$ is not a polynomial due to power of x at one place is $\frac{1}{2}$.

6. $\because 1058 = 2 \times \overline{23 \times 23}$
Hence 1058 is not a perfect square.

7. $\because 3087 = 3 \times 3 \times \overline{7 \times 7 \times 7}$
$\therefore$ Required number is 3.

8. $$\left(\frac{625}{81}\right)^{\frac{1}{4}} = \left(\frac{5\times5\times5\times5}{3\times3\times3\times3}\right)^{\frac{1}{4}}$$
$$= \left[\left(\frac{5}{3}\right)^4\right]^{\frac{1}{4}} = \frac{5}{3}$$

9. Let the marked price be ₹ 100
$\because$ C.P. of the watch
$= 100 - 20 = ₹\ 80$
and S.P. $= ₹\ 100$
$\therefore$ Profit $= 100 - 80 = ₹\ 20$
$\therefore$ Gain% $= \frac{20}{80} \times 100 = 25\%$

10. Compound interest $= 8000\left[\left(1+\frac{10}{100}\right)^3 - 1\right]$
$$= 8000\left[\frac{11}{10}\times\frac{11}{10}\times\frac{11}{10} - 1\right]$$
$$= 8000\left(\frac{1331-1000}{1000}\right)$$
$$= \frac{8000 \times 331}{1000} = 8 \times 331$$
$= ₹\ 2648$

11. Area of a rhombus $=$ side $\times$ altitude
$= 6.5 \times 4$
$= 26\ \text{cm}^2$

12. Area of an equilateral triangle
$$= \frac{\sqrt{3}}{4} \times (\text{side})^2$$
$$= \frac{\sqrt{3}}{4} \times (20)^2$$
$$= 100\sqrt{3}\ \text{cm}^2$$

13. $\because$ Circumference of the wheel
$$= 2\pi r = 2 \times \frac{22}{7} \times 35 = 220\ \text{cm}$$
Hence, required number of revolutions
$$= \frac{110}{220} = \frac{1}{2}$$

14. Here, $2\pi rh = 4.4\ \text{m}^2$
$\Rightarrow 2 \times \frac{22}{7} \times 0.7 \times h = 4.4$
$\therefore h = \frac{4.4 \times 7}{2 \times 22 \times 0.7} = 1\text{m}$

15. Given $\frac{5x-7}{3x} = 2$
$\Rightarrow 5x - 7 = 6x$
$\Rightarrow 6x = 5x - 7$
$\Rightarrow 6x - 5x = -7$
$\therefore x = -7$

16. $x = 60°$ (Corresponding angles)
$\because 60 + y = 180°$ (Linear pair)
$\Rightarrow y = 180° - 60°$
$\therefore y = 120°$

17. Given, PAQ || DE || BC
$\Rightarrow \frac{AE}{EC} = \frac{AD}{BD}$
$\Rightarrow \frac{AE}{8} = \frac{3}{6}$
$\therefore AE = \frac{8 \times 3}{6} = 4\ \text{cm}$

18. Here, chord AB = 6 cm
$\therefore AC = \frac{1}{2}AB = 3\ \text{cm}$
Now in rt. angled Δ ACO.

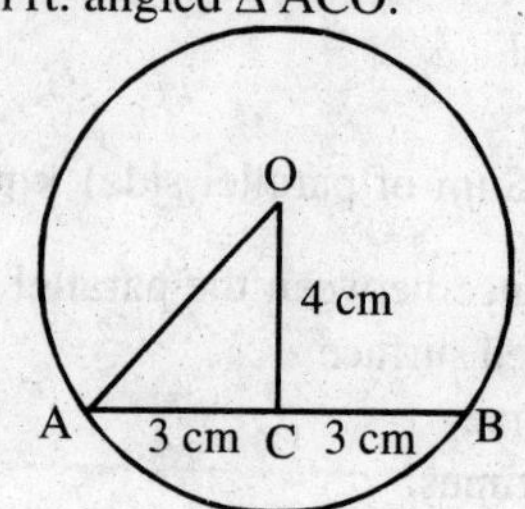

$$AO^2 = OC^2 + AC^2$$
$$= (4)^2 + (3)^2$$
$$= 16 + 9 = 25$$
$\therefore$ $AO = \sqrt{25} = 5$ cm

$\therefore$ Radius = 5 cm

19. Here, $\angle AOC + \angle BOC + \angle AOB = 360°$

$\Rightarrow$ $\angle AOC + 110° + 90° = 360°$

$\therefore$ $\angle AOC = 360° - 110° - 90°$
$$= 360° - 200°$$
$$= 160°$$

Hence $\angle ABC = \frac{1}{2}\angle AOC$
$$= \frac{1}{2} \times 160°$$
$$= 80°$$

20. From the figure,

$\angle ABC + \angle BCA + \angle CAB = 180°$

$\Rightarrow$ $\angle ABC + 45° + 55° = 180°$

$\therefore$ $\angle ABC = 180° - 100°$
$$= 80°$$

Here, ABCD is a cyclic quadrilateral

$\Rightarrow$ $\angle ADC + \angle ABC = 180°$

$\therefore$ $\angle ADC = 180° - \angle ABC$
$$= 180° - 80°$$
$$= 100°$$

21. Let the number be x and y

Here, $x - y = 36$ ...(i)

and $\frac{x}{y} = 4$

$\Rightarrow$ $x = 4y$ ...(ii)

Putting the value of x in eq (i)
$$4y - y = 36$$
$$y = \frac{36}{3} = 12$$
and $x = 4 \times 12 = 48$

Hence the required positive integers are 48 and 12.

22. Area of the parallelogram $= 25 \times 10$

and also area of the parallelogram $= 20 \times x$

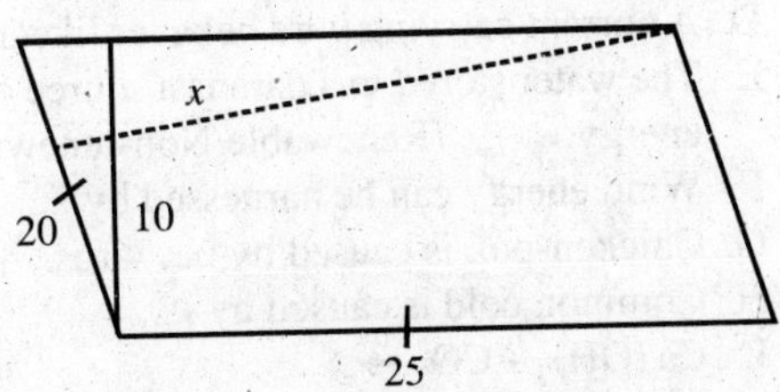

(Here, x is the altitude on other side)

$\Rightarrow$ $20x = 250$

$\therefore$ $x = \frac{250}{20}$
$$= 12.5 \text{ cm}$$

23. Area of the isosceles rt. angled $\Delta = \frac{1}{2}$ (base)^2
$$= \frac{1}{2} \times (40)^2$$
$$= \frac{1}{2} \times 1600$$
$$= 800 \text{ cm}^2$$

24. Area of the circular pit $= \pi r^2$
$$= \frac{22}{7} \times (100)^2$$
$$= \frac{22}{7} \times 10000$$
$$= \frac{220000}{7} = 31428\frac{4}{7} \text{ m}^2$$

25. Let the speed of the motor boat in still water be x km/hr, then speed of motor boat in downstream and upstream will be $(x + 2)$ and $(x - 2)$ km/hr respectively.
$$6(x - 2) = 5(x + 2)$$
$\Rightarrow$ $6x - 12 = 5x + 10$
$$6x - 5x = 10 + 12$$
$$x = 22 \text{ km/hr.}$$

26. Difference between their circumferences
$$= 2\pi R - 2\pi r$$
$$= 2\pi(R - r)$$

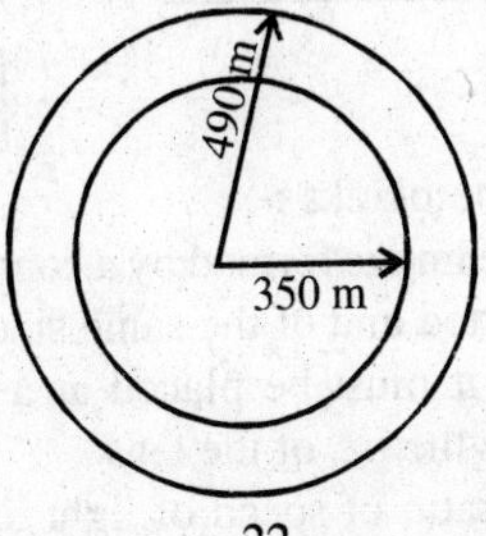

490 m

350 m

$$= 2 \times \frac{22}{7}(490 - 350)$$

$= 2 \times \frac{22}{7} \times 140$
$= 2 \times 22 \times 20$
$= 880$ m.

27. Total surface area of the cone

$= \pi r(l + r)$

$= \frac{22}{7} \times 12 \times (16 + 12)$

$= \frac{22}{7} \times 12 \times 28$

$= 22 \times 12 \times 4$

$= 1056 \text{ cm}^2$

28. Here, Radius of the Moon (r)

$= \frac{1}{4} \times$ radius of the earth

$= \frac{1}{4} \text{R}$

Hence, $\frac{\text{Volume of the Moon}}{\text{Volume of the Earth}} = \frac{\frac{4}{3}\pi r^3}{\frac{4}{3}\pi \text{R}^3}$

$= \frac{\left(\frac{1}{4}\text{R}\right)^3}{\text{R}^3}$

$= \frac{1}{64}$

29.

	0. 0 91
9	0. $\overline{00}$ $\overline{82}$ $\overline{81}$
	81
181	181
	181
	×

Hence, square root of 0.008281 = 0.091

30. $\left(\frac{32}{243}\right)^{\frac{-4}{5}} = \left(\frac{2^5}{3^5}\right)^{-4/5}$

$= \left(\frac{2}{3}\right)^{-4} = \left(\frac{3}{2}\right)^4$

$= \frac{3^4}{2^4} = \frac{81}{16}$

31. C.P. of 100 blankets = 2000 × 100
= ₹ 200000

S.P. of 10 defective blankets
= 10 × 1200 = ₹ 12000

Total S.P. at 14% profit

$= 200000 \times \frac{114}{100}$
= ₹ 228000

∴ Remaining S.P. = 228000 – 12000
= ₹ 216000

Now, No. of remaining blankets
= 100 – 10 = 90

Hence, Rate of S.P. of each remaining blanket

$= \frac{216000}{90} =$ ₹ 2400

32. Let required time be n years

then, $378 = 1800\left[\left(1+\frac{10}{100}\right)^n - 1\right]$

$\Rightarrow \frac{378}{1800} = \left(1+\frac{10}{100}\right)^n - 1$

$\Rightarrow \left(\frac{11}{10}\right)^n = \frac{21}{100} + 1$

$\Rightarrow \left(\frac{11}{10}\right)^n = \frac{121}{100} = \left(\frac{11}{10}\right)^2$

Hence, $n = 2$ years

Part 'B' — Science

1. Fill in the blanks :

A. If the image formed by a convex lens is real, inverted and of the same size as the object, then it must be placed at a point that ..... times the ..... of the lens.

B. The ratio of speed of light in two media is expressed as ..... of the one medium with respect to the other.

C. Our eyes make an image of objects at the .....

D. A current carrying wire behaves like a .....

E. The water stored in a dam is a source of ..... energy. (Renewable/Non-renewable)

F. Wind energy can be harnessed by .....

G. Chicken-pox is caused by ..... virus.

H. Common cold is caused by .....

I. $Ca(OH)_2 + CO_2 \rightarrow$ .....

J. The three fundamental particles of the atoms are .....

2. State True or False :

A. Stars are celestial bodies that do not emit own light heat (T/F)

B. The phases of moon occur due to relative position of the moon, earth and the sun (T/F)

C. Soil erosion can be prevented by growing trees and reclamation of ravines (T/F)

D. Air is a mixture of several gases. Nitrogen is found in small quantity in air (T/F)

E. Greenhouse effect is dangerous for human being. (T/F)

F. Decomposition of a substance can be termed as chemical reaction (T/F)

G. Loss or gain of electron from or to an atom leads to the formation of ions. (T/F)

H. Atoms of an element having the same atomic number but same mass number are called isotopes (T/F)

I. Metals like aluminium, magnesium react with acids. (T/F)

J. Concave lens are used as a magnifying glass and also in making telescopes and microscopes. (T/F)

3. Briefly explain "Solar System".

4. Define Coulomb's Law.

5. What is difference between conductors and Insulators? Give example.

6. Two cells of 1.25V and 0.75V are connected in parallel. What will be the effective voltage?

7. An object is placed at a distance of 25 cm from a convex lens of focal length 20 cm. Draw a ray diagram to show the position and size of its image formed by the lens.

8. Give two examples of scalar quantities and vector quantities.

9. The capacity of a conductor is 1 farad. What is meant by this?

10. What do you understand by Nitrogen Cycle?

11. Differentiate between oxidation and reduction reactions. Give example.

12. What do you understand by ionic compounds? What happens when these are dissolved in water?

13. Briefly explain 'Isomerism'.

14. What is 'CNG'?

15. Why carbon dioxide is known as green house gas?

16. Complete the following equation—

A. $xCO_2 + xH_2O \xrightarrow{\text{(Sunlight)}}$ .....

B. $2NaHCO_3 \xrightarrow{\text{(Heat)}}$ .....

C. $CaCO_3 + 2HCl \rightarrow$ .....

D. $CH_4 + 2O_2 \rightarrow$ .....

E. $ZnO + C \rightarrow$ .....

17. Match the items in column A and B—

Column (A)	Column (B)
A. $NaNO_3$	(i) Baking soda
B. $Na(NH_4)HPO_4$	(ii) Washing soda
C. $NaHCO_3$	(iii) Chile salt petre
D. $Na_2CO_3, 10H_2O$	(iv) Microcosmic salt

18. What are noble gas? Name them.

19. Match the items in column A and B :

Column (A)	Column (B)
A. Coal	(i) Hydroelectric power Station
B. Water in dam	(ii) Bus
C. Diesel	(iii) Cooking
D. Wind	(iv) Thermal Power Station
E. LPG	(v) Windmill

20. Which type (form) of water is mostly used by plants?

21. Name two coal based fuels, which have higher calorific value?

22. Describe the functions of the following

(i) Liver ....

(ii) Vocal cords ....

(iii) Nephron ....

23. Name the micro-organism that causes following diseases:

(i) Plague ....

(ii) Leprosy ....

(iii) Tetanus ....

24. What is the normal blood sugar level of human?

25. Name the location of pituitary gland.

ANSWERS WITH EXPLANATIONS

1. A. is two, focal length
B. refractive index
C. retina
D. magnet
E. renewable
F. windmills
G. varicella
H. rhino virus
I. $CaCO_3 + H_2O$
J. electron, proton and neutron.

2. A. False B. True
C. True D. False
E. True F. True
G. True H. False
I. True J. False

3. Solar System: The sun and all the objects which are orbiting it, including the planets, asteroids, comets and meteors form the solar system. The nine known planets in the solar system are—Mercury, Venus, Earth, Mars, Jupiter, Saturn, Uranus, Neptune and Pluto. It is known that the solar system has at least 1,00,000 asteroids and 100 billion comets.

4. Coulomb's Law: It states that the force between two charged objects is directly proportional to the product of their charges and inversely proportional to the square of the distance between them.

$$F = 9 \times 10^9 \times \frac{q_1 \times q_2}{r^2} \quad \text{(In S.I. system)}$$

5. Substances that allow electrons to pass freely through them are called conductors; eg; silver and copper. But when a substance that does not allow electron to move through them freely, is called insulators. e.g.; Hard rubber, glass, mica, porcelain are all good insulators.

6. Here, $E = E_1 - E_2$
$= (1.25 - 0.75)$ V
$= 0.50$ V

7.

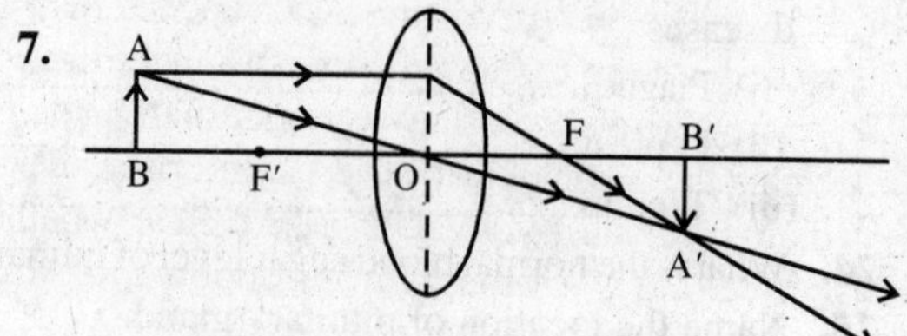

8. Scalar quantities—Distance, speed
Vector quantities—Displacement, velocity.

9. The capacity of a conductor is 1 farad means 1 Coulomb charge is required to increase the potential of conductor by 1 volt.

10. Nitrogen Cycle: The sequence of processes in which nitrogen and its compounds are utilized in nature. This is also the cycle of chemical changes that keep nitrogen flowing through the biosphere in soil and air.

11. Oxidation: (i) Reaction of oxygen with another substance (example $2\,Zn + O_2 \rightarrow 2\,ZnO$). (ii) A chemical reaction in which a compound or radical loses electrons (example $Cu \rightarrow Cu^{2+} + 2e^-$).

Reduction: (i) Reaction of hydrogen with another substance (example : $Br_2 + H_2 \rightarrow 2HBr$) (ii) Chemical reaction in which an element gains an electron (example, $Zn^{2+} + e^- \rightarrow Zn^+$).

12. Compounds are combinations of positive and negative ions; Magnesium chloride, for example, is formed from Magnesium ions (Mg^+) and chloride ions (Cl^-). If such a compound is disolved in water, it breaks up into ions.

13. Those compounds which have the same molecular formula but different structural arrangement of atoms in them, are known as isomers and the phenomenon is known as isomerism. All members of Alkanes, except first three members methane, ethane and propane can have more than one structural formula.

```
     H   H   H   H
     |   |   |   |
  H—C—C—C—C—H
     |   |   |   |
     H   H   H   H
```

n–Butane

```
              H
              |
           H—C—H
   H          |
   |          |
H—C————C————C—H
   |          |          |
   H          H          H
```

14. The natural gas is mostly methane having small amounts of ethane, propane and butane in decreasing order. If this natural gas is compressed to a limit degree, then this gas is known as Compressed Natural Gas (CNG).

15. Carbon dioxide plays a significant role by absorbing radiant heat, acting as the glass wall of a green house. Therefore carbon dioxide and other heat trapping gases are known as green house gases.

16. A. $(CH_2O)x + {}_xO_2$
(Carbohydrate)
B. $Na_2CO_3 + H_2O + CO_2$
C. $CaCl_2 + H_2O + CO_2$
D. $CO_2 + 2H_2O$
E. $Zn + CO$

17. A. $NaNO_3 \rightarrow$ Chile salt petre
B. $Na(NH_4)HPO_4$—Microcosmic salt
C. $NaHCO_3$—Baking Soda
D. $Na_2CO_3 . 10H_2O$—Washing Soda.

18. The noble gases are inactive in normal condition. They are—
Helium (He), Neon (Ne), Argon (Ar), Krypton (Kr), Xenon (Xe), Radon (Rn).

19. A. (iv) B. (i) C. (ii) D. (v) E. (iii)

20. Capillary form of water

21. Two coal based fuels having high calorific value are—
(i) Coal gas—calorific value of 450-500 B. Th. U.
(ii) Water gas—calorific value of 280-310 B. Th. U.

22. (i) Liver—Bio chemical laboratory phagocytic in function.
(ii) Vocal cords—Sound production
(iii) Nephron—The structural and functional unit of kidney

23. (i) Yersinia pestis
(ii) Mycobacterium leprae
(iii) Clostridium tetani.

24. Normal level of blood sugar is 60-100 mg/100 ml. of blood.

25. Pituitary gland is located at the base of brain in a cavity, the sella turcica of sphenoid bone of skull. Which is connected by a short infundibular stalk to the ventral wall of diencephalon of the brain.

PAPER-II—LANGUAGE AND SOCIAL STUDIES

Part 'A' — English Language

1. The following sentences have ERRORS. Select the part in which the error lies and encircle its letter I, II or III. If there is no error, encircle IV. (10 Marks)

A. (I) Ram and Shyam are old friends/(II) does every-thing together whenever they/(III) meet/(IV) No error.

B. (I) I walk fastly when/(II) I go for my morning/(III) walk/(IV) No error.

C. (I) Sainik School is/(II) one of the best/(III) schools of the country/(IV) No error.

D. (I) I and she/(II) read in/(III) the same class./(IV) No error.

E. I always/(I) prefer/(II) tea to coffee in/(III) my breakfast./(IV) No error.

2. Read the following passage carefully and complete the sentences given below— **(20 Marks)**

How Coffee was discovered

According to an ancient Arab legend, coffee was discovered in Abyssinia in the 3rd century AD by some Christian monks, who observed how their sheep and goats, after browsing on a certain shrub, were wakeful and full of energy at night when they should have been sleeping. Prior picked and ate some of the fruits of the shrub and he, too, felt an unusual sense of exhilaration and wakefulness. Another version of the story is that a goat herd called Kaldi, who lived in Ethiopia in the 9th century AD, watched his animals as they ate the bright red berries from a tree growing wild in the pasture; they were unusually active after eating the berries. He too tried the berries and enjoyed their stimulating effect. It is not clear whether the coffee tree was brought from Ethiopia to Arabia or whether it was also native to Arabia.

The word 'coffee' is derived from the Arabic word 'qahwah' which means wine or a brew, the coffee beverage, some say it has its connections with the province in South-West Ethiopia, called Kefa or Kaffa. Until the end of the 17th century all coffee came from Arabia. It was shipped from Mocha, the port of Yemen; the Arabs long maintained coffee as a national monopoly. For centuries they exported large quantities of beans but did not permit a fertile seed or seedling to leave their territories. Only in 1690, the Dutch managed to obtain a few plants and placed them in botanical gardens in the Netherlands. From there they were sent to Java and other botanical gardens in Europe. Eventually the coffee plant reached Brazil in the 1720s. Today most of the world's output comes from South and Central America. Brazil is by far the largest producer; it not only produces two-thirds of the world's coffee, but also its best.

A. Some Christian monks observed that after having browsed on a certain shrub the sheep ______

B. The effect the shrub had on Prior was ______

C. Encircle the correct alternative. Coffee was discovered—
 (i) After research in labs
 (ii) Accidentally
 (iii) By mixing various concomitants

D. Coffee acts as—
 (i) An intoxicant
 (ii) A stimulant
 (iii) A sedative

E. In Ethiopia a goat by name Kaldi observed ______

F. He cross checked the effectiveness of the barries by ______

G. Qahwah literally means ______

H. The Arabs for long maintained ______

I. The enterprising Dutch ______ and spread its use

J. From 1720 Brazil had the good fortune of ______ and today it is ______

Find ANTONYM (Opposite in meaning) to the following words: (10 Marks)

3. **Determined**
 A. Fickle B. Easy
 C. Committed D. Slow

4. **Quiet**
 A. Silent B. Noisy
 C. Cool D. Abusive

5. **Graceful**
 A. Disgraceful B. Incorrect
 C. Grateful D. Awful

6. **Anger**
 A. Reckless B. Sorrow
 C. Happy D. Calm

7. **Sleepy**
 A. Active B. Careless
 C. Healthy D. Tired

8. **Change the narration– (10 Marks)**
 A. Ram said to Sita, "He wants to marry her" ______
 B. He asked me, "Where are you going?" ______
 C. Mary said, "how clever I am!" ______
 D. "Call the first witness," said the judge ______
 E. He asked me, "Do you want a pen?" ______

Encircle A, B, C or D for correct spelling– (5 Marks)

9. A. Demokracy B. Democrazy
 C. Democracy D. Demokrazy

10. A. Enlightenment B. Nlightenment
 C. Enligtment D. Lightenment

11. A. Cigarette B. Cigarete
 C. Cigerettee D. Cigareete

12. A. Pneumonia B. Pnemonia
 C. Nemonia D. Pnemunia

13. A. Coperation B. Co-operation
 C. Copperation D. Coooperation

14. Change the sentences as directed— **(10 Marks)**

A. The cat killed the mouse (Passive Voice)

B. Ram has been playing cricket (Simple Present)

C. She is fond of music (Interrogative)

D. He does not like to fight (Affirmative)

E. She plays football (Simple Future)

Fill in the blanks— **(20 Marks)**

15. Although he worked hard ..... he failed.

16. In ..... short time, he rose to the rank of General.

17. He is taller ..... her.

18. He is the man whom I was talking .....

19. All Indians have great respect ..... the country.

20. I was angry ..... him.

21. Shyam died ..... fever.

22. Are you blind ..... your own interests?

23. Shelly and Hary ..... walking since morning.

24. A cashier is liable to render account ..... the money received.

25. Zaheer hit a ball right ..... of the house.

26. He jumped ..... the river.

27. First listen ..... him and then decide.

28. According ..... the rules he should have been adjudged first.

29. Police stopped him ..... the entrance.

30. There is no death ..... trained man in India.

31. ..... umbrella costs more in rainy season.

32. He is senior ..... him in service.

33. He has gift ..... God.

34. I ordered for ..... cup of tea in the restaurant.

35. Write a letter to your father stating that you need Rs. 100 to buy books for your forthcoming Sainik School Entrance Examination. Assume details. **(15 Marks)**

ANSWERS WITH EXPLANATIONS

1. A. (II) B. (I) C. (I) D. (I) E. (IV)

2. A. were wakeful and full of energy at night when they should have been sleeping.

B. that he felt an unusual sense of excitement and wakefulness.

C. (ii)

D. (ii)

E. that as his animals ate the bright red berries from the tree growing wild in the pasture they were unusually active after eating the berries.

F. eating them himself.

G. wine or brew.

H. coffee as a national monopoly.

I. managed to obtain a few plants.

J. being the largest producer of coffee.

3. (A) **4.** (B) **5.** (A)

6. (D) **7.** (A)

8. A. Ram told Sita that he wanted to marry her.

B. He asked me where I was going.

C. Mary exclaimed with wonder saying that she was very clever.

D. The judge ordered someone to call the first witness.

E. He asked me if I wanted a pen.

9. (C) **10.** (A) **11.** (A)

12. (A) **13.** (B)

14. A. The mouse was killed by the cat.

B. Ram plays cricket.

C. Is she fond of music?

D. He liked to fight.

E. Will she play football?

15. yet. **16.** a **17.** than

18. about **19.** for **20.** with

21. of **22.** to **23.** have been

24. for **25.** at the **26.** into

27. to **28.** to **29.** at

30. of **31.** an **32.** to

33. from **34.** a

35.

Hostel
W.H.S. School Madhubani
12-9-05

My Dear Papa,

I am well with my health and study and hope you will be the same. As per you wish I am preparing for the forthcoming Sainik School Entrance Examination. I am doing my bit, but I have great need of some books. At present I have no money since I spent the money you gave on paying the hostel charges. Please send Rs. 100 immediately in order to buy some books. Rest is OK. My pranam to Mummy and love to Saurabh

Yours affectionately,
Sameer

Part 'B' — Social Studies

State True or False

1. Henry Ford was instrumental in popularising automobiles. (T/F)
2. The decline in the monopolistic power of the medieval church enabled the progress of more liberal ideas (T/F)
3. Battle of Buxar was fought in 1764 (T/F)
4. The first Indian to enter the Indian Civil Service was Mr. Satyendra Nath Tagore (T/F)
5. Nawab Mir Kasim shifted his capital to Murshidabad (T/F)
6. It shall be the duty of every citizen of India to uphold and protect the soverignty, unity and integrity of India (T/F)
7. Seven years' war (1757-1763) was fought between America and Canada (T/F)
8. Countries involved in the First Opium war were India and Pakistan (T/F)
9. Nadir Shah brought the Peacock Throne to Delhi. (T/F)
10. The Marathas had strong naval force to counter the Europian naval might (T/F)
11. The demand for Swaraj or self-government emerged by the beginning of the 20th century (T/F)
12. Gopal Krishna Gokhale was the political guru and mentor of Gandhiji (T/F)
13. Quit India Movement call was given at Calcutta during 1938. (T/F)
14. Azad Hind Fauz was raised by Captain Mohan Singh (T/F)
15. In March 1947, Lord Wavell replaced Mountbatten as the Viceroy of India (T/F)
16. Arya Samaj was established by Swami Brahmanand. (T/F)
17. Swami Vivekananda's original name was Narendra Nath Dutta (T/F)
18. Brahmo Samaj of India was organised by Raja Ram Mohan Roy (T/F)
19. Consequent to 1857 revolt, the power of ruling over India was transferred from the British East India Company to the Crown in 1858. (T/F)
20. "Bande Matram" was written by Bhartendu Harishchandra (T/F)
21. Population, food Production and poverty are interlinked.
22. Terrorism challenges territorial integrity and governance of a nation (T/F)
23. In India, death rate is more than birth rate (T/F)
24. Earthquake is caused due to heavy rainfall. (T/F)
25. Literacy rate in developing countries is 100% (T/F)

Fill in the blanks—

26. Deforestation and overgrazing lead to soil ________
27. Recycling can help conserve ________ resources.
28. ________ cells convert sunlight directly into electricity.
29. About 90% of the world's population occupy roughly ________% of its land area.
30. Non-renewable resources are minerals ________ fuels.
31. Four aims in the governance of India are Justice, Liberty, Equality and ________
32. United Nations came into existence on ________
33. Bal Gangadhar Tilak proclaimed ________ as our birthright.
34. ________ is an essential part of terrorism.
35. Globalisation gives thrust to liberalisation and ________
36. Theosophical society of India was founded by ________
37. Swami Vivekananda was the disciple of ________
38. ________ was appointed as the Governor of Bengal in 1772.
39. The Mughal Empire was founded in India by ________ in 1526.
40. The term 'Middle Age' was first used by ________ Scholar.
41. Respiratory diseases such as bronchitis and pneumonia increase due to ________ pollution.
42. The full form of CBSE is ________

43. The ________ Commission was appointed by the British Government in 1927 to assess India's fitness for self-rule.
44. Gandhiji was made to shift to lower class compartment in ________ (country).
45. Muslim League was formed in the year ________
46. Tantia Tope was killed during ________ for independence.

Match the following—

47.	HQs of UN	(A) Switzerland
48.	HQs of UNESCO	(B) Hague, Netherlands
49.	HQs of World Bank	(C) Paris
50.	HQs of WHO	(D) New York
51.	HQs of International court of Justice	(E) Washington DC

Match the following—

52.	Discovery of Direct Sea Route of India	(A) Telephone
53.	James Watt	(B) Road
54.	John Macadam	(C) Vasco-da-Gama
55.	A.G. Bell	(D) Steam Engine

Match the following—

56.	The 11 Sep	(A) Gandhiji
57.	Satyagrah	(B) President
58.	Supreme Commander of Indian Armed Forces	(C) USA
59.	Indian National Museum	(D) Hyderabad
60.	Charminar	(E) Kolkata

Answer Briefly **(3 marks each)**

61. List three causes of poverty.
62. What is meant by resource depletion?
63. Define Human Rights.
64. Write any three "Fundamental Rights" guaranteed by our Constitution to all citizens.
65. What is Terrorism?

ANSWERS WITH EXPLANATIONS

1. True **2.** True **3.** True
4. True **5.** False **6.** True
7. False **8.** False **9.** False
10. False **11.** True **12.** True
13. False **14.** True **15.** False
16. False **17.** True **18.** True
19. True **20.** False **21.** True
22. True **23.** False **24.** False
25. False **26.** Erosion **27.** Natural
28. Solar **29.** 30%
30. and other geological **31.** Fraternity
32. Oct. 24, 1945
33. Swarjya **34.** Violence **35.** Privatization
36. Mrs. Annie Besant
37. Swami Ram Krishna Paramhans
38. Warren Hastings
39. Babar **40.** European
41. atmospheric
42. Central Board of Secondary Education
43. Simon **44.** South Africa
45. 1906 **46.** Ist war
47. (D) **48.** (C) **49.** (E)
50. (A) **51.** (B) **52.** (C)
53. (D) **54.** (B) **55.** (A)
56. (C) **57.** (A) **58.** (B)
59. (E) **60.** (D)

61. I. Illiteracy
II. Unemployment.
III. Non-exploitation of resources.

62. The term resource depletion is related to non-renewable resources which are limited. The continued use of these resource leads to their depletion, is called resource depletion.

63. Human Rights are those conditions of social life without which no man can seek to be himself at his best.

64. I. Right to Equality.
II. Right to Freedom.
III. Right to Freedom of Religion.

65. Terrorism is an anti-social activity, usually associated with violence, indulged in by an individual or a union to subserve the questionable ends.

Previous Paper (Solved)

Sainik School Exam, 2004

(Class-IX)

PAPER-I—MATHEMATICS AND SCIENCE

PART–A : Mathematics

1. Evaluate the following algebraically
107×103

2. Write the following in expanded form
$(9x + 2y + z)^2$

3. Divide $8a^3 - 27b^3$ by $2a - 3b$.

4. Anita borrowed a sum of ₹ 2000 from a bank to purchase a machine. If the rate of interest is 5% per annum, calculate the compound interest that Anita has to pay to the bank after three years.

5. Sophia wants to secure an annual income of ₹ 1500 by investing in 15% debentures of face value ₹ 100 each and available for ₹ 104 each. If the brokerage is 1%, what sum of money should she invest?

6. Find the least number which must be subtracted from 194491 to make it a perfect square.

7. Find the square root of 0.00053361.

8. What is the smallest number by which 675 may be multiplied so that the product is a perfect cube?

9. Find the cube root of 157464.

10. Write the cube root of $\frac{31}{216}$. [Hint: $(3.141)^3 \cong 31$]

11. Solve the equation : $\frac{2x-3}{3x+2} = \frac{-2}{3}$

12. The ages (in years) of Mahesh and Ram are in the ratio 5 : 7. If Mahesh was 9 years older and Ram 9 years younger, the age of Mahesh would have been twice the age of Ram. Find their ages.

13. The base of an isosceles triangles is 48 cm and its perimeter is 108 cm. Find the area of the triangle.

14. Given that carbon 14 decays at a constant rate in such a way that it reduces to 50% in 5568 years, find the age of an old wooden piece in which the carbon is only $12\frac{1}{2}\%$ of the original.

15. Divide the polynominal :
$6x^5 + 4x^4 - 27x^3 - 7x^2 - 27x - 6$ by $2x^2 - 3$.

16. Fill in the blanks–

(i) The angle of an arc of a circle subtends at the _____ is double the angle it subtends at any point on the _____ part of the circle.

(ii) A quadrilateral is said to be _____ quadrilateral, if its vertices lie on a circle.

17. Fill in the blanks–

(i) A tangent to the circle at a point is _____ to the radius and touches at the _____ of radius at circle.

(ii) The two tangents to a circle from an external point are equally ___ to the line joining the point to the centre of the circle.

18. The parallel sides of a trapezium are 15m and 8m and the distance between them is 14m. What is the area of the trapezium?

19. The sides of a triangle are 11m, 60m and 61m. Find the altitude to its largest side.

20. The distance between the two stations 'A' and 'B' is 230 km. Motorist and Cyclists start simultaneously from A and B in the opposite directions and the distance between them after three hours is 20 km. If the speed of the cyclist is less than the other by 10 km/hr., find the speed of each.

21. Factorize the expression :
$8x^3 + 27y^3 - z^3 + 18xyz$

22. The denominator of a rational number is greater than its numerator by 4. If numerator is increased by 11 and the denominator is decreased by 1, the new number becomes $\frac{7}{3}$. Find the original number.

23. The following scores were obtained by 20 students in a mathematics test:

69 48 54 84 76 39 50 60 71 91
41 56 73 78 36 57 69 70 78 94

Prepare a frequency distribution table.

24. ABCD is a quadrilateral inscribed in a circle. Diagonals AC, BD are joined. If ∠ACB = 45° and ∠CAB = 40° what is ∠ADC?

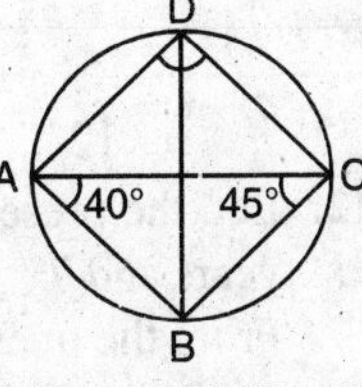

25. The population of a certain city is 125000. If the annual birth rate is 3.3% and the annual death rate is 1.3%, calculate the population after 3 years.

26. A storage tank consists of a circular cylinder, with a hemisphere adjoined on either end (see fig.). If the external diameter of the cylinder be 1.4 m and its length be 5 m, what will be the cost of painting it on the outside, at the rate of ₹ 10 per square metre?

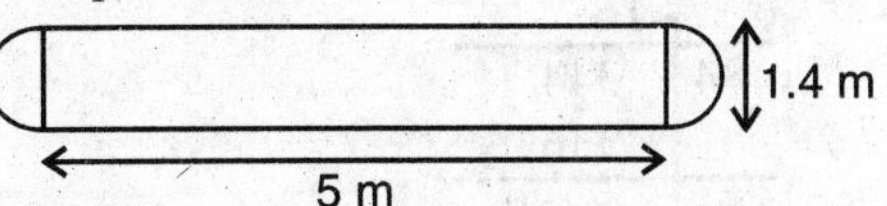

27. A conical cup 18 cm high has a circular base of diameter 14 cm. The cup is full of water, which is now poured into a cylinder vessel of circular base of diameter 10 cm. What will be the height of water in the vessel?

28. Find the value of :

(i) $64^{-\frac{2}{3}} \times 27^{-\frac{2}{3}}$ (ii) $16^{\frac{5}{2}} \div 16^{\frac{1}{2}}$

29. Find the value of $a^3 + 8b^3$ if $a + 2b = 10$ and $ab = 15$.

30. The digit in the tens place of a two digit number is three times that in the ones place. If the digits are reversed, the new number will be 36 less than the original number. Find the number.

EXPLANATORY ANSWERS

1. $107 \times 103 = (100 + 7)(100 + 3)$
$= 10000 + (7 + 3) \times 100 + 21$
$= 10000 + 1000 + 21$
$= 11021$

2. $(9x + 2y + z)^2$
$= (9x)^2 + (2y)^2 + (z)^2 + 2(9x) \times (2y) + 2(2y) \times z + 2(9x) \times z$
$[\because (a + b + c)^2 = a^2 + b^2 + c^2 + 2ab + 2bc + 2ca)]$
$= 81x^2 + 4y^2 + z^2 + 36xy + 4yz + 18zx$

3.
$$
\begin{array}{r|l|l}
2a - 3b & 8a^3 - 27b^3 & 4a^2 + 6ab + 9b^2 \\
 & 8a^3 - 12a^2b & \\
 & (-) \quad (+) & \\ \hline
 & +12a^2b - 27b^3 & \\
 & +12a^2b - 18ab^2 & \\
 & (-) \quad (+) & \\ \hline
 & 18ab^2 - 27b^3 & \\
 & 18ab^2 - 27b^3 & \\
 & (-) \quad (+) & \\ \hline
 & \times &
\end{array}
$$

4. Here, $\text{C.I.} = P\left[\left(1+\frac{R}{100}\right)^n - 1\right]$

$= 2000\left[\left(1+\frac{5}{100}\right)^3 - 1\right]$

$= 2000\left[\left(1+\frac{1}{20}\right)^3 - 1\right]$

$= 2000 \times \left[\frac{21}{20}\times\frac{21}{20}\times\frac{21}{20} - 1\right]$

$= 2000\left[\frac{9261}{8000} - 1\right]$

$= 2000 \times \frac{1261}{8000}$

$= \frac{2522}{8} = ₹\ 315.25$

5. Now ₹ 15 is income on ₹ 105

$\therefore$ ₹ 1500 is income on ₹ $\frac{105 \times 1500}{15}$

= ₹ 10500

6.

	4 4 1
4	$\overline{19}\ \overline{44}\ \overline{91}$
	16
84	344
	336
881	891
	881
	10

Hence, Required number = 10.

7.

	0.0 2 3 1
2	$0.\overline{00}\ \overline{05}\ \overline{33}\ \overline{61}$
	4
43	133
	129
461	461
	461
	×

Hence, square root of 0.00053361 = 0.0231

8.

3	675
3	225
3	75
5	25
	5

$675 = \overline{3\times3\times3}\times5\times5$

Hence, required number = 5

9.

2	15 74 64
2	7 8 7 32
2	3 9 3 6 6
3	1 9 6 8 3
3	6 5 6 1
3	2 1 8 7
3	7 2 9
3	2 4 3
3	81
3	27
3	9
	3

$\therefore$ 15 74 64

$= \overline{2\times2\times2}\times\overline{3\times3\times3}\times\overline{3\times3\times3}\times\overline{3\times3\times3}$

Hence, Cube root of 157464 = $2\times3\times3\times3 = 54$

10. Cube root of $\dfrac{31}{216} = \dfrac{\sqrt[3]{31}}{\sqrt[3]{216}}$

$= \dfrac{3.141}{6} = 0.5235$

11. $\dfrac{2x-3}{3x+2} = -\dfrac{2}{3}$

$\Rightarrow 6x - 9 = -6x - 4$

$\Rightarrow 6x + 6x = 9 - 4$

$\Rightarrow 12x = 5$

$\therefore\ x = \dfrac{5}{12}$

12. Let, the present age of Mahesh and Ram be $5x$ years and $7x$ years respectively.

From the question,

$2(7x-9) = 5x+9$

$\Rightarrow 14x - 18 = 5x + 9$

$\Rightarrow 14x - 5x = 9 + 18$

$\Rightarrow 9x = 27$

$\therefore\ x = 3$

Hence, Mahesh's age and Ram's age are 15 years and 21 years respectively.

13. Each equal side of the isosceles Δ

$= \dfrac{108-48}{2} = \dfrac{60}{2} = 30$ cm

$\therefore\quad S = \dfrac{108}{2} = 54$ cm

Hence, Area of Δ

$= \sqrt{54(54-30)(54-30)(54-48)}$

$= \sqrt{54\times24\times24\times6}$

$= 3\times6\times24$

$= 432\ \text{cm}^2$

14. Here, Half life of carbon = 5568 years

Now, $\dfrac{x}{2} = x\left(1+\dfrac{r}{100}\right)^{5568}$

$\therefore\ \dfrac{1}{2} = \left(1+\dfrac{r}{100}\right)^{5568}$ ...(i)

Again, $\dfrac{x}{8} = x\left(1+\dfrac{r}{100}\right)^{n}$

$\Rightarrow \dfrac{1}{8} = \left(1+\dfrac{r}{100}\right)^{n}$

$$\Rightarrow \left(1+\frac{r}{100}\right)^n = \left(\frac{1}{2}\right)^3$$

$$\Rightarrow \left(1+\frac{r}{100}\right)^n = \left(1+\frac{r}{100}\right)^{3\times5568} \quad \text{From eqn. } (i)$$

$\therefore \; n = 16704$ years

15. Dividing $6x^5 + 4x^4 - 27x^3 - 7x^2 - 27x - 6$ by $2x^2 - 3$:

Quotient: $3x^3 + 2x^2 - 9x - \frac{1}{2}$

$$
\begin{array}{l}
6x^5 + 4x^4 - 27x^3 - 7x^2 - 27x - 6 \\
6x^5 \quad -9x^3 \\
(-) \quad (+) \\
\hline
4x^4 - 18x^3 - 7x^2 - 27x - 6 \\
4x^4 \quad - 6x^2 \\
(-) \quad (+) \\
\hline
-18x^3 - x^2 - 27x - 6 \\
-18x^3 \quad +27x \\
(+) \quad (-) \\
\hline
-x^2 - 54x - 6 \\
-x^2 \quad + \frac{3}{2} \\
(+) \quad (-) \\
\hline
-54x - \frac{15}{2}
\end{array}
$$

16. (i) Centre, Circumference
(ii) Cyclic

17. (i) Perpendicular, end
(ii) Equal

18. Here, Area of Trapezium $= \frac{1}{2}\times(15+8)\times14$

$= \frac{1}{2}\times23\times14 = 161$ sq. m.

19. Here, $s = \frac{11+60+61}{2} = 66$ m

Area of $\Delta = \sqrt{s(s-a)(s-b)(s-c)}$

$= \sqrt{66\times(66-11)(66-60)(66-61)}$

$= \sqrt{66\times55\times6\times5}$

$= \sqrt{2\times3\times11\times5\times11\times2\times3\times5} = 2\times3\times5\times11$

$= 330$ m^2

Let, the Altitude to its largest side be x m

then, $\frac{1}{2}\times61\times x = 330$

$\Rightarrow x = \frac{330\times2}{61} = 10.82$ m

20. Let, the speed of the cyclist be x km/hr

then, the speed of motorist = $(x + 10)$ km/hr

From the question,

$3x + 3(x+10) = 230 - 20$

$\Rightarrow 3x + 3x + 30 = 210$

$\Rightarrow 6x + 30 = 210$

$\Rightarrow 6x = 180$

$\therefore \; x = \frac{180}{6} = 30$ km/hr

Hence, speed of motorist and cyclist are 40 km/hr and 30 km/hr respectively.

21. $8x^3 + 27y^3 - z^3 + 18xyz$

$= (2x)^3 + (3y)^3 + (-z)^3 - 3(2x)(3y)(-z)$

$= (2x + 3y - z)[(2x)^2 + (3y)^2 + (-z)^2 - 2x\times3y - 3y(-z) - (2x)(-z)]$

$= (2x + 3y - z)[4x^2 + 9y^2 + z^2 - 6xy + 3yz + 2zx]$

22. Let, the numerator be x then denominator will be $x + 4$.

From the question,

$\frac{x+11}{x+4-1} = \frac{7}{3}$

$\Rightarrow \frac{x+11}{x+3} = \frac{7}{3}$

$\Rightarrow 7x + 21 = 3x + 33$

$\Rightarrow 4x = 12$

$\therefore \; x = 3$

Hence, original rational number

$= \frac{x}{x+4} = \frac{3}{3+4} = \frac{3}{7}$

23.

Marks of Maths	No. of Students
31 – 40	2
41 – 50	3
51 – 60	4
61 – 70	3
71 – 80	5
81 – 90	1
91 – 100	2

24. In Δ ABC,

$\angle ABC = 180° - (40° + 45°) = 180° - 85° = 95°$

Hence, $\angle ADC = 180° - 95° = 85°$

25. Here, annual increase rate = 3.3 – 1.3 = 2%

$\therefore$ Population after 3 years $= 125000\left(1+\frac{2}{100}\right)^3$

$= 125000 \frac{51}{50}\times\frac{51}{50}\times\frac{51}{50}$

$= 51 \times 51 \times 51$

$= 132651$

26. Area of the surface to be painted $= 2\pi rl + 4\pi r^2$

$= 2\pi r(l + 2r)$ (Here $l = h$)

$= 2 \times \frac{22}{7} \times 0.7\,(5 + 2 \times 0.7)$

$= 4.4 \times 6.4$

$= 28.16\ m^2$

Hence, cost of painting = 28.16 × 10

= ₹ 281.60

27. Volume of water $= \frac{1}{3}\pi \times 7^2 \times 18 = 294\pi\ cm^3$

Area of the base of the cylinder $= \pi \times 5^2$

$= 25\pi\ cm^2$

Hence, height of water in the vessel $= \frac{294\pi}{25\pi}$

$= 11.76$ cm

28. (i) $64^{-2/3} \times 27^{-2/3} = (4^3)^{-2/3} \times (3^3)^{-2/3}$

$= 4^{-2} \times 3^{-2}$

$= \frac{1}{16}\times\frac{1}{9} = \frac{1}{144}$

(ii) $16^{5/2} \div 16^{1/2} = (16)^{5/2-1/2} = (16)^2$

$= 16 \times 16 = 256$

29. $(a + 2b)^3 = (10)^3$

$\Rightarrow a^3 + 8b^3 + 3 \times a \times 2b\,(a + 2b) = 1000$

$\Rightarrow a^3 + 8b^3 + 6 \times 15 \times 10 = 1000$

$\Rightarrow a^3 + 8b^3 + 900 = 1000$

$\therefore a^3 + 8b^3 = 1000 - 900 = 100$

30. Let, the number be $10x + y$

and also, $x = 3y$

$\Rightarrow x - 3y = 0$ ...(i)

Now, $(10x + y) - (10y + x) = 36$

$\Rightarrow 9x - 9y = 36$

$\Rightarrow x - y = 4$ ...(ii)

$x - 3y = 0$

(–) (+) (–)

$2y = 4$

$y = 2$

$\therefore x = 2 \times 3 = 6$

Hence, number $= 10 \times 6 + 2$

$= 62$

Part 'B' — Science

1. The sure test of magnetism is ..... and not attraction.

2. A fuse should have .... resistance and .... melting point.

3. The resistance of a body to fight against the diseases is known as ....

4. Total resistance of three resistances R_1, R_2 and R_3 connected in parallel combination is ....

5. Name the micro-organisms that causes following diseases :

(i) Typhoid *(ii)* Measles *(iii)* Ringworm

6. Methane is also called ...... gas.

7. In vacuum or free space, the speed of light is ...... km/sec.

8. An instrument used to see very small objects is called .... and an instrument used to see distant objects is called ....

9. Unit of pressure in S.I. system is ....

10. At surface of earth one cubic metre of air weighs 1.29 kg and one litre of air weighs .... gm.

11. State Ohm's law.

12. Give the chemical formula of the following ores:

(i) Rock salt (halite) ....

(ii) Bauxite ....

13. What are hydrocarbons?

14. Name the constituent metals of following alloys:

(i) Brass *(ii)* Steel *(iii)* Bronze

15. Velocity of light in glass is equal to 180,000 km/sec. Calculate the refractive index of glass.

16. Calculate the reistance of wire 110 cm long and 0.2 mm in diameter. Given specific resistance of wire 49×10^{-8} ohm-m.

17. Match the following :

Column A	Column B
A. Phyllode	1. Bryophyllum
B. Food storage	2. Calotropis
C. Tendril	3. Australian Acacia
D. Chemical defence	4. Pea
E. Vegetative propagation	5. Onion

A.→ B.→ C.→ D.→ E.→

18. What are biodegradable substances? Name two substances.

19. Give two conditions which are necessary for Rusting.

20. Complete the equations :

1. $CO_2 + H_2O \rightarrow$ .... (When dissolved)
2. $Na_2CO_3 + 2HCl \rightarrow H_2O +$ .... $+ CO_2$
3. $Na_2CO_3 +$ .... $\rightarrow H_2O + Na_2SO_4 +$ ....
4. $Fe_2O_3 +$ .... $\rightarrow$ .... $+ 3CO_2$
5. .... $+ CO_2 \rightarrow Na_2CO_3 +$ ....

21. Write the chemical formula of the following compounds:

(i) Copper Sulphate ....

(ii) Iron Silicate ....

(iii) Lead oxide ....

(iv) Calcium Carbonate ....

(v) Sodium Chloride ....

(vi) Sodium Hydroxide ....

22. Describe the modifications that have enabled desert plants to adapt themselves to the environments.

23. What are noble metals? Name them.

24. What kind of image is formed by a convex lens, when the object is placed beyond focus.

25. Why are the electric switches made of plastic?

EXPLANATORY ANSWERS

1. repulsion

2. high, low

3. immunity

4. Here, $\frac{1}{R} = \frac{1}{R_1} + \frac{1}{R_2} + \frac{1}{R_3}$

$$= \frac{R_2R_3 + R_1R_3 + R_1R_2}{R_1R_2R_3}$$

Hence, $R = \frac{R_1R_2R_3}{R_1R_2 + R_2R_3 + R_3R_1}$

5. *(i)* Bacterium *Salmonella typhi*

(ii) Rubeola virus

(iii) Trichoplayton

6. Marsh

7. Velocity of light in vacuum or free space

$C = 3 \times 10^8$ m/s

$= 3 \times 10^5$ km/s

8. Microscope, Telescope

9. newton/metre^2

10. $\because$ 1 m^3 = 1000 l

Here, wt. of 1000 l = 1.29 kg

$\therefore$ Wt of 1 $l = \frac{1.29}{1000}$ kg

$= \frac{1.29 \times 1000}{1000}$ gm

$= 1.29$ gm

11. Ohm's Law states that ratio of the potential difference at the ends of a conductor and current flowing through it is constant, provided that the physical state of the conductor does not change.

12. (i) NaCl

(ii) $Al_2O_3 . 2H_2O$

13. Hydrocarbons are organic compounds consisting of hydrogen and carbon, as methane, ethane, benzene, etc.

14. *(i)* Copper and Zinc

(ii) Iron and Carbon

(iii) Copper and Tin

15. $_a\mu_g = \frac{3 \times 10^5 \text{ km/s}}{1.8 \times 10^5 \text{ km/s}} = \frac{30}{18} = \frac{5}{3} = 1.67$

16. Here, resistence of wire

$$R = \rho \times \frac{l}{A}$$

$$= 49 \times 10^{-8} \times \frac{1.10}{\frac{22}{7} \times \frac{0.1}{1000} \times \frac{0.1}{1000}}$$

$$= \frac{49 \times 10^{-8} \times 1.10}{\frac{22}{7} \times 10^{-8}} = \frac{49 \times 7 \times 1.10}{22} = \frac{34.3}{2}$$

= 17.15 ohm

17. A. →3 B. →5 C. →4 D. →2 E. →1

18. The chemical degradation by living organisms of substances introduced into the environment are known as biodegradable substances.

Examples— Plant wastes, Vegetables wastes

19. Rusting on iron is the combined effect of air, water and carbon dioxide.

The conditions which are necessary for Rusting:

I. Presence of moisture.

II. Presence of air.

III. Presence of weak acidic atmosphere (as CO_2 gas)

IV. Presence of impurities in the iron.

20. 1. H_2CO_3

2. 2NaCl

3. H_2SO_4, CO_2

4. 3CO, 2Fe

5. 2NaOH, H_2O

21. *(i)* $CuSO_4$ *(ii)* $FeSiO_3$ *(iii)* PbO

(iv) $CaCO_3$ *(v)* NaCl *(vi)* NaOH

22. A plant which can grow in very dry conditions and is able to withstand periods of drought. The adaptations has an ability to store water, waxy leaves and leaves reduced to spines to avoid water loss through transpiration.

23. Noble metals do not rust or tarnish in air or water and not easily attacked by acids. Noble metals are—silver, gold and platinum.

24.

S. No.	Position of object	Nature of Image
1.	At infinity	Image at focus, real, inverted, highly diminished
2.	Beyond 2*f*	Image between *f* and 2*f*, real, inverted, diminished
3.	At 2*f*	Image at 2*f*, real, inverted, same size
4.	Between *f* and 2*f*	Image beyond 2*f*, real, inverted, magnified

25. Plastic is insulator of electricity. So, plastic switch are quite safe.

PAPER-II—LANGUAGE AND SOCIAL STUDIES

Part 'A' — English Language

Directions (Q. 1-15): *Each question is followed by three or four alternatives. Select the correct answer and encircle its letter. You are not required to write that choice in the blank.*

1. Is there ...... at the door?
A. someone B. anyone
C. somebody

2. We have ...... chairs in the library.
A. much B. many
C. a little

3. He is ...... honourable man.
A. an B. a
C. none of these

4. Copper is ...... useful metal.
A. an B. a
C. none of these

5. Honest men speak ...... truth.
A. a B. the
C. none of these

6. Trust ...... God and do the right.
A. on B. in
C. at D. upon

7. I differ ...... you on this point.
A. from B. of
C. with D. at

8. Let me congratulate you ...... your success.
A. in B. for
C. on D. at

9. He is blind ...... his defects.
A. for B. to
C. of D. at

10. He has put an appeal ...... the judgement.
A. for B. from
C. to D. against

11. She jumped off the bus while it–
A. moved B. had moved
C. is moving D. was moving

12. When we went to cinema, the film–
A. already started
B. had already started
C. would already start
D. is starting

13. I ...... answer the letter tonight.
A. am B. have
C. shall D. was

14. The farmer ...... cutting the corn, which has ripened.
A. was B. had been
C. is D. will have been

15. He ...... here for the last five years.
A. worked B. is working
C. has been working D. could be working

Directions (Q. 16-20): *Select the appropriate ANTONYM (Opposite in meaning) to the word given in the following questions–*

16. Rationed
A. Incapable B. Intolerable
C. Untidy D. Unrestricted

17 Obstinate
A. Grateful B. Intelligent
C. Co-operate D. Vengeful

18. Joyous
A. Redundant B. Poignant
C. Melancholy D. Simple

19. Acquittal
A. Entrusted B. Convicted
C. Freed D. Burdened

20. Affinity
A. Friendship B. Enmity
C. Discordance D. Frequency

Directions (Q. 21-25): *Select the appropriate SYNONYM, which is nearest to the meaning of the given words in the following questions–*

21. Illuminate
A. Swell up B. Light up
C. Praise D. Point deep

22. Invaluable
A. Of no value B. Without limit
C. Of great value D. Generous

23. Detergent
A. Arresting quick movement
B. Cleaning agent
C. Not urgent
D. Disinfectant

24. Majestic
A. Religious
B. Unusual
C. Tall
D. Stately and dignified

25. Proton
A. Sunspot
B. Part of atom's nucleus
C. Nerve connection
D. Food element

Directions (Q. 26-30): *Out of the given alternatives choose the correct word which is very close to each definition–*

26. One who does not believe in God–
A. Agnostic B. Theologist
C. Atheist D. Ascetic

27. A person who rarely speaks the truth–
A. Crook B. Liar
C. Scoundrel D. Hypocrite

28. Persons witnessing a thing or an event–
A. Boot-legger B. Misnomer
C. Spectator D. Transient

29. Something through which we can see through–
A. Translucent B. Opaque
C. Transparent D. Triumvirate

30. Medical examination of a dead body–
A. Post-marital B. Diagnosis
C. Analysis D. Post-mortem

Directions (Q. 31-35): *Choose the correct spellings from the given four choices and encircle the spelling choice number you find correct–*

31. A. Plesant B. Pleasant
C. Pleasent D. Plasant

32. A. Aggregate B. Agregate
C. Aggrigate D. Agreegate

33. A. Humrous B. Humorus
C. Humorous D. Humoros

34. A. Endeavour B. Endavour
C. Endevour D. Endeavuor

35. A. Auspecious B. Auspiceous
C. Auspecious D. Auspicious

Directions (Q. 36-40): *Rearrange the following group of words and make meaningful sentences, write your sentence in the space provided–*

36. all courtiers, told, the Queen, she was, how beautiful, all day long.

37. they left, where, they had been, the hotel, in a motor car, staying.

38. He visited, was defeated, Napoleon, where, the battle field, holidays, in his.

39. only, work, they, when, no money, have, they.

40. a gentleman, a dog, has, to sell, wishes, who abroad, to go.

Directions (Q. 41-45): *In the following sentences some sentences have ERRORS. Select the part in which the error lies and encircle its letter A, B or C. If there is no error encircle D.*

41. (A) He has not undergone any technical training in games / (B) but he plays well than / (C) most of the professionals./ (D) No error.

42. (A) As she was tired off / (B) after a long walk / (C) she went to bed early. / (D) No error.

43. (A) Even if it takes me six months / (B) I am determined / (C) for finishing job. / (D) No error.

44. (A) I lived in Delhi / (B) for five years / (C) and earned a lot. / (D) No error.

45. (A) Vinod's brother / (B) as well as his son / (C) was present at the variety show. / (D) No error.

Driections (Q. 46-50): *Change the Voice of the following–*

46. He will finish the work in a fortnight.

47. Who did it?

48. Why did your father write such a letter?

49. One should keep one's promises.

50. Help the poor.

Directions (Q. 51-55): *Change the Narration of the following sentences–*

51. " Are you going to help me? " he asked me.

52. My teacher often says to me, "If you do not work hard, you will fail."

53. He said to him, "Please wait here till I return".

54. He asked Ram to go with him.

55. He asked me if I would accompany him.

Directions (Q. 56-60): *Read the following passage carefully and answer the questions given below–*

National integration is, therefore, the need of hour. India has already suffered centuries of servitude and enslavement. Perhaps India is the only country in the world, which has suffered foreign rule for more than seven hundred and fifty years. The internal dissensions among the Rajput kings and princes allowed the Muslim invaders to establish their foothold in India, which was prolonged as long as five centuries. Then there was once again a time when destiny gave India a chance to be united in bonds of unity but the British ingeniously succeeded in creating a rift between different kings and princes and enabled themselves to establish theirs way which was overthrown only when the different links of Indian nationhood were joined together, again by Indian leaders of unparalleled political acumen, who were not creations of history but creators of history. They had realized fully well that India's sorrow had originated from disunity and the ugly spirit of mutual rivalries. They made the herculean efforts to weld his country again into strong bonds of unity. But their resourcess efforts were pitted against a power which on the strength of her abundant resources and her ugly policy of divide and rule had prevented the different communities of India from being united in close bonds of unity. The mighty efforts of these leaders succeeded and India achieved independence, but India's heart had already been vivisected in the creation of Pakistan.

Answer the following–

56. India has suffered foreign rule for how much period?

57. Why could Muslim invaders establish rule over India?

58. Who succeeded in a big way to establish their rule over India after the Muslims?

59. Which factor prevented the different communities in India from being welded into close bonds of unity?

60. How did India succeed in throwing off her bondage of slavery?

Directions (Q. 61-65): *Rewrite the following sentences as directed–*

61. He is so young that he cannot understand (Use 'too' in the sentence. Make any other change if necessary).

62. This razor is not as sharp as that one (Rewrite the sentence using comparative degree of sharp without changing the meaning of the sentence).
63. He told me to work hard (Change into interrogative sentence).
64. What an intelligent fellow he is! (Change this exclamatory sentence into Assertive sentence).
65. He was astonished when he saw me. (Change this complex sentence into simple sentence).
66. Write a passage in about 150 words on 'The T.V. serial I like the most'.
67. You are Arun. You have received Rs. 300 as a birthday present from your uncle. Write a letter thanking him and telling him how you propose to spend it. (Not more than 300 words)
68. Construct a readable story from the outlines– An old lady becomes blind .... calls in a doctor ..... agrees to pay large fee if cured but nothing if not cured ..... doctor comes daily ..... wants to take away lady's furniture .... delays the cure .... everyday takes away some of her furniture ...... at last cures her ...... demands his fee ...... lady refuses to pay ..... saying cure is not complete ...... doctor goes to the court ...... judge askes the lady why she will not pay ...... she says sight not properly restored ...... she cannot see all her fruniture ...... judge gives verdict in her favour.

ANSWERS

1	2	3	4	5	6	7	8	9	10
B	B	A	B	B	B	C	C	B	D
11	12	13	14	15	16	17	18	19	20
D	B	C	C	C	D	C	C	B	B
21	22	23	24	25	26	27	28	29	30
B	C	B	D	B	C	B	C	C	D
31	32	33	34	35	41	42	43	44	45
B	A	C	A	D	B	A	C	D	D

EXPLANATORY ANSWERS

36. All courtiers told the Queen all day long how beautiful she was!
37. They left the hotel, where they had been staying, in a motor car.
38. He visited the battle field, where Napoleon was defeated in his holidays.
39. They work only when they have no money.
40. A gentleman who wishes to go abroad has a dog to sell.
41. Change 'well' to 'better'.
42. Delete 'off'.
43. Change 'for finishing the job' to 'to finish the job'.
46. The work will be finished by him in a fortnight.
47. By whom was it done?
48. Why was such a letter written by your father?
49. Promises should be kept.
50. Let, the poor be helped.
51. He asked me if I was going to help him.
52. My teacher often tells me that if I do not work hard, I shall fail.
53. He requested him to wait there till he returned.
54. He said to Ram, "Go with me".
55. He said to me, "Will you accompany me?"
56. India has suffered foreign rule for more than seven hundred and fifty years.
57. The internal dissensions among the Rajput kings and princes allowed the Muslim invaders to establish their rule over India.
58. The British ingeniously succeeded in a big way to establish their rule over India after the Muslims.
59. The ugly policy of divide and rule of the British prevented the different communities in India from being welded into close bonds of unity.
60. The great Indian leaders made the herculean efforts to weld this country again into strong bonds of unity. Hence, India succeeded in throwing off her bondage of slavery.

61. He is too young to understand.

62. That razor is sharper than this one.

63. Did he tell me to work hard?

64. He is a very intelligent fellow.

65. He was astonished to see me.

66. Now a days so many serials shown on the T.V. I like 'Dishayen' the most. My father also likes it the most. It is the story of two families which become victims to inhospitable condition. Colonel Sharma has two daughters Nikita and Neha. They are young girls of the marriageable age. Col. Sharma fixes the engagement of the elder daughter Nikita with Rajiv in a good family. The two sisters are twins and hence, resemble each other very closely. Nikita wants to make her career in the films. So, she leaves the home and goes to Mumbai. Col. Sharma marries the younger daughter Neha to Rajiv. Rajiv and his mother do not recognise the difference because both Nikita and Neha are close resemblance to each other. Hence, the entire story is powerful in effect and the suspense element is very strong, so much. So, the spectators would await the telecast of the successive episodes seriously.

67. 11/269, Vasundhara
Ghaziabad
U.P.
Date.......

My Dear uncle,

I am well with my health and study and hope you will be the same. I received your M.O. for Rs. 300 as a birthday present just yesterday. I value your M.O. not only for its monetary value but also it is a indication of your love and affection for me.

I believe that you expect me to put the money sent to me to the best use. I would spend about Rs. 100 in purchasing a small English-Hindi dictionary. I would make it a point to memorize 5 new English words and their meanings every day in order to build up my vocabulary which is suggested by my English teacher.

Out of the remaining two hundred rupees I would spend Rs. one hundred for an alarm clock. Although I am trying my best to rise early in the morning. The alarm clock will help me to wake up early in the morning without fail.

I would spend Rs. 50 in purchasing almonds which will help in sharpening my memory and strengthening the brain power. My mother advises me to save Rs. fifty for future use. I would put fifty rupees in my savings account.

In this way I propose to spend Rs. three hundred sent by you, Hope you would approve of my plan. In the annual examination I have topped the class with your blessings.

Rest is O.K. Please convey my best regards to aunt and my heartiest love to Sonu. With the best of regards.

Yours affectionately,
Arun.

68. An old lady became blind. She called in a doctor. She agreed to pay a large fee if she was cured, but nothing if not cured. The doctor used to come to her home daily. He wanted to take away some of her furniture, so, he delayed the cure of her blindness. He would everyday take away some of her furniture. At last he cured her and demanded his fee. The lady refused to pay. She said him that the cure was not complete. The doctor went to the court. The judge asked the lady why she would not pay the doctor's fee. She answered that her sight was not properly restored because she could not see all her furniture in the house. The judge gave the verdict in her favour.

Part 'B' — Social Studies

SECTION-I (One Mark each)

1. The famous battle between English and Sirajud-daulah, the Nawab of Bengal is known as battle of ________

2. 'SEPOY MUTINY' against British rule in India broke out in the year ________.

3. The first Governor General of India was ______.

4. European traders came to India to sell their goods and take with them gold and silver from here. Is the statement correct? ______

5. The first railway was started in India in the year ______.

6. In a Secular State, there is ______ discrimination against any religion.
7. In a DEMOCRACY, the government is elected by ______.
8. In the original caste system, there used to be only four Varnas : the Brahmins—the Vaishyas and the Shudras.
9. ______ is the movement which began the modern age in Europe.
10. The East India Company was formed by ______
11. British adopted policy of 'Divide & Rule' to create differences between Hindu and ______
12. The British Government encouraged the cultivation of cotton to feed the Indian textile industry. True/False.
13. The battle of Buxar was fought in ______ A.D.
14. People who can fulfil their minimum needs are __.
15. To determine goals and to establish priorities is the responsibility of ______ Commission.
16. Raja Ram Mohan Roy was responsible for abolition of ______
17. The Pitt's India Act was passed in the year______.
18. Arya Samaj was founded by ______ in 1875.
19. General Dyer was responsible for ______ massacre.
20. The Industrial Revolution gave birth of two new classes in the society known as the ______ and the ______.
21. The Capital of Nagaland is ______.
22. Most populated country of the world is ______.
23. Babri Masjid is located at ______.
24. Humayun was the son of great ______.
25. India is a permanent member of UN Security Council. True/False.
26. First five year plan came into effect in the year ______.
27. ______ is the Supreme Commander of the Indian Armed Forces.
28. The inner core of the earth comprises iron and ______.
29. ______ is the policy of racial discrimination.
30. The rank of the Chief of the Air Staff is ______
31. National Anthem was composed by ______
32. Muslim leader who insisted for creation of separated country (Pakistan) was ______
33. Devanagari is the script of ______
34. Remains of plants and animals in the soil is known as ______.
35. India fought against ______ in 1962.
36. Highest Court of India is known as ______ Court.
37. The Indian National Congress was founded by ______
38. Quit India Movement was started by ______
39. The Russian Revolution occurred in ______.
40. First Indian Scientist to get Nobel Prize was ______.
41. Latest State is ______
42. SAARC stands for ______
43. Indian National Army was formed by ______
44. The main objective of the UNO is to establish ____ in the world.
45. The point of the earth's surface directly above the focus is called the ______ of the earthquake.

SECTION-II (3 Marks each)

46. What is glacier?
47. What do you understand by Delta?
48. What are the six fundamental rights? Enumerate.
49. Define sex ratio.
50. Who were the three freedom fighters popularly known as Lal, Bal & Pal?
51. What is Socialism?
52. What do you understand by the term 'Doctrine of Lapse'?
53. Give two reasons of rapid population growth.
54. Define weathering.
55. What is National Integration?

EXPLANATORY ANSWERS

1. Plassey
2. 1857
3. Lord William Bentinck
4. Yes
5. 1853
6. No
7. The People
8. Kshatriya
9. Industrial revolution
10. European countries

11. Muslims
12. False
13. 1764
14. Medium class people
15. Planning
16. Sati Pratha
17. 1784
18. Swami Dyanand Sarswati
19. Jalianwalla Bagh
20. Developed and developing
21. Kohima
22. China
23. Ayodhya
24. Babar
25. False
26. 1951
27. The President
28. Nickel
29. Apartheid
30. Chief Air Marshal
31. Rabindranath Tagore
32. Mohammad Ali Jinnah
33. Hindi
34. Fossils
35. China
36. The Supreme
37. Sir A.O. Hume
38. Indian National Congress
39. 1917
40. Sir C.V. Raman
41. Jharkhand
42. South Asian Association for Regional Co-operation.
43. Netaji Subhash Chandra Bose
44. Peace
45. Epicentre
46. Glacier is the mass of ice which flows outward from ice caps or down from above the snow-line. They cover about one-tenth of the earth's land area. Glaciers originate in areas above the level where snow does not melt completely during the summer. They are classified as continental glaciers, valley glaciers and piedmont glaciers.
47. Where river discharges into a sea, a large fan-shaped accumulation of sediment deposited at the mouth of a river is known as delta. It forms when the river's flow is slowed down on meeting the comparatively static sea. The river is increasingly divided by the deposition into channels.
48. There are six fundamental rights provided in the constitution of India. Which are– (I) Right to Equality, (II) Right to Freedom, (III) Right to Freedom of Religion, (IV) Right against Exploitation, (V) Cultural and Educational Rights and (VI) Right to Constitutional remedies.
49. Sex ratio is known as number of females per thousand males. The sex ratio in the country has always remained unfavourable to females. Present sex ratio of India is 933. Hence, sex ratio is an important social indicator to measure the extent of prevailing equality between males and females in a society of a given point of time.
50. The three great freedom fighters are—Lala Lajapat Rai, Bal Gangadhar Tilak and Vipinchandra Pal and they are popularly known as Lal, Bal and Pal.
51. Socialism is a kind of society which opposed to individualism and capitalism. The society takes precedence over the individual in socialism. It believes in the existence of classes in the difference between physical and mental labour, and also in the difference between government and cooperative organisations. It accepts the existence of the state. Under socialistic kind of society no one will be able to explain only one else. There shall be maximum possible economic equality and every body will get social justice.
52. The term doctrine of lapse propounded by Lord Dalhousie, in which many Indian states whose rulers had no heirs were taken under British rule. The British government of India didn't accept the adopted sons as heirs.
53. (a) Illiteracy.
    (b) Fall in death-rate due to availability of better medical facilities.
54. Weathering is largely a response to lower temperatures and pressures and thus the effects of air and water. Most rocks were formed under conditions in which pressures and temperatures were higher than those to which they are now exposed.
55. National integration provides a feeling of belonging to one nation among all citizens of the country. The people of the country have feelings loyalty to the country irres-pective of their place of birth, caste, creed, religion etc.